PHOTO ICONS

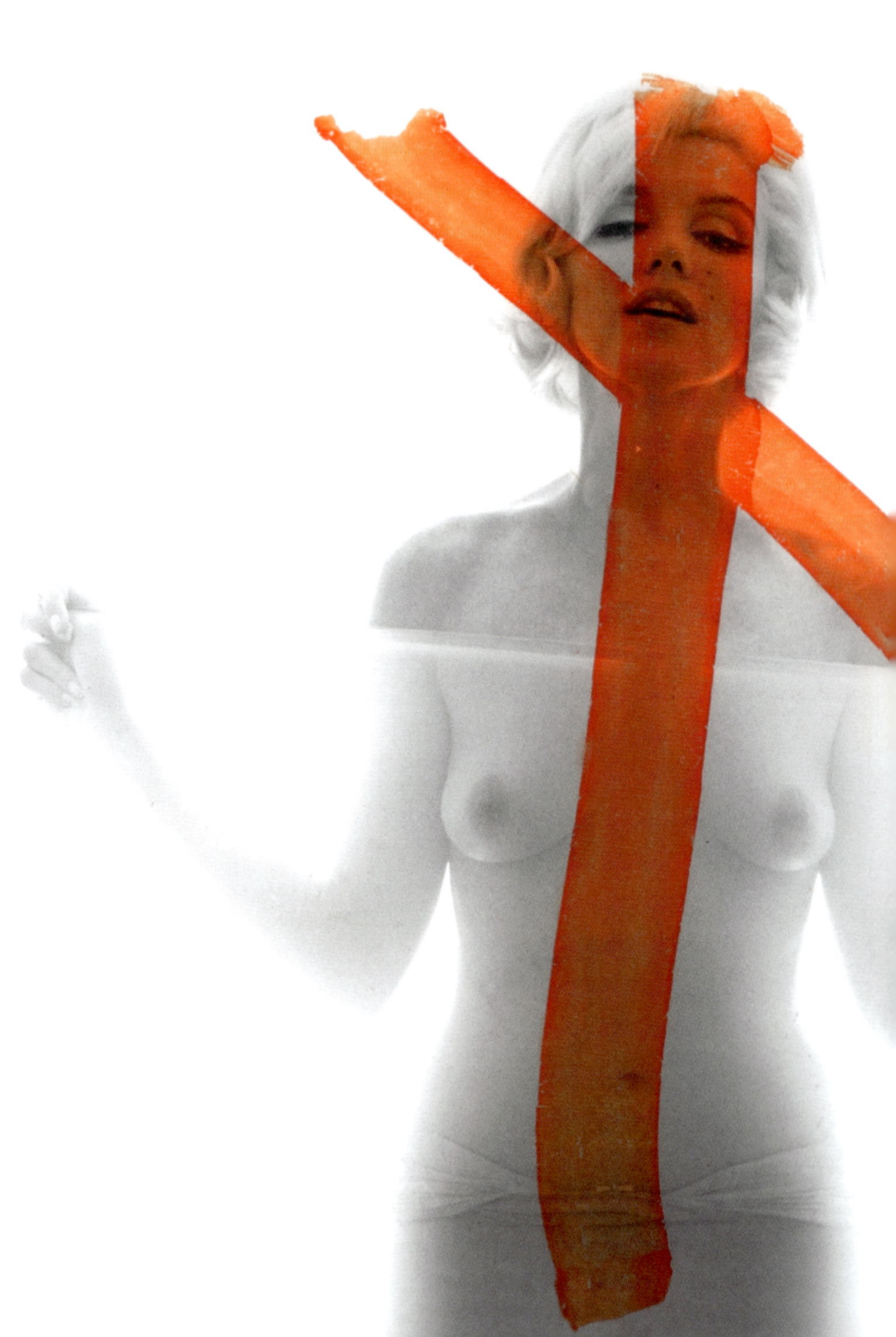

HANS-MICHAEL KOETZLE

PHOTO ICONS

50 Landmark Photographs and Their Stories

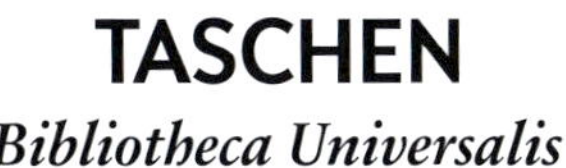

Contents

Reading Pictures
Hans-Michael Koetzle

The photographic era was heralded in 1827 by a camera image produced by an exposure lasting over several hours, using a simple bitumen-coated plate. Now billions of digital photos are being taken every day, to be deleted, saved, or sent instantly around the world via the Internet. There can be no doubt about it: we are living in an age of technically produced images. Photographs, pictures from films, television, video, and digital media all compete for our attention. They try to seduce us, to manipulate, eroticize, and even at times to inform us. People talk of how we are being deluged by images, which sounds threatening, but at heart this points above all to a phenomenological problem: How do we deal with all of these images? How do we select between them? What do we manage to take in? And what, moreover, still has a chance of entering our collective, global memory?

We find ourselves at the moment in a paradoxical situation. While photography as a visual means is losing its influence in its traditional territories, such as photojournalism, the medium is becoming increasingly the object of a public discourse. Photographic images are now an accepted fact in art galleries and museums, at art fairs and auctions. The question as to whether photographs are art appears to have answered itself. Six-figure sums paid for key works from the history of photography, or for works by contemporary photo-artists, have long since ceased to be a rarity. A young generation has discovered in photography the same thing that previously investors found in antiques. Photography is starting to reach a ripe old age, and yet is more relevant now than ever before. As a medium of the more contemplative kind, it has found – in unison with mostly flickering images – a new, forward-looking role.

The media theorist Norbert Bolz has spoken in this connection of the "large, quiet image" that grants something like a secure foothold in the current torrent of data. Where television, video, or the Internet at best produce a visual "surge," the conventional photographic image – as the "victory of abstraction" – is alone in having the power to take root in our minds and engender something akin to a memory. The doyen of advertising, Michael Schirner, put this to the test in the mid-1980s in his exhibition *Bilder im Kopf* (Pictures in Mind). The show simply presented black squares with captions added in negative lettering: *Willy Brandt Kneeling at the Monument to the Heroes of the Warsaw Ghetto*, for instance. Or *The Footprint of the First Man on the Moon*. Or *Albert Einstein Sticking out His Tongue*. Photography, as the Düsseldorf photographer Horst Wackerbarth puts it succinctly, is "the only genre that can achieve a popular effect on the immediate, visible level, and also an elitist one after its initial impact on a deeper, more subtle level."

This book presents photographs from some 180 years, arranged in chronological order. And every one of them is a key image from the history of the medium: images that have pushed photography forward in terms of its technology, aesthetics, or social relevance. There is a tradition to viewing "icons" such as these by themselves, each on its own. Best known in this context is John Szarkowski's classic book *Looking at Photographs,* first published in 1973. But going beyond Szarkowski's associative, journalistic style, the present volume also provides in-depth analyses of the contents. With the history of a picture's reception, we arrive at the question of when and in what way the motif became exactly what it is: a visual parameter for central categories of the human experience. Almost every technical approach and every major field of application (from portraiture to landscapes, from the nude to the snapshot) has been included here, making this book a "potted history of photography." This prompts us to read pictures critically, to look at them more attentively and with greater awareness. As early as the 1920s, Moholy-Nagy pointed to the dangers of visual illiteracy. That applied to the era of silver salts in the photographic lab. Yet it applies more than ever to the age of satellite TV, video, and the Internet.

Nicéphore Niépce
View from the Study Window
1827

Traces in Bitumen

The public announcement of Louis Jacques Mandé Daguerre's photographic process in August 1839 is usually accepted as the birth date of photography. But in fact, Daguerre's compatriot Nicéphore Niépce had succeeded in fixing images with a camera obscura a good decade earlier.

The view must have been very familiar to the photographer. After all, what does a thoughtful person do when the flow of ideas is blocked, and they merely spin in circles around the problem without advancing further? One looks out the window, beyond the limitations of one's own desk, and seeks new ideas and inspiration from the distance. The study of Joseph Niépce – who signed himself Niépce, but by the end of 1787 had adopted a second forename, Nicéphore – was located on the second floor of his family estate Maison du Gras, in the village of Saint-Loup-de Varennes, about six kilometers (nearly four miles) from the village of Chalon-sur-Saône in French Burgundy. Just how often Niépce must have glanced out the window of this room we can only guess, but what he saw is a matter of absolute certainty: to the right is an at least partially visible barn roof; somewhat to the left, a dovecote; to the far left, a recessed baking kitchen; and finally, in the background, the pear tree, whose leafy crown nonetheless allows a clear glimpse of the sky to show through in two places, even in the summer months. And what he saw, he captured with the camera. *View from the Study Window* at Maison du Gras, taken in June or July 1827, is in all probability the first permanent – although mirror-reversed – image in the history of photography.

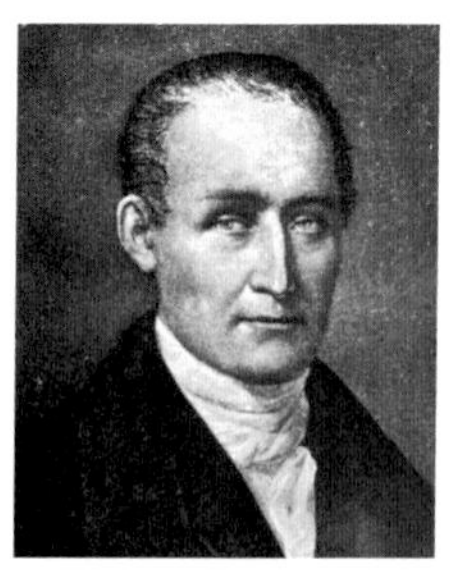

Nicéphore Niépce

Born ***1765*** *in Chalon-sur-Saône, France, the son of a royal tax-collector. Works as a teacher.* ***1792–94*** *lieutenant in the Revolutionary Army. From* ***1801*** *administers the family's country estate at Chalon. At the same time develops a ship engine (pyréolophore) together with his older brother Claude. From* ***1813*** *explores the possibilities of lithography.* ***1816*** *first experiments with a camera obscura. From* ***1822*** *on, his first successes with photochemical reproduction of images.* ***1827*** *meets Daguerre on his way to England. Gives a report on heliography to the Royal Society.* ***1829*** *forms a partnership with Daguerre.* ***1833*** *dies unexpectedly of a stroke.*

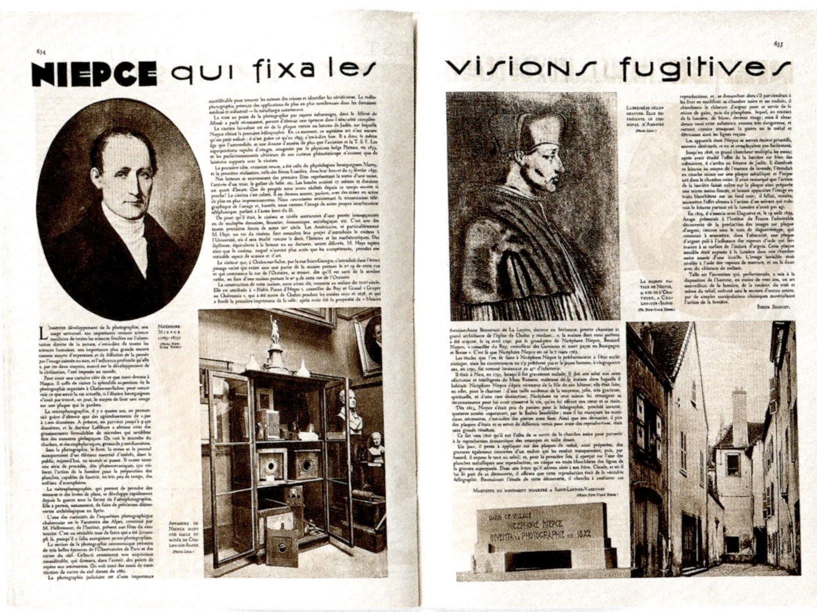
NIEPCE qui fixa les visions fugitives

A long way from permanent camera images

Nicéphore Niépce had returned to Burgundy in 1801 after a number of years spent in Italy, on the island of Sardinia, and in Nice. Now, as a gentleman-farmer, he raised beets and produced sugar; financially, however, he was in fact independent, for in spite of the vicissitudes of the French Revolution and the Napoleonic era, his inheritance was large enough to support him comfortably. With the years, he increasingly devoted his time to scientific experiments, busying himself as a private scholar and developing (together with his brother Claude) the so-called pyréolophore, a combustion engine meant to revolutionize human locomotion, but which in fact turned into a financial debacle. Furthermore, Niépce attempted to find a substitute for indigo, which had become scarce as a result of the Continental Blockade, invented a kind of bicycle, and determined to fixing the fleeting of the camera obscura.

Niépce had already produced his first heliographs, as he called the results of his experiments, in the spring of 1816. And already at this point, it was precisely the view from the window that he attempted to depict in his 'sun drawings.' One wonders what motivated Niépce again and again specifically to aim the eye of his camera from his study down onto his property in Le Gras. Was it sentimentality? Or did the experiment of capturing precisely the view that he knew so well appeal to him because its very familiarity would make it easier for him to check its precision and accuracy – the qualities that he was most striving for? In all probability, the reason lies elsewhere: Niépce could work with his camera on the window sill at length, without interruption and without having to answer the questions of the curious – and without alerting possible competitors to the progress of his experiments. For he knew that discovery was in the air. "My dear friend," he wrote in May 1816 with unusual candor to his brother Claude, now

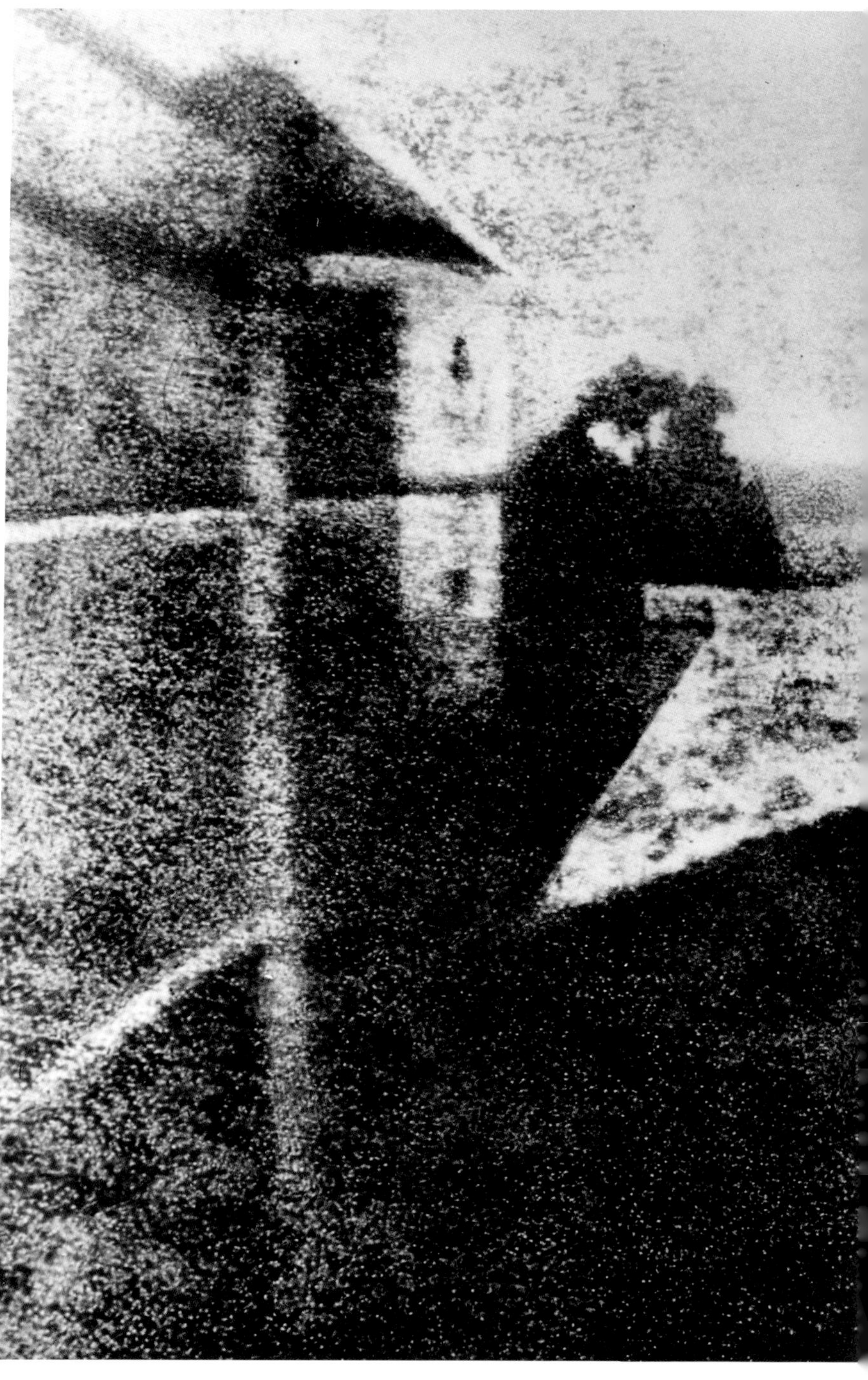

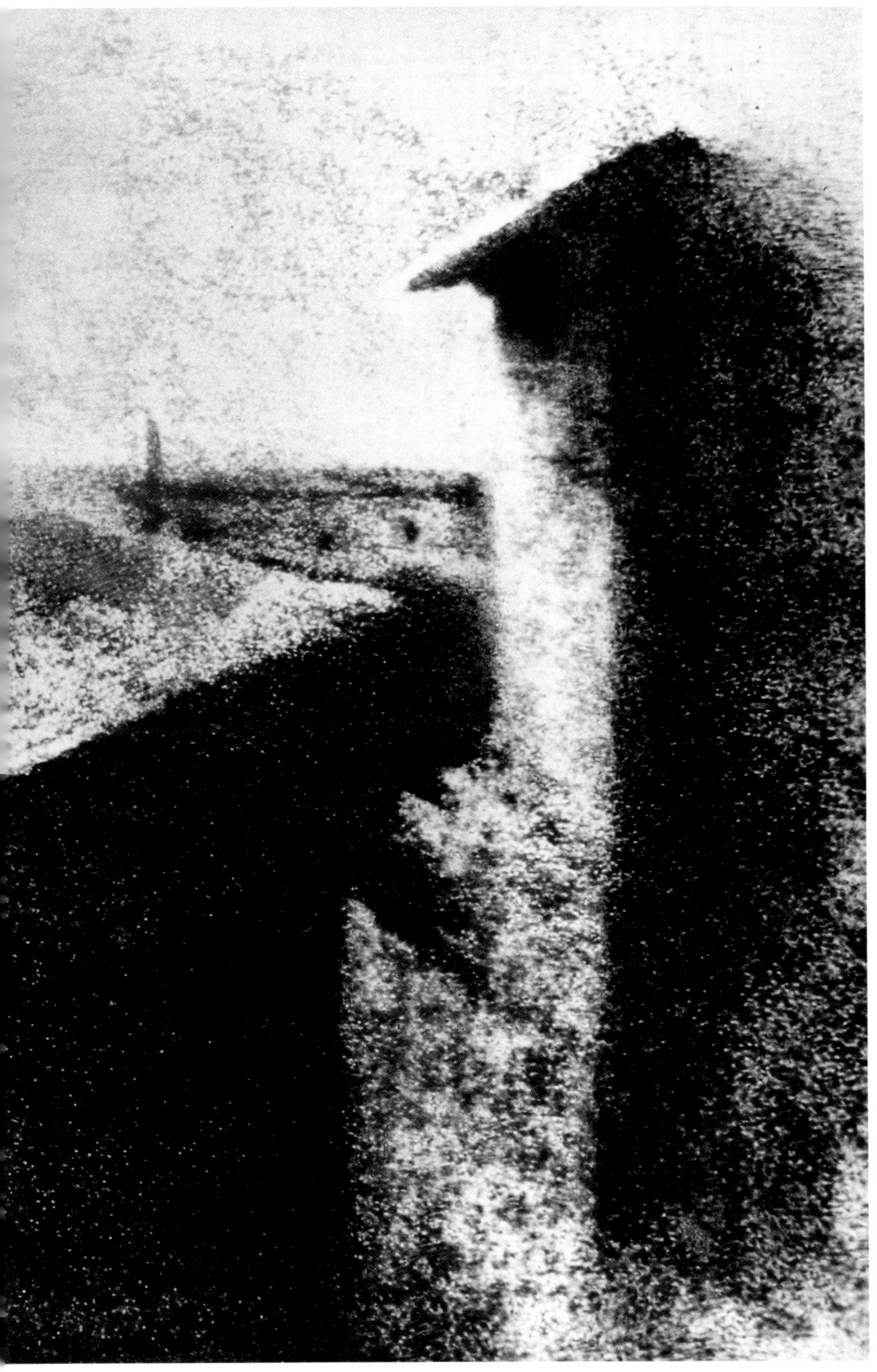

living in Paris, "I am rushing to send you my four latest test results. Two large and two small ones, all considerably clearer and more exact, which I succeeded in making with the help of a simple trick: namely, I reduced the aperture of the lens by means of a piece of paper. Now less light makes its way into the interior of the camera, so that the image becomes more lively, and the outlines as well as the light and shadows are clearer and better illuminated."

And what does Claude see in the pictures, insofar as he can make out anything at all? For Nicéphore has not yet found a means of permanently fixing the silver-chloride images made with the help of his home-made camera obscura. Together with Nicéphore, he gazes out the window of their hereditary Maison du Gras: before him are the two wings already described, the dovecote, the dominating slate roof of the baking kitchen. Admittedly, all that he sees is reversed from left to right; similarly, the shadows and light appear as negative images; and the whole is merely black and white. Niépce is still a long way from either positive or permanent camera images. At the same time, he remains confident and confides in his brother in order to convince himself of his own progress. He has no inkling that it will take him another ten years to produce a permanent photographic image.

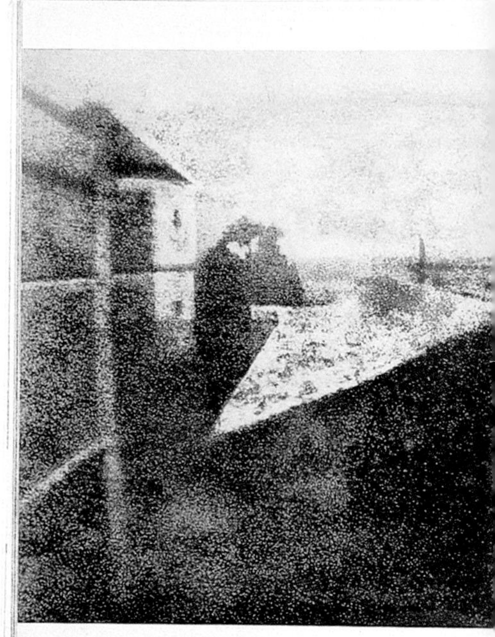

DIE ERSTE PHOTOGRAPH

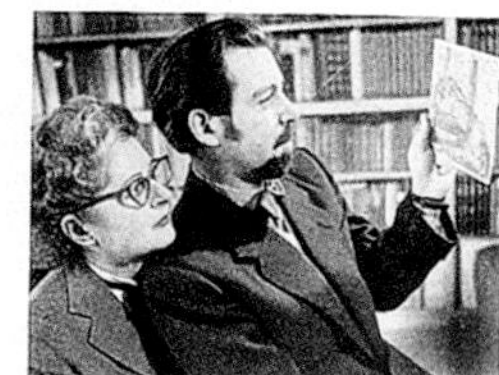

Soeben gelang es *Hel*
Photographie – das Urp
den. Er wußte, es muß
sein. *Nicephore Niepce*
nommen. Es zeigt den
Gras bei Chalon-sur-Sa
übernahm sofort die n
an diesem letzten und
unterscheiden sich die
ren Sammlern: jeder ne
prüft und sorgfältig dok
Daß wir dieses stark ver
zeigen können, ist den
torium zu danken, dem
lang, eine druckfähige

38

Page 11: Homage to Niécpe: *double-page spread from* Miroir du Monde, *17 June 1933. His* View from the Study Window *had not yet been discovered.*

Above: *"The First Photograph in the World." This article in* Fotomagazin *(May 1952) is probably the first reference to the sensational discovery in a German specialist publication.*

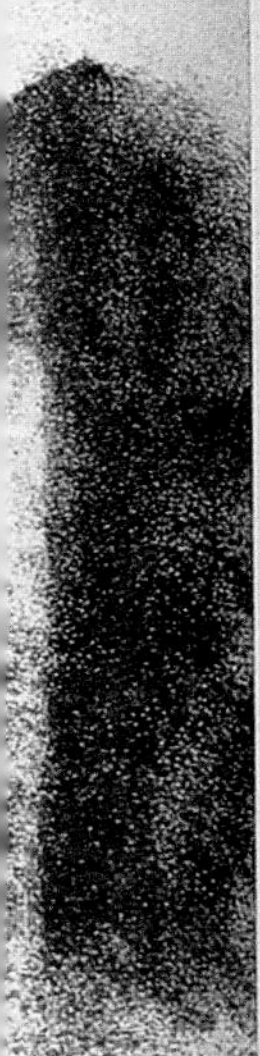

ER WELT

die älteste
– aufzufin-
vorhanden
1826 aufge-
Fenster in
Gernsheim
hungsarbeit
gerade darin
vielen ande-
gründlich ge-

seren Lesern
ungs-Labora-
Arbeit ge-
herzustellen.

GUSTAV SCHENK

RHYTHMEN IN DER WASSERSPUR

Im Naturerleben, im Nachdenken über die Gestaltenfülle in der Natur, taucht immer wieder eine zentrale Frage auf: Wie wird Gestalt? Die Wasserringe und Wellenfurchen auf dem See, die ebenmäßigen, rhythmisch so wohlgeordneten Sanddünen, die Wogen der Schäfchenwölkchen und der Zirren, die Vollkommenheit der Prägung auf Muschel- und Schneckenschalen, die Anordnung der Farben auf Pfauenfedern, selbst die Verteilung der Adern unter der Haut — was für eine Macht hat sie gerade so und nicht anders geschaffen? So wenig auch die unterschiedlichen Gestaltungen miteinander zu tun haben, etwas einigt sie: Sie sind nicht ungestaltet, sie bilden keine amorphen, strukturlosen Massen. Eine unsichtbare Kraft hat sie sinnvoll, richtend geordnet, und ihre Ordnung ist rhythmisch. Rhythmische Gestaltung war in der überwältigenden Anschauungsfülle scheinbar eine gemeinsame Richtung, in der Naturbewegungen sich dynamisch vollziehen konnten.

•

Es war seit langen Jahren mein Wunsch, rhythmische Gestaltung vor meinen Augen, auch gelenkt von mir, sichtbar in handlichen Maßen entstehen zu sehen und sie eindrucksvoll deutlich im Lichtbild festzuhalten.

Es gab viele erprobte physikalische Versuche mit Sand, Flüssigkeiten, Dämpfen oder Gasen, die eine solche rhythmische Gestaltung bewegt sichtbar machten. Für bestimmte technische Prüfungen und Untersuchungen waren sie oft ganz unentbehrlich. Nur erforderten sie meistens große Mittel, komplizierte Apparaturen, und die Ergebnisse gaben jedesmal nur ein einseitiges, stets sich wiederholendes Bild.

Mit dem schwierigen, schwer zu lenkenden Material Wasser war schließlich aber auf die allereinfachste Weise der ganze Reichtum rhythmischer Naturgestaltung in handlicher, übersichtlicher und einfacher Weise darzustellen.

Die einfachste, doch vollkommene Anschauung ergibt ein Versuch mit dichtem, lückenlosem, quarzreichem Tonschiefer (der Wasserstein des Handels für Messerschleifen), dessen eine Seite angeschliffen ist. Mit einem Aufreiber aus gleichem Gestein und gleich glattgeschliffener Oberfläche reibt man den mit Wasser benetzten Tonschiefer so lange, bis die von ihm abgeschliffenen Teile aus Glimmer, Feldspat und Quarz eine Körnchenaufschwemmung ergeben. Diese „Suspension" bedeckt dann als dünnen Flüssigkeitsspiegel den Tonschiefer. Auf das Tonwasser setzt man den Aufreiber. Das Wasser haftet innig zwischen beiden Steinflächen. Wenn man nun plötzlich den Aufreiber nach oben hin hochreißt, dann überwindet man ruckartig die Haftspannung, und die Flüssigkeitshaut wird zerrissen. Nach dem Verdunsten des Wassers trocknet der mineralische Rückstand auf und hebt sich als weiße Zeichnung von außerordentlicher Feinheit vom grauen Grund des Tonschiefers ganz deutlich ab.

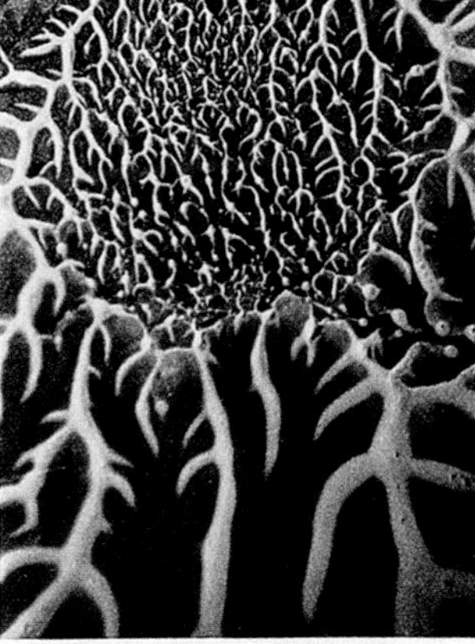

Hier schon enthüllte sich deutlich auch auf dem kleinen Raum von nur wenigen Millimetern Umfang eine echte rhythmische Gestaltung, bei der von wissenschaftlich-physikalischer Sicht aus vieles im Geheimnis ruhen bleibt.

Die Überführung des gestaltlosen Flüssigkeitsspiegels zwischen den Steinen in geordnete Gestalt ging spontan in einem Augenblick vor sich. Die Zerlegung der Wasserfläche geschah ja nicht auf Grund einer periodischen Überwindung von Haftspannungen. Aus der ungestalteten flüssigen Schicht sprang in allen Teilen sofort fertig als ein Ganzes die rhythmische Gestalt. Dieses spontane Werden ohne ein gerichtetes „Nacheinander" einzelner physikalischer Prozesse ist wunderbar und kaum zu analysieren. Es ist aber in den meisten rhythmischen Gestalten der Natur mit offenem Auge wiederzufinden.

•

Ich verfeinerte aber den einfachen Versuch ein wenig, um die Ergebnisse für die photographische Abbildung deutlicher und plastischer zu machen.

Die Körnchenaufschwemmung, die ich durch das Schleifen gewann, verdünnte ich stark mit Wasser. Die Rückseite abgewaschener photographischer Platten bestrich ich mit Asphaltlack. Auf der blanken, nun tiefschwarzen Glasoberfläche trug ich das Tonwasser auf, setzte den kleinen Aufreiberstein darauf und riß ihn plötzlich nach oben. Sehr rasch verdunstete das Wasser, und der mineralische Rückstand trocknete schneeweiß auf dem schwarzen Glase auf. Durch die Menge der Flüssigkeit und durch den Gehalt an Gesteinsstaub waren die Bilder zahllos zu variieren. Aber gerade in ihrem kleinsten Umfang, bis hinunter zu einem Quadratmillimeter, gewannen sie oft die stärkste Ausdruckskraft. Dabei war zu bedenken, daß keine zähe, dicke Masse sich so gestaltete, sondern praktisch wirklich nur Wasser, denn der Gesteinsstaub-Zusatz war verhältnismäßig überaus gering.

•

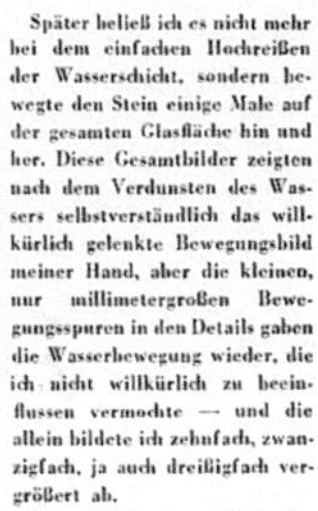

Später beließ ich es nicht mehr bei dem einfachen Hochreißen der Wasserschicht, sondern bewegte den Stein einige Male auf der gesamten Glasfläche hin und her. Diese Gesamtbilder zeigten nach dem Verdunsten des Wassers selbstverständlich das willkürlich gelenkte Bewegungsbild meiner Hand, aber die kleinen, nur millimetergroßen Bewegungsspuren in den Details gaben die Wasserbewegung wieder, die ich nicht willkürlich zu beeinflussen vermochte — und die allein bildete ich zehnfach, zwanzigfach, ja auch dreißigfach vergrößert ab.

Diese Bilder nun offenbarten auf dramatische Weise den Ablauf von Bewegungsverhältnissen innerhalb winziger Wasserteile. Sie gaben kein Chaos ungestalteter Wasserspuren wieder, sondern zeigten gleichsam Pulsationen von höchster Kraft, sie waren völlig durchtränkt von spontaner rhythmischer Gestaltung.

39

View from the Study Window, 1827

Searching for a new technology

Nicéphore Niépce, born the scion of a wealthy family in March 1765, was not the only one searching at the turn of the nineteenth century for a new technology that would produce images appropriate to the new positivistic age. It had been four hundred years since Gutenberg introduced a true textual revolution. In contrast, the development of the visual image had stagnated, at least in the technical sense. Of course Alois Senefelder's invention of lithography (1797) signified an important flat-printing process for the graphic arts. But here also – and in this, lithography did not differ from woodcuts or copper engraving – the active hand of the artist remained necessary to the creation of a picture. Still missing was a quasi-automatic process that would be both fast and inexpensive. Above all, the new technology had to be dependable, objective, and precise in detail – in short, it must correspond to a rational age oriented to exactitude. To this end, research and systematic experiments were being conducted in almost all the lands of Europe, but nowhere more intensively than in England and France. After all, the principles behind an analogue process for producing pictures were already long familiar: the operation of the camera obscura, known from the Renaissance, and Johann Heinrich Schulze's discovery of the light sensitivity of silver salts in 1727. It was only necessary to combine the physical and the chemical.

Views according to nature

In his quest, Niépce was a child of his age; his research was not at all directed toward the discovery of a new medium of artistic expression. He strove for a pictorial mass medium: quick, cheap, and dedicated to the realistically oriented Zeitgeist of a bourgeois age. Niépce had actually begun quite early to employ various acids for etching transitory images onto metal and stone. "This kind of engraving," claimed Niépce in 1816, "would be even better than the [the silver chloride images] because they can be so easily replicated and because they are unalterable." In the end, however, his efforts, whether to obtain a direct positive image or to produce plates that could be used for printing, remained unsuccessful. Not until 1822 did Niépce discover in bitumen, an asphalt-like substance used by both copper engravers and lithographers, a medium capable of holding an image. He realized that bitumen eventually bleaches out and, more importantly, hardens under the influence of light; on the other hand, bitumen kept in the shade remains soluble and can be rinsed away. Niépce succeeded in copying a portrait of Pius VII by using oil to make the copperplate print transparent, placing it on a bitumen-coated glass plate, and laying it in the sunlight. After two or three hours, the exposed portions had hardened to such an extent that the shadowed areas could be rinsed away with a solution of lavender oil and turpentine.

On the advice of his brother, Niépce soon replaced the glass plates with copper or, often, tin, which reflected more light and was thus more suited to his intention of creating "views according to nature." Now, with his discovery of the missing clue, Niépce took up his earlier experiments with the camera obscura again around 1825, replacing his home-made camera in February 1827 with a 'professional' model that had double convex lenses using bitumen-coated tin plates. In the summer he succeeded in making a 16.5 × 20.5 cm (6½ × 7¾ inch) direct positive image with left-to-right reversal. In the picture, the lustrous bitumen rendered the light, while the tin, washed clean with lavender oil, reproduced the shadows. His shooting point was his study in Le Gras, and experts have calculated that the exposure time must have been more than eight hours. It is for this reason that the two opposite wings of the building are both in sunlight. Clearly recognizable at the edges of the picture are the curved and out-of-focus vertical lines produced by the lenses.

What we are looking at – and here historians of photography are unanimous – is clearly the world's first photograph. Initially, Niépce left it behind in Burgundy when he journeyed to England in September 1827 to visit his seriously ill brother Claude, who was now living in Kew, near London. Among the acquaintances he made on the visit was that of the botanist Francis Bauer, who immediately took a strong interest in Niépce's heliographic experiments and proposed making a report on the process before the Royal Society. Niépce sent at once for his pictures, including *View from the Study Window*, and immediately drew up a memorandum, point-blank identifying himself as the inventor of what he called "heliography": a process of "capturing the pictures reflected in the camera obscura in gradated tones from black to white solely with the help of light."

Niépce avoided, however, giving precise information about his method of procedure, a reticence which led the Royal Society to reject the report. Niépce returned home to France, undoubtedly disappointed, in January 1828, having turned over all his experimental pictures to Francis Bauer as a gift. The botanist was well aware of the significance of the seemingly insignificant objects: "Monsieur Niépce's first successful experiment of fixing permanently the Image of Nature," he inscribed on the back of the picture which makes its way into every history of photography as *View from the Study Window*.

After Bauer's death in 1841, Niépce's pictures and other documents passed first into the ownership of Dr. Robert Brown for a sum of 14 pounds 4 shillings, and later into the hands of J. J. Bennett, both of whom were members of the Royal Society. Bennett subsequently sold one portion of the legacy to the photographer Henry Peach Robinson, and a second to Henry Baden Pritchard, the publisher of *Photographic News*. In 1898, the heliographs surfaced once again within the framework of a photographic exhibition in the London Crystal Palace. And then they disappeared without a trace into the depths of history. We would still probably be speculating about the content and whereabouts of Niépce's view of Le Gras today if Alison and Helmut Gernsheim had not set out on a seemingly hopeless search for the pictures a few years after the end of the Second World War. In April 1948, the two researchers published a brief report in the London *Times* with all their findings gathered up to that point, but the article found no immediate resonance. Two years later, they made a second attempt, and this time the aged son of Henry Baden Pritchard responded in a corresponding article in the *Observer* – without, however, offering any information on the whereabouts of the pictures, last seen in 1900. Months passed until Mr. Pritchard Jr. was heard from again at the end of 1951: tucked between books and clothing, Niépce's picture (in the meantime framed) had turned up in the family attic in a suitcase belonging to his mother, who had died in 1917. The joy at the discovery was muted, however, because the motif was hardly discernible to the naked eye, and was furthermore not reproducible. There followed long and arduous attempts by the research department at Kodak until a certain P. B. Watt finally succeeded in photographing the image in such a way that the picture – today owned by the University of Austin, Texas – became legible: the contours of the buildings at Le Gras emerge recognizably behind the initially reflective surfaces. Niépce's *View from the Study Window* had thus been exposed, so to speak, a second time.

Louis Jacques Mandé Daguerre
Boulevard du Temple
1838

The Loneliness of the Shoeshine Man

Around 1835, Louis Jacques Mandé Daguerre succeeded for the first time in fixing permanent photographic images through the process that later became known by his name. His most famous daguerreotype, almost certainly taken in the spring of 1838, was long thought to be the first photographic image of a human figure.

The image was anything but perfect – its creator realized this full well. The painter, inventor, and diorama owner Louis Jacques Mandé Daguerre belongs – together with Niépce and Talbot – to the great triumvirate of photographic history. Of the three, however, Daguerre was surely the most skilled tactician, possessing what we would today call a highly developed sense of PR. Ever since the 1820s, Daguerre had been looking for a process to enable the technical production of pictures based on the images produced by the camera obscura. Finally, in 1835 he achieved success, and now the issue became how best to exploit the potential of the new medium. Daguerre's view of the Boulevard du Temple was intended to be a link in a visual chain of argumentation for his new process. Admittedly, as remarkable as his picture was for the conditions of his time (or rather, for the limitations of his process), his 12.9 × 16.3 cm (5 × 6½ inch) format image remained nonetheless modest in comparison with what painting, drawing, or graphics could offer. In short, from the very beginning, photography had to compete with the 'fine arts'. And in this contest, the new medium labored under numerous disadvantages: Daguerre's photograph, for example, reproduced the reality it sought to capture in very small format – and 'merely' in black and white (as the early critics noted with disappointment as early as 1839). Furthermore, the photograph, which consisted of a single direct plate, was necessarily a reverse image, and on top of this, the reflecting surfaces of the plate itself interfered with viewing the image: according to how one held the daguerreotype, the picture

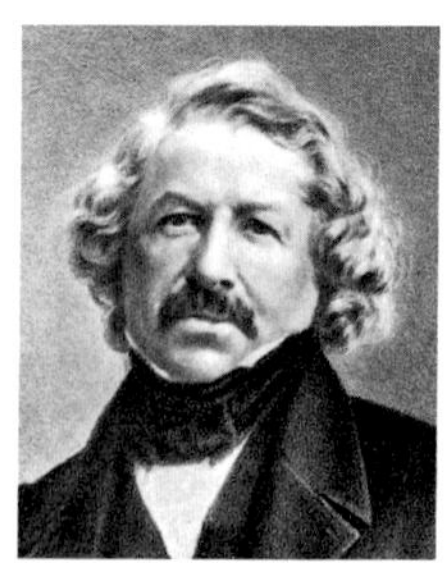

Louis Jacques Mandé Daguerre
*Born **1787** in Cormeilles-en-Parisis, France. **1801–03** trains in an architect's practice in Orléans. From **1803** in Paris. **1816–22** works as a scenic artist. **1822–30** builds and runs a diorama. **1829** forms a partnership with Niépce. **1839** the diorama is destroyed in a fire. Public presentation of the daguerreotype that same year. The state purchases the rights to the method. **1841** returns to the country. **1844** last daguerreotypes. Dies **1851** in Bry-sur-Marne.*

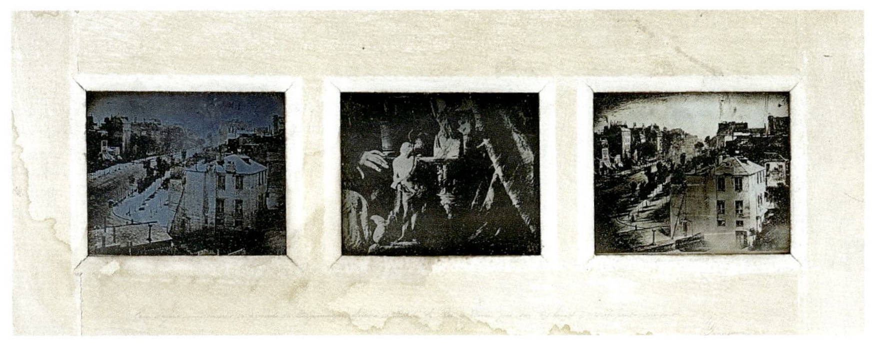

flipped from a positive to a negative image. But perhaps worst of all was the fact that nothing was to be seen of the pulsating life of the Boulevard with its trade and activity and traffic, in the form of carts and horse-drawn wagons. These were left to be imagined. The deadening effect of the daguerreotype is evident in an encyclopedia entry for "Paris" written in 1866, which describes precisely this length of the Boulevard as the former "main square for the true life of the people of Paris… [where] quacks, somnambulists, rope-dancers, etc., compete with lots of larger and smaller theaters, whose audiences as a rule found entertainment in such blood-curdling pieces that the street was called the boulevard du crime." Our picture, however, conveys none of this. In the left foreground is merely a gentleman in a frock coat, a tiny figure, apparently having his shoes polished – and even contemporaries suspected that Daguerre had hired two people to play the parts by maintaining a pose for the still lengthy exposure time of several minutes. As Jean-Pierre Montier once put it, their shadows were "impregnated" onto the plate. Whatever the case, this picture remains the first photographic image of a human being, or rather, two of them – if one omits the recently discovered portrait of a certain "M. Huet," dated 1837, also attributed to Daguerre.

Curious onlookers are unwelcome

A view out the window. A view from above down into a world that now existed to be photographically explored, investigated, exploited, and recorded. Niépce had already gazed out of the window of his estate in Le Gras. Talbot, the inventor of the negative-positive process and Daguerre's true competitor in the struggle for the copyright to photography, had already bequeathed us even more than a view from a window: perhaps the most famous of his works is his calotype of the Boulevard des Capucines. As so often in the early stages of photography, the photographers here, too, consciously turned to a theme that had already been formulated by traditional panel and canvas painting. In the early days of photography, when a photographer aimed a camera out of a window – whether from his house (Niépce), his room (Daguerre), or even a hotel (Talbot) – he had a completely pragmatic reason, beyond that of iconographic reverence for the traditions of painting. These early researchers feared too much publicity and sought to exclude a curious audience from taking note of their endeavors. This was one reason they searched out a photographic 'hiding place'. Furthermore, their work was easier if they could conduct it close to the home laboratory; more precisely, the lab was what

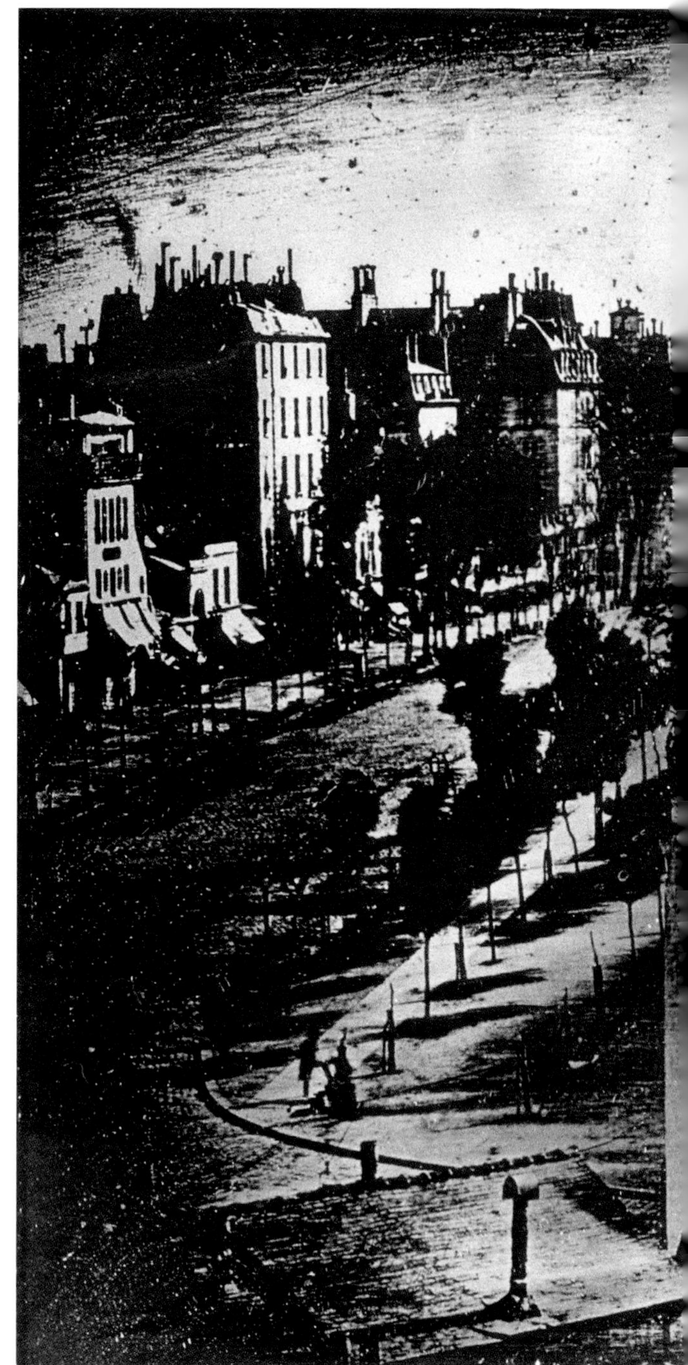

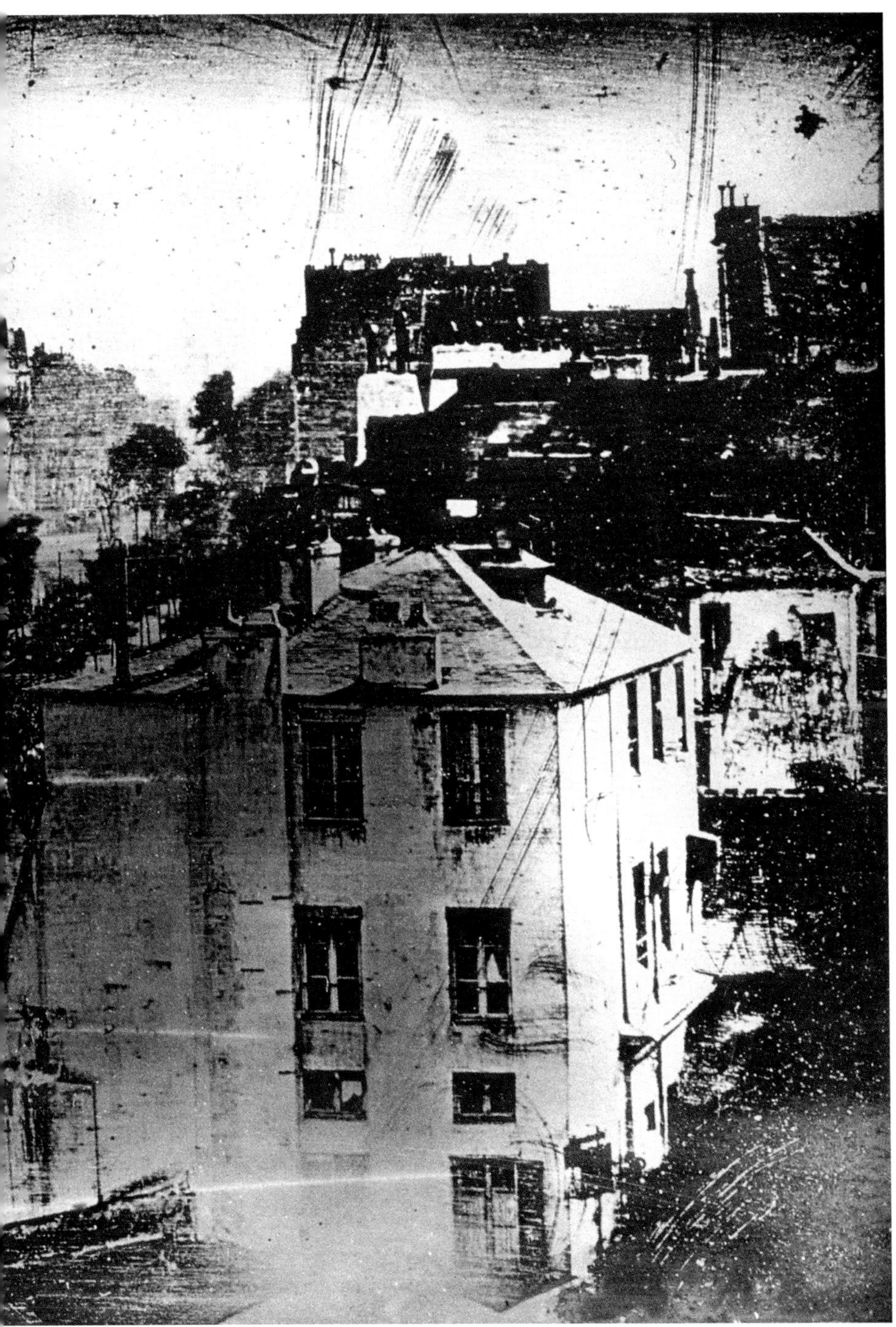

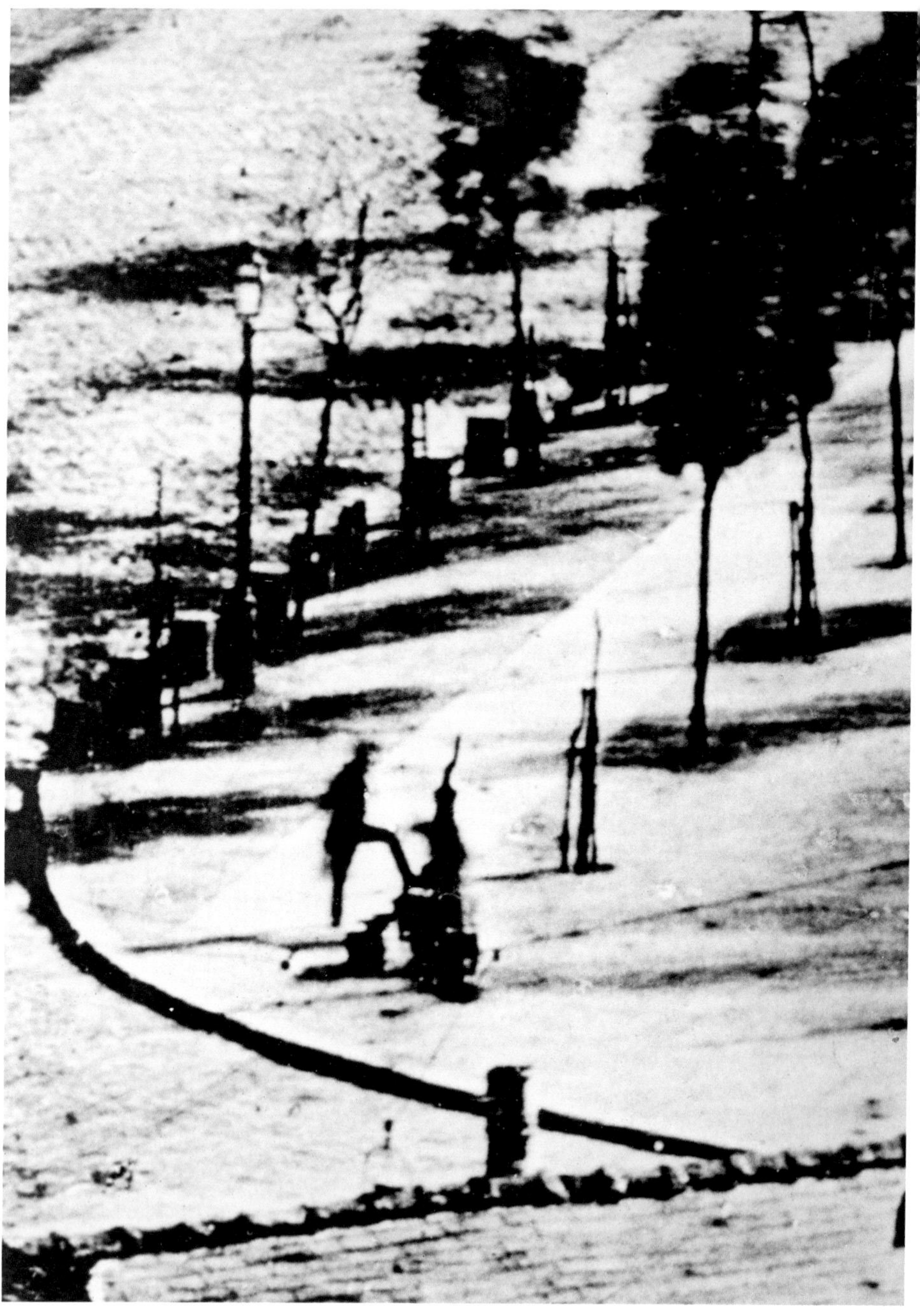

made early photography possible in the first place. The French science minister François Arago estimated that the preparatory work for a single daguerreotype amounted to 30–45 minutes – and Daguerre wanted always to make three exposures in a row for the sake of underlining the usefulness of his process, so to speak: one taken in the morning, one at noontime, and one in the afternoon.

We find ourselves at 5 rue des Marais. We can be fairly certain that it was from the window of his private apartment that Daguerre made his three exposures, of which only two have survived, albeit in heavily damaged condition. Anyone looking for the house today is on a fool's errand, for the rue des Marais, like so many tranquil – or, phrased negatively, dim – corners of old Paris fell victim to the colossal urban renovations of Baron Haussmann. But we can imagine the house to be approximately where the Boulevard de Magenta runs into the Place de la République, that is, in the 10th arrondissement. In Daguerre's day, Paris housed around 800,000 inhabitants. The city limits in the west were defined by the Champ de Mars, in the east by the Père Lachaise cemetery, in the south by the Montparnasse cemetery, and in the north by today's Pigalle. This is the Paris of Balzac and Hugo, Ingres, Delacroix, and Dumas *fils* – the Paris in which Rodin would be born in 1840, Sarah Bernhardt in 1844. All this makes the city sound like the world art capital – which the city certainly was in the nineteenth century. But Paris was something else as well, namely narrow, dark, close, dirty, and in this age before sewers, filled with what was then called a miasma. As the writer Maxime Du Camp pertinently remarked, "Paris as it existed on the eve of the Revolution of 1848 had become unlivable."

A pictorial diversion for the broad masses

In the spring of 1838, Daguerre tuned the lens of his camera obscura, which had been built by the Paris opticians Charles and Vincent Chevalier, down onto the Boulevard du Temple. He was not at all interested in a nostalgic look at 'Old Paris' threatened with (possible) extinction; that is a theme that such photographers as Atget would explore decades later. Instead, Daguerre, wholly in the role of a technician and inventor, sought within the panorama of his city a picture that would be at once as rich in detail, as sharp and effective, and as large as possible (in spite of the very small aperture) – and that at the same time that could function as a metaphor of the cradle of the invention. And in fact it was the many tiny objects in the picture that captivated the first viewers of the photograph. Among these was no less a figure than the American painter and inventor Samuel F. B. Morse, who looked up Daguerre in Paris in March 1839 "to see these admirable results." Morse expressed himself charmed "by the exquisite minuteness of the delineation" but noted at the same time: "Objects moving are not impressed. The Boulevard, so constantly filled with a moving throng of pedestrians and carriages was perfectly solitary, except an individual who was having his boots brushed."

The Parisian inventor, born Louis Jacques Mandé Daguerre in 1787, already had several careers behind him as a scenic artistic, stage and costume designer, and the creator and director of a diorama, before he developed an interest in the possibility of permanently

---

Enlarged detail from Boulevard du Temple. *The image of the shoeshine is regarded as the first successful depiction of a person (or rather: two people) in photography.*

Page 19: *Triptych with three daguerreotypes for King Ludwig I of Bavaria.*

capturing the fleeting images produced by the camera obscura. Daguerre was what we might today call a media person – someone who recognized the need of his times for pictures and sought to commercialize this need in as many ways as possible. Whereas the diorama offered an almost archaic form of the cinema – a pictorial diversion for the broad public, a spectacle produced by means of illusionistic painting united with skilled lighting effects – the new medium of photography, which still remained to be invented, sought a process of picture-making that would correspond to the positivist age: a process at once fast and exact, economical and objective. Daguerre, who had worked together with Nicéphore Niépce, had realized the light sensitivity of silver iodide already in 1831, a discovery which in turn led him to an improvement in the process that bears his name. A popular anecdote claims that in 1835 it was merely by chance that Daguerre discovered the so-called latent image, which meant that the exposure time could be reduced to a sensational 20 to 30 minutes – thus raising Daguerre's hopes for the genre of picture that was of greatest interest to him, namely the portrait.

The delicacy of the contours, the purity of the forms

The daguerreotype, however fascinating, has always been termed a dead end of photography – an accusation that refers primarily to the production of a single, irreproducible plate, in contrast to the real aim of an economical mass medium. The daguerreotype has in fact neither predecessors nor successors. All of this may be true, but nevertheless overlooks the importance of daguerreotypy as the first truly practical photographic process, which in some countries – such as the USA – remained viable until into the 1860s. From the technical point of view, the daguerreotype is a direct positive image in a (then) maximum full-plate format of 21.5 × 16.5 cm (8½ × 6½ inches). To produce a picture, a silvered copper plate was sensitized with iodine vapor, exposed in the camera obscura, developed in mercury steam, and finally fixed in a solution of salt or sodium thiosulfate. The result was a reflective and one-of-a-kind image, whose finely chiseled lines, even down to tiny details and shadings of tone, produced a picture of the world that addressed the scientific interests of the time.

Daguerre's discovery placed him on the horns of a dilemma. His process was still far from mature, especially because portraits, which at this point continued to require an exposure time of ten minutes in sunlight, remained more or less out of the question. On the other hand, the inventor was involved in an international race, and he felt intense pressure to go public with his process. Therefore, in the autumn of 1838, Daguerre appealed to leading scientists for help in interesting the government in his invention. He found his chief supporter in François Arago, the secretary of the Academy of Sciences. It would also be Arago who convinced the French Parlement to buy the rights of the process and to make it internationally available. On 19 August 1839, the two official bodies held their memorable meeting in which the technical details of daguerreotypy were presented. The age of photography had begun.

The initial reports concerning the announced discovery appeared early in 1839, and the photographs of the Boulevard du Temple became the focus of amazement among contemporary scholars and journalists. The *Pfennig Magazin*, for example, announced in 1839 that in one of the pictures, a man could be seen "having his boots polished," and continued, "He must have held himself extremely still, for he can be very clearly seen, in contrast to the shoeshine man, whose ceaseless movement causes him to appear completely blurred and imprecise."

What intrigued John Robinson, the secretary of the Royal Society of Arts, were the differences between the three plates caused by the changes in light. In addition, "delicacy of the outlines, the purity of the forms, and the precision and harmony of the tones, the aerial perspective, the thoroughness of even the smallest details" also earned praise (Eduard Kolloff, 1839). Daguerre's invention was clearly greeted as a sensation. Soon 'daguerreotypomania' spread throughout France and the rest of Europe.

Excitement among artists and art-lovers

We do not know precisely what moved Daguerre late in 1839 to send a sample of his 'artworks' to the ruling houses of Russia, Prussia, and Austria. Gernsheim (1983) speculates about an initiative of the French foreign minister; in any case, the list of selected monarchs included the Bavarian King Ludwig I, who received – along with a dedication by Daguerre – what were even then already the world's most famous photographs, namely two of the three views of the Boulevard du Temple and, in the middle of the framed triptych, a still life which has not survived, along with an inscription by Daguerre. "Midi" (noon), wrote the photographer in his own hand under the picture on the left. "Huit heures du matin" (eight o'clock in the morning) is legible below the photograph with the shoeshine man – information that later formed the basis of the attempt to determine the exact date of the picture. Using contemporary maps and diagrams, and taking into account the length of the shadows and the camera position 15.70 meters (51½ feet) above the street, Peter von Waldhausen has been able to date the view of the boulevard to the period between 24 April and 4 May 1838. The identity of the shoeshine man and his customer, however, remain matters for speculation.

In October 1839, the three daguerreotypes arrived in Munich, where they were on display at the Arts Association after 20 October. They immediately caused excitement, particularly among "artists and art-lovers." According to commentary in the *Allgemeine Zeitung*, the pictures were absolutely free of error and "by demonstrating all the advantages and wonder of the invention, they teach us also about its relation to art." After the exhibition closed, the daguerreotypes returned to the private royal household, and after the regent's death became part of the collection at the National Museum of Bavaria. The pictures, however, received no special attention, at times being included in the permanent exhibition. As a part of this collection, they were evacuated for storage during the Second World War, and were heavily damaged. In any case, by the time the plates were turned over by the National Museum to the Munich Photography Museum as a permanent loan, they were suffering so severely from oxidation that the still life in the center – a picture contradictorily described by contemporaries – was totally beyond recognition. An inexpert attempt at cleaning Daguerre's two remaining plates in the 1970s succeeded only in erasing their content. Thus, one hundred forty years after their creation, nothing more of the Boulevard du Temple was to be seen. The photo-historian Beaumont Newhall, however, had earlier made reproductions of the plates for an exhibition at the New York Museum of Modern Art entitled *Photography 1839–1937*. Based on these plates, Peter Dost of Nuremberg and Bernd Renard of Kiel were able to produce facsimiles. Our *Boulevard du Temple* as seen on these pages is thus no more than a technical (i.e., screened) translation of the original daguerreotype based on one of the modern reproductions of the original plate. As cynical as it may sound as far as the cultural loss is concerned, photography as a technical pictorial medium nonetheless won the day.

Hippolyte Bayard
Self-Portrait as a Drowned Man
1840

A Temporary Demise

Around 1830, scientists and artists alike were fascinated by the dream of finding a means of permanently preserving the fleeting image produced by the camera obscura. One of the pioneers in the effort was the Frenchman Hippolyte Bayard, who not only succeeded in producing photographic images, but who was also one of the most versatile photographers of the early nineteenth century.

In the center of the picture is a man, not particularly young but not yet marked by life, probably in his mid-thirties. His torso is naked to the navel. Hardly of athletic build, he appears rather to be someone who spends his time at a desk – but his browned hands and equally tanned face tell us that he also must spend long hours outdoors in the sun. A long, heavy, large-patterned piece of cloth serves both as a comfortable underlay for his head and back, and drapes his loins, thighs and knees to cover the lower part of his body. The nameless man appears to be lost in thought, his hands resting on his lap. Is he asleep? Is he dead? The theme and design of the picture seem at first to provide an answer: this early photograph unmistakably reflects Christian iconography, which typically presents the Deposition of Christ in a similar manner. Even the traditional shroud, or burial cloth, is present and plays an important role in the composition, in this case by emphasizing the powerful diagonal running from the lower left to the upper right. This line is contrapuntally picked up by the wide-brimmed straw hat on the wall as well as by a shadowy, barely recognizable vase in the lower right of the picture.

A great deal of honor, but not a single penny

The paper print with an original format of approximately 19.2 × 18.8 cm (7½ × 4½ inches) bears an inscription on the reverse – an extensive quill-and-ink commentary that seems to

---

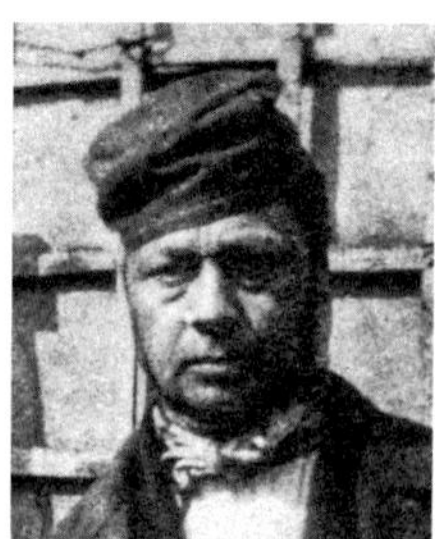

Hippolyte Bayard
*Born **1801** in Breteuil-sur-Noye, France, the son of a justice of the peace. Tax official in Paris. Early **1839** first photographic experiments: daguerreotypes, calotypes, later also wet-plate collodion and albumin exposures. **1840** publication of his own photographic methods. **1851** becomes a founder member of the Société héliographique and **1854** of the Société française de photographie. The latter also came to be entrusted with his estate of 900 exposures. Dies **1887** in Nemours.*

Le cadavre du Monsieur que vous voyez ci-derrière est celui de M. Bayard, Inventeur du procédé dont vous venez de voir, ou dont vous allez voir les merveilleux résultats. À ma connaissance il y a à peu près trois ans que cet ingénieux et infatigable chercheur s'occupait de perfectionner son invention.

L'Académie, le Roi et tous ceux qui ont vu ses dessins, qu'il lui trouvait imparfaits, les ont admirés comme vous les admirez en ce moment. Cela lui a fait beaucoup d'honneur et ne lui a pas valu un liard. Le Gouvernement, qui avait beaucoup trop donné à M. Daguerre a dit ne pouvoir rien faire pour M. Bayard et le malheureux s'est noyé. Oh! Instabilité des choses humaines! Les artistes, les savans, les journaux se sont occupés de lui pendant longtemps et aujourd'hui qu'il y a plusieurs jours qu'il est exposé à la Morgue, personne ne l'a encore reconnu, ni reclamé. Messieurs et Dames passons à d'autres, de crainte que votre odorat ne soit affecté, car la figure du Monsieur et ses mains commencent à pourrir, comme vous pouvez le remarquer.

HB

18 Octobre 1840.

address the questions raised by the picture itself: "The body of the man you see in the picture on the other side," reads the French text, "is that of Mr. Bayard, inventor of the process whose glorious results you have just seen or are about to see. To the best of my knowledge, this talented and untiring scientist has been working for about three years on perfecting his invention. The academy, the King, and all those who have seen this picture, were full of admiration, just as you yourselves are, although [the artist] found the picture unsatisfactory. It has brought him a great deal of honor, but not a single penny. The government, which has granted so much to M. Daguerre, claimed it was unable to do anything for M. Bayard. As a result, the unfortunate man drowned himself. Oh, human fickleness! Artists, scientists, and newspapers have taken an interest in him for a long time, but today, after he'd been lying in the morgue a few days, no one recognized him or claimed his mortal remains. Ladies and gentlemen, let us now move on to other matters for fear that your olfactory organs will be affected, for as you have noticed, the face and hands of the gentleman have already begun to decay." The lines are dated 18 October 1840.

Peter Weiermair has designated the picture, taken a good year after the announcement of the daguerreotype process (August 1839), as the first male nude in photography. It is wise to exercise restraint in using superlatives in the history of photography, above all in the area of erotic photography, for precisely here we may be certain that there are many pictures that have remained unpublished. What we can say about the present picture, however, is that it represents an early photographic falsification: it is a fake, so to speak, made with the conscious intention of misleading the observer, the person reading the picture and text. In short, at the time the photograph was taken, the protagonist was anything but dead. Spurred by resentment, worry, or fury at the lack of recognition for his pioneering role in the development of photography, Hippolyte Bayard staged himself in the photograph as the victim and tragic hero of a scene of his own creation – and indeed not without a touch of irony, for the accompanying text is signed "H. B."

The history of photography accepted Bayard's self-evaluation at face value and continues to do so today. Thus Jammes terms him an "unrecognized inventor"; Newhall considers him the "most luckless pioneer," and Gernsheim sees him as an "unfortunate inventor" who moreover deserved "greater respect" than he received. In fact, none of the photographic processes bear his name. The life and work of this early photographer have given rise to more speculation than fact, and as far as the invention of photography is concerned, Bayard is rarely mentioned with the trinity comprised of Niépce, Daguerre, and Talbot. And yet Bayard discovered on his own an independent direct-positive process on paper. Furthermore, in contrast to Daguerre, Bayard left behind a multi-faceted œuvre that made use of practically all the early processes (daguerreotypy, calotypy, albumin and collodion prints). Last but not least, he played an important role as a founding member and secretary (1861–80) of the Société française de photographie.

Milieu of painters, writers, and lithographers

The literature on the subject relates that Hippolyte Bayard, born on 20 January 1801 in Breteuil-sur-Noye (Département Oise), had come into contact already as a youth with the 'photo-graphic' phenomena in the literal sense of the words ('light' + 'drawing'). According to legend, his father, who was a proud garden owner, was passionately devoted to cultivating peaches. Before they ripened, he sometimes pasted cutouts of his initials on the fruit, causing these places to remain white. Probably a good deal more important, and of a more lasting impression, was the milieu of painters, writers, and lithographers into which Bayard, a trained notary clerk and later tax assessor, fell after moving to the French capital. By the mid-1830s, 'photography' (the medium had as yet not acquired a universally recognized name) – in particular the experiments of Daguerre – had become the talk of interested Parisian circles, and by early 1839 at the latest, Bayard had begun his own experiments. According to the journal of his experiments, he began work on 1 February

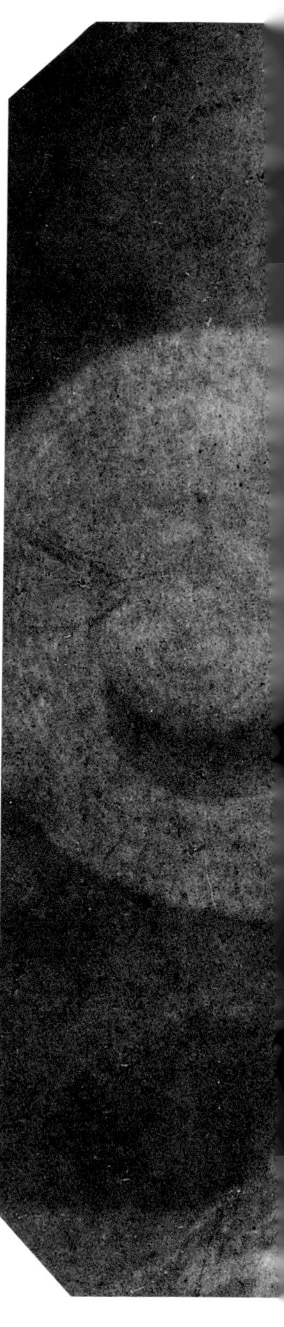

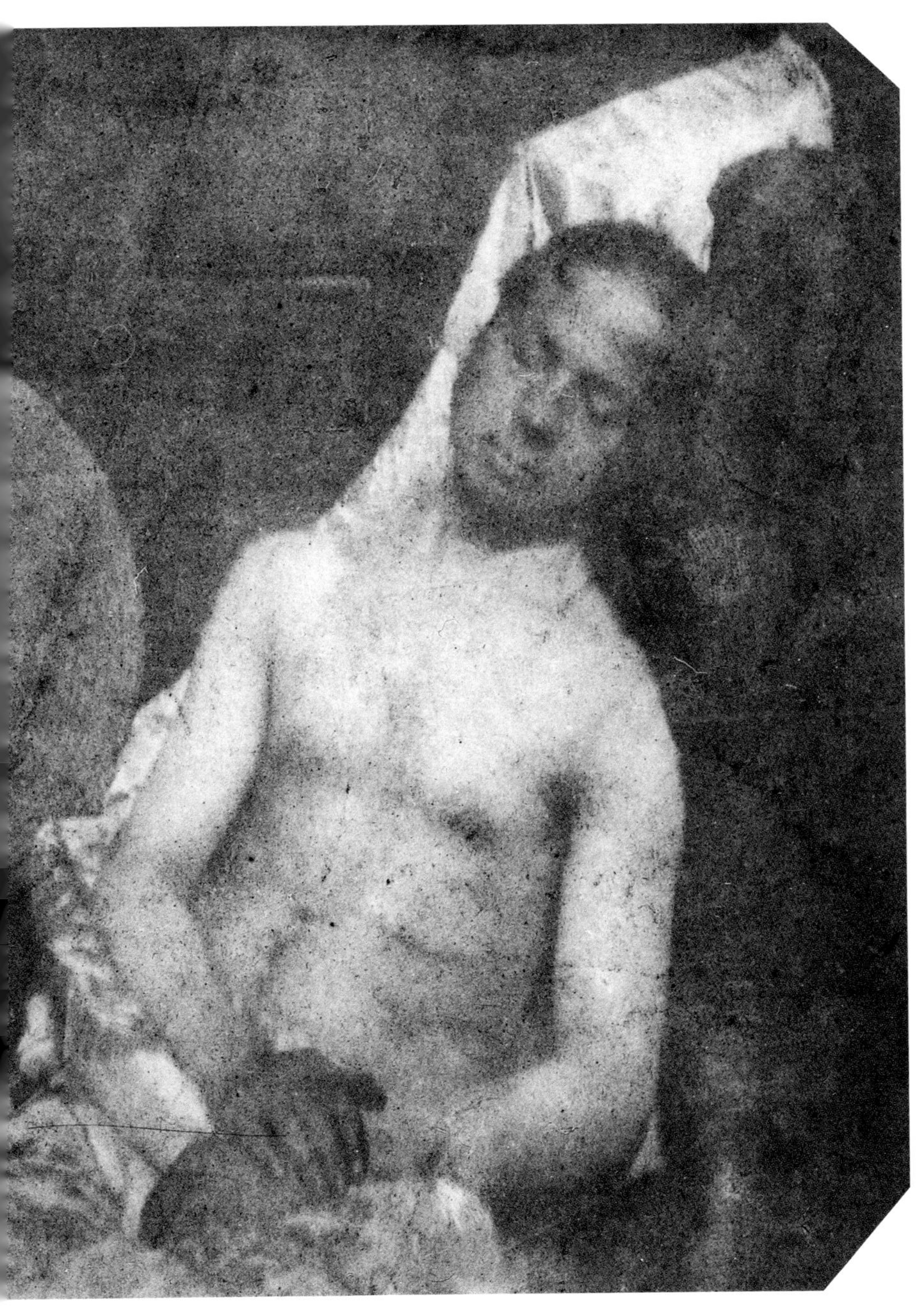

Self-Portrait as a Drowned Man, 1840

1839. "On 20 March," he noted, "obtained direct positive image with the camera obscura." By June, his diary records that he had succeeded in taking photographs of statues using an exposure time of a quarter of an hour, and of a landscape in twenty minutes. Thus, according to his biographer André Jammes, Bayard had mastered "the principles of the technique within forty days."

Bayard's use of factory-made paper as a vehicle for the photosensitive layer shows foresight. Nonetheless, the search for a direct-positive process eventually revealed itself to be a dead end, for the future of the medium resided in the production of a negative that could in theory be reproduced an unlimited number of times. In the direct-positive approach, Bayard's process resembled Daguerre's, although the latter had already won over François Arago, the Secretary of the Academy of Sciences, and convinced the French government to purchase his process in return for a lifetime pension. "Until today," protests Bayard in a declaration addressed to the Academy of Sciences, "I have postponed the publication of the photographic process which I invented because I wanted first to make it as perfect as possible. But because I was not able to prevent some information from leaking out, I believe I dare not postpone the announcement of the process any longer, in order to prevent anyone from disputing my rightful claim to the discovery or possibly profiting from my work." Bayard published these lines on 24 February 1840. By then, the detailed publication of daguerreotype process had already been a matter of history for half a year.

Advantageous on long journeys

Thus, in Hippolyte Bayard, we meet an inventor who arrived too late – who introduced his process after the political die had long been cast in Daguerre's favor. Technically, however, Bayard's procedure was not intrinsically more complicated than Daguerre's. Bayard exposed his blackened silver chloride paper to natural light, dipped it in a potassium iodide solution, and then exposed it in the camera obscura. The treatment caused the paper to bleach out at the appropriate places during the exposure period. Afterwards, he fixed the image in a solution of sodium hyposulfate. Raoul Rochette, secretary of the Academy of Arts, particularly stressed in his evaluation of Bayard's process the importance of the fact that the photography paper could be prepared ahead of time – as it were, manufactured: "How advantageous it might be during the course of a longer or shorter journey always to have at one's disposal a supply of these prepared sheets that are ready for use at any time." Nonetheless, in the end the field was won by the daguerreotype process, whose finely chiseled details unquestionably appealed to the precision-oriented positivistic age. An exhibition in June 1839 containing approximately thirty photographic samples produced by Bayard's method probably mark the high point of Bayard's work as scientist and inventor.

Hippolyte Bayard died a natural death in Nemours on 14 May 1887. Popular histories of photography commonly skip over his name and role in the early, pioneering phase of the medium. To this day, Louis Jacques Mandé Daguerre is celebrated together with the date of his announcement, 19 August 1839. Serious research, however, knows better. "Photography," argues

---

Page 27: *Bayard's pretend farewell letter dated 18 October 1840, facsimile.*

Right: **Hippolyte Bayard:** Self-Portrait in Studio, *after 1850.*

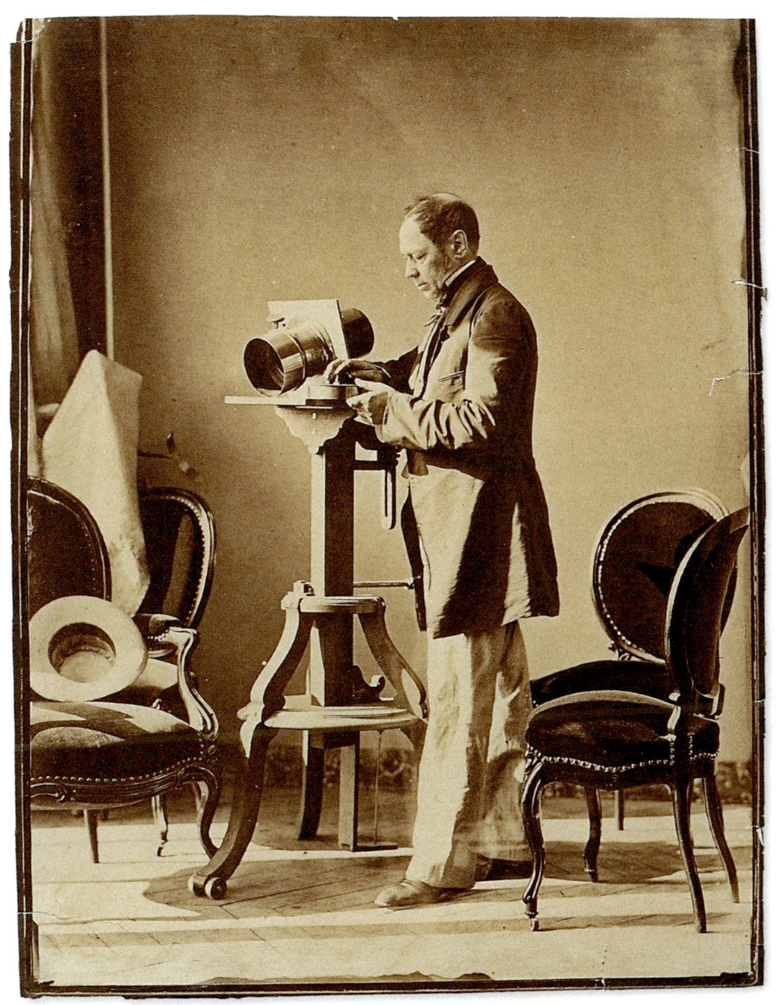

Wolfgang Kemp, "is the outgrowth of a broad spectrum of energies moving along in the same direction in philosophy, art, science, and economy; realism, positivism, and materialism are some of the terms for these epochal tendencies." In other words, photography is a child of numerous fathers, and Hippolyte Bayard is one of them.

Alois Löcherer
Torso of Bavaria
1850

An Allegory in the Making

The casting, transportation and installation of the colossal statue of Bavaria in Munich pushed the bounds of what was technically feasible in the years around 1850. The Munich photographer Alois Löcherer followed the sensational project with his camera. His documentation bears important witness to early event photography in Germany.

True, the picture has somewhat faded. The one hundred and fifty years since it was taken have not passed without leaving their mark. Although not erased completely by bleaching (a nightmarish problem much discussed by pioneer photographers in the period around 1850), the image has clearly suffered a loss of contrast – something that does nothing, however, to lessen the visual appeal of this pictorial invention from the era of the calotype. On the contrary, the 'gray veil' over the motif only seems to sharpen our attention and lends the picture an additional charm that underlines the bizarre – or as it is occasionally described, surreal – element of the composition.

Fourteen people, all of them male, are discernible in the picture. They are gathered around what can be made out as the torso section of a colossal, still unfinished statue of a woman. Some are sitting, some standing in relaxed poses. Others are miming strenuous effort, while making sure that the camera can still see their face. Others again are ascending like mountaineers towards the start of the enormous sculpture's neck. Another, lastly, has even used a ladder to climb up to the large, headless woman's left breast, which is clad in a bearskin. Erotic connotations are present and probably played a role – whether overtly or not – in the composition of the photograph. The director of the scene and his fellow 'actors' may well have been inspired, moreover, by Jonathan Swift's *Gulliver's Travels*, published in 1726 and widely read in

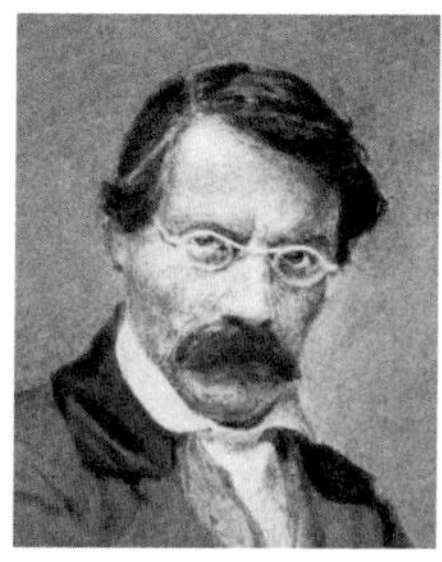

Alois Löcherer

Born in Munich in ***1815****, the son of weighhouse official Ludwig Löcherer.* ***1837–39*** *studies chemistry and pharmacy.* ***1840*** *introduced to the daguerreotype process by an itinerant photographer.* ***1844*** *first calotypes.* ***1848*** *gives up his job as a pharmacist to devote himself to photography. Opens a studio.* ***1849*** *first exhibition in the Munich Kunstverein.* ***1850*** *photos of the colossal statue* Bavaria *created by Ludwig Schwanthaler.* ***1852*** *first appearance as a photographer in the Munich trade directory. Trip to Paris. Also in* ***1852****, first photographs using the wet-collodium process.* ***1854*** *takes part in the first General Exhibition of German Industry in Munich's Glaspalast. Dies* ***1862*** *in Munich.*

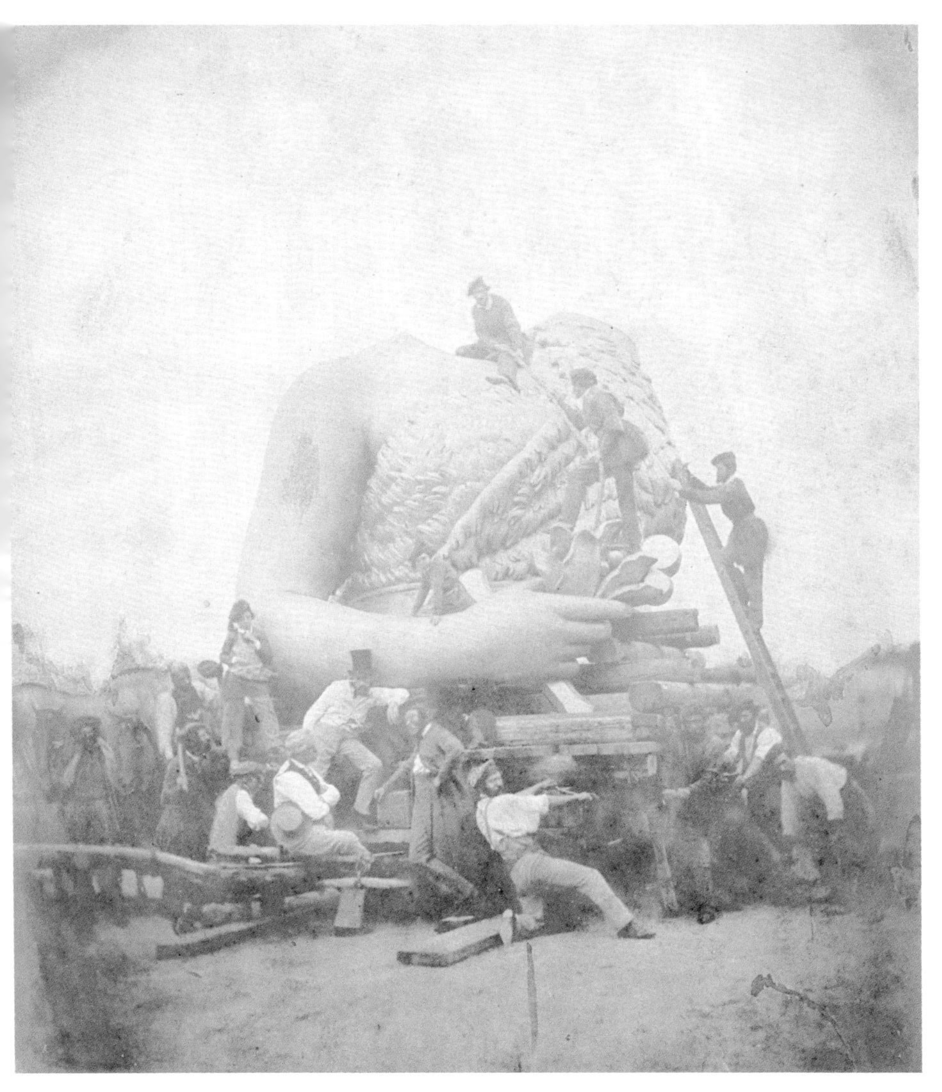

Torso of Bavaria, 1850

German-speaking circles. We might recall the passage in Chapter 6, where Gulliver describes how no fewer than three hundred tailors were employed to make him a new suit of clothes. "I kneeled down," Swift's hero relates, "and they raised a ladder from the ground to my neck; upon this ladder one of them mounted, and let fall a plumb-line from my collar to the floor."

Age of contradictions

Literary references such as these cannot be ruled out. First and foremost, however, the image was intended as a visual document of a feat of design and engineering whose scale, sensational for its epoch, could only be visualized through the inclusion of concrete points of comparison. And who or what could be more appropriate for this – in an ironic refraction, so to speak, of professional group portraits – than those who were directly involved in the *Bavaria*'s planning, casting, and installation? Namely the artists, engineers, and workers, of whom at least three have been identified to date. Standing in the center in his frock coat and peakless cap is Ferdinand von Miller, who took charge of the casting of the figure following the death of Johann Baptist Stiglmaier. Seated to his left is Franz Xaver Schwanthaler, responsible for the organization of the project and a nephew of Ludwig von Schwanthaler, court artist to Ludwig I, who provided the original design for *Bavaria*. The man behind him in the top hat is the painter Joseph Petzl. Nor should we overlook the two boys on the statue's forearm, said to be von Miller's two sons, Ferdinand and Fritz. The picture was taken by the Munich photographer and calotypist Alois Löcherer. The location can be assumed to be the courtyard of the Royal Metal Foundry, which at that time lay outside Munich's city limits, near Nymphenburger Strasse. Precisely when the picture was taken remains unknown. What is certain is that the torso was cast in 1845 and the transportation of the six finished sections of the statue from the foundry to the Theresienwiese began on 20 May 1850. The picture must therefore have been taken somewhere between these two dates, most likely towards the end of the 1840s.

Löcherer's photograph takes us back to the reign of King Ludwig I of Bavaria, an epoch characterized by the striking antagonism between scientific and industrial progress on the one hand, and on the other an enthusiastic return to classical antiquity, in whose Greco-Roman style the art-loving Ludwig saw an ideal model for the present. The statue of *Bavaria*, plans for which were first formalized in 1837, unifies precisely these two opposites: technical innovation and artistic revival, progress and retrospection. What represented a superlative, internationally acclaimed masterpiece of technical design and engineering remained derivative and second-rate from an artistic point of view and is noteworthy today solely for its political implications. The commission for an ensemble comprising a hall of fame and a *Bavaria* statue was originally awarded to Leo von Klenze, and it was he who lent the allegory of the Bavarian nation clearly Hellenistic traits. The design of the statue was ultimately entrusted to the young Ludwig von Schwanthaler, however, who instead of recreating the *Athene Promachos* proposed by Klenze gave his figure an unmistakably Germanic appearance – including such Teutonic attributes as an oak wreath and a bearskin. Schwanthalter thereby took up the idea of a Bavaria occupying an elevated position within a larger Germany, a notion that would only became a reality one generation later. The statue stood almost 16 meters (over 52 feet) high. When it was unveiled on 9 October 1850, it was the largest monumental figure since antiquity (the New York *Statue of Liberty* was inaugurated only in 1886). Almost fifteen years separated the earliest designs for the *Bavaria* and its final installation. During this period, both Schwanthaler and Stiglmaier – in

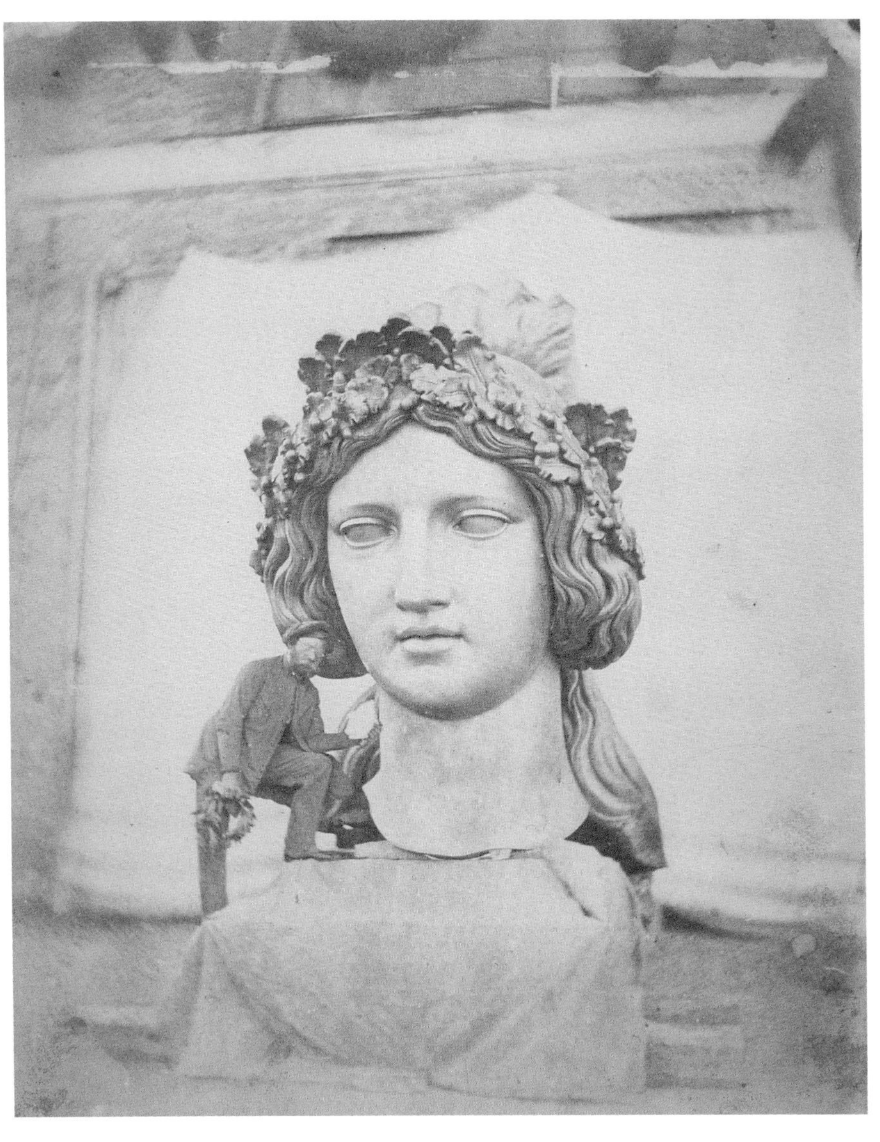

Alois Löcherer: *Head of* Bavaria *in the courtyard of the Royal Metal Foundry. On the left is Ferdinand von Miller with the death mask of Ludwig von Schwanthaler, 1850.*

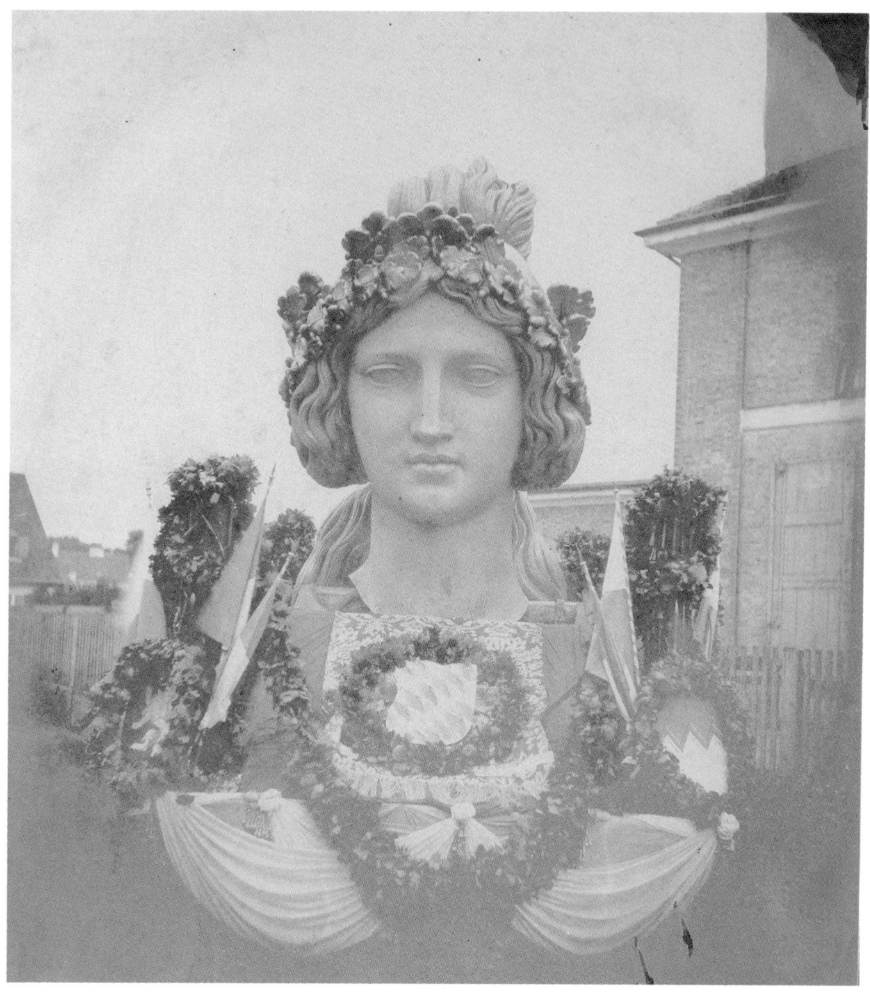

charge of the casting – died. Nor did Ludwig I see the completion of the statue, at least not in his capacity as king: in 1848 he was forced to abdicate by an outraged public following his scandalous affair with the dancer Lola Montez. "Nero and I," he had boasted a few years earlier with regard to "his" *Bavaria*, "are the only ones to have produced something so enormous; no one has managed it since Nero."

An example of early event photography

The *Torso of Bavaria* is not the only photograph that Alois Löcherer took of the statue. Five motifs and their variations have come down to us, including views of the head seen frontally

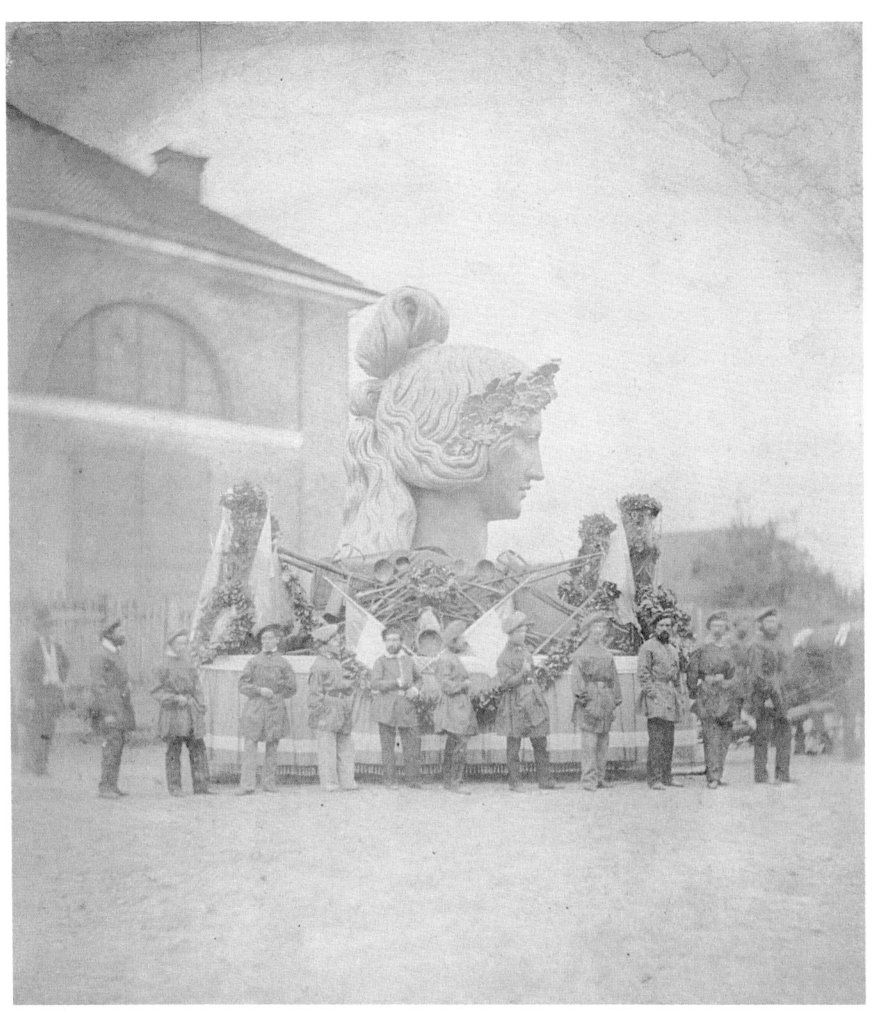

Left: **Alois Löcherer:** Bavaria *was completed by Ferdinand von Miller and represents the most ambitious bronze cast since antiquity. The head of the colossal statue was festively decorated for its journey to Munich's Theresienhöhe. 7 August 1850.*

Above: **Alois Löcherer:** *Art reproduction, event coverage and industrial photography: Löcherer's pictures embraced three of the new medium's spheres at once. Here the transportation of the head of* Bavaria *from the Royal Metal Foundry to the Theresienhöhe. 7 August 1850.*

and in profile, and shots of the head, festively decorated, on the carriage on which it was to be moved. This last picture is thereby the only one in the series that can be dated with certainty, namely to 7 August 1850, the day on which the last section of the statue was transported to the Theresienwiese. "The installation of the *Bavaria*," noted the Munich *Neueste Nachrichten* newspaper on this occasion, "the colossal bronze statue through which King Ludwig has further embellished the Bavarian capital and royal residence, will be completed this week. If the weather is fine, the final piece – the head, weighing some 200 hundredweight – will be moved this Wednesday the 7th, ceremonially escorted by the workforce concerned, to its destination – the Hall of Fame at the top of the Theresienwiese." Before it left the foundry, Löcherer took a photograph of the carriage adorned with flags, wreaths, and tools; posing in front of it are the foundry workers, from whom the photographer must have requested a few moments of frozen attention.

This is undoubtedly the very early photographic record of an event. Something that has regularly prompted later commentators to view the series in terms of photojournalism. Thus the photography historian Erich Stenger, in his book *Siegeszug der Photographie* (1939/50), treats the *Bavaria* series in a chapter devoted to press photography, visual reporting, and documentary photography. Taking their cue from Stenger, Helmut Gernsheim (1955/83) and Heinz Gebhardt (1978) speak in their respective publications of the earliest or "one of the earliest" reportages in the history of the medium. Quite apart, however, from the fact that photographs could only be reproduced via wood engravings in the years around 1850 (the autotype process of halftone printing was invented only around 1900), the *Bavaria* pictures were never used to illustrate contemporary accounts in the press. Löcherer, it is now suspected, did not create the series in the spirit of modern photojournalism, in other words with the intention of publishing it, but as a private commission for von Miller. The only known reproduction of the *Bavaria* dating from the 19th century remains a cabinet card bearing the head of the colossal figure, issued around 1890 by the publisher F. Finsterlin. This is not counting an exhibition in the Munich Kunstverein, a society for the promotion of the fine arts that provided Löcherer with a regular exhibition platform between 1849 and 1854. Five images from the *Bavaria* series went on show at the Kunstverein from 15 August 1850: three photographs of the face seen frontally and in profile, the carriage used to transport the festively decorated head, and our torso shot (or a variant of it). We know about the presentation thanks to an article in the *Neueste Nachrichten*, which mentions amongst other things the "magnificent photographs by Löcherer," which merited "heightened interest as true commemorative prints" both in terms of "the sequence of the subject of their representation" and in the "happy results" thereby obtained. In other words the choice of motif and the quality of the pictures were enough to astound the contemporary public and without question helped to cement Löcherer's position as the leading photographer in what was then the Kingdom of Bavaria. He is today considered a "key figure" in the early history of photography; indeed, he is celebrated as "the most important German calotypist." This is regardless of the fact that, of the 24,000 Löcherer photographs mentioned in the press of his day, only some five hundred have, as yet, come to light. His daguerreotypes are lost, and his nude photos – *académie*s that were discussed in contemporary journals in France – have also yet to be found. The question of whether the series of five motifs described here represents Löcherer's complete documentation of the *Bavaria* must, for the moment at least, remain unanswered.

Alois Löcherer was twenty-four years old when, in August 1839, the invention of the daguerreotype was announced in Paris and details of the process were released. He had previously studied chemistry and pharmaceutics in Munich and had already worked for a few years as a pharmacist's assistant. It seems, however, that he was fascinated by photography from an early stage and in particular by the calotype patented by its British inventor, William Fox Talbot. A calotype is a salted-paper print from a waxed or unwaxed paper negative. As a photographic process, it was clearly more modern than the daguerreotype: for the first time, it brought within the bounds of practical possibility the concept of an image that could in principle be reproduced as many times as desired. But the calotype had disadvantages: prints were a lusterless brownish color and the fibers of the paper negative left them with a coarse grain. They also lacked the fine detailing achieved by the daguerreotype, which also held the advantage of being more widely known. In addition, the calotype was patented: it was necessary to purchase a license to use Talbot's process, which – being still fairly unrefined – promised success only to those budding photographers with an adequate knowledge of chemistry. This Alois Löcherer possessed. He also had sufficient foresight to abandon the daguerreotype and devote himself, both from a technical and aesthetic point of view, to the negative–positive process.

He appears to have submitted "photographs on paper" to the Polytechnic Society of the Kingdom of Bavaria for the first time in 1847, where none less than Carl August von Steinheil noted their "substantial advances over Talbot's pictures." The following year Löcherer resigned from his position with the pharmacist Ludwig Widnmann and set himself up as a freelance specialist in "portraits from life or from paintings," as he announced in an advertisement placed in the *Neueste Nachrichten* in June 1849.

Portraits indeed seem to have formed the chief focus of his activity and reflected the demand for pictures amongst members of the bourgeoisie, for whom a photographic portrait was first and foremost a means of affirming their identity. Löcherer's clientele also included the Duchess Elisabeth of Bavaria (later Empress Sisi), the painters Wilhelm von Kaulbach and Anselm Feuerbach, the scientist Justus von Liebig and the author and composer Count Franz Pocci – eminent individuals whose names are still familiar to us today. Löcherer also photographed views of Munich, however, including a remarkable interpretation of the Siegestor (Victory Gate).

Löcherer also broke new ground with his idea of a photographic pantheon of well-known contemporaries. He did the same with his *Bavaria* series, which as a "genre picture of art in the age of technology" (Rudolf Herz) remains unique, at least in the Germany of the mid-1800s. Interest in the photographic documentation of technological progress only seems to have increased following the advent of the wet collodion process, whose crisp, large-format prints held much greater commercial potential. Around 1854 Franz Hanfstaengl – Löcherer's 'pupil' and later competitor – made several wet collodion photographs of the Munich Glaspalast (Glass Palace) under construction. In 1854 he photographed the front façade of Munich's main railway station and in 1857 the Grosshesseloher Bridge under construction. That same year Löcherer published the essay "The Production of Negative Collodion Photographs on Glass," one of many such practical articles that he wrote during his career. From an artistic point of view, however, he produced nothing more of note in this new process. Löcherer died in August 1862. His death went largely unremarked by the general public.

Eugène Durieu/Eugène Delacroix
Nude from Behind
ca. 1853

Charm and Quiet Modesty

Paris, June 1854: working together, the painter Eugène Delacroix and the amateur photographer Eugène Durieu completed a series of nude photographs. The nearly three dozen studies that have survived constitute one of the artistic high points of early nude photography.

We know neither her name nor her age. In all probability, she is a professional model. She averts her face in a movement that may be partially interpreted as calculated caution, as a conscious attempt at anonymity. Nonetheless, there are three other variations in the series in which the narrow, serious, young face is visible. The turning away from the camera is therefore part of a carefully thought-out scene. The combination of revealing and concealing, charm and quiet modesty, lasciviousness and humility, eroticism and innocence succeed in achieving a rare balance. Even a hundred and fifty years after the photograph was made, the image seems amazingly modern: simple in concept, superb in lighting, radical in its rejection of ornamentation or typical contemporary accessories. Only a self-confident photographer, sure of his style and obeisant only to his own taste, could have created an image of such timeless validity in the middle of the nineteenth century. Eugène Durieu, so the story still goes, handled the camera, while the painter Eugène Delacroix directed the scene. This constellation would go a long way in explaining the excellence of the result. But the real ground for the photograph's success may lie elsewhere.

Eugène Delacroix: the quintessential Romantic and antithesis to Ingres; the painter once described by Baudelaire as a volcano whose crater was artfully hidden by a bouquet – a remark that elegantly highlights the unparalleled productivity of this great nonconformist to French art of the nineteenth century. When Ferdinand-Victor-Eugène Delacroix died at

---

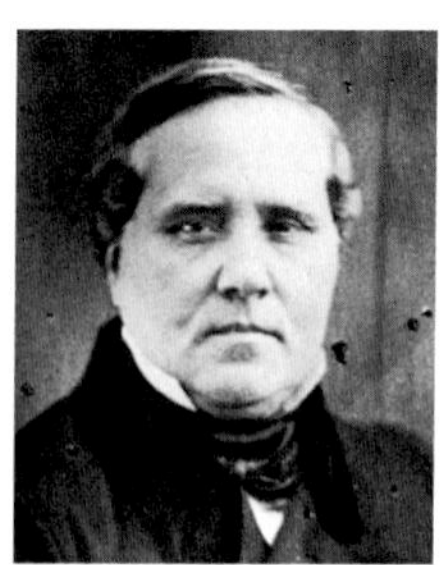

Jean Louis Marie Eugène Durieu
*Born **1800** in Nîmes, France. Lawyer in government service. Around **1845** astrophotography in collaboration with Baron Gros. From **1848** first calotypes. **1851** founder member of the Société héliographique. **1854** founder member of the Société française de photographie (S.F.P). **1855–58** chairman of the S.F.P. **1856** represented with his works at the World Exposition in Brussels. Dies in Paris in **1874**. His works are now in the Bibliothèque Nationale, Paris, the collection of the S.F.P., and the George Eastman House, Rochester.*

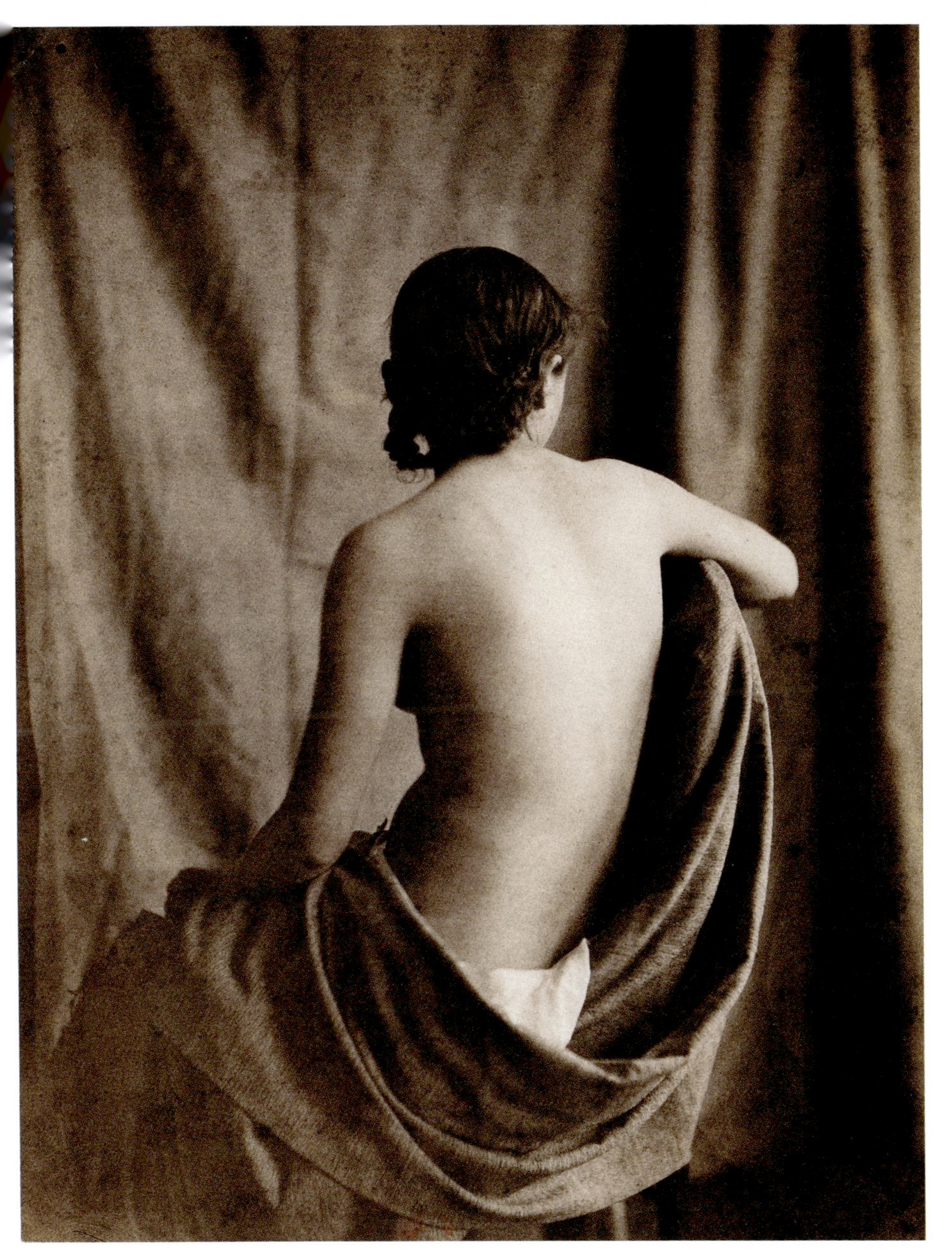

Nude from Behind, ca. 1853

age sixty-five in his studio on the Place de Furstenberg on 13 August 1863, he left behind 853 paintings, 6,629 drawings, 24 etchings, 109 lithographs, and 1,525 watercolors, ink drawings and pastels. In addition, his estate included more than 60 sketch books, an impressive number of writings important for art history, and one express wish: in no case, decreed the artist, should a death mask, drawing, or photograph be made of his face: "I expressly forbid it." The last testament comes as a surprise. For one thing, it was entirely customary to photograph the deceased in the nineteenth century. In addition, during his lifetime Delacroix had done everything he could to foster his own image and guarantee himself lasting fame. As far as his own photographic portrait was concerned, by 1842 – only a few years after the announcement of the photographic process – Delacroix had himself daguerreotyped several times by Léon Riesener, only to claim later that, "If we take a closer look at daguerreotype portraits, we must admit that among a hundred, not one is tolerable."

Delacroix's attitude toward the new pictorial medium was markedly ambivalent. The painter was thoroughly appreciative of photography as a handmaiden to the artist that provided a fast and comfortable process for capturing an image. Photography had, as Jean Sagne emphasizes, "enriched [Delacroix's] vision and strengthened his mode of working." But the artist was reticent in approving photography as an independent artistic form of expression. In his essay On the Art of Drawing, he admits, "daguerreotypy is certainly a good purveyor of the secrets of nature," but, he continues, when it comes to bringing us closer to certain truths, a photograph is nonetheless not an independent work. For Delacroix, photography was an ancillary medium, a visual lexicon – but its productions could never be more than a cold and artificial imitation of reality.

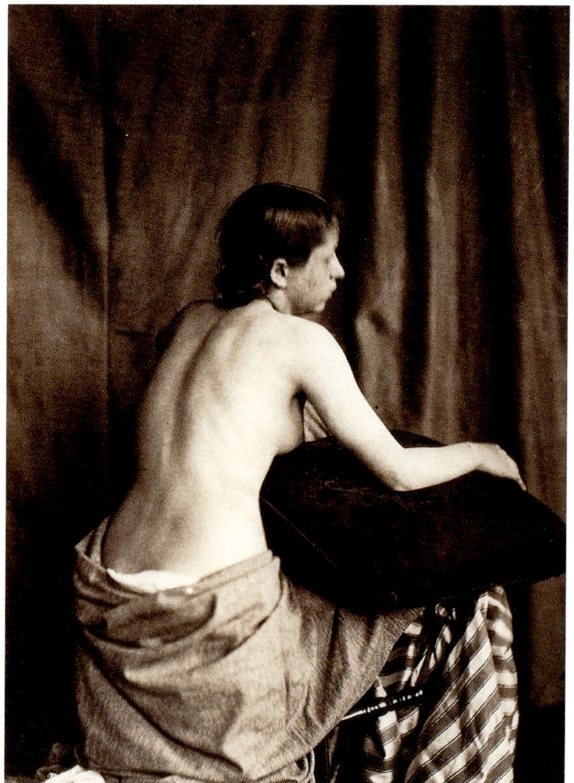

Drawn and painted from photographs

Did Delacroix himself take photographs? In all probability, he did not; at any rate, there are no photographs from his own hand. Furthermore, the estate auction held in 1864 contained no technical equipment that would point to photographic experiments of any kind. Delacroix was too busy as a painter; why would he have additionally involved himself in the still very complicated and time-consuming pictorial medium of photography, especially when he maintained friendly contact to well-known photographers such as Riesener and Durieu, who regularly provided him with photographs, including, often enough, nude studies? Delacroix used these photographs to sketch from and to train his hand at drawing. He clearly carried nude photographs along to the popular bathing resort Dieppe in 1854, for example – and into the Church of Notre Dame as well, where it is said he had drawn from nude photographs during the Mass. In short, Delacroix maintained a sober and pragmatic approach to the medium. He did not join the public polemic against photography, begun in 1862 when Ingres, together with such prominent artists as Flandrin, Fleury, and Puvis de Chavannes, declared war on the new medium. To the contrary, in 1851 Delacroix became the sole painter to become a founding member of the Société héliographique. A slap in the face to Ingres and his supporters? Perhaps. "Which of them," Delacroix is reputed to have asked, "would be capable of such perfection of line and such delicacy of modeling? But no one may speak about this aloud."

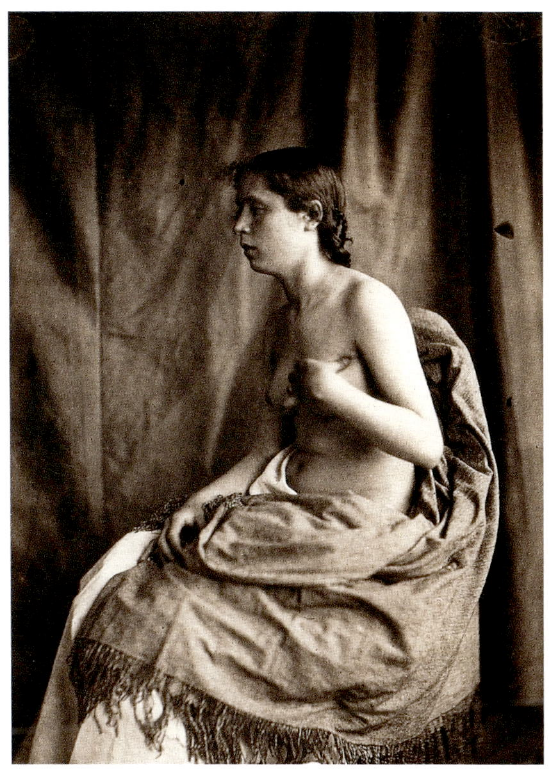

How Delacroix reacted to the sensational news of Daguerre's process in August 1839 is not known. His diary is silent on the years between 1824 and 1849; but we may well assume that the artist paid close attention to the emergence of this new, quasi automatic pictorial medium. After 1850, numerous, if scattered, entries in his journal indicate an alert, engaged, and at times amazed interest in photography, such as for 13 August 1850: "Read in Brussels that someone in Cambridge set up an experiment to photograph the sun, moon, and even the stars. They

---

Left: **Eugène Durieu/Eugène Delacroix:** *Plate XXXII from the from the Uwe Scheid Collection, albumin print, ca. 1853.*

Above: *This female nude is also attributed to Eugène Durieu. Albumin print, ca. 1855, from the Uwe Scheid Collection.*

obtained prints of the constellations Alpha and Lyra [with stars] the size of pinheads. The report also includes a true but curious insight: if one assumes that the light of the daguerreotyped stars has taken around twenty years to reach us, then it follows that the beam that engraved itself into the plate had left the heavens long before Daguerre made his discovery."

Delacroix's short-term interest in the cliché-verre process that he learned from Constant Dutilleux remained merely a passing episode. Delacroix was an avid collector of photographs, but he used them only for purposes of study. (That he had his portrait taken a number of times in the 1850s by photographers such as Pierre Petit or Nadar is noted only for the sake of completeness.) As far as Delacroix's relation to photography was concerned, what was most important was his collaboration with his friend Jean Louis Marie Eugène Durieu (1800–74), an administrative official and – beginning in 1848 at the latest – an enthusiastic amateur photographer with a studio in Paris located at 10 rue des Beaux-Arts. On 18 and 25 June 1854, Durieu and Delacroix scheduled an appointment with male and female models at the studio to take a series of nude photographs. "Eight o'clock at Durieu's," Delacroix noted in his journal. "Had them pose the whole day. Thévelin sketched, while Durieu took photographs, one or one-and-a-half minutes per picture."

The results of this early collaboration have survived in the form of an album of thirty-two photographs that the art critic Philippe Burty, whom Delacroix appointed administrator of his estate, bought from the estate auction. The note on the half-title stems from Burty's hand: "I bought the following series of photographs at the posthumous sale of the studio of Eugène Delacroix. He often used the pictures as models. And the folders held a considerable number of pencil drawings based on precisely these photographs." Today, in the Musée du Louvre, Paris, or in the museums in Besançon and Bayonne, for example, one can find entire series of small-format pencil drawings from these photographs. Delacroix also took inspiration for his oil paintings from the album. Apparently Plate XXIX served as the model for the small odalisque today in the Niarchos Collection in London. Delacroix had begun to conceive the painting already in October 1854: "Painted a little on the odalisque from the photograph," he wrote in his journal, "but without much energy."

At Philippe Burty's death, the album passed into the hands of Maurice Tourneux, who in turn bequeathed the outwardly unassuming notebook to the National Library in Paris in 1899. There it was duly entered as Gift No. 9343 in the collection of the Cabinet des Estampes. On a number of occasions since the 1970s, portions of the series – in particular our nude from the rear – have been reproduced and exhibited. Jean-Luc Daval used the image on the cover of his work, *La photographie, histoire d'un art* (*Photography: The History of an Art*), Paris. Beyond this, the picture has appeared in almost every exhibition of the nude in photography. The complete sequence was first shown at the exhibition *L'art du nu* in 1997 at the Bibliothèque nationale de France, after the album had been disassembled by art experts. It is probably not too much to claim that the series today presents the best-known contribution to the theme of the nude in early photography – although it is likely that Delacroix's name has contributed significantly to the reception of the photographs. But what part did the painter really play in the series?

Let's take a closer look at the sequence of thirty-two photographs in various formats. The smallest is 10 × 11.5 cm (4 × 4½ inches); the largest 19.5 × 13.5 cm (7¾ × 5¼ inches). Plates I through XXIX were processed as calotypes, that is, as waxed and unwaxed salted paper prints made from paper negatives.

Plates XXX to XXXII, however, are albumin prints produced from wet-collodion negatives, a process which explains their clearly improved sharpness and brilliance of half-tones. There are eighteen male and five female nudes, with the combination of a male and a female models occurring nine times. In the first twenty-nine plates, the poses do not at all seem to be a matter of chance: we may assume they were taken at the direction of the painter to suit his concrete needs. Jean Sagne has compared the photographs with other works of Durieu, such those in an album now residing in the George Eastman House in Rochester, New York: "The props in the form of rocks or draperies constitute a well thought-out form of setting a scene. The Bibliothèque nationale has no prints which compare with these. Dutilleux insists quite properly on the substantial influence of Delacroix, who may well have posed the bodies and determined the lighting. Durieu's role was certainly that of an operator, his actual contribution, that of a clever technician."

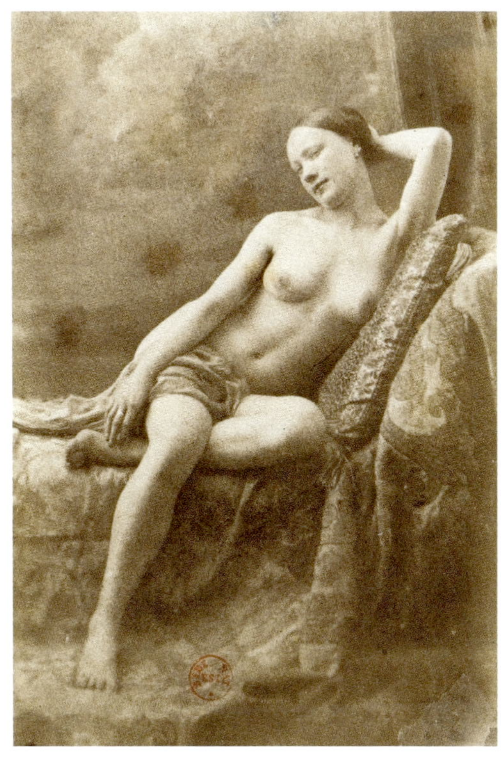

Rest zones for the eye

Beyond this, Sagne speaks of the thirty-two photographs as a series that is generally homogenous – a position contradicted by Sylvie Aubenas in a recent study. The curator of the Bibliothèque nationale argues that in terms of their technical production alone, the first twenty-nine photographs distinguish themselves from the last three. What is remarkable in this connection is that Durieu remained true to calotypy until far into the 1850s. There are also clear indications that Delacroix also preferred the glaze of the salted paper to the brilliance of the wet-plate process. Quite decidedly he adopted a position against the detailed richness of daguerreotype and glass negatives in favor of "an ineffableness, a rest zone for the eye, that prevents it from concentrating too much on individual details." What also must be not overlooked is that Plates XXX to XXXII are clearly carefully formulated, consummate images of decisively classical composition. In contrast, Plates I to XXIX are clearly 'academy photographs', that is,

Plate XXIX from the total of 32 motifs in the series. Calotype, ca. 1853.

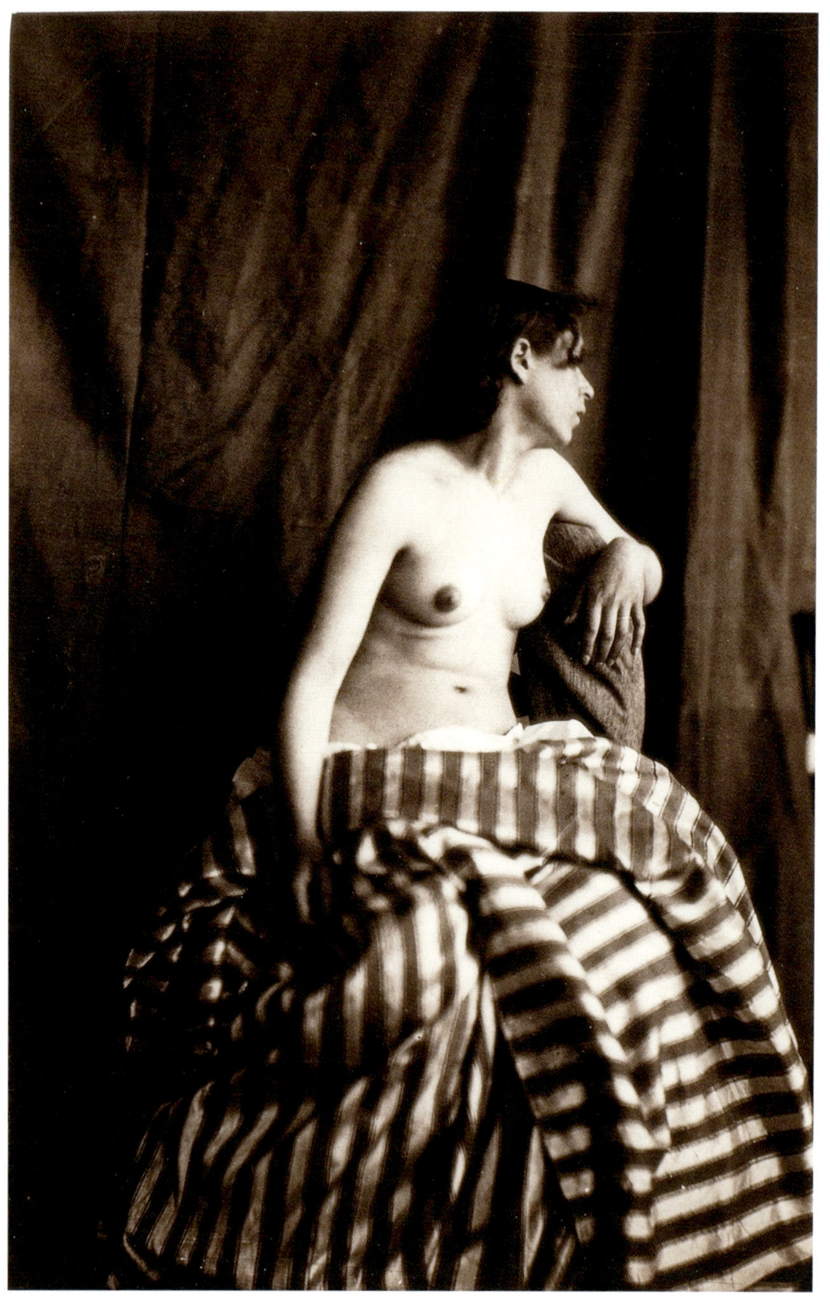

Eugène Durieu/Eugène Delacroix

studies of the human body produced for artists. In addition, the pictures possess a clearly experimental character, play with various degrees of focus, indistinct contours, and movement. Interestingly, after the last three nude photographs, whose composition is more reminiscent of an Ingres or David, Delacroix stopped drawing. In contrast, the pencil sketches based on the majority of the salted paper motifs have survived. And something else is puzzling: Durieu, the amateur, never tried to sell his photographs. Examples of his work are extremely rare, and those resulting from his collaboration with Delacroix are known only from our album – with the exception of precisely the last three, which are in the collections of the Getty Museum (Plate XXX), or of Uwe Scheid (Plates XXXI, XXXII, and variation), or of Robert Lebeck (Plates XXX and XXXI). Is it therefore possible that our rear nude is by a third, heretofore unknown, photographer? But who could have been the photographer of such a picture? The album has been only recently restored. In the process, photographs were removed from their backgrounds, but contain no stamp or signature. That contemporary nude photographers such as Moulin, Belloc, or Vallou de Villeneuve could have produced them is out of the question: their creations are too enamored of decoration and trimmings. Closest in style to the nude are the photographs of a nude from the rear by Paul Berthier (1865) or Nadar's portrait study of the actress Marie Laurent (1856), a picture which Sophie Rochard once described as a "miracle of charm."

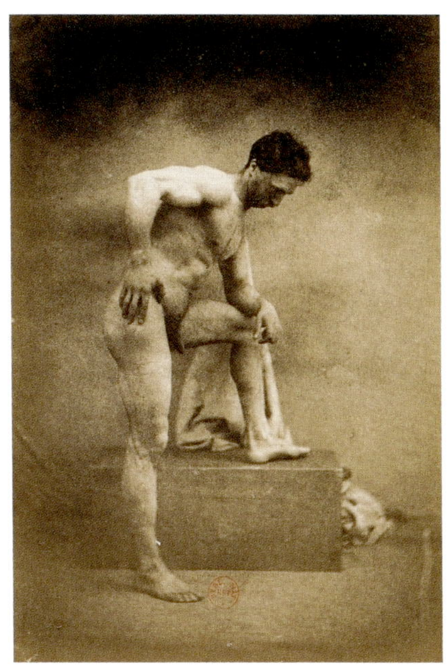

But we are nonetheless brought back to Durieu by a child nude ascribed to him, which was auctioned at Beaussant Lefèvre in Paris in 1993. The simplicity of the picture, the reduction of accessories to a piece of cloth, the interplay between concealing and revealing all resemble our rear nude rather closely. But even more decisively, it is clear that the albumin print of 19.6 × 11.7 (7¾ × 4½ inches), today in the Manfred Heiting Collection (Amsterdam/Houston), was taken before the same neutral curtain and with the same lighting. Moreover, the folds of the background are of such astonishing similarity that one must conclude that the picture was created not only in the same ambient as our motif: if one assumes that a soft, movable curtain can hardly hold its shape for a longer period of time, the nude must have been made close to the same time as the albumin print. But the reverse of the child nude bears neither date nor signature. In the face of many questions, one point is certain: whoever the creator of our nude from the rear may be, he succeeded in creating a true "miracle of charm."

Left: **Eugène Durieu/Eugène Delacroix:** *Plate XXXI from the Uwe Scheid Collection, albumin print, ca. 1853.*

Above: **Eugène Durieu:** *Male nude with crate: Plate XXII of the Delacroix album, Bibliothèque nationale, Paris, calotype, ca. 1853.*

Duchenne de Boulogne
Contractions musculaires
1856

A Grammar of Feeling

The French medical doctor Guillaume Duchenne de Boulogne may not have been the first to seek and discover applications for the new pictorial medium in the realm of medicine. But, unlike his predecessors, he had a conceptual grasp of the medium and moreover sought to establish a bridge to the fine arts.

Why is he looking at us? Why must he peer into the camera like that? Wouldn't Dr. Duchenne de Boulogne, on the right of the picture, not have been better advised to concentrate on the subject of his experiment? To take care that the two electrodes maintain their contact, and thus produce the desired effect. It is of course possible that an operator in the foreground is giving him directions, but that would be possible also without eye contact, especially since this is not the first photograph that has been produced on the basis of pre-formulated guidelines. Nonetheless, this is the sole exemplar from the almost one hundred photographs in which Dr. Duchenne is wearing this unique cap that hides his 'high forehead'. "Look at me," his face seems to say, with a trace of vanity. "Here I am: Dr. Guillaume-Benjamin-Armand Duchenne, known as Duchenne de Boulogne, medical doctor, scientist, member of the Société de médecine in Paris, specialist in the field of electrophysiology, and at this moment conducting precisely the experiment with which I hope to change both the history of medicine and of photography."

In 1856, the year in which the photograph was supposedly taken, the technical processes of photography had already been in use for around a decade and a half. The age of the daguerreotype and the calotype was drawing to an end. With his wet-collodion process, the Englishman Frederick Scott Archer had given the photographic world not only a more sharply defined process based on glass negatives, but also a technology which was twenty times more sensitive to light than the earlier processes. Instantaneous photographs now became at

---

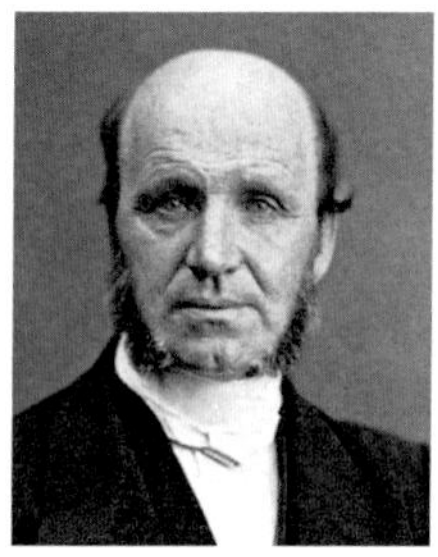

Duchenne de Boulogne
Born Guillaume-Benjamin-Armand Duchenne at Boulogne-sur-Mer, France, in ***1806****. From* ***1826*** *studies medicine in Paris.* ***1831*** *doctorate and return to Boulogne. From* ***1842*** *back in Paris.* ***1847*** *embarks on his scientific researches in the field of electrotherapy.* ***1851*** *member of the Société de médecine in Paris.* ***1857*** *and* ***1864*** *applies unsuccessfully for the Prix Volta.* ***1862*** *publication of his (photographically illustrated) work* The Mechanism of Human Physiognomy. ***1871*** *correspondence with Darwin. Numerous photographs by Duchenne are included by Darwin in his* The Expression of the Emotions in Man and Animals *(****1872****). Dies* ***1875*** *in Paris.*

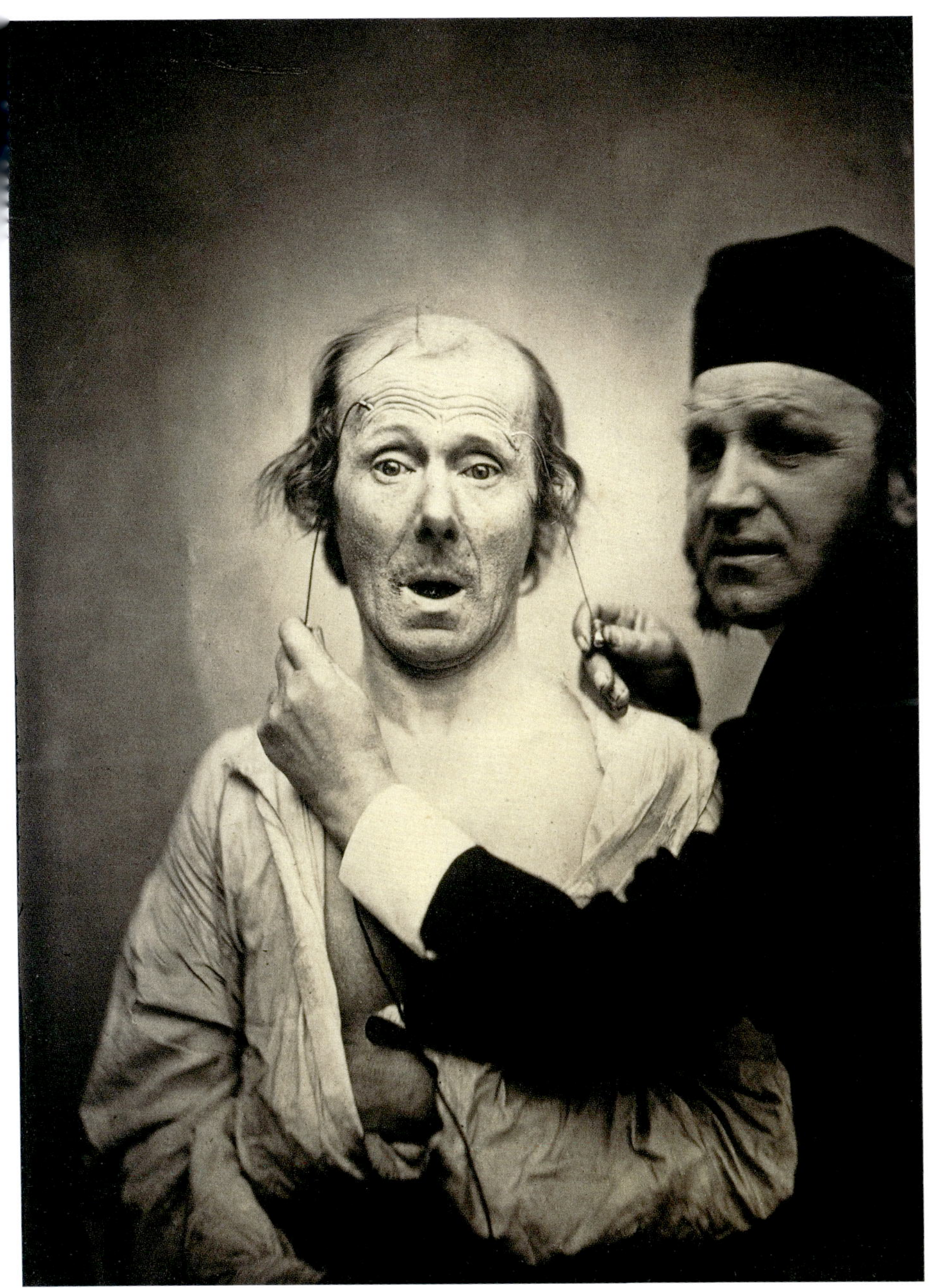

Contractions musculaires, 1856

least theoretically possible. Photography was being applied to more and more fields. The positivist notion of inventorying the world by means of the purely 'objective' medium of photography seemed to have taken a bold and irrevocable step forward. Photography appeared to be useful in all possible areas of life – becoming the medium of seduction in nude photography, of memory in the portrait, of inventories in ethnic studies, of reflection in death portraits, and of identification in criminal photography, to mention just a few of the ways in which photography was being applied specifically to the human body. It was bound to be only a matter of time before the medical sciences also would take up the medium. And in fact, Duchenne de Boulogne, born in 1806, was not the first to place photography at the service of medical research. In 1844 Léon Foucault had succeeded in making daguerreotypes of human blood corpuscles. But this early exploratory attempt – moreover by means of a process whose results consisted of one-of-a-kind, saucer-sized reflecting plates – was hardly suitable for conveying the desired knowledge in a comprehensible manner. Moreover, doctors were divided over the use of photography as a pictorial medium. For a long period, many medical experts held that the traditional kind of illustration that had been in use since the Renaissance was preferable to photography because it allowed the presentation of finer distinctions and hierarchies. From this standpoint, Duchenne de Boulogne, although not the first medically trained photographer, was nonetheless the first modern doctor to use photography scientifically, in that he worked conceptually; in other words, he arranged his subjects with a view toward the medium. De Boulogne thought beyond the successful individual picture in terms of the larger connections. He thus reflected the communicative function of photography, and last but not least, he understood and accepted the medium on its own terms, including the principles of cropping, perspective, and light. In fact, his well-composed scenes and subtly illuminated pictures provide far more than merely an early visualization of certain bodily phenomena for purposes of study. Not only do his physiognomies *au repos* pass for excellent portraits, but also his experimental pictures evoke nothing less than amazement, even today, 150 years later. One cannot help but wonder what was really going on here.

Duchenne de Boulogne began his experiments, which were rooted in a combination of anatomy, physiology, psychology, and art, in the early 1850s. The way had already been pointed out by the writings of Lavater, whose *Essai sur la physiognomie* (1781–1803) – a much respected work in its age, and praised by Goethe – described the art of reading character from facial features. In the realm of art, character typologies had existed since the seventeenth and eighteenth centuries, and were a part of the standard program in academic instruction, as is evident from painters such as Charles Le Brun and Henry Testelin. The technical basis of de Boulogne's work lay in the discoveries of Luigi Galvani, who was the first to prove the existence of electrical currents in muscles, and also in the work of Michael Faraday, whose discoveries in the area of electromagnetic induction (1831) proved directly beneficial to Boulogne's experiments. It is highly unlikely, however, that Duchenne de Boulogne would have been familiar with the anatomical studies and drawings of Leonardo da Vinci residing in the library of Windsor Castle (these would become available to the broader public only later, through the carefully prepared edition by Théodore Sabachnikoff, *I manoscritti di Leonardo da Vinci della Reale Biblioteca di Windsor,* 1898).

A slight anesthesia in the region of the head

Joy and fear, wonder and disappointment, horror and amusement – these constitute fundamental human states of being that communicate themselves in a universally understandable manner through facial expressions. The impulses behind these expressions are provoked by certain muscles. If one stimulates these muscles systematically, one after the other, then one should be able to produce a kind of grammar of the feelings, an atlas of the emotions – thus Duchenne's hypothesis.

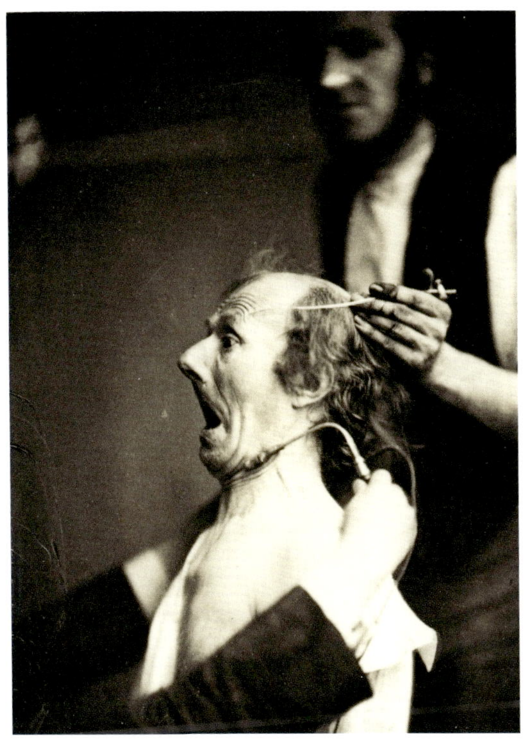

Beginning in 1852, five volunteers stood available to the doctor as guinea pigs: two women, one younger, one older; a young anatomy student named Jules Talrich (who was also able to mime feelings without induction current); an alcoholic worker; and, as the central figure in the series of experiments, a former shoemaker, whom Duchenne himself described as "old and ugly." The man was furthermore intellectually handicapped and suffered under a slight 'anesthesia', or lack of feeling, of the head, a condition which presumably helped to make the application of electric current painless. According to Duchenne, he selected the man as a subject because the age wrinkles in his face responded well to the effects of the current, and thus provided especially clear delineation of facial expressions. The man's gauntness additionally increased the clarity of the facial creases and made the precise points for the placement of the electrodes easier.

Between two and four electrodes were used to stimulate the muscles, the source of the electric current being a generator (today in the Parisian Musée d'histoire de la médecine), which we may imagine to be located to the lower left, just outside the frame of the photograph. Duchenne's experiments, which are looked at askance by experts, are one thing; their photographic documentation, however, is another issue. Might Duchenne have been inspired to his efforts by the experiments of his colleague H. W. Diamond, who daguerreotyped mentally ill patients in British asylums? Probably not. What is certain, is that beginning in 1852 Duchenne sought the advice of respected photographers in Paris, possibly including Gustave Le Gray, Alphonse Poitevin, and even Louis Pierson.He certainly had contact with Nadar's younger brother, Adrien Tournachon.

Tournachon had studied medicine for a while and might therefore have already been acquainted with the doctor. We may suppose that the young man introduced Duchenne to the technology of photography; but what is certain is that the younger Tournachon photographed some of the motifs – otherwise why would the stamp 'Nadar Jne' appear on eleven prints in the Archives nationales? Beyond this, Duchenne claimed sole authorship for most of the photographs; "I myself," he wrote in the second edition of his *Mécanisme*, "have produced the majority of the seventy-two pictorial examples in the scientific portion of the work, or was at least present [as they were made]." Proof of the claim exists also in the clearly visible (also evident in our photograph) black fingernails, revealing the unattractive, but unavoidable, evidence of the professional photographer in the age of the wet-collodion process. Duchenne described the method of exposure: "The light was so placed that the creases stimulated by the electric impulse would be defined as clearly as possible… An assistant sensitized the plate with wet collodion. Before placing it in the camera, the photographer, with the help of the assistant, attempted to find a pose that would illustrate the subject in sharp detail, without disturbing the already sharp focus of the subject… At an agreed sign the assistant opened and closed the lens. Finally, the experimenter himself did the developing."

We have no information about where our motif was taken. In other photographs, Duchenne's private apartment at 33 boulevard des Italiens, where it is known that the doctor maintained a *laboratoire*, is recognizable. In the case of our picture, a completely neutral background provides an atmosphere at once concentrated and anonymous. The lighting indicates the direct influence of Nadar, whereas the posture of the subject, whose left hand disappears into his simple white shirt, could be read as a reference to the Second Empire, for Louis Napoleon, the nephew of Napoleon I, had dissolved the National Assembly and had taken over the government in 1851 in the course of a coup. That the ambitious emperor was particularly interested in supporting the sciences and industry is well known, and the revival of the Prix Volta for pioneering practical research in electrophysics was a result of his initiative. Duchenne de Boulogne applied for the attractive prize with its award of 50,000 francs with his works on "human physiognomy" in both 1857 and 1864, but without success.

Duchenne's investigations and his photographs – including our motif, which represented the emotion 'surprise' – appeared in a work published in 1862 under the title *Mécanisme de la physiognomie humaine ou analyse électro-physiologique de l'expression des passions applicable à la pratique des arts plastiques*; that is, they were presented in a book whose visual and educational material was primarily directed toward artists in the fine arts. But Duchenne's pasted-in albumin prints chiefly depicting a debilitated old man apparently interested the creative sector that the doctor had in mind just as little as they impressed his colleagues in the field of medicine. The book remained almost wholly without a public, a circumstance that no less a figure than Charles Darwin remarked upon in the introduction to his *The Expression of the Emotions in Man and Animals* in 1872 when he noted that Duchenne's work had either not been taken seriously by his fellow countrymen, or had been completely ignored. In fact, the first French translation of Darwin's study created a certain level of attention for Duchenne de Boulogne. In 1875, one year after the publication of the French title, the doctor died in Paris. In the context of a questionnaire à la Proust, Duchenne de Boulogne was once asked what he most liked to do. His answer: "To research." His photographically illustrated *Mécanisme de la physiognomie*, which straddles a bizarre line between science and art, is without a doubt the most original contribution to its field.

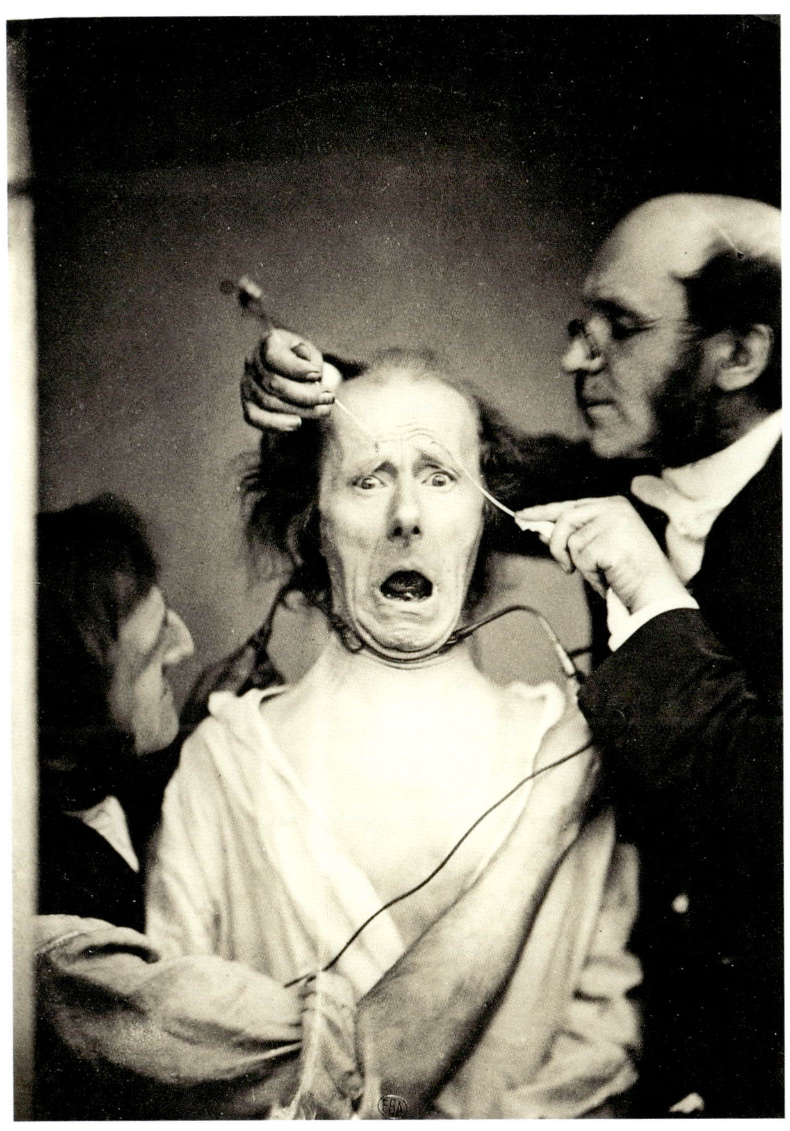

Page 51: **Duchenne de Boulogne:** Effroi, sujet vu de profil (Fright, subject viewed in profile), *Plate 42 from Duchenne's* Album personnel, *1855–56.*

Above: **Duchenne de Boulogne:** Effroi, mêlé de douleur, torture (Fright, pain, agony), *Plate 45 from Duchenne's* Album personnel, *1855–56.*

Robert Howlett
Isambard Kingdom Brunel
1857

Moloch on the Thames

The *Great Eastern* was one of the largest steamships of the nineteenth century – a dream-turned-steel of overcoming the elements. The builder of the ship, which originally bore the name *Leviathan*, was the imaginative and resourceful engineer Isambard Kingdom Brunel, whose portrait is part of one of the earliest industrial photographic reports.

Let's not deceive ourselves: the top hat is still an integral element in the wardrobe of a British gentleman – and the same is true for the half-length frock coat, vest, and bow tie above the collar that, unlike today, would never be left open. One might almost speak of 'full dress' in the sense of the combination of matched and co-ordinated elements, if it were not for the emphatically relaxed posture of the figure – or the wrinkles in the vest, caused by the upper button, instead of the prescribed lower one, having been left open; or the hands stuffed into the remarkably high trouser pockets; or, above all else, the unmistakably filthy shoes and trouser legs. And this is not even to mention the cigar jauntily tilting out of the right corner of his mouth, which lends our protagonist a rakish air – although one must remember that the gesture of smoking together with the aura it created was considered, from George Bryan Brummel to Oscar Wilde, as the *arbiter elegantiarum*, and thus signified the complete opposite of lassitude and nonchalance. But in the role of the 'rake' or 'dandy', insofar as these terms implied a sense of self-admiring vanity, was probably not how the man here pictured, Isambard Kingdom Brunel, would have seen himself. Not that he wasn't both vain and full of self-regard; however, this master builder, architect, and engineer did not define himself by his persona, but rather by the industrial 'monuments' that he had created. With these amazing productions of the capitalist age, the bourgeois world of the nineteenth century sought to link itself almost

---

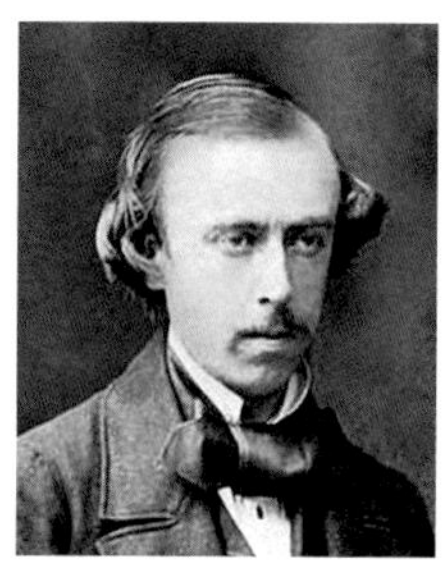

Robert Howlett
Born ***1831****. Makes his name in London during the* ***1850s*** *as a successful commercial photographer. Partner in the firm Cundall and Downs. Distinguishes himself by his portraits of Crimean War veterans, for instance, and interior views of Buckingham Palace.* ***1857–58*** *pictures of the launching of the* Great Eastern. *Portrait of its builder, Isambard Kingdom Brunel. 16 January* ***1858*** *pictorial report in the* London Illustrated Times *using his photographs. Dies the same year. His photographs are to be found in the collection of the Victoria and Albert Museum, London, as well as of the Gilman Paper Company, USA.*

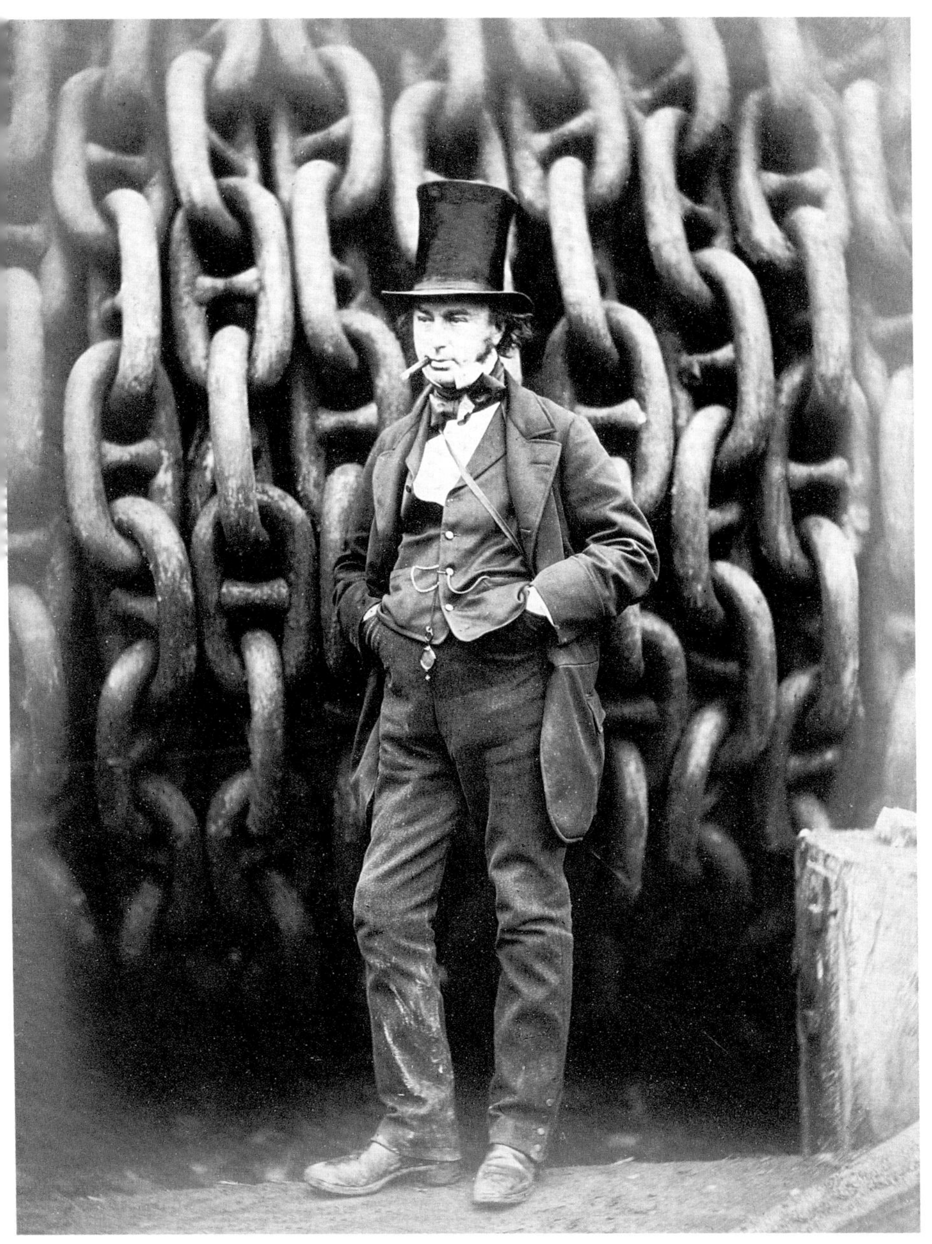

Isambard Kingdom Brunel, 1857

seamlessly to the world wonders of antiquity. Looked at from this perspective, the dirty boots and trousers can be interpreted as entirely in keeping with the required uniform expressing the ideas of making and creating. To this uniform also belonged the folded monocle and, especially, the watch affixed to a long chain: the watch, after all, was the medium that could turn human achievement into a measurable quantity.

In November 1857 the young London photographer Robert Howlett made a portrait of Isambard Kingdom Brunel. Unusually enough, he shot the portrait in the open air, and even more surprisingly flaunted the expectations of contemporary bourgeois self-confidence, which normally preferred an antiquating decor as backdrop to lend the picture a classic air. Instead, Howlett selected as background the mighty anchor chain of the ship with which the engineer Brunel was to leap beyond all norms and dimensions of shipbuilding that had held valid till that time. There is something undeniably Babylonian about the picture. The human figure, low in height, fragile in comparison to the power suggested by the rolled iron links, nonetheless stands proud in the knowledge of being the creator of all this might. The photograph, like the great ship itself, must have surprised contemporaries and moved them to a sense of wonder. The *London Illustrated Times*, which published an illustrated report on the completion of the floating monster, significantly named *Leviathan*, also offered original prints for sale, which presumably found a multitude of ready buyers. How else can one explain the fact that precisely this exposure, for example, is owned by the American private collector

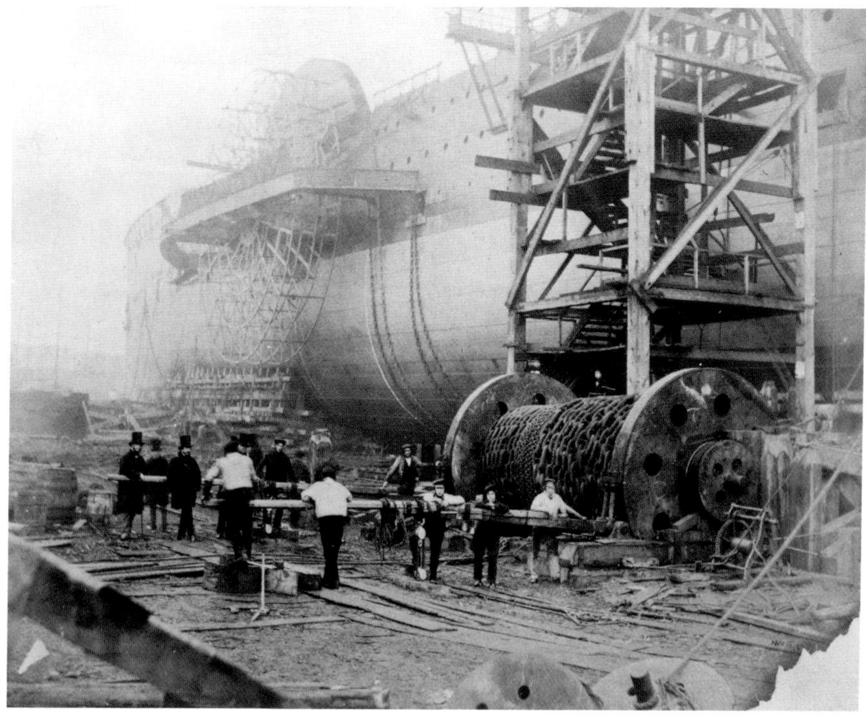

Paul F. Walter? The Gilman Paper Company also calls a particularly fine copy their own, as well as the Amsterdam collector Manfred Heiting, whose print - in the original format 28.2 × 21.6 cm (11 × 8½ inches) - we were allowed to reproduce here. The list of copies furthermore includes various British and American collections and archives, to mention just a few. In other words, the photograph numbers among the better-known incunabula of early British photography - an astonishing portrait that retains the full force of its suggestive power even today.

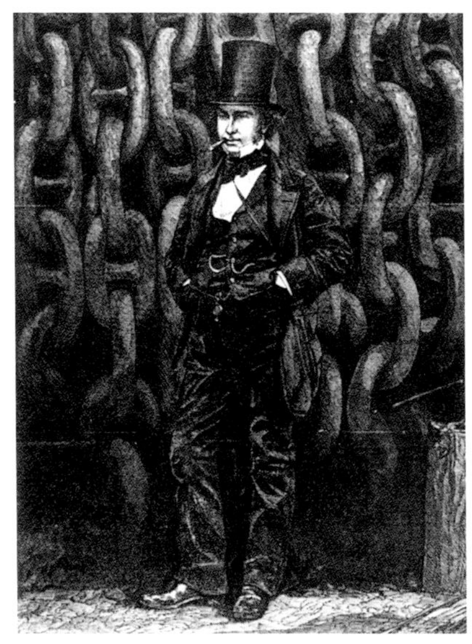

To be precise, the picture is part of a larger series, what we would today call a photo-report, that Robert Howlett completed under commission from the Illustrated Times immediately before the *Leviathan* - or, as the ship soon came to be popularly called, the *Great Eastern* - was finished. Mind you, as a technical pictorial medium, photography had been in use for only a decade and a half. With the wet-collodion process invented by Frederick Scott Archer in 1851, glass could now for the first time be practically employed as the vehicle for the colloid. This meant that the negatives were more clearly defined than the calotype, or paper negatives that had been used up until then. Just as important was the reduced exposure time. On the other hand, because the collodion plates that were about to be exposed were wet, they required considerably more technical and logistical work. One can easily identify at least eighteen different steps in the process, ranging from the sensitizing of the plate to the completed exposure. As a result, the self-confident engineer Isambard Kingdom Brunel likely found himself facing an equally self-confident photographer. Robert Howlett would also have seen himself as a pioneer and innovator of the industrial age, albeit in the completely different area of photographic technology and aesthetics.

Leaving few, but therefore all the more impressive, traces

We know comparatively little about Robert Howlett - a surprising situation, in view of the high evaluation today accorded him and his works. Mark Haworth-Booth, for example, calls him "one of the leading professional photographers of the mid-1850s," and Waeston

---

Left: **Robert Howlett:**
Construction of the "Great Eastern", *albumin print, 1857. Unmistakle on the right hand side is the rolled-up anchor chain Brunel posed in front of for the photographer.*

Above: *Brunel as a woodcut; only via this circuitous route could a half-tone be printed prior to 1900. From* The Illustrated Times, *London, 16 January 1858.*

Neaf recognizes him as "one of the daring innovators in British photography of the 1850s." Nonetheless, data concerning Howlett remains sparse. On the one hand this vagueness may result from the fact that research into nineteenth-century photography is still in its infancy; on the other hand, it may be because Howlett died at age of twenty-seven, leaving few, but therefore all the more impressive, traces.

Born in 1831 as the son of a Norwegian pastor, Howlett is supposed to have been for a time the partner of the photographer Joseph Cundall (1818–75). Under the title *On the Various Methods of Printing Photographic Pictures upon Paper* (1856), Howlett authored a widely used photographic text book. In addition, he developed a portable darkroom tent that was probably especially helpful to him in his work at the London docks. Most importantly, however, Howlett was open to the most various applications of the still young medium. Still extant are his portraits of Crimean War veterans, which he supposedly made at the behest of Queen Victoria; in addition, he completed landscapes and architecture studies. Howlett was also active in the area of art reproduction, and produced photographs meant to serve artists as models. The painter William Powell Frith, for example, is reputed to have referred to works by Howlett in the composition of his celebrated painting *Derby Day* (1858). Admittedly, however, Howlett's most famous work is his series on the launching of the *Great Eastern*, photographed precisely one year before his unexpected death in November 1858 – whether this was from typhus or, as is occasionally argued, from careless handling of the sometimes dangerous chemicals that were a part of these early years of photography, remains an open question.

Was Robert Howlett a friend of Isambard Kingdom Brunel? It has occasionally been claimed, and if true, would explain why the engineer appears in almost every photograph in the series. At the same time, it must be stressed that Brunel was something of a star engineer, and his presence in a picture would certainly contribute to the public's interest in a newspaper article. In an age when the limits of the feasible served as a constant challenge in the struggle for progress, Brunel functioned more or less as the prototype of an uninterrupted belief in progress. With truly breathtaking speed, a society whose commerce was primarily determined by agriculture and hand-production had transformed itself into a capitalist industrial economy, a process in which England could rightly claim a leading role. New materials (above all, iron), new sources of energy (in particular coal, and the resultant steam), and new technologies now determined the rhythm of progress, which in turn lead ultimately to the creation of new way of life, new social levels and classes – as well as to the class antagonisms later described by Karl Marx and Friedrich Engels in their works.

Born in 1806, Brunel's father was the famed engineer Mark Isambard Brunel. A pure technocrat, the son had little interest in the social implications of his accomplishments: for him, the art of engineering meant the conquest of the elements, a battle which could never be pursued far enough. At Brunel's death on 15 September 1859, the *Morning Chronicle* appropriately noted: "The history of invention holds up no other example that great innovations can be so keenly conceived and so successfully implemented. Had he been less bold, he would have been less successful… Brunel was able to create an epic of engineering epic, but not a sonnet of engineering. If he could not exert power, he was absolutely nothing…"

He had built tunnels and harbors, involved himself in the railroads, and, in particular, designed, financed and built ships. British historian Francis D. Klingender begins the history of steamship travel with Brunel's *Great Western* (1838); five years later, his 3,000-ton *Great Britain*

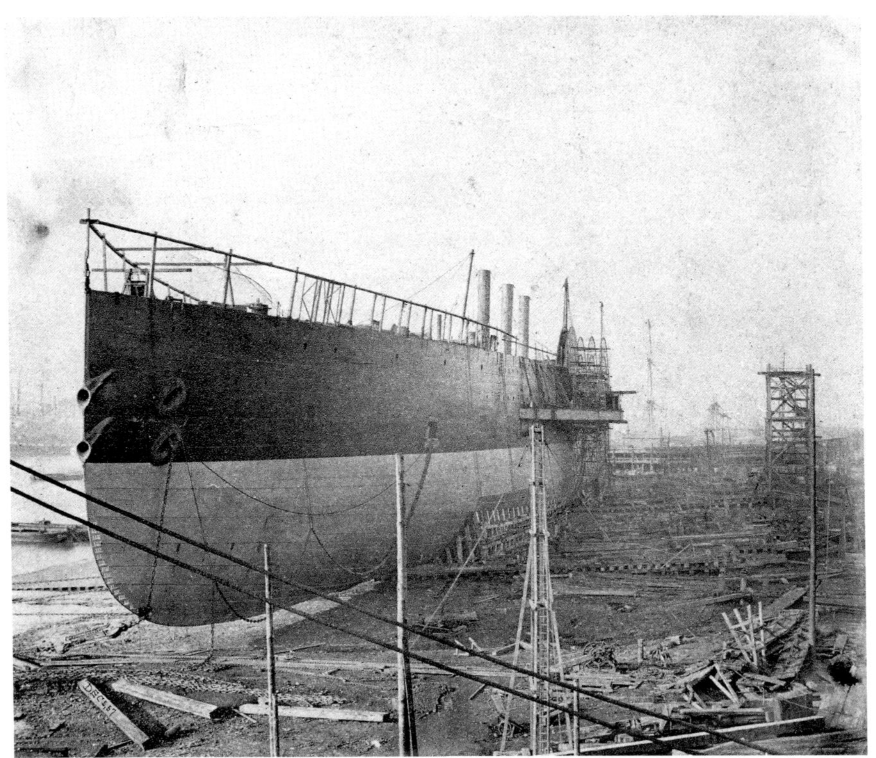

was launched – for its time, a mighty vessel, but modest in comparison to the *Great Eastern*, which gradually took shape on the mud banks of the Thames beginning in 1852. The records speak of a water displacement of twenty-seven thousand tons, a length of 211 meters (692 feet), and a breadth of 25 meters (82 feet). The ship was planned for four thousand passengers, sported six masts and five stacks. A steam engine with eleven thousand horsepower turned a paddle wheel almost sixty feet in diameter. In addition, there was stowage for approximately 15,000 tons of coal; that meant that the ship could cross the Atlantic without having to load fuel on route. Contemporary reports turned to the map of London to convey their readers an idea of the dimensions of the ship: "Neither Grosvenor nor Belgrave Square could take the *Great Eastern* in; Berkeley would barely admit her in its long dimension."

From the very beginning, it was the task of photography to testify to the (nearly) incredible. The mechanical, semi-automatic, aspects of the photographic process lent

---

Robert Howlett:
The Bows of the "Great Eastern",
albumin print, 1857.

photographs their power as evidence, without reference to aesthetic demands that were laid upon the medium from the other direction. Although the series of pictures that Howlett made in November 1856 of the construction of the *Great Eastern* possesses uncontested aesthetic value – and in this sense it constitutes one of the great achievements of early photography – the photographer was primarily interested in the visualization of an event. Because of the complexity of the photographic process, instantaneous exposures were impossible. Therefore, Howlett placed the protagonists, in particular Isambard Kingdom Brunel, at the center of the striking setting provided by the powerful new ship – no doubt with the request to stand still. We do not know how many plates Howlett exposed, but in any case, the surviving images prove his skill in analyzing a theme into individual aspects in order to tell a story, quite in keeping with today's understanding of reporting that tells a story. Howlett repeatedly placed the engineer in front of imposing backdrops, at times photographing close up, at times at a distance, an approach which emphasized the size of the ship. In the collection of the J. Paul Getty Museum in Malibu, there is a particularly impressive group portrait, dated 1857, of dark-clothed men, presumably taken before the launching of the ship. Howlett must therefore have followed the construction of the ship over a period of time. The *Illustrated Times* published a report with photographs by Howlett and Cundall in its issue of 16 January 1858. Because half-tone print could not be directly printed, the original was first copied as a wood engraving. The portrait of Isambard Kingdom Brunel was rendered fairly exactly in front of the large anchor chain. Only the dirt on his trousers and shoes fell victim to the correcting stylus of the engraver.

Marxist aesthetics in particular has found fault with the absence of workers in Howlett's pictures. And in fact, workers, when they appear at all, are small, relegated to the background, and usually blurred. The reigning concept of the age was still that of patriarchs, to whom all industrial progress owed its being. From this standpoint, Robert Howlett's photograph of the self-confident engineer reveals the ideology of a century that saw bourgeois heroes as the focal point of historical interest. That Brunel himself did not live to see the maiden voyage of his ship is one of the tragic aspects of the picture, an image which stands almost emblematically for the technological enthusiasm of the early nineteenth century. In 1867 the *Great Eastern* put to sea; among the passengers was no less a figure than the writer Jules Verne. Through him the utopias of Isambard Kingdom Brunel found their apotheosis, even though 'merely' an artistic one.

Robert Howlett:
Isambard Kingdom Brunel, *albumin print, 1857. The ingenious inventor in one of the less common versions of the photograph.*

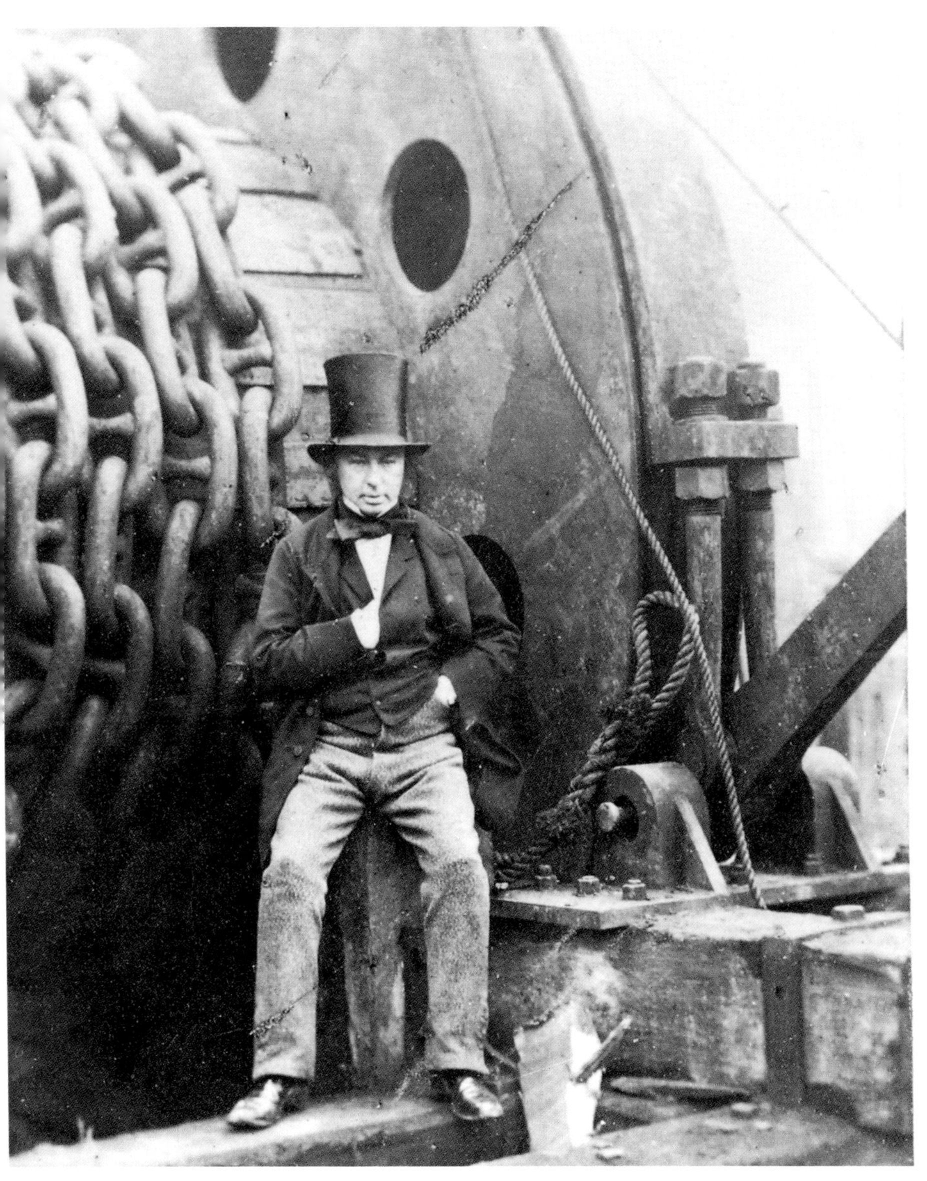

Isambard Kingdom Brunel, 1857

Auguste Rosalie Bisson
The Ascent of Mont Blanc
1862

The Architecture of the Alpine Peaks

The eighteenth and nineteenth centuries - the age of industry and technology - discovered nature anew. The idealized landscapes of classical painting were replaced by scenes of an environment as perceived through the analytic eyes of science, and photography came into its own as a pictorial medium suited to the needs of the age. In the new, realistic interpretation of landscape, the younger of the two Bisson brothers was a leading pioneer.

They photographed architecture – ever and again architecture. Along with Édouard-Denis Baldus, Gustave Le Gray, and Henri Le Secq, they number among the most important architectural interpreters of the nineteenth century. Their large-format photographs manifest an amazing feel for the power of light, for the modulations produced by the interplay of light and shadow. In short, the photographs of the Bisson brothers represent an attempt to convey the reality of architecture in the form of a two dimensional image. But what is it that lent their unpeopled topographies such clarity and artistic power? Was it the slowness of their large plates? The complexity of the photographic process? Or the atmosphere of an age capable of greater concentration than ours? After 1860, at any rate, the name of the firm, "Bisson frères," was known even beyond the borders of France as a synonym for the quickly growing genre of architectural photography. But the brothers did not rest with views of the Louvre, Paris or the cathedrals of Chartres or Rheims. They undertook lengthy journeys to Italy, Spain, and Germany. In Heidelberg they used a platform to achieve a new and unfamiliar view of the castle ruins; in Paris, the towers of Notre Dame offered the opportunity to formulate several views of the city from the airy heights. A panorama with the astounding dimensions of 45 × 105 cm (17¾ × 41½ inches), composed of three negatives depicting the interior of the Musée du Louvre in Paris won a positive review from the

---

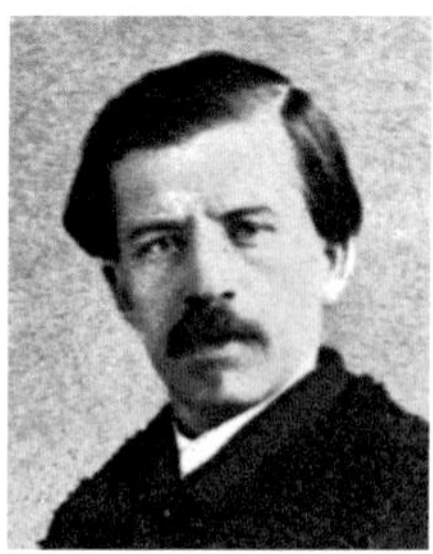

Bisson brothers

__1814__ Louis Auguste Bisson born in Paris. __1826__ Auguste Rosalie born in Paris. __1843__ Louis Auguste and Bisson senior open up a portrait studio in Paris. __1848__ Auguste Rosalie opens a studio. From __1852__ the two brothers work openly together ("Bisson frères"). __1854__ first presentation of large format views of monuments. Become founder members of the Société française de photographie. __1858__ views of the Mont Blanc range by Bisson the younger. __1861__ views of the peak of Mont Blanc. __1862__ second successful ascent of Mont Blanc. __1863__ the firm goes bankrupt. __1876__ death of Bisson senior, __1900__ death of Bisson the younger in Paris.

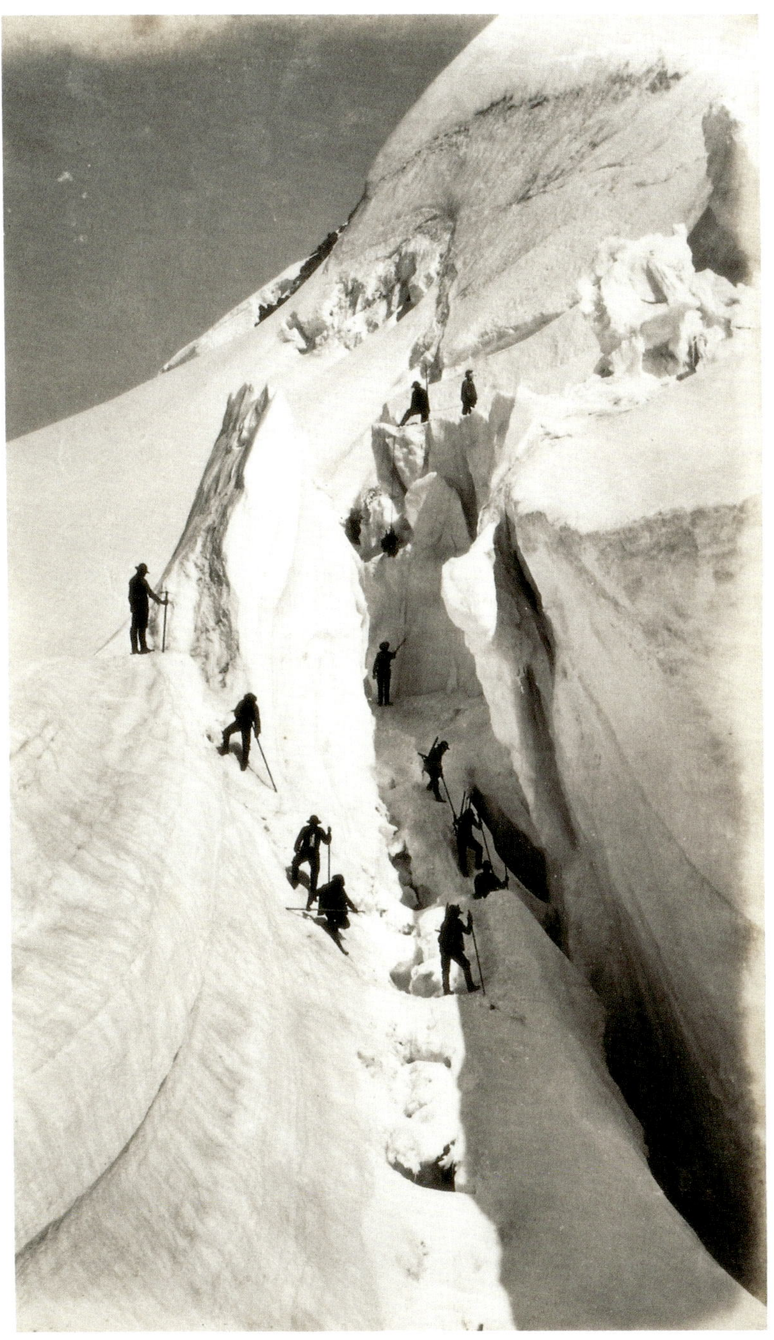

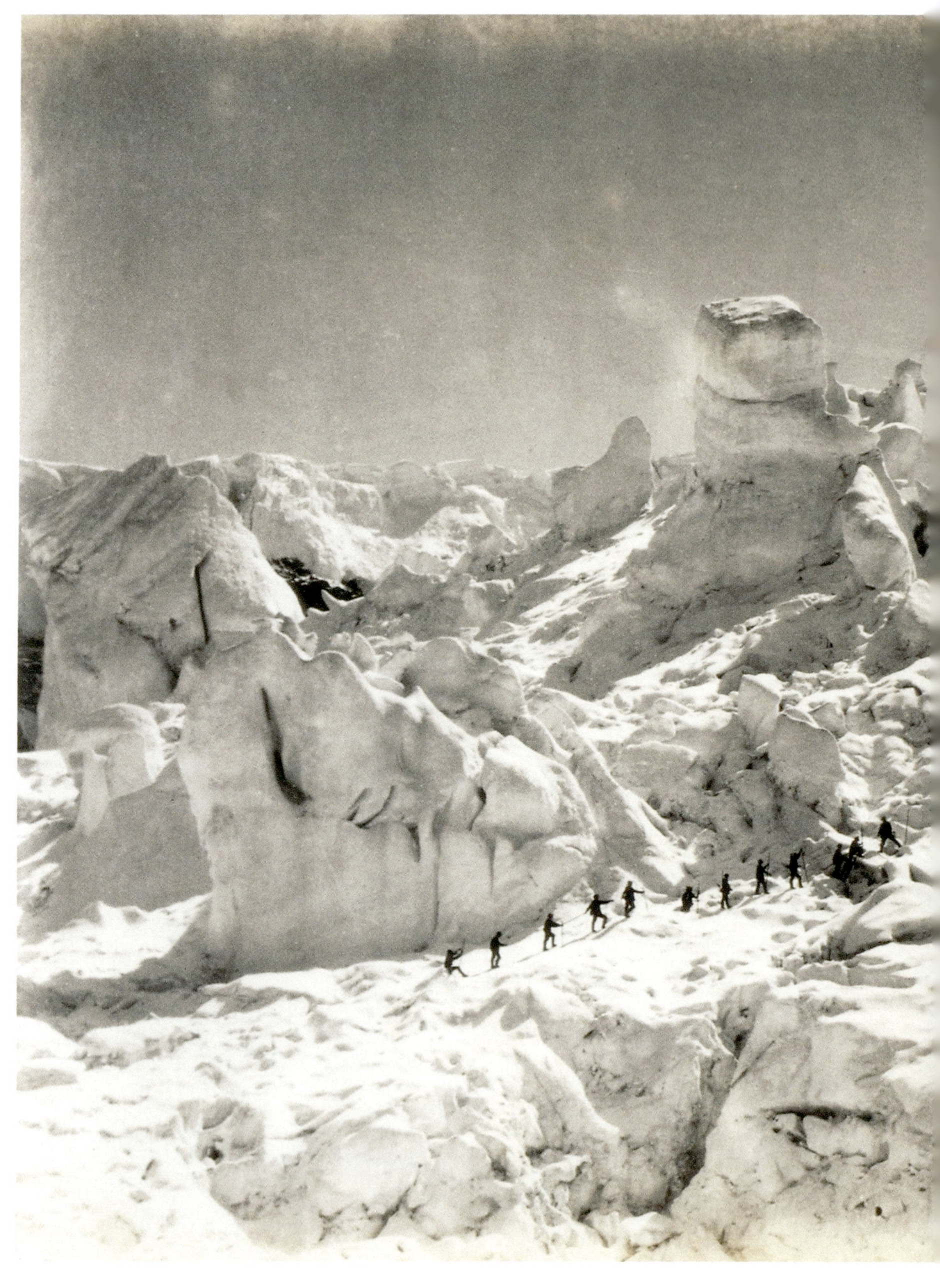

Auguste Rosalie Bisson

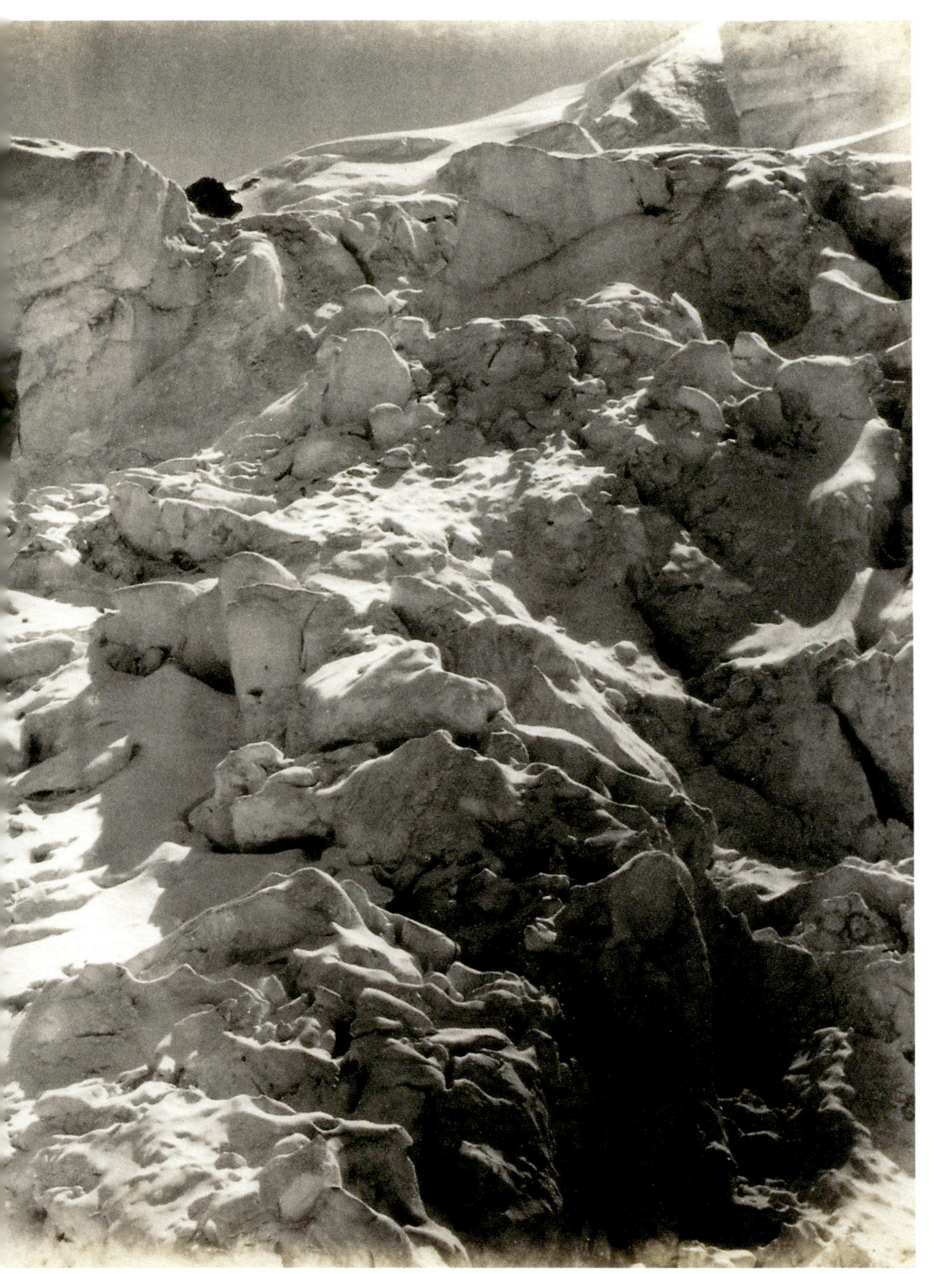

photography journal *La Lumière*: one must praise the "great harmony of light, and all the fine and numerous details of this sculptural jewel," which was here "reproduced with rare harmony." For the sake of completeness, it must be noted that the brothers also produced daguerreotypes, fulfilled portrait contracts, photographed art works, and also placed their talents at the service of science. But most importantly, theirs were the first successful photographs of the peak of Mont Blanc in 1861 – an impressive achievement in terms of skill both in mountaineering and photographic technology. Their achievement not only caused much excitement at the time, but it also constituted an important contribution to the history of photography and secured the Bisson brothers a place among the six most important French photographers of the pioneer age: Bernard Marbot, Nadar, Nègre, La Gray, Baldus, and finally, the Bisson brothers themselves, who, as "diligent pilots of a large firm," were thus also intermediaries between industry and art.

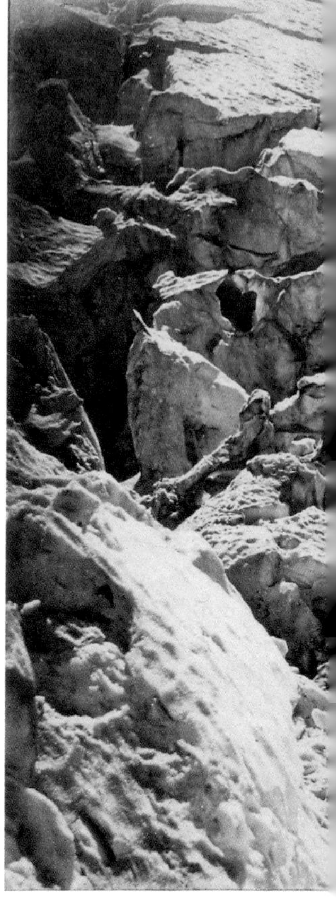

Two brothers: Louis Auguste, born in 1814 and Auguste Rosalie, twelve years younger. It was intended that Louis Auguste become an architect, but in fact he worked for twelve years in the Paris city administration before turning to daguerreotypy in the early 1840s – a surprising decision from today's point of view. But we must remember, at that time, the medium, still young, was a playground for any entrants into the field who could demonstrate courage, a readiness to take risks, an interest in pictures, and the spirit of an inventor. Reviewing the original professions of the early photographers, Hans Christian Adam came up with a list that included portrait painters, scientists, lithographers, and even a coal dealer. The Bissons' father, Louis François Bisson, was a ministerial official who painted coats-of-arms on the side, before he took up the still-young process of daguerreotypy in 1841. The family was thus from the very beginning a part of that much-cited 'daguerreotypomania' that took root in France and elsewhere after 1840. It is therefore not surprising that Auguste Rosalie also soon gave up his job as an official in the Office of Weights and Measures and turned to photography. He began with portraits, but also reproduced paintings, and gave instruction in photography. By 1849 at the latest, the two brothers were working together as partners and in 1852 they opened a joint studio, initially located at 50 rue Basse du Rempart, then at 62 rue Mazarine, and finally at 8 rue Garancière, where they occupied a total of twelve rooms on three stories for their private and professional needs.

Although the Bisson frères, as they were officially known as a firm after 1852, were active in all the early genres of photography except the nude, their real domain remains that of architectural photography. They advertised an impressive selection of offerings, including "photographic reproductions of the most beautiful examples of architecture and sculpture of antiquity, the Middle Ages, and the Renaissance." The photographs were pasted into books or albums, or

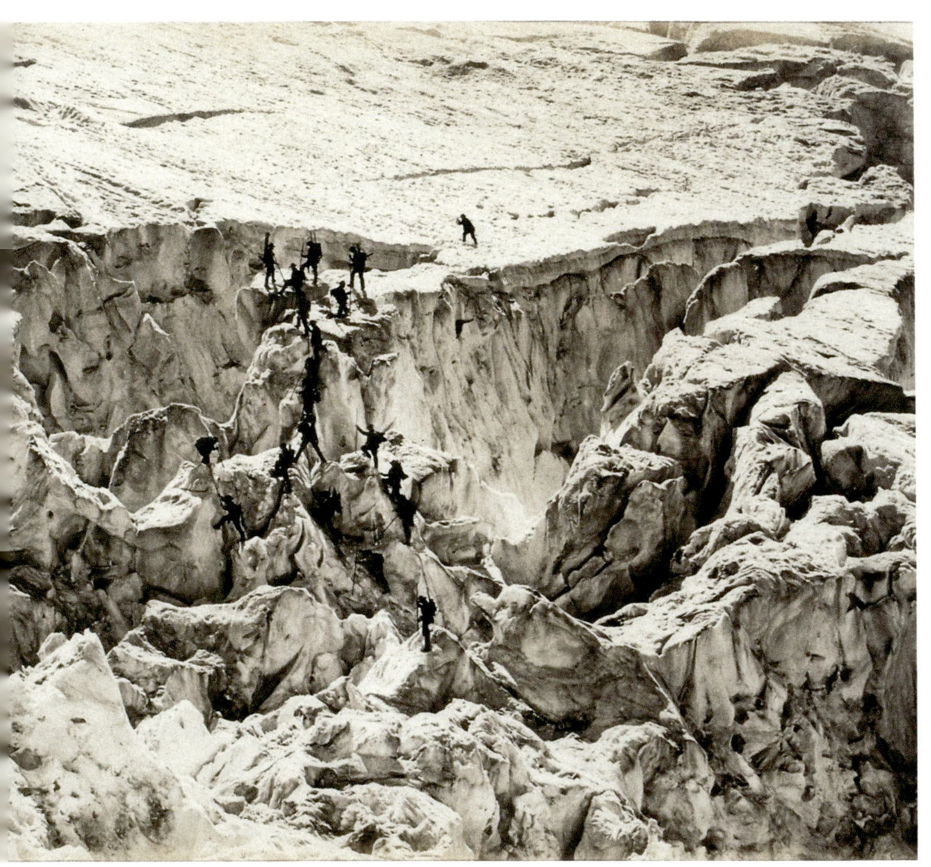

alternatively were made available to the educated public in the form of original single sheets. In addition to all this, at the beginning of the 1850s the brothers began to take an interest in landscape photography. A 1.85 meter (six foot) long panorama of the Pavillon de l'Aar probably represents their first zenith as photographers of nature – and is said to have moved the Alsatian clothing-manufacturer Daniel Dollfus-Ausset to buy his way into the Bisson brothers' firm as a limited partner for a sum of one hundred thousand francs. Dollfus-Ausset took a lively interest in Alpine glaciers, and felt confident that in Louis August and August-Rosalie Bisson he had finally found a team who could guarantee him the photographic exploration of the mountain world. Dollfus-Ausset's affinity for the mountains heights must be understood in the context of

---

Page 63: **Auguste Rosalie Bisson:** Ascent of Mont-Blanc (Via a Crevice), *albumin print, 1862.*

Above: **Auguste Rosalie Bisson:** Meeting Point of the Bossons and Taconnaz Glaciers (Abandoned Attempt to Ascend Mont Blanc), *albumin print, 1859.*

the new understanding of nature. Beginning with Jean-Jacques Rousseau at the latest, the traditional, normative concepts of nature had begun to dissolve: the traditional image of the ideal landscape as found in literature and the fine arts was now being replaced by an empirical model. This approach had already entered the sciences, and by the time of the Napoleonic wars, had increasingly made its way into the military. It is no accident that fields such as geology, geodesy, and geomorphology blossomed for the first time precisely during these years of increasing nationalism and imperialism.

Photography in the cold, thin mountain air

Even before establishing his connection with the Bisson brothers, Daniel Dollfus-Ausset had already spurred other photographers on to make pictures of the high ranges of the mountains. Thus, Jean Gustave Dardel was the first to succeed in taking photographs of the Alpine landscape, producing approximately a dozen pictures in 1849. Similarly on the initiative of Dollfus-Ausset, Camille Bernabé made daguerreotypes of several Alpine glaciers and peaks in August 1850. The midpoint of the century also found other photographers such as Friedrich von Martens, Aimé Civiale, Édouard-Denis Baldus, and the Ferrier brothers at work in the mountains. Although Auguste Rosalie Bisson was not the first to set up his camera in the high Alpine ranges, he was the first photographer to succeed in conquering the heights of Mont Blanc. Furthermore, unlike the majority of the photographers cited above, he employed the more modern, albeit more complex, wet-collodion process, which, it must be added, had not yet been tested under the extreme weather conditions of the mountain heights. What he brought back from his successful expeditions of 1861 and 1862 was more than a mere 'I-was-there' variety of proof: Auguste Rosalie Bisson's large-format negatives and prints also conform to the highest aesthetic standards.

In August 1859, Auguste Rosalie Bisson started his first attempt to ascend to the peak of Mont Blanc. It is difficult for us today to imagine the difficulty of such an undertaking. In the first place, in 1850 mountain climbing was still in its infancy, the equipment of the mountain climbers had not yet been perfected, and the participants as a rule were insufficiently trained. But even without all this, Mont Blanc represents a particularly dangerous and moody peak, which had been first conquered only in 1786, and significantly bore the nickname *montagne maudite*, or 'damned mountain'. Furthermore, the challenge facing the younger Bisson was not merely to reach the nearly 4,810-meter (16,000-foot peak, he also wanted to take photographs there – specifically using the wet-collodion process that was as yet untested in the thin mountain air and extremely cold temperatures. The collodion process, announced in 1851 by the Englishman Frederick Scott Archer, was the most complex of all the early black-and-white photographic processes, calling for a glass plate as the vehicle for the photographic layer. The use of the glass plate offered the advantages of considerably increased light sensitivity and a more brilliant and precise image. The disadvantage lay in the no fewer than eighteen various steps that the process required, from the sensitizing the plate with a fluid mixture of ether alcohol, collodion, iodine and bromide salts, through the exposure of the plate in the camera, and ending in the development and fixing of the negative. Because the plates had to be exposed while still wet, a traveling photographer had to carry along – in addition to the camera, tripod, glass plates and chemicals – a complete darkroom tent. In reality, no fewer than twenty-five men accompanied Auguste Rosalie Bisson on his excursion; in addition to the necessary porters, there were also experienced mountain guides such as Mugnier and Balmat.

Aesthetic of the high mountains

On 16 August 1859, the party set out from Chamonix. Initially, the weather looked promising, but worsened considerably in the course of the day. A hut on the glacial lake served as their quarters for the night. Now it started to snow and the temperature sank to ten degrees Fahrenheit; nonetheless, Bisson and four guides reached the final rock face before the summit on the next day. Buffeting winds and whirling snow prevented the final ascent, however, and taking photographs was out of the question. The first attempt was given up without result. A year later, on 26–27 July 1860, a second attempt also resulted in Bisson's retreat from the peak without pictures. It was not until the third try on 24 July 1861 that the photographer finally succeeded in climbing "the giant among mountains with his equipment," as *La Lumière* commented with admiration. Once again, the weather seemed favorable. The group set off from Chamonix on the morning of 22 July. By evening they reached the Grand Moulets at a height of more than ten thousand feet. They rested for an hour, and reached the great plateau around six o'clock in the morning. Proceeding to the Petits Moulets at a height of more than fifteen thousand five hundred feet, the group was greeted with storm winds and snow, and was forced to turn back. Some of the men began to give out; they were sent back to Chamonix, and replacements were sent up. Toward midnight of the second day, they set off again, finally attaining the peak at morning. "The tent was erected," as described in a contemporary report, "the camera placed on the stand, the plate coated and sensitized, exposed, and the view was taken. And what a view! What a panorama! As the picture was being developed, there was no water at hand to rinse it. It was assumed one could melt snow with the lamps, but in this atmosphere, the lamps burned only with a very small flame… One man was assigned to the lamps, to keep them burning; he fell asleep. Another replaced him, but the same thing happened. Finally M. Bisson himself managed to obtain enough of the precious substance. He hurried to his tent, at whose door only Balmat was still standing, and completed processing his negative."

In this first successful expedition to the summit of Mont Blanc, Bisson succeeded in taking a total of three photographs. On a second ascent in 1862, he brought back six more. These were not to be his last pictures from the mountains, but they remain his most spectacular: in the technique, aesthetics, and logistics of the entire process, these stand as milestones of early photography. Whether or not Bisson used a green filter to even out the extreme differences in contrast in the negative, we do not know. Nor do we have information about the exact format of the plates, the camera, or the lenses that he used. What stands out in the pictures is their aesthetic content, undoubtedly wrung from Bisson's routine architecture interpretations; his sure sense of style; his experience with light, composition, reduction, and the golden section – from all of which he could profit. Bisson, as Milan Chlumsky rightly has said, was the first to prove that the "deserts of snow possess unmistakable aesthetic qualities. He was the first to capture the majesty of the Alps by photography."

We know that the Bisson brothers had assumed they would make money from the spectacular undertaking. But ironically, more than a year after the second ascent of Mont Blanc, the firm went bankrupt and went under the auctioneer's hammer on 7 April 1864. The buyer, a certain Émile Placet, paid the ridiculously low sum of 15,000 francs for the entire inventory, the negatives, and the rights to the pictures – including the legendary photographic conquest of Mont Blanc.

Nadar
Sarah Bernhardt
ca. 1864

Lady at Ease

She was a true child of the age of photography. Fascinated with the new pictorial medium that photography represented, Sarah Bernhardt understood how to use photography to foster her growing fame.

At some point in the course of 1864, the young Sarah Bernhardt had her portrait taken in the studio of the Paris photographer Félix Tournachon, known as Nadar. The precise day and month have not been recorded but researchers nevertheless have agreed. At the time, Henriette Rosine Bernhardt, the daughter of a Dutch Jewish mother, was twenty years old, and it would be an exaggeration to term her a famous actress. At this point even the word 'promising' might be too much – although she had been a conscientious student at the Paris Conservatory, and had passed the final exams as the second in her class. But even so, coming directly from school, she would never have been engaged by the Comédie Française – at that time still the leading theater in France – without the support of her mother's influential friends. One cannot speak, however, of the beginning of a brilliant career; in fact, rather the opposite. "Her debut," writes Cornelia Otis Skinner, one of Bernhardt's biographers, "was not at all sensational; it wasn't even good." In particular, the stage fright from which she was to suffer throughout her life weakened her self-confidence during her performances. Accordingly, the critics responded with restraint. Francisque Sarcey, for example, initially commented positively on the way the young actress carried herself and spoke in her first appearance in Racine's *Iphigénie* – but shortly afterward rescinded his faint praise. Similarly, the influential critic of *Le Temps* found her performance unsatisfactory. If she seem to have made an impression at all, then it was thanks to her appearance: "Mademoiselle Bernhardt… is a tall and pretty young person of slender build and very pleasant facial expression. The top half of her face

---

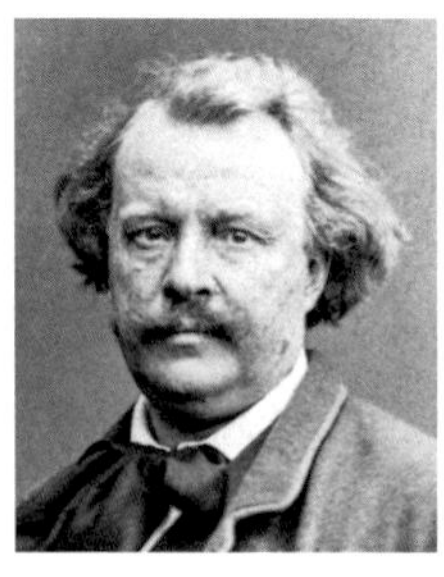

Nadar
*Actually Gaspard-Félix Tournachon. Born **1820** in Paris. Studies medicine, without finishing. **1838–48** unsettled bohemian life. Friends with Henri Murger and Baudelaire. First caricatures. **1851** works preliminary work on a pantheon of famous contemporaries. **1854** turns to photography, opens a studio. **1858** first exposures using electric light. **1860** founds Atelier Nadar on Boulevard des Capucines. **1861** pictures of the Paris catacombs. **1887** ceases studio work. **1897–99** new studio in Marseille. Dies **1910**, and buried in Père-Lachaise cemetery, Paris.*

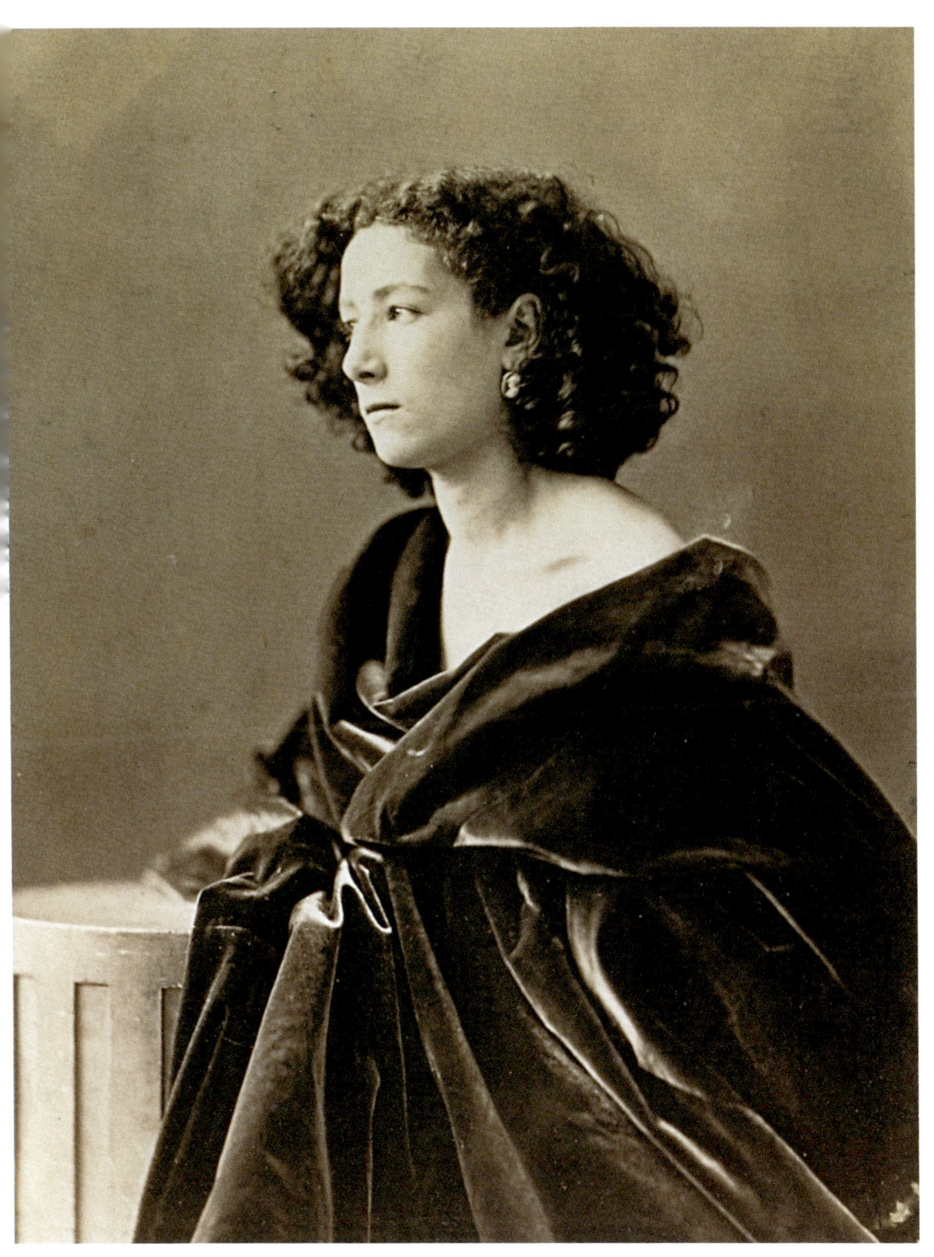

Sarah Bernhardt, ca. 1864

is remarkably beautiful; her posture is good and her pronunciation completely clear. More," according to Sarcey, "cannot be said at this point." By 1864, Sarah Bernhardt had two years of stage experience behind her. She had appeared in pieces by Molière and Racine, and had also held her own in now-forgotten plays by writers such as Barrière, Bayard, Laya, and Delacourt. But until the time of the photograph, she had garnered more attention from a certain extravagance of clothing and appearance, as well as a series of moderate-sized scandals, which initially were anything but helpful to the progress of her career. A slap she delivered on the public stage in early 1863 gained her not only dismissal from the Comédie Française but the reputation of being difficult, stubborn, and arrogant. She was, and remained, without permanent engagement. On top of all this, she was now pregnant. The child – a son named Maurice – was born in December 1864 on the wrong side of the blanket. All in all, the young actress was not in an enviable position. "This young person," her teacher at the Conservatory is said to have prophesied, "will either be a genius or a disaster." In 1864, the latter seemed the more likely prognosis.

In precisely this unpromising year, the young actress determined to visit Nadar's atelier. The studio was not just any of the by-then numerous photography establishments in Paris: it was the largest and probably the best known. Opened in 1860 at 35 Boulevard des Capucines, the studio tended to draw customers of name and rank, if not precisely the power elite of the Second Empire, from whom the republican sympathizer Nadar kept a critical distance. Instead, his clientele included the members of the bohemian circles from which Félix Tournachon himself had arisen, even if his meanwhile well-developed sense for business distinguished him from the "water-drinkers," as he called them.

Pantheon of prominent personalities

Gaspard-Félix Tournachon, who began to style himself 'Nadar' in 1838, had started his career as a theater critic, writer, publisher of literary magazines, draftsman, and caricaturist. His project of creating a lithographic *Pantheon of Famous Contemporaries*, begun in 1851, won him attention, even though financial problems prevented him from producing more than a first issue. In the same year, Nadar also turned to the still-young field of photography, a decision that at first glance seems logical for technical reasons: photography was faster and cheaper than lithography, thus making it easier to construct his 'pantheon' of prominent personalities, for example. Furthermore, a new process had just become available that, although rather complicated, was many times more sensitive to light: the wet collodion process, which Félix Tournachon set to immediate use in his very first photographs. Nadar began making portraits of family members; soon, however, his artist friends were also stepping in front of his camera: Baudelaire, Champfleuri, Doré, Delacroix, Rossini, and Berlioz – a collection of simple, concentrated studies that "even today still retain their directness" (Françoise Heilbrun). Within a very short time, Nadar refined his portraiture to a remarkable level, a feat for which no doubt his familiarity with his subjects, his years of work as a caricaturist, as well as his "general curiosity about human beings" (Heilbrun) proved of great value. Nadar himself was thoroughly conscious of his abilities – of his own 'genius' – as demonstrated in a sensational civil suit against his own brother Adrien, who was in competition with him. During the trial, the self-assured Nadar declared that in photography, one could learn much for oneself, but not everything; excellent portraits, in particular, depended chiefly on the talent of the artist behind the camera. This evaluation was picked up by

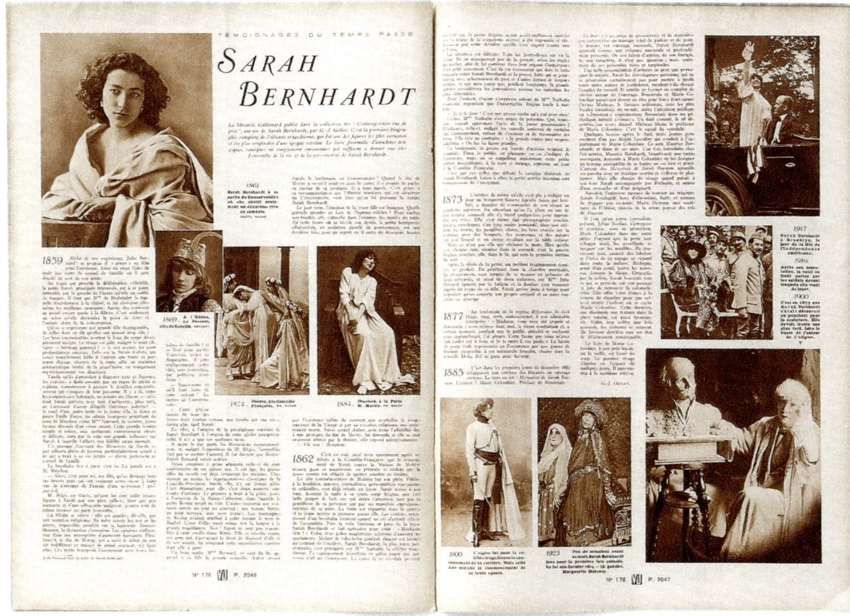

TÉMOIGNAGES DU TEMPS PASSÉ

SARAH BERNHARDT

1861

1859

1869

1874

1884

1862

1873

1877

1885

1917

1916

1900

1909

1923

Nº 178 VU P. 2046

Nº 178 VU P. 2047

Philippe Burty in his criticism of the photographic Salon in 1859: "M. Nadar," as he wrote in the *Gazette des beaux-arts*, "has made his portrait photographs into unquestionable works of art in the truest sense of the word specifically through the manner in which he illuminates his models, the freedom with which they move and assume their postures, and in particular by his discovery of the typical facial expression of each. Every member of the literary, artistic, dramatic, and political classes – in short, the intellectual elite – of our age has found its way to his studio. The sun takes care of the practical side of the affair, and M. Nadar is the artist who supplies the design."

For almost a decade, portraiture seems to have engrossed Nadar's artistic energies. Afterwards, so the story goes, he became bored by photography, although not to such an extent that he gave it up entirely. In 1861 he took impressive photographs of the catacombs of Paris using artificial light, and later he also photographed from balloons. Furthermore, he remained involved in portraiture, although his large new studio which opened in 1861 was primarily devoted to the quasi-'mechanical' production of photographs that had become almost universally popular. The process introduced by Disdéri allowed the production of up to twelve saucer-size portraits quickly and cheaply. Nadar's answer to the commercial challenge was his new studio in the Boulevard des Capucines that is supposed to have cost an unimaginable sum of two hundred thirty thousand francs – of borrowed money. Rumor has it further that he

---

Above: *"Sarah Bernhardt after Leaving the Conservatory," an article in the French glossy* Vu, *12 August 1931. The date of Nadar's photograph is given here as 1861.*

Page 75: **Nadar:** Sarah Bernhardt, *ca. 1864.*

employed fifty workers, who could finish up to ten portraits a day; until that time, the upper limit had been three. It is not difficult to imagine why this 'mass production' was unable to achieve the desired 'character balance' sought-after in more 'intimate portraits'. If Nadar's studio was still important in the 1860s, it was chiefly because of its size and his advertising methods, which were unusual for the age. Attached to the façade of the building facing the boulevard was the owner's name in red script, which was furthermore illuminated at night. Nadar and his young client Sarah Bernhardt at least shared the feel for the grand entrance.

New food for his lens

Sarah Bernhardt had visited Nadar's studio for the first time in 1862. The proof is a visiting card in the Bibliothèque nationale that already evinces all the signs of the standardized portrait. Whereas Nadar had rejected the use of props in his early portraits, such accessories, considered indispensable accouterments in the photography studios of this age of rapid commercial expansion, now began making their way into Nadar's studio, too. The typical example of these studio props was the supposedly antique-looking stump of an ancient column, made if necessary of papier maché and left unlacquered to avoid reflections. Such a column is clearly evident in the well-known Bernhardt portrait of 1864, and was present in the photograph of 1862 as well. In the older photograph the pose is conventional, the lighting unconvincing. The picture is, in short, flat, like the scene itself. The light-colored drape across the actress's shoulders emphasizes the thinness of her arms, a 'fault' which had often been ridiculed in her stage appearance, just she had often been teased as a child for her thick, curly hair. For the portrait, the 'blond Negress', as she was sometimes called, had combed her dark hair back into a braid and bound it. If there is anything that this insignificant photograph of Sarah Bernhardt does not exude it is precisely the quality that later characterized her whole being, namely, self-confidence and pride to the point of defiance. It is no accident that her chosen life-motto was *Quand même* – "Despite everything."

It is highly unlikely that Nadar personally took this first photograph; on the other hand, we may well assume that it was precisely he who undertook two years later to portray Sarah Bernhardt's often-praised beauty so convincingly in a single sitting. Art critics reckon the photograph of the young, still unknown actress to be among Nadar's "most inspired" works (Silvie Aubenas), and one of his best after 1860. The background of the portrait is neutral; the stump of a column hidden behind a pose that seems purely natural. The transfigured gaze is directed into the distance; there is no jewelry to complement her beauty – the small cameo on her left ear in the photograph is hardly noticeable. She is wearing her hair loose; the burnoose that she has thrown off emphasizes the pyramidal composition of the entire photograph. This time, the actress's slim upper torso is skillfully presented, with only the tip of the left shoulder showing, to give the picture a suggestive note. There is here both a clearer contrast between dark and light elements and a selectively sharper focus that together increase the sculptural effect of the picture. Only on a few, rare occasions, according to Françoise Heilbrun, one of the leading experts on Nadar's work, did Nadar again achieve a portrait of this quality: in his later years, only when he was fascinated by the subject – or, more precisely, the person. Three versions of the Bernhardt portrait have survived, and each may well be accounted successful in terms of offering a convincing image of the actress's personality. In all three, the actress is presented in a half-length portrait, leaning against the remains of a column. Her hair is loose, the burnoose is on one occasion replaced by a black velvet drape. In any case, Nadar succeeded in eliciting the touching

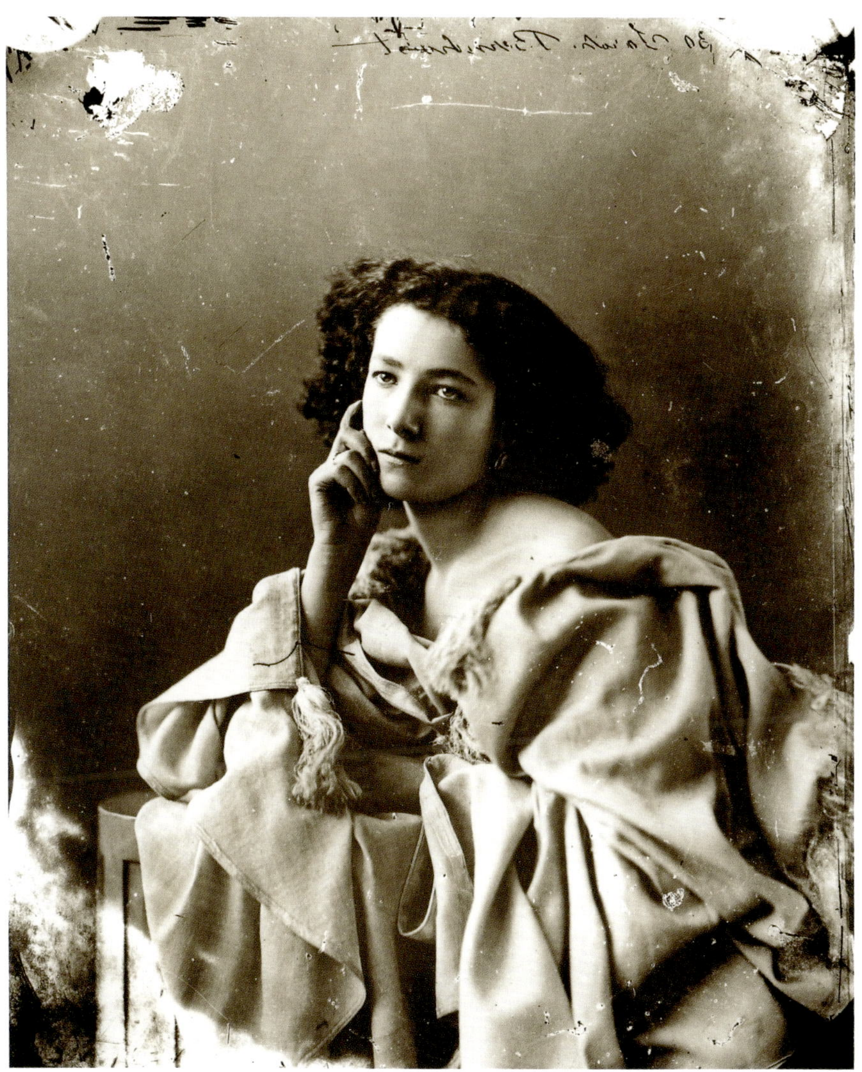

beauty of the young actress, whether en face or in three-quarters profile, for viewers even a hundred and thirty years later. That no contemporary print (vintage print) of the photographs exists is explained by the fact that the twenty-year-old was still unknown. On the other hand, this public insignificance seems to be precisely what provided a particular challenge to the photographer. "Our photographic hero finds the greatest joy and an unimaginable enthusiasm there where his lens makes out an unknown food," wrote one of Nadar's contemporaries. Once the 'divine' Sarah Bernhardt had become a legend, she was no longer of interest to the photographer.

***Sarah Bernhardt*, ca. 1864**

François Aubert
Emperor Maximilian's Shirt
1867

Decision in Querétaro

François Aubert stood at the side of the unfortunate Emperor Maximilian of Mexico as court photographer. The photographs he made of the final phase of the *imperio* were of particular interest to many of his European contemporaries, and are even said to have served Édouard Manet in the creation of his famous historical paintings.

In the summer of 1867, the news broke like a bombshell in the carefree Parisian salons: the emperor Maximilian of Mexico, together with his generals Mej'a and Miramón, had been executed in Querétaro. In spite of the numerous foreign dispatches that had alerted to the danger, in spite of appeals for mercy from figures like Giuseppe Garibaldi and Victor Hugo, the news came as a shock. To the nineteenth-century understanding of justice, execution was a thoroughly accepted concept, and ever since the French Revolution the violent death of a monarch was of course recognized as one of the possible outcomes of the historic process. What shook the self-confidence of great European powers, especially Austria and France, was the fact that in this case the "upstart," Benito Juárez García, was of Indian background. He had successfully challenged the Old World and had put a definitive end to at least the French attempt at hegemony in Central America. Rumor had it that Napoleon II spontaneously broke out in tears when the news reached him on 30 June. After all, it had been he who had sent Maximilian to Mexico, but then left him to his own devices, without military or political support. Prince and Princess Metternich demonstratively walked out of a fête associated with the Paris World Exhibition. The Count of Flanders and his wife did not even appear. Emperor Franz Joseph of Austria probably greeted the news with mixed feelings. He had always mistrusted the political instincts of his younger brother, but had also more or less encouraged him to undertake what was in any case a very risky venture.

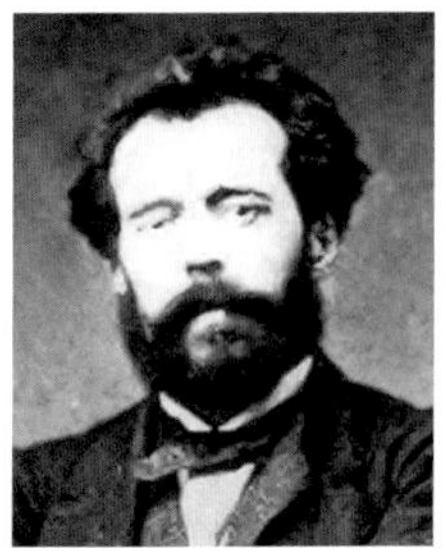

François Aubert
*Born **1829** in Lyon, France. Studies at the École des Beaux-Arts, under, among others, Hippolyte Flandrin. **1851** participates in the Salon. Emigrates to Central America. **1864** opens a studio in Mexico City. **1864–69** portraits of French, Belgian, and Austrian soldiers. Unofficial pictorial chronicler at the court of Emperor Maximilian. **1867** present as photographer at the capture and execution of Emperor Maximilian. **1890** return to Algeria, where he photographs the battle fleet. Dies **1906** in Condrieu, Rhone Département.*

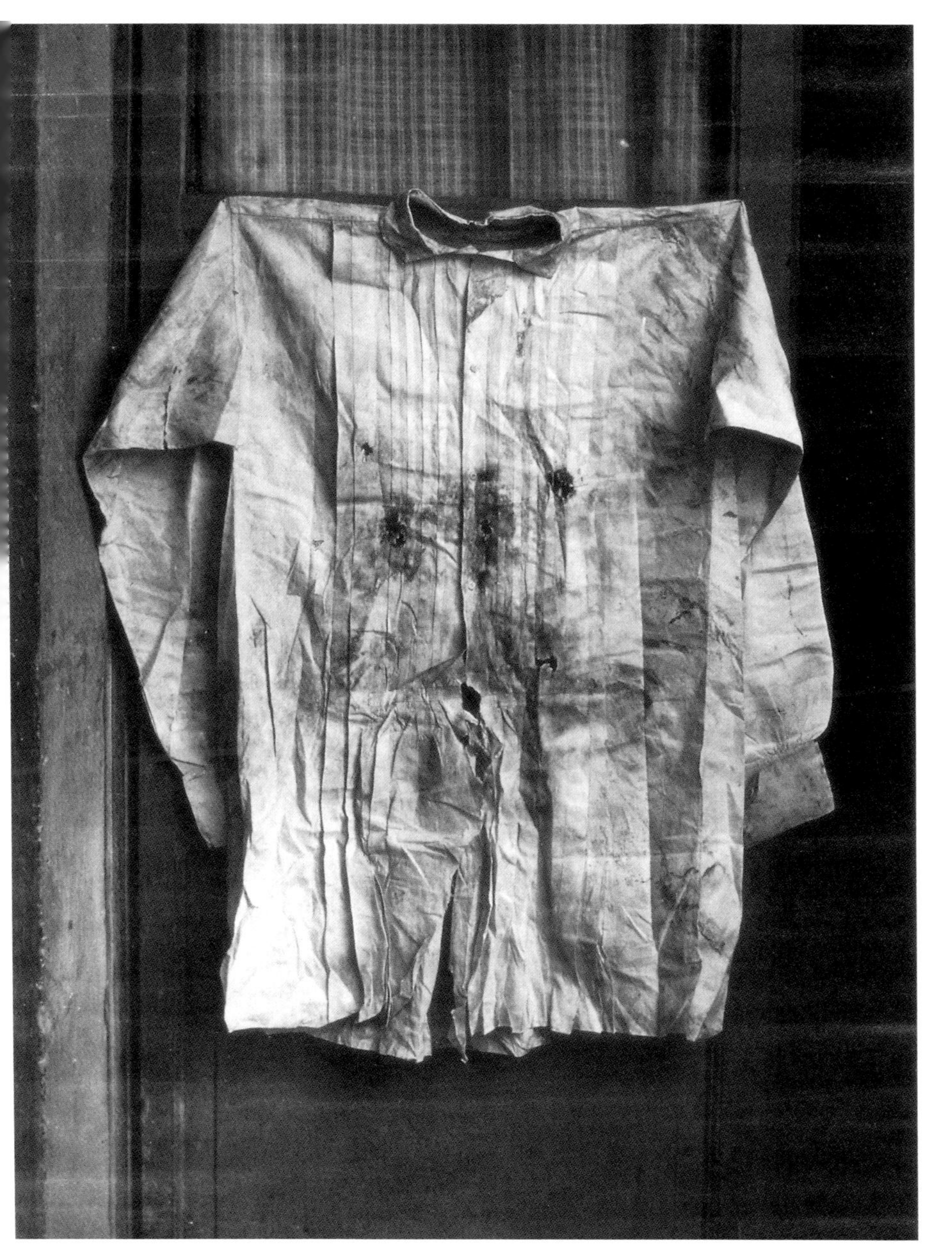

Emperor Maximilian's Shirt, 1867

Maximilian's doomed mission to Mexico might be understood as a strategic diplomatic power play for political influence. But it was also a personal debacle of a passionate and emotional man, who was literally destroyed by the interests of clever tacticians working according to different plans. And because the fate of individuals moves the thoughts and feelings of contemporaries more powerfully than abstract political configurations, Maximilian succeeded in becoming one of the great tragic figures of the nineteenth century, his fate being a matter of interest, at least in Europe, for a considerable length of time. It was hardly by chance that Édouard Manet, upon learning that the death sentence had been carried out, immediately began working on a large-format painting of the scene – a painting that remains not only one of his most important works but also an apotheosis of historical painting.

Today it is generally accepted that Manet, one of the leading Impressionists, derived much inspiration from photographs – although it must be borne in mind that the painter was not primarily concerned with the simple portrayal of historic events. If we nonetheless 'read' the painting as a document – as the title, *The Execution of Emperor Maximilian*, suggests – then it is chiefly because the photograph itself does not offer us the decisive moment. François Aubert was denied permission to document the execution photographically. In spite of this, in the early morning of 19 June 1867, Aubert, a trained painter, hurried off to the Cerro de las Campanas, the so-called 'Hill of Bells', to capture the scene at least by pencil. His small-format sketch, today in the possession of the Musée Royal de l'Armée in Brussels, offers in fact the most authentic visual witness to the moment of execution.

Born in 1829 in Lyons, France, François Aubert graduated from the local art academy, studied under Hippolyte Flandrin, and by 1864 was active as a photographer in Mexico. In addition to his private work, he also served as court photographer to the Emperor Maximilian – although he hardly had to undergo the formalities that normally surrounded such an appointment in the courts of Europe. Soon after the arrival of the designated monarch in Mexico, Aubert began to make portraits of him, the court, and his staff of generals. We might well picture Aubert – a powerful figure with a broad face, bearded and with a full head of hair – more as an itinerant photographer and adventurer than as a serious courtier. Furthermore, he was a clever reporter and an instinctive businessman who knew how to take commercial advantage of the growing public interest in photography. Although Aubert wasn't allowed to photograph the actual execution, he at least managed to document the 'scene of the crime' afterwards: the site of execution is marked with wooden crosses and an iron-wrought 'M' with a crown. Also clearly evident on the photograph are parts of the clay wall that had been hastily erected for the execution – a backdrop that also appears in two of Manet's four versions of the scene. In addition, Aubert photographed the execution squad, and the embalmed and freshly dressed corpse of Maximilian in his coffin; nor was Aubert shy of capturing the bullet-ridden, blood-spattered clothing of the emperor for a curious public. He photographed the emperor's black frock coat, vest, and blood-flecked shirt before as

---

Pages 82–83: **François Aubert:** The Place of Execution at Querétaro, Mexico, *albumin print, 1867. Maximilian and his generals were executed at this spot.*

Right: **François Aubert:** Maxmilian's Embalmed Body in His Coffin, *albumin print, 1867. A doctor, Vicente Licea of Querétaro, was responsible for fitting the corpse with blue glass-eyes.*

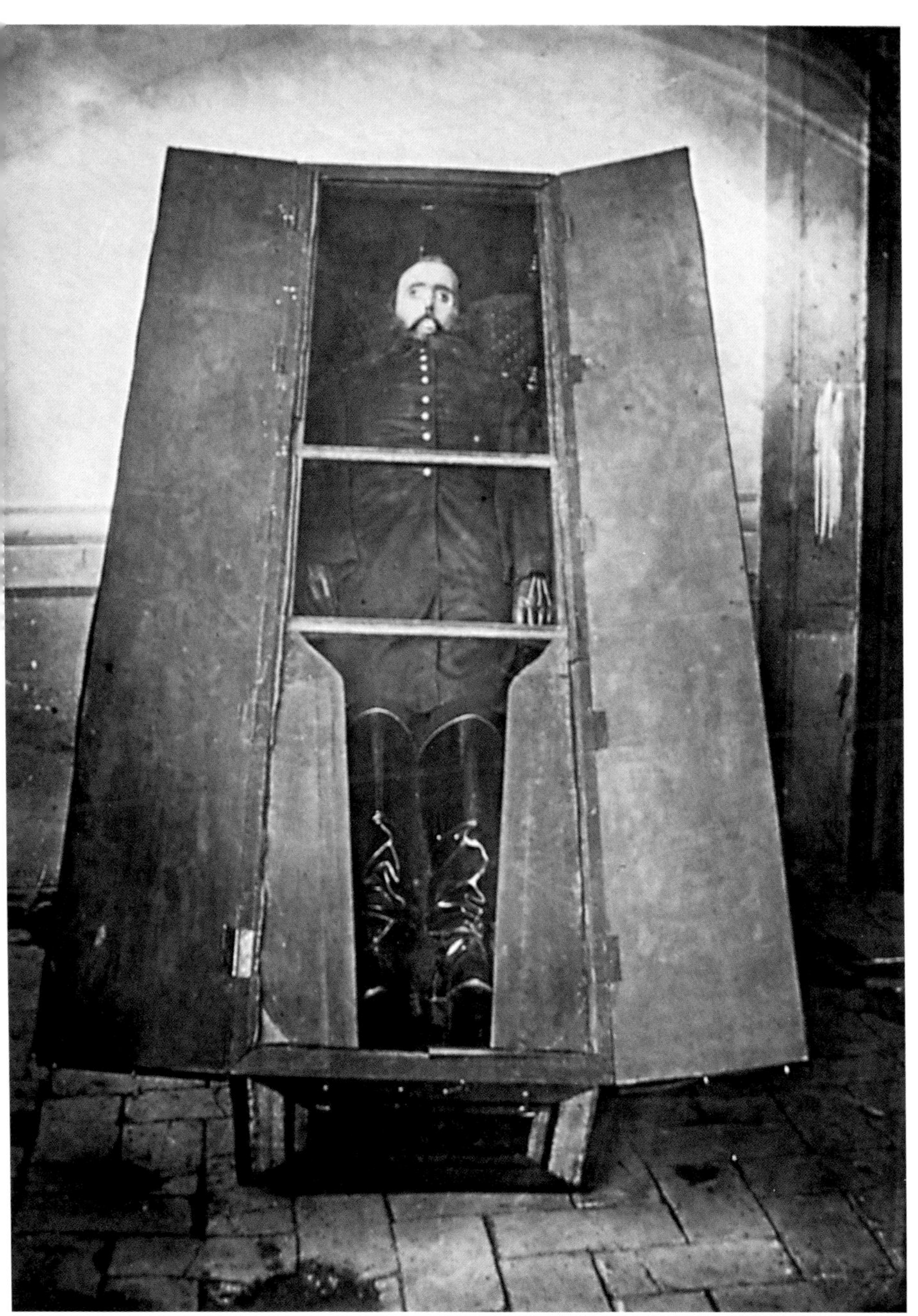

neutral a background as possible. The photographs were subsequently distributed and sold internationally by the firm A. Pereire, which had presumably purchased the photographic plates and rights from the photographer.

A cosmopolitan with liberal tendencies

In the tradition of Christian reverence for relics, Aubert placed the emperor's shirt in the center of his composition, thereby making it into the determining element of his photograph. The dark door frame in the background, the window, and the curtain behind it serve to concentrate the observer's attention on the most important artifact. The photographer attached the shirt to the door with two nails in such a manner as to make the pleated front clearly visible; having less interest in the presentation of the arms, he allowed them to fall rather more carelessly to the side. Clearly visible also are six circular bullet holes at chest level. According to Maximilian's personal physician, Dr. Basch, the bullets had all passed through the emperor's body, puncturing heart, lungs, and the large arteries: "From the nature of these three wounds, the death struggle of the emperor must have been extremely short." Aubert's photographs substantiate the doctor's statement and relegate rumors that Maximilian died only after receiving a *coup de grace* to the realm of legend – although it must be stressed that Aubert did not at all consider his work to be forensic. Instead, he was concerned with producing commercial icons – images that would satisfy the visual curiosity of an international public and thus allow them to participate in the fate of a young man who had failed in his endeavors. A brilliant conversationalist, gallant social figure, talented dancer, art collector, and belletrist who expressed himself in the form of travel accounts and poetry; a cosmopolitan with liberal tendencies, who could converse in at least four languages – so runs the description of Maximilian, born the second son of Archduke Franz Carl and his wife Sophie of the noble house of Wittelsbach in 1832. Maximilian enthusiastically devoted his energies to the creation of a modern Austrian fleet on the British model, incorporating the newest technology, including steam power, screw-driven propellers, and iron hulls. In addition, he founded a marine museum and hydrographic institute and furthered the construction and fortification of a new shipyard in Pola. Appointed rear admiral at age twenty-two, he shortly thereafter was named supreme commander of the navy as well, and was subsequently designated governor-general of the Lombard-Venetian kingdom. When his sober-minded brother withdrew these important offices from him in 1859 under threat of impending war with France, Archduke Maximilian came to feel the weakness of his position at home. This made him all the more susceptible to an offer from Paris, where Napoleon III had sought a candidate for the imperial throne he wanted to establish in Mexico – by today's standpoint an absurd idea.

Walking to his death with an upright posture

The background of the Mexican experiment was the attempt of several European powers to revive Old World influence in Central and South America and simultaneously to "balance the Protestant-republican power of North America with the counterweight of a Latin-Catholic empire" (Konrad Ratz). A unilaterally imposed moratorium on the repayment of the overdue Mexican state debt declared by President Benito Juárez García provided France, Spain, and England with a welcome excuse for immediate military intervention and the establishment of Maximilian's *imperio*. For his part, the Archduke of Austro-Hungary made his agreement dependent on the outcome of a plebiscite – which Napoleon and his Mexican vassals quickly served up. Thus Maximilian considered himself to have been "elected by the people," and on 10 April 1864 accepted the crown in the palace of Miramar. Four days later he set sail from Triest aboard his favorite ship, the *Novara*, headed for Vera Cruz. What turned out in the end to be merely a short Central American regency reflects the internal contradictions of a monarch who swung oddly between court etiquette and liberal sentiments, between a zeal for reform and de facto highly authoritarian decisions. In an attempt to satisfy all parties – monarchists, republicans, liberals, and the Catholic Church – he placed himself politically between various political positions without having a firm basis of his own. On top of this, he faced an increasingly hopeless military situation. The end of the American Civil War had provided Benito Juárez García – who in any case was far from defeated on his own turf – with an unexpected ally in the form of the USA. Simultaneously, Napoleon, succumbing to internal pressures, lost interest in his American adventure and withdrew his troops from Mexico. As a result, Maximilian's twenty thousand imperial troops – in part recruited by force – confronted what eventually amounted to more than fifty thousand republican soldiers. Maximilian's offer to negotiate remained unanswered. As a result, everything depended on a swift military solution to the problem.

It is 14 May 1867. Since February, Maximilian and his remaining troops have been entrenched in the small Mexican city of Querétaro, 200 kilometers (125 miles) northwest of Mexico City. The strategy, particularly supported by the Indio General Tomás Mej'a, was to gather all forces for a final and decisive blow to the republican troops far from the capital. In fact, however, the imperial troops had maneuvered themselves into a trap, which they now planned to break out of on the morning of 15 May. It is no longer a matter of debate that Colonel Miguel Lopez betrayed the plan from a sense of wounded honor, and allowed Juárez's troops to infiltrate the city the night before. Within a few hours, the streets of Querétaro were in republican hands, Maximilian and his officers were captured. A trial lasting several days was held, and the emperor was sentenced to death on the basis of the "Law of Punishment for Crimes Against the State," which had been decreed by Juárez in 1862. On the morning of 19 June 1867, Maximilian and his generals Miguel Miramón and Tomás Mejía faced an eight-man firing squad under command of nineteen-year-old Simón Montemayor. "I forgive all and ask all to forgive me. May the blood we lose be of benefit to the country. Long live Mexico, long live independence!" are reputed to have been his last words.

Reports by the few eye-witnesses who remained loyal to the emperor are contradictory in their details. It seems certain, however, that Maximilian walked to his death with an upright posture and amazing serenity. However self-contradictory, fickle, naive, and indecisive he may have been in the short course of his life, he now faced death with bravery and pride. He granted General Miramón the place of honor in the middle of the trio; Maximilian himself, contrary to Manet's interpretation, stood at the far right. The distance from the firing squad is said to have been five steps. To each of the soldiers he is supposed to have bequeathed an ounce of gold with the request not to aim at his head. Then, at 6:40 am, he turned his gaze to the heavens, and stretched out his arms. Maximilian's final gesture was substantiated by the testimony of his adjutant Prince Felix zu Salm-Salm: the emperor compared himself to Jesus Christ in the end, who had also been betrayed into the hands of his enemies. François Aubert, with his photograph of the blood-spattered shirt, bequeathed us the icon corresponding to his martyrdom.

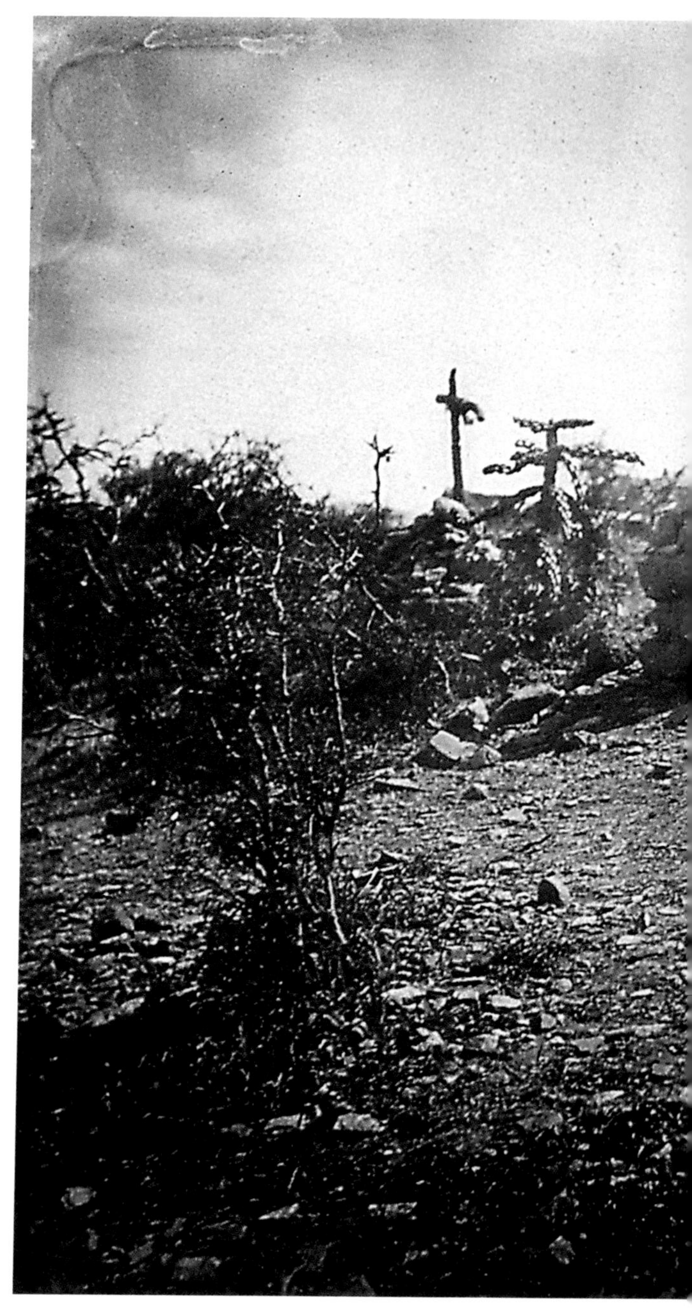

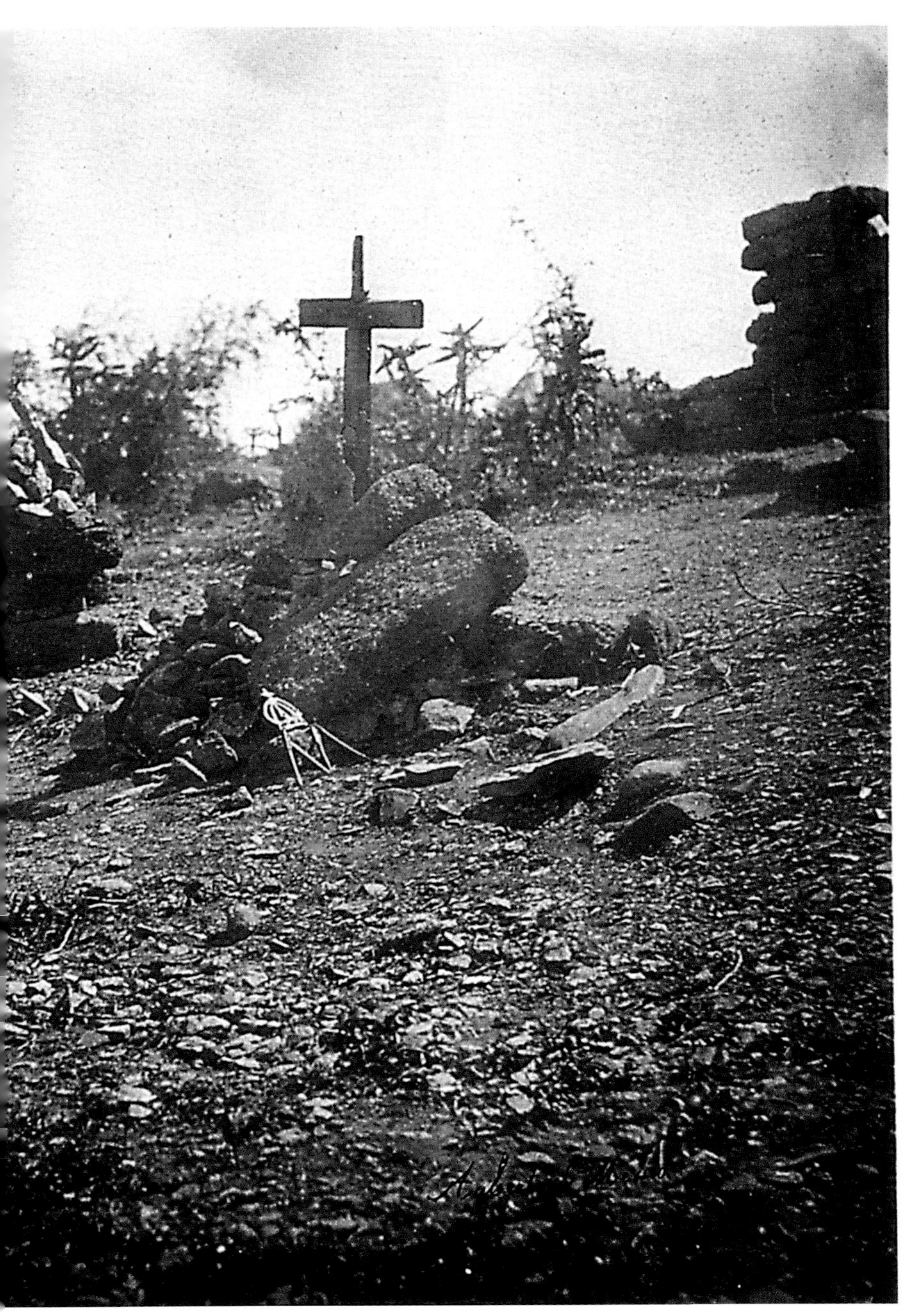

André Adolphe Eugène Disdéri
Dead Communards
1871

The End of a Utopia

Historians are still in disagreement: Was the Paris Commune of 1871 merely an outburst of chaos and anarchy, or was it the first proletarian revolution in history? In either case, the uprising resulted in even more casualties than the French Revolution of 1789. It was a civil war, as bloody as it was brief, in which photography defined a new field for itself.

Someone had distributed slips of paper, had given them numbers. Perhaps that is what is most shocking in this picture that breaks with taboo in two senses, consciously offending against the accepted rules of decency and morality. First, it makes the wounded, desecrated, defenseless human body into a pictorial object, and second, it subjugates suffering to a cool arithmetic. But why, one asks, were these twelve male bodies in plain coffins made of raw spruce boards laid side by side and provided with hand-written numbers? Whoever did it could not have been following any imaginable principle. One may speculate about a coded message, but such a theory is really rather improbable. It remains astonishing that the row of numbers begins with a 'six' and ends with a 'one'; 'four' was assigned twice; 'twelve' is missing. The sum amounts to 70 – but that can hardly be significant. Literature concerning the picture has sometimes claimed that the numbers could have served for later identification of the corpses. But this, too, seems hardly plausible if one considers the fate of the men: anonymous members of the Commune, presumably arrested after 21 May 1871, shot by unknown soldiers of the regular troops, quickly buried – but first provided with a 'portrait' beforehand. Who could have been interested in identifying them? And if someone were, then why don't the numbers follow some kind of understandable logic. Don't the physiognomies provide enough evidence on their own?

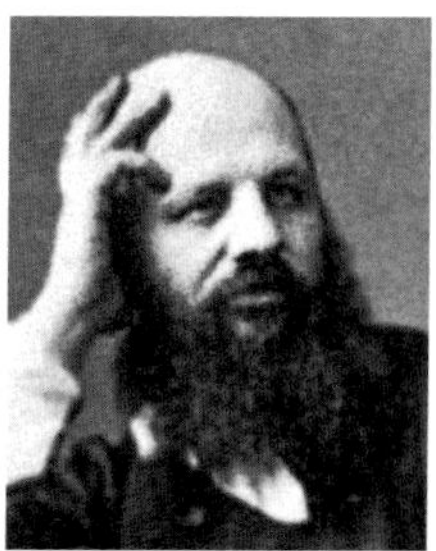

André Adolphe Eugène Disdéri
Born ***1819*** *in Paris. First dedicates himself to painting and theater.* ***1847*** *turns to photography. Initially active in Marseille, Brest, Nîmes.* ***1854*** *sets up a studio in Paris. In the same year files a patent for a fast and reasonably priced form of portrait (known as* carte de visite*).* ***1855*** *founding of the Société du Palais de l'Industrie.* ***1860–62*** *portraits of prominent contemporaries for a Galerie des contemporains. Branches in Nice, Madrid, and London.* ***1871*** *takes photos during the Commune.* ***1877*** *sells his business. Moves to Nice.* ***1889*** *returns to Paris. Dies* ***1889*** *in the Hôpital Sainte-Anne in Paris, deaf, blind, and totally impoverished.*

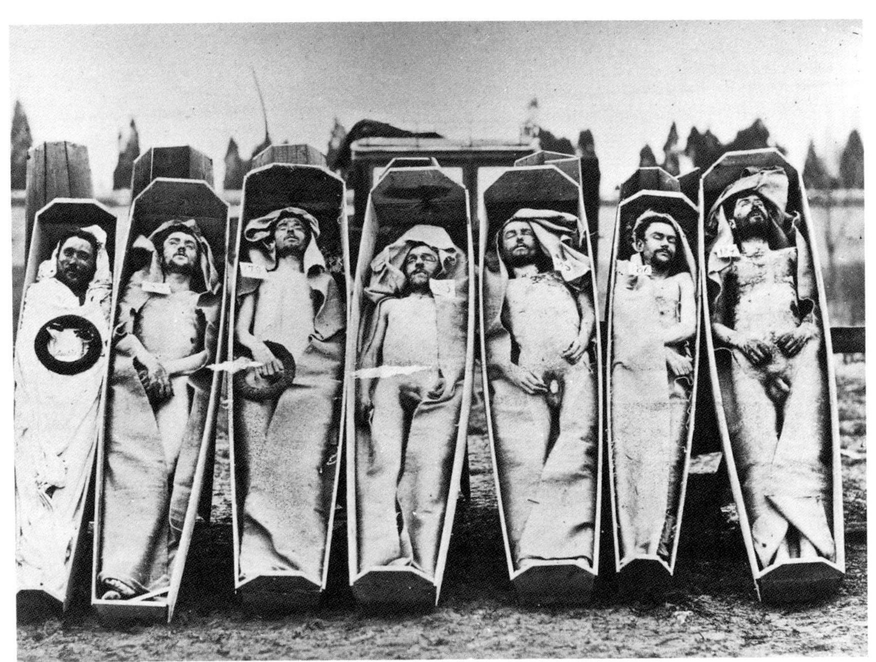

The picture is beyond a doubt a document of power – the power of the living over the dead, who can no longer remove themselves from such degrading exhibition and classification. The power of the victor over the vanquished, the bourgeoisie over the defeated proletariat. "Hard years for the amputated, the debt-ridden, the working class, under surveillance and suspicion – these years under Thiers and MacMahon," as Michelle Perrot describes the situation in her book *Les ouvriers en grève*. "Paris had lost approximately 100,000 workers: 20,000 to 30,000 had probably been killed, 40,000 imprisoned, and the rest fled..."

Mountains of bodies round the Jardin du Luxembourg

To make it clear from the beginning: we know little about this photograph, whose original is now in the possession of the Musée Carnavalet, the municipal museum of Paris. The lightly bleached-out albumin print bearing the archive entry 9951 is 21 × 28.2 cm (8¼ × 11 inches) in size, pasted onto grey cardboard, and was a private donation, as the handwritten remark, "Legs Hauterive," testifies. Neither does the photograph provide further information on its reverse about the place and time it was taken, nor does it identify the names of the executed.

André Adolphe Eugène Disdéri:
Shot Communards, *Gernsheim Collection, The University of Texas at Austin. This picture from 1871 is also now attributed to Disdéri.*

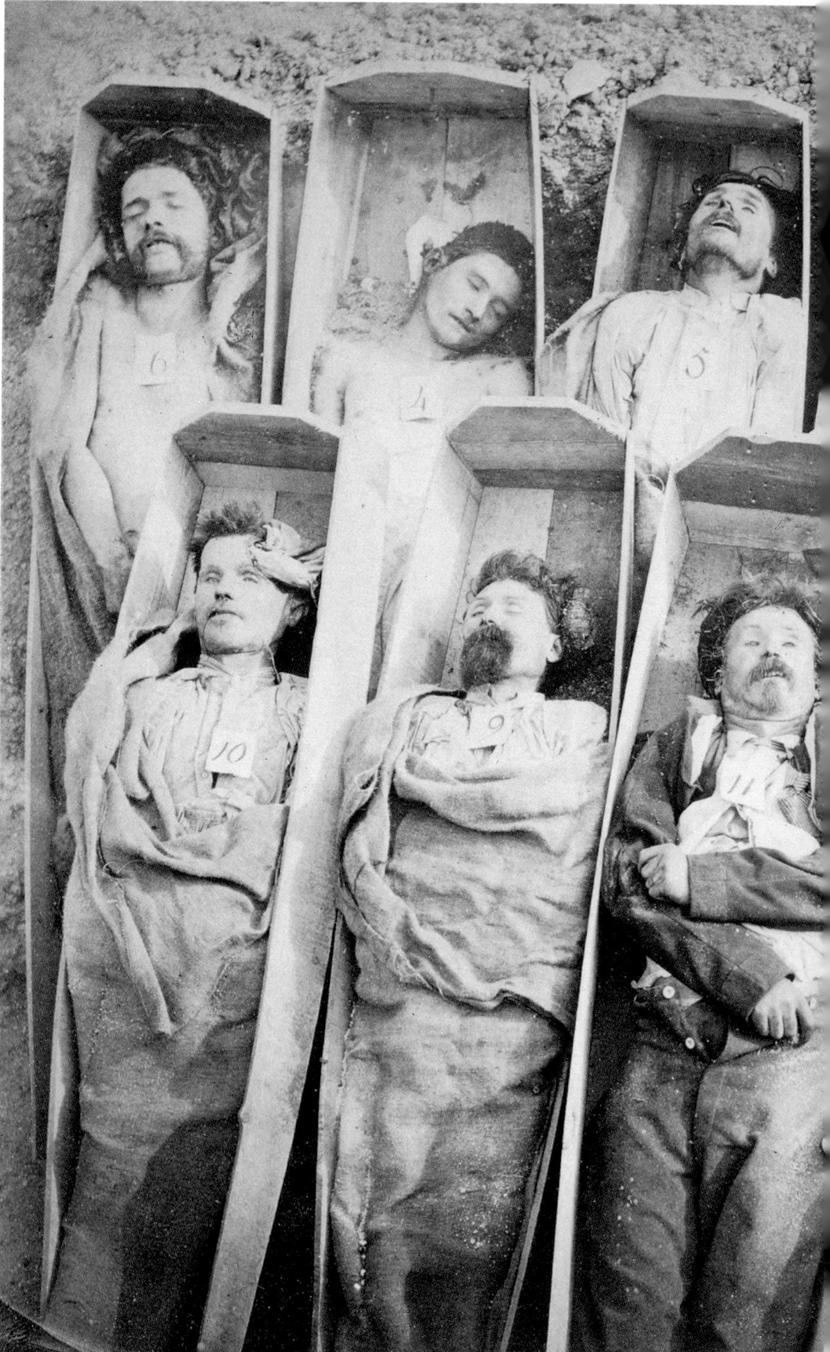
6
4
5
10
9
11

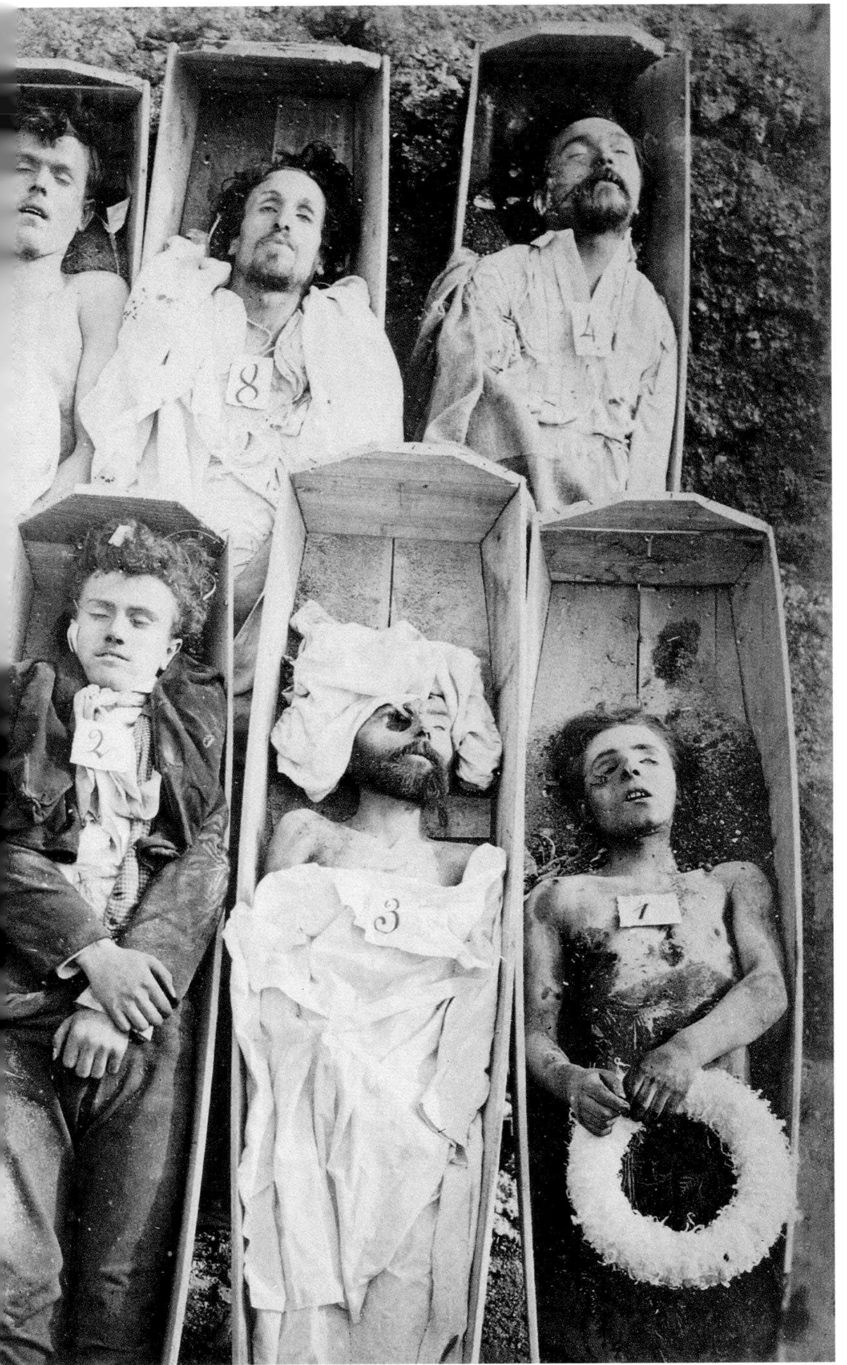
8
4
2
3
1

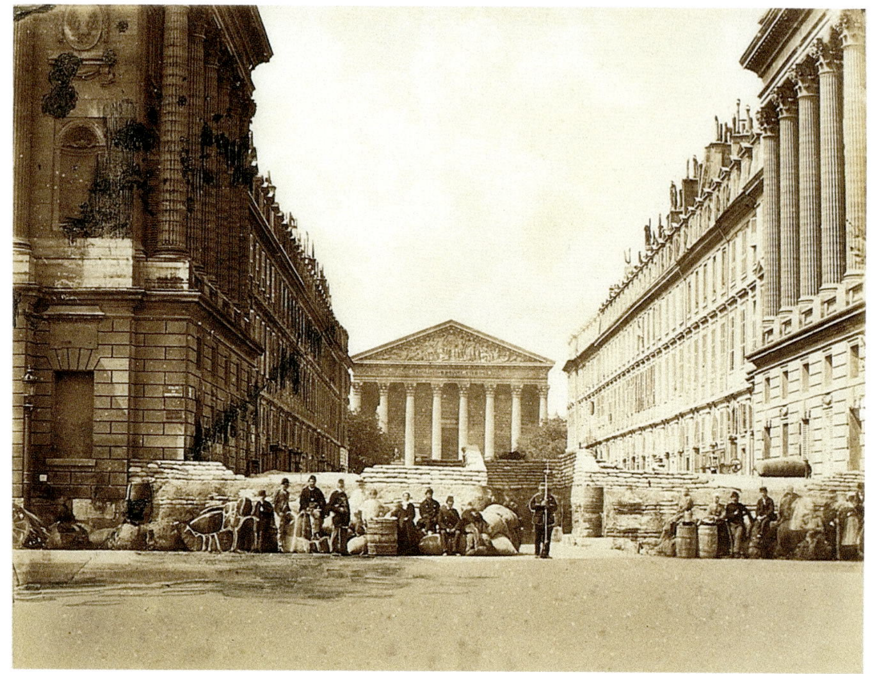

Only the small stamp at the bottom right on the front puts us on the trail of the photographer: namely, Disdéri.

In all probability, the photograph was taken immediately after 21 May 1871, that is, during the so-called Bloody Week during which most of the revolutionaries – or men who were held to be such – were shot by Thiers's merciless troops and buried in mass graves. The location of the picture might be the Père Lachaise cemetery, at the time the center for the executions, or the walls around the Jardin du Luxembourg, where "mountains of bodies" were also reported. The naked torsos of the corpses one, three, four, six, and seven may be an indication that they died heroically with their chests bared. The slightly dandyish clothing of corpses two and eleven suggests that they were of the bohemian world, and in fact there are supposed to have been an above-average number of intellectuals and artists who sympathized with the Commune. Research speaks of 1,725 members of the liberal professions who were arrested after the Bloody Week. Among them, perhaps the most prominent of them, was the painter Gustave Courbet, who miraculously survived the 'cleansing', but was fined an annual sum of

---

Above: **Émile Robert:** Barricades in Front of the Madeleine, *albumin print, 1871. A version of this picture was included in the* Match *report of June 1939.*

Right: **Franck (François-Marie-Louis-Alexandre Gobinet de Villecholles)**: The Demolished Vendôme Column, *albumin print, 1871.*

10,000 francs in the course of a sensational trial. The money was used for the re-erection of the column damaged by the Commune on the Place Vendôme.

Through Paris with a darkroom on wheels

Why did André Adolphe Eugène Disdéri photograph the twelve executed Communards? Probably not from 'artistic' motives – nor because he wanted to test the limits of his medium. Disdéri, born in 1819, was above all a businessman – not always a fortunate one, as Helmut Gernsheim points out, but with at least a strong commercial interest and the readiness to seek out his advantage wherever his nose led him. Although he had not invented the *cartes- de-visite*, as is often claimed, he had, more importantly, popularized them. It was his Paris studio that fostered the breakthrough of the aesthetically unambitious portraits that were, however, fast and cheap to produce. "In 1861," writes Gernsheim, "Disdéri was already accounted the richest photographer in the world. In his Paris studio alone, he took in an 1,200,000 francs annually. This means that at a price of twenty francs for a dozen portraits, his etablissement was serving on average 200 customers per day." Disdéri, who had started as a landscape painter, fabric maker, bookkeeper, and actor, was correspondingly interested in photography as a mass medium. It was he who recognized the wish of the broad majority of the bourgeoisie for portraits, and knew how to satisfy them. Whereas the Franco-Prussian War of 1870–71 was not of interest to the majority of the studio photographers of Paris (Nadar, Carjat, Reutlinger, Thiébault),

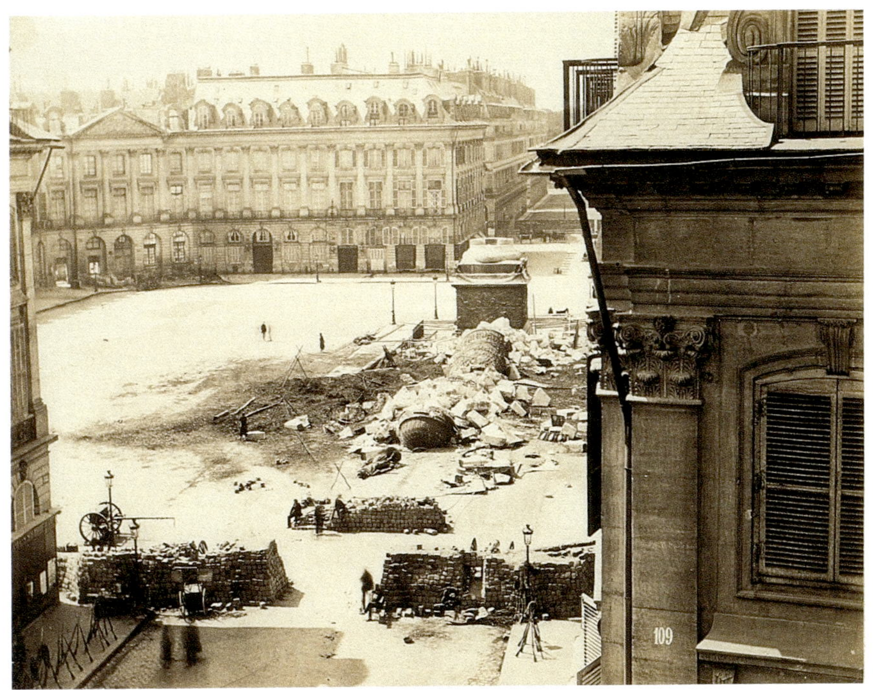

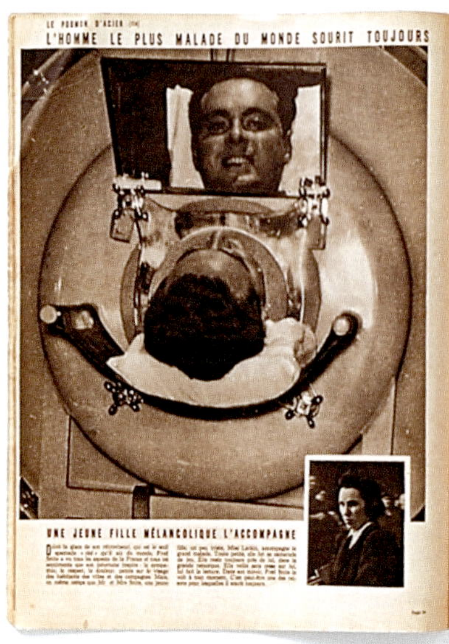

L'HOMME LE PLUS MALADE DU MONDE SOURIT TOUJOURS

UNE JEUNE FILLE MÉLANCOLIQUE L'ACCOMPAGNE

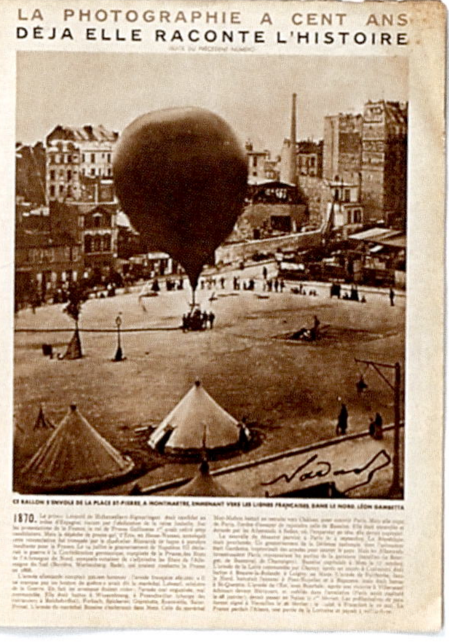

LA PHOTOGRAPHIE A CENT ANS
DÉJA ELLE RACONTE L'HISTOIRE

CE BALLON S'ENVOLE DE LA PLACE ST-PIERRE, A MONTMARTRE, EMMENANT VERS LES LIGNES FRANÇAISES, DANS LE NORD, LÉON GAMBETTA

1870.

Disdéri rode through Paris with a darkroom on wheels, documenting war damage, photographing the destroyed Tuilleries, the burned-out city hall, Thiers' house, destroyed by the Communards, and the Vendôme column. After the end of the riots, he published a book with the title *Ruines de Paris et de ses environs*. But our picture of the executed Communards does not appear on its pages, nor does a variant (now at the University of Texas in Austin), depicting seven Communards, this time unclothed, in their coffins. Anne McCauley suspects that Disdéri was at the time commissioned by the police to record the faces of the Communards – but evidence is lacking. Later, the picture is said to have been distributed by other studios as a stolen copy, and if so, that is a clue that there was no other picture available that responded to the increased public interest. Disdéri himself seems not to have commercialized the photograph. Or might it be possible that he was not the true creator of the photograph? After all, the modest stamp on the cardboard only indicates that the print had at one point or another passed through Disdéri's studio. "If his studio indeed made these negatives," argues McCauley, "its owner must have either been desperate for money or felt little sympathy for the Commune."

Jacobin dreams of a popular uprising

The photography of the period of the Paris Commune – a still largely unresearched field – was determined by the ideological interests of its photographers. The pictures mirrored the technical possibilities of a medium that hardly allowed instantaneous shots in the sense of today's photojournalism. The photographs of the Commune can be fairly exactly dated between the 18 March and end of May 1871, the beginning and the bloody end of a popular proletarian revolt, whose life span as a social utopia lasted around 70 days. The

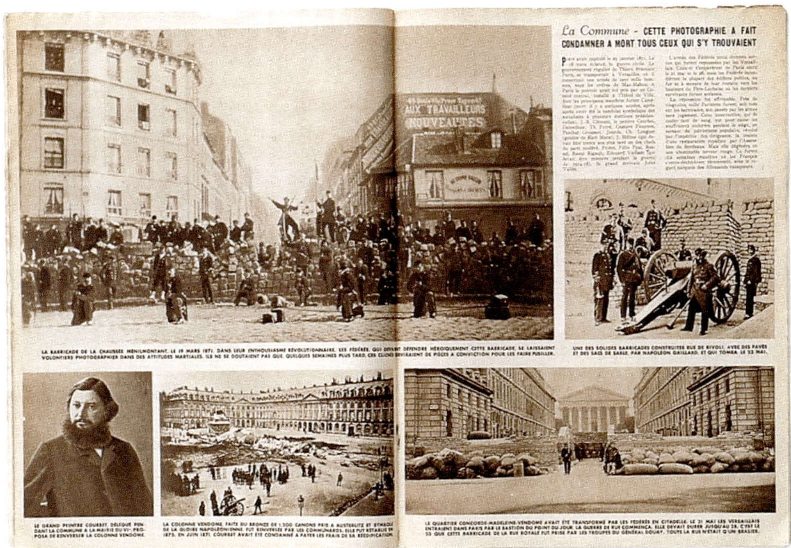

La Commune - CETTE PHOTOGRAPHIE A FAIT CONDAMNER A MORT TOUS CEUX QUI S'Y TROUVAIENT

LA BARRICADE DE LA CHAUSSÉE MÉNILMONTANT, LE 19 MARS 1871. DANS LEUR ENTHOUSIASME RÉVOLUTIONNAIRE, LES FÉDÉRÉS, QUI DEVAIENT DÉFENDRE HÉROÏQUEMENT CETTE BARRICADE, SE LAISSAIENT VOLONTIERS PHOTOGRAPHIER DANS DES ATTITUDES MARTIALES. ILS NE SE DOUTAIENT PAS QUE, QUELQUES SEMAINES PLUS TARD, CES CLICHÉS SERVIRAIENT DE PIÈCES A CONVICTION POUR LES FAIRE FUSILLER.

UNE DES SOLIDES BARRICADES CONSTRUITES RUE DE RIVOLI, AVEC DES PAVÉS ET DES SACS DE SABLE, PAR NAPOLÉON GAILLARD, ET QUI TOMBA LE 23 MAI.

LE GRAND PEINTRE COURBET, DÉLÉGUÉ PENDANT LA COMMUNE A LA MAIRIE DU VIe, PROPOSA DE RENVERSER LA COLONNE VENDÔME.

LA COLONNE VENDÔME, FAITE DU BRONZE DE 1.200 CANONS PRIS A AUSTERLITZ ET SYMBOLE DE LA GLOIRE NAPOLÉONIENNE, FUT RENVERSÉE PAR LES COMMUNARDS. ELLE FUT RÉTABLIE EN 1875. EN JUIN 1871, COURBET AVAIT ÉTÉ CONDAMNÉ A PAYER LES FRAIS DE SA RÉÉDIFICATION.

LE QUARTIER CONCORDE-MADELEINE-VENDÔME AVAIT ÉTÉ TRANSFORMÉ PAR LES FÉDÉRÉS EN CITADELLE. LE 21 MAI LES VERSAILLAIS ENTRAIENT DANS PARIS PAR LE BASTION DU POINT DU JOUR. LA GUERRE DE RUE COMMENÇA. ELLE DEVAIT DURER JUSQU'AU 28. C'EST LE 23 QUE CETTE BARRICADE DE LA RUE ROYALE FUT PRISE PAR LES TROUPES DU GÉNÉRAL DOUAY. TOUTE LA RUE N'ÉTAIT QU'UN BRASIER.

historical background is well known. The starting point, or rather the catalyzer, of the uprising was the loss of the war against Germany. The Prussians had been occupying Paris since 18 September 1870; capitulation and the conclusion of a peace seemed inevitable. In fact, the National Assembly, dominated by monarchists and clerics, which met together in Bordeaux on 12 February 1871 decided upon an immediate and unlimited peace. Paris flaunted the decision with nationalistic, chauvinistic slogans, and Jacobin dreams of a popular uprising filled the air. For the first time since 1848 red flags began to appear. On the night of 17 March, it came to armed conflict when 'regular' troops attempted to take the approximately one hundred cannons stationed on the mound of Montmarte under their control at the order of the designated prime minister, Adolphe Thiers. But the half-hearted raid was foiled by the rebel troops. Thiers's band was driven from the city as the rebels occupied the city hall and other public buildings. A municipal council operating out of Versailles now assumed power as a countergovernment to Thiers. Its program included such resolutions as the separation of church and state, the confiscation of property belonging to religious orders and cloisters, the official adoption of the red flag, and a law forbidding bakers to bake at night. Certainly this was no revolution in any real sense of the term, but rather a pack of Jacobin or Proudon-inspired measures that would serve to solidify the later reputation of the Commune as a proletarian revolt. Already on 2 April, conflict exploded again between the followers of Thiers and the Commune. The Paris Guard behind the ubiquitous barricades understood well enough how to fight, but problems ranging from quibbles over domains of competence, to lack of leadership, military disorganization, and to dilettantism soon allowed the superiority of the regular troops to emerge clearly. On 21 May, they succeeded in overcoming the Paris defensive wall at an unguarded point. What followed has gone down in the annals of history as a

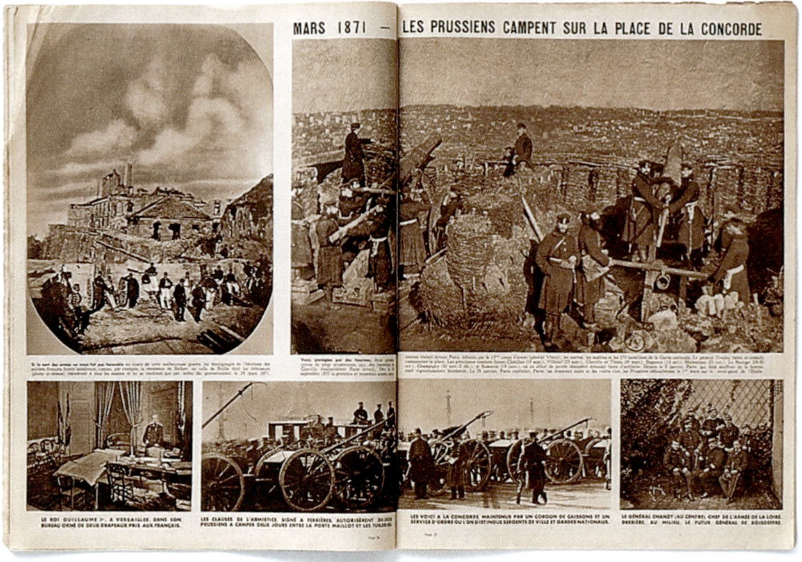

MARS 1871 — LES PRUSSIENS CAMPENT SUR LA PLACE DE LA CONCORDE

LE ROI GUILLAUME Iᵉʳ, A VERSAILLES, DANS SON BUREAU ORNÉ DE DEUX DRAPEAUX PRIS AUX FRANÇAIS.

LES CLAUSES DE L'ARMISTICE, SIGNÉ A FERRIÈRES, AUTORISÈRENT 30.000 PRUSSIENS A CAMPER DEUX JOURS ENTRE LA PORTE MAILLOT ET LES TUILERIES.

LES VOICI A LA CONCORDE, MAINTENUS PAR UN CORDON DE CAISSONS ET UN SERVICE D'ORDRE OU L'ON DISTINGUE SERGENTS DE VILLE ET GARDES NATIONAUX.

LE GÉNÉRAL CHANZY (AU CENTRE), CHEF DE L'ARMÉE DE LA LOIRE. DERRIÈRE, AU MILIEU, LE FUTUR GÉNÉRAL DE BOISDEFFRE.

"semaine sanglante" (bloody week) – a week of denunciations, persecutions, mass executions, and merciless terror such as had not been seen since the Revolution of 1789 (with its 12,000 casualties throughout the entire nation). The estimates for 1871 range between 20,000 and 40,000 Communards killed or executed. We have more precise numbers on the losses at Versailles: official records counted almost 900 dead and 7,000 wounded.

The Commune was a time of many photographs – and few. Many if one looks at the troublesomeness of the then standard wet-collodion process, in which a plate had to be sensitized and developed on location; few, if one considers the number of photographers then active in Paris. Gernsheim speaks of 33,000 persons in 1861 who "earned their living by photography or in businesses that served it." Ten years later, the number certainly would not have been less. But those who remained seem, as Jean Claude Gautrand has expressed it, to have exchanged "the velvet of the studios" for the street rather unwillingly. The only photographers who stand out for larger collections of pictures are in fact Alphonse Liébert, Hippolyte-Auguste Collard, Eugène Appert, and Bruno Braquehais, whose series of a total of 109 photographs were dutifully handed over to the Bibliothèque nationale in late 1871 and represent the most remarkable contribution to Commune photography.

Meeting of the proletariat and photography

From a Marxist perspective on art history, the photography of the Commune has at times been evaluated as the predecessor of the later development of working-class photography. The days of the Commune had, according to Richard Hiepe, brought about "the first meeting of the proletariat and photography" – which can at most apply to the early pictures of the barricades with posing Communards, though it worth emphasizing that those

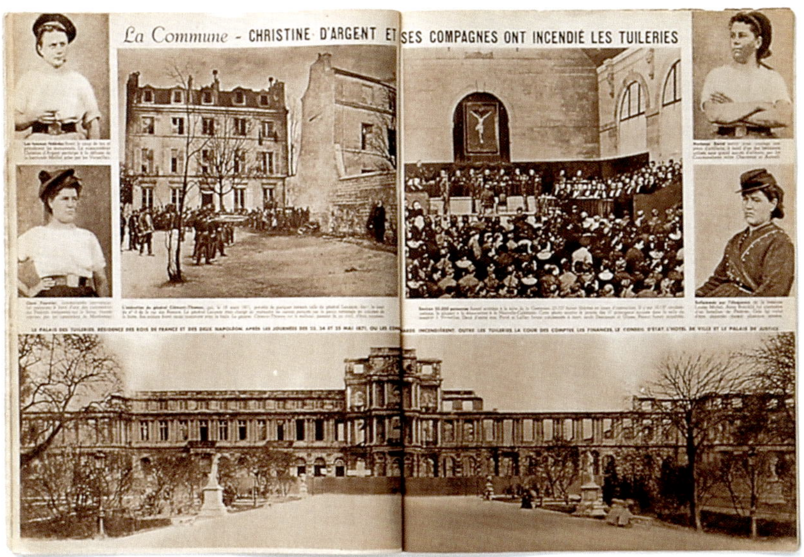

La Commune - CHRISTINE D'ARGENT ET SES COMPAGNES ONT INCENDIÉ LES TUILERIES

taking the photographs were and remained members of the bourgeoisie. In no sense does the term "proletarian photography" apply to the large majority of the pictures, which range from the innumerable views of war-ravaged Paris (and express a clearly critical position toward the Commune) through to the tendentious photomontages of an Eugène Appert, or to his photographic inventory of the approximately 40,000 imprisoned Communards, which constitutes an early form of the information-gathering approach to photography later refined by Alphonse Bertillon. What is missing, surprisingly enough, between the pictures of the barricades and the ruins, are photographs of the dead; as if they never existed, the twenty to thirty thousand victims left hardly a trace on the photographic plates. For photography, as Christine Lapostolle rightly claims, "there was no semaine sanglante, and as a result, no painful pictorial return of the wounded and dead after the battles before the gates of Paris. Nothing of the misery that tortured the people remained to be seen." Even if there were one or another picture of victims in addition to Disdéri's images of the dead Communards, quantitatively and qualitatively the 'proceeds' would be comparatively modest. And thus it is no accident that precisely this photograph has been able to attain symbolic status in the course of time. Whether Disdéri himself took the photograph or not, this status will not disappear. What is important is that the photograph has become an icon, a pictorial metaphor for the end of a short-lived utopia.

Pages 90–93: *Photo report in* Match, *1 June 1939. Even 70 years later, the Commune still haunted the minds of the French.*

Maurice Guibert
Toulouse-Lautrec in His Studio
ca. 1894

The Artist and His Photographer

At some point in the mid-1890s – presumably in 1894 – Maurice Guibert photographed his friend Toulouse-Lautrec in the latter's studio. Although the amateur photographer was simply following one of the common photographic conventions of the turn of the century, his ironic perspective on the subject drew emphasis to the special position of the already internationally known artist.

He has laid his brush and palette aside, his hands in the pockets of his trousers. It's a little as if he is standing there because the director of the photograph wanted him in the picture only for the sake of a vague symmetry. And yet, he is the protagonist of the scene, even if the gaze of the unprejudiced viewer is caught initially, and is probably held for some time, by the unclothed woman to the left in the picture. That she is standing barefoot and completely naked may at first seem rather curious. Her nudity acquires a 'deeper' significance, however, when one realizes that around 1900, artists – both painters and sculptors – often had themselves photographed with their models in the studio. Usually the camera 'caught' them at their work: the visualization of the breath of genius, a literal transformation of transitory flesh into 'eternal' art, as it were. But here, there is no question of work, and, furthermore, the studio appears remarkably orderly. The presentation of what are recognizably seven panel paintings reminds one rather of a kind of informal *vernissage* in which the naked muse, not only unclothed but also holding a lance in her hand, does not really seem to fit. Even her supposed role as 'model' is questionable if one looks more closely at the pictures on the floor and on the easels: there is not a single nude in the academic sense among them. Further doubts about the role of this 'model' arise when one considers that this genre did not really constitute the creative center of the work of

---

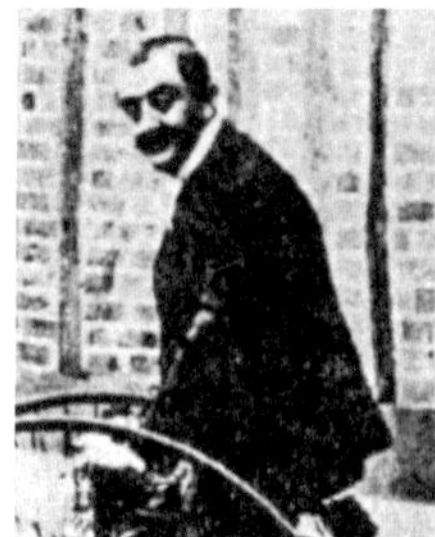

Maurice Guibert
Born ***1856****. Active member of the Société française de photographie as well as the Société des excursionnistes photographes. Autodidact and amateur. By profession a representative of the champagne company Moët et Chandon.* ***1886–95*** *photographic diary entitled* Ma vie photographique. *Becomes acquainted and then friends with Toulouse-Lautrec. The artist's first exposures around* ***1890****. August* ***1896*** *beach holiday in Arcachon together with Toulouse-Lautrec, where he takes snapshots of the latter swimming in a light-hearted mood.* ***1951*** *essay by Jean Adhémar on Guibert in the journal* Aesculape, *the first and only work to date on the committed hobby photographer's life and works. Dies* ***1913****.*

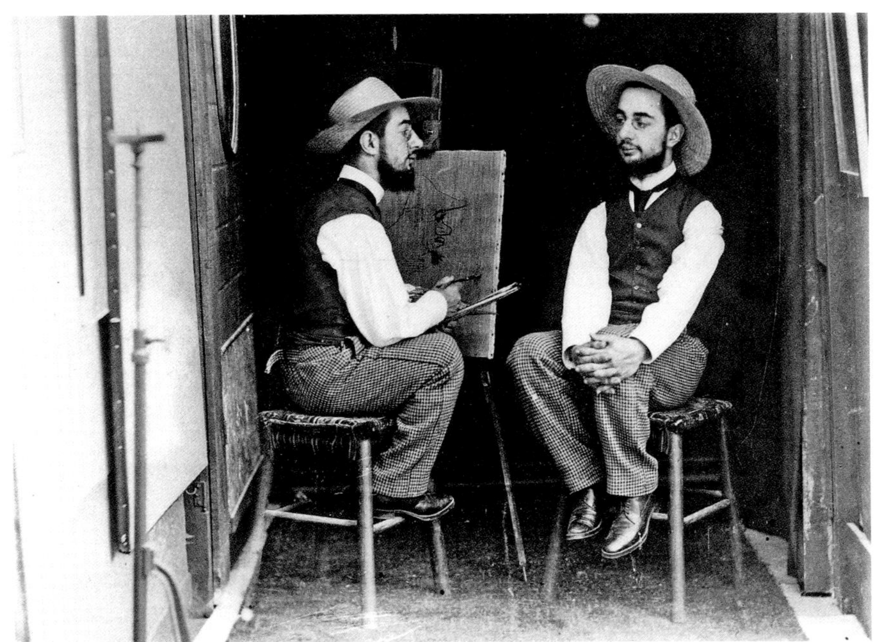

our artist, Henri de Toulouse-Lautrec, painter, draftsman, poster artist and, by the time of the photograph, a both celebrated and castigated personality of *fin de siècle* art.

Bourgeois clothing of English cut

Toulouse-Lautrec has donned formal attire, wearing long trousers, a dark vest, a white shirt with stand-up collar and tie. It is rumored that he also owns a suit cut from green billiard-table felt – but this seems rather to be only a gag reserved for special occasions. As a rule, the artist tended toward bourgeois clothing of English cut, irrespective of his affinity for what we would today refer to as the 'subculture'. What his contemporaries may well have found odd, however, was that even in closed rooms, he never removed his hat. The brim, as he took care to explain his foible, eliminated glare when he was painting. In addition, the hat made him appear a little taller – and also covered a deformity in the formation of his head, one that nobody spoke about: a fontanelle where the bones had not grown together properly. According to recent medical research, this – together with the many other bodily infirmities that the child born Henri Marie Raymond de Toulouse-Lautrec in the southern French town of Albi in 1864 suffered from in the course of his short life – resulted from the long history of incestuous

---

Toulouse-Lautrec Paints Toulouse-Lautrec, *photomontage, ca. 1892. This picture, now popularized by postcards, was also one of Maurice Guibert's ideas.*

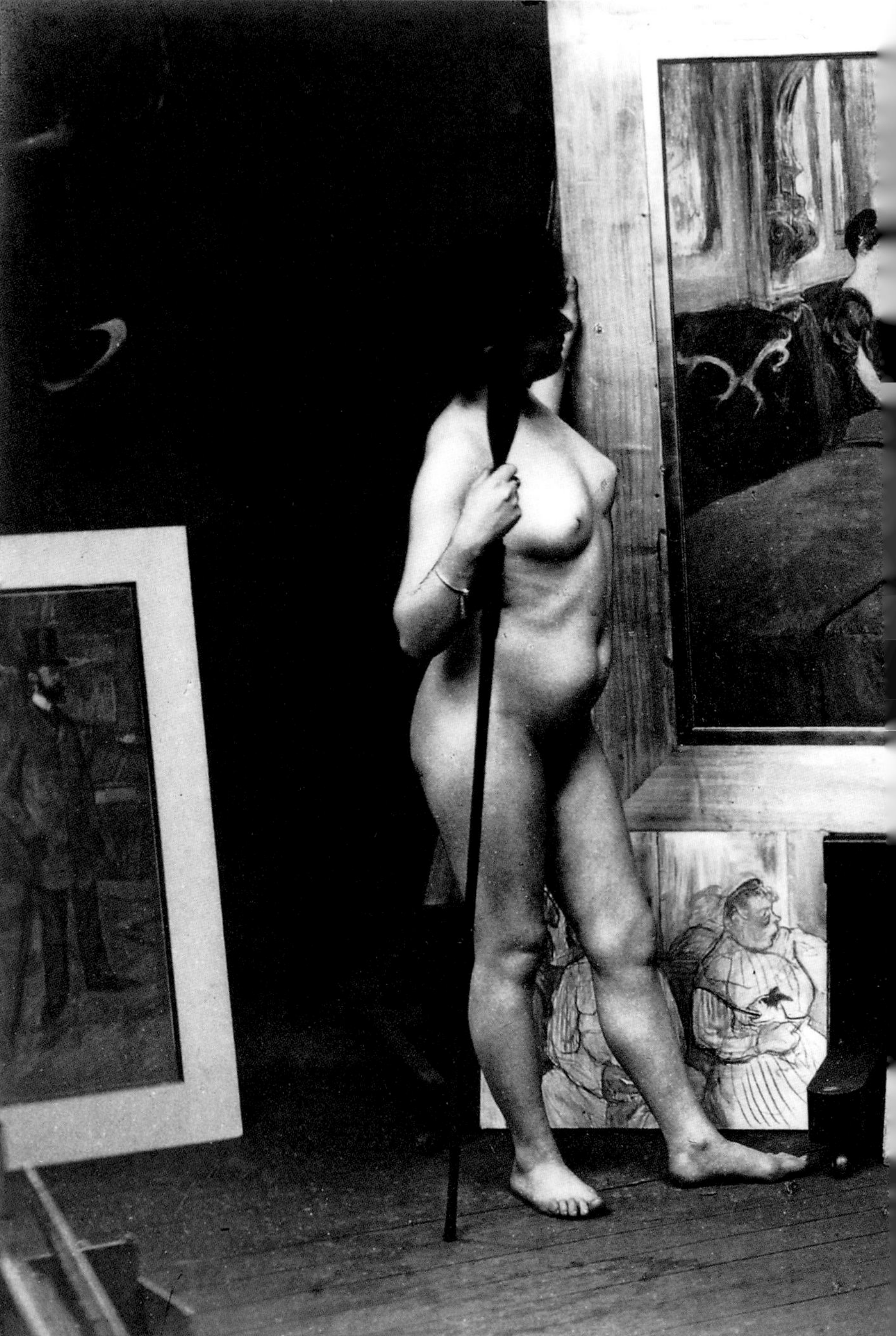

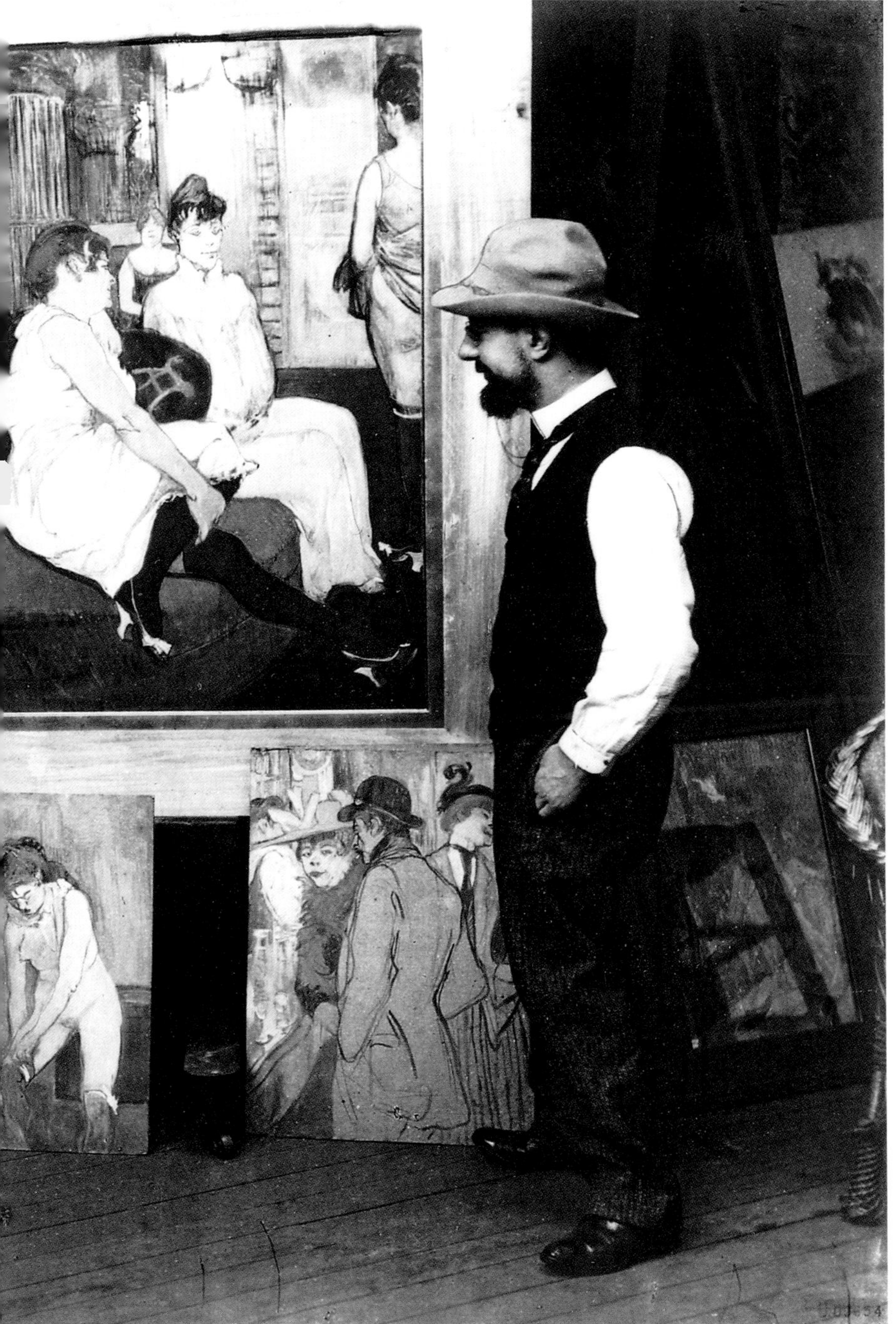

marriages entered into by his noble ancestors. The artist lisped, was short-sighted, and spoke with a marked stentorian voice – but these were only the smaller problems. He had large and clearly protruding nostrils, a receding chin, and abnormally thick red lips that he concealed behind his dark beard. On a more serious level, he suffered from a generally weak constitution combined with pyknodystosis, a rare from of dwarfism. In addition, two broken legs that he suffered at age thirteen and fourteen ensured that Toulouse-Lautrec would move about only awkwardly and painfully for the rest of his life. "I walk badly," he liked to say, with a touch of self irony, "like a duck – but a runner duck."

Henri de Toulouse-Lautrec was short: five feet in height, to be exact. He was a cripple, fleeing from the many virtues extolled particularly by his father, a passionate rider and huntsman, not to mention lady-killer. The son sought refuge in the bohemian world of Paris during the Belle Epoque, in the demimonde of Montmartre, where he found friends of both sexes, and which became a spiritual home, and almost a family, to him. He had been in the city on the Seine – at first with interruptions – since 1878, studying with the animal painter René Princeteau, and later with Léon Bonnat and Fernand Cormon, both of whom were recognized exponents of an academic style. If their salon painting did not really further the talented young man artistically, at the same time neither did it interfere with the development of his free brush strokes – nor does it particularly seem to have placed obstacles in his incipient interest in the world of the bordello, cabaret, and café concert. During the same period, Émile Bernard and Aristide Bruant became his friends and important sources of inspiration for him, as did the ten-year-older Vincent van Gogh, whom Lautrec immortalized in a remarkable pastel in 1887. A year earlier, in 1886, he had rented a spacious studio on Montmartre at 7 rue Tourlaque at the corner of rue Caulaincourt 27 (today no. 21). It was in this studio, where he stayed approximately ten years, that he probably finished the majority of his œuvre of 737 paintings, 275 watercolors, 5,084 drawings, as well as 364 graphic works and posters. Our photograph, too, bearing the title *Toulouse-Lautrec dans son Atelier*, was certainly taken here, even if we do not know precisely when. But the fact that his large-format painting *Au Salon de la rue des Moulins* (a major work of which several studies and variations exist), which dominates the composition, was completed only in 1894 offers at least a vague reference point for the photograph.

The myth and cliché of the Belle Epoque

To the left in the photograph, although partially cut off, we see the full-length portrait of Georges-Henri Manuel, which has been dated 1891 (today in the Bührle Collection, Zurich). A little further to the right, half visible through the legs of the unclothed young woman, is a sketch titled *Monsieur, Madame et le chien*. The bordello scene *Femme tirant son bas*, painted in 1894 (today in the Musée d'Orsay), constitutes the striking center point of the works displayed on the floor. Finally, to the right, is the last of the identifiable tableaus, *Alfred la Guigne*, painted in 1891 (today in the National Gallery of Art in Washington). Who arranged the pictures for display and why precisely these? Who is the woman with the seemingly meaningless lance? Is she perhaps to be interpreted as a parody of William-Adolphe Bouguereau's painting *Vénus et l'Amour* of 1879: a prostitute who recognizes herself in the large panel painting – an interior of the well-known bordello in the rue des Moulins, in which Lautrec is supposed to have lived for a time? The fact that she presents herself naked before the camera, the manner

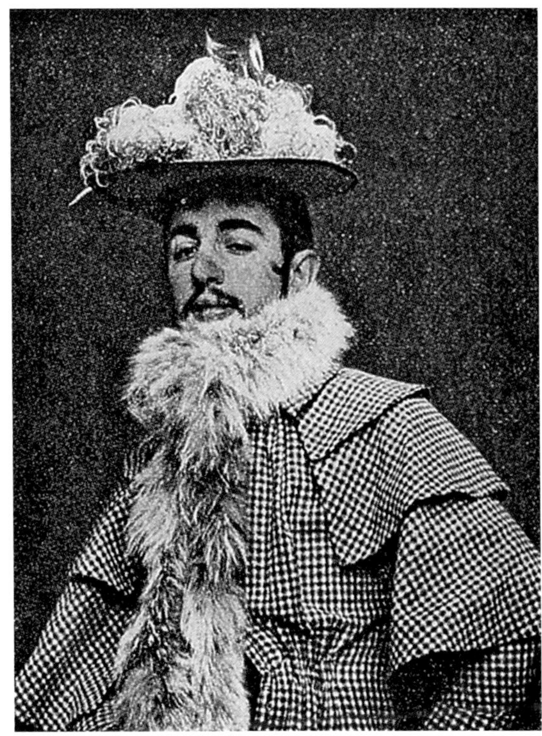

in which she inspects the painting, as well as her, so to speak, thoroughly non-academic measurements, which do not at all correspond to the ideal of an artist's model, argue for this possibility. Admittedly we don't know the answer, for neither Toulouse-Lautrec nor 'his' photographer, Maurice Guibert, commented on the picture. All we have is a fairly large original print of 24 × 35 cm (9½ × 18¾ inches) that stems from Guibert's estate and was donated to the Paris National Library by his granddaughter. Art-lovers and visitors to Paris are familiar with the photograph as a postcard, in which format the picture has become a bestseller, effortlessly taking advantage of several clichés: Paris as a city that is both art-minded and generous, lascivious and open to sensual joys – a Paris in which the Belle Epoque has become a myth, a regular ideal of the pleasures of bourgeois life.

Toulouse-Lautrec, like Maurice Guibert, knew nothing of a 'Belle Epoque', a term that arose only in the 1950s. But no one disagrees that before 1900 both were part of the merry and carefree society centered in Montmartre, although Lautrec seems to have maintained a special relationship to Guibert. In letters to his mother, Toulouse-Lautrec is always speaking of his "friend, Maurice Guibert" (July 1891) or the "faithful Guibert" (August 1895), who seems in fact to have been something of an elongated shadow of the artist in the Paris years. There is also evidence of several journeys jointly undertaken, for example to Nîmes; the castles on the Loire; Malromé, the estate of his mother, located near Bordeaux; Arcachon; and, in 1895, a ship voyage from Le Havre to Bordeaux, during which Guibert was able only with great exertion to restrain the painter, blinded with love for a young beauty, from following her to Africa. Lautrec accorded Guibert no such impressive portrait as the one he painted of

---

Above and page 101: *Guibert took Lautrec's portrait in the most outlandish of costumes: Dressed as a woman, with Jane Avril's famous boa hat on his head (1892), as Pierrot (1894), and as a Japanese man (1892).*

another photographer, namely Paul Sescau (1891, now in the Brooklyn Museum, New York), but Guibert appears in no fewer than six other paintings and twenty-five drawings as exactly what he in fact was for Lautrec: a drinking partner, a friend who could hold his alcohol well and who accompanied the artist on nightly romps, a companion on visits to the legendary *maisons closes* – in short, a bon vivant whose stout figure is easy to identify in pictures such as *À la Mie* (With the girlfriend, 1891), and *Au Moulin Rouge* (1892–93). Little more is known about Maurice Guibert, except that he was born in 1856, died in 1913, lived in a handsome inherited estate in the rue de la Tour, was primarily employed as the representative of the champagne firm Moët et Chandon, and indulged in a remarkable hobby in his free time –photography. Guibert was an active member of the Société française de photographie and the Société des excursionnistes photographes, a loose association of amateur photographers with a penchant for hiking, to which the well-known science photographer Albert Londe also belonged. Several albums in the possession of the National Library in Paris, including a volume with the thematic title *Ma vie photographique* (1886–95), provide proof of Guibert's photographic interests, which – remarkably enough – were not at all aimed at ennobling the art of the camera by means of artistic photographic techniques, as the international community of the pictorialists were striving for at the time. Instead, Guibert pursued a kind of privately defined 'snapshot' photography characterized by wit and a sense of fun in setting up scenes. The dry gelatin plates that came into use in the 1880s, which made amateur photography in our modern sense possible for the first time, proved of course very useful to Guibert and his ultimately artistically unambitious approach.

Costumed in front of the camera

The relevant lexicons remain silent on the photographer Maurice Guibert. And without a doubt he and his small œuvre would have been forgotten, if the playboy and boon companion of Toulouse-Lautrec had not in the course of the years become something of a 'family and court photographer' to the painter. Lautrec himself seems to have taken an interest in photography from early on, although it must be said that his relation to photography on the whole still awaits a proper analysis. What is certain is that Toulouse-Lautrec, like many contemporary painters – one needs only to think of Degas or Bonnard – used photographs as patterns for his painting; in contrast to these other artists, however, Lautrec was himself not an ambitious photographer. In a photograph depicting the tipsy Maurice Guibert at the side of an unknown woman – the pictorial basis of *À la Mie* – Lautrec may have released the shutter of the camera. But basically he seems to have left the medium to Paul Sescau or, more precisely, to Maurice Guibert, who seems to have advanced around 1890 to becoming the private and unofficial pictorial chronicler of Henri de Toulouse-Lautrec. What have survived are photographs of Lautrec swimming naked during a sailing meet on the sea by Arcachon (1896). In a letter to his mother from November 1891, the artist speaks of "wonderfully beautiful photographs of Malromé" that Guibert will send to her. It was above all Guibert who urged his friend to have his portrait taken repeatedly – and in the most ridiculous clothing: Lautrec dressed as a woman, wearing Jane Avril's famous hat decorated with boa on his head (1892); Lautrec as a squinting Japanese in a traditional kimono (also 1892); or as Pierrot (1894) – a sad clown who apparently needed little by way of costuming to create a convincing image. Jean Adhémar has subjected this portfolio to searching analysis: "Thanks to Guibert," writes the

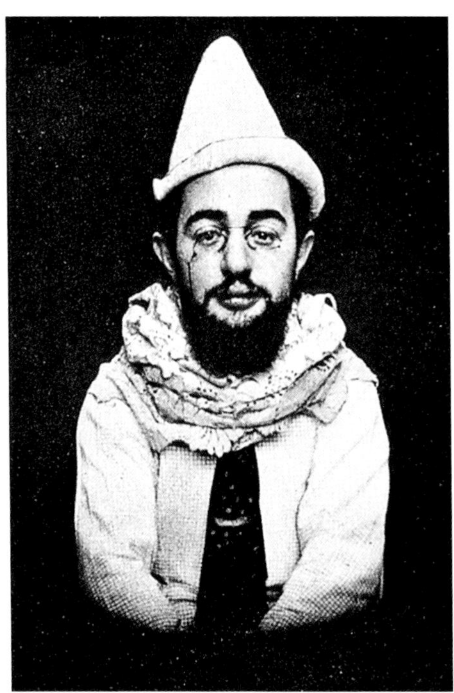

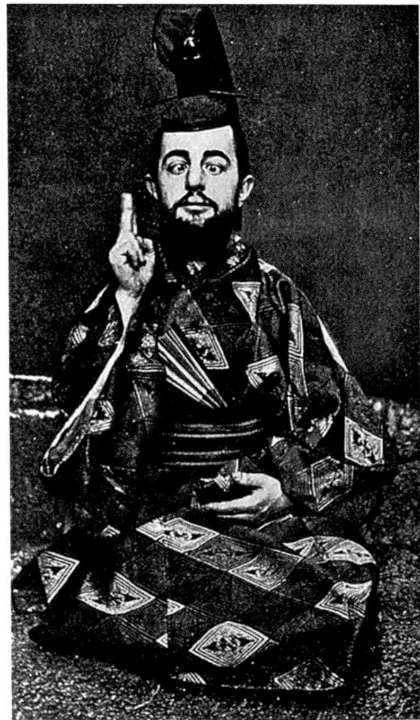

former curator of the Bibliothèque nationale, "we accompany Lautrec from 1890 to his death. One sees him in the most various surroundings and in all possible poses. It is particularly striking, however, that we meet a natural Lautrec at most only two or three times. The artist always poses himself; aware that he is being photographed, he places himself in a scene. He never seeks to hide his deformities. On the contrary, he presents them openly, expressly emphasizing his ugliness and his dwarfish stature." Why does he engage in these travesties? Adhémar finds a logical explanation: "When Lautrec underlines his infirmity to such an extent, then it is very simply because he was suffering from it – more than we realize. In this sense, his form of masochism becomes a distracting maneuver. He would like to laugh about himself before others do so, or rather: to give his audience occasion to make jokes about something that in fact has nothing to do with his physical defects." It would have been very simple for Henri de Toulouse-Lautrec to have visited one of the prominent Paris photography studios to ensure, with the help of a practiced portraitist exploiting the photographic means at his command – lighting, pose, framing, perspective, retouching of the negative and positive – a pleasing half- or three-quarters portrait. Instead, the artist left in the hands of a friend and amateur the task of creating the photographic witness that still today defines our image of the tragic genius: Toulouse-Lautrec in his studio. Not at work. Not painting before an easel, but in visual dialogue with a naked prostitute(?). In other words, the loner of Montmartre pursued his own course also in his dealings with photography.

Max Christian Priester/Willy Wilcke

Bismarck on His Deathbed

1898

The Humanization of a Legend

Shortly after Otto von Bismarck's death, a death photograph that the public had never in fact seen led to a sensational trial in Hamburg, Germany. The defendants were two photographers who had secretly and illicitly captured the deceased founder of the German Reich on film. Not until years after the end of the Second World War was the photograph finally published.

A great man has died. Think what one may of Bismarck – and historians are still divided today over whether he was a visionary or reactionary, a "white revolutionist" (Lothar Gall) or a "daemon" (Johannes Willms) – one thing is certain: he was one of the great figures in nineteenth-century politics, and for a time he was the most powerful man in Europe. This claim remains true even under the Hegelian understanding of history, in which even the most influential individuals are at best the 'business managers' of a predetermined 'purpose', that is, mere assistants in the fulfillment of the inevitable course of history. The majority of Germans, however, would have looked at the matter differently around 1890. For them, Bismarck was the founder of a German Reich with well-defined borders, the creator of a nation under Prussian leadership. In those days, people still felt unreserved admiration for the Junker stemming from the lands east of the Elbe, and throughout the country Bismarck towers and Bismarck memorials made of bronze or stone reinforced the idea. On a popularity scale, Bismarck surpassed both Wilhelm I and the reigning monarch Wilhelm II – a fact which the latter realized all too well. In response, the young kaiser therefore repeatedly sought some kind of reconciliation with the aged chancellor whom he had disgracefully dismissed from office in 1890. But to no avail. Otto von Bismarck nursed a resentment that might well be termed hatred and that was to have repercussions even after his death.

Max Christian Priester

Born ***1865*** *in Altona, Germany.* ***1894*** *opens his own photography shop in Hamburg. From* ***1895*** *photographic reports from Friedrichsruh.* ***1898*** *takes photographs together with Wilcke of the deceased Bismarck. Trial for trespassing. Jailed for five months. Dies* ***1910*** *in a mental asylum.*

Willy Wilcke

Born ***1864*** *in Wismar. Apprenticeship in Wismar. Afterwards works as a photographic assistant.* ***1887*** *opens a photography shop in Ratzeburg.* ***1889*** *moves to Hamburg, opens a larger shop. From* ***1893*** *photographs Bismarck receiving homages in Friedrichsruh.* ***1898*** *takes photos of the dead Bismarck with Priester. Jailed for eight months. Dies* ***1945****.*

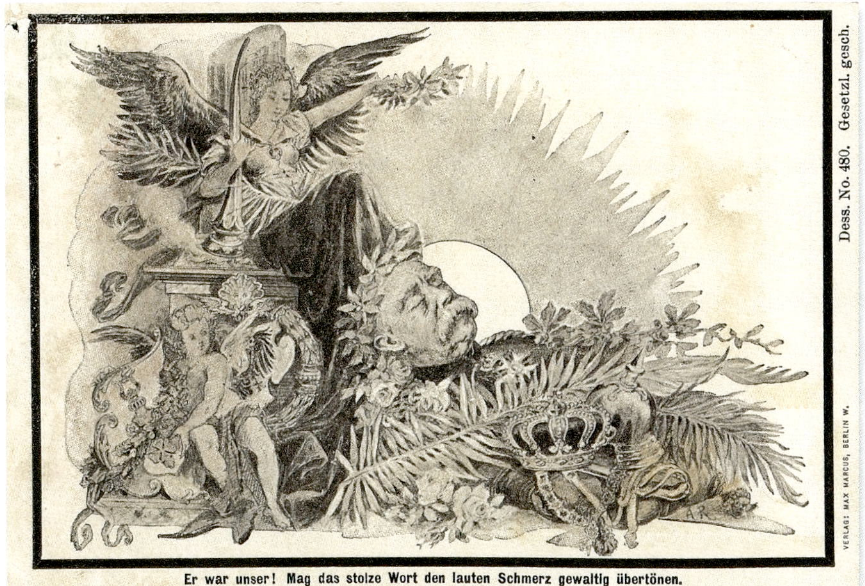

Wilhelm was in no case to be allowed to view Bismarck's mortal remains. By the time the kaiser, who had been intentionally misled by those around him about Bismarck's true condition, finally arrived in Friedrichsruh near Hamburg, the coffin had already been sealed: Bismarck had thus effectively delivered an insult from beyond the grave.

Assembly line pictures of the Chancellor

In fact, there were very few who had been allowed to say farewell to Bismarck – family members, house servants, a handful of neighbors from Friedrichsruh. Reinhold Begas was refused permission to make a deathmask, the painter Franz von Lenbach, a death portrait. Similarly, in the beginning no one seems to have thought about photographing the deceased – understandably from today's point of view, although it must be remarked that the photographing of the dead remained a completely common practice until the end of the nineteenth century. One needs only to think of Ludwig II, whose picture lying in an open coffin provoked almost no interest among the public. After Bismarck's death, however, there was to be no picture that contradicted the official iconography of the chancellor – in particular the image that had been professionally formulated by Lenbach, that Munich-based prince of painters, who had immortalized the Iron Chancellor in a number of oil and chalk works (as if on an assembly line, according to the ironic opinion of the painter's contemporaries). In any case, Lenbach's chancellor was a man of power, determination, and vision: a statesman in uniform, or sometimes in

Bismarck in the eye of the imagination. Picture postcards of this kind went into circulation shortly after the death of the Chancellor.

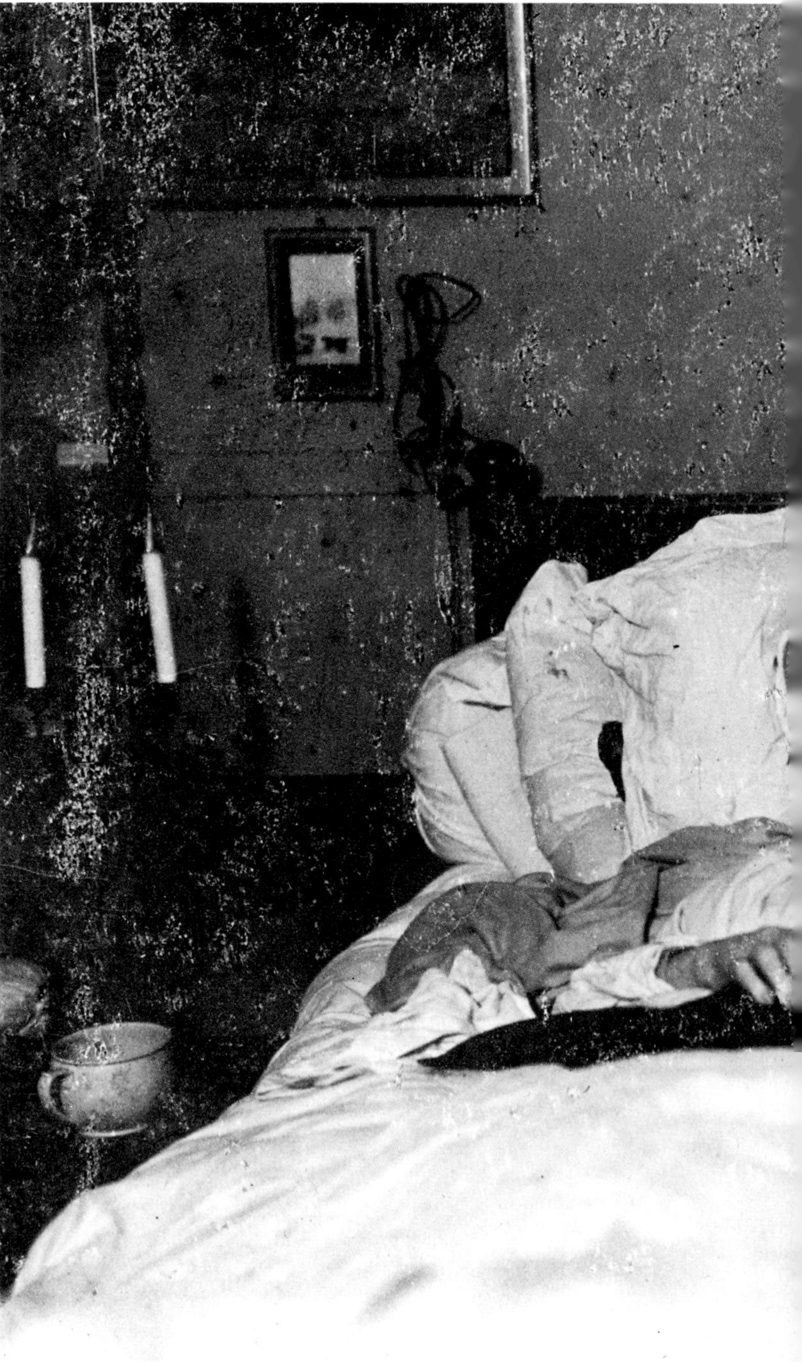

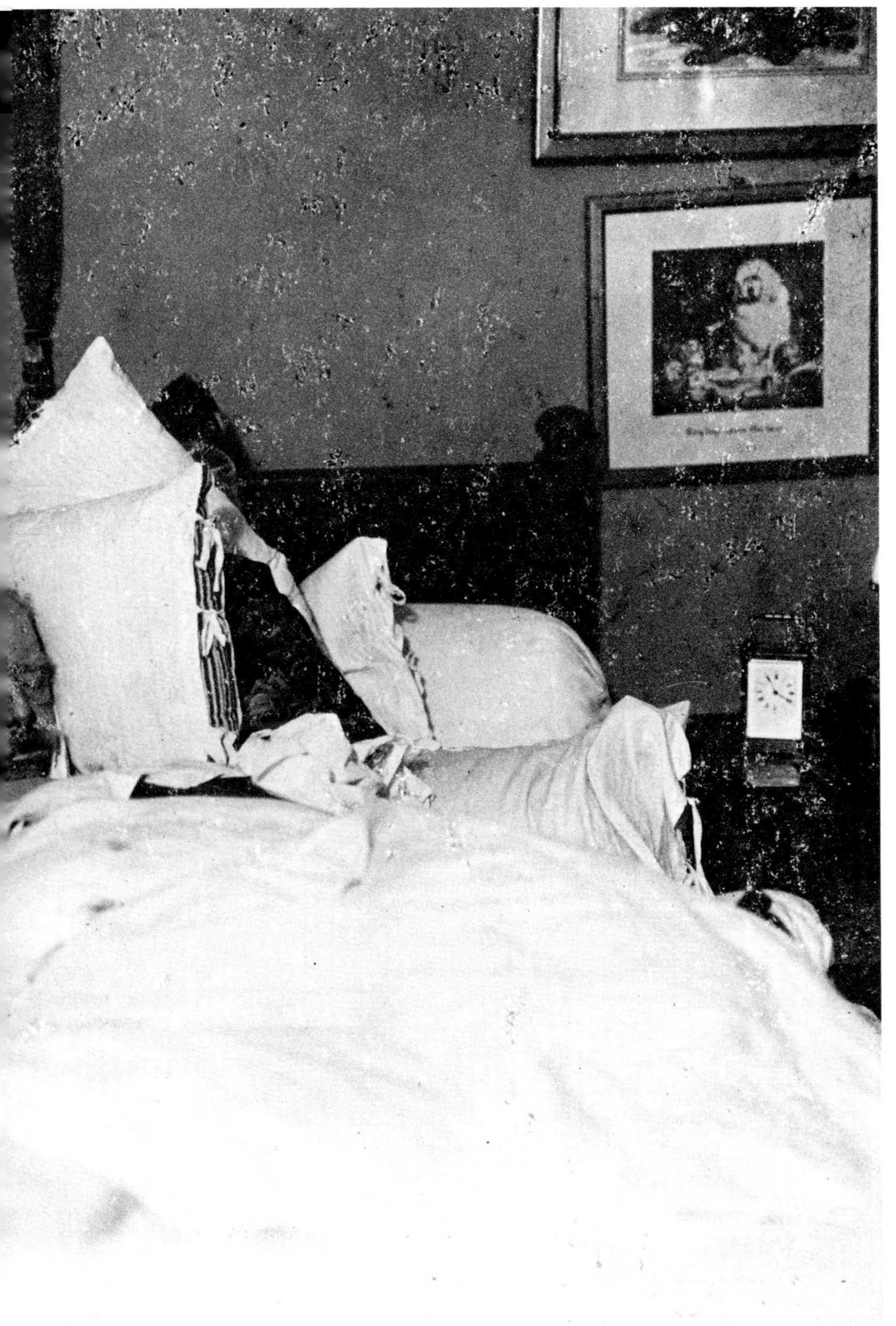

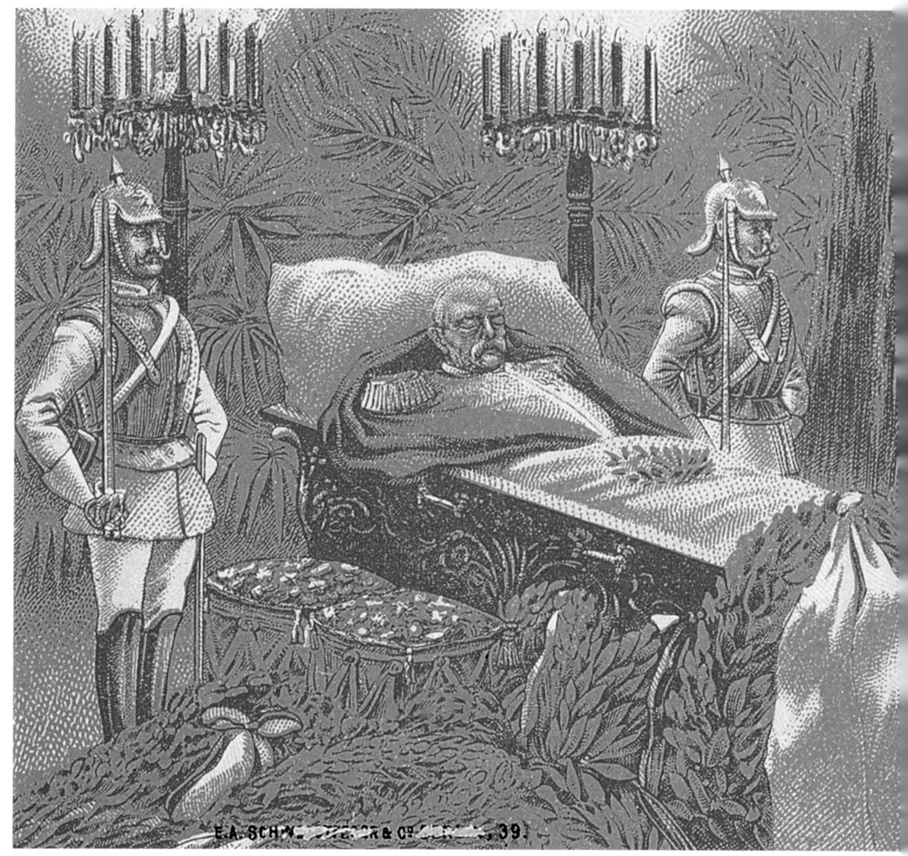

black civilian dress; a great figure in the literal physical sense. And now this travesty: a photograph of the deceased chancellor – the legendary Bismarck – sunk into an unmade bed, the absolute opposite so to speak of the familiar impressive figure exerting a powerful influence on the observer in Lenbach's portraits. To make matters worse, the photograph revealed a veritably shabby ambiance that one would hardly have imagined possible of the former chancellor, with the chamber pot adding an almost vulgar note to the scene. "Pure realism," as the Bismarck scholar Lothar Machtan appropriately pointed out, and thus a possible corrective to the stylized image that had been proffered by Bismarck himself – to the presentation of himself according to the motto "nothing is truer than the appearance" (Willms). For the kaiser, on the other hand, the photograph would have seemed like a belated revenge.

"In Remembrance of the Death of the Great Chancellor." Picture postcard, before 1900.

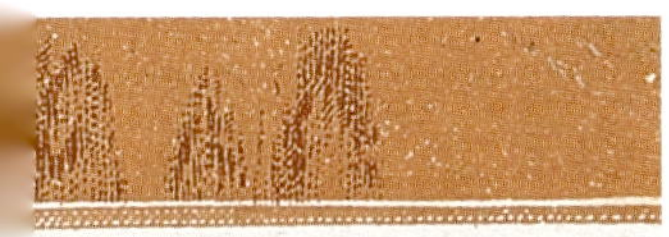

The photograph had been taken by the professional Hamburg photographers Max Priester and Willy Wilcke the night that Bismarck died – admittedly without the family's permission. The term 'paparazzo' had not yet been coined (Fellini introduced it in his film *La Dolce Vita*), but Priester and Wilcke were consummate paparazzi in the modern sense, motivated neither by personal curiosity nor even by a sense of 'art'. Like the paparazzi of today, what they wanted was money, and the ingredients for success were the same then as now, namely, the interest of the public in the private lives of the prominent. As a vehicle for conveying pictorial information, however, the illustrated press of the day was at best in a relatively archaic state. For technical reasons, photographs often made their way into the press only by way of woodcuts. But in Bismarck's case, the process never got that far. A civil suit, to be discussed below, together with the prior confiscation of all pictures, including "negatives, plates, prints, and other reproductions," by the police – meant that the pictorial material was effectively removed from the public sphere. The picture was in fact not published until approximately two generations later in the *Frankfurter Illustrierte* (No. 50/1952), a German magazine appearing from 1948 to 1962. On another occasion, *Die Welt* (No. 270, 19 November 1974) printed the photograph in connection with a review of a book, *Oevelgönner Nachtwachen*, by the Hamburg author Lovis H. Lorenz, in which he relates his version of the photograph's history. Four years later, the picture appeared once more, this time in the *ZEIT-magazin* (4 August 1978), accompanied by a text from Fritz Kempe. It may be tempting to interpret the publication of the once-taboo picture in a widely circulated magazine ten years after the student rebellions of the late 1960s as a further stage in the process of the Bismarck's demythification process. But in fact, the picture probably contributed even more to the humanizing of Bismarck. The photograph reveals that the circumstances of Prince Otto von Bismarck's death were in fact rather trivial: in death he became one of us.

The air was full of rumors that Bismarck was dying. The old man, increasingly depressed, had been ailing for quite some time. When gangrene set in, it was clear that his days were numbered. In other words, a media event, as we would term it today, was about to occur – and this in turn required the 'right' pictures; that is, the most recent pictures had to be rounded up for publication – and what could be more recent than a picture of the deceased founder of the Reich. Two Hamburg photographers had determined to obtain the necessary image: Max Priester and Willy Wilcke, who had bribed a reliable informant in the person of Bismarck's forester, Louis Spörcke. Now they had only to wait for the moment of death. An hour before midnight on 30 July 1898 Otto von Bismarck died – according to historians, after drinking a glass of lemonade. Then, "with a cry of 'Forward!', he sank back into the pillows and died" (Willms).

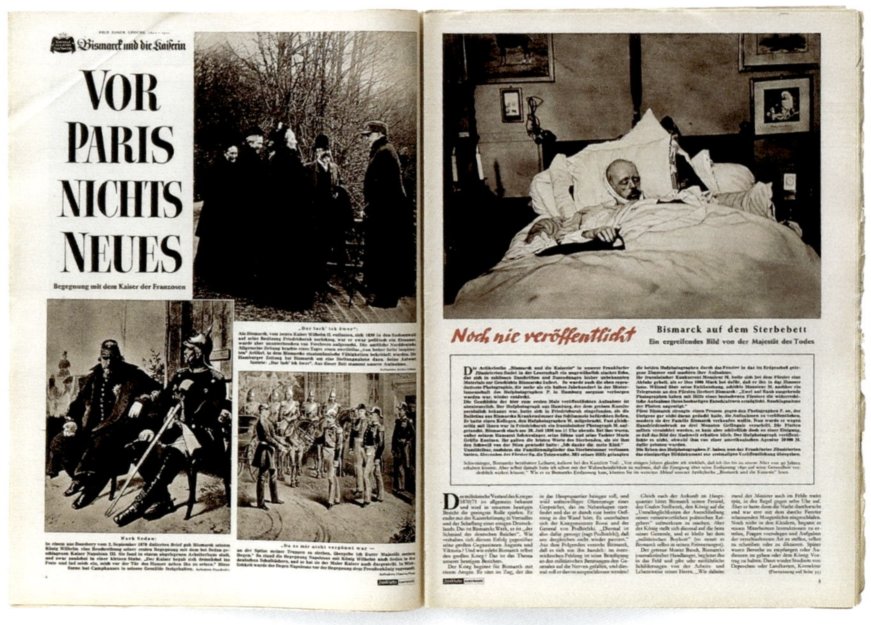

Bismarck und die Kaiserin

VOR PARIS NICHTS NEUES

Begegnung mit dem Kaiser der Franzosen

Noch nie veröffentlicht

Bismarck auf dem Sterbebett

Ein ergreifendes Bild von der Majestät des Todes

Spörcke, who had kept the night watch, informed Priester and Wilcke, lodging nearby and fully on the alert: the forester would leave the garden gate and ground-floor window open for them. Toward four in the morning the pair made their way in the house, exposed several plates with the help of the magnesium flashes that were usual at the time. The whole procedure supposedly lasted less than ten minutes, and on the following morning, they returned to Hamburg and attempted to make money as quickly as possible from their – as we would say today – scoop. But that, as it turned out, would not be as easy as they thought.

The incriminating materials confiscated

They advertised for interested parties with money. "For the sole existing picture of Bismarck on his deathbed, photographs taken a few hours after his death, original images, a buyer or suitable publisher is sought," ran the announcement in the *Tägliche Rundschau* of 2 August 1898. A Dr. Baltz, owner of a German publishing house, replied that he was prepared to pay as much as thirty thousand marks plus twenty percent of the profit for the images. All that was necessary now was for the photographers to obtain the family's permission to publish. In response, Priester and Wilcke quickly produced a retouched version of the picture, showing a clearly younger-looking Bismarck, without headband or patterned handkerchief. The light-colored chamber pot also fell victim to the practiced stroke of the retoucher. It is quite possible that the Bismarcks might have granted permission to publish, but in the meantime, a jealous competitor, Arthur Mennell, had already stumbled upon the plan, and denounced Priester and Wilcke to the family. The Bismarcks responded swiftly. By 4 August they had already managed

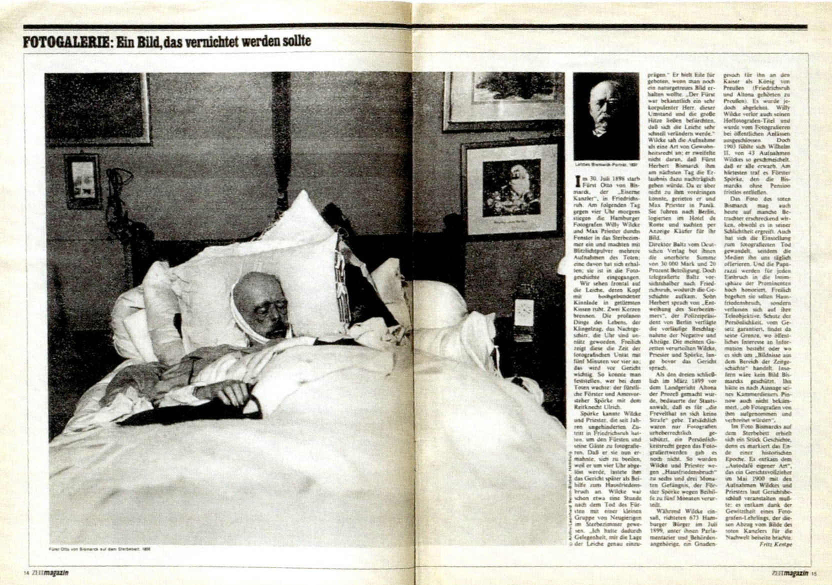

FOTOGALERIE: Ein Bild, das vernichtet werden sollte

Fürst Otto von Bismarck auf dem Sterbebett, 1898

Letztes Bismarck-Porträt, 1897

Am 30. Juli 1898 starb Fürst Otto von Bismarck, der „Eiserne Kanzler", in Friedrichsruh. Am folgenden Tag gegen vier Uhr morgens stiegen die Hamburger Fotografen Willy Wilcke und Max Priester durchs Fenster in das Sterbezimmer ein und machten mit Blitzlichtpulver mehrere Aufnahmen des Toten; eine davon hat sich erhalten; sie ist in die Fotogeschichte eingegangen.

Wir sehen frontal auf die Leiche, deren Kopf mit hochgebundener Kinnlade in geflimmten Kissen ruht. Zwei Kerzen brennen. Die profanen Dinge des Lebens, der Klingelzug, das Nachtgeschirr, die Uhr sind unnütz geworden. Freilich zeigt diese die Zeit der fotografischen Untat mit fünf Minuten vor vier an; das wird vor Gericht wichtig. So konnte man feststellen, wer bei dem Toten wachte: der fürstliche Förster und Amtsvorsteher Spörke mit dem Reitknecht Ulrich.

Spörke kannte Wilcke und Priester, die seit Jahren ungehinderten Zutritt in Friedrichsruh hatten, um den Fürsten und seine Gäste zu fotografieren. Daß er sie nun ermahnte, sich zu beeilen, weil er um vier Uhr abgelöst werde, lastete ihm das Gericht später als Beihilfe zum Hausfriedensbruch an. Wilcke war schon etwa eine Stunde nach dem Tod des Fürsten mit einer kleinen Gruppe von Neugierigen im Sterbezimmer gewesen. „Ich hatte dadurch Gelegenheit, mir die Lage der Leiche genau einzuprägen." Er hielt Eile für geboten, wenn man noch ein naturgetreues Bild erhalten wollte. „Der Fürst war bekanntlich ein sehr korpulenter Herr, dieser Umstand und die große Hitze ließen befürchten, daß sich die Leiche sehr schnell verändern werde." Wilcke sah die Aufnahme als eine Art von Gewohnheitsrecht an; er zweifelte nicht daran, daß Fürst Herbert Bismarck ihm am nächsten Tag die Erlaubnis dazu nachträglich geben würde. Da er aber nicht zu ihm vordringen konnte, gerieten er und Max Priester in Panik. Sie fuhren nach Berlin, logierten im Hotel de Rome und suchten per Anzeige Käufer für ihr Bild.

Direktor Baltz vom Deutschen Verlag bot ihnen die unerhörte Summe von 30 000 Mark und 20 Prozent Beteiligung. Doch telegrafierte Baltz vorsichtshalber nach Friedrichsruh, wodurch die Geschichte aufkam. Sohn Herbert sprach von „Entweihung des Sterbezimmers", der Polizeipräsident von Berlin verfügte die vorläufige Beschlagnahme der Negative und Abzüge. Die meisten Gazetten verurteilten Wilcke, Priester und Spörke, lange bevor das Gericht sprach.

Als den dreien schließlich im März 1899 vor dem Landgericht Altona der Prozeß gemacht wurde, bedauerte der Staatsanwalt, daß es für „die Frevelthat an sich keine Strafe" gebe. Tatsächlich waren nur Fotografien urheberrechtlich geschützt, ein Persönlichkeitsrecht gegen das Fotografiertwerden gab es noch nicht. So wurden Wilcke und Priester wegen „Hausfriedensbruch" zu sechs und drei Monaten Gefängnis, der Förster Spörke wegen Beihilfe zu fünf Monaten verurteilt.

Während Wilcke einsaß, richteten 673 Hamburger Bürger im Juli 1899, unter ihnen Parlamentarier und Behördenangehörige, ein Gnadengesuch für ihn an den Kaiser als König von Preußen (Friedrichsruh und Altona gehörten zu Preußen). Es wurde jedoch abgelehnt. Willy Wilcke verlor auch seinen Hoffotografen-Titel und wurde vom Fotografieren bei öffentlichen Anlässen ausgeschlossen. Doch 1903 fühlte sich Wilhelm II. von 43 Aufnahmen Wilckes so geschmeichelt, daß er alle erwarb. Am härtesten traf es Förster Spörke, den die Bismarcks ohne Pension fristlos entließen.

Das Foto des toten Bismarck mag auch heute auf manche Betrachter erschreckend wirken, obwohl es in seiner Schlichtheit ergreift. Auch hat sich die Einstellung zum fotografierten Tod gewandelt, seitdem die Medien ihn uns täglich offerieren. Und die Paparazzi werden für jeden Einbruch in die Intimsphäre der Prominenten hoch honoriert. Freilich begehen sie selten Hausfriedensbruch, sondern verlassen sich auf ihre Teleobjektive. Schutz der Persönlichkeit, vom Gesetz garantiert, findet da seine Grenze, wo öffentliches Interesse an Information besteht oder wo es sich um „Bildnisse aus dem Bereich der Zeitgeschichte" handelt. Insofern wäre kein Bild Bismarcks geschützt. Ihn hätte es nach Aussage seines Kammerdieners Pinnow auch nicht bekümmert, „ob Fotografien von ihm aufgenommen und verbreitet würden".

Im Foto Bismarcks auf dem Sterbebett erhielt sich ein Stück Geschichte, denn es markiert das Ende einer historischen Epoche. Es entkam dem „Autodafé eigener Art", das ein Gerichtsvollzieher im Mai 1900 mit den Aufnahmen Wilckes und Priesters laut Gerichtsbeschluß veranstalten mußte; es entkam dank der Gewitztheit eines Fotografen-Lehrlings, der diesen Abzug vom Bilde des toten Kanzlers für die Nachwelt beiseite brachte.

Fritz Kempe

14 ZEITmagazin — ZEITmagazin 15

to have the incriminating materials confiscated. A civil and criminal court case ensued, today remarkable in that the crime of trespassing was not the sole charge: the question of the right to one's own picture was also at issue. The case was decided in favor of Bismarck; the photographers had not acted for the sake of the German people, but merely in their own interest. The sentences handed down on 18 March 1899 were correspondingly harsh: five months for Spörcke, who also lost his position as forester; eight months for Willy Wilcke along with the loss of his title as court photographer; five months for Max Priester, who died at age 45 in an institution for the mentally ill. The 'evidence' disappeared into the Bismarcks' safe, "never to be turned over to the public," according to the express wish of the family. A clever photography assistant named Otto Reich, however, had already made a print, and from him Lovis H. Lorenz obtained possession of the picture, so he claimed, after the war. Lorenz in turn handed the photograph over to the Hamburg State Educational Institute, which kept the picture in their own collection. What had clearly caused a scandal in 1898 was hardly capable creating a public stir a decade after the Second World War. People had other concerns. Paradoxically, the picture of the dead chancellor helped to keep the otherwise distant and alien Bismarck alive, if not to bring him closer. The photograph proved taht Bismarck, too, had died a completely normal, perhaps even trivial, death. A legend had been humanized.

Left: Frankfurter Illustrierte, *No. 50, 1952: this magazine was the first to publish the confiscated Bismarck photograph.*

Above: *"A picture that was supposed to be destroyed." Fritz Kempe's analysis of the photograph in* ZEIT magazine, *4 August 1978.*

Heinrich Zille
The Wood Gatherers
1898

Wood Sale in Grunewald

Heinrich Zille, the well-known graphic artist who depicted proletarian conditions of life around 1900, was also a photographer, but his camera work was not discovered until the mid-1960s. His œuvre of more than 400 photographs is now appreciated as an important contribution to modern photography.

Autumn in Charlottenburg, a small town outside Berlin. Two women, possibly mother and daughter, are pulling a cart loaded high with brushwood across the sandy ground typical of the region, one woman with the right hand, the other with the left clasped around the shafts of the simple vehicle whose left wheel seems to be set none too surely on its axle. The two wood gatherers have in addition yoked themselves with a shoulder band to distribute the load and are literally putting themselves in harness to bring their harvest home quickly. Home – it may be Charlottenburg itself – whose western outskirts are recognizable to the left in the picture as a lightly sloping strip between the grassy fields and the sky. In 1900, the city with its approximately 190,000 inhabitants is still an independent community; it willnot be incorporated into Greater Berlin for another two decades.

The two wood gatherers have already put a few kilometers between themselves and the forest of Grunewald. Their clothing, consisting of skirt, blouse, and apron, indicates their status as peasants. "In Grunewald, in Grunewald there's a wood sale" – the popular old street ditty looks back to the days when the forest, then located far to the west of Berlin, was an important source of natural raw materials for working-class families. Wood was used not only for heating, but also in cooking stoves, for which brushwood and sticks were the cheapest form of fuel – as dramatized by the important role such wood plays in Gerhard Hauptmann's comedy *The Beaver Pelt.*

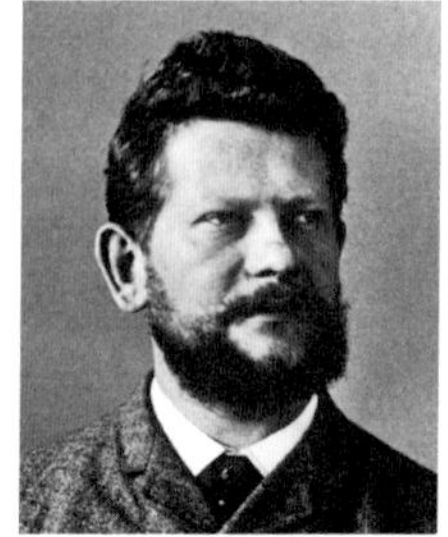

Heinrich Zille
Born Rudolf Heinrich Zille in ***1858*** *in Radeburg near Dresden, Germany.* ***1872–75*** *apprenticeship in lithography in Berlin.* ***1877–1907*** *works as a lithographer for the Berlin Photographische Gesellschaft. Around* ***1890*** *friendship with Max Liebermann.* ***1892*** *moves to Charlottenburg. First etchings in the same year under the influence of literary Naturalism. From* ***1903*** *member of the Berlin Secession. Published in magazines such as* Simplicissimus, Lustige Blätter, Jugend. ***1907*** *first illustrated book,* Kinder der Strasse *(Children of the Streets).* ***1924*** *awarded a professorship. Dies* ***1929*** *in Berlin. Photographic estate is in the keeping of the Berlinische Galerie, Berlin.*

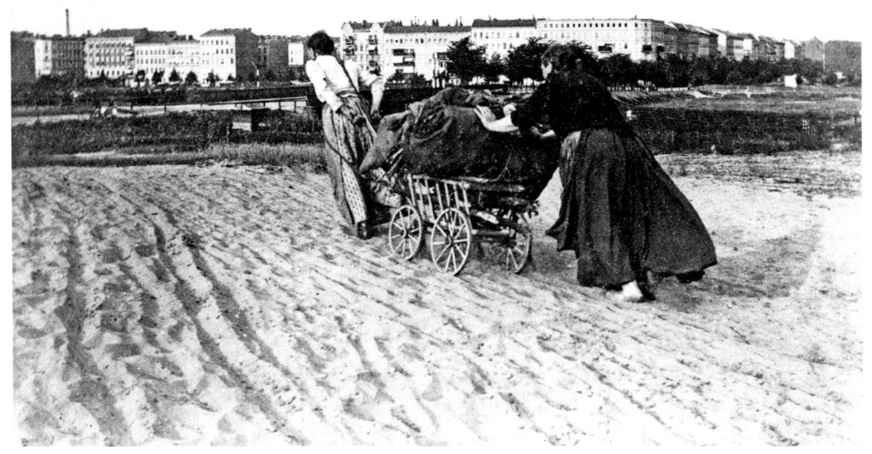

Eyes to the ground and swinging their arms

Although they constitute the central theme of the picture, which presumably was taken in 1898, the two women are not the only people in the oblong-format photograph. Between the smaller woman in the background and the wagon with its high load we recognize, half hidden, a baby carriage typical of the times, which is also loaded with wood and a jute sack. And yet a further person intrudes into the picture: the photographer himself, whose long shadow stands out clearly in the bottom right against the bright dune. Somewhere in the background, but not visible in this photograph, there must be the Ringbahn, or circular railway around the city, which in those days more or less functioned as the boundary between city and countryside, that is, between Charlottenburg and Grunewald. Somewhat further to the right, one can imagine today's radio tower and the Berlin exhibition center. The goal of the two women may well be the Knobelsdorff Bridge. From this point the path leads across the track into the western end of Charlottenburg. It is evident that the photographer is wearing a hat, but whether or not he is using a camera stand for his work cannot be determined. What is certain is that he is looking eastward; the sun must therefore be standing in the west, indicating that the time of the photograph is late afternoon or early evening. The two women are thus making their way back from a daytime outing, which indicates the completely legal nature of their undertaking. In reality,

---

Heinrich Zille: *Third series from* The Wood Gatherers, *5th image:* View towards Knobelsdorff Bridge, *Fall 1898.*

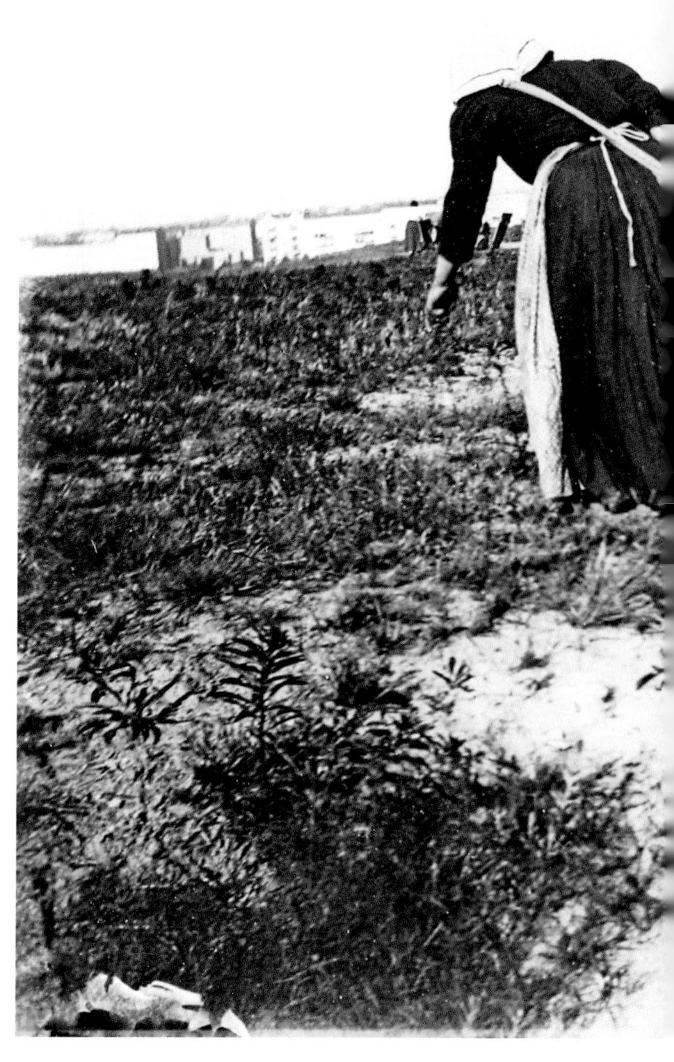

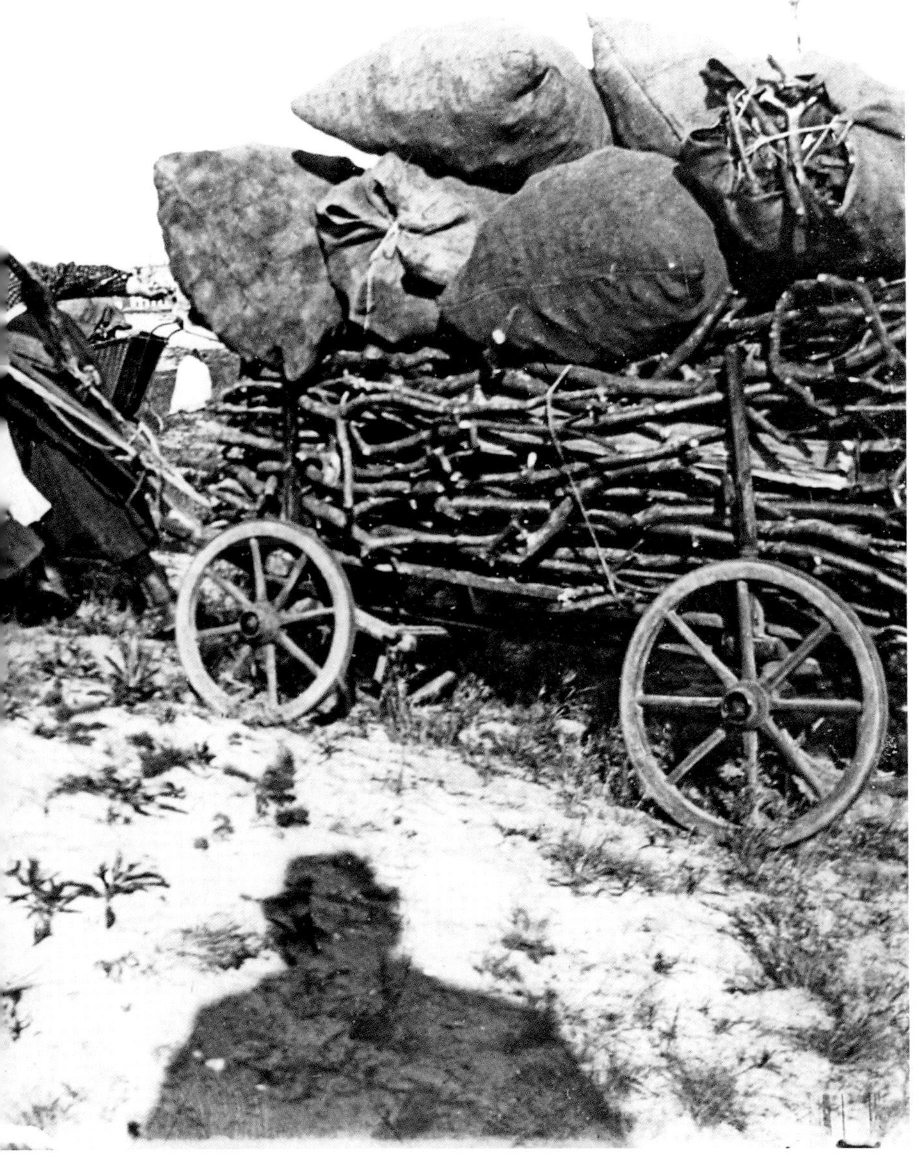

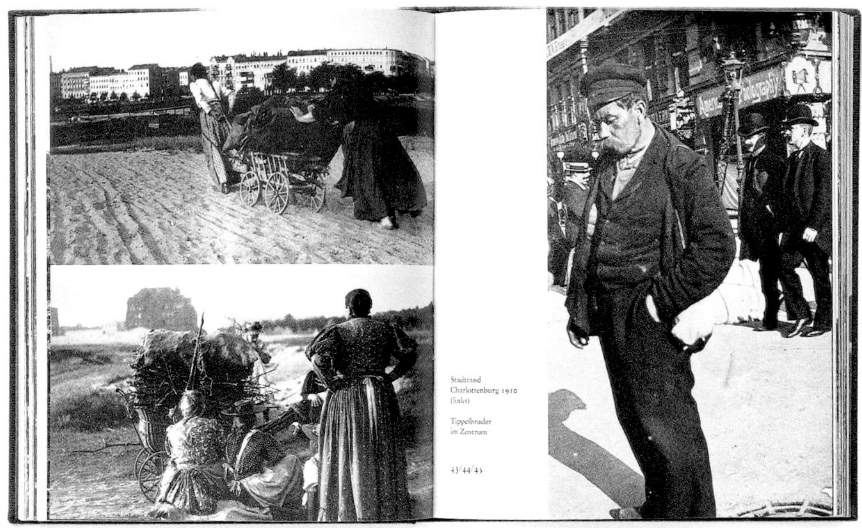

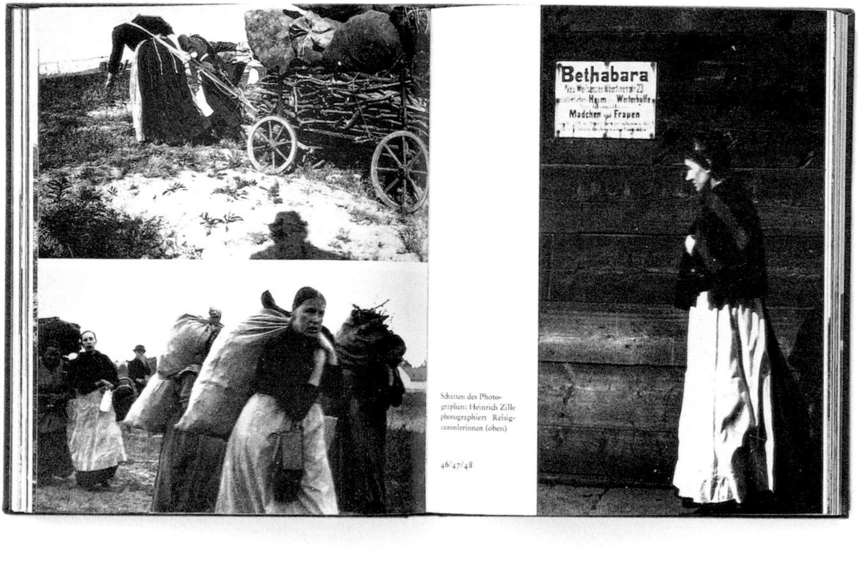

Mein Photo-Milljöh *(My photographic 'nvironment): the book publication edited 1967 by the Berlin theater critic Friedrich Luft first drew attention to Heinrich Zille as a photographer.*

women collecting wood must have been a part of daily life in western Berlin, a situation which explains why none of the court or amateur photographers active in or around the Reich's capital hit upon the idea of capturing a scene such as this, without at least an attempt at idealizing the 'simple life'. But in this picture, there is no trace of romanticism. The women are pulling with their full strength against the harness to keep the wagon rolling, and in the process are swinging their free arms strongly, their eyes to the ground.

Max Liebermann as engaged patron and friend

Heinrich Zille was neither a professional photographer nor an amateur in the sense of being merely a hobby photographer with artistic pretensions, a type that was occasioning much international discussion around 1900. Born in 1858 in Radeburg in Saxony, Zille was primarily a graphic artist known for his tragi-comic sketches of simple people. His work appeared in various magazines and newspapers beginning in 1903, and five years later, was also published in book form. Zille had already achieved popularity within his own lifetime – but his was a controversial fame. Kaiser Wilhelm II, for example, discredited Zille's work, oriented as it was toward the naturalism of the age, as "gutter art." The Berlin Secessionists on the other hand valued his drawing. Particularly in Max Liebermann the trained lithographer found both a prominent and engaged patron and friend.

Zille never made a secret of his photographic activity; at the same time, he did not emphasize it. Like many artists of the turn of the century – Stuck, Lenbach, and Munch are perhaps the best known – Zille also drew from photographs that he had taken himself. Unlike his famous colleagues, however, he seems to have followed this practice, commonly employed by painters and graphic artists of the day, rather rarely. Also of note are the intimacy of Zille's gaze, his particular mode of perception, and his joy in experimentation, all of which are far removed from any kind of commercial photography. One may rest assured that for Zille, the camera served primarily as a means to assimilate reality in a new way.

His contemporaries were aware of Heinrich Zille's work with the camera. Nevertheless, by the time of his death in 1929 this aspect of his work had sunk into oblivion. Not until 1966 was a cache of somewhat more than four hundred glass negatives and approximately one hundred and twenty original prints discovered in his estate, out of which a selection was offered to the public for view for the first time by the Berlin Theater critic Friedrich Luft in 1967. The legacy indicates that after 1882, Heinrich Zille photographed exclusively with large-format glass-plate cameras which he may have borrowed from the Photographic Society, his employer of at the time. Surviving are also 12 × 16, 13 × 18, and 18 × 24 cm (4¾ × 6¼, 5½ × 7, and 7 × 9½ inch) negatives, along with positives in the form of contact prints.

Interest in banal, everyday life

The spectrum of Zille's themes was remarkably broad, even if the majority of his œuvre, which was largely concerned with the realities of daily life among the simple working class, consists of views of old Berlin – rear courtyards, alleys, narrow houses reached by high staircases, shops and stores. In addition, Zille's legacy contains portraits and self-portraits, family pictures, nudes, scenes of fairgrounds and beaches, and – oddly enough – trash dumps, which Zille photographed a number of times. Practically absent in Zille's work are panoramic views of the quickly growing Wilhelmine Berlin, such as those produced by contemporary photographers such as Max Missmann, Waldemar Titzenthaler, and Hermann Rückwardt. Similarly, photographs of the German Reichstag, the Victory Column (Siegessäule), or the Brandenburg Gate constitute the exception in an œuvre centered on paradigms of daily life.

In keeping with his interest in banal, everyday life, Zille often made wood-gathering women the object of his lens. All in all, it is possible to distinguish four cycles, in the first of which, taken in 1897, Zille would still have had to combat the inconveniences that were a part of short-exposure photography. The pictures are not sharp, and the framing unsatisfactory – or the women are looking toward the camera, a circumstance that Zille, who strove for 'discretion', always sought to avoid. In this area, Zille, still very much the amateur, worked to refine his techniques, rubbing his nose in his chosen theme, which clearly interested him until 1898.

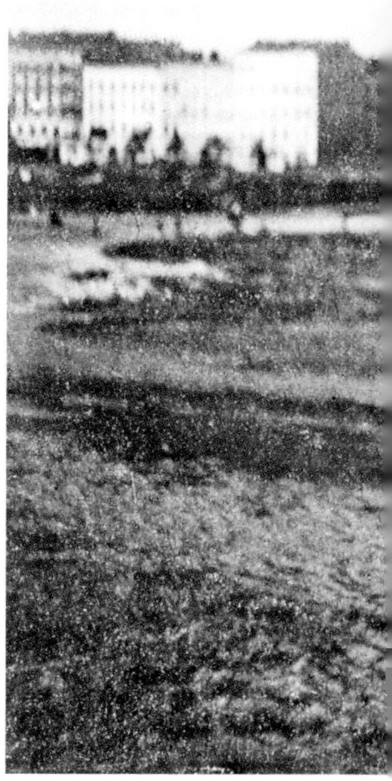

Precisely why Zille specifically made the theme of daily female labor the center of his cycle, we don't know. One thing is certain: the wood gatherers had become a more or less daily sight for Zille after he moved from Rummelsburg to Sophie-Charlotte Street in 1892, where such women passed every evening on their way back from collecting wood. "A tranquil peace settled on the street," according to Zille's son Hans, describing his parents' new apartment. "From the apartment windows, one's gaze ranged over the open land. On the other side of the street, the sandy soil was cultivated; in the middle, there was a large area for drying laundry that was ringed with bushes and trees. Behind the Ringbahn stretched fallow land, partially covered with low-growing pines, and finally came the first trees of the Grunewald and the outskirts of the suburban villas of the West End."

From the open window of his apartment, Heinrich Zille had photographed the grounds of the Ringbahn with the Knobelsdorff Bridge to the southwest as early as 1893. Four years later, he went out into the fields and turned his camera onto the women returning home from picking wood, almost as if looking over the same scene from the other direction. Only a few pictures show them at rest. All his later pictures also avoided the direct gaze into the camera. Zille photographed the women from behind, thus making them 'faceless' but lifting their personal trials and tribulations onto the level of a generalizable condition.

That Heinrich Zille used the photographs from his series on wood gatherers as illustration models does not diminish their value as independent artistic achievements. Already in 1903, his drawing *Wünsche* (Wishes) appeared in *Simplicissimus*, which an editor, referring to Zille's origin, probably supplied with a text in pseudo-Saxon dialect: "If only I had won big time, just once! I woulda had myself a fine cart and then I coulda carried that brush wood back home

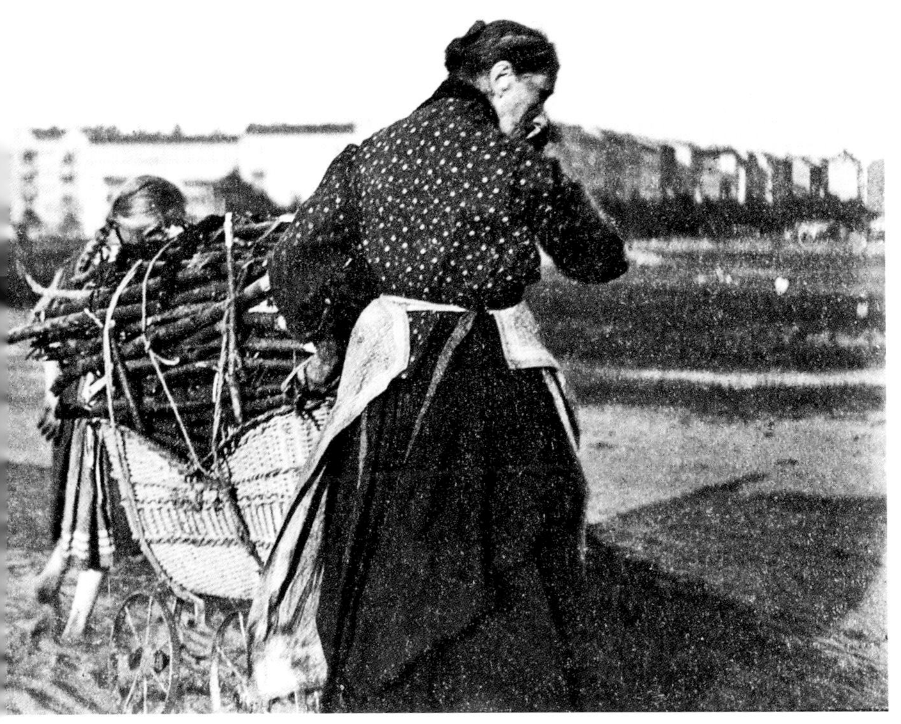

right comfortable." Today, the completely unsentimental directness of the photograph lends it credibility, in contrast to the drawing. Zille's radical gaze bluntly captures the essential, and he intuitively applies photography in terms of its intrinsic characteristics. Decades before the proclamation of the New Objectivity, Heinrich Zille was pursuing the idea of photography as unembellished documentation with his *Wood Gatherers*. In this sense, he is properly seen as an ancestor of the modern spirit in photography.

Heinrich Zille:
Woman with Child Pushing a Pram Loaded with Brushwood, with Knobelsdorff Bridge in the Background, *Fall 1897.*

Karl Blossfeldt
Maidenhair Fern
ca. 1900

A Herbarium from the Darkroom

Toward the end of the 1920s, Karl Blossfeldt's plates, published as *Urformen der Kunst*, became one of the most-discussed photographic books of the interval between the wars. His plant studies, originally completed with a view to the commercial art classes, fascinated the contemporary avant-garde, and still influence both conventional and conceptual photographers today.

Occasionally he stood before the camera himself, as in Italy in 1894. Or a year later, still lingering on the peninsula, this time wearing a simple felt hat, a white collarless shirt, and a plain light-colored suit of coarse material. His right hand is resting in his suspenders; his gaze, looking straight and resolutely into the camera. The combination of his wide mustache and a very relaxed posture makes abundantly clear that we are not looking at someone concerned with the socially impressive pose of a bourgeois citizen. This not-quite-middle-aged man is in fact engaged in substantiating himself as an artist. The two portraits have a good deal in common: both were taken out-of-doors with available lighting, and both are close to nature. And something more: the protagonist is always alone – not that he necessarily intended to imply that this solitude was a matter of principle. Nonetheless, the stance is noteworthy in this age during which the avant-garde was vociferously withdrawing itself from the traditional business of art – and forming itself into secessions, or at least groups, whose members accordingly often posed themselves for group portraits in front of a camera. There can be no doubt about it: Karl Blossfeldt was an isolated figure in the bustling art world of the turn of the twentieth century. But perhaps he was not even this, if one uses the term 'isolated' to designate an individual who is first and foremost devoted to his own artistic will. What was Blossfeldt, then? A sculptor and modeler, a talented artist who primarily wanted to have his work – illustrations, plaster casts,

---

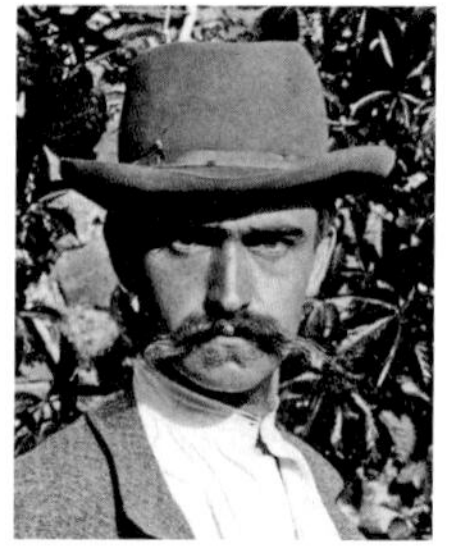

Karl Blossfeldt
*Born **1865** in Schielo, Lower Harz, Germany. Apprenticeship as sculptor and modeler. Lives from **1889** in Italy, Greece, North Africa. During this period he commences his systematic documentation of plants. **1896** return to Berlin. **1898** teaches at the Institute of the Arts and Crafts Museum. **1921** appointment as professor. **1926** first exhibition at the Nierendorf Gallery, Berlin. **1928** publication of his book* Urformen der Kunst. *1929 participates in the* Film und Foto *exhibition in Stuttgart. Dies **1932** in Berlin.*

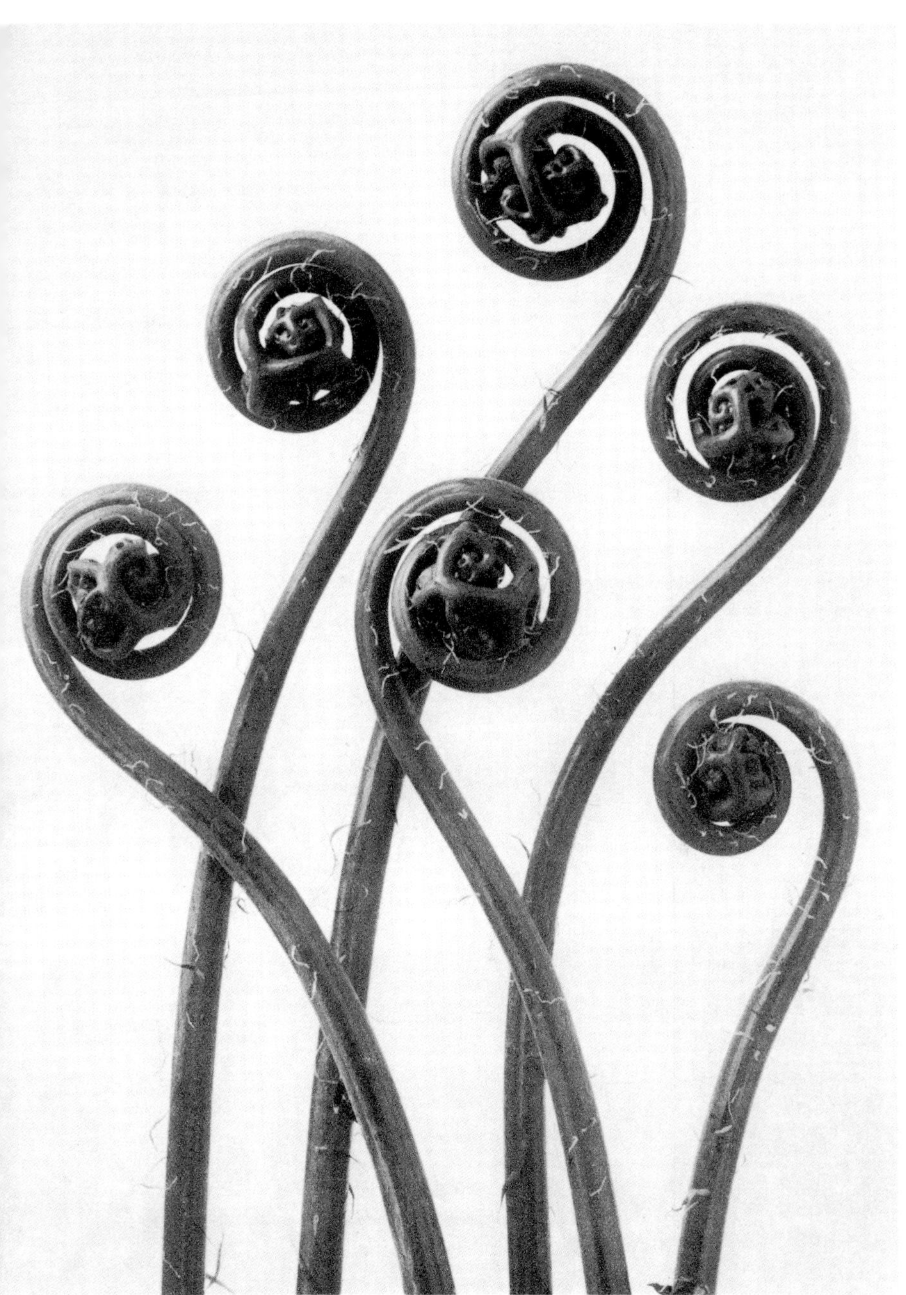

Maidenhair Fern, ca. 1900

photographs – comprehended within the context of learning and education. Until the mid-1920s, he was completely unknown as a photographer. In this connection, Gert Mattenklott even speaks of an "odd ball" who attempted to "make porcelain, but accidentally produced gold with his left hand," the porcelain in this case standing for photography and the gold for a book which overnight placed the inconspicuous Blossfeldt on a level with Sander and Renger-Patzsch as the most prominent representative of the New Objectivity in German photography.

Who was this Karl Blossfeldt, whose photographic plant studies, published in book form in 1928, achieved international recognition? We know something of the answer, even if the verifiable data of his active life, spent in the waning years of the Wilhelmine era and the Weimar Republic, are comparatively sparse and leave many questions open. In 1865, Blossfeldt was born into simple family circumstances in the town of Schielo in the Harz Mountains of Germany. He attended secondary school (Realgymnasium) in Harzgerode, and later completed an apprenticeship as a modeler in a foundry for art casting in Selketal. The attentive eye of the local pastor, combined with a state scholarship, enabled Blossfeldt subsequently to study art in Berlin. In 1884 he transferred to the teaching institute of the Royal Museum of Commercial Art, where Professor Moritz Meurer was particularly impressed with Blossfeldt's talent. Inspired by Gottfried Semper and the writings of Erich Haeckel, the professor was exploring new

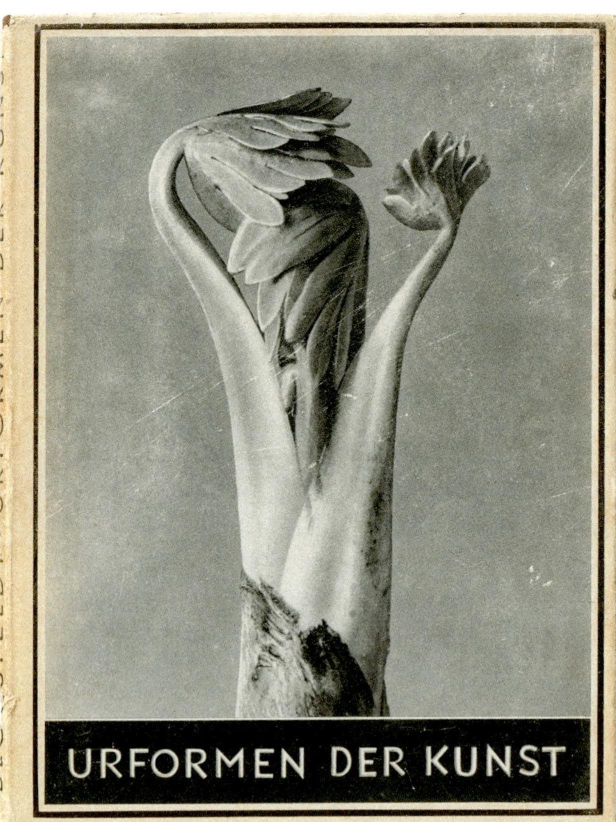

Urformen der Kunst, *published in the English-speaking world as* Art Forms in Nature, Examples from the Plant World Photographed Direct from Nature. *Cover of the 4th German edition, Berlin 1948 (above), and double-page spread (right).*

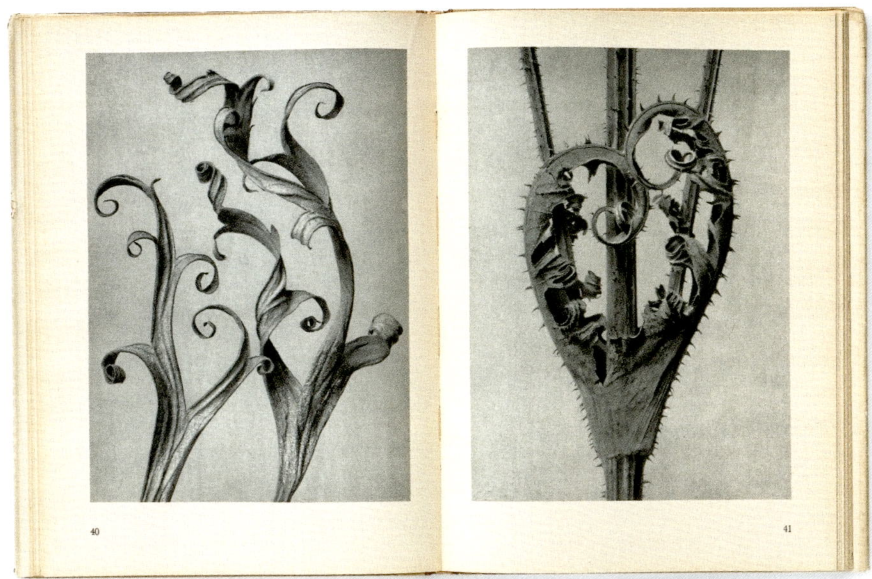

paths in art teaching, and placed the replication of biological *Urformen*, or basic forms, at the center of his practically oriented pedagogy. This approach had its roots in the idea that nature provided important pre-formulated building blocks, so to speak, for architecture and product design. To build up a methodical collection of studies, the professor journeyed to Italy in 1890, accompanied by six graphic artists and modelers, including Karl Blossfeldt.

Purity of design

Their main task was to gather pedagogical material by drawing and modeling plant parts that had been dried or pressed. We may assume that the technical possibilities offered by photography were soon enlisted in the work parallel to more traditional forms of reproducing images from nature. That the task of photography was handed over to Blossfeldt makes two points clear: he was already working with photography at the end of the nineteenth century, and, more importantly, his photography was not by any means the outgrowth of an autonomous desire to be an artist, but rather stood in the service of a serious pedagogical project whose scope and content had not yet been formulated. Blossfeldt's inspiration was therefore not the Pictorialism that was being vehemently discussed and pursued at the time in contradistinction to commercial photography. If the autodidactic photographer Blossfeldt sought anywhere for inspiration in his work with buds, leaves, and blossoms, then it was in the herbaria and plant books produced from the Middle Ages to the Renaissance. These old illustrations, in their attempt to demonstrate the compatibility of natural forms, evinced a purity of design that may well have pointed Blossfeldt in the direction of a similar photographic direction, which – without his initially desiring it – anticipated the pictorial language of what later came to be called the New Objectivity.

***Maidenhair Fern*, ca. 1900**

A technical herbarium in black and white: cool, clear

Blossfeldt remained in Italy for six years. Returning to Berlin in 1896, he first worked as an assistant to Professor Ernst Ewald at the Royal Art School and shortly thereafter became a private lecturer at the Museum of Commercial Art, where a course of instruction, "Modeling from Living Plants," had been set up at the initiative of Moritz Meurer. To the fragile preserved specimens and plaster models that were already a part of the program, we may be certain that Blossfeldt soon added photographic studies of the plants. Blossoms, buds, stems, leaves and umbels: Karl Blossfeldt patiently conjured plants and more plants onto the plates, using, it is said, a self-made camera for 6 × 9, 9 × 12, and 13 × 18 cm (2¼ × 3½, 3½ × 4¾, and 5⅛ × 7 inch) glass negatives. For Blossfeldt, photographing the plants signified work, and nothing more than work, as Rolf Sachsse has emphasized, for the artist was interested neither in cutting an artistic profile for himself nor in gaining revenue from the project. Only for teaching purposes did he use his pictures, in the form of large-format slides or prints pasted on the classroom walls. In short, until their publication in the middle of the 1920s, Blossfeldt's photographs enjoyed only a very modest and very temporal publicity.

There is also another sense in which taking the photographs was work, especially when one associates the term with a certain tiresome monotony. From the beginning, Blossfeldt followed a standardized form of arrangement. The plants are always placed against a neutral background and are illuminated by diffuse and evenly directed daylight that brings out their volume and three-dimensionality. He aims the camera directly, that is, vertically, at his subjects, from which he has removed visually disruptive shoots and leaves, as well as the roots. These are the photographic hallmarks that characterize his work: this is how he creates his specimens that are then enlarged between three and fifteen times – forty-five times on occasion, if necessary – to fill the pictorial space. In this manner, between 1890 and 1930, Karl Blossfeldt completed 6,000 photographs, creating an enormous technical herbarium in black and white: cool, clear, and – without the artist realizing it – surrealistic. Anyone who wishes may claim to find an extrapolation of the Art-Nouveau interest in floral designs in Blossfeldt's eight-fold enlargement of the fronds of a maidenhair fern (scientific name: *Adiantum pedatum*), or in the winding tendrils of a pumpkin, the base of an aristolochia stem, or a forsythia bud. But no interpretation could be more false. Both Blossfeldt and the turn-of-the-century reform movement that he supported were opposed precisely to Art Nouveau's "fashionable playing with mindless curlicues" (Richard Graul, 1904). Although perhaps not so vehement as Adolf Loos, whose equation of "ornamentation and crime" has become a slogan, Blossfeldt desired a turning away from the ubiquitous aestheticizing and decoration of the objects of daily life. If patterns were to be sought in nature, then let it be in the form of basic biological shapes whose tectonics were seen as providing a model for the combination of a 'natural' technology and aesthetics, of economics and material-social justice. This alone was what Blossfeldt attempted to illuminate through his visual researches. Half a century earlier, Semper's *Science, Industry, and Art* (1852) had recommended making the study of nature a duty for design of every sort. Now Blossfeldt was responding to this demand with a unique documentation deriving from possibilities offered by photography – a documentation whose influence is still evident today, perhaps even more in conceptual photography than in commercial art.

In the 1920s, Karl Nierendorf, founder of a Berlin art gallery as well as the *Catacombs* cabaret, became aware of Blossfeldt's work. Just how the clever Nierendorf – who had started his career

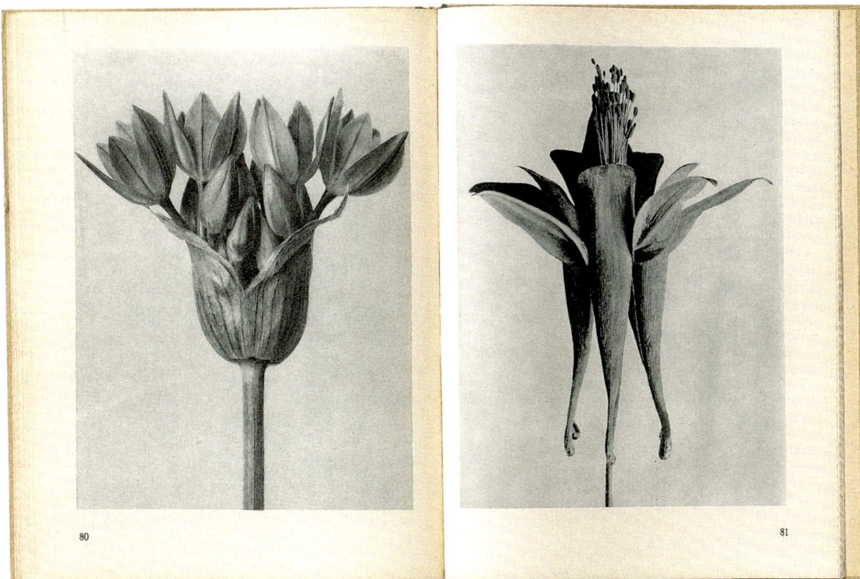

as a banker in Cologne – discovered Blossfeldt for the realm of art remains hidden in the depths of history. All we know is that the first gallery exhibition of Blossfeldt's plant studies was mounted in April 1926; until that point – and this is worth emphasizing – the photographs had never passed beyond the walls of the educational complex located in Berlin's Hardenbergstrasse. Through Nierendorf, Blossfeldt's photographic works appeared for the first time in an artistic context, and in this context they would later be received by the public. Although the response in the popular press ranged from positive to euphoric, the exhibition itself did not yet constitute the great 'breakthrough'. It was not until two years later that the renowned Berlin architectural publisher Ernst Wasmuth brought out Blossfeldt's book *Urformen der Kunst.* The effect was like a "thunderclap," in the words of a contemporary. The book "was to be seen in all the book stores, and the man whom many in the Hardenbergstrasse had looked upon as a friendly specimen of an extinct species – and whom some would gladly have chased out [of the academy] because they thought his two studios were a waste of space – this man had now become famous."

Friends throughout the world

"The first edition," Karl Nierendorf announced proudly in the foreword to the popular edition of *Urformen*, "was taken up by the public in a manner that exceeded all expectation. The German edition was soon succeeded by an English and a French, and throughout the world the work found so many friends that the publisher has now determined to release a popular

---

Double-page spread from Blossfeldt's Urformen, *1948.*

edition." This first popular edition appeared in 1935, ironically a year in which important artists of the New Objectivity – a term first used by G. F. Hartlaub in 1925 – had already fallen into disgrace. Nonetheless, this was not to be the last time *Urformen* would be brought to press. After the war, the book was again printed a number of times, and is said to have influenced commercial art teaching in West Germany into the 1950s.

The public's positive reaction to the work found resonance in the euphoric reception by the critics, who immediately claimed Blossfeldt as a protagonist of a new manner of perception. Leading the pack of critical reviews was no less a figure than Walter Benjamin, whose critique appeared in the *Literarische Welt* of 23 November 1928, and became "probably the most cited review" (J. Wilde). Critics, including such figures as Franz Roh, Julius Meier-Graefe, Max Osborn, and Curt Glaser, as well as authors such as Arnold Zweig and Hans Bethge, also discussed the work. The book, whose first edition moreover had sold out in eight months, also received some negative criticism, particularly from the political left. Stanislav Kubicki, for example, writing in the *a–z*, a Rhineland magazine that reflected a socially progressive position, identified the basic assumptions behind *Urformen* in an understanding of form that was oriented on supposedly "natural principles of construction"; the truth is, he countered, that "almost all architectonic form derives from practical application... from the materials used, and from the purpose [behind it]. If we today discern a similarity between a Doric column and an enlarged photograph of a segment of horsetail, it is not at all because the horsetail constitutes the basic form of the Doric column. Rather, we have before us an accidental, quite amusing, but insignificant parallelism that tells us absolutely nothing." What Kubicki's commentary overlooks, however, is that Blossfeldt's book, with its one hundred twenty full-page plates printed as greenish copper intaglio prints (*Maidenhair Fern* is Plate LV), had long since exceeded the author's initial didactic aim and had become a signal of visual modernity. Moholy-Nagy in particular expressed his reverence for the accomplishment when he presented Blossfeldt's botanic studies in the section of the epochal *Film and Foto* exhibition (1929) in Stuttgart. Whether Blossfeldt himself appreciated the radical newness of his activity is doubtful, when we look at the foreword he wrote to his second book, *Nature's Garden of Wonders* (1932), where he speaks of nature offering a model for the "healthy development of art," offering "fruitful inspiration," and providing an "inexhaustible fountain of youth." It is therefore, so to speak, only against the grain of Blossfeldt's philosophy of nature that postmodern photographers have adopted his work as a model, whether in terms of his conceptual, accretive, and comparative method of procedure, or in terms of his camera approach, which unconsciously conforms to the ideals of so-called Straight Photography. What is certain is that neither the comparative approach of Bernd and Hilla Becher, nor the cool plant studies of Irving Penn, Robert Mapplethorpe, Reinhart Wolf, or recently, Kenro Izu, would be conceivable without the creative preliminary groundwork of Karl Blossfeldt. For this reason, Klaus Honnef has rightly granted him a place in the pantheon of twentieth-century photography: Karl Blossfeldt, an amateur photographer, untrammeled by the rules of the craft or the norms of art, was open to a new kind of perception that corresponded to a rational age.

Karl Blossfeldt:
Saxifraga Willkommiana, *ca. 1900.*

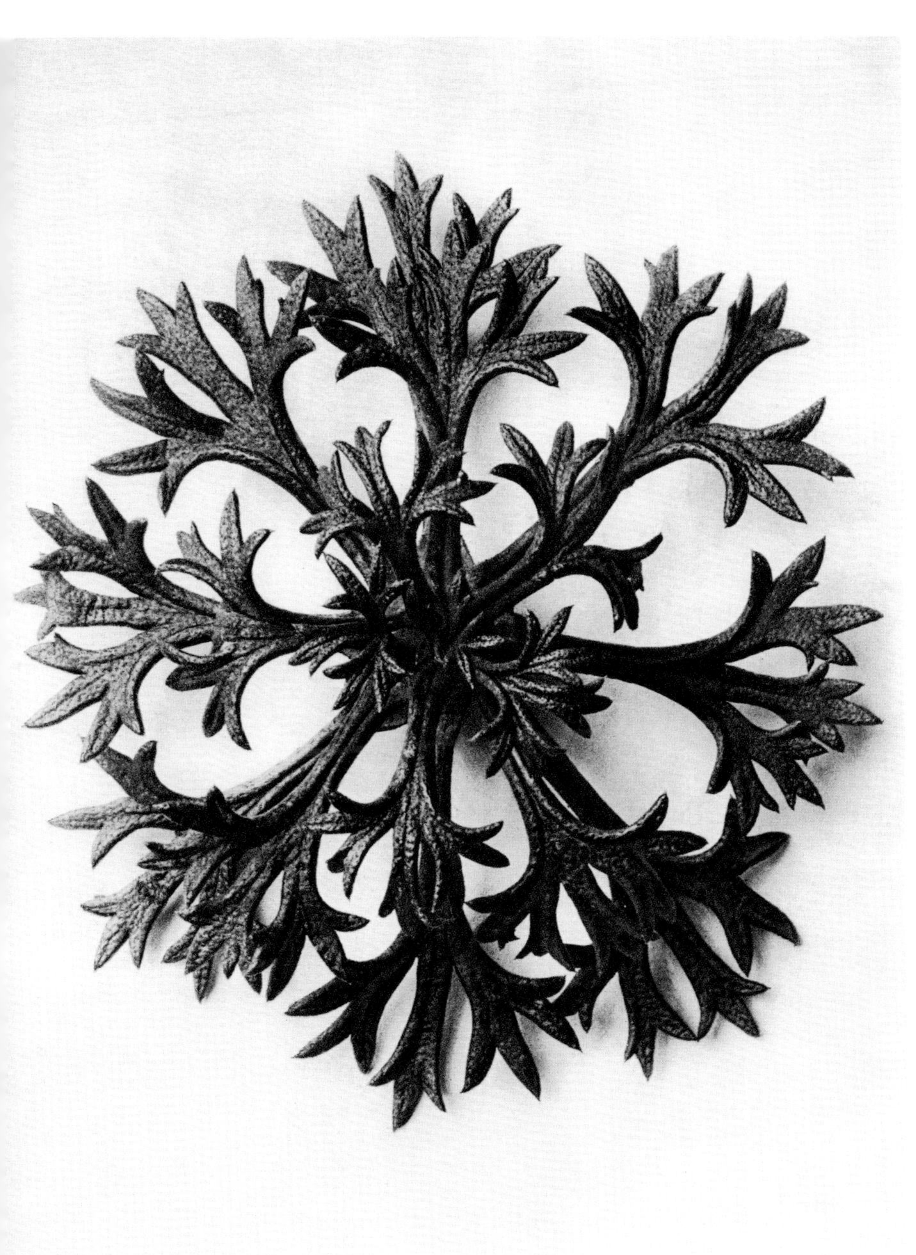

Maidenhair Fern, ca. 1900

Alfred Stieglitz
The Steerage
1907

Class Excursion on the High Seas

It is his most well-known, and in his opinion most important, image. During a voyage from New York to Le Havre in the spring of 1907, Alfred Stieglitz photographed the steerage deck of the trans-Atlantic steamer *Kaiser Wilhelm II*. The aesthetic of the picture boldly anticipated what came to be called the New Objectivity in photography.

One gazes at the gentleman wearing the straw hat approximately in the center of the upper third of the picture. This brightly gleaming headgear seems to have functioned as an especially important compositional element for Alfred Stieglitz: after all, he repeatedly made the so-called 'boater', which had become fashionable around 1880, into an unmistakable component of his pictures. One needs only to recall his photograph *The Ferry Boat* of 1910, where an entire group of young hat-wearers perhaps set off his desire to take a picture. Or a more successful variation of the motif, in which the light-colored headgear competes with a row of wooden bollards, painted white. Not that Alfred Stieglitz had any special interest in the hat styles of his age: to the contrary, the material world tended to leave him cold, unless it offered him usable 'raw material' for a photograph he was interested in taking. Stieglitz was no documentarist; the here-and-now had only a limited value for him. And if he once claimed that photography was his passion, and the search for the truth an obsession, then he was certainly not equating 'truth' with the quest after the internal contradictions of an age, society, or political system that contemporary photographers such as Jacob Riis or Lewis W. Hine were concerned with. For Stieglitz, truth implied rather a balance, a rightness, an equanimity within the picture itself; in other words, it was an aesthetic concept. Not that the social aspect failed to move him: according to his own testimony, it was precisely the sense of surfeit inherent in

---

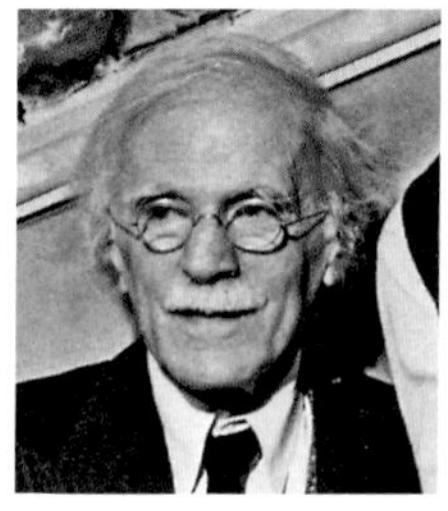

Alfred Stieglitz
*Born **1864** the son of wealthy German immigrants in Hoboken, New Jersey. Studies in Berlin (engineering, photochemistry). **1883** first exposures. **1890** returns to New York. From **1893** editor of the journal* American Amateur Photographer. ***1902** editor of* Camera Notes. ***1902** founding of the Photo Secession. **1903–17** editor of the seminal periodical* Camera Work. ***1905** opens the Little Galleries. **1907** tours Europe. Meets among others Heinrich Kühn. **1925–29** directs the Intimate Gallery. **1929–46** directs the gallery An American Place. Dies **1946** in New York.*

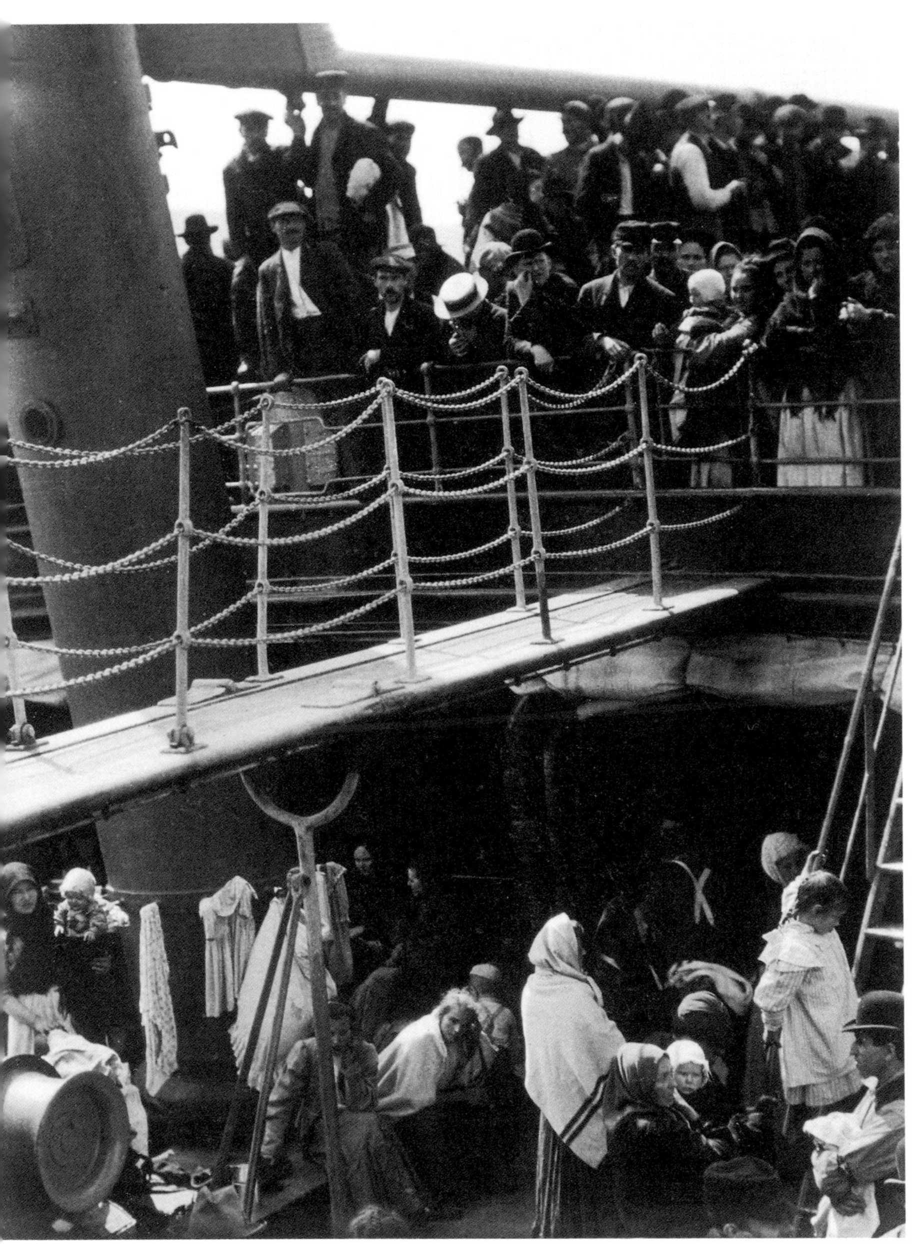

The Steerage, 1907

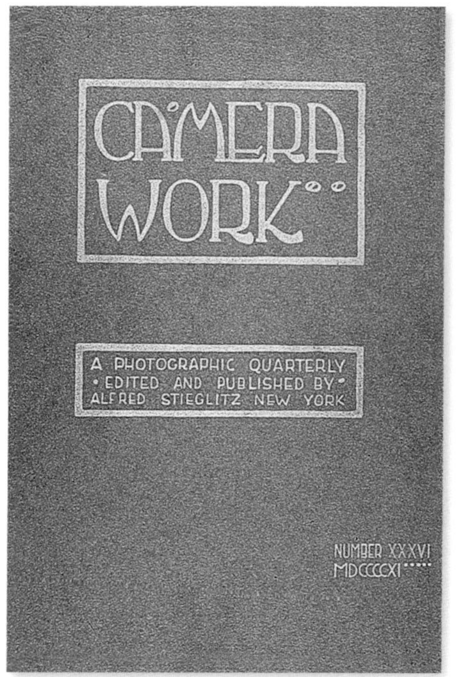

the bored atmosphere of the First Class that was a part of what moved him during the steamship passage to Europe in 1907 to seek out the 'tween-decks of the Second and Third Class, where he took what is perhaps his most famous photograph, *The Steerage*. Typically, however, Stieglitz kept his distance, photographing downward from an elevated position. And, decades later, when he provided a remarkably comprehensive commentary to his picture, he was concerned exclusively with compositional, technical, and aesthetic questions. The social extremes evident in the picture in other words were the trigger, but not the goal, of his pictorial exploration. Stieglitz sought not to penetrate but to aestheticize the world by means of photography. He understood himself chiefly as an artist, an apologist for an autonomous photography, that served nothing and no one but the duty to be art.

Alfred Stieglitz was born in 1864 in Hoboken, New Jersey, into a German-Jewish family, his father having emigrated from Münden, near Hanover. The son possessed a contradictory spirit. He himself sensed these contradictions, and raised them consciously to the sine qua non of his restless, lifelong devotion to art, specifically, photography. In every person who is truly alive, he once declared, these contradictions are to be found; moreover, "where there are no contradictions, there is no life." In this sense, Stieglitz was an apologist for photography but, as an elitist in thought and deed, he lacked any real desire to popularize it. Stieglitz was an avant-gardist with an almost nostalgic leaning toward craftsmanship; he was doctrinaire, but without a unified doctrine; he was feared, but ultimately powerless. As a critic, editor, publisher, gallerist, curator, go-between, instigator, impresario, and collector, he was probably the most brilliant figure in American art business in the new twentieth century. His role as a midwife to modern art in the broadest sense of the term is uncontested. In his excellent biography of the photographer, Richard Whelan claims that Stieglitz "is perhaps the most important figure in the history of the visual arts in the USA." Therefore, in the 1950s and 1960s, when New York finally replaced Paris as the world art capital, the revolution unquestionably owed its thanks to Alfred Stieglitz as the long-term result of his influence and effort, so to

Camera Work, *1911 edition, in which* The Steerage *was first published. Edward Streichen did the typography for the cover.*

speak. It was he who introduced America to the European avant-garde, and in turn fostered and encouraged American artists. But in spite of all this, he understood himself first and foremost to be a photographer. "When I'm finally judged," he once said, "I should be evaluated primarily in terms of my own photographic work."

Between applied art and conceptual art

As a photographer, Stieglitz is a giant. In today's market; his works easily bring in three hundred thousand dollars – when they come to market at all, that is. His œuvre is discussed in practically every history of the medium. And yet, his photographic creations still stand under the shadow of the artists that he publicized and fostered as his protégés: Edward Steichen, Edward Weston, Paul Strand, to name only three. Stieglitz does not appear in the 'pantheon' of the thirty most important photographers of the twentieth century established in 1992 by Klaus Honnef, who characterizes Stieglitz's work as "commercial photography – though of a high degree": a surprizing evaluation, insofar as Stieglitz succeeded in establishing Pictorialism in the USA while he was almost simultaneously anticipating Straight Photography in works like *Winter, Fifth Avenue* (1893), *From the Back-Window, 291* (1915), or – precisely – *The Steerage*. In other words, at least twice Stieglitz was the leading figure in the artistic avant-garde. Furthermore, it was he who raised the metropolis, modern civilization itself, to an object for art, introducing it into polite company, as it were. Skyscrapers, city canyons, rail and ship traffic all appear as motifs on an equal basis with classical themes such as landscape, genre, and nude photography. Stieglitz's œuvre even comprises examples of conceptual photography, if one considers his portraits of Georgia O'Keeffe, one of his later lovers, shot over a period of years, or his cloud studies, his so-called *Equivalents*, that he pursued almost obsessively. Admittedly absent from Stieglitz's photographs is the radicalism that his contemporaries such as Evans or Strand brought to their work. In a sense, Stieglitz remained a pictorialist, above all interested in adapting the classical rules of art to photography and to creating an elegant print. All of this applies specifically to *The Steerage*, a work at once ambivalently radical and affirmative. Stieglitz published the picture for the first time in 1911 in his magazine *Camera Work*; years later he designated it among his most important works. "If all my photographs were lost, and I were to be remembered only for *The Steerage*," he once said, "I would be satisfied."

In the spring of 1907 Alfred Stieglitz was forty-three years old. We can picture the artist, of whom so many portraits exist, as a respectable middle-aged gentleman with thick hair and a dark mustache, wire-rimmed glasses, and the skeptical gaze of the restrained misanthrope who has not yet given up the struggle against ignorance and poor taste. Although born in the USA, Stieglitz was strongly influenced by spending a number of school and university years in Germany. In particular, the lectures by Hermann Wilhelm Vogel, the inventor of orthochromatic film, greatly furthered his interest in photography. Stieglitz's first experiments with the camera stem from his Berlin period beginning 1882. He began to submit his work to photography contests and to write knowledgeable essays on the subject for international magazines. Upon his return to the USA, initially as editor of the journal *American Amateur Photographer* and later of *Camera Notes*, he became the apologist of an 'autonomous' photography, free from the service to any particular goals. His association with *Camera Work* (beginning 1903) and the Little Galleries at 291 Fifth Avenue (beginning 1905) provided him with influential forums for broadcasting his ideals. By 1907 he had also opened his doors to the fine arts, in particular to the work of artists like Rodin, Toulouse-Lautrec, Matisse, and Picasso. In the same year, Stieglitz himself undertook a voyage to Europe. In early June, acceding to the wishes of his wife, Emmy, he boarded the *Kaiser Wilhelm II*, the luxurious flagship of the Norddeutsche Lloyd lines. Along with his wife, daughter Kitty, and a governess, he brought along a Graflex for 4 × 5 inch (10 × 12.7 cm) glass negatives, and a single unexposed plate with which he was later to capture his famous 'tween-decks picture.

For photographers to speak about their individual creations is more the exception than the rule. Nonetheless, in 1942 – four years before his death – Stieglitz provided *The Steerage* with a longish commentary, which Wilfried Wiegand once with justice termed "the most precise description… ever offered on the creation of a masterpiece." Stieglitz begins his discussion with a description of the atmosphere in the First Class, which he hated: faces that "would cause a cold shudder to run down the spine," led him to spend the first few days at sea in a lounge chair on deck with his eyes closed. "On the third day," he continued, "I couldn't take any more. I had to get away from this society."

The artist moved "as far forward as the deck allowed." The sea was calm, the sky clear with a sharp wind blowing. "Reaching the end of the deck, I found myself alone, and looked down. In the steerage were men, women and children. A narrow stairway led up to a small 'tween-deck above, directly over the prow of the ship. To the left was a slanted chimney, and from the 'tween deck, a gleaming, freshly painted gangway hung down." Stieglitz noticed a young man with a round straw hat and the funnel leaning left, the stairway leaning right, "the white drawbridge with its railings made of circular chains – white suspenders crossing on the back of a man in the steerage below, round shapes of iron machinery, a mast cutting into the sky, making a triangular shape… For a while I stood there as if rooted, looking and looking. Could I photograph what I was feeling…?" Stieglitz hurried back to his cabin, grabbed his Graflex, and hurried back "out of breath and afraid that the man in the straw hat might have moved. If he had left his place, then I no longer had the picture than I had imagined earlier. The relation between the forms that I wanted to capture would have been destroyed, and the picture would have been gone." But the man was still standing there. Furthermore, neither the man wearing the suspenders nor the woman with her child on her lap had altered their positions. "Apparently," claimed Stieglitz, "no one had changed position. I had only one cassette with a single unexposed plate. Would I be able to capture what I saw and felt? Finally I pressed the button. My heart was pounding. I had never heard my heart beating before. Had I gotten my picture? If the answer was yes, then I knew I had reached a new milestone in photography, similar to *Car Horses* in 1892 or *Hand of Man* in 1902, both of which had introduced a new epoch in photography and perception."

In comparison with the euphoria that he later expressed, Stieglitz seems not to have been so certain in the beginning about the quality of the picture. How else can one explain the fact that the work that he designated as a milestone of photographic art appeared neither in the art photography exhibition in Dresden in 1909, nor in the Albright Gallery in Buffalo a year later. *The Steerage* was published for the first time in 1911 as a 19.7 × 15.8 cm (7¾ × 6¼ inch) photogravure in Number 36 of the legendary magazine *Camera Work* that Stieglitz edited. Earlier, the photographer thought he recalled showing the photograph to his friend and colleague Joseph T. Keily. "'But Stieglitz', he protested, 'you took two pictures, one above and

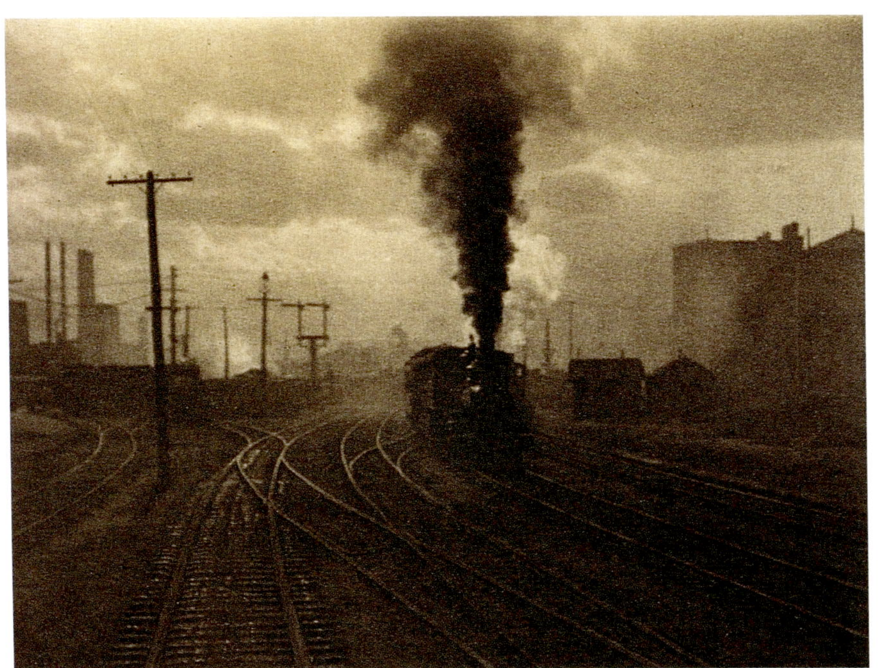

one below'... It became clear to me that he did not rightly see the picture that I had taken." Even today, the photograph is regularly misunderstood as a visual witness to the masses of immigrants that were streaming to the USA around the turn of the twentieth century. In fact, however, the ship is sailing in the opposite direction, and the people traveling in steerage were in fact 'migratory birds' – manual workers and craftspeople who, as Richard Whelan writes, "made the crossing between Europe and the New World in two-year cycles." Stieglitz himself did not comment on them – just as he did not seem interested in the entire social aspect of his photography. He placed forms and structure above any possible human implications – at any rate, the latter were not the subject of his reflections. Thus, on the eve of the First World War, 'pure' art was able to celebrate itself once more. Afterwards, it would be forced to redefine its role in a new age and a new world.

Alfred Stieglitz:
The Hand of Man, *1902.*

Lewis W. Hine
Girl Worker in a Carolina Cotton Mill
1908

Moments of Childhood

The work of the American photographer Lewis W. Hine unites moral perspective and social engagement with a media-conscious application of photography. Especially in his cycle on child labor in the USA, he rose beyond pictorial journalism to create an early model for a humane photojournalism.

He is said to have been always extremely exact with the inscriptions on his photographs. For he realized that only when all coordinates passed muster – place, time, situation, etc. – would his photographs be believed, and only then could he defy the skeptics and doubters, of which American politics and economy seemed to provide so many. To undertake all that was necessary so that his work might produce results – this was the so-to-speak motive force behind his at times mortally dangerous, and in any case physically and intellectually grueling, activity. "There were two things I wanted to do," the artist once explained: "I wanted to show the things that had to be corrected. I wanted to show the things that had to be appreciated." In these terms, Lewis W. Hine numbers among the leading figures of socially oriented documentary photography.

An interpretation of nature

Girl Worker in a Carolina Cotton Mill is the simple authorized title of the original 4½ × 6½ inch (11.8 × 16.8 cm) photograph. Specific mention of the name of the factory or the date and hour of the photograph are absent. Hine's concern here is with the condition in general: the presentation of child labor in factories, coal mines, saw mills, southern cotton fields, and northern urban streets and squares. What is most important for him is that the situation appear believable, that the photograph be accepted as evidence, as a document

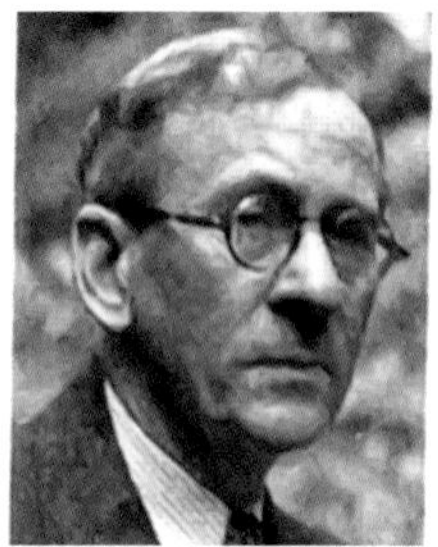

Lewis Wickes Hine

Born ***1874*** *in Oshkosh, Wisconsin, USA. His father dies in an accident during his early childhood. From* ***1892*** *various jobs, including heading a team of cleaners. Teacher training at the University of Chicago. Moves to New York. Supply teacher at the Ethical Culture School.* ***1903*** *turns to photography.* ***1904*** Immigrants on Ellis Island *is his first major project with an educational purpose.* ***1908*** *quits teaching. A large scale survey commissioned by the National Child Labor Committee on the topic of child labour.* ***1918*** *documentation for the Red Cross on the impact of the war on Europe.* ***1930*** *photo-reportage on the building of the Empire State Building.* ***1932*** *publication of* Men at Work. *Dies* ***1940*** *in New York.*

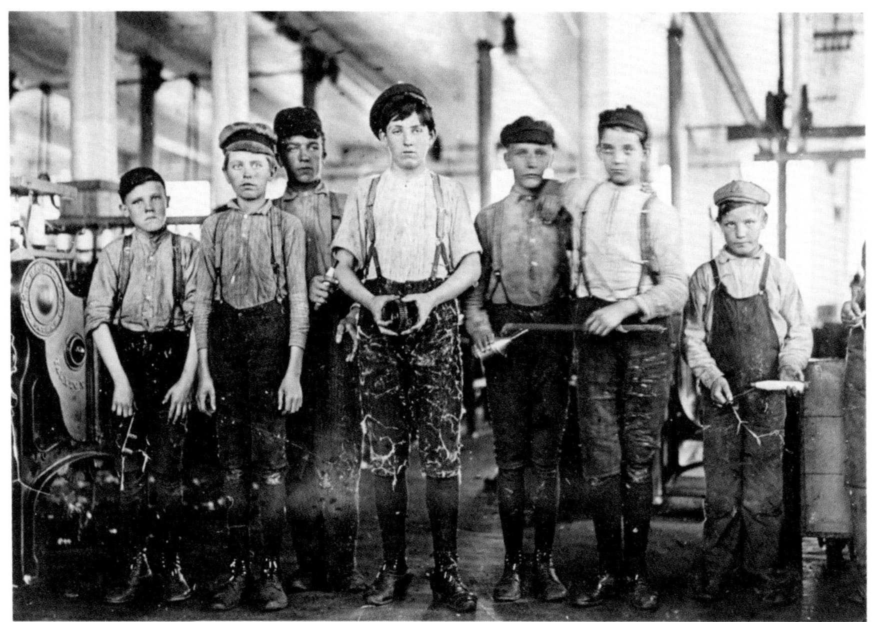

of record – a term that, moreover, first arose in the middle of the 1920s in John Gierson's review of Robert Flaherty's film *Moana* in the *New York Sun* of 8 February 1926, in which a similar impulse is termed a 'documentary'. Hine himself never used the expression. "A good photograph," as he once defined it, "is not a mere reproduction of an object or a group of objects – it is an interpretation of Nature, a reproduction of impressions made upon the photographer which he desires to repeat to others."

With this statement, Hine gives a hint that he was to some extent willing to set up a scene. In the end, he was not simply seeking the naked pictorial evidence, but rather an effect in the sense of a clear, but moving, emphasis. Even in his very first series of photographs of immigrants on Ellis Island he had focused on individuals or couples from the mass of people, arranged them before a neutral background, and – one suspects – asked them to hold still a moment until the heavy Graflex camera was ready for the take and the flash powder was in the pan. Beyond a doubt, the complexity of the equipment itself required a certain level of the photographer's attention. In addition, however, Hine was always concerned also with composition, a fact that is often forgotten in the face of the simplicity of his pictures. "Certainly, Hine was conscious also of the aesthetics of photography," writes Walter Rosenblum, one of the top experts on Hine's work. "His files contain beautiful prints as well as

---

Lewis W. Hine:
Untitled, *1908.*

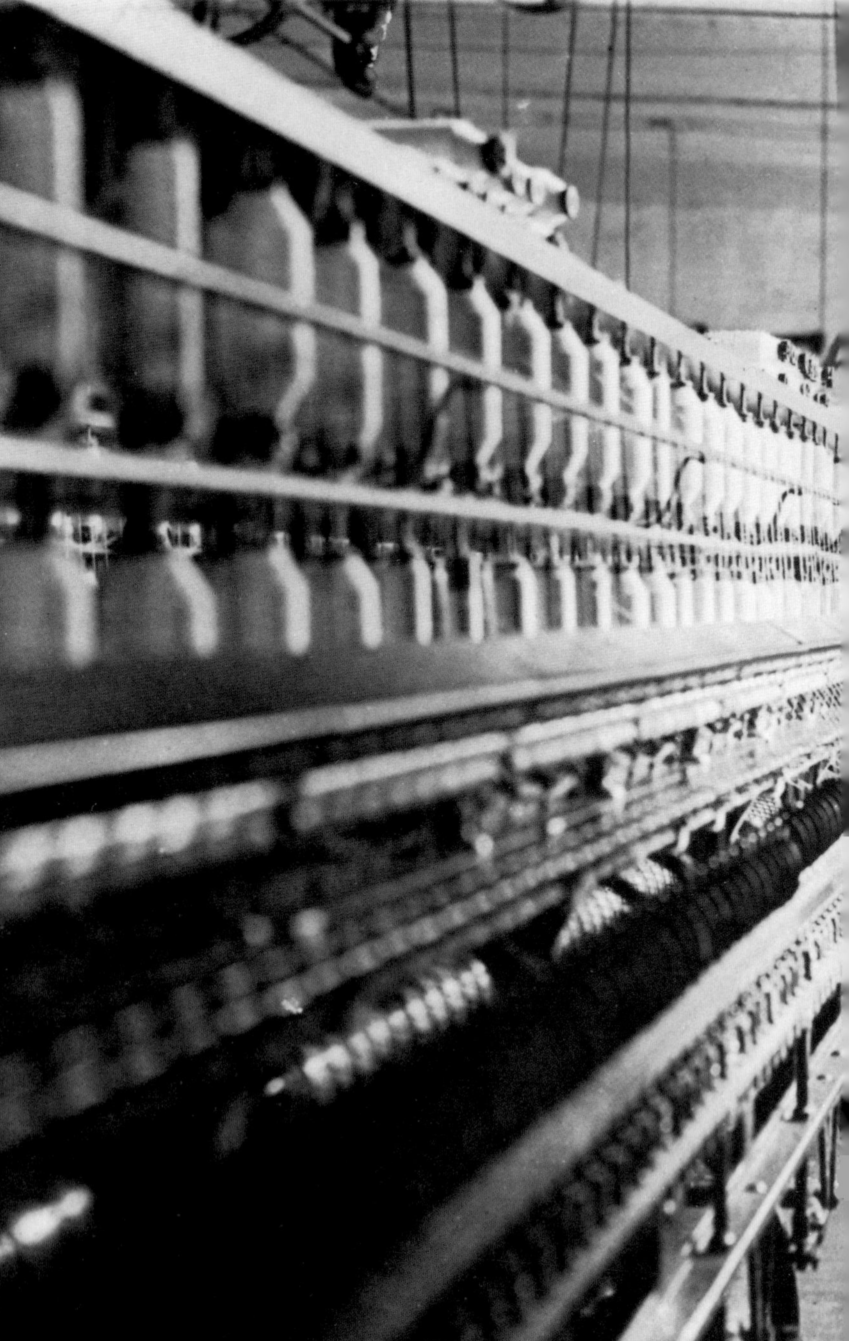

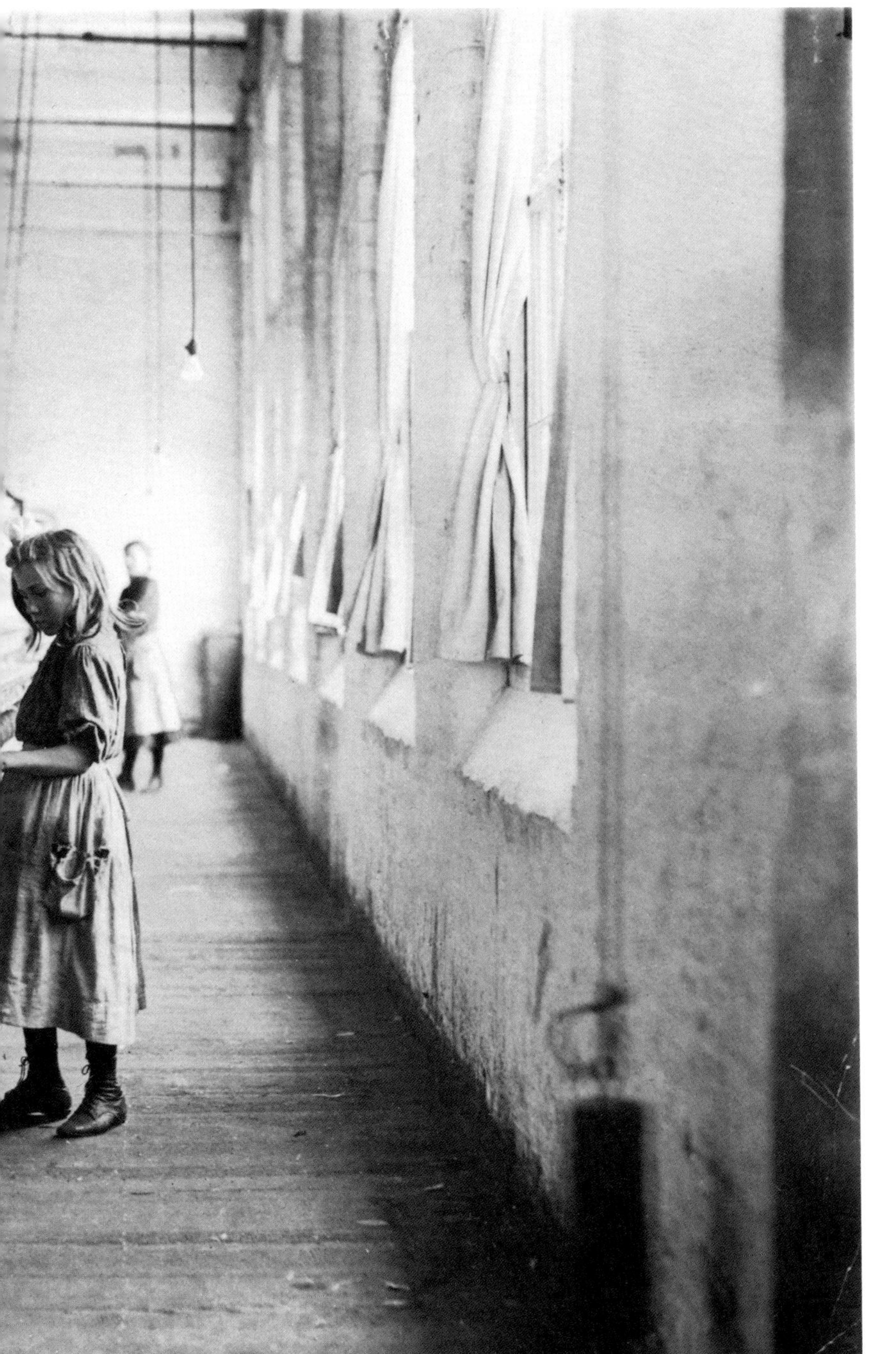

mediocre ones. But when he organized a photograph, the effect was right. Considering the range of subject matter, the difficulties of site and execution, his vision is always fine and often superb."

A girl standing in front of a spinning machine. We can only guess at her age, for Hine did not reveal it, even though he often conducted short interviews with the subjects of his photographs, inquired about their circumstances, and asked their age. Sometimes he measured the size of the children he photographed against the buttons on his vest in order at least to estimate their ages later. This child, whom we could well imagine at a school desk, is probably between eight and ten years old. Technically, she is not alone in the photograph, but the grown woman in the background plays no role in the scene, even if she seems to be attentively watching the process of taking the photograph. The child herself is unselfconsciously working at the so-called ring spinning machine, a device invented in the USA at the beginning of the nineteenth century. The fact that at the moment of the photograph the child has paused in her work deprives the picture of none of its authority. She is hardly looking happily into the camera, nor does the state of her apron indicate any especially blessed living conditions.

In 1907, that is, shortly before Hine made his photograph, a government inquiry reported that there were no fewer than 1,750,178 children between the ages of ten and fifteen years working in American factories, mines, farms, or what we would today designate as service industries (such as shoeshine, newspaper and errand boys). Moreover, sixty-hour weeks were no rarity, in spite of child labor being forbidden by law in many of the states. In Pennsylvania, for example, children under the age of fourteen could not work in the mines, and in other fields a minimum age of nine years had been set. Such regulations, however, were constantly being evaded, on the one hand because the booming economy required much labor, and on the other because the sheer poverty widespread among urban and city dwellers caused many families to rely on even their youngest members for financial help. For these reasons, proof-of-age certificates were forged, or false information was provided by the parents. Hordes of underage children drudged away as 'breaker boys' in mines where accidents were a common occurrence, and where darkness, cold, wet, and bad air leading to life-long health problems were a certainty; these Hine also addressed in his pictures. "Whatever industry saves by child labor," Hine recognized very early, "society pays over and over."

The worst form of institutions exploiting children

Some of the very worse conditions seem to have existed in the cotton mills of the American South – in North Carolina, South Carolina, and Georgia – where official statistics record that almost fifty percent of all workers were approximately ten years old. The cotton mills are "the worst form of institutions exploiting children" according to the newspaper *Solidarity*, the "Official Organ of the Worker, Health, and Death Insurance of the United States of America," in 1907. The paper cited also the large rate of illiteracy among the children: 18.8 per cent of all working children between the ages of ten and fourteen were designated

---

Lewis W. Hine:
Spinner in New England Mill, *1913*.

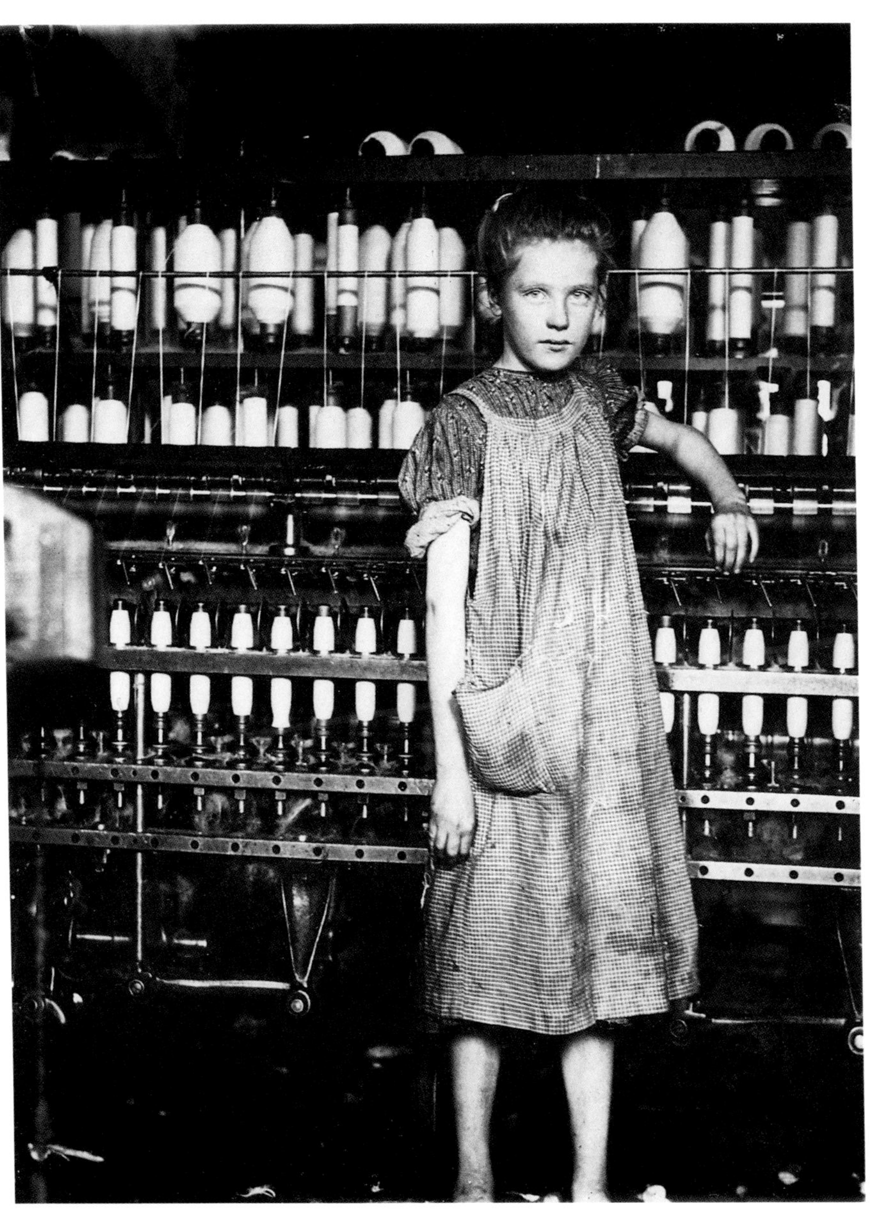

Girl Worker in a Carolina Cotton Mill, 1908

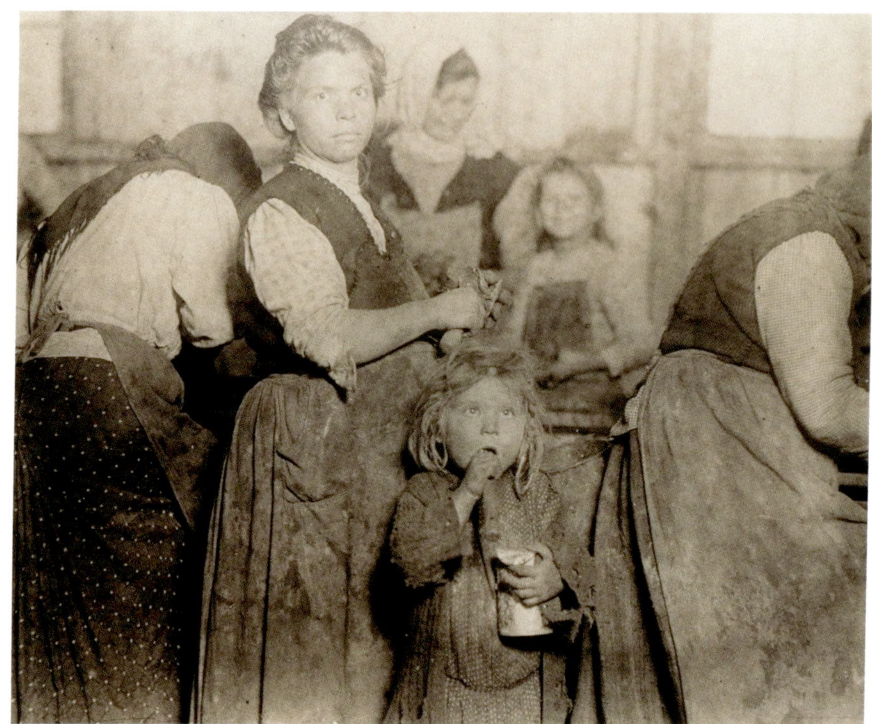

as illiterate, that is, they could neither read nor write. "How many of these innocent children, created as human beings in order to populate this planet, cannot attend school because they lack shoes, and above all, enough to eat! Because the mothers must go to work in place of the thousands of fathers who have been killed in the factories, and cannot look to their children's nourishment!"

The problem of child poverty and child labor was known, statistically proven, and the object of public debate. In 1904, the National Child Labor Committee (NCLC) under the direction of Owen R. Lovejoy had formed a private organization with waving banners against the "greatest crime of modern society," the enslavement and exploitation of minors. A jointly issued journal bearing the title *The Survey* was founded to create the necessary publicity, but seems in fact to have drawn little attention to itself before Hine appeared. It was only with the help of his photographic testimony that the opposition to the often-excoriated evil gained the momentum necessary for reforms, new laws, and stricter oversight, and finally the abolition of child labor. "Although we cannot attribute a specific reform to a certain

---

Lewis W. Hine:
Oyster Openers, *1913*.

photographic image, the mass of Hine's powerful photographs could not have failed to make an impact" (Stephen Victor).

Commissioned by the NCLC, Hine produced more than five thousand photographs between 1906 and 1918. He took his pictures in the factories of Cincinnati and Indianapolis, visited the glass works and mines of West Virginia and the textile mills of North Carolina. He visited home-workers in New York, and observed the night newspaper-sellers in New England. And this was not his first and largest photographic inquiry. As early as 1904 Hine had documented the arrival of European immigrants on Ellis Island. We can assume that Lewis W. Hine, born into modest circumstances in Oshkosh, Wisconsin, in 1874, and orphaned at an early age, had refined his self-taught photographic knowledge while attending the New York Ethical Culture School – that is, he learned the use of the Graflex and Fachkamera for 9 × 12 and 13 × 18 cm (3½ × 4¾ and 5⅛ × 7 inch) glass negatives, the handling of the rather dangerous flash powder, and in particular the dialogue with those whom he intended to portray in the midst of the fateful circumstances of their lives. In this effort, his humor, wit, human understanding, and love of mankind undoubtedly aided him – together with his often-noted dramatic talent that is supposed to have gained the versatile Hine entry into factories whose doors were officially closed to outsiders. There are stories that he regularly assumed the role of a Bible salesman, an insurance agent, or an industrial photographer to ease his way around the occasionally militant factory guards. After all, "to most employers, the exploitation of children was so profitable that nothing could be permitted to end it" (Walter Rosenblum).

Hine's photographs appeared in the publications of Hine NCLC, in particular in *The Survey*. They became the motif for posters and appeared in exhibitions and slide-lectures with whose help Hine and the NCLC attempted to reach a broader public. Hine's photographs, in other words, were part of an advanced concept in a double sense: they looked to modern media to effectively raise the desire for social reform.

Photography as a contemporary visual means of communication

More recent photographic criticism customarily poses Hine as the antithesis of Alfred Stieglitz – an opposition that is only partially justified. Stieglitz attempted to create recognition for photography as a modern art form by arguing for elaborate noble-metal processes and an elegant finish. Exactly these qualities seem not to have interested Hine, at least not in the sense of an artful photographic practice. "When he became school photographer in 1905, he didn't know anything about cameras, lenses, technics," according to his biographer Elizabeth McCausland. "Even today, at 64, he will say with a naiveté both lovable and sad: 'How is it that you make so much better prints than I do? Is it because your enlarger is better than mine?'"

To attempt to conclude that Hine was not interested in technical photographic questions would be false, however. What fascinated him was photography as a contemporary visual means of communication; what he ignored was the concept of the 'fine art print' as defended by the photographic community oriented on Stieglitz and his circle. And precisely here may lie the explanation for the low estimation that Hine and his work have received up to the present time. For example, Edward Steichen, chief curator for photography at the Museum of Modern Art in New York, showed no interest in 1947 in Hine's estate after his death in 1940. And even the evaluation of Susan Sontag, who held Walker Evans to be the most

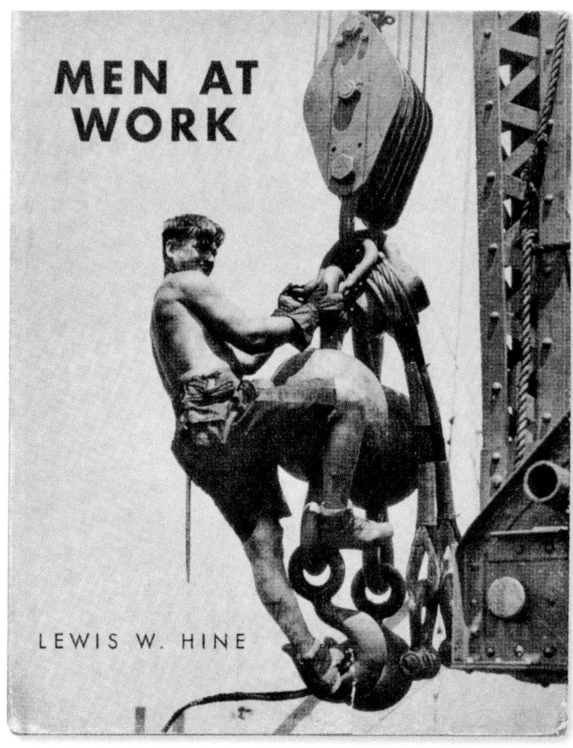

important photographic artist to have concerned himself with America, reveals something of the skepticism that art criticism has shown toward Hine's œuvre primarily directed to social criticism. And yet Hine was in fact interested in formal and aesthetic questions and had, moreover, developed a visual vocabulary that could hold its own at the height of art-photography debates, being wholly based on the qualities intrinsic to the medium. In particular his early workers' portraits, according to Miles Orvell "endow their commonplace subjects with a dignity not in terms of an art-historical tradition, but in terms of a new vocabulary of representation that erased the existing ethnographic and documentary traditions of portraiture and established a new procedure for representing working-class character." But there were very few who recognized this truth during Hine's lifetime, not even a Roy Stryker, who roundly rejected Hine's application for work with the FSA project. Thus Lewis Hine died in 1940 impoverished and forgotten. He who had devoted himself lifelong to the social welfare of others finally become a welfare case himself.

Above: Men at Work *was the primary, life-long theme of Lewis W. Hine's photography. The first edition of his book of the same name appeared in 1932 in the US.*

Right: *Spreads from* Men at Work. *The book's design orients itself more closely to the dynamic layout of magazines than to classic volumes of photography.*

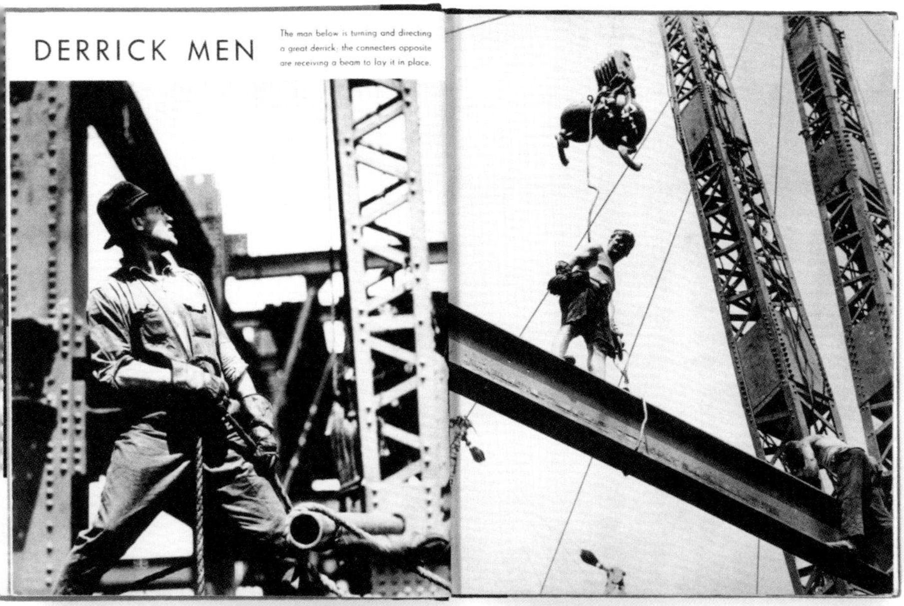

DERRICK MEN

The man below is turning and directing a great derrick; the connecters opposite are receiving a beam to lay it in place.

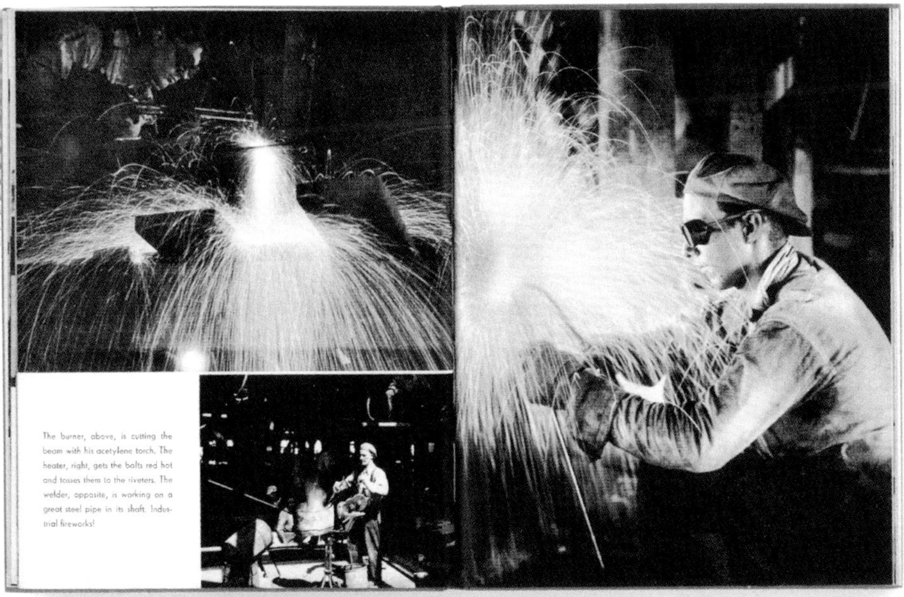

The burner, above, is cutting the beam with his acetylene torch. The heater, right, gets the bolts red hot and tosses them to the riveters. The welder, opposite, is working on a great steel pipe in its shaft. Industrial fireworks!

Jacques-Henri Lartigue
Grand Prix de l'A.C.F.
1912

The Tempo of Our Times

Automobile racing was a keenly watched spectacle at the turn of the 20th century. Roaring down the open highways, various makes of autos strove to demonstrate their performance ability. At the Grand Prix of the Automobile Club of France (A.C.F.) in 1912, the young Jacques-Henri Lartigue succeeded taking a photograph that we interpret today above all as a metaphor of the speed of the technological age.

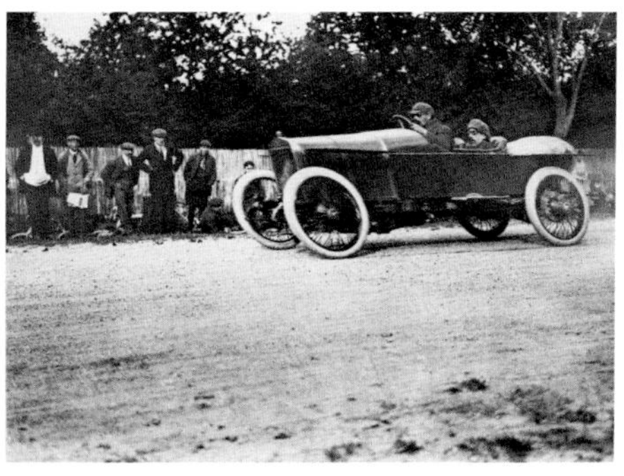

He loved classy automobiles – but what boy of his age doesn't? He watched as the first aviators swooped boldly through the skies, witnessed the advent of unheard-of technical innovations, and was fascinated by the age's intoxication with speed. Unlike most of his contemporaries the small Jacques-Haguet-Henri Lartigue (as he was christened) participated directly in the events. His family was wealthy – for a time, it was accounted the eighth richest in France – and his father, a well-known railroad director, banker, and publisher, exhibited a marked interest in novelty. As early as 1902 the family acquired their first automobile, a Krieger, followed by a Panhard-Levassor designed by Million Guiet. Next came a Peugeot, and finally, as the high point of the private fleet, a Hispano Suiza – before the family's wealth melted away after the First World War. But for now we're looking at a happier age. It was the fabulous

---

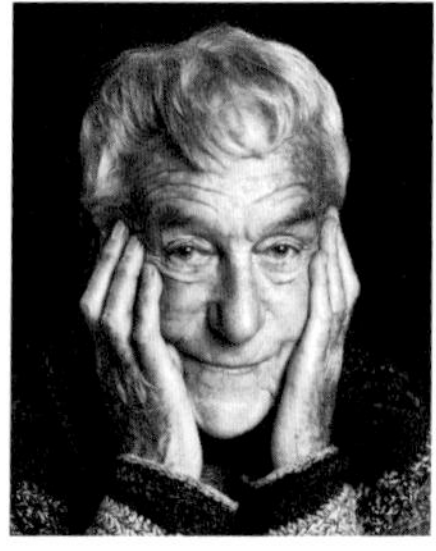

Jacques-Henri Lartigue

Born the scion of a wealthy Parisian family in ***1894*** *at Courbevoie. First camera at age eight, first exposures of his own at age ten.* ***1915*** *studies art in Paris. Numerous exhibitions in* ***1930****s Paris. Friendship with among others Picasso and Cocteau.* ***1963*** *first exhibition of his photography at the Museum of Modern Art, New York. First exhibition in Germany in* ***1966*** *at the* photokina. ***1970*** *publication of* Diary of a Century, *edited by Richard Avedon.* ***1979*** *donates his photo archive to the French state.* ***1984*** *culture prize of the DGPh German photography society.* ***1986*** *officer of the Légion d'Honneur. Dies* ***1986*** *in Nice.*

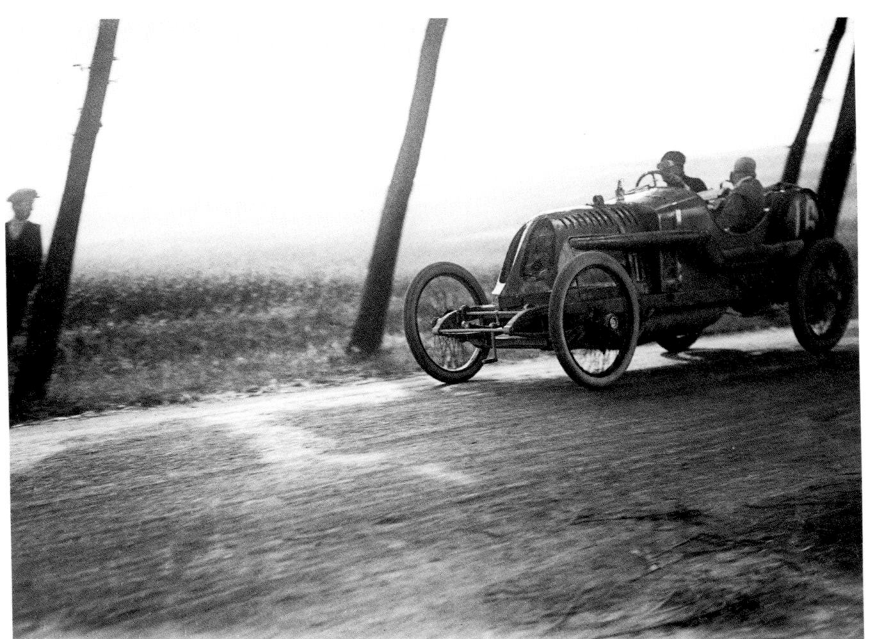

era of the Belle Epoque, and the Lartigue family entertained itself with all the diversions appropriate to their class: Sundays spent in the Bois de Boulogne or, often enough, at the auto races conducted on the periphery of Paris. And here, if the enjoyment proved to be fleeting, it could at least be captured on film.

A thing one must love immediately

Père Lartigue himself was apparently an enthusiastic amateur photographer. "Papa makes pictures," wrote Jacques-Henri in his *Mémoires sans Mémoire*. "Photography is a mysterious affair. A thing with an odd smell, bizarre and peculiar to itself – a thing one must love immediately." In 1901, at age seven, Lartigue received his first camera. "Papa," he noted, "seems like Dear God to me. He says, 'I'll give you a regular photography apparatus as a present'." This gift proved to be a heavy wooden camera for 13 × 18 cm ($5^{1}/_{8}$ × 7 inch) glass negatives, a device typical for the times, but in reality much too cumbersome for the slight and delicate Lartigue. But he quickly grasped his new medium as a technical refinement of that "angel trap," as he called it, by which Jacques-Henri, almost as soon as he learned to walk, had begun to record images of the visible world around him: "I blink my eyes quickly three times, spin myself around, and whoosh!, the picture is mine." In this way, photography very soon became an important tool of visual exploration for him; it was not merely a pastime, but the young boy's serious

Top left: **Jacques-Henri Lartigue:**
Grand Prix de l'A.C.F., *12 July, 1913.*

Above: **Jacques-Henri Lartigue:**
Course de côte de Gaillon, *6 October, 1912.*

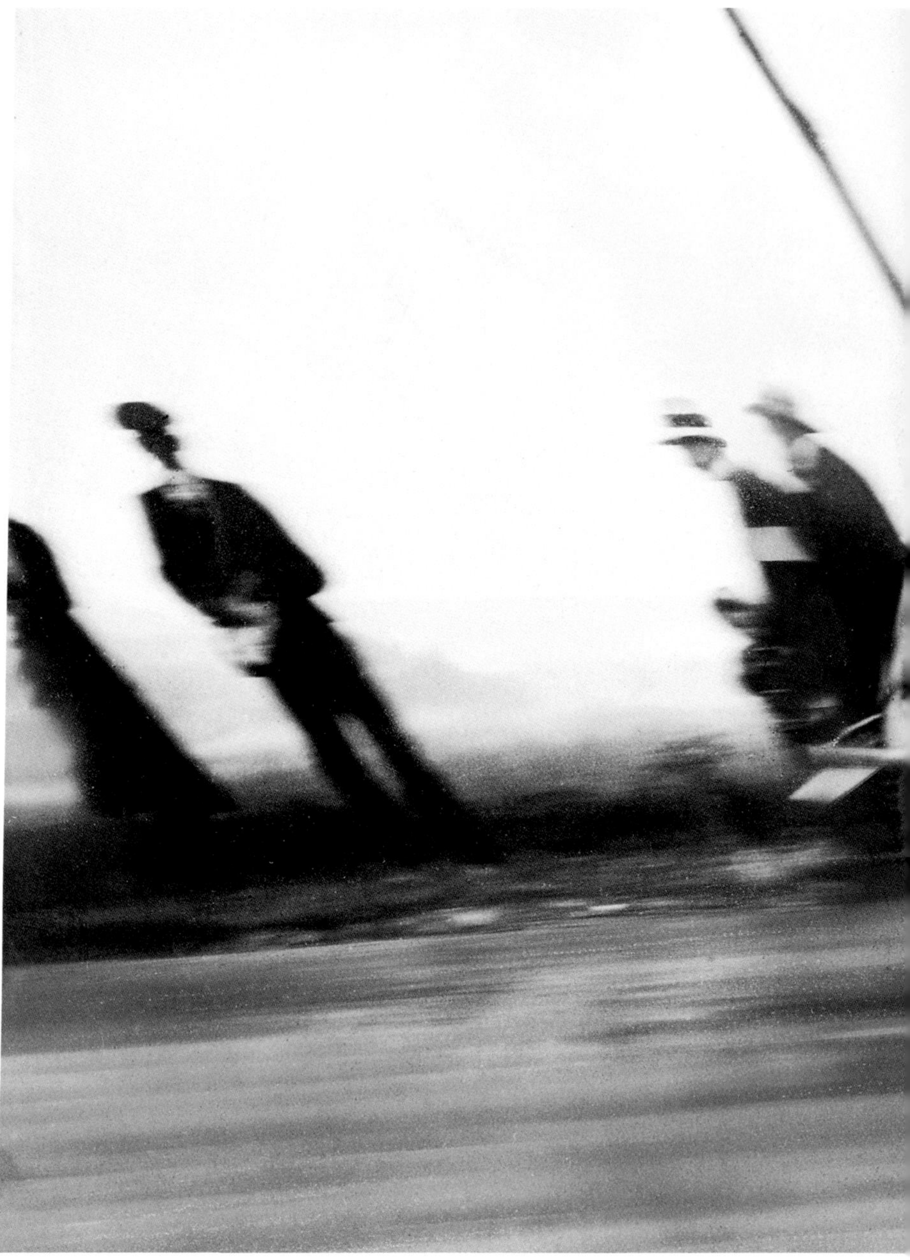

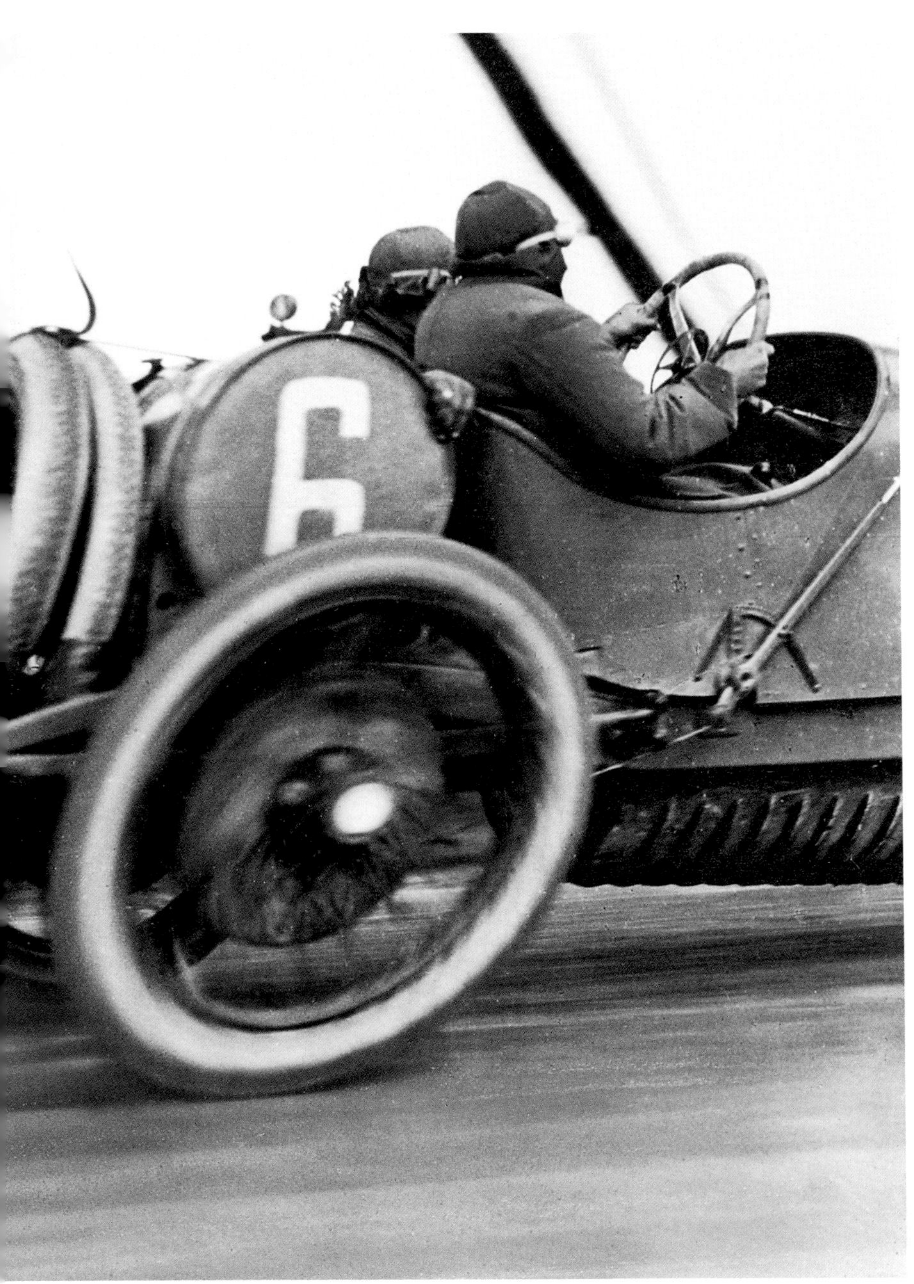
6

endeavor, which already extended from carefully composed exposures through the development and enlargement processes in the dark room.

With inexhaustible enjoyment and a remarkable eye

Lartigue photographed his own room, his toys, and furniture; then came the house, garden, servants, Mama, Papa, and his older brother Zissou. He broadened his horizons constantly. This is, after all, what he had always sought to do: to stop the process of things, to be able to apply the brake to the speed of time, to be allowed to remain a child for whom, so to speak, the world of technology unfolded itself as an over-sized arsenal of toys. Lartigue photographed automobiles – again and again automobiles. He captured airplanes on his plates. And zeppelins. And he did all this with inexhaustible enjoyment and a remarkable eye – but above all with an amazing, seemingly intuitive understanding of the iconographic characteristics of his medium. Decades later, no less a figure than John Szarkowski would claim, "These pictures are the observations of genius: fresh perceptions, poetically sensed and graphically fixed."

Lartigue was eighteen years old when he succeeded in shooting what has since become his probably most famous photograph. The date is 25 June, 1912. The family has set out to watch the Grand Prix of the Automobile Club de France near Le Tréport. At this time, France was still the leading automobile nation: more than two hundred auto manufacturers courted the favor of prospective customers. In comparison, the USA sported about a hundred such firms, England around sixty, and Imperial Germany slightly more than thirty. Until the end of the 1920s, France would remain Europe's largest producer of motorized vehicles and, until the start of the First World War, its most important exporter. France also presided over the publication of the first journal devoted to the automobile, *L'Auto* in October 1900 – a publication to which, one might add, Jacques-Henri Lartigue held a subscription since 1908. Moreover, it was also in France that the first highway races took place. The Paris–Rouen race (1894) is generally accounted as the first of its kind. Additional races and test runs stretched from Paris to Toulouse, or from Paris to Ostend and Vienna. The routes were laid out on the dusty, largely unsurfaced country roads. As a result, flat tires – caused by the horseshoe nails that littered the roads – were the norm, and broken axles were no rare occurrence. Even fatal accidents were often an unavoidable part of the spectacle that Lartigue – in spite of tragic incidents – could not tear himself away from. "At 2 pm," he confided to his diary under the heading of 25 June 1912, "no more cars in sight. The race is over for today. In the hotel we were informed that Hemery is alive and well. It got Colinet. He's hurt, his mechanic dead."

A picture accorded no significance for many years

Grand Prix de l'A.C.F. – so the official title of the picture – was taken during the course of 26 June 1912. This was the second day of the Grand Prix, and the photograph is one of a total series of one hundred sixty-nine shots. Lartigue was now photographing with an Ica Reflex for 9 × 12 (3½ × 4¾ inch) glass negatives. The original camera bears the serial number 489955 and sports a Zeiss Tessar 1:4.5 150 mm objective. The peculiarity of this comparatively large camera with a top-mounted focusing screen is its horizontal focal-plane shutter, which accounts for the elliptical form of the rear wheels in the photograph. Obviously Lartigue followed the motion with his camera. This is why the surroundings are blurry, whereas in contrast the body of the automobile and the two drivers are sharply in focus. That the entire radiator of the Schneider-made

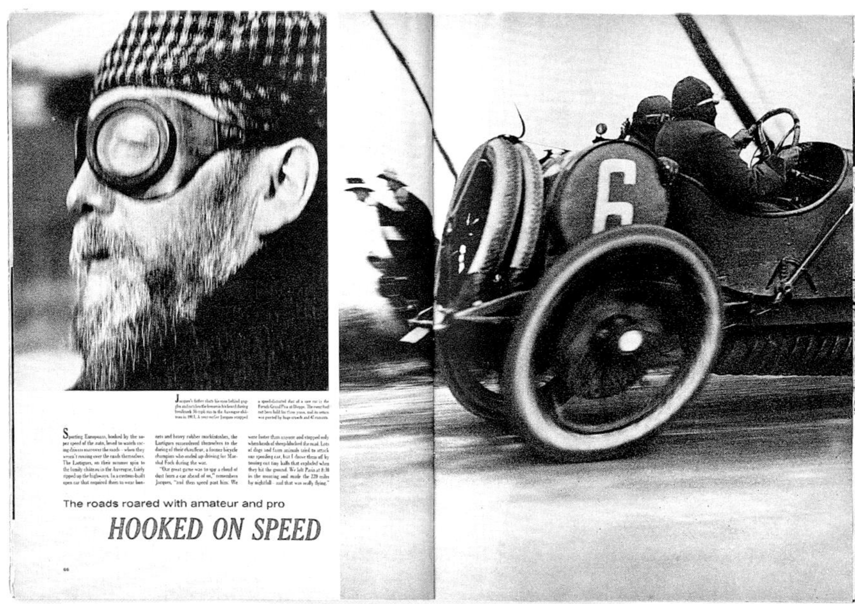
The roads roared with amateur and pro

HOOKED ON SPEED

automobile is sacrificed to the framing of the shot can hardly have been the intention of the auto-maniac Lartigue, who otherwise always strove for the total image.

It seems that for many years the photographer accorded no significance to the picture. Moreover, he even judged it a mistake. How else can one explain the fact that only a single, badly processed print, which furthermore is strongly clipped on one corner, has survived? The small 11.5 × 17.1 (4½ × 6¾ inch) vintage print is today in the possession of the Gilman Paper Company in the USA. A further, clearly later print is included in an early volume of Lartigue's carefully kept albums. But the years between 1919 and the 1960s were rearranged and expanded in the album: one cannot exclude the possibility that the he added the picture in the context of its increasing international fame.

At the beginning of the 1960s, Jacques-Henri Lartigue was, true to his philosophy of life, a happy individual – and was utterly unknown. As a photographer, he was an amateur in the literal sense of the word, a person who, without aiming at 'art', explored his personal environment. As a painter, he had won recognition only to the extent that occasionally one of his works found a courageous buyer. An invitation drew Lartigue to the USA in 1962. And what happened here is something that Lartigue's third wife, Florette, would later refer to as a "miracle." She accompanied her twenty-six-year-older spouse on the passage to the USA. And because she understood how boring life can be on board a freighter, Florette Lartigue carried along a stack of photographs

---

"Hooked on Speed." Lartigue's Grand Prix de l'A.C.F. *as the lead for the* Life *portfolio, 29 November 1963.*

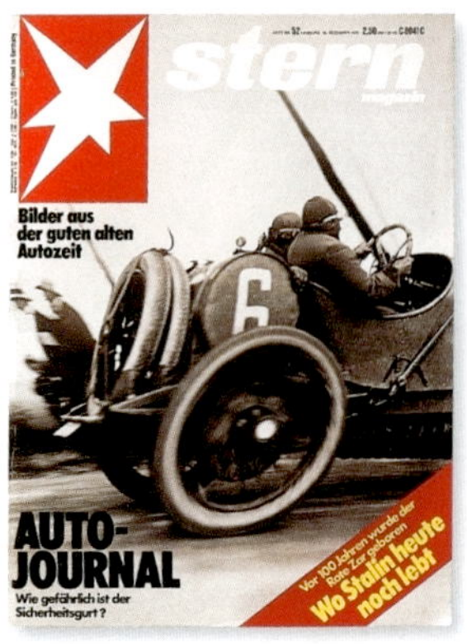

in order to retouch them on board. Upon arrival in New York, the couple met with Charles Rado, who had operated a photo agency in France before the war and now worked as an agent in the USA. "In the course of conversation," recalled Florette Lartigue, "the discussion turned to photography, and Jacques mentioned that he himself had been taking photographs since childhood." Charles Rado's interest was aroused; the Lartigues handed over to him the stack of photographs the couple had brought. And Rado promised to publicize them. In fact, on the very same day, he offered them to the illustrated magazine *Life*. A little later he showed them to John Szarkowski, who had recently stepped into Edward Steichen's shoes as director of the photographic department at the Museum of Modern Art. Looking back, Szarkowski described his first encounter with the works: "What I then thought to be the œuvre consisted of two large scrapbooks and a sheaf of fifty-two loose prints; the scrapbooks contained a wide variety of prints – little yellowing contacts and bigger prints, including enlargements, on a wide variety of papers… The prints were plunked down on the pages of the album with concern chiefly for the maximum utilization of every square centimeter of the sheet, and with a heartwarming freedom from obedience to any design principle that I knew of, either traditional or modern. The pictures themselves seemed to me astonishing, primarily because of the simplicity and grace of their graphic structure. They seemed – like a fine athlete – to make their point with economy, elegance, and easy precision. It seemed that I might be looking at the early, undiscovered work of Cartier-Bresson's papa…."

Szarkowski was swept away by the material and immediately decided – even though it was the work of an entirely unknown sixty-eight-year-old amateur photographer – to devote a single-man show to Jacques-Henri Lartigue at the Museum of Modern Art. In the first place, Szarkowski reckoned, as a young director he could offer a truly new discovery right from the start. And secondly, Lartigue's photography provided the argumentative groundwork for the development of a new symbolic language for which Szarkowski would later become the apologist. Lartigue, as he reasoned consequently in the catalogue, "saw the momentary, never-to-be-repeated images created by the accidents of overlapping shapes… This is the essence of modern photographic seeing: to see not objects but their projected images."

Accidents and miracles

Lartigue's first exhibition, or, as we would call it today, his coming-out as a photographer, opened on 1 July 1963 at the New York Museum of Modern Art and subsequently went on tour to sixteen other cities in the USA and Canada. The slim exhibition catalogue containing a total of forty-three photographs presented the *Grand Prix de l'A.C.F.* on page 27. The picture was also featured, although strongly cropped, by the illustrated magazine *Life*, which devoted a comprehensive section to Lartigue in its issue of 29 November. But the end was not yet in sight of the 'accident' – 'miracle' – of Lartigue's equally sudden and world-wide fame as chronicler of the Belle Epoque (as he was initially termed, at any rate). On 22 November 1963, John F. Kennedy was assassinated in Dallas. "We responded to the news with a shock in which there was also a mixture of disappointment," recalled Florette Lartigue. "We were certain that the

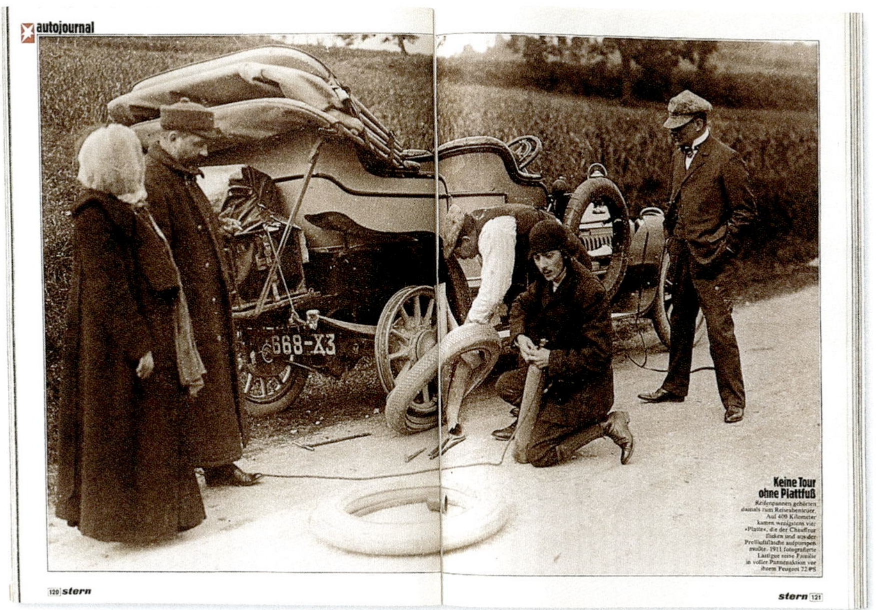

autojournal

668-X3

Keine Tour ohne Plattfuß

Reifenpannen gehörten damals zum Reiseabenteuer. Auf 400 Kilometer kamen wenigstens vier »Platte«, die der Chauffeur flicken und aus der Preßluftflasche aufpumpen mußte. 1911 fotografierte Lartigue seine Familie in voller Pannenaktion vor ihrem Peugeot 72 PS

120 stern

stern 121

pages intended for Jacques would now be sacrificed to the dramatic events of this autumn of 1963. In fact, however, photographs of the tragedy in Dallas and Jacques' untroubled pictures shared the pages of *Life*. Precisely because of the title story, this issue now sold like wildfire." Moreover, as Mary Blume underscores, it was one of the highest-selling issues of *Life* ever. Thus Jacques-Henri Lartigue advanced, in a sense overnight, to become "one of the world's most famous photographers, and its best loved." Since then, particularly his photograph *Grand Prix de l'A.C.F.* has been repeatedly reprinted and reproduced. The picture is to be found in practically every work on Lartigue. Almost as a matter of course it provides the cover motif of the small Lartigue issue in Robert Delpire's paperback edition *Photo Poche*. The German magazine *Stern* (52/1979) selected the picture as the title page to announce a special automobile issue. Recently, the picture has been increasingly in demand by mathematicians, psychologists, and phenomenologists, who have used it to illustrate particular facets in their respective areas. Even company reports have often had recourse to the picture in order to visualize the dynamics of economic life. For Lartigue himself, however, the shot was merely one of approximately one hundred thousand. As a child, he had once complained: "I am sad not to be able to photograph odors." Nonetheless, he succeeded in capturing the times. The *Grand Prix de l'A.C.F.* remains a primary exemple of the power of perception, of our ability to see in an age of supersonic speed: an image for the tempo of our modern technological times.

Lartigue's famous picture was used for Stern *52/1979 as both the cover and the lead for a portfolio.*

August Sander
Young Farmers
1914

A Profile of the People

In 1910, August Sander began a systematic attempt to portray and typologize his fellow countrymen. The project, undertaken wholly at his own initiative and expense, found support only among his painter friends in the Rhineland area of Germany. His book *Antlitz der Zeit* was outlawed and partially destroyed by the Nazis in 1936, but Sander's ambitious undertaking today ranks among the most outstanding contributions to the New Objectivity in photography.

The parameters are fairly clear: August Sander titled his picture *Young Farmers,* 1914, thus indicating both the date of the photograph and the social status of the subjects. But whether the picture was made before or after the outbreak of the First World War, felt by many of his contemporaries to mark the end of an epoch, seems not to have been particularly important to Sander. Where the three young men are coming from, or where they are headed, also remains unknown. Are they brothers? friends? neighbors? It has often been claimed that the three are on their way to a dance in town – which at first seems a reasonable assumption. But surely the weekend or even the end of the workday offer additional grounds for 'young farmers' to wash themselves, shave, comb their hair, and draw the dark suit out of the closet. At any rate, we can be sure that the trio have a common goal. But for the moment they let it slip from their minds, as they stop and turn, looking at us directly almost as if on command – and thus make us aware of another person, also present in the photograph without being visible: the man behind the camera.

At the time of the photograph, August Sander was thirty-eight years old. As the Wilhelmine Empire neared its end, he had the reputation – along with Hugo Erfurth and Hugo Schmölz – of being one of the leading photographers in Cologne. In Bavaria or Prussia, he probably

---

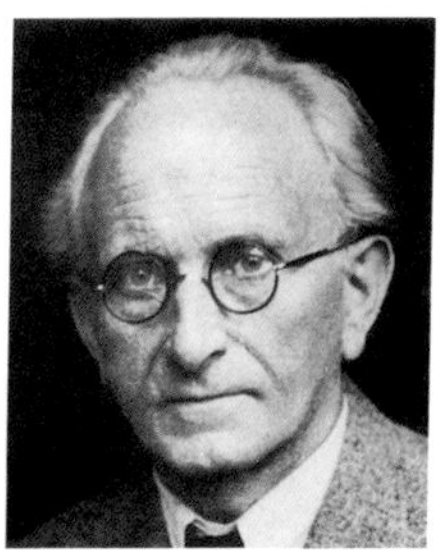

August Sander
*Born **1876** in Herdorf, Siegerland, Germany. **1890–96** works as a pit boy at the iron mines. First contact with photography. Works in a photographic studio in Trier. Years of travel. **1901–09** first studio, in Linz, Austria. **1910** moves to Cologne. Studio in Cologne-Lindenthal. **1914–25** military service. Contact with the Rheinische Progressive. Conceives his long-term project* People of the 20th Century. ***1929** publication of* Antlitz der Zeit. ***1945** studio in Cologne destroyed during WWII. **1951** solo exhibition at* photokina *in Cologne. **1955** takes part in* The Family of Man *exhibition, Museum of Modern Art, New York. **1961** culture prize of the DGPh German photography society. Dies **1964** in Cologne.*

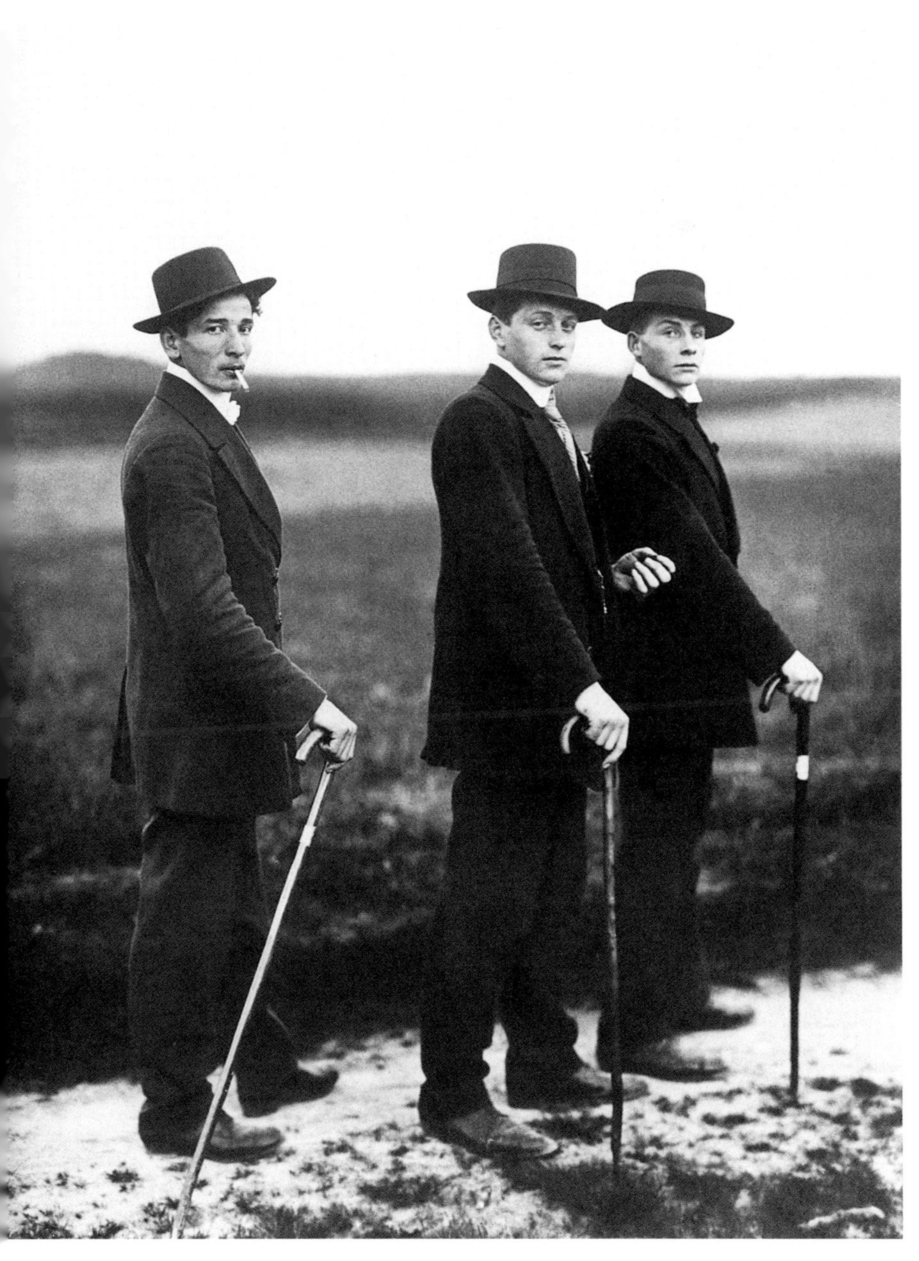

Young Farmers, 1914

would have sought the status of court photographer; in the bourgeois Rhineland, however, he attempted to prove that he was among the best through the quality of his work and the correspondingly high prices he could ask for it. Was it the loyalty of the Rhineland bourgeoisie to the older, long-established studios, or was it Sander's understanding of the recompense he deserved for his photographs, that soon forced him to look for customers outside of Cologne? In any case, it is certain that Sander increasingly found his clientele in the nearby Westerwald region – a situation that could hardly have displeased him, since Sander, who had come from a simple background himself, had a great understanding and appreciation for the area and undoubtedly struck up a sympathetic relationship with the farmers who lived there.

Whether the negative numbered 2648 was the response to a portrait commission, we do not know. Nonetheless, the name of a certain Family Krieger is known – and nothing else, except that they were to be sent a dozen copies of the photograph: "12 cards" is noted by hand on the negative – probably a reference to printing them in the approximately 10 × 15 cm (4 × 6 inch) cabinet format. What might at first glance be misunderstood as 'instantaneous' photography is therefore actually the result of a carefully composed scene, probably preceded by Sander's intensive preparatory conversation with the subjects. In other words, he and the young farmers would have chosen the location of the photograph, decided in favor of a group portrait, and set the specific day and time. Neither the fact that the photograph was made in the open air, nor the make and age of the camera – which first had to be carried to the site, fastened to a stand, and set up for the photograph – probably struck the men, inexperienced as they were with standard photographic practice, as unusual. Sander himself explained nothing: in his remarks and theoretical explanations he was always remarkably reticent. In 1959, however, at an exhibition in the Cologne Rooms of the German Society for Photography, Sander, asked to comment on his picture, offered only technical details about the camera and chemical processes – not at all unusual for the times, but amazing for the "artist" August Sander. "Ernemann portable camera 3/18," he noted about the *Young Farmers,* 1914; "built-in Luc-shutter release – time exposure no diaphragm – lens: Dagor, Heliar, Tessar, old lenses – Westendorf-Wehner plates – development meteol-hydrochinon or pyro daylight."

Clothes as an expression of social change

Sander's *Young Farmers,* 1914, (original negative format: 12 × 16.5 cm/4¾ × 6½ inches) contains a good many oddities and contradictions. But these characteristics are probably precisely what make the picture so interesting and have made it into the most-reproduced and most well-known of Sander's photographs. Sander, it is often said, constructed his pictures in archetectonic fashion, giving his subjects sufficient time to present themselves in an arrangement that felt right to them. Oddly, the group portrait of the three young farmers creates a simultaneously static and active impression, almost with a trace of the cinematic about it. A cigarette is still hanging loosely from the lips of the young farmer to the left; the one in the center is holding a cigarette in his hand, and the young farmer on the right has possibly already thrown his away. The young man to the left appears as if he had just stepped into the picture,

---

August Sander: Pastry Cook, *1928,*
from: People of the 20th Century.

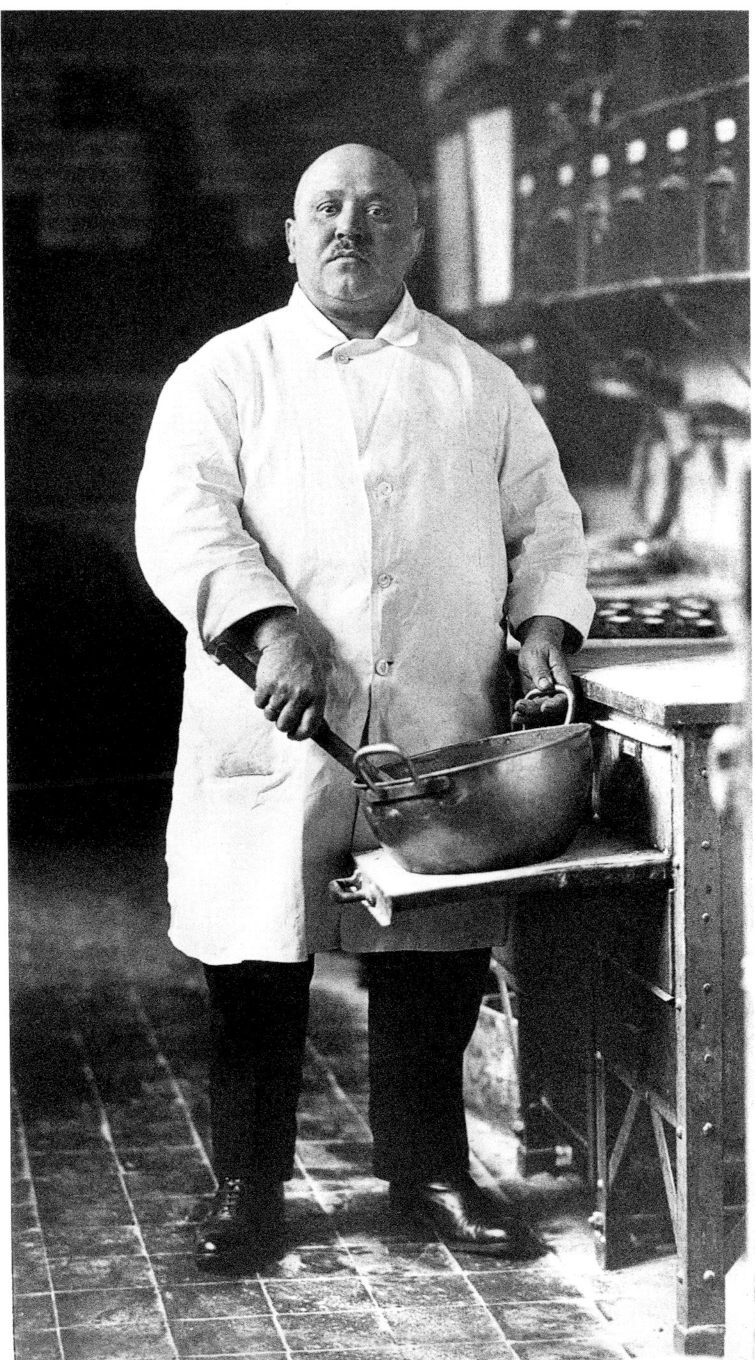

an impression underlined by his walking-stick held at a slant, whereas the young farmer in the background seems petrified into a pillar, his cane boring perpendicularly into the earth, his gaze steadfast, even dogged. Whereas the other two have just arrived, he is already a making a face as if he wants to move on.

Contemporary art critic and theorist John Berger, who has subjected the photograph to a penetrating analysis, points out another peculiarity: the dark suits of the three young men. In terms of cultural history, the suit is an 'invention' of the bourgeois era. The replacement of courtly dress by a special costume developed specifically in England is above all a reflection of deep social changes. With the 'suit', the new bourgeois elite had created an appropriate uniform for itself: simple, practical, and egalitarian. At least for men, what was now important was less social prestige, as signified by an elaborate wardrobe, than economic success in capitalist competition. The suit is, as Berger expresses it, a costume for the "serene exercise of power," in which a man with a powerful build developed through hard bodily labor appears "as if he is physically deformed." And yet, as Berger correctly emphasizes, "no one had forced the farmers to buy these pieces of clothing, and the trio on their way to a dance are obviously proud of their suits." They are even wearing them with a certain dash in Berger's interpretation – an attitude which nonetheless does not relieve the contradiction, but rather lends an ironic accent to the picture.

The real end of the nineteenth century

The year 1914, when this photograph was taken, undoubtedly marks a break in modern history. This was the year in which Sigmund Freud published his outline *On the History of the Psychoanalytic Movement*, Duchamp was developing his 'ready-mades', Walter Gropius had designed the Fagus factory, which was to be so important for modern architecture, Albert Einstein developed his theory of general relativity, and Charlie Chaplin made his first movie. For many historians, the first year of the war marks the real end of the nineteenth century and the beginning of the increasing technological development, rationalization, speed, and loss of individuality that characterize modernity. August Sander was almost certainly well aware of the change of paradigms – all the more so because leading exponents of what later came to be known as the "Rhine Progressives" – Heinrich Hoerle, Franz Seiwert, Anton Räderscheidt – numbered among his closest friends. Sander was born in 1876 as the son of a mine carpenter and small farmer in Siegerland. Whereas in his early years as a professional photographer he had subscribed entirely to an artistic approach to photography devoted to painterly ideals, by the time he moved to Cologne in 1910 he had transferred his allegiance to what he called "exact photography," without softening effects, retouching, or other manipulations. These principles hold both for his commercial photography and for his ambitious portfolio *Menschen des 20. Jahrhunderts* (*People of the 20th Century*), that has long been recognized as one of the most significant contributions to the New Objectivity photography of the 1920s.

August Sander:
The Artist (Anton Räderscheidt),
Cologne, *1926, from:*
People of the 20th Century.

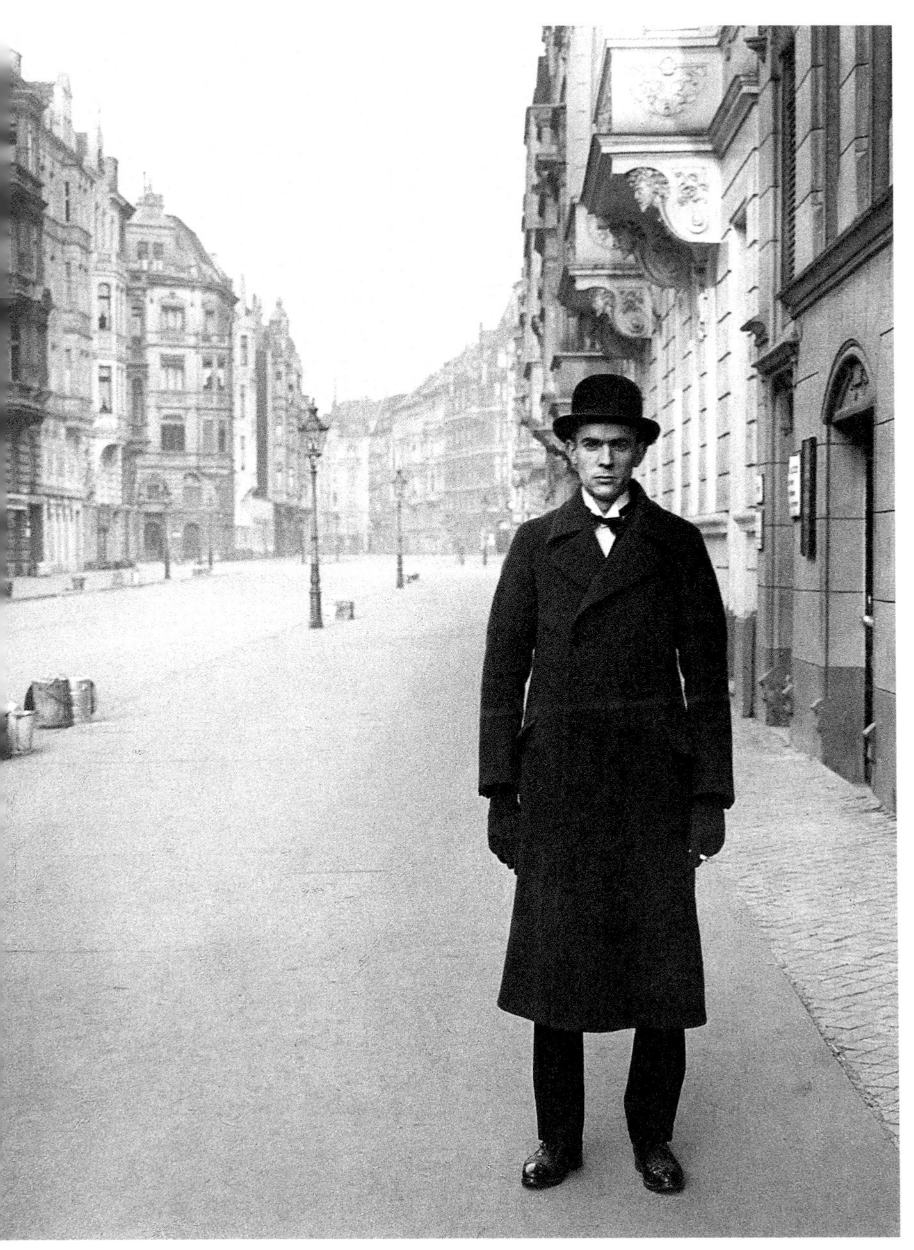

Young Farmers, 1914

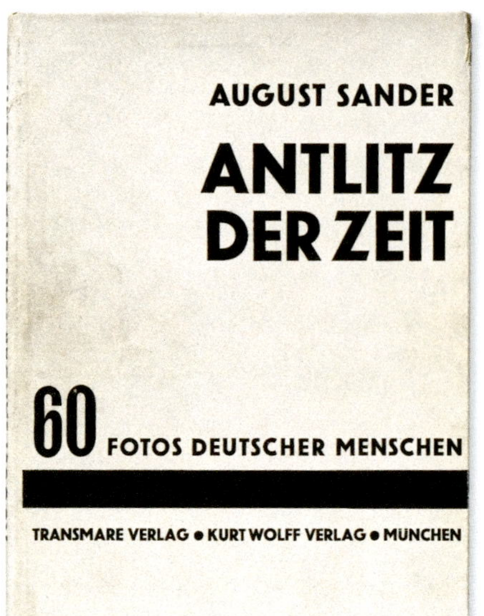

The idea of creating a cycle of portraits was not necessarily new. Nadar, Étienne Carjat, and the German photographer Franz Hanfstaengl had already introduced the ancient idea of a pantheon of important contemporaries to photography. At the beginning of the twentieth century, Erna Lendvai-Dircksen and Erich Retzlaff were pursuing 'folk' or pseudo-racial investigations, while their contemporary Helmar Lerski experimented with the formal vocabulary of photographic Expressionism in his *Köpfe des Alltags* (Ordinary Heads). August Sander's intentions were considerably more modern that those of his forerunners, in that he not only took notice of the immense social transformations that had occurred during the process of industrialization, but also made them precisely the basis of his social inventory of the German people. Sander has long been criticized for not organizing his work according to the latest knowledge of modern social sciences, but rather arranging his social inventory into seven groups and forty-five folders according to a more or less antiquated model of professional distinctions and hierarchies. The high number of representatives of certain 'types' does not at all correspond to the social reality of the Weimar Republic. In fact, the labor force as such is hardly included in Sander's concept, whereas farmers, taken as a group that the photographer respected as 'fundamental', were clearly over-represented. The Cologne newspaper *Sozialistische Presse*, for example, apostrophied the figure of a huntsman as "ripe for a museum" and posed the question whether the work really had anything to do with representative examples of the twentieth century. Sander's work, which remained unfinished, may in the end deserve particular criticism in view of the photographer's claim to ('pseudoscientific') neutrality (Susan Sontag). But as a contribution to photography it remains unique.

Approximately as the First World War drew to a close, August Sander turned his attention seriously to his self-appointed task, which he soon provided with the ambitious and encyclopedic title *People of the 20th Century*. Later he explained: "People often ask me how I came up with the idea of creating this work. Seeing, observing, and thinking – that answers the question. Nothing seemed more appropriate to me than to use photography to produce an absolutely true-to-nature picture of our age." Different from the artistic photographic portrait, Sander's work was not an attempt to visualize inner values, but of interpreting social reality by photographic means. Farmers, craftsmen, laborers, industrialists, officials, aristocrats, politicians, artists, 'travelers', to name a few of Sander's categories, step before the camera. Most of his subjects he found in his immediate Rhineland environment, a fact which today gives his work a slight regional flavor. Formally Sander followed his own, self-determined standards, which do not necessarily make the photographs similar, but lend them a compatibility to each other.

That is, he photographed by available light, and usually in a setting in which the subject felt at home. He handled his subjects as complete figures, selected a wide frame, and avoided extreme upward or downward shots that were popular in photography at the time. That in the case of *Young Farmers*, 1914, as with the majority of Sander's motifs, only a single negative plate exists indicates that the photographer was relatively self-assured in his visual dialogue with his protagonists.

Commercial harbinger of the larger projected work

August Sander first gained attention through an exhibition in the Cologne Arts Association in 1927. Whether *Young Farmers*, 1914, was on display in the show we do not know. But it is certain that older works, originally created as commissioned portraits, were in the meantime being gathered and selected with a view toward the creation of a portfolio that was already in the works. Sander now came to the attention of Kurt Wolff, who had previously published Renger-Patzsch's highly regarded book *Die Welt ist schön* (*The World Is Beautiful*), and in 1929 *Antlitz der Zeit* (*Faces of our Time*) appeared as a first volume, intended as a commercial harbinger of the larger projected work to follow. According to an advertisement sheet included with the work, the volume of selections was able "to convey only a weak idea of the extraordinary size and range of Sander's full achievement. What is does show, however, is the ability of the photographer to get to the core of the people that he places in front of his camera, excluding all poses and masks, and instead fixing them in a completely natural and normal image." In *Antlitz der Zeit*, a full-page print of *Young Farmers* appears as Plate VI. In other words, Sander had already selected the picture to be a part of the core of the œuvre that in the end was supposed to comprise approximately five thousand plates. Exactly what caused the National Socialists to destroy the printing plates and the remainder of *Antlitz* in 1936 still remains somewhat unclear; similarly, we do not know why, after the war, Sander did not bring his project to a conclusion that would have satisfied him. It is clear that the photographer, now in his seventies, no longer possessed the same energy as earlier. Furthermore, his post-war living quarters in Kuchhausen, with only modest laboratory equipment, were certainly not the ideal place to finish a portrait work of this dimension in an appropriate manner. Nonetheless, Sander continued to work on the project for the rest of his life, taking up old photographs into the collection, and rearranging them all. In the process, he was accompanied by an increasingly interested public. The *photokina* fair exhibitions of 1951 and 1963, as well as Sander's participation in Steichen's *The Family of Man* project (1955), were important early stations in his more recent reception. That the world had changed since the conception of the project can hardly have escaped Sander's notice. Where youthful gestures of protest might express themselves in 1914 through cigarettes and a hat askew, the world after 1945 sported chewing gum, rock and roll, jeans, and petticoats as signs of the modern spirit. In a certain sense, August Sander had lost hold of 'his' people.

Antlitz der Zeit (Faces of Our Time), *featuring "60 German People." Here the cover of Sander's first book, as published 1929 by Transmare/Kurt Wolff Verlag in Munich.*

Paul Strand
Blind Woman
1916

Manhattan People

"Strand is simply the biggest, widest, most commanding talent in the history of American photography" – thus has Susan Sontag described her countryman Paul Strand. Especially in his early work, he transcended the limits of Pictorialism and thus prepared the way for modern photography in the USA.

New York, autumn 1915. A young man enters Gallery 291 on Fifth Avenue. This is not his first visit: he had become acquainted with the legendary gallery while he was a student at the Ethical Culture School, and perhaps even now he might have been thinking of his former teacher, Lewis W. Hine, who had initiated the class excursion of young amateur photographers to the gallery Decades later, Paul Strand would report that Hine "took us all down to a place called the Photo-Secession Gallery at 291 Fifth Avenue, where there was an exhibition of photographs. I walked out of that place that day feeling, This is what I want to do in my life... That was a decisive day."

In 1915, Paul Strand was twenty-six years old. He had graduated from the Ethical Culture School, and was earning a living in his father's import business. In addition, he already spent a *Wanderjahr* in Europe and was now a member of the New York Camera Club. He was sure of his goal, but he had not succeeded in establishing himself as a commercial photographer or through his independent work. He had returned from Europe with well-composed landscapes in the painterly tradition of pictorialist photography. With his *Garden of Dreams/Temple of Love* (1911) he had won praise from fellow amateurs at exhibitions in New York and London. Realizing that such artistic ventures were hardly sufficient, the self-critical Strand sought advice from recognized exponents of artistic photography such as Clarence H. White and Gertrude Käsebier. "They were very sweet to me as a young fellow, but not very helpful." It was in fact

---

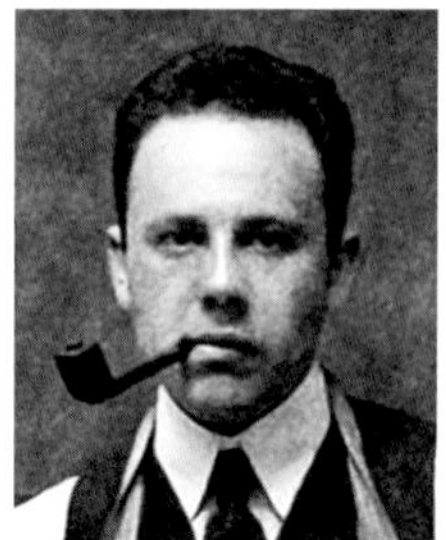

Paul Strand

*Born **1890** in New York as the son of Bohemian immigrants. Works till **1911** in his parents' shop. During this time devotes his attention to photography. **1909–22** member of the Camera Club. **1916** first exhibition in Stieglitz's Gallery 291. **1917** major presentation of his photos in* Camera Work *(in its last issue). **1920** experimental film* Manhatta. ***1922–32** works chiefly as a freelance camera man. **1932–34** Mexico. **1935** Moscow.* Time in New England *as his last photographic project in the USA. **1950** moves to France. **1952–54** Italy. **1954** Hebrides. Devotes especial attention during his later years to nature studies around his home in Orgeval. Dies there **1976**.*

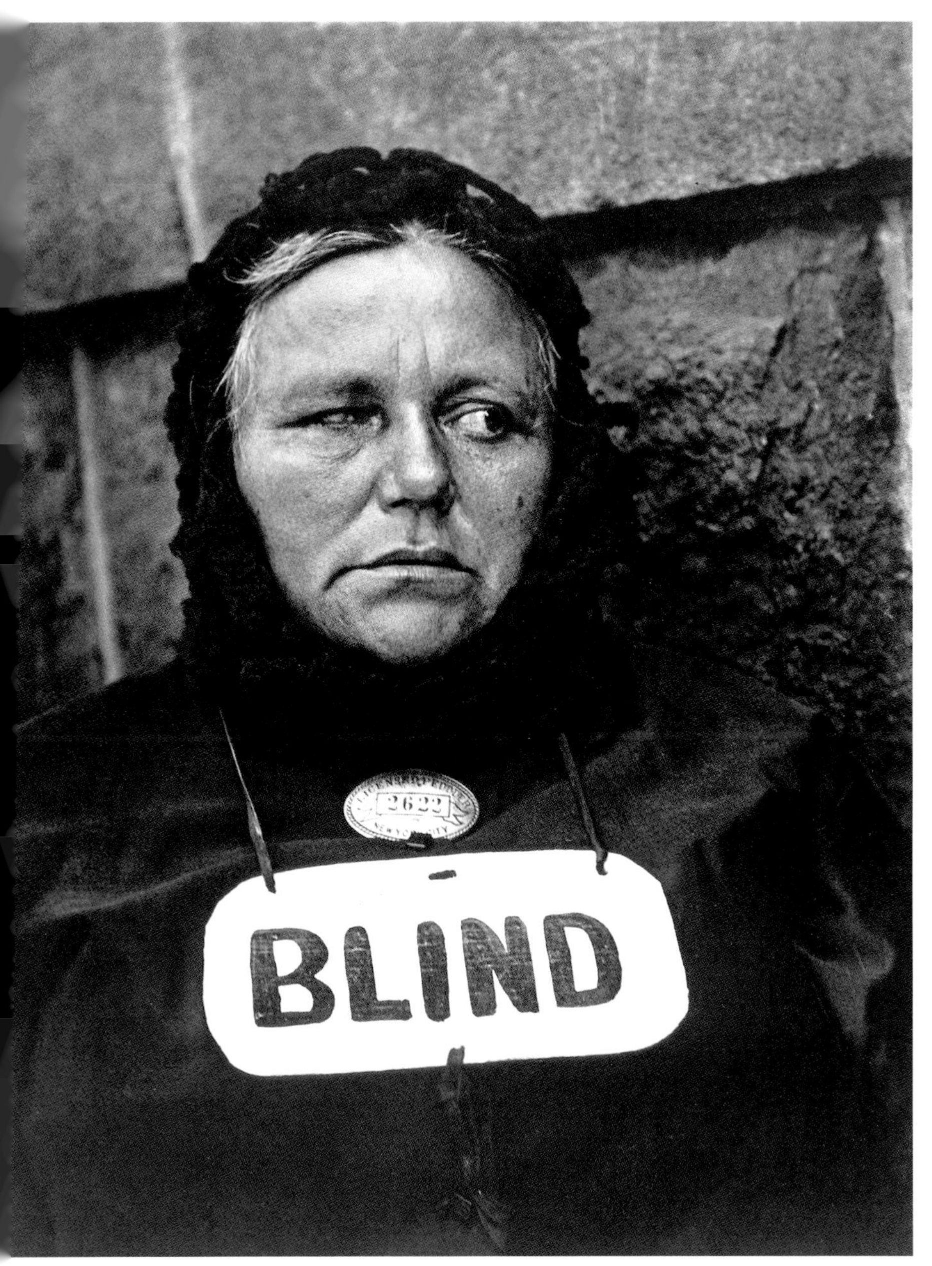

Blind Woman, 1916

Alfred Stieglitz himself, the great apologist of artistic photography in the USA, who became an important mentor and helpful adviser to the young man. "I used to go and see Stieglitz about once every two years. I did not go there to bother him unless I had something to show. He was a great critic for me."

In this autumn of 1915, Strand had reached that point once again. He selected a number of more recent works to show Stieglitz. Since his last visit, the young photographer had visited the path-breaking Armory Show with works representing the European modern and had furthermore acquainted himself with the art of Vincent van Gogh, Paul Cézanne, Pablo Picasso, and Georges Braque. Influenced by Cubism as well as the documentary projects of Lewis W. Hine and the advice of Alfred Stieglitz, who was himself coming ever nearer to a straight photography, Strand had turned to urban themes and a more rigorous way of seeing. Of course, by this time, cityscapes were nothing new to photography; one has only to look as the works of Karl Struss (*New York*, 1912), for example, or Alvin Langdon Coburn (*House of a Thousand Windows*, 1912), or Alfred Stieglitz (*The City of Ambition*, 1910).

Strand, however, was the first to create a valid synthesis of contemporary themes and artistically mature vision appropriate to the photographic medium. His pictures, as Maria Morris Hambourg once stated: "were tough, surprising, and had intimate weight." We have a pretty clear idea just which motifs Paul Strand presented to his mentor on this autumn day in 1915: *Fifth Avenue and 42nd Street*, *City Hall Park*, and *Wall Street*. And we also know Stieglitz's reaction. "We were alone in the Gallery," recalled Paul Strand. "He was very enthusiastic and said: 'You've done something new for photography and I want to show these'." Stieglitz kept his word; shortly thereafter, in March 1916, Paul Strand had his first exhibition at the 291 gallery – the gallery that one can justly claim to be the most important forum of the avant-garde in the USA. For Strand, it was, so to speak, the breakthrough. For the art of the camera in the USA, in the words of Helmut Gernsheim, it was the beginning of a new epoch: the "era of modern photography."

The search for the greatest degree of objectivity

Europe was already caught in the throes of the war in which the USA became an active participant in 1917. The mood of the country had already begun to change: out of the dismay, there emerged a growing self-confidence. "In the ferment of World War I, there was also a great deal of unrest in America," recalled Paul Strand. "It was a time of new thinking and new feeling about various forms of culture, sharpened later by the catastrophic Crash of 1929." We can only speculate about what might have inspired Strand in this age of intellectual upheaval to begin portraying anonymous people in the streets of New York. He himself always defended the series, which many consider his best work, with the desire to photograph people "without their being aware of it." But it is hardly imaginable, according to the critic Milton W. Brown "that this series of memorable and psychologically probing studies could have been the by-product of a technical gimmick." Are these photographs indeed concerned merely with

---

Page 163: **Paul Strand:** Man in a Derby, *1917.*

Right: **Paul Strand:** Blind Woman *and* Abstraction, Porch Shadows, Twin Lakes, Connecticut, *in:* Camera Work, *1917.*

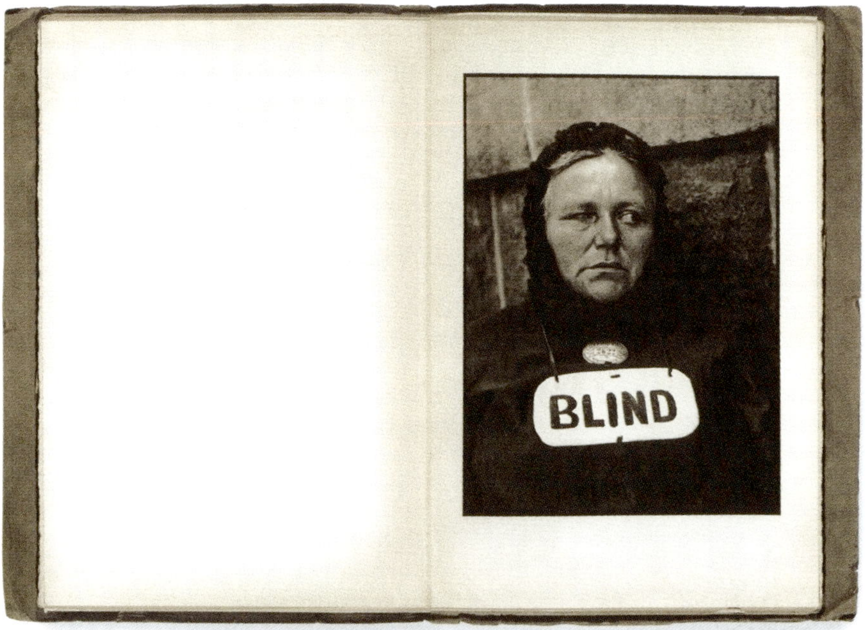

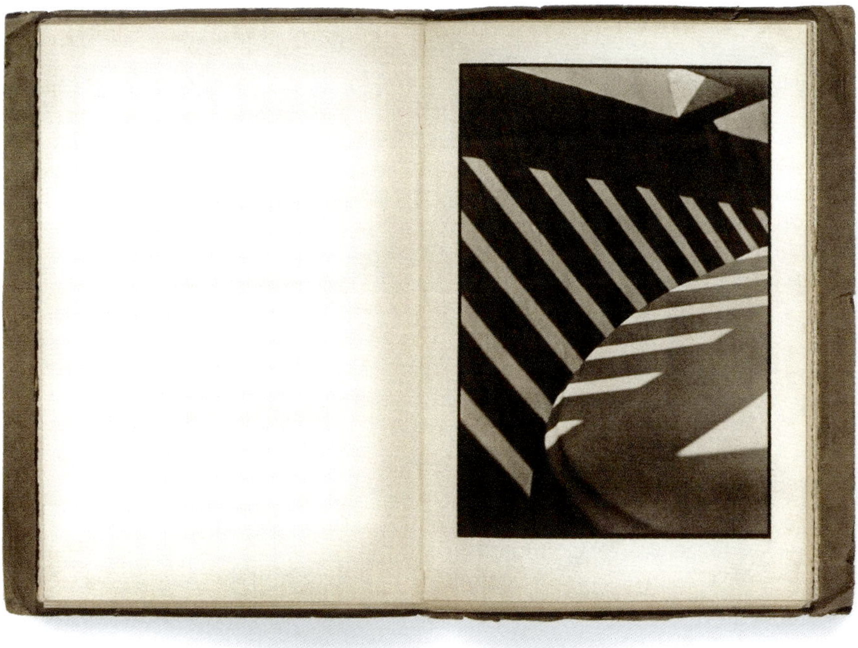

Blind Woman, 1916

a cheap effect? Insofar as Strand in a sense "stole" his portraits, had he not freed himself from traditional portrait standards: interaction, visual dialogue, the possibility of setting one's own scene? What is certain is that Strand, with the help of specially fitted cameras (initially with a side-mounted objective, later with a prism lens) was largely able to photograph without being noticed. And this anonymity also became the guarantee of what he was meanwhile striving for: the greatest possible degree of objectivity. But Strand was neither concerned with creating a sociogram of New York society (the series is too small in scope), nor did he make a claim to journalism (for this, the images are too indefinite in their historical context). Strand sought and found characters of everyday life, drew simple people into the center of his photographic attention, thus making them the unconscious 'object' of a psychological investigation.

Strand opened his cycle in Five Points, the slum where Jacob Riis had also worked. He photographed on the Lower East Side and around Washington Square. Seventeen of Strand's portraits have survived, including *Man in a Derby* and *Blind Woman*, a picture that Walker Evans termed brutal, but in a positive, cathartic sense: nothing, according to Evans, had as great an influence on his own photography as Paul Strand's work. In a somewhat exaggerated comparison, one might say that just as the First World War caused a break in painting – a turning away from the pictorial aesthetic that had exhausted itself in formalism – Strand single-handedly brought about a new era in the USA with the Cubist-inspired structure of his photographs: machines pulled into the frame, unposed portraits. Strand's work, according to Alfred Stieglitz, is 'pure': "It does not reply upon tricks of process… The work is brutally direct. Devoid of all flim-flam; devoid of trickery and of any 'ism'; devoid of all attempt to mystify an ignorant public, including the photographers themselves. These photographs are the direct expression of today."

Excluding all situational or anecdotal perspective

A blind woman with a cardboard sign hanging from her neck. What is more disturbing here – the obvious physical deficit, or the written notice calling attention to it? In one sense, the picture is tautological, but there is a system to the tautology. In a hectic age, and specifically in a metropolis, anyone wanting to call attention to her infirmity must provide it with an exclamation point. Cynical as that may sound, the cynicism redounds upon the head of the society that gives the handicapped no other choice but to assure survival through public demonstration of her 'fault' – in other words, to make capital out of the infirmity. Stanley Burns in *A Morning's Work* calls attention to the dramatic situation of amputees and other cripples – for example all those injured in work-related accidents – in America at the turn of the twentieth century. Many of these people were forced to earn their income by selling their own photographic portraits; the public always took an interest, according to Burns, in the misfortune of others. Whether the blind woman is in fact selling something or only holding her hand out we don't know. The photographer intentionally kept the frame of the photograph small, thus excluding all situational or anecdotal perspective – an approach which at the same time eliminates any feel of pity such as otherwise might be aroused by the sight of a forlorn blind soul amid the stone canyons of New York. The photograph decisively turns its back on all that is sentimental or maudlin. The picture is also 'straight' in its reduction to only a few determining formal elements. There is for example the simple sign, dominating the composition like a title added to the photograph and reminiscent of the denunciatory 'INRI' hung over Christ in the

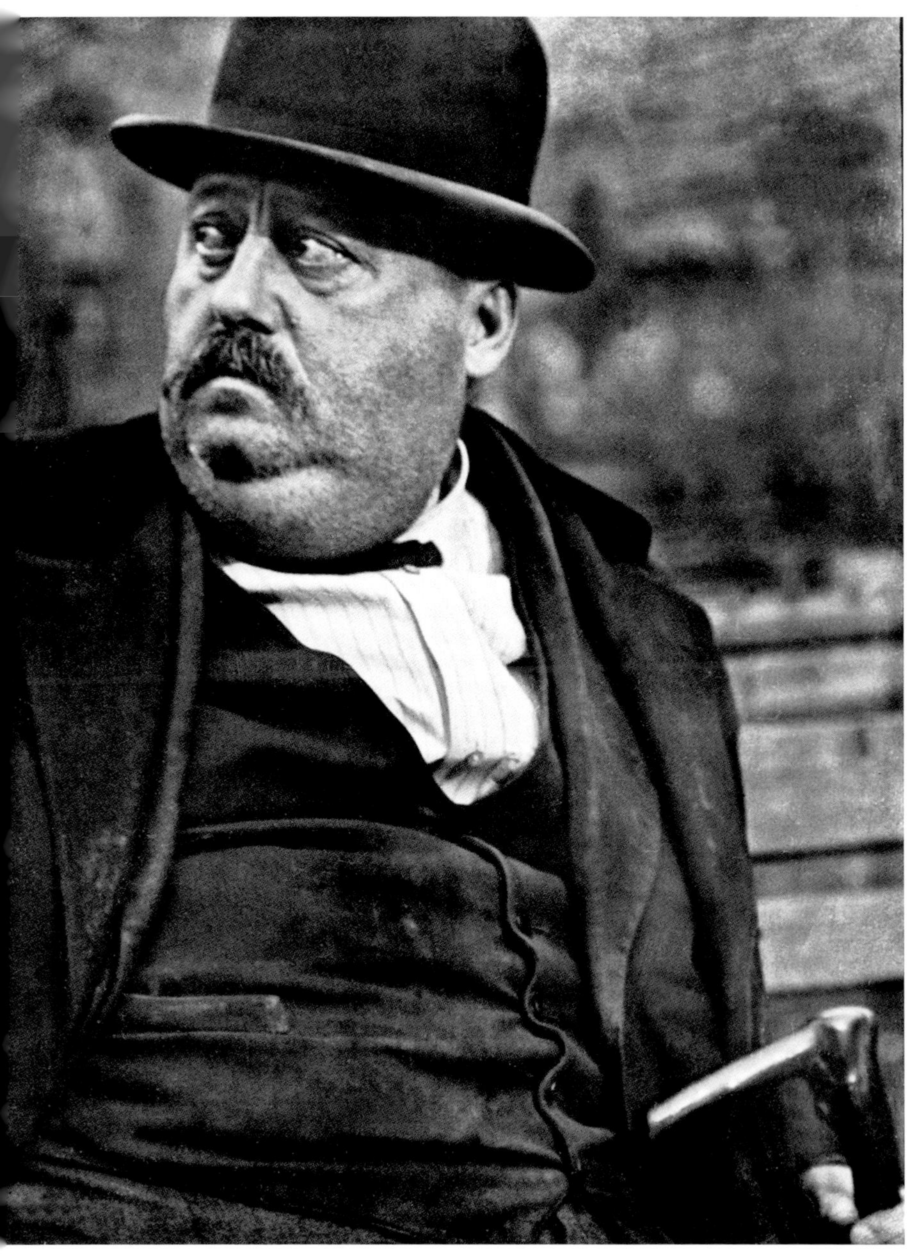

Blind Woman, 1916

Christian topos of the Crucifixion. Similarly, there is the comparatively modest oval of the metal license tag bearing the number 2622, which was issued by the City of New York, and gave the recipient the right to sell door-to-door. And finally there is the fleshy, clearly asymmetric face, darkly vignetted by some sort of shawl, and the lifeless eyes. These elements, in combination with the photograph's directness, without any attempt at photographic beautification, constitute a drastic presentation that would have shocked contemporaries viewers, accustomed as they were to non-committal Pictorialism. Decades later, Strand remained impressed by the woman's dignity and recalled that she had "an absolutely unforgettable and noble face." He did not inquire after her name or story.

It is doubtful that Strand – in contrast to Lewis W. Hine, for example – intended to make a symbolic gesture for social reform. Although the artist always understood himself to be a politically thinking man, open toward movements of the times (it is well known that he later took an interest in Communism), the context in which the picture first appeared, in the form of a 34 × 25.7 cm (13 3/8 × 10 1/8 inch) platinum print (today in the Metropolitan Museum, New York), suggests that Strand's only interest in revolt was in the realm of art. The *Blind Woman* was not a part of the first Paul Strand exhibition organized by Stieglitz at his 291 gallery in 1916; but in the following year the picture already reached a broader international public when Stieglitz devoted the entire final double edition of his influential journal *Camera Work* to Paul Strand. In addition to *Blind Woman*, the final Number 49/50 presented five further street portraits, views of

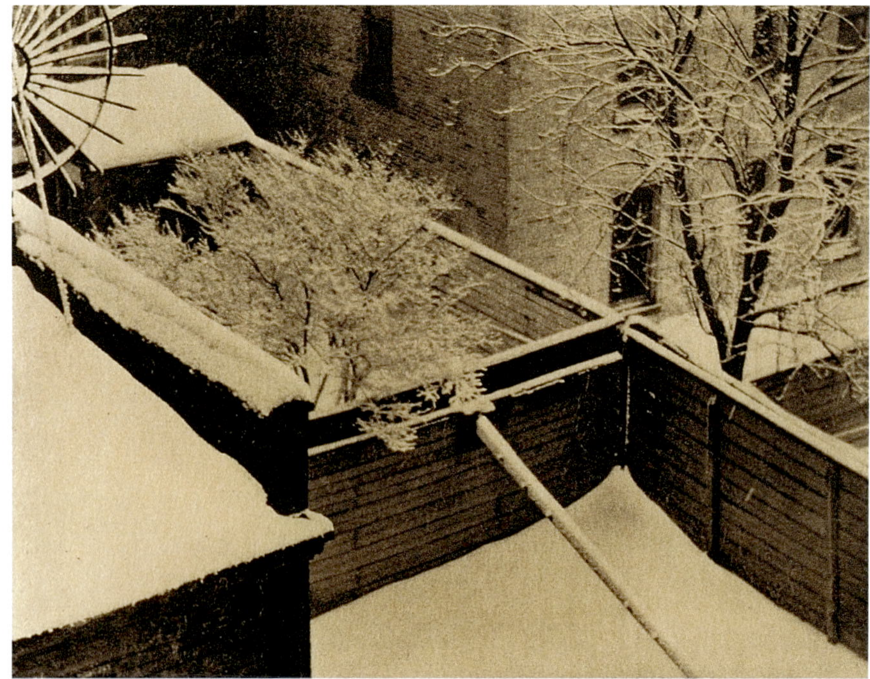

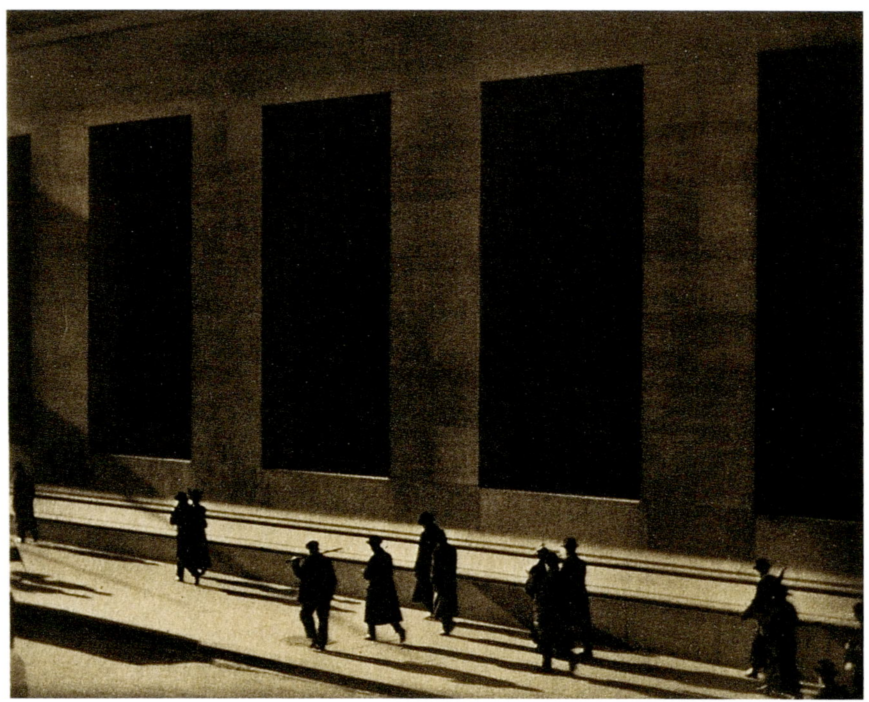

New York, graphically conceived object studies, and an essay in which the photographer formulated his aesthetic credo. Strand's belief in an unfalsified, unmanipulated straight photography was not necessarily new, for the art critic Marius de Zayas had argued in 1913 for a use of the camera composed for "the objective condition of the facts." But Strand's explanations and arguments were delivered simultaneously with convincingly believable images.

Since its first publication in *Camera Work* in 1917, *Blind Woman*, together with the photographer's other street portraits have been accounted as "Strand's most exciting work," in the words of Alan Trachtenberg. Helmut Gernsheim called them "living fragments from the great kaleidoscope of everyday life." Similarly, in his history of street photography, Colin Westerbeck claimed that every street photographer surely knows *Blind Woman* and has learned from it. The question arises then, why the young Paul Strand gave up this kind of photography as early as 1916, never to return in later years. Did working with a 'hidden camera' suddenly seem immoral to him, as one critic surmises? One thing is certain: "His later images are magnificent," according to Milton Brown, "yet they don't have the journalistic quality that the early ones have."

Paul Strand:
New York, *in:* Camera Work, *1916.*

Man Ray
Noire et blanche
1926

Kiki with the Mask

Painter, graphic artist, writer, experimenter with 'ready-made' art – throughout his life, the American artist Man Ray oscillated among various disciplines. Nonetheless it was primarily as a photographer that he achieved fame as the creator of a richly varied œuvre in which the photograph serves less to illustrate reality than to express the artist's surrealistically inspired images, fantasies, and visions.

This picture is found in every catalogue, every exhibition of Man Ray's work. In addition to *La Prière, Violon d'Ingres, Les Larmes,* and a series of more-or-less experimental portraits of Ray's Paris artist friends, the image is among his best-known photographs. The picture was already included in the catalogue of 1934, Man Ray's first programmatic summary in book form. The artist himself accounted the originally square photograph, cropped into various formats, as one of the core works of his photographic production of the 1920s and early 1930s – an evaluation still shared today by exhibition organizers, writers, art dealers, and gallery owners. When Klaus Honnef put together his *Pantheon of Photography in the Twentieth Century*, Man Ray was represented by *Noire et blanche* as a matter of course; similarly in the catalogue to the large and highly respected Man Ray retrospective in 1998 in the Grand Palais in Paris, where *Kiki with the Mask* formed the upstroke as it were to a discriminating aesthetic discussion of his photographic œuvre. And as far as the international art market is concerned, by the middle to end of the 1990s, Noire et blanche had turned up at auctions on three occasions, making the headlines every time. In the process, that had undergone fairly minor cropping print brought in a prodigious $206,000 at Christie's in 1995, just as the year earlier an unnamed buyer had paid $320,000 for Man Ray's probably most prominent photograph as a vintage print. Last but not lease, in 1998, a collector – once again at Christie's – was prepared to pay no less than

---

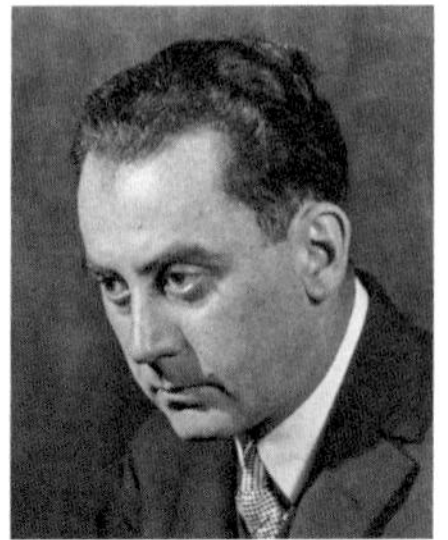

Man Ray

Born Emmanuel Radnitzky ***1890*** *in Philadelphia, Pennsylvania.* ***1911*** *moves to New York. Friendship with Stieglitz and Duchamp. First photographic reproductions of his art works.* ***1916*** *first portraits.* ***1921*** *moves to Paris.* ***1922*** *opens a studio in Montparnasse. First Rayographs.* ***1929*** *first solarisations.* ***1934*** *publication of his book* Man Ray: Photographies. ***1935–44*** *fashion shots for* Harper's Bazaar. ***1940*** *return to the USA. His interest in photography wanes. From* ***1951*** *back in Paris.* ***1966*** *culture prize of the DGPh German photography society. Dies* ***1976*** *in Paris.*

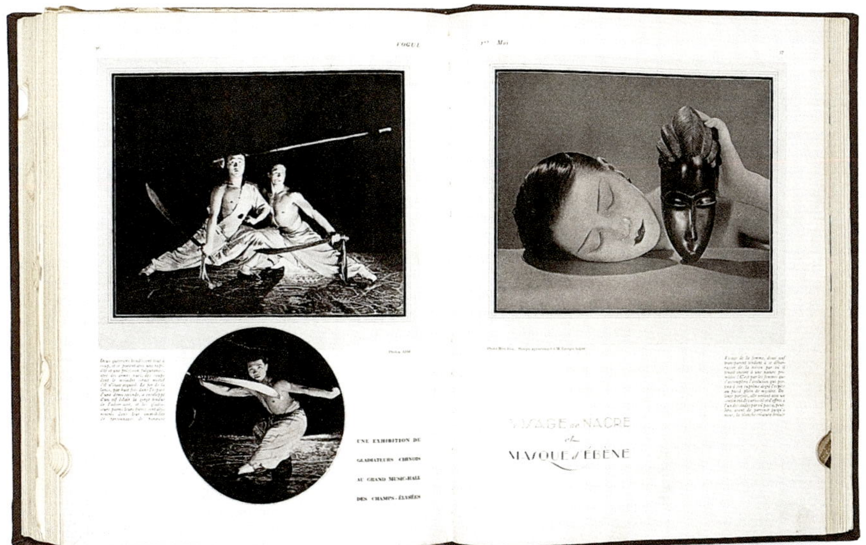

$550,000 for the motif in the form of a diptych, making *Noire et Blanche* into one of the most sought-after treasures in the international photographic trade.

The same sleep and the same dream

About the picture itself and its creation we know little. Man Ray, born Emmanuel Radnitzky in 1890 in Philadelphia, was by no means an artist who spoke willingly about his work. Even his comprehensive autobiography published in 1963 avoided discussing concrete pieces. It is clear, however, that the photograph was made at the beginning of 1926 in Man Ray's studio at 31 rue Campagne Première, which the now-successful portrait artist had opened four years earlier in Paris, his adopted city of residence. The photograph was first published on 1 May 1926 in the French *Vogue* under the title *Visage de nacre et masque d'ébène* (Pearl Face and Ebony Mask). The picture appeared again two months later in the Belgian Surrealist magazine *Variétés* (No. 3, 15 July 1928), now under the title *Noire et blanche* (Black and White), and once more, in November of the same year, in *Art et décoration*, this time with a text by Pierre Migennes: "The same sleep and the same dream, the same mysterious magic seem to unite across time and space these two female masks with closed eyes: one of which was created at some point in time by an African sculptor in black ebony, the other, no less perfect, made up yesterday in Paris."

Visage de nacre et masque d'ébène*: Man Ray's photograph first appeared under this title in the French edition of* Vogue *in May 1926.*

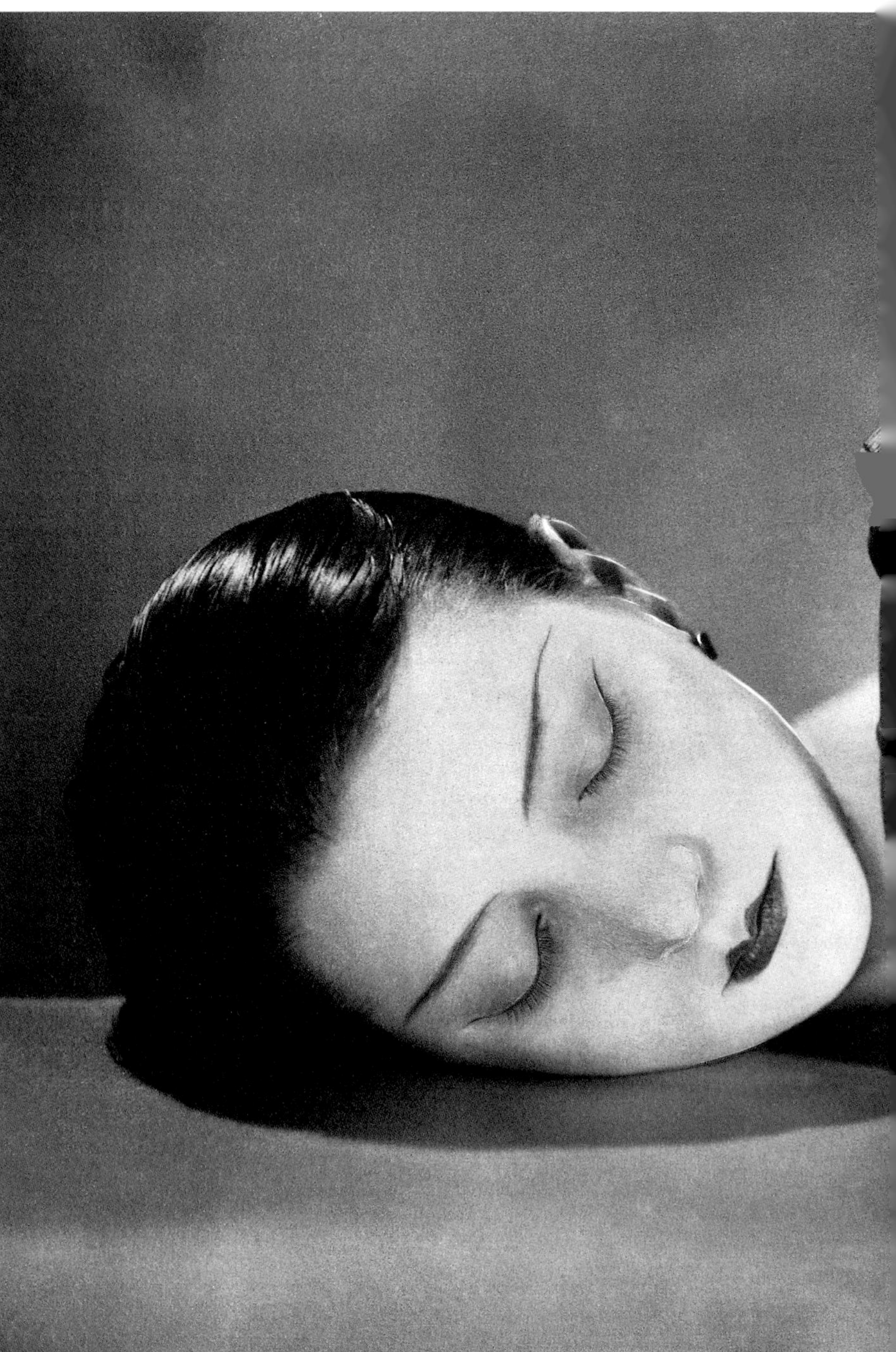

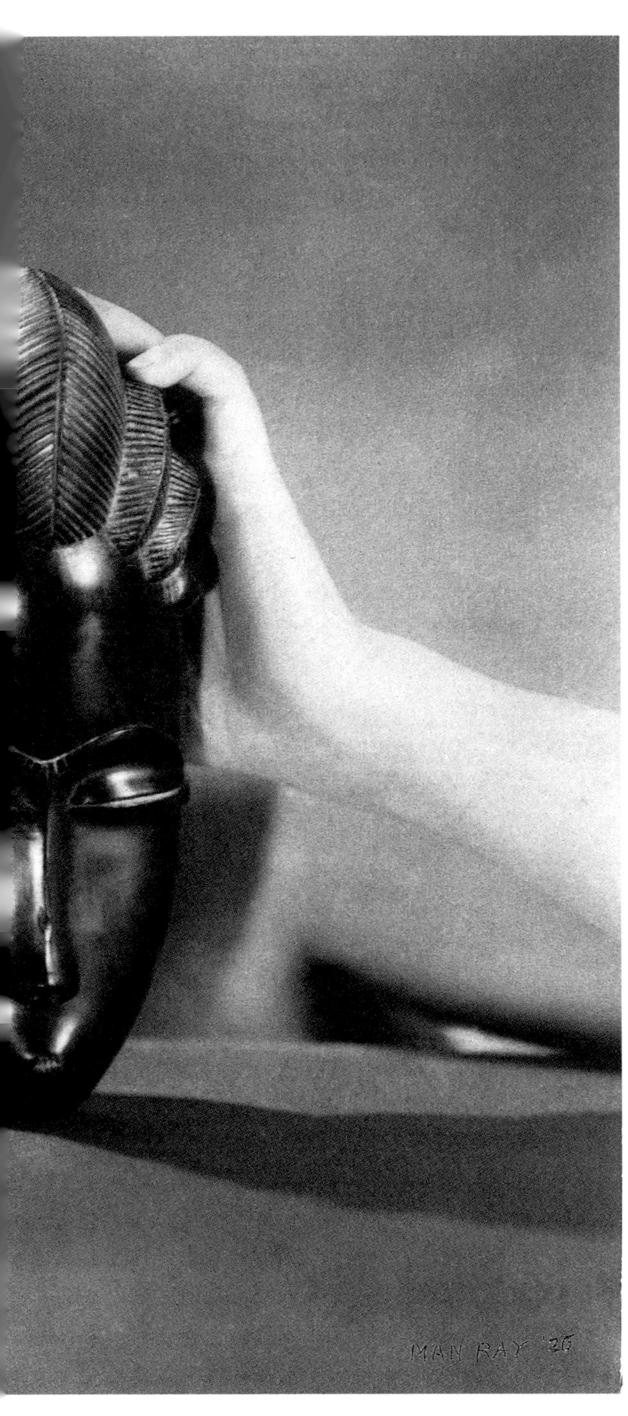
MAN RAY '26

The opposite of a rapid-fire shooter

Man Ray was in the habit of giving his photographic and all other creations ringing titles ever since he had visited the legendary New York Armory Show in 1913. Á propos Marcel Duchamp's *Nude Descending a Staircase*, Man Ray had concluded that without its provocative title, the picture would hardly have received all the attention that the press and public paid it. Whereas *L'enigme d'Isidore Ducasse*, *Retour à la raison*, and *À l'heure de l'observatoire* belong in this sense to the most striking and inventive of Man Ray's titles, at first glance *Noire et blanche* seems in contrast to be hardly more than a simple description, even if, from the perspective of Western culture, which normally 'reads' from left to right, the correct reference would have to be *Blanche et noire* – a title valid in fact for the negative of the picture (which of course presents the image in reverse).

Man Ray, who began photographing as an autodidact in 1914, was initially concerned with achieving an adequate reproduction of his own painting and art objects. As a photographer, he was cautious – the opposite of a 'rapid-fire shooter', as Emmanuelle de l'Ecotais points out. Even his preference for working with a 9 × 12 cm (3½ × 4¾ inch) plate camera required a carefully thought-out and economical method of procedure. Especially in the face of these hindrances, May Ray must be accounted an extraordinarily productive photographer: no fewer than twelve thousand negatives and contact prints were turned over alone by Man Ray's last wife, Juliet, to the French nation. Among them were several variations of Kiki with the Mask – pictures that prove that Man Ray had in this case been initially unsure of the valid formulation of his pictorial idea and that he reached the final composition only after passing several versions.

This was not the first time that Man Ray gave West African art a determinant role in his work. As early as 1924 in the creation of La lune brille sur l'"le de Nias, he had photographed an unidentified young woman next to a sculpture of a Black African, admittedly without reaching a convincing formulation of an image that barely arose above the illustrative. Two years later, *Noire et blanche* confirmed his continuing interest in the art of 'primitive' peoples, which in fact had had an extremely great influence precisely on the avant-garde after 1900 (Expressionists, Fauvists, Cubists). Man Ray himself had first become acquainted with African art around 1910 in Alfred Stieglitz's New York gallery 291, and in his autobiography, African art is significantly mentioned in the same breath as the artistic expressions of Cézanne, Picasso, and Brancusi. The mask in this case, moreover, is a work in the Baule style, supposedly one of those cheap replicas which even in those days were available everywhere.

In the studio, Man Ray gave form to his dialogue between 'white' and 'black', between an inanimate object and a supposedly sleeping female model (Kiki, in reality Alice Prin, once more taking on the role), in front of a neutral background. Shortly after moving from New York to Paris in 1921, Man Ray had become acquainted with the young woman, a favorite nude model in artistic circles, whose defiant charm was precisely such as to appeal to Man Ray. In his memoirs, the photographer described at length his first meeting with 'Kiki de

---

Pages 172–173: **Man Ray:** Noire et blanche, *1926. Interestingly Man Ray also produced a reverse print from the negative.*

Right: **Man Ray:** Noire et blanche. *A rarely reproduced and thus little known variant from the cycle.*

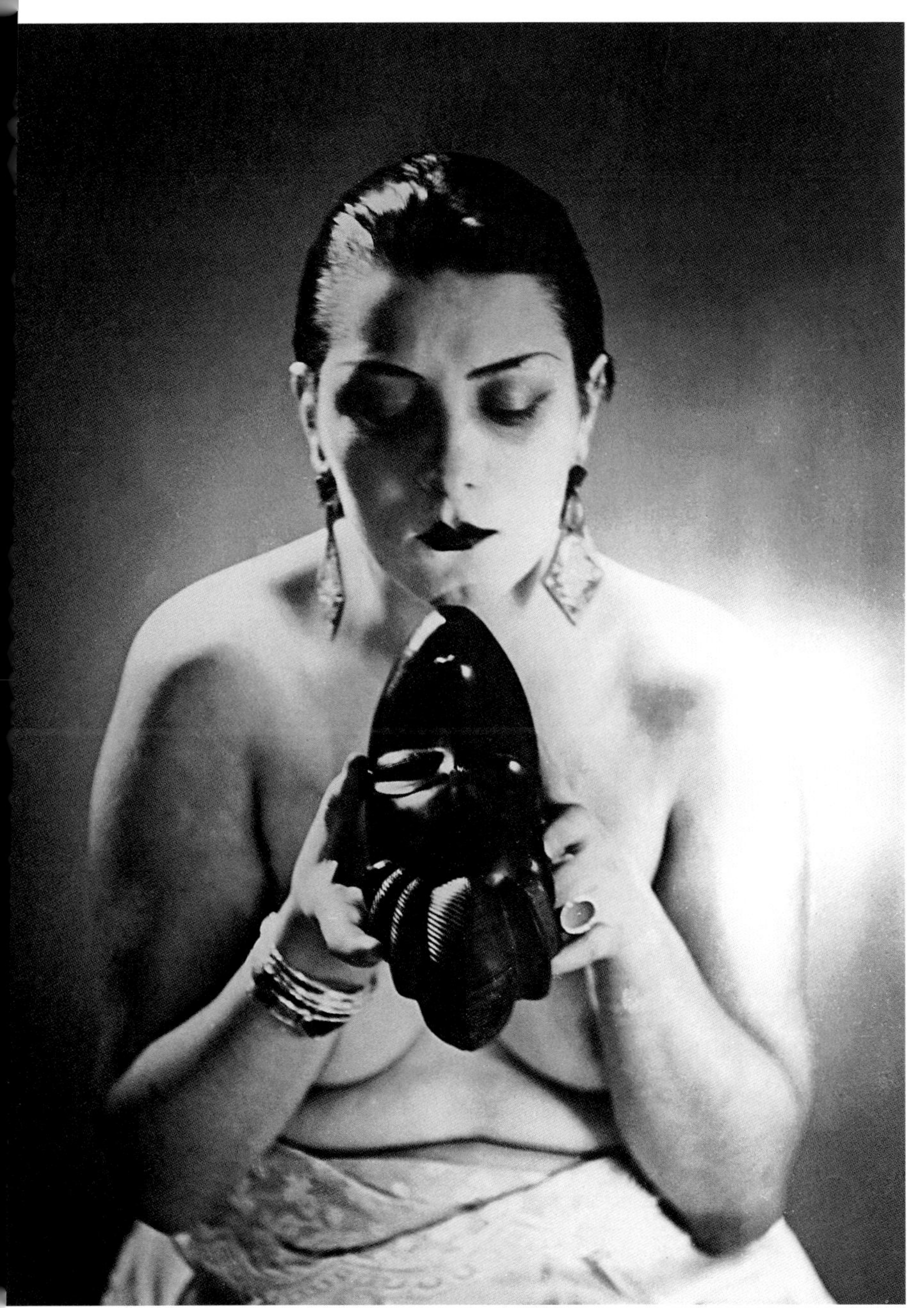

Noire et blanche, 1926

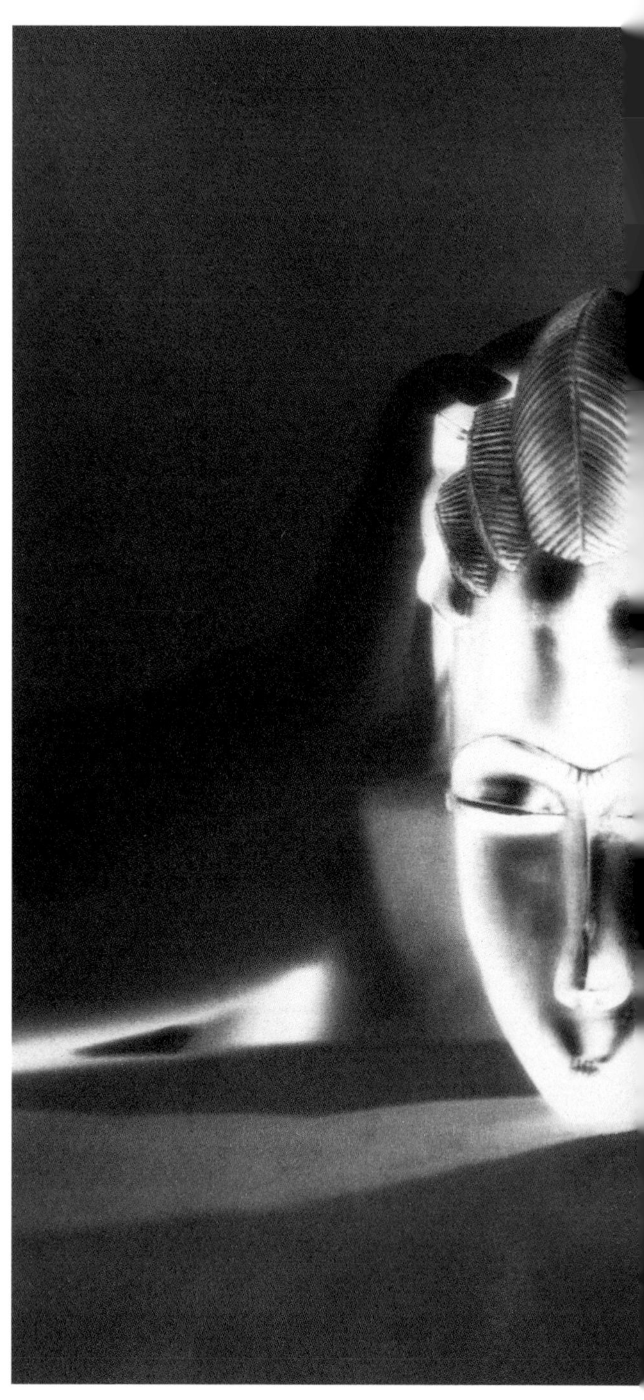

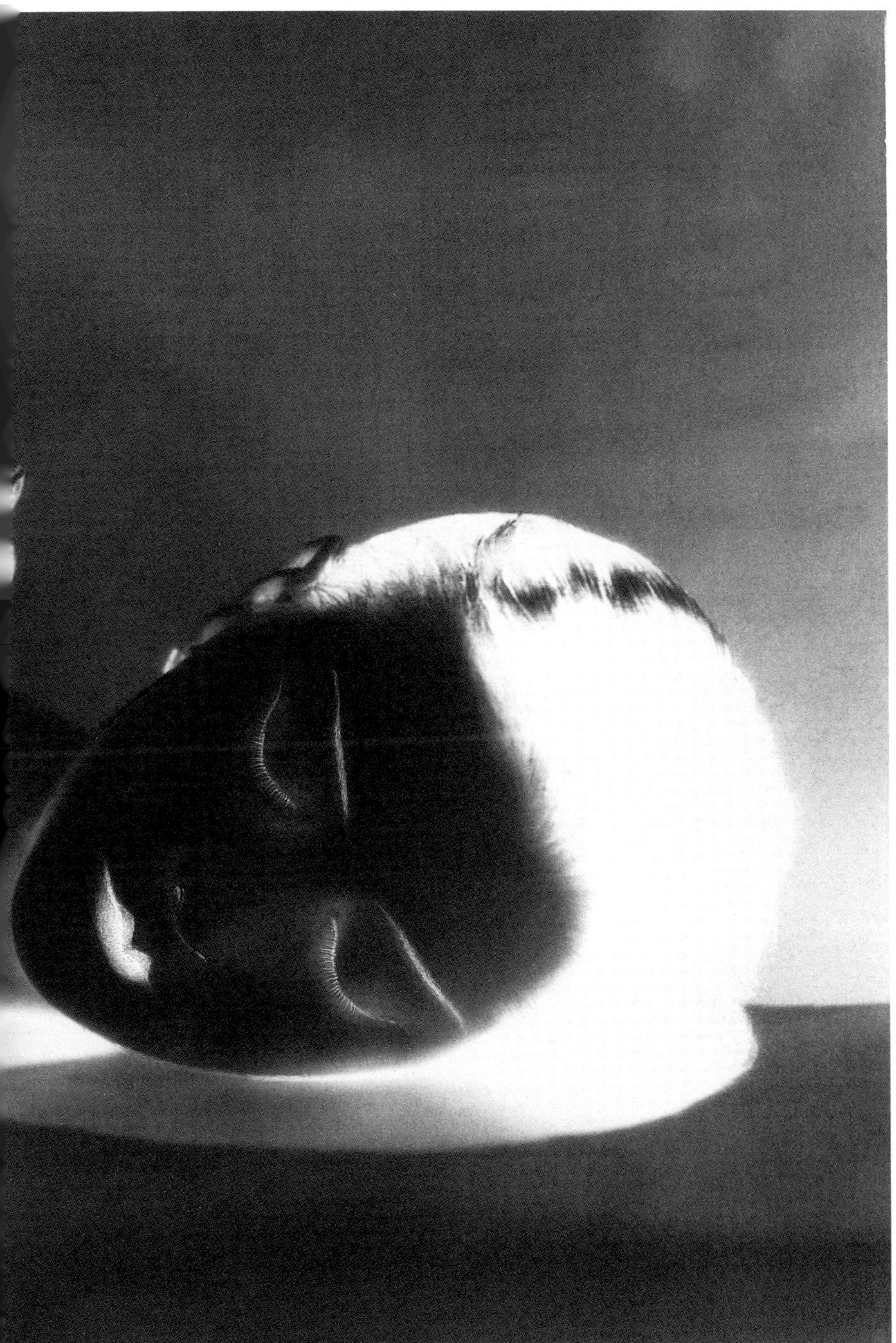

Montparnasse': "One day I was sitting in a café Soon the waiter appeared to take our order. Then he turned to the table of girls, but refused to serve them: they weren't wearing hats. A violent argument arose. Kiki screamed a few words in a patois I didn't understand, but which must have been rather insulting, and then added that a café is after all not a church, and anyway the American women all came without hats... Then she climbed onto the chair, from there onto the table, and leapt with the grace of a gazelle down onto the floor. Marie invited her and her friends to sit with us; I called the waiter and in an empathic tone ordered something for the girls to drink."

First lover during the years in Paris

Before long Kiki became the first of Man Ray's lovers during his early years in Paris. For him she was a model, a source of inspiration, and also an antagonist in turbulent scenes. In ever-new portraits and nude photographs, Man Ray succeeded after 1922 in capturing something of the irascible spirit of this legendary sweetheart of artists. Perhaps the most famous of these photographs is a portrait from 1926, which may have been made on the same day as *Noire et blanche*. In any case, the pale complexion, clearly contoured lips, and the pomaded, tightly combed-back short hair suggest the proximity.

Kiki is holding the mask to her cheek, supporting it with both hands and casting a dreamy look sideways toward the art object – a shot in vertical format, which apparently satisfied the artist just as little as the symmetrically composed, markedly static version in which Kiki's chin is set against that of the mask as a so-to-speak mirror image. Numerous details in the photograph – clothing, jewelry, Kiki's naked bust – distract from the real intention. Only the addition of the table as a stable, space-defining horizontal element, combined with narrower framing, provided a formally convincing solution. Now the horizontal stands unmistakably against the vertical, black against white, living against lifeless, European against African: the equality of the cultures is underlined by the negative print. Moreover, the subtle use of light, which emphasizes the strong geometry of the composition, plays a convincing role.

Man Ray had already published a photo titled *Black and White* on the cover of the magazine *391*, edited by Francis Picabia, in 1924. In that work, a classical statuette contrasted with an African sculpture; now, as if in a further development of the same concept, Man Ray set a human face against a 'primitive' mask. In the earlier work, Man's English title implied no reference to the sex of the subjects. With *Noire et blanche*, on the other hand, there can be no doubt: what is portrayed is, so to speak, a purely feminine dialogue that, in best Surrealist tradition, knows how to remain somewhat mysterious. There can be no doubt that *Noire et blanche* is more than a merely formal game. At the very least, according to Emmanuelle de l'Ecotais, the work is exemplary for one of Man Ray's fundamental dictates: *provoquer la réflexion*.

Man Ray:
Photographies 1920–1934 Paris,
published by Cahiers d'art, Paris 1934.
Two double-spread pages.

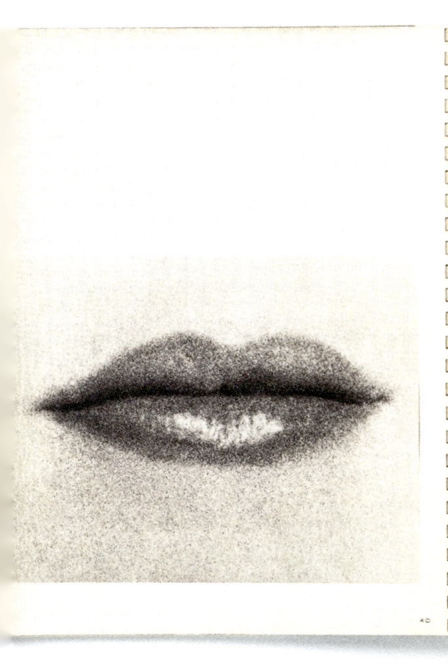

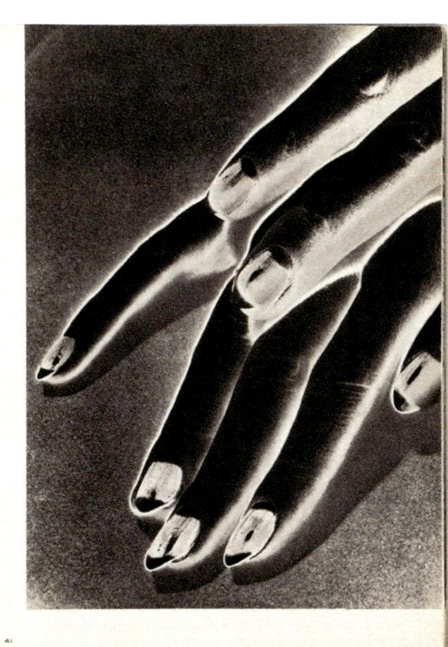

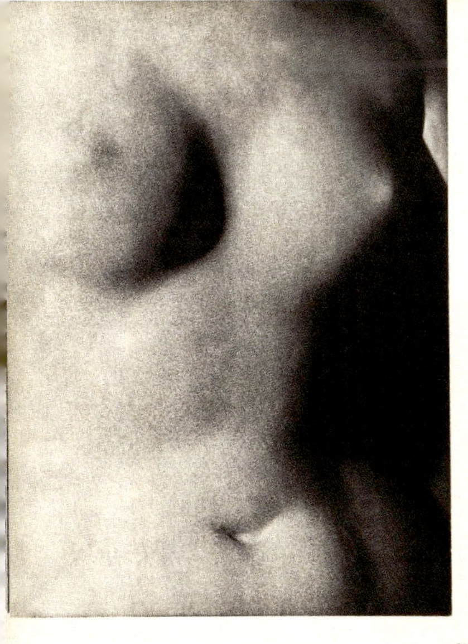

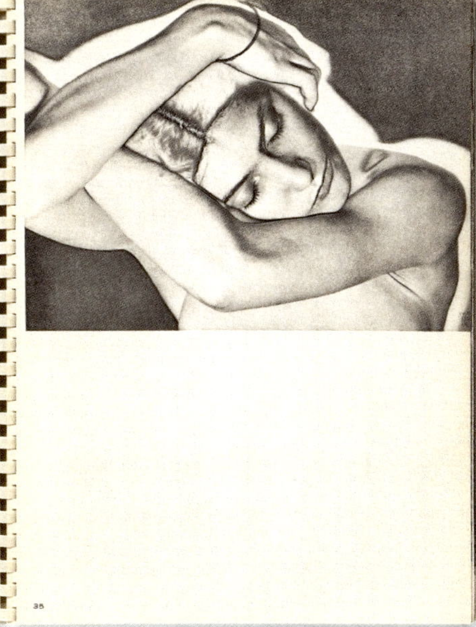

Noire et blanche, 1926

Konrad Ressler
Bertolt Brecht
1927

The Dramatist and his Photographer

At the end of the 1920s, the young Bertolt Brecht had himself photographed in his native city of Augsburg. The thirty-two glass negatives from that portrait sitting were only rediscovered in the mid-1980s - a sensation at the time. They are now part of the holdings of the photography collection of the Münchner Stadtmuseum.

Bertolt Brecht has taken a seat. He's waiting to appear before the camera in the studio of royal Bavarian court photographer Konrad Ressler. The atmosphere on the first floor of the rear building at Bahnhofstrasse 24 is familiar to him. It was here that Eugen Berthold Friedrich Brecht had his very first childhood portrait taken – at the age of barely eighteen months. Konrad Ressler was a friend of the family and took most of the other, later, shots for the Brecht private album: visiting cards, photographs in cabinet format, and postcard-size group portraits of the Augsburger Liedertafel choir, whose members included both Bert Brecht's father and Konrad Ressler.

Probably in the summer of 1927, Brecht once again sought out Ressler's studio, situated not far from Augsburg railway station. He was now twenty-nine years old. A rising writer for the stage, determined to conquer the theaters of the Weimar Republic with his plays. Two – *Drums in the Night* and *In the Jungle of Cities* – had already been staged and had divided the professional critics within the German art scene. Alfred Kerr voted against Brecht, but Herbert Ihering supported and encouraged him, and helped to secure him the prestigious Kleist Prize as early as 1922.

Brecht himself was full of confident optimism during these years. "I know how to write," he stated years earlier; "I can write plays for the theater better than Hebbel, wilder than Wedekind." When the pictures were taken, he was working on a *Singspiel*, a sort of anti-opera,

---

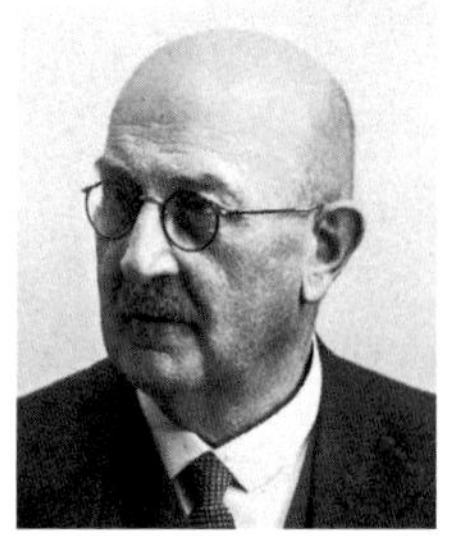

Konrad Ressler
*Born **1875** in Donauwörth, Germany. **1878** family moves to Neuburg (Upper Bavaria). His father opens a photographic studio. From **1881** primary and secondary school. Apprenticeship under his father. Years of travel with stays in Riga, Petersburg, and Bucharest. **1900** takes over the Gebrüder Martin in Augsburg. Meets Berthold Friedrich Brecht, father of the writer. **1907** Court Photographer. **1914–18** takes part in the First World War. Subsequently turns to industrial, architectural and commercial photography. **1927** portrait session with Bertolt Brecht. **1937** tribute to Konrad Ressler in the* Neue Augsburger Zeitung. ***1944** studio suffers war damage. Dies **1960** in Augsburg.*

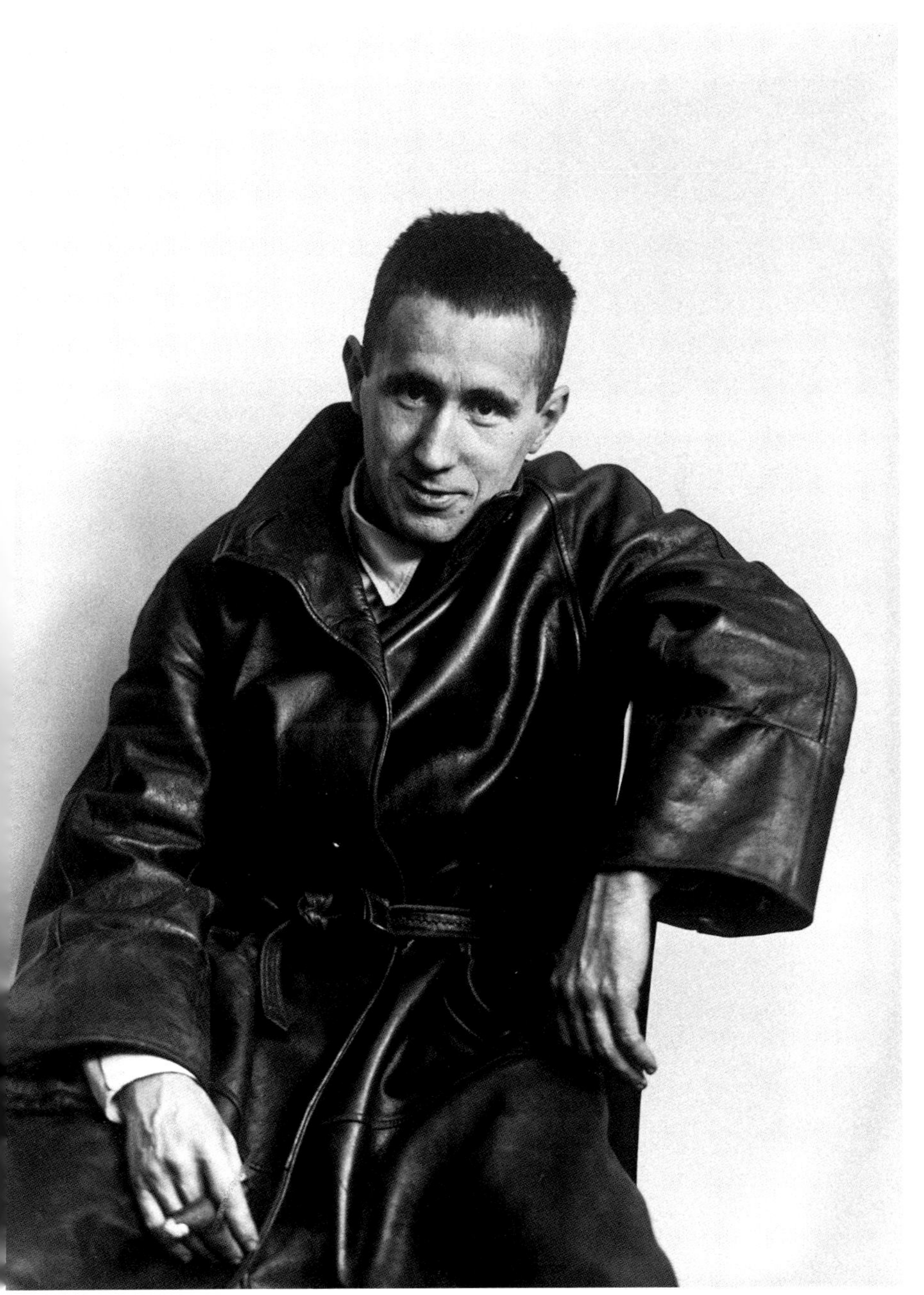

Bertolt Brecht, 1927

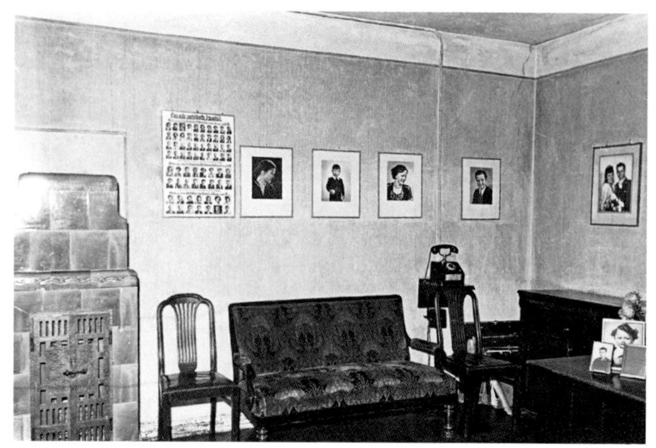

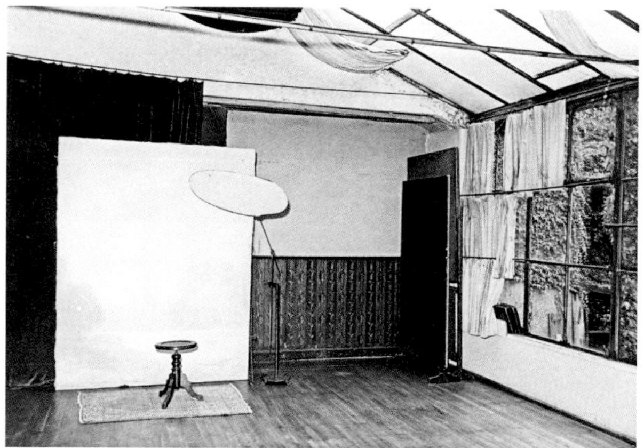

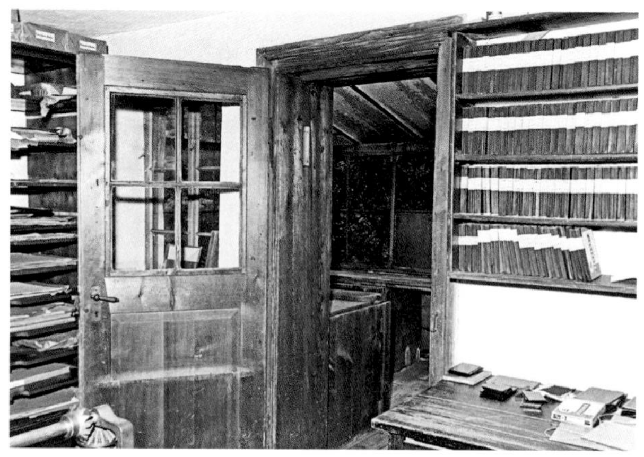

which in one year's time would be premiered at the Berlin Theater on Schiffbauerdamm as *The Threepenny Opera* – and make Brecht probably the most talked-about playwright in the Weimar Republic.

An ambivalent attitude towards his own appearance

What prompted Brecht, in 1927, to pose no less than thirty-two times for the camera of the established Augsburg photographer Konrad Ressler, is not clear. What we do know is that Brecht had a somewhat ambivalent attitude towards his own appearance. He disliked having his photograph taken. "I know I look stupid," he is supposed to have confessed on one occasion. On the other hand, he was well aware of the publicity value of a picture seen in print. "The 'face' of the author," he wrote, "belongs to the 'worth' of a poem." Which may explain why, in the 1920s and 1930s, he regularly allowed photographers engaged in most cases in journalism – Ellen Auerbach, Grete Stern, Fred Stein, Gisèle Freund, and Josef Breitenbach amongst them – to take portraits of him.

Commercial photographic studios were still plentiful after 1900, and those who visited them were as a rule interested in a picture that would underline their rank and reputation, their position in society. Smart dress, an immaculate appearance, an upright posture and a resolute gaze that was usually directed past the camera into the distance – these were the constants of the genre. Backgrounds and a selection of props served to reinforce the desired impression of respectability. Lighting, pose, composition and angle were more or less standardized and thus meant that customers could visualize the result – one characterized as much by illusion as by reality (or rather, *more* by illusion than by reality). This balance was cautiously adjusted by photographers with artistic ambitions in order to enhance expression and character.

Little or nothing of this has made its way into the portrait of Bertolt Brecht. The young author is quite unashamedly lolling against his chair. He has not even laid aside his lit cigar, which instead seems to form a firm part of the cocky attitude he presents to the camera. The image is emphatically provocative and thereby simple, almost modern, in its compositional means. Nothing similar survives either amongst the known (photographic) portraits of Brecht or in the estate of his photographer: Konrad Ressler, born in 1875 in Donauwörth and the owner from 1900 of the Gebrüder Martin studio in Augsburg's Bahnhofstrasse. A solid craftsman whose name, were it not for his portraits of the young Brecht, would undoubtedly have been forgotten.

The dramatist as dandy

Vignetted by the dark borders left by the plate-holder, Brecht's figure appears slightly off-center within the portrait-format print. His pose describes a diagonal. The light falls from the right-hand foreground, with a fill-in light on the left. The background is neutral. Nothing distracts from the main character in his thoroughly relaxed pose. Blurred areas in the folds of the

---

Konrad Ressler's studio (formerly owned by the Martin Brothers), 1954. From top to bottom: the reception room, the studio, and the plate store.

leather coat – which, as the button tape reveals, must have been a woman's coat – lend volume to the aggressive item of clothing. "In those days," recalled Marieluise Fleisser, "he used to wear leather jackets, in which his fine-boned physique virtually disappeared." Just what we see here. His forehead is smooth, his round eyes dark. His gaze is directed straight into the lens of an aging studio camera. Brecht, who is very present in this picture, gives the viewer a slight grin. We gain a sense, or so it feels, of the poor posture so often associated with him. In a moment he will stand up and fasten the collar of his coat or present himself to the camera – now against a black background – in profile and head-and-shoulders views. There is no doubt that we are witnesses to an experiment, the playful exploration of a face, the search for a 'valid' portrait in which the young writer and dandy hopes to recognize himself. A process that might be described as a visual dialogue, in which – so it is to be suspected – Konrad Ressler was responsible for the technical production and Brecht for the theatrical direction.

In the spirit of New Objectivity

In Berlin one year previously, Bert Brecht had his portrait painted in oils by Rudolf Schlichter, an artist close to New Objectivity. The canvas, measuring 75.5 × 46 cm (29¾ × 18 inches) is today in the collection of the Städtische Galerie im Lenbachhaus in Munich. Schlichter shows the author as a self-confident figure with a cropped haircut and a narrow face, holding an extinguished cigar in his overly large right hand. Here, too, he is clad in black leather. The Schlichter painting thereby seems to anticipate the Ressler studies both in its overall layout and in the sitter's pleasure in projecting an image designed to shock and outrage the middle classes. Did Brecht and Schlichter talk, as one sat and the other painted, about portraiture and about formal means of representing the human individual in a contemporary manner? Astonishingly, neither the painter nor the playwright makes a single mention of any portrait sittings in their diaries or letters. The chronology of events is enough to suggest, however, that Brecht was at least thinking about his hours spent with Schlichter when he began stage-managing his photographic portraits in the studio and trusted presence of Konrad Ressler.

In 1924 Brecht moved to Berlin. He regularly returned to his native Augsburg, however, in order to be able to work undisturbed. It must have been during one of these visits that Ressler's series of portraits, comprising thirty-two negatives in a 12.5 × 16.5 cm (5 × 6½ inch) format together with one original bromoil print – were taken. Whether the photographer was speculating on publishing his successful images, we do not know. Whatever the case, at the time they were taken, Brecht was not yet famous and certainly not popular enough. Only after the success of *The Threepenny Opera* was one of the images published. It accompanied an article on Brecht featured in the *Augsburger Neuesten Nachrichten* in May 1929 and entitled "Born in Augsburg – Internationally Active – Known Around the World." The photographer was not credited. It would remain the only picture by Konrad Ressler published during his lifetime. He died in 1960 and thus did not live to see Bert Brecht's renaissance in the theaters of West Germany.

Poster for the first exhibition of the Brecht series in the Fotomuseum im Münchner Stadtmuseum in Munich. Staged in July 1986, this exhibition brought the portraits to international attention.

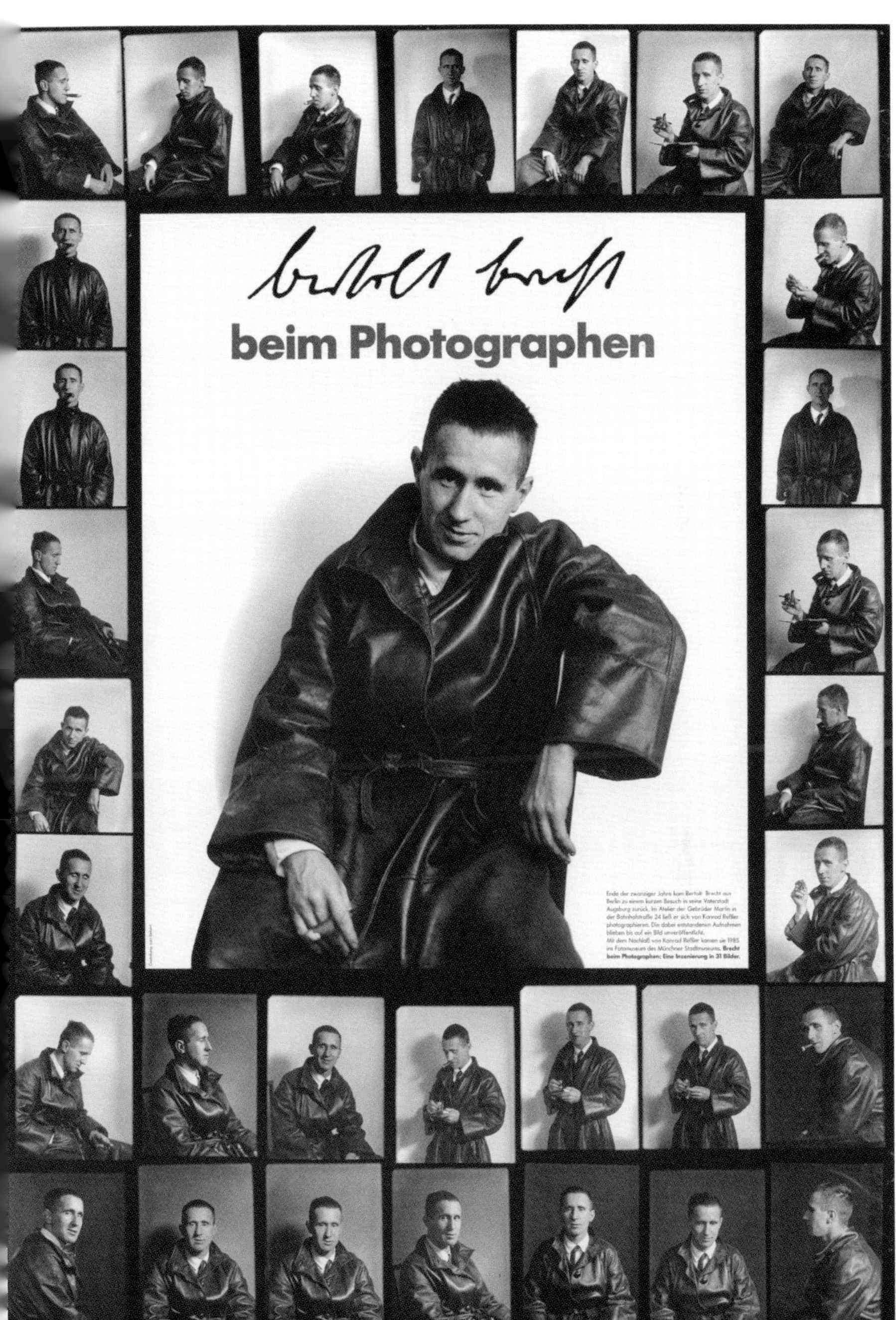

Bertolt Brecht, 1927

André Kertész
Meudon
1928

The Poetry of the Street

He always saw himself as a realist and documentary photographer. But during his time in Paris, the Hungarian-born André Kertész had in fact matured into artistic greatness. Just how strongly he was also influenced by the Cubist and Surrealist developments of his age is clear in *Meudon*, taken in 1928.

At least in titling his photographs, the great poet among twentieth-century photographers was fairly prosaic: the names of what are today probably his best known works – *Chez Mondrian*, *Danseuse satirique*, and *Fourchette* – merely designate what is to be seen in the photograph. And also in christening this photograph *Meudon*, Kertész was referring to an actual place, a suburb to the southwest of Paris, approximately halfway to Versailles. Just when in 1928 the picture was taken we do not know, but from the leafless tree in the background, it must have been either at the beginning or end of the year, even though the photograph wasn't published until 1945, a good decade and a half after Kertész took it.

The New York publishing house of J. J. Augustin brought out *Day of Paris*, edited by George Davis and designed by Alexey Brodovitch, in a 24 × 18 cm (9½ × 7 inch) format, with 148 pages containing 102 illustrations – in what was a halfway decently printed volume, even though it was quite modest by today's standards. Nevertheless, for André Kertész, the publication was an important event, not so much because the design of the book had been taken over by the man who was probably the most important art director of the day, but because Kertész's collection of Paris shots taken between 1925 and 1936 formed a reminiscence of what he always referred to later as artistically the most fruitful and most beautiful period of his life. Moreover, the publication constituted a piece of publicity during a phase that otherwise must undoubtedly be regarded as the low point of his career.

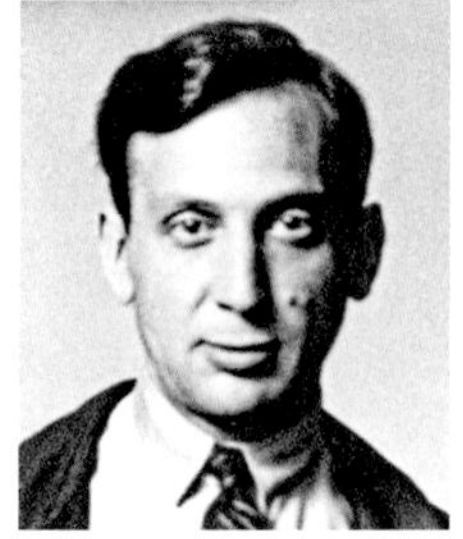

André Kertész
*Born **1894** in Budapest and named Kertész Andor. Works initially as a book-keeper at the Budapest stock exchange. **1914** military service. **1917** publication of first photo. **1925** moves to Paris. **1929** participates in the* Film und Foto *exhibition. **1929** first distortions in mirrors. **1936** moves to New York. Publications in* Harper's Bazaar, Vogue, Coronet. ***1944** American citizenship. **1945** publication of his book* Day of Paris. ***1946** exclusive contract with* House and Garden. *Dies **1985** in New York. **1986** estate (100,000 negatives) donated to the French state (Patrimoine Photographique). **2010** major retrospective at Jeu de Paume, Paris.*

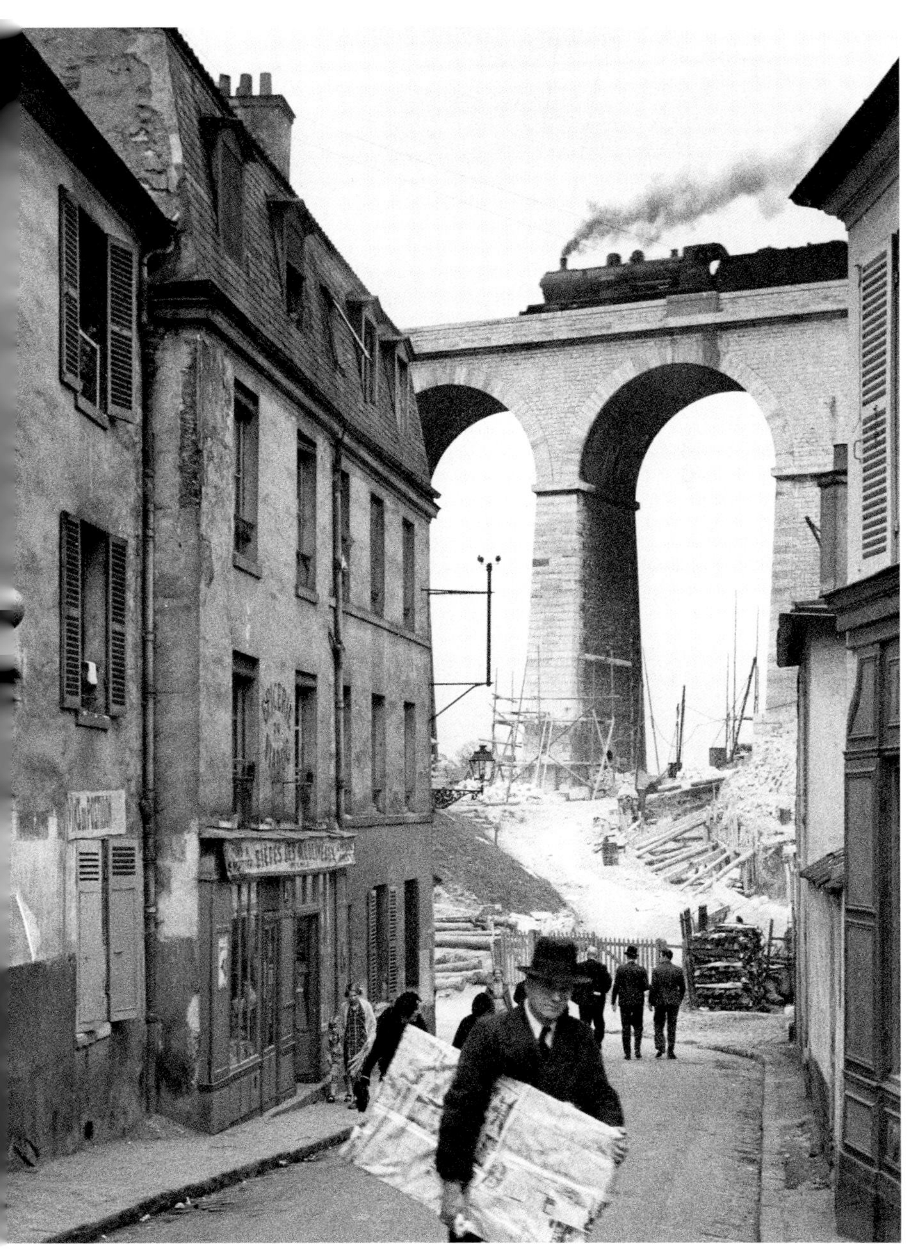

Meudon, **1928**

The greater part of his pictorial archive in his bags

André Kertész emigrated from Paris to New York in 1936, lured by an offer of the Keystone Agency – although it is possible that the photographer, scion of a Jewish Hungarian family, was also motivated by political developments in Europe. In his baggage, Kertész had carried along the greater part of his pictorial archive – a fact which suggests that he had determined to spend a longer time in the USA. This material was to form the basis of *Day of Paris* more than a decade later. The rest of the story is well-known – an almost immediate falling-out with Keystone; the artist's more-or-less unsuccessful attempts at finding work with all the various publishers and presses; his classification as an unfriendly alien in 1941, resulting in a ban on publication of his work; his jobbing after the war in magazine photography. Looking back, Kertész always designated his move to the USA as a mistake, and his work for magazines such as *House and Garden* and *Vogue* as a waste of time. Why he therefore remained in the USA remains a riddle; what is certain is that the artist, who had been active on numerous projects between the wars in Europe, could not gain recognition in the USA for his work, steeped as it was in the formal language of Surrealism. In an often-told story of his failure to acquire a foothold in *Life*, which had been founded in the year of his arrival in America, it is said that the editors told him that his pictures told too much: a highly telling comment when it comes to our picture.

Contradictions that create both the visual interest and the oddity of the image

The publication of the monograph in 1945, the year that the war ended, must therefore have seemed to Kertész to be a priceless recompense, all the more so because it also made amends for an even earlier blow. The title of the book, *Day of Paris*, may have seemed to many like a counterpart to Brassaï's warmly received *Paris de Nuit* of 1933, but in fact the publisher had originally offered the theme to Kertész. In view of the meager stipend, however, Kertész refused the commission, thus opening the door for his somewhat younger Hungarian colleague. No less a figure than Paul Morand had composed the foreword to Brassaï's first published work. *Day of Paris*, by contrast, was served with extended captions, supposedly written by the editor George Davis. *Meudon* appears as a full-page plate on page 83. "The sharp unreality of stage-sets. Like a toy an engine crosses the viaduct in a suburb," reads the caption – which indicates that the image had already irritated and alienated its contemporaries.

A train, coming from the right, is crossing a viaduct. In the foreground, as if accidentally, a man in a dark coat wearing a hat is crossing the street, while further behind, nine figures, two of them children, are heading off in various directions. Nothing in the picture is unusual in itself: there is no 'event' here, no 'transgression' of borders in the sense of the artistic theory promulgated by Structuralism. And yet the effect of the vertical black-and-white photograph is somehow disturbing. Does this feeling originate in a simultaneity of

---

André Kertész:
Meudon, *1928. A total of three negatives (the published shot and two variants, right and page 187) have survived in André Kertész' estate.*

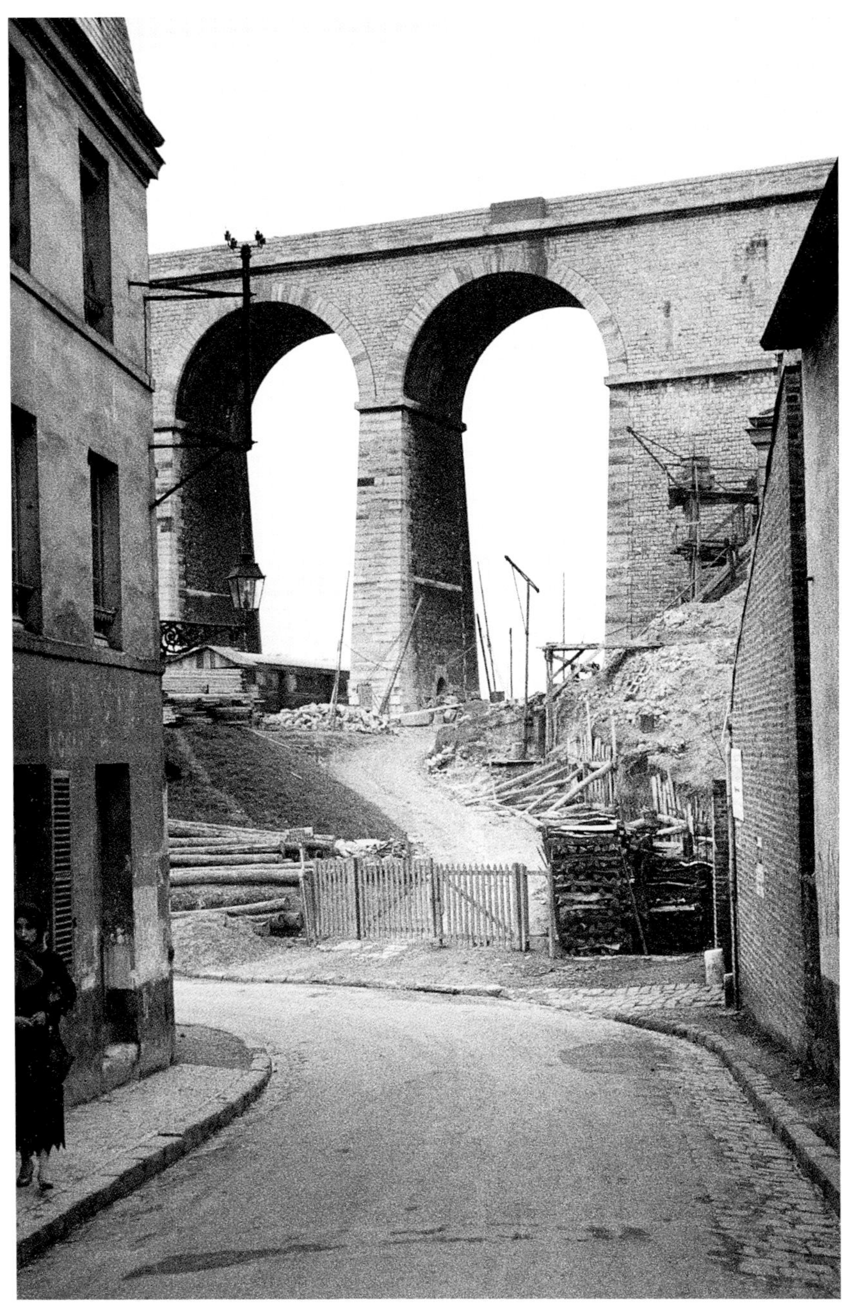

Meudon, 1928

dissimilar things, which captures the observer's gaze, surprises them, leaves questions unanswered? Normally, photography presents connections, reveals causalities, gives insights. But this picture explains nothing; it seems to be torn from some kind of unknown context. And on top of this, it is loaded with an entire series of clearly obvious contradictions that constitute the visual interest, but also the oddity, of the image. There is, for example, the massive viaduct and equally imposing steam locomotive that appear as if in miniature in the photograph, as if taken over from a model train set. And then there is the well-groomed gentleman, whose dark coat together with his tie and Homburg don't quite fit into the otherwise rather shabby surroundings. What is a man like him, whom we would rather expect to find strolling on one of the boulevards in the center of the city, doing out here in the suburb of Meudon – and furthermore, 'caught' with a newspaper-wrapped object which the 'suspect' seems to be transporting like booty from left to right through the picture. Even though it depicts a scene clearly drawn from everyday life in Paris, something surreal clings to the photograph, something reminiscent of the paintings of de Chirico, or the inventions of a Balthus or René Magritte, or of certain scenes in the films of Luis Buñuel. More than anything else, the photograph resembles a still taken from a film; the architecture, diminishing in size as the receding street curves away to the left, and the viaduct in the deep background, lend the picture a tangibly stage-like quality.

Friends with the avant-garde circles of Montparnasse

At the time he made the picture, the Hungarian-born Kertész, age thirty-four, was a well-known and successful photographic artist in Paris. No less a figure than Julien Levy would soon designate him as a "prolific leader in the new documentary school of photography." Strictly speaking, Kertész was a member of the large Hungarian-Jewish Diaspora whose innovative work was making a major contribution to the development of a new look to photography around 1930. In this context one can name Robert Capa, Stefan Lorant, Martin Munkácsi, as well as Brassaï, born Gyula Halász, who had moved to Paris in 1924. Kertész's first photographs date from 1914, and his journalistic publications had already gained him a certain degree of fame in Hungary of the early 1920s. Why he moved to Paris in 1925 we do not know; after all, the majority of his photographic compatriots were drifting to Berlin, at that time the uncontested center of a dynamically growing photographic press. What is certain is that in Paris he soon found his way into the artistic avant-garde circles of Montparnasse. Although he seems to have had only a loose connection with the reserved Man Ray, he was in regular contact with more-or-less well-known Hungarian artists such as Lajos Tihanyi, Josef Csáky, István Beöthy, and even Brassaï. Kertész regularly met his colleagues in the Café du Dôme, which, located on the corner of the boulevards Montparnasse and Raspail, soon became the center for the informal group of artists.

Opened in September 1840, the 145 meter (476 feet) long and 32 meter (105 feet) high railway viaduct at Meudon was considered the greatest feat of engineering in its day. Nevertheless, it seems unlikely that André Kertész traveled solely on its account to the outskirts of Paris.

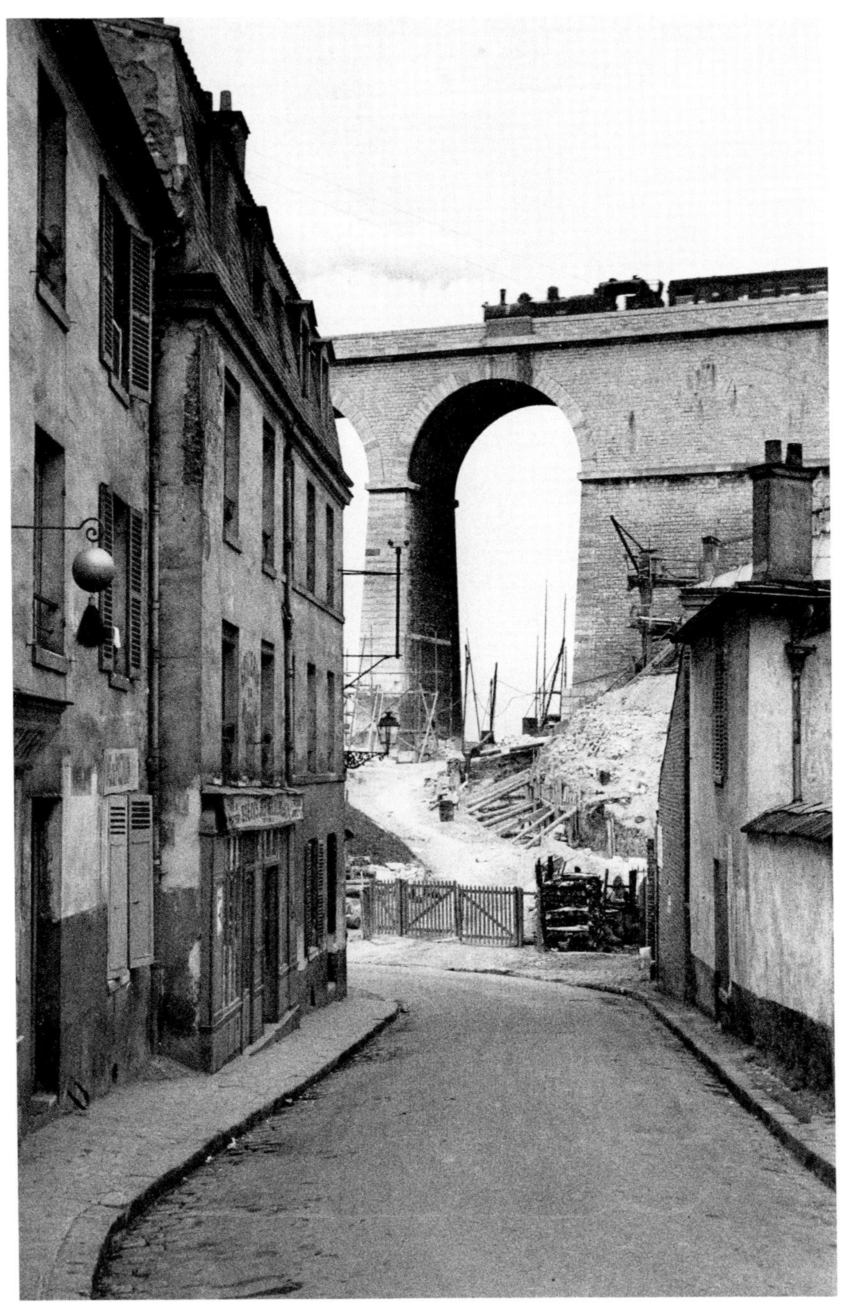

Meudon, 1928

In addition to achieving a respectable measure of success in these years as a photojournalist, especially for German and French papers, Kertész still had enough time and energy to pursue freelance projects directed toward developing his personal photographic style – one which is moreover not to be defined with any of the traditional vocabulary. According to Jean-Claude Lemagny, his pictures "have something restrained, dampened, soft, about them." Kertész was perfectly aware of the artistic tendencies of his age, especially Cubism and Surrealism, "but neither dominate his work; both remain subservient to the actual photographic task at hand ... Kertész is surrealistic only to the extent that reality itself is. With every step in the real world, an abyss of poetry can open up."

The ideal tool for the artist

Meudon came into being at an important moment in Kertész's life, for this was the year in which he purchased his first Leica. The small-format camera, which had been available on the market since 1925, proved to be the ideal tool for the artist. The 35-mm camera, at once handy and discreet, made Kertész's particular approach as a strolling photographer considerably easier. In addition, the 36-exposure rolls allowed pictures to be taken in sequence, thus allowing a visually more experimental approach to a valid pictorial formula – an advantage which, as we shall see, played an important role also in the conception of *Meudon*.

Portraits of his artist friends; including Mondrian, Foujita, and Chagall; interiors, as well as everyday objects and street scenes, were among Kertész's more common themes in those early years in Paris. Nonetheless, from the beginning, Kertész's visual exploration of the metropolis on the Seine occupied the center of his artistic interest. In these years, according to Sandra S. Phillips, he often strolled through areas like Montmartre and Meudon. Gaining familiarity with the traditional artist-quarter of Montmartre was, of course, a part of the required task of every newcomer to the Paris scene. Meudon, in contrast, was not a place that a strolling photographer would visit as a matter of course: one must intentionally board a streetcar to get there. But what might have drawn Kertész to Meudon in 1928?

At this point, the survival of a total of three small-format negatives, distributed on two nitrate films, becomes significant. One image is without people or train, and lacks both date and frame number on the roll. Two more images, including the published version, were taken one directly after the other. Which was the first exposure? Presumably the scene without people or train, for it seems unlikely that the visually experienced Kertész would have followed the dramatic composition of our picture with a comparatively boring variation without human figures. In any case, the photographer made two visits to Meudon. The diminishing wood pile and the alterations in the scaffolding of a building indicate that a good deal of time must have elapsed between the first shot and the two succeeding ones. If Kertész had traveled out to Meudon for the sake of the viaduct, however imposing it might be, he would undoubtedly have been satisfied with his first picture, in which the bridge is clearly evident – or he would have immediately attempted another shot. Consequently, there must have been another motive that drew Kertész to Meudon, where the critical picture was made almost in passing, as it were.

Kertész's exhibition at the gallery Sacre du Printemps in 1927 undoubtedly marked an important station in the artist's professional career. Not only was the show one of the first exhibitions emphasizing the art of photography in general, but it also constituted the first large summary of his work in progress, with which he hoped to establish connections to better known photographers, in particular Man Ray. A group photograph also dating from 1927 reveals just how much a part of the international art circle in Paris Kertész had already become. On the picture titled *After the soirée* we see Piet Mondrian, Michel Seuphor, Adolf Loos, Ida Thal, and in the background the German artist Willi Baumeister who, in his own words, had met with "recognition and very great interest on the part of the French artists" and even toyed for a time with the idea of moving to France. At least on one other occasion Kertész did a portrait of Baumeister: in 1926 in Mondrian's studio together with Gertrud Stemmler, Julius Herburger, Piet Mondrian, Michel Seuphor, and Margit Baumeister. In other words, Kertész and Baumeister had met at the latest by 1926. Taking a closer look at the group portrait of 1926, there is an astounding similarity between Baumeister and the gentleman in a dark coat, whose shadowed face nonetheless emerges as powerful and broad – and who likewise seems to be wearing glasses.

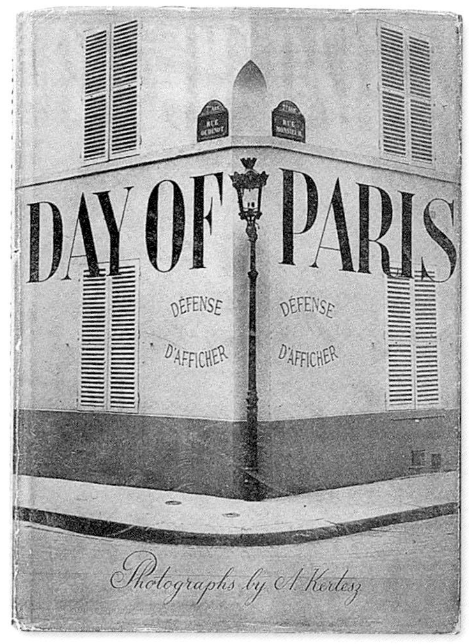

Never rearranged a subject

We know that Willi Baumeister visited Paris in 1926, 1927, and 1929, even if there is no direct evidence for 1928. In a letter to Oskar Schlemmer dated 2 November 1928, now privately owned, the German artist speaks of a certain "Miss whom I met in Paris" – a statement that certainly does not constitute proof of a visit to the city during the year in question, but which makes it nonetheless more probable. If we assume that Willi Baumeister in fact was in the French capital during the course of the year, what might have led him to Meudon? A visit to his friend and fellow-painter Hans Arp, whose studio was in fact located in Meudon at this time? Clearly, there is at least some evidence to support the hypothesis that the photograph presents us with the figure of the constructivist Willi Baumeister – whom Kertész had accompanied to Meudon and captured on film as he crossed the street. The flat, newspaper-wrapped package also suggests the possibility of a painter. But if the figure is in fact

---

Day of Paris*: The book, designed by Alexey Brodovitch, was published 1945 by J. J. Augustin of New York, and was Kertész's first book offering in the USA.*

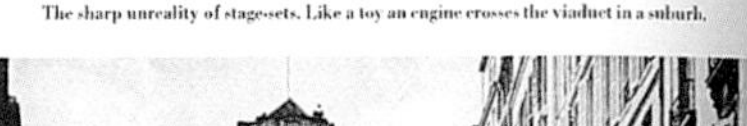

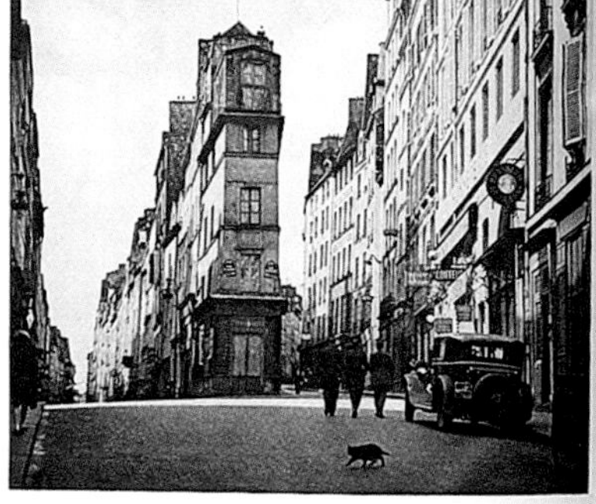

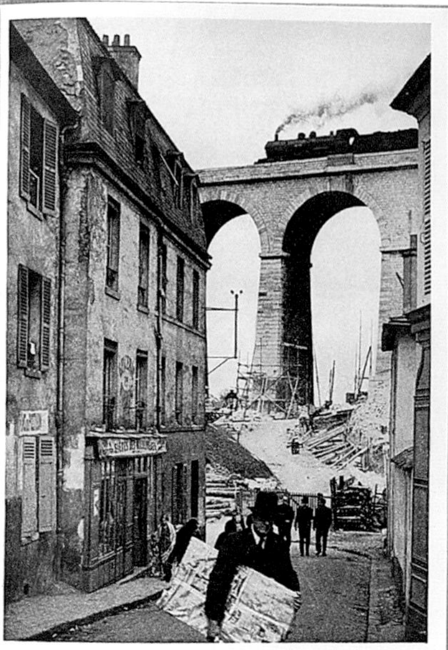

that of his friend Baumeister, why then did Kertész not identify him in the caption beneath the picture? The explanation is simple: "The difference between Kertész and Bourke-White, as well as many others who did photographs on assignment to satisfy editorial needs, is that she would sometimes rearrange a subject; Kertész never would," declared Weston Naef. But the idea of staging a scene would certainly have occurred to Kertész's 'teammate' Willi Baumeister, who appears, moreover, as a complete figure in the uncropped photograph. The possibility of staging is all the more realistic since Kertész was demonstrably working toward an ultimate composition for his picture – as evidenced by the three 'stages' through which the photograph passed. Moreover, a reference to Baumeister in the photograph would have led to an inevitable hierarchizing of the elements in the picture. The balance among viaduct, train, and man-with-hat would shift in the direction of the human figure, and we would therefore understand the picture solely as a portrait of Willi Baumeister – and a none too good one at that. Only insofar as the photograph keeps its secret does it also retain its visual power and surrealistically inspired poetry.

Day of Paris*: Double-page spreads,* Quartier Saint Denis *and* Meudon *(above)*; Tuileries Gardens *(top right);* Kiki of Montparnasse *and* Montparnasse, Studio *(bottom right).*

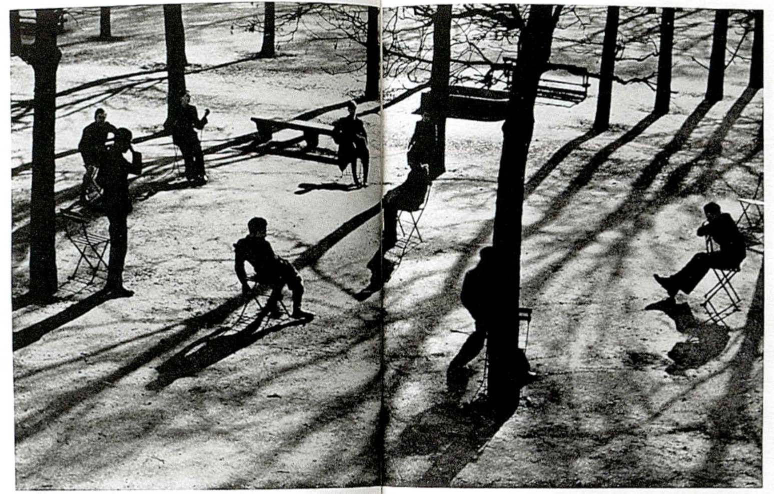

Perhaps the children of the Medici played this same passionately subtle game.

114

115

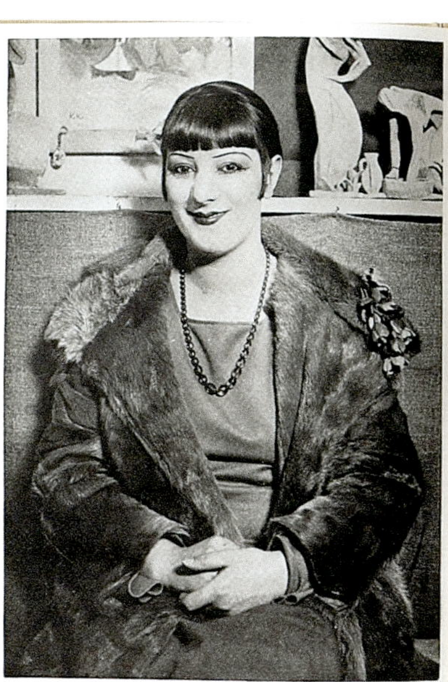

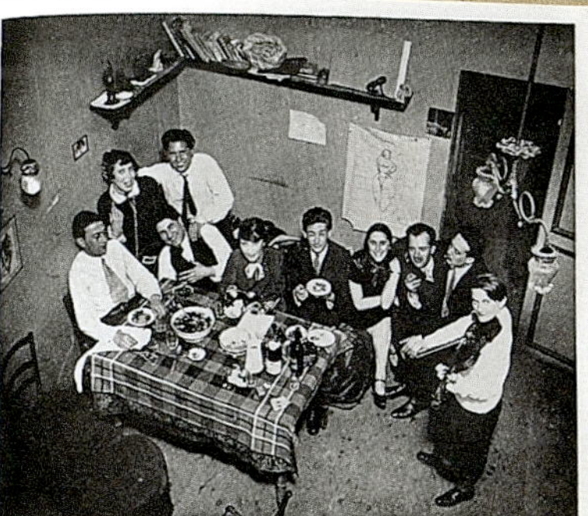

She is proud that her fame has spread all over the world as Kiki of Montparnasse, model, mistress and crony of artists; she is even prouder that she has never grown pubic hair. She has, like the celebrants above, the innocence of the classic bohemian.

137

Robert Capa
Spanish Loyalist
1936

Córdoba Before the Fall

Robert Capa was more than a war photographer, even if it was his war scenes that made him famous. In the end, his estate comprised more than 70,000 negatives – but that of his most famous picture is accounted lost.

Finally, he has acquired a name. For decades, he was merely an unknown soldier, a nameless victim of war. He, or rather his picture, stood symbolically for the millions of deaths lost to war and violence. The caption affixed to the image was as brief as it was general: *Loyalist Soldier* was the most usual title. Or *Falling Soldier*, or even *Loyalist Militia* – but this reference to the Anarcho-Syndicalists who fought on the Republican side of the war attempted a more exact identification than the picture really allowed. For, as many critics have rightly noted, this photograph drew, and still draws, its power precisely from its generalization of death. Only insofar as the photograph stands for a reality that passes beyond time can it function as an icon of dying in a higher sense. As late as 1984, the writer Peter Härtling, in his lectures on poetics given in Frankfurt-am-Main, addressed the issue of the "absence of data on the soldier" and asked whether it was proper to create something like an identity for him. According to Härtling, "He cannot have been a soldier after the model of a Malraux or Hemingway, but rather one of those who were buried – nameless among thousands of nameless – in the Cemeteries of the Moon, as Georges Bernanos described them in helpless protest." Härtling answered his own question: "No, I would not give him a name." But now some think they know his name: They say he was called Federico Borrell García, was just 24 at the time and had come from Alcoy in southern Spain. He apparently lost his life on the Córdoba front near Cerro Muriano on 5 September 1936. His death was documented in the files of the military archive of Salamanca – that's something we'll talk about later.

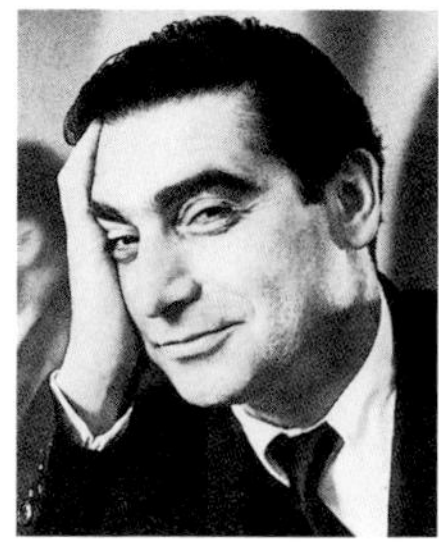

Robert Capa
Born Endre Ernö Friedmann ***1913*** *in Budapest, Hungary.* ***1931*** *moves to Berlin. Studies at the liberal German College for Politics.* ***1932–33*** *lab assistant at the photo agency Dephot.* ***1932*** *first photos are published.* ***1933*** *moves to Paris. Acquainted among others with Gisèle Freund and Henri Cartier-Bresson. From* ***1936*** *photo-journalism on the Spanish Civil War for the magazines* Vu *and* Regards. ***1938*** *war correspondent in China. Moves* ***1939*** *to the USA. Works for* Collier's *and* Life. *Highly acclaimed reportages on the European theaters of war.* ***1947*** *founder member of Magnum.* ***1954*** *in Indochina for* Life. *Killed that same year by a mine.*

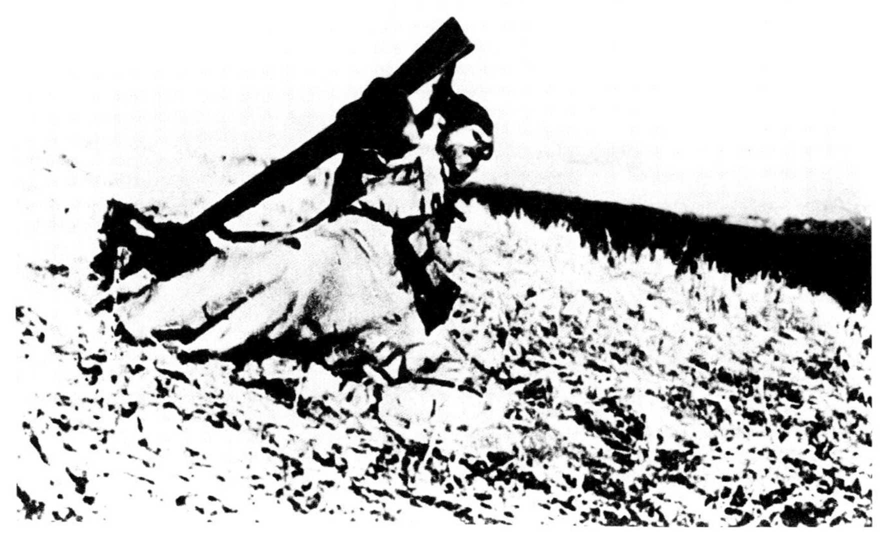

The most exciting shot of battle action

The photographer Robert Capa, who was 22 at the time, captured the moment of death, thereby taking what is undoubtedly his most famous photograph. There is no information about the picture; not even Magnum, the agency co-founded by Capa and which still holds the rights to the picture under entry number CAR 36004 W000X1/ICP 154, has data about its circulation and reception. Nonetheless, historians and biographers agree on the unique status of this picture. To cite just a few voices: the Capa scholar Richard Whelan speaks of "the most exciting and immediate shot of battle action" ever taken; Russell Miller in his recent book on Magnum declares it to be "the greatest war photograph ever taken"; the German illustrated *Stern* (41/1996) termed the photograph "a symbol of the Spanish Civil War and later the ultimate image for the anti-war movement"; and finally, Rainer Fabian, in his article on more than 130 years of war photography, speaks of "the most legendary and most-published war picture in history." According to Fabian, "War photography is the use that one makes of it"; that is, a war picture defines itself primarily through the way it is used.

Robert Capa's photograph of the Spanish Loyalist was not the first picture to emerge from a war, but it stands as "the first compelling action shot taken during wartime" (Carol Squiers). One tends to treat such superlatives with skepticism; after all, many photographs and films also emerged from the First World War, at a time when Capa's preferred working camera,

Robert Capa:
Comment sont-ils tombés (How They Fell).
It was under this title that Vu *magazine first published Capa's* Spanish Loyalist, *on 23 September 1936, together with this lesser known photograph of a falling soldier.*

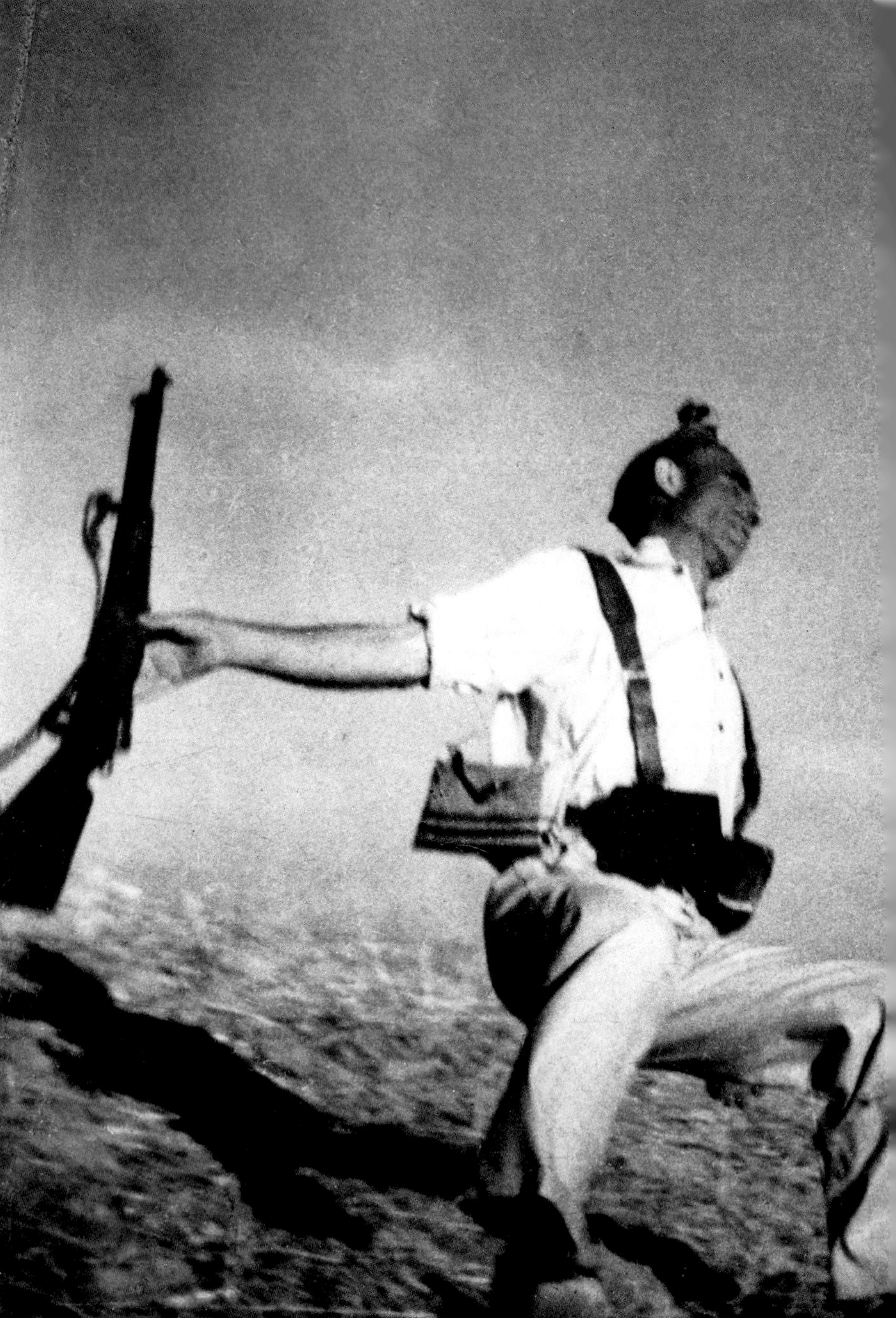

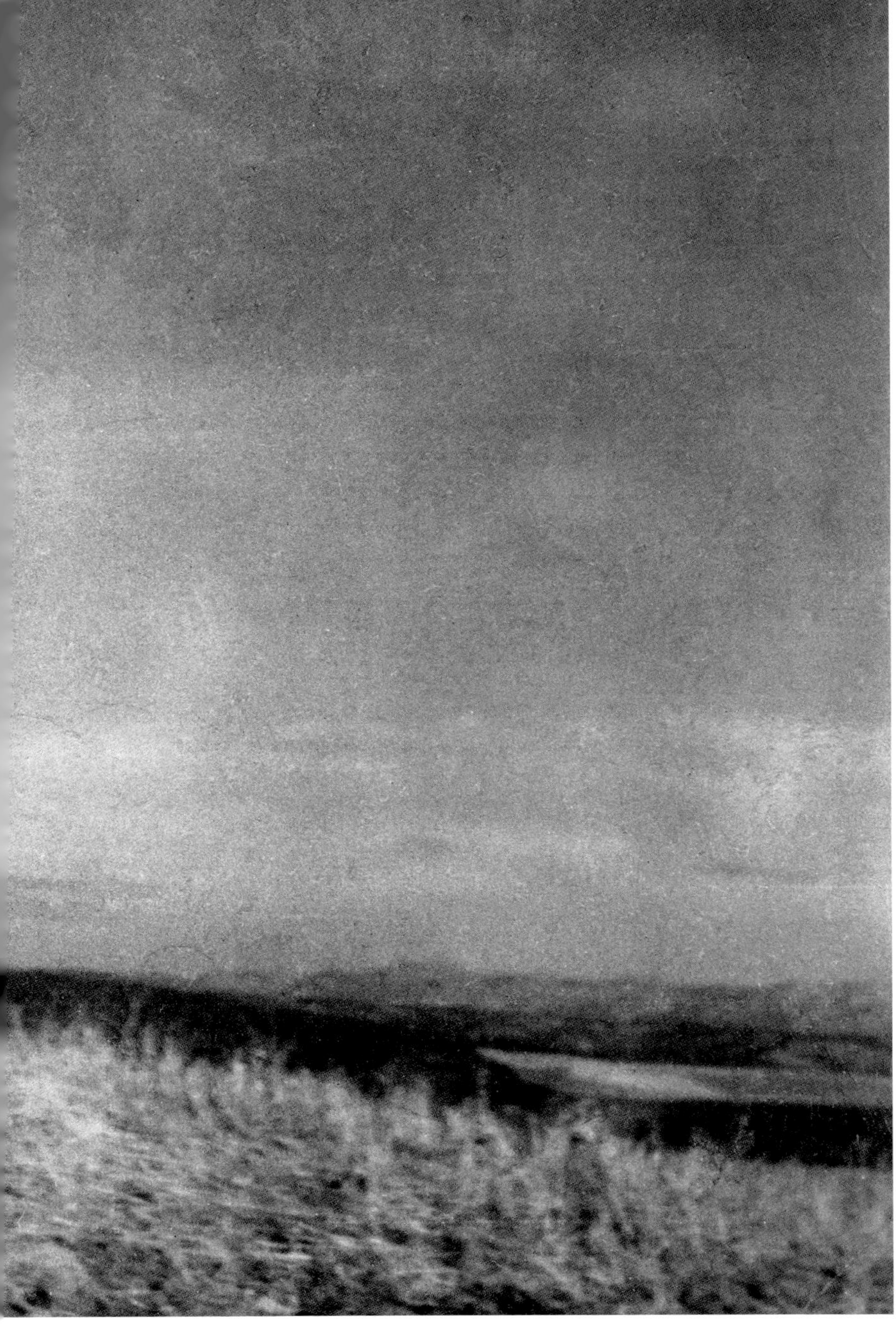

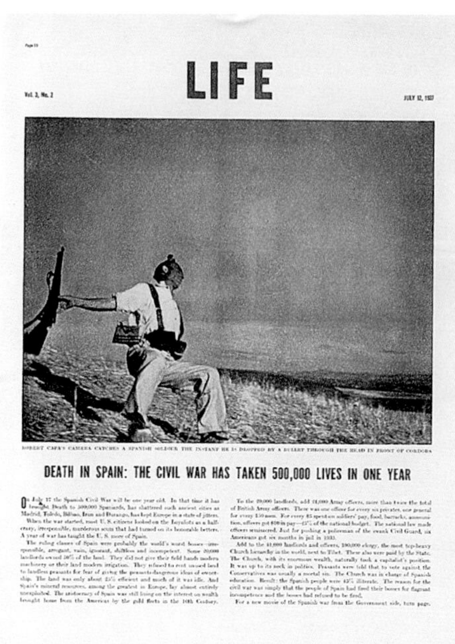

Vol. 3, No. 2 **LIFE** JULY 12, 1937

ROBERT CAPA'S CAMERA CATCHES A SPANISH SOLDIER THE INSTANT HE IS DROPPED BY A BULLET THROUGH THE HEAD IN FRONT OF CORDOBA

DEATH IN SPAIN: THE CIVIL WAR HAS TAKEN 500,000 LIVES IN ONE YEAR

the Leica, was not yet on the market. In those days, photojournalists had comparatively large and clumsy cameras, weak lenses, and glass negatives that debarred quick reactions or sequences. Notwithstanding, one cannot exclude the possibility that among the many thousands of photographs taken, there might be a picture of a death that is at least the equal of Capa's. What had certainly changed since the end of the First World War, however, was the situation of the media. War pictures were now treated differently, as photographs found a forum in the newly created illustrated press. As a result, there was now a demand and, in many lands, a largely uncensored public sphere. In short, a change in paradigms had taken place.

The blossoming new genre of illustrated magazines

The specific character of the Spanish Civil War must also be kept in mind. For most Europeans, it was a distant civil war which one nonetheless regarded with curiosity because here – quasi symbolically for the rest of the world – the struggle between the Left and the Right, between Communism and Fascism, was being fought out. In other words, in this age before television there was a strong and international interest in pictures that the new genre of illustrated magazines, which had blossomed into being since the 1920s, knew how to satisfy. Advances in printing techniques, new forms of distribution, and revolutionary layout techniques allowed the improved reproduction of images more quickly and attractively than had been possible earlier, and supplied them to the readers. In addition, a new generation of photographers had appeared: equipped with faster cameras and a new understanding of their role. The field now included photojournalists, adventurers, and parvenus who personally stood – or were supposed to stand – for the originality, seriousness, and authenticity of a story. It is not by chance that reports became more and more personalized. When the English illustrated *Picture Post* devoted all of eleven pages to Robert Capa's civil war photographs

---

Above: **Robert Capa:**
Spanish Loyalist, *which appears over the title "Death in Spain," a feature in* Life, *12 July 1937.*

Right: *Double-page spread from* La Revue du Médecin, *30 September 1936: the first issue of the magazine for doctors and pharmacists published Gerda Taro and Capa's pictures (including the variant from page 193) in an exceptionally avant-garde layout.*

in December 1938, the cover clearly proclaimed him to be the greatest war photographer in the world. This was not the first publication of pictures from Spain, but it was the start of a myth that is still effective today.

He was young and obviously ambitious, a photographer with leftist sympathies, a charmer, a ladies' man, gambler, and adventurer all in one – thus we can imagine Capa in those years. In addition, he was undoubtedly a "concerned photographer," who above all believed in himself, his talent, skill, and courage to take good pictures. His real name was Endre Ernö Friedman, and he had been born in Budapest in 1913, the second of a tailor's three children. Even as a boy, he was alert and knew how to take his life in hand. In 1931 he moved to Berlin, studied at the Academy for Politics, and earned a bit of money at the legendary Dephot agency, where he carried coal, handled the laboratory work, and at some point was also permitted to take a camera into his own hands. Photographs of the camera-shy Leon Trotsky are said to be the beginning of his career as a photographer. Even here, Capa already succeeded instinctively and with a good deal of chutzpah in a brilliant report. "If your pictures are no good," he is reported to have said, "you didn't get close enough."

The first to recognize the visual power of the photograph

Hitler's takeover hindered the further development of Capa's career, at least in Nazi Germany. Like so many of the photographic guild – Stefan Lorant, Martin Munkácsi, Simon Guttmann, to name only Capa's fellow Hungarians – Capa, who was Jewish, felt forced to emigrate. Only after he moved to Paris did the talented novice with a sense for themes

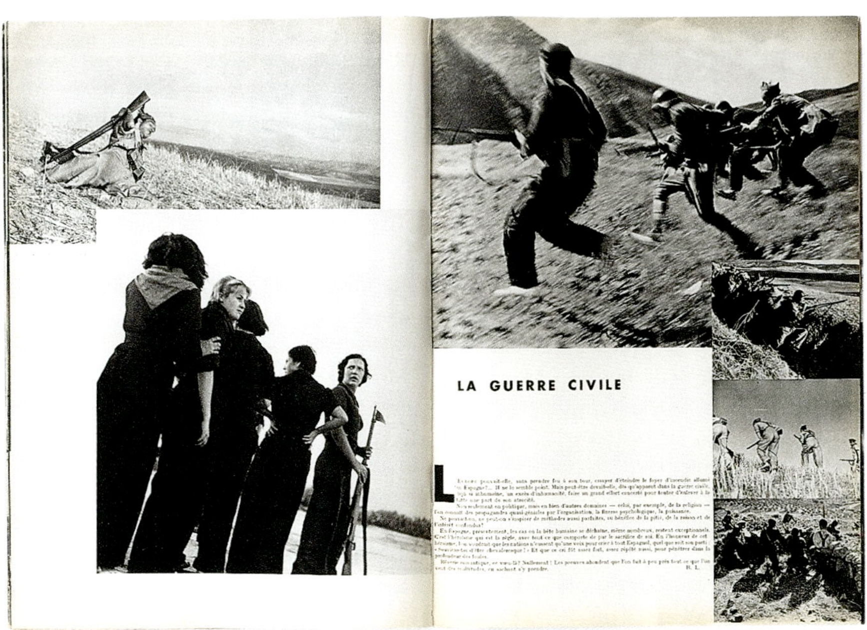

LA GUERRE CIVILE

L[illegible] pouvait-elle, sans prendre feu à son tour, essayer d'éteindre le foyer d'incendie allumé en Espagne?... Il ne le semble point. Mais peut-être devait-elle, dès qu'apparut dans la guerre civile, déjà si inhumaine, un excès d'inhumanité, faire un grand effort concerté pour tenter d'enlever à la lutte une part de son atrocité.

Non seulement en politique, mais en bien d'autres domaines — celui, par exemple, de la religion — l'on connaît des propagandes quasi géniales par l'organisation, la finesse psychologique, la puissance.

Ne pouvait-on, ne peut-on s'inspirer de méthodes aussi parfaites, au bénéfice de la pitié, de la raison et de l'intérêt confondus?

En Espagne, présentement, les cas où la bête humaine se déchaîne, même nombreux, restent exceptionnels. C'est l'héroïsme qui est la règle, avec tout ce que comporte de par le sacrifice de soi. En l'honneur de cet héroïsme, l'on voudrait que les nations n'eussent qu'une voix pour crier à tout Espagnol, quel que soit son parti : « Souviens-toi d'être chevaleresque ! » Et que ce cri fût assez fort, assez répété aussi, pour pénétrer dans la profondeur des foules.

Rêverie romantique, est-ce-là? Nullement ! Les preuves abondent que l'on fait à peu près tout ce que l'on veut des multitudes, en sachant s'y prendre.

R. L.

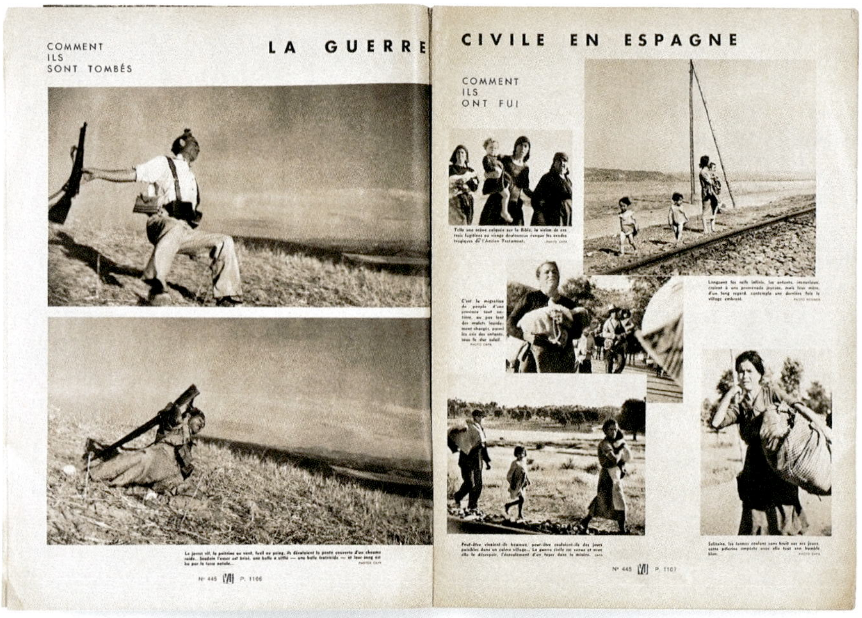

COMMENT
ILS
SONT TOMBÉS

LA GUERRE CIVILE EN ESPAGNE

COMMENT
ILS
ONT FUI

N° 445 VU P. 1106

N° 445 VU P. 1107

change his name to Robert Capa – a man whose work was in fact not at all limited to war photography, even if it was primarily his war reports that carried him to fame.

These were restless times politically. Spain was caught up in civil war since July 1936. An alliance of right-wing generals, large landowners, nobles, and the Catholic Church had risen up against the elected popular-front government. Political upheaval was also threatening France, with workers on strike since May to force the leftist government under Léon Blum to undertake social reform. Precisely where Capa stood politically is unknown, but a picture published in the left-oriented illustrated *Vu* from 3 June 1936 testifies to his interest in the workers' strike. Similarly, during the Spanish Civil War we can identify at least a modicum of sympathy for the Left in Capa, who had been inspired by Karl Korsch and his ideals of a people's front in Berlin. What in any case is certain is that in early August, Capa and his long-term companion Gerda Taro set out for Spain to document the two-week-old conflict from the perspective of the Anarcho-Syndicalists. Capa photographed in Barcelona and on the Aragón front, then went on to the Huesca front, until he finally arrived at Córdoba, where he took the picture that would be his most famous.

The *Spanish Loyalist* initially appeared in *Vu*, No. 445, on 23 September 1936. The picture occupies the upper left half of a double-page spread entitled "La Guerre Civile en Espagne."

"La Guerre Civile en Espagne." A feature in the French magazine Vu, *No. 445, 23 September 1936.*

Responsible for the layout was Alex Liberman, later art director of the American *Vogue*, who thus was the first to recognize the visual power of the photograph. Under the picture, Liberman also placed a variant, thus conveying the rhythm of a film to the sequence of images – although close observation indicates that there are really two protagonists depicted here. There is no reference to place, time, or even the names of the dead. The caption remains general in content, speaking in pathos-filled tones about the whistle of a bullet and blood being drunk by the native soil. The next to publish the picture was *Life*, in its issue from 12 July 1937. Under the heading "Death in Spain," the magazine marked the first anniversary of the beginning of the war and spoke of the victims – *Life* reported half a million lives had been lost. The article opened with Capa's photograph in large format, although slightly cropped on the right. Two days later, the Communist magazine *Regards*, which had already published several of Capa's reports, also published the photograph. Capa himself gave it a prominent position on the cover of his book *Death in the Making* (New York, 1938), along with other photographs he and Gerda Taro had taken in Spain. He still, however, absolved himself of the duty to provide data on the location, time, or circumstances of the picture.

Soon the photograph began to provoke questions; doubt as to its authenticity began to make the rounds. *Life* commented on the moment in which the solder is struck by a bullet in the head. But even a close examination of the picture fails to reveal a bullet wound anywhere on the body. One also might ask oneself how a man hit by a bullet while he is storming down an incline can fall backwards. Speculation also arose over the blossom-white uniform, hardly appropriate for the battle field. Furthermore, it is strange that Capa photographed the soldier from the front: wouldn't this necessarily imply that he had rushed ahead of the militiaman? On the other hand, there is just as much that argues against the thesis that Capa staged the photograph, including his very professionalism as a photographer. It hardly would have been necessary for him to have staged such a picture. And that one of the members of the Confederación National del Trabajo (CNT) should have stooped to act out his own death appears equally implausible. Nonetheless, in the course of several interviews, the British journalist O'Dowd Gallagher re-ignited the discussion over the credibility of the photograph in the 1970s when he declared that he had shared a hotel room with Capa near the French border at the time the photo was made, and that later, Loyalist soldiers staged useful photos for the press. Elsewhere, however, Gallagher speaks of Franco's troops in Loyalist uniforms who carried out the deception. But, as Richard Whelan points out, aside from the journalist's self-contradictory testimony, Capa as a Jew and a self-declared anti-fascist would have found it difficult to work together on a project with the Falangists.

The key picture of a longer sequence

Neither can the original negatives offer further information, for they have disappeared. Capa himself spoke about the picture only once, in an interview on 1 September 1937. According to a paraphrase by a journalist for the New York *World Telegram*, Capa and the militiaman had both been left behind by the troops: "Capa with his precious camera and the soldier with his rifle. The soldier was impatient. He wanted to get back to the Loyalist lines. Time and time again he climbed up and peered over the sandbags. Each time he would drop back at the warning rattle of machine-gun fire. Finally the soldier muttered something to the effect that he was going to take the long chance. He climbed out of the trench with Capa

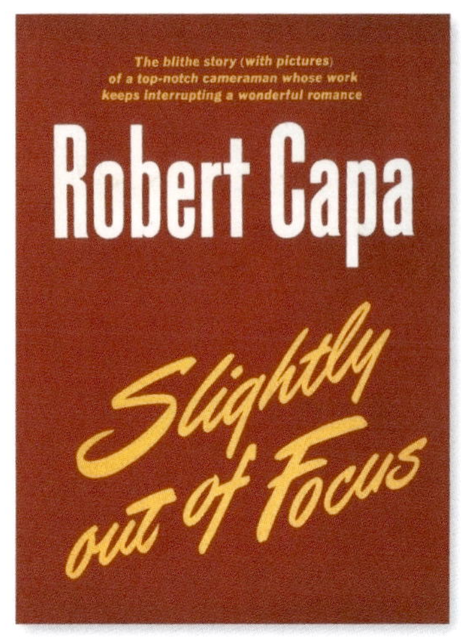

behind him. The machine-guns rattled, and Capa automatically snapped his camera, falling back beside the body of his companion. Two hours later, when it was dark and the guns were still, the photographer crept across the broken ground to safety. Later he discovered that he had taken one of the finest action shots of the Spanish war."

Was Capa really alone with the militiaman? His biographer Richard Whelan expresses doubts on this point. After all, the key picture is one of a larger sequence in which several pictures clearly depict both of the soldiers who were later killed – one in the midst of a momentarily care-free group of CNT militiamen, and another in a leap over a trench. Furthermore, in the battle our protagonist is clearly recognizable. But there is something else that is suspicious: the two photographs of a wounded and a falling soldier published in the *Vu* issue of 1936 must have been taken at approximately the same time, judging by the unchanged cloud formations. The perspective is also identical. Finally, the argument for the existence of two militiamen is supported by a more exact look at their clothing. One of the soldiers is wearing a white shirt and trousers; the other, a kind of worker's overall. On one soldier, the leather suspenders follow a straight line down to the trousers; the other soldier wears them crossed. "If one then looks closely at the ground in the *Falling Soldier* photograph and in the variant image," argues Richard Whelan in his biography of Capa, "and compares the configuration of prominently upstanding stalks, it becomes obvious that the two men are shown falling on almost precisely the same spot. (The *Falling Soldier* is about one foot closer to the photographer than is the man in the other picture.) We may well then ask why it is that although the two men fell within a short time of each other... in neither picture do we see the body of the other man on the ground."

The truth is the best picture

Neither Whelan nor Capa's younger brother Cornell, who administered the estate left by Capa after he was killed by a mine in 1954 in Indochina, have ever allowed a doubt to be raised about their belief in the truth of the documentary photograph. Furthermore, according to Whelan, it's "a great and powerful image... To insist upon knowing whether the photograph actually shows a man at the moment he has been hit by a bullet is both morbid and trivializing, for the picture's greatness ultimately lies in its symbolic implications, not in its literal accuracy as a report on the death of a particular man."

Whelan's biography of Capa was published in the USA in 1985. Exactly ten years later the amateur historian Mario Brotóns Jordá edited and self-published his memories of the Spanish Civil War under the title *Retazos de una época de inquietudes*. He initially recognized the leather bullet pouches in Capa's famous picture; these were only manufactured in this way in Alcoy, Spain, and were only carried by militiamen from Alcoy. Using clues in Capa's picture, Whelan dated the photograph to 5 September, believing it to have been taken in the region

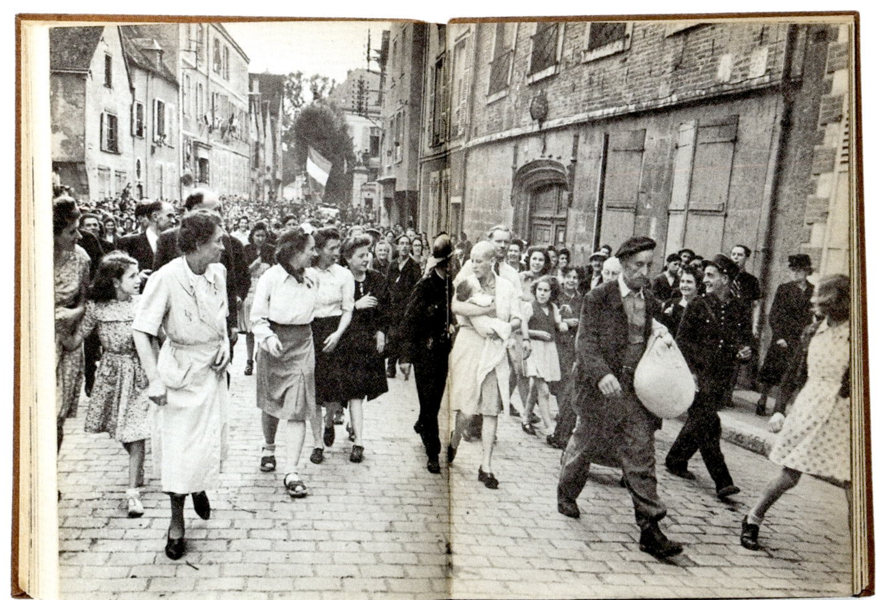

around Cerro Muriano. In actual fact, as Brotóns allegedly discovered in the state archive in Salamanca, only one militiaman from the Alcoy brigade fell on the Cordóba front near Cerro Muriano on 5 September 1936: Federico Borrell García. However, Mario Brotóns Jordá never visited the archive in Salamanca, as the historian Alex Kershaw proved in his book *Blood and Champagne* (2002). Did the newspaper *Stern* cheer too soon when it wrote that Capa's loyalist "really had fallen in battle", following Jordá's revelations? Even forensic experts such as Robert L. Franks, the chief homicide detective of the Memphis police force, were asked to examine the picture. Franks believed that the left hand pulled together as a fist was strong evidence that the militiaman was really dying: anyone who is simulating will try to cushion the fall with flat hands.

As Capa expressed it at the time in an interview with the *World Telegram*: "No tricks are necessary to take pictures in Spain. You don't have to pose your camera [i.e., pose your subjects]. The pictures are there, and you just take them. The truth is the best picture..."

Robert Capa's most important book – Slightly out of Focus *– appeared in 1947 in New York. A slender volume by today's standards, it nevertheless helped to cement Capa's reputation as a go-getter and globally active war photographer. Cover and double-page spread.*

Dorothea Lange
Migrant Mother, Nipomo, California
1936

Madonna for a Bitter Age

Stock market crash, economic crisis, and catastrophic drought in the southern states: with good reason the decade following 1929 came to be known in the USA as 'the bitter years'. It was during this period that Dorothea Lange made a portrait of a female migrant worker and her children, thereby creating an image that has established itself as a timeless metaphor for human suffering.

Her name is Florence Thompson; she is 32 years old, married, with no permanent address and seven children to feed. What would constitute no mean feat even in times of economic prosperity now threatens to bring the family to the brink of disaster during the Great Depression in the USA. Florence Thompson is one of the many migrant workers, as they came to be called during these dark times, who traversed the land seeking any work they could find. But it turns out that now, in March 1936, the pea harvest is once again poor, and that means no work – and therefore no income – for the pickers. Florence Thompson has found lodgings for the time being, in a camp for pea pickers in Nipomo, California. "Of the 2,500 people in this camp," noted Dorothea Lange; "most of them were destitute."

One of the most-cited pictorial images of our times

We know surprisingly much about the woman in the photograph, in part thanks to the comparatively precise information that the photographer provided on the back of at least the early prints. From another source we also know that one of the daughters (left in the picture) later made a futile attempt in court to stop the publication of the photograph. Furthermore, in 1983 there was a public appeal for contributions for Florence Thompson, ill with cancer. The 'bitter years', as they have been made real to us particularly in the works of

---

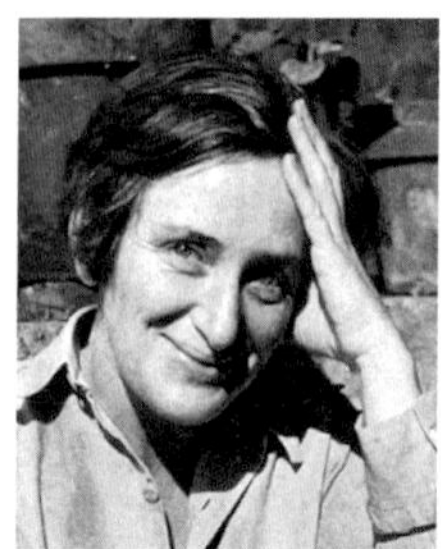

Dorothea Lange

*Born **1895** in Hoboken, New Jersey. **1913** drops out from high school and turns to photography. **1917** courses under Clarence H. White. **1919** opens a portrait studio in San Francisco. After **1930** turns to social topics. **1935** marries the social scientist Paul Schuster Taylor, who puts her in contact with the Resettlement Administration (from 1937 the FSA). Works for the organisation until **1939**. **1939** publication of* An American Exodus. ***1943–45** works for Office of War Information. **1955** participates in* The Family of Man *exhibition. Dies **1965** in San Francisco of cancer.*

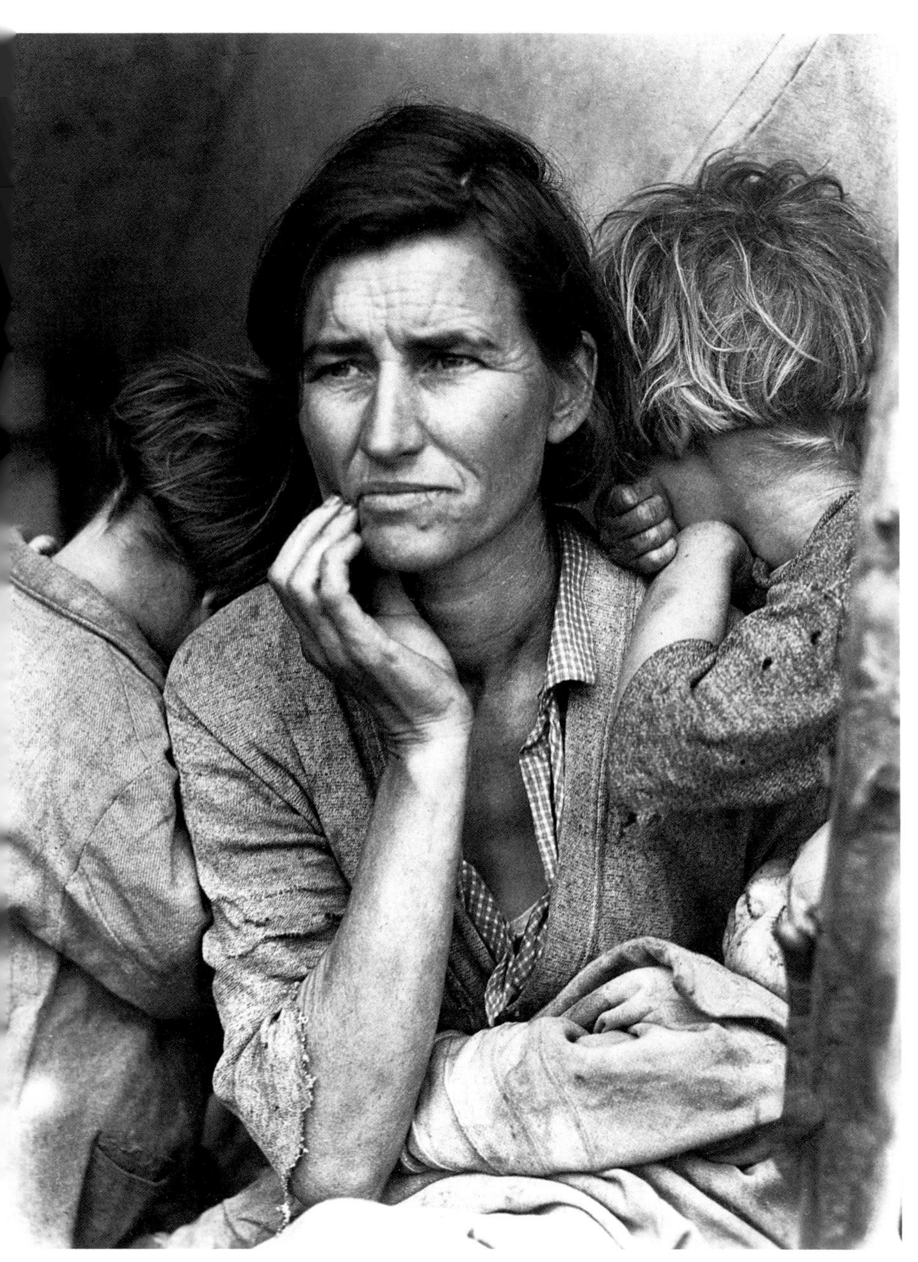

Migrant Mother, Nipomo, California, 1936

John Steinbeck and John Dos Passos, now lie well over a half a century in the past, and few people can recall the Great Depression from first-hand experience. The portrait of the young Florence Thompson, however – thin-lipped, care-worn, gazing emptily into the distance – is familiar to almost everyone. Since its appearance in *The Family of Man* exhibition (1955), conceived by Edward Steichen and viewed by more that nine million people around the world, the photograph has become a part of the collective memory. Originally designated in 1955 simply as "U.S.A: Dorothea Lange Farm Security Adm.," the photograph is now known as *Migrant Mother*, a much more gripping title that raises the concrete historical circumstances to a level of timeless contemplation. The picture, intended as a documentary, has understandably become one of the most-cited pictorial images of our century.

Through the years, there have been numerous attempts to subject *Migrant Mother* to art-historical analysis. Comparison has often been made to images, common since the Renaissance, of the Mother of God with the Christ Child. Other interpretations explain the success of the picture through its balanced composition, or refer to the: "dignity and essential decency of the woman facing poverty" (Denise Bethel), or to the picture's "simplicity of means, its restrained pathos, and its mute autonomy of language" (Robert Sobieszek). Whatever the reasons may be, what remains certain is that Dorothea Lange largely ignored all such theoretical motives when she took the photograph. As she herself once described her approach to her work: "Whatever I photograph, I do not molest or tamper with or arrange… I try to [make a] picture as part of its surroundings, as having roots… Third - a sense of time… I try to show [it] as having its position in the past or in the present…" Ironically, the framing actually chosen by Lange here is so narrow that the tent in the background is not even recognizable. Furthermore, the image is fairly indefinite temporally: only with difficulty can one conclude – based on the children's haircuts – that the picture dates from the 1930s. As far as setting up a ‚scene' is concerned – or rather, the attempt to avoid doing this – we know that Lange approached the family slowly, taking pictures all the while, thus giving the family members the chance to pose themselves. In fact, in the initial photographs, the children are looking into the camera; only in the

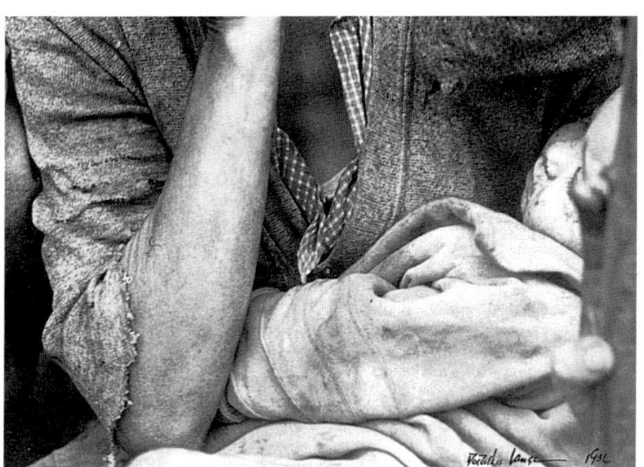

Close-up of Migrant Mother*: a thumb is clearly visible on this print (right edge of the picture). It seems to have bothered the photographer, for later she removed it from the negative.*

final photo of the sequence do they turn away, thus demonstrating their condition as social outsiders that Lange had first documented in 1933 with her photograph *The White Angel Breadline*.

Making human suffering into an aesthetic object

A further modest but important detail is often overlooked in the discussion of Dorothea Lange's *Migrant Mother*: namely, the thumb that appears in the lower right of the picture and that remains vaguely recognizable even in the retouched version. Dorothy Lange retrieved the picture from the archives of the Farm Security Administration approximately two years after it had been shot, which is to say in 1938. In an action that remains controversial to this day – and one which elicited furious protest especially from Roy Stryker, Lange's immediate superior at the FSA – Lange eliminated the image of the thumb, whose owner remains only a matter for speculation, although it may belong to Florence Thompson herself. Whatever the case may have been, the incident illustrates Lange's ambivalent understanding of 'documentary', which for her implied not merely demonstrating, but also convincing; that is, in addition to the simple registration of reality, her concept also includes moving the observers – in a double sense, for Florence Thompson is supposed to have in fact thanked her survival to the published picture.

In other words, Dorothea Lange was seeking visual evidence, but also quite consciously a suggestive image. In making human suffering into an aesthetic object, the photographer discovered a way of stimulating attention, interest, and sympathy in a world saturated with optical images. As once formulated by John R. Lane, she carried "the concept of documentary photography far beyond the purely pragmatic domain of record-making." Lange's *Migrant Mother* exemplifies precisely this understanding, and probably for this reason it became the single best-known motif of the FSA campaign. The visible thumb, however, would have spoilt the overall composition, and invested the photograph with an unintentional humor – the reason why Lange broke with her own principles to remove it.

When Dorothea Lange took the picture in 1936, she was forty years old, a committed photographer, and herself the mother of two children. Divorced from her first husband, the painter Maynard Dixon, she had now been married for a year to the sociologist Paul Schuster Taylor. Born in Hoboken, New Jersey, Lange had quit school at age eighteen more or less on the spur of the moment, in order to devote herself to photography. She studied first under Arnold Genthe and afterward with the no-less-renowned Clarence H. White. In the years following 1900, Pictorialism was still at its zenith – a school of art photography which pursued the model provided by painting, and of which Clarence White (described by Lange as extremely helpful and inspiring) was one of its leading representatives. Lange's early photographs, insofar as any have survived, still reveal overtones of the pictorial approach, although, as stressed by Sandra S. Phillips Lange encompassed a social interest that reached beyond the formal principles of the pictorial approach. At age seven, Lange suffered from polio, which resulted in a deformity of her right leg, and five years later her father abandoned the family. Thus, concludes Phillips, "[Lange's] great ability to identify with the outsider was shaped by these two emotionally shattering events, disability and desertion."

An eye focussed on the social realities

Intending to widen her horizon, Lange set off on a world tour in 1918, but she and her friend got no further than San Francisco before being robbed of their savings. So Lange took a job in the photographic department of a drugstore to supply the funds necessary for survival. The following year, Lange established herself in the city with her own photographic studio, which she maintained until 1934. The collapse of the New York stock market in 1929 and the ensuing economic crisis caused a professional break in a double sense for Lange, who by then had long been a successful portraitist. On the one hand, there were now fewer customers who could afford a studio portrait, and on the other hand, especially in the agricultural American South, the unemployed, the homeless, and the migrant workers increasingly became a part of the street scene. This was the phenomenon that Lange captured with her camera: her view of the down-and-out and needy waiting in front of a soup kitchen set up by a wealthy woman, known under the title of *The White Angel Breadline*, stands as the turning point in her photographic œuvre. From that time on, it was the social realities in an increasingly industrial America that dominated her artistic work.

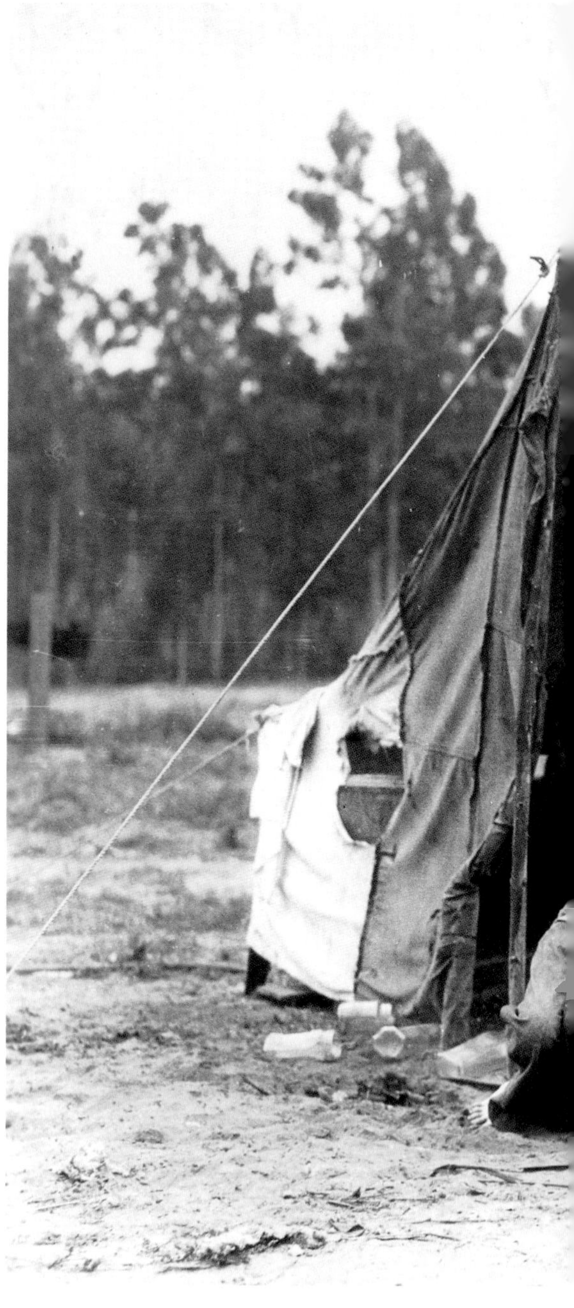

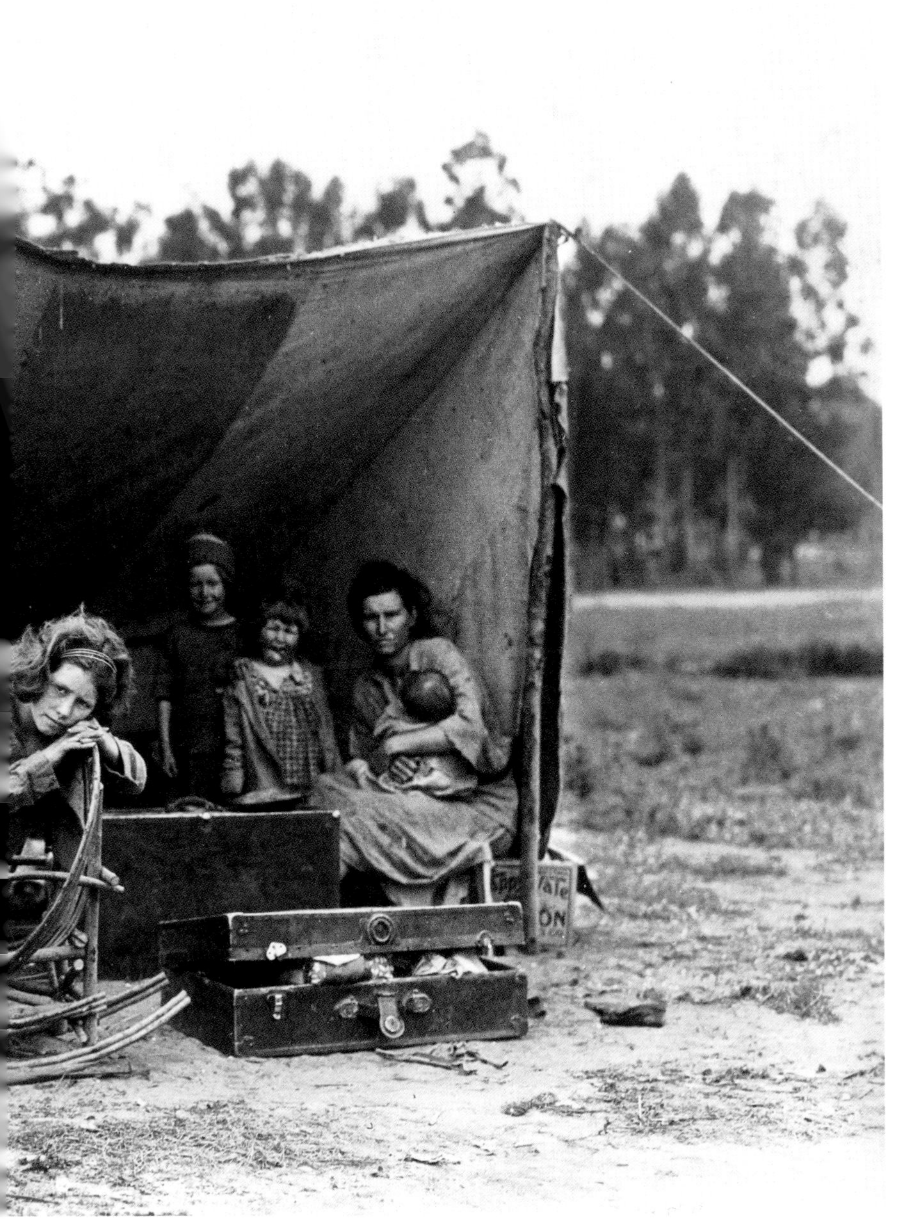

Migrant Mother, Nipomo, California, 1936

The Crash of 1929 had hit agriculture in the American South perhaps even harder than industry. The prices for farm products had been declining since the early 1920s, and increasing mechanization had brought unemployment to thousands of farm laborers. On top of this came the droughts that transformed once-rich farmland into deserts. According to one official estimate, in 1936 approximately six hundred and fifty thousand farmers were attempting to wring a living from almost two hundred and fifty million acres of parched and leached-out land. *A Record of Human Erosion*, the subtitle of Dorothea Lange's most important book (1939) thus bears a double meaning.

The end of a long, hard winter

Franklin D. Roosevelt's New Deal aimed at consolidating the economy, industry, and agriculture. A great variety of state measures – which admittedly first had to be pushed through Congress – finally resulted in an unparalleled state-controlled relief program. The Historical Section of the Resettlement Administration (RA; known as the Farm Security Administration after 1937) was created to propagandize the new initiative, as it were. Headed by Roy Stryker, the chief task of the Section was to document the disastrous situation in rural America. Photographers such as Ben Shan, Walker Evans, Carl Mydans, Arthur Rothstein, Russell Lee, and Jack Delano were hired for this purpose. Dorothea Lange joined the group in 1935, but left four years later after disagreements with Roy Stryker. In total the FSA bequeathed around 170,000 negatives and 70,000 original prints to posterity.

Even before starting her work for the FSA, Dorothea Lange was already actively photographing in southern California. Her husband, Paul Taylor, had been assigned by the State Emergency Administration (SERA) to investigate the situation of needy migrants in California, and his wife accompanied him to the pea harvest in Nipomo. In other words, the photographer was already familiar with the camp in which a year later, in March 1936, she would take her most famous photograph. In was the end of a long, hard, winter, she recalled – and simultaneously the conclusion of several weeks of working with the camera. She was on her way back home in the car. It was raining. A sign on the side of the road announced the camp of the pea harvesters. But, according to Lange: "I didn't want to remember that I had seen it." She drove past, but could not put it out of her mind. Suddenly, approximately twenty miles later, she turned the car around:

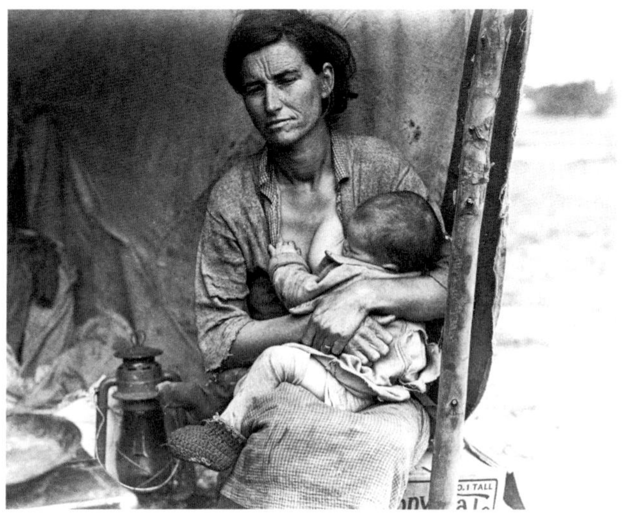

"I was following instinct, not reason." She drove back to the rain-soaked camp, parked her car, and got out. Already from the distance she saw the woman, a "hungry and desperate mother," an apparition that drew her like a magnet. "I do not remember," said Lange later in a conversation with Roy Stryker, "how I explained my presence or my camera to her, but I do remember she asked no questions. I took five shots, coming ever closer. I did not ask her name or history. She told me her age, that she was thirty-two. She said that they had been living on frozen vegetables from the surrounding fields, and birds that the children killed. She had just sold the tires from her car to buy food. There she sat in that lean-to tent with her children huddled around her, and seemed to know that my pictures might help her, and so she helped me."

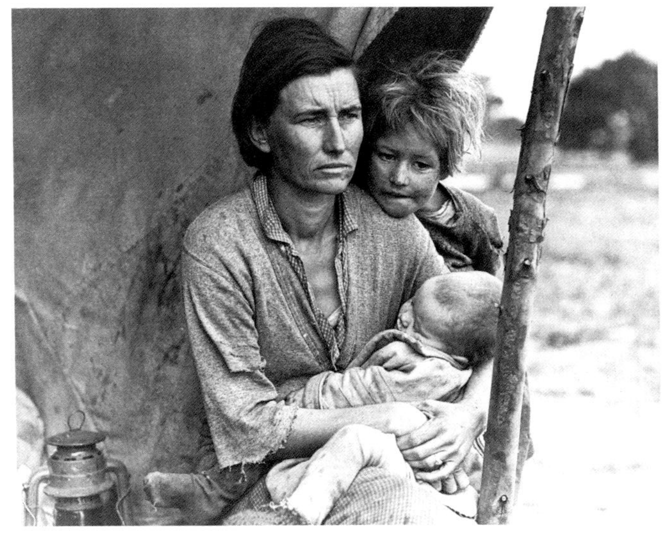

As early as 6 March 1936, two versions from the series appeared in the *San Francisco News* – and in response the federal government immediately ordered food to be sent to the affected region. The key image itself was first published in *Survey Magazine* in September 1936, and was included in an exhibition of outstanding photographic achievement organized by the magazine *U.S. Camera* in the same year. Dorothea Lange therefore understood full well the suggestive power of this modern Madonna. That the picture some day would be treated as an art object, however, was hardly foreseeable: the most spectacular, if not the first, auction of an early (unretouched) print of *Migrant Mother* took place in 1998 at Sotheby's in New York, where the Paul Getty Museum in Malibu, California, bid $244,500 for this 13½ × 10½ inch (34.3 × 26.7 cm) vintage print.

Pages 206–207: **Dorothea Lange:** Migrant Mother, Nipomo, California. *Here the situation as a whole. According to her statements, the photographer took a total of five exposures.*

Left: **Dorothea Lange:** Migrant Mother: *a lesser-known version of the key portrait.*

Above: *A further variant of Lange's image. It's clear just how she resolutely approached the family with her camera.*

Sam Shere
Lakehurst, New Jersey, USA
1937

A Legend in Flames

It was the end of a dream. The pride of the German Zeppelin fleet was not the only thing that went up in flames on 6 May 1937. The idea of the Zeppelin as a whole was cast into question. Not least because there were shocking pictures. Images that contrasted the proud vision of flying in comfort with pure apocalypse. Undoubtedly the most spectacular photo was taken by the American reporter Sam Shere. His shot of the end of the LZ 129 *Hindenburg* also represents an early example of disaster reporting immediately after the event.

To be able to fly is one of humankind's age-old fantasies. To become light. Weightless. To possess the capacity to take off from the ground and leave this "vale of tears" far below. As long ago as Greek antiquity, the dream of flying was lent wings in the shape of Daedalus and Icarus. When Icarus flew too close to the sun, the heat melted the wax of his home-made wings and he plummeted to earth. Since then, falling out of the sky has been an inseparable part of the vision. For if flying remains the dream, falling remains the ultimate nightmare. It is no coincidence that air travel disasters fascinate more than any other civil catastrophe. Which may be connected with the fact that the height of the fall from such a shattered fantasy is – quite literally – so great and so conspicuous. From Albrecht Berblinger, the legendary "flying tailor of Ulm," to the crew of the American Challenger space shuttle that exploded in the stratosphere, failed flights are part of the global inventory of tragedies that are narrated, described and discussed again and again. They haunt our thoughts. Stimulate our imagination. Pursue us deep into the night. Why? Because vision and failure, flight and fall are nowhere more dramatically held up to the light than in aviation.

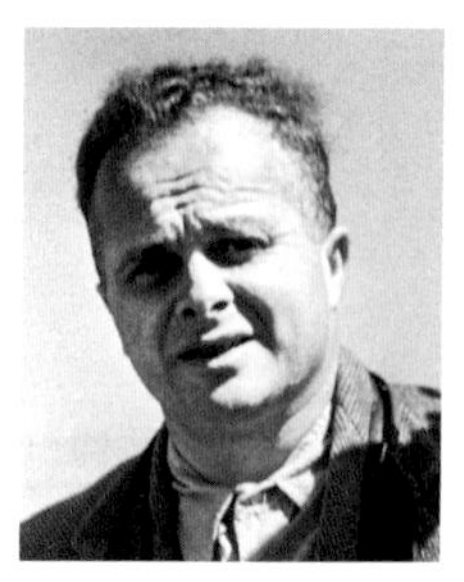

Sam Shere
*Born **1904** in Belarus. Emigrates to the USA, where he works for the Hearst Corporation. War correspondent for* Life *during the Second World War. His later photography is primarily concerned with everyday life in America. Dies **1982**.*

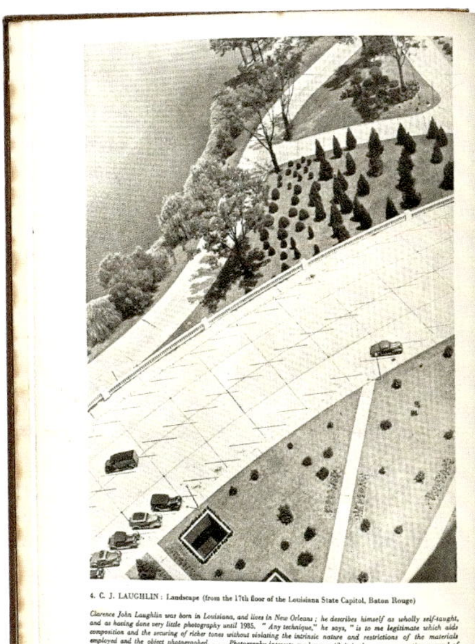

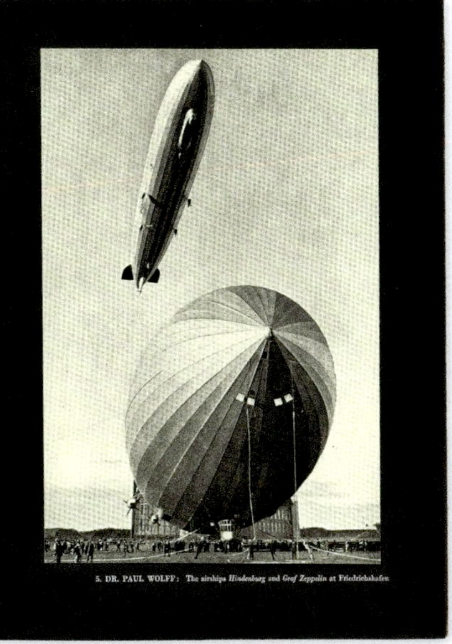

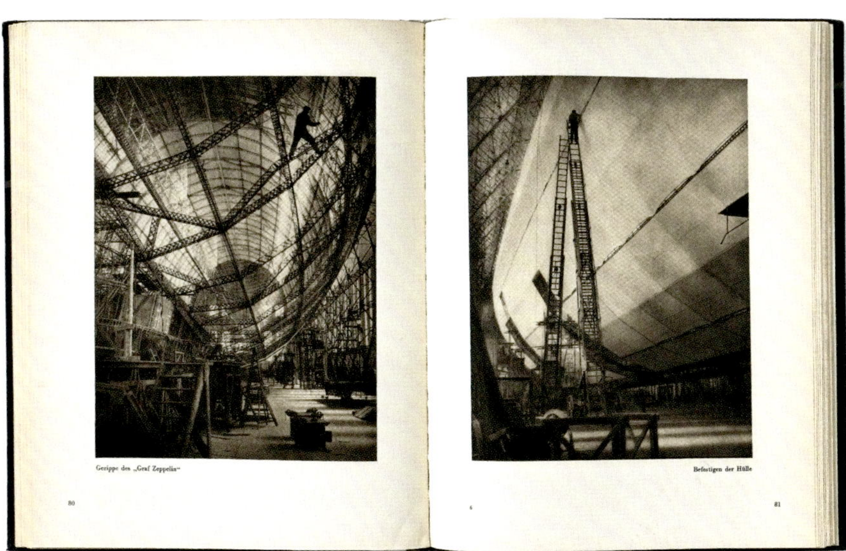

The Zeppelin legend: Paul Wolff: The Airships Hindenburg and Graf Zeppelin at Friedrichshafen, *in* Modern Photography, *1937/38 (top right). Emil Otto Hoppé:* Skeleton of the Graf Zeppelin *and* Attaching the Hull, *in* Deutsche Arbeit, *Berlin 1930 (above).*

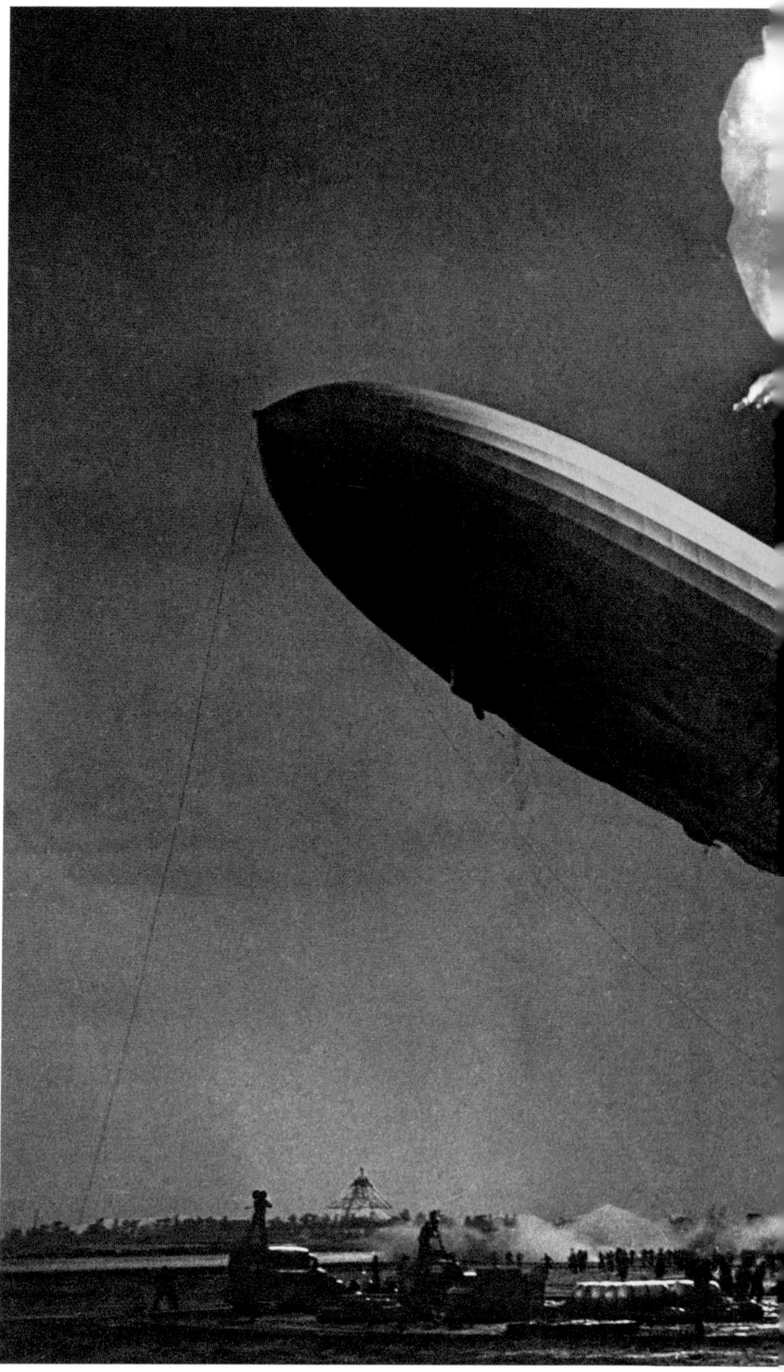

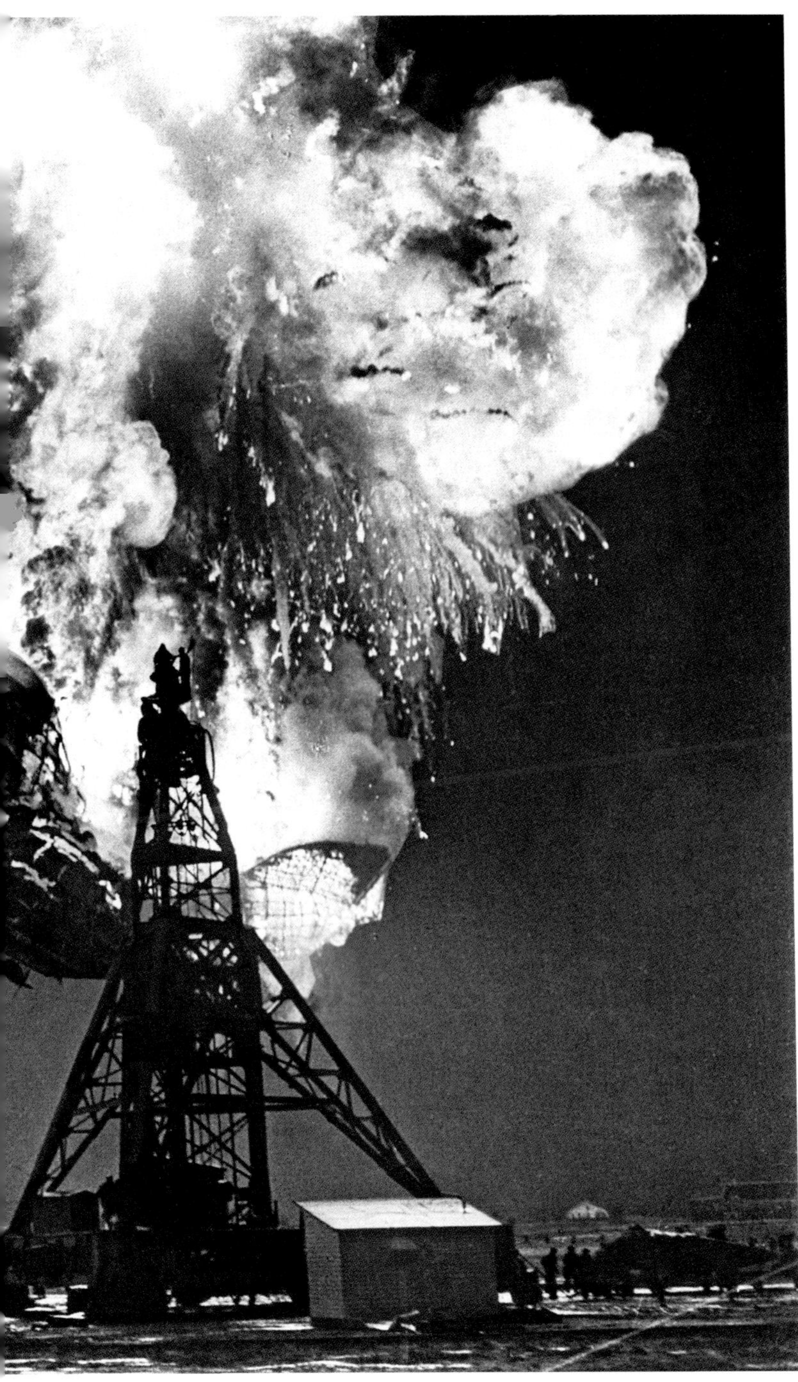

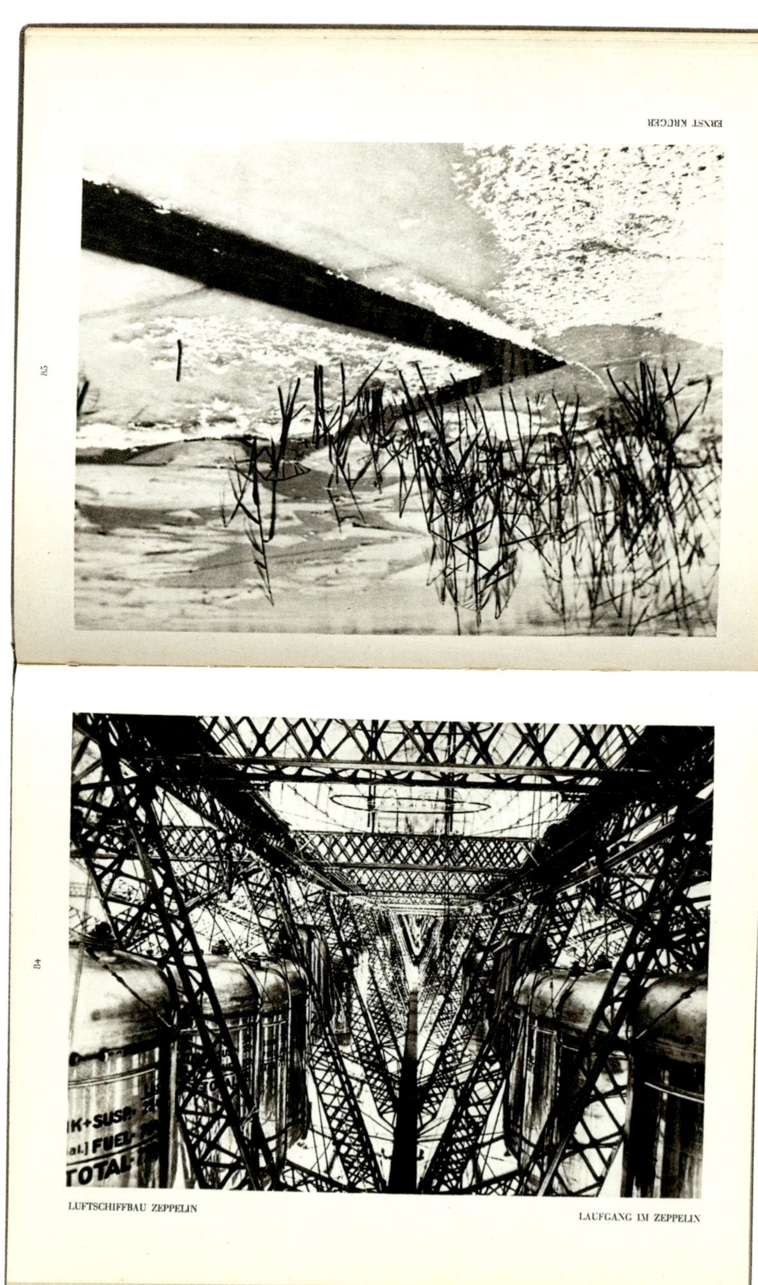
ERNST KRUGER
85
84
LUFTSCHIFFBAU ZEPPELIN
LAUFGANG IM ZEPPELIN
TOTAL
FUEL

Luxury and propaganda

Lakehurst, New Jersey, 6 May 1937. It's late afternoon and the weather anything but clement. A heavy downpour at 6 o'clock had already made it impossible for the airship LZ 129 *Hindenburg* to land first time. But conditions were improving; the wind had dropped and the barometer was rising. A crowd had gathered at the landing site. Marines and civilian helpers, newspaper reporters and radio journalists, including the young, later celebrated Herbert Morrison, a journalist working for the WLS radio station in Chicago. Just to remind ourselves: in 1937, the era of mass air travel remained a long way off. Transatlantic flights were still a major event, especially when in the form of a vast and regal airship. And so the arrival of an airship such as the *Hindenburg* attracted plenty of media coverage. "Well, here it comes, ladies and gentlemen," Morrison began his radio report. "And what a great sight it is, a thrilling one, just a marvelous sight. It's coming down out of the sky, pointed directly towards us and toward the mooring mast. The mighty diesel motors just roared, the propellers biting into the air and throwing it back into a gale-like whirlpool. No wonder this great floating palace can travel through the air at such a speed, with these powerful motors behind it. Now and then the propellers are caught in the rays of sun, their highly polished surfaces reflect. The sun is striking the windows of the observation deck on the eastward side and sparkling like glittering jewels on the background of black velvet."

There was something that Morrison overlooked. Or did he simply think it insufficiently important to be worth mentioning? The *Hindenburg*'s tailfins were painted with huge swastikas that were impossible to miss. The airship was of course first and foremost a magnificent feat of engineering. But it was also the instrument of a well-oiled propaganda machine. Spreading propaganda for Nazi Germany. And propaganda for the megalomania of a system that, two and a half years later, would declare war on the rest of the world. The National Socialists seized upon Count Zeppelin's invention at an early stage. It was they who made the construction of the *Hindenburg* financially possible and, following its baptism in 1936, used it for overtly political purposes. As soon as it was commissioned, the *Hindenburg* was used to drop leaflets over Germany's major cities. During the 1936 Olympic Games, the *Hindenburg* floated impressively in the skies over Berlin. Nor was the largest airship ever built absent from the Nazi rally in Nuremberg. The LZ 129 was indeed the biggest airship of all time and the pride of the German Zeppelin Transport Company. With a length of 245 meters (804 feet), the *Hindenburg* was no less than twice as long as the very first airship commissioned in 1900. The cigar-shaped body had a diameter of 41.2 meters (135 feet) and a tare weight of no less than 118 tons. The Hindenburg was powered by four specially developed Daimler-Benz diesel engines with a capacity of 1,000 hp each. The airship was able to achieve a maximum speed of 125 km/h (76 mph) and had a range of 16,000 kilometers (10,000 miles). It held compartments and tanks for 11 tons of post, freight and luggage, 88,000 liters (19,350 gallons) of diesel and 40,000 liters (8,800 gallons) of water.

Zeppelin Airship: Gangway
Inside a Zeppelin, *in* Das Deutsche Lichtbild, *1937 (bottom).*

The superlative reputation of the *Hindenburg* went before it, even if its standards of luxury could not match those of classic transatlantic steamers. The two passenger decks integrated at the rear of the ship nevertheless offered a considerable degree of comfort. There were showers, a bar, and a smoking saloon. Music-lovers were entertained by a Blüthner grand piano, and the dining menus with their accompanying fine wines must similarly have helped the trip across the Atlantic, which on average took sixty hours, pass pleasantly.

On that 6 May 1937, 97 people were on board the *Hindenburg*. The list of passengers included, amongst others, a tea merchant, a photographer, two stockbrokers, an arms manufacturer, a sales agent, several members of the military, an acrobat, and an heiress. Shortly after 7 p.m., and despite a light drizzle, the decision was taken to land. People waved from the promenade deck as, in the landing area below, 231 ground staff were busy fastening the mooring ropes and pulling the airship towards the mooring mast. Helmut Lau would be the first to hear it: a muffled hissing, like the burner of a gas stove being turned on. Fire, an explosion. A moment later the stern of the LZ 129 *Hindenburg* burst into flames. An inferno that would ultimately claim the lives of 36 people. Looking back, it is a miracle that anyone at all survived the crash. But what triggered the catastrophe? Experts continue to argue over its cause even today. A faulty hydrogen tank, say some. The problematic chemical composition of the coating on the outer skin, say others. One thing is certain: the *Hindenburg* catastrophe is one of the legendary disasters of the 20th century, comparable with the sinking of the *Titanic*.

But in contrast to the loss of the *Titanic* far out at sea, the end of the *Hindenburg* is well documented in reports and images. For one thing, there was Herb Morrison's dramatic radio broadcast. And for another, there were the photographs by Sam Shere, who captured the decisive moments as the airship was engulfed by fire. No less than thirty journalists, including twenty-two cameramen, watched the *Hindenburg* disaster unfold. But it would be the images by Shere, who was working for the Keystone agency, that traveled around the world in the days that followed and which continue to shape our mental picture of the disaster even now. A specially chartered plane flew the material straight to Europe, where Shere's pictures appeared on the front covers of French newspapers on 12 May. From the point of view of media history, this was the start of the coverage of disasters as soon as possible after the event. With regards to the history of the Zeppelin, it meant the abandoning of plans for an international fleet of airships. The LZ 129 *Hindenburg* had completed 63 flights and 37 transatlantic crossings within just two years. It had traveled more than 300,000 kilometers (186,420 miles) and thereby carried over 3,000 passengers. But Lakehurst spelled the end of all such high-flying projects. In hindsight, the explosion of the *Hindenburg* may also be interpreted as a warning to its political sponsors: almost eight years to the day after the Lakehurst disaster, the Second World War ended. And with it the apocalyptic megalomania of Nazi Germany.

Top: *Paul Wolff's best-selling manual on photography would have been incomplete without a picture of a Zeppelin:* Zeppelin Landing at Frankfurt Airport, *in* Meine Erfahrungen mit der Leica, *Frankfurt am Main 1934 (right-hand page).*

Bottom: *Lotte Reichmann:* Untitled, *in* Das Deutsche Lichtbild, *1935 (right-hand page).*

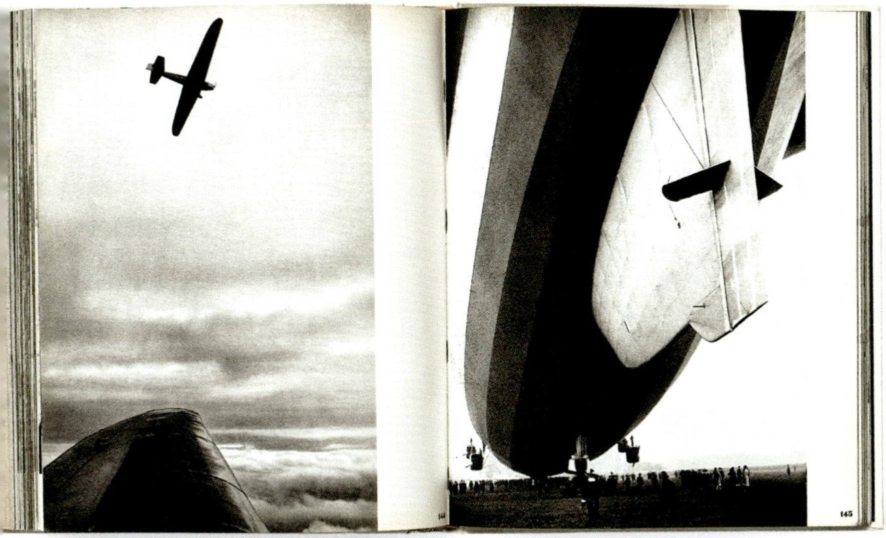

144

145

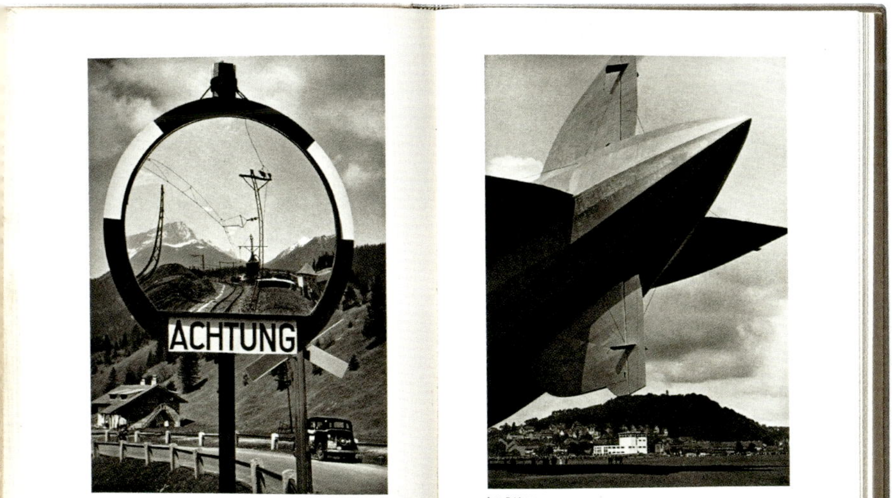

ACHTUNG

Hans Nordhoff

78

Lotte Reichmann

79

Horst P. Horst
Mainbocher Corset
1939

Eros Reined In

In August 1939, on the eve of the Second World War, Horst P. Horst took his famous photograph of the Mainbocher Corset in the Paris Vogue studios on the Champs-Elysées. The picture, which marked the end of his work for some time, later became his most cited fashion photograph.

There's no question: it's a "great silent picture," to borrow the expression of the media scholar Norbert Bolz – a picture that literally lends form and, by means of photography, permanence to the beautiful phantasm of fashion. Many consider the photograph to be Horst P. Horst's best work – an opinion that the photographer himself would probably agree with, for otherwise, how is one to explain that he chose the motif almost as a matter of course for the cover of his autobiography *Horst: His Work and His World*? Timeless beauty, balance, an interplay of modesty and charm, eros and humility, provocation and subtle elegance are simultaneously at play in the photograph, not to mention the flattering light and dramatic shadows. After all, wasn't the photographer called a master of dramatic lighting?

Horst P. Horst photographed his *Mainbocher Corset* in the studios of the Paris *Vogue* in 1939. Only a few years earlier, Martin Munkácsi had let a model in light summer clothing and bathing shoes run along the dunes of a beach – freedom, adventure, summertime, sun, air, movement, sporty femininity – all caught by a photographic technique schooled in photojournalism. Munkácsi's picture, first published in the December 1935 issue of *Harper's Bazaar*, caused a sensation. Its carefree dynamism marks, as it were, the opposite pole to the aesthetics of Horst – who was, after all, a man of the studio – and of well thought-out staging, in which light was more than a mere necessity to call an object forth from darkness. With Horst, there were always settings, constructions, parts of an architecture built for the moment. Munkácsi

---

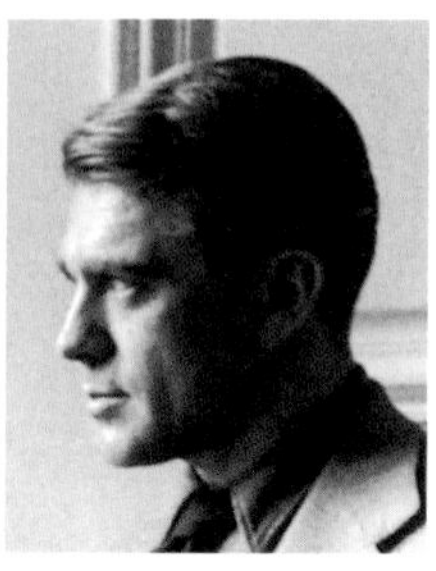

Horst P. Horst
*Born **1906** in Weissenfels, Germany, as Horst Paul Albert Bohrmann. Studies at the Hamburg School of Commercial Arts. **1930** moves to Paris. Internship under Le Corbusier. Makes the acquaintance of Hoyningen-Huene. **1931** first shots for French, **1932** American* Vogue. ***1939** moves to the USA. **1943** American citizenship. **1951** closure of the* Vogue *studios, followed by opening of own studio. Intensive work for* House and Garden. ***1961** photo series on the lifestyle of international high society. Dies **1999** on Long Island.*

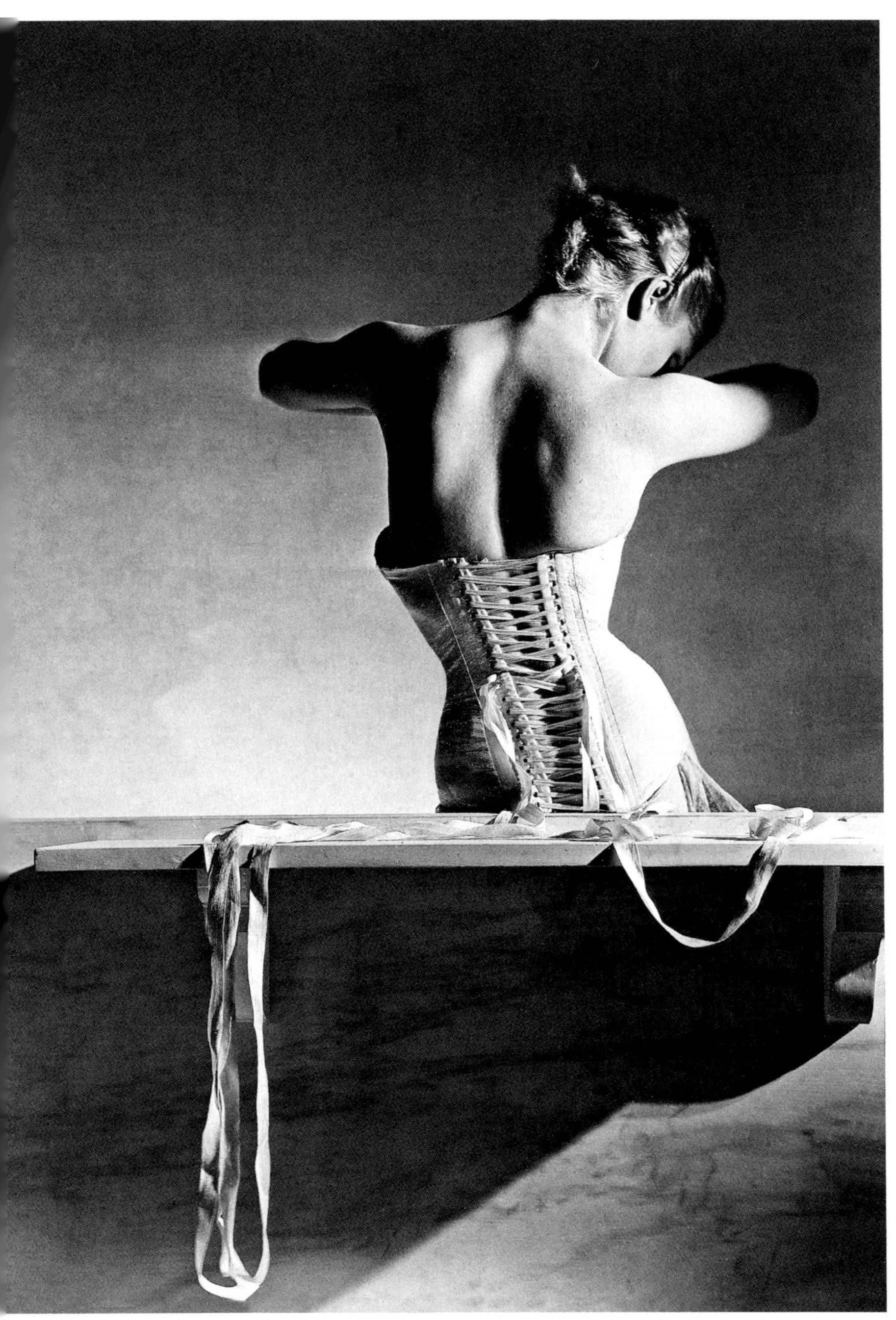

Mainbocher Corset, 1939

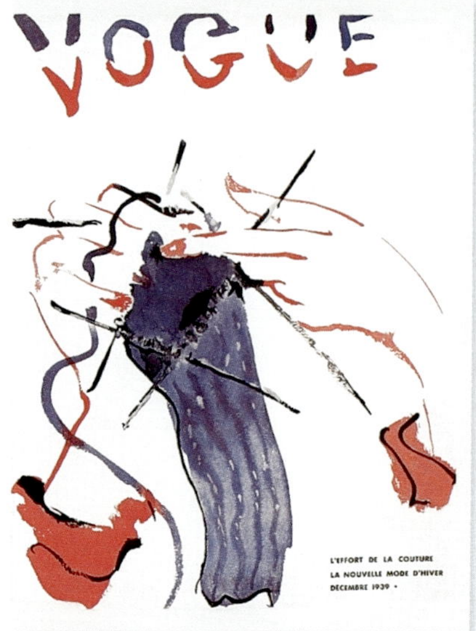

photographed with a medium-sized camera from his hand, and the photographer moved to keep up with the moving object. Horst in contrast favored the large camera mounted on a stand and a focusing screen that allowed him to calculate his photograph down to the last detail. In other words, Horst sought to produce elegance as the outgrowth of intuition and hard work. How long did he pull at the bands, turn and twirl them, until they arrived at the right balance on an imaginary scale between insignificance and the determining factor in the picture! Roland Barthes, the great French philosopher, structuralist, and prognosticator of photography, might well have discovered his 'punctum' precisely here, that is, the apparently insignificant detail of a photograph that gives the picture its fascination and charm, and ultimately what awakens our interest. Horst P. Horst would probably have described the effect differently. Occasionally he spoke of "a little mess" that he carefully incorporated into his pictures. In later years, when he photographed the interiors of rich and prominent Americans for *House and Garden*, this 'point' might be a not-quite-fresh bouquet of flowers, or pillows on the sofa that suggested that someone had already been comfortably seated there. Or, as rumor once had it, a full ashtray – but one searches his pictures futilely for anything of the sort: even the planned accident had its limits in the productions of a Horst.

Representative of both the old and the new age

Horst P. Horst – his real name was Horst Paul Albert Bohrmann – had initially come to Paris in 1930 to work voluntarily for Le Corbusier. In fact Horst developed into the super-aesthete among the fashion photographers of the age. He seized the artistic tendencies of those years, amalgamated them into a new aesthetic rooted in traditional ideals, and thereby provided an orientation in taste for an age that was flagrantly questioning tradition across international borders. Born in 1906 in Weissenfels on the Saale River in Germany, Horst studied briefly in Hamburg at the School of Commercial Arts before migrating to the Seine, where the young, blond, handsome photographer soon felt himself at home. Significantly, it was not the impoverished bohemia of exiled Hungarians, Russians, or avant-gardists such as Man Ray that appealed to Horst; instead, he sought his friends among the high bourgeoisie with an interest

---

Above: *Cover of the French edition of* Vogue, *December 1939 issue.*

Right: *Double-page spread from the French edition of* Vogue, *December 1939. Due to the War, neither the October nor the November issues appeared. Consequently, the unpublished pages (including the one with Horst's* Mainbocher Corset*) were offered in reduced format in the last issue of the year.*

in art, or among precisely those commercial artists who were especially successful in fashion and fashion publicity. The Baltic Baron von Hoyningen-Huene, already one of the great fashion photographers of his time, became a particularly important and influential friend to Horst. The younger photographer, well built but somewhat short, often stood as model for Hoyningen-Huene, and thus gradually established a foothold in fashion photography for himself. Unmistakable in Horst's early pictures are the influences of Hoyningen-Huene's typically polished approach to photography, oriented on geometric Art Deco principles. In addition, Horst was also clearly influenced by the photography of the Bauhaus, whose principles he often consciously adopted – without attempting to explore the limits of the medium, however, as did an artist like Moholy-Nagy, for example. Horst furthermore admired Greece and the classical world, an interest that he shared in turn with Herbert List, and was also open to the Surrealists, without really becoming one. He always photographed 'straight', thus placing himself in the ranks of those who had overcome 'applied' Pictorialism, such as was cultivated by Baron de Meyer or the early Stieglitz. Paradoxically, Horst was a representative of both the old and the new age.

Horst's work was first published at the beginning of the 1930s in the French *Vogue*. Later he devoted a book to the decade, which one can justly call his most creative period: Salute to the Thirties. Published in 1971 with photographs of both Horst and Hoyningen-Huene, the book oddly does not include the *Mainbocher Corset*. On the other hand, the volume does includes a sensitive foreword by Janet Flanner, in which the legendary Paris correspondent of the New Yorker described once more the atmosphere that came to an end with the Second World War. Horst had photographed his famous study on the very eve of the coming catastrophe. "It was the last photograph I took in Paris before the war," he later recalled, "I left the studio

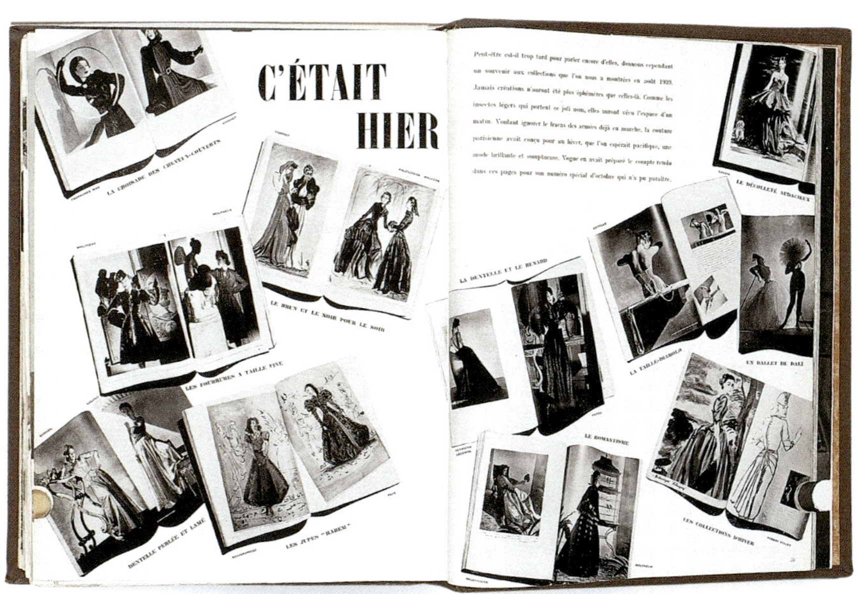

C'ÉTAIT HIER

Peut-être est-il trop tard pour parler encore d'elles, donnons cependant un souvenir aux collections que l'on nous a montrées en août 1939. Jamais créations n'auront été plus éphémères que celles-là. Comme les insectes légers qui portent ce joli nom, elles auront vécu l'espace d'un matin. Voulant ignorer le fracas des armées déjà en marche, la couture parisienne avait conçu pour un hiver, que l'on espérait pacifique, une mode brillante et somptueuse. Vogue en avait préparé le compte rendu dans ces pages pour son numéro spécial d'octobre qui n'a pu paraître.

***Mainbocher Corset*, 1939**

at 4:00 a.m., went back to the house, picked up my bags and caught the 7.00 a.m. train to Le Havre to board the *Normandie*. We all felt that war was coming. Too much armament, too much talk. And you knew that whatever happened, life would be completely different after. I had found a family in Paris, and a way of life. The clothes, the books, the apartment, everything left behind. I had left Germany, Heune had left Russia, and now we experienced the same kind of loss all over again. This photograph is peculiar – for me, it is the essence of that moment. While I was taking it, I was thinking of all that I was leaving behind."

Highlights and deep shadows

Horst remained the classicist among photographers. Women, he once said, he photographed like goddesses: "almost unattainable, slightly statuesque, and in Olympian peace." Stage-like settings along with all kinds of props and accessories emphasize his affinity to the classical world – although under Horst's direction, plaster might mutate into marble and pinchbeck into gold. In his best pictures, he limited himself to a few details. In our present case, a balustrade suggesting marble skillfully turns the rear view of the semi-nude into a torso. In addition, it is the light – the direction from which it falls, forming highlights and deep shadows – that gives the photograph the desired drama. "Lighting," Horst once admitted, "is more complex than one thinks. There appears to be only one source of light. But there were actually reflectors and other spotlights. I really don't know how I did it. I would not be able to repeat it." The rear view of the nude clearly looks back to the great French achievements in art – we need only think of Ingres or, later, Degas, or the nineteenth-century photographic nudes of Moulin, Braquehais, or Vallou de Villeneuve, not to mention the ancient models. Horst, however, ironically comments on the ideal of the well-formed female body in a choice pose by means of a decidedly erotic accessory, namely the corset. The suggestiveness of the pose is increased by the loosened bands that almost invite the virtual observer to enter the game of concealing and revealing. After all, there are always two involved with a corset: the woman wearing it and someone who laces it. And in terms of the effect of the photograph on a female observer, the equally elegant and relaxed staging suggests that the proverbial torture of wearing a corset cannot really be as great as it is made out to be. Few viewers notice that the wasp waist was achieved with the help of a bit of light retouching.

So here it was again: the corset. Enlightened doctors had warned against it; Coco Chanel had combated it. In the eyes of the reform movement of the 1920s, the corset was nothing less than a relict of feudal times and the expression of a highly unhealthy way of life. But now, suddenly, on the eve of the Second World War, it had reappeared. More precisely, it appeared in the fashion shows of 1939. Dresses, coats, jackets once again showed a waist, thus making a corset a necessary item for all those for whom, as *Vogue* formulated it, things were not quite comme il faut. At first glance, it may seem absurd to attempt to locate in the corset a reference to the political situation around 1940. But fashion has always been the expression of its time, and is it not worth noting that the corset reappeared precisely at the moment when half of Europe had fallen under totalitarian rule (and the other half maintained at least sympathy for the right wing). Whatever the answer may be, the French edition of *Vogue* had the job of 'selling' its readers the idea of the corset. "Oh," said a commentary in the September issue of 1939, "stop complaining that the corset is uncomfortable. In the first place, the modern stays are well designed: one can sigh and even breathe properly. And secondly, comfort is not really

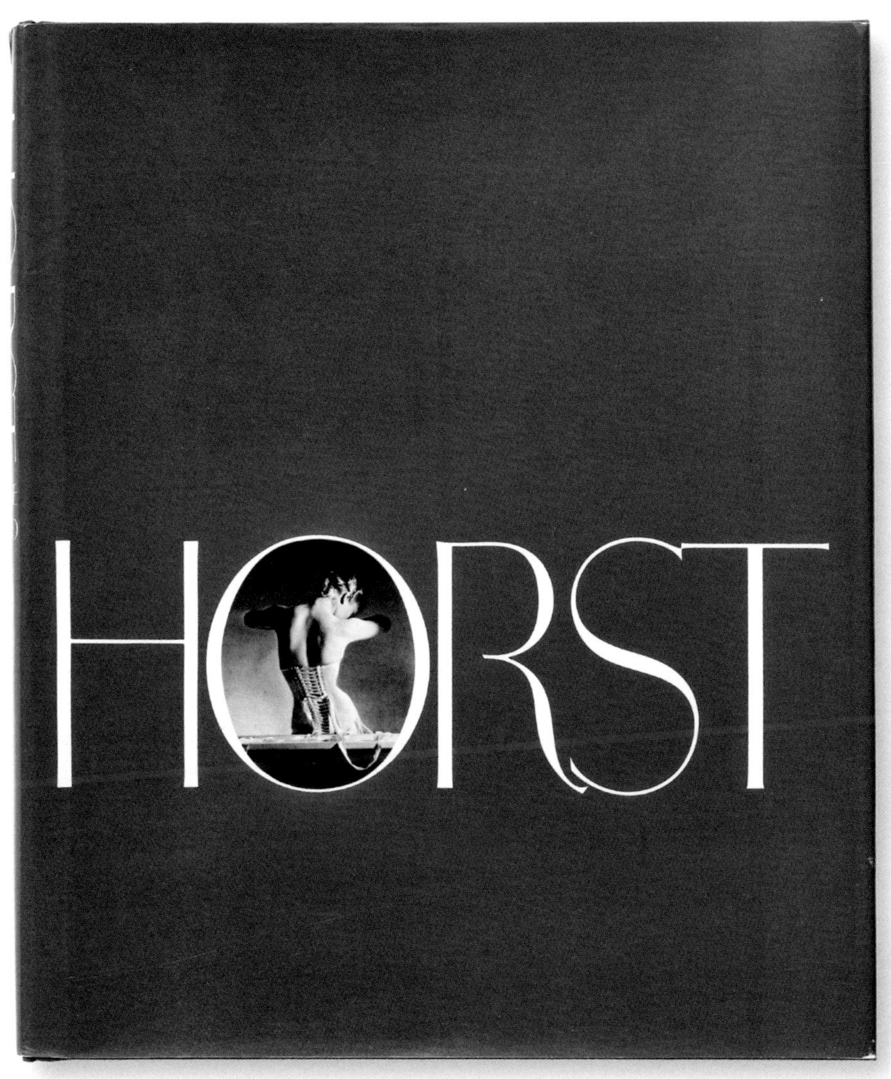

Horst: His Work and His World. *This large monograph, edited by Valentine Lawford and published 1984, gave pride of place to the* Mainbocher Corset *on the title page.*

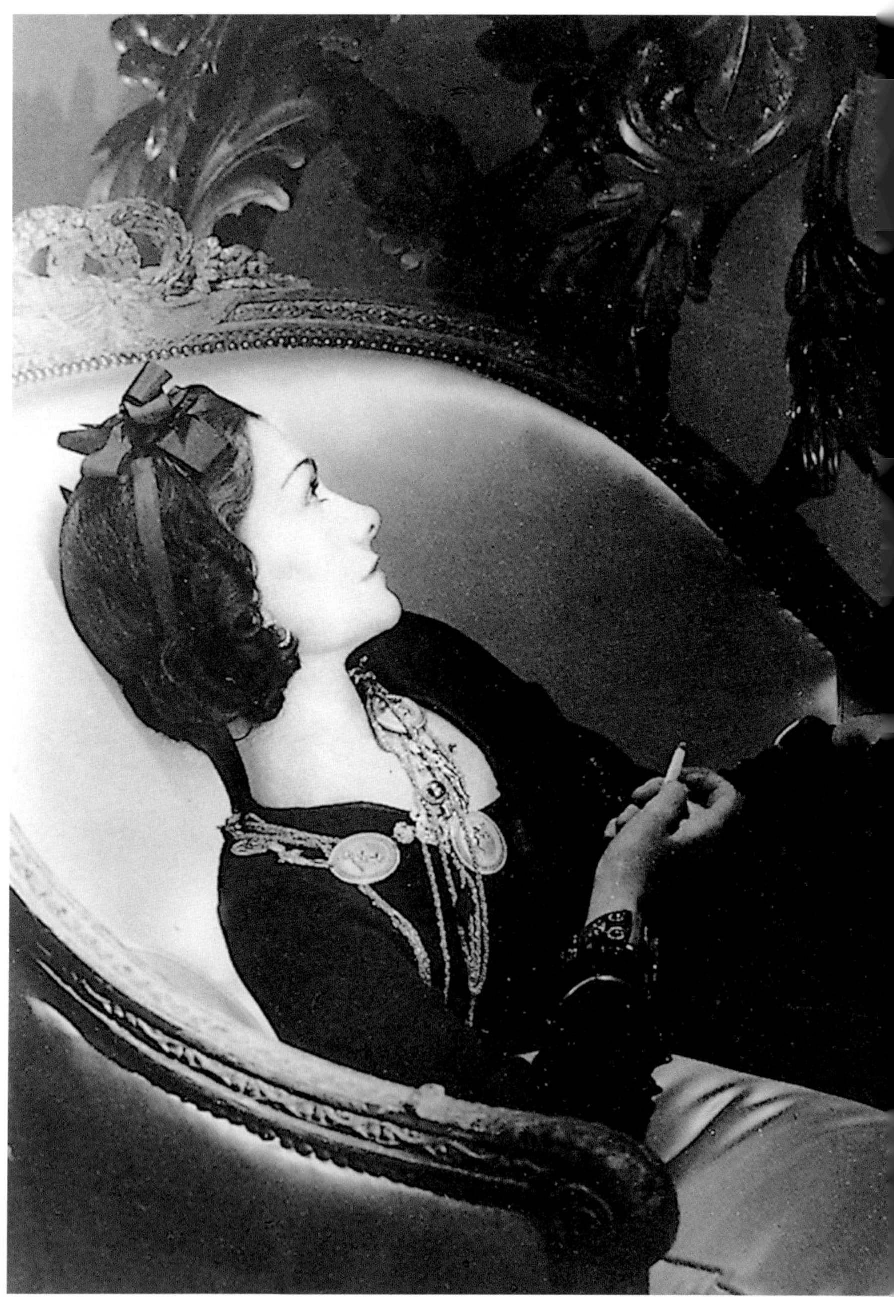

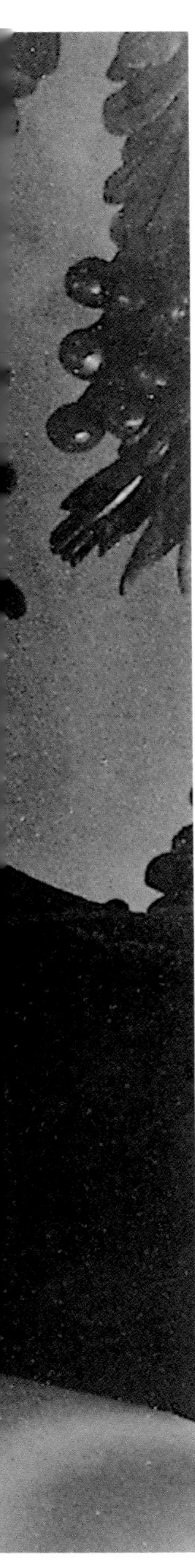

the issue, but rather acquiring the bodily proportions of a siren. Or those of Tutankhamun in his golden sarcophagus."

Making themselves useful at least through work

In the spring of 1939, Horst had traveled with Hoyningen-Huene through Greece. Upon his return to Paris, he met with Jean Cocteau and Thornton Wilder. In August he photographed the corset creation of Mainbocher. A few days later, on 1 September, Hitler attacked Poland and the Second World War began. Horst's photograph had actually been intended for a *Vogue* special in October 1939. The pictures were ready, and the layouts were finished. But in the present situation, did anyone still have an interest in fashion? England and France had already declared war on Germany, and *Vogue* did not appear in October. The November issue of the French *Vogue* also failed to appear. Not until December was the magazine again delivered to the kiosks. Business as usual? Not entirely. *Vogue*, too, could not escape the shadow of war. "Must it be, you will perhaps ask, that in these dark hours, frivolity has come in again?" asks an editorial, and then continues: "Whoever makes this argument is forgetting that the French clothing industry is the second most important sector next to metal-working..." This real issue is therefore jobs and the question of proper behavior during a state of "total war." This meant "that the entire nation finds itself at war and must fight back on all fields and in all areas. Those who are not called to the dubious glory of fighting with weapons can at least make themselves useful through work..." Furthermore, the article continues, one might ask oneself whether it is not outmoded to speak now about the fashion shows from the previous August. Rarely, according to the anonymous editorial, were the fashion creations more ephemeral than in that year. "Like mayflies they lived hardly more than a single morning." To convey the readers an impression of the fashions, the editors decided to copy the already laid-out, but unprinted and undelivered, pages of the October issue. Thus Horst's Mainbocher Corset appears reduced to the size of a postage stamp – on page 35 of the December issue of the French *Vogue*. By this time, the photographer had already been in the USA for some time, and in the following year, he would apply for American citizenship. Similarly, Mainbocher, who had still managed to make an impression through "a memorable collection" in 1939, closed its Paris house in 1940 and also moved to America. Thus Horst's magnificent rear nude unwillingly became the apotheosis of an age and of a profession. "The Thirties," as Janet Flanner later laconically observed, "were over."

Horst P. Horst:
Coco Chanel, *Paris 1937.*

Alfred Eisenstaedt
VJ Day
1945

A Stolen Kiss

The war is over. Not just any war. What came to end on 15 August 1945 with the formal capitulation of Japan was the most ferocious, most deadly, most devastating war in the history of humankind. A global struggle that, with the deployment of the atom bomb, had assumed a whole new dimension in terms of technology, too. If there is one picture that expresses the joy released by the longed-for declaration of peace, it's the one taken by the American *Life* photographer Alfred Eisenstaedt. His shot fuses nothing less than private exuberance and world history.

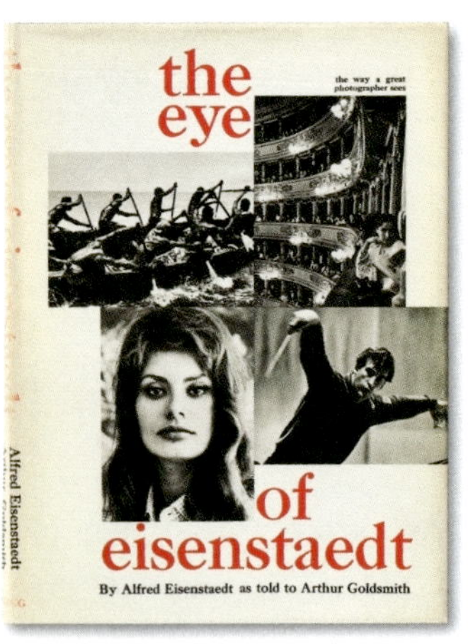

New York, Times Square, 15 August 1945. A young man is kissing a young woman. To judge from the drama of the image, he has more or less grabbed her in the middle of the street. He grasps her waist with his right hand, brings her head into position with his bent left arm and kisses her resolutely on the mouth. Is she resisting? Perhaps. But her right arm is trapped between her chest and his upper body, while her left hand makes a fanning movement at hip height. The girl is smartly dressed. Done up. Or is she wearing a uniform? Whatever the case, she is all in white: a white dress, white shoes, and white stockings with a seam, clearly visible, running from her ankle to her upper thigh. She seems to be toppling backwards; at all events, she is trying to steady herself with her right foot, toe pointed, lending the picture a risqué note that

---

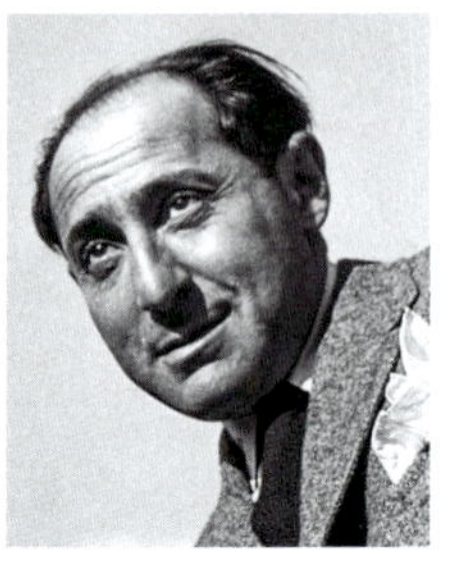

Alfred Eisenstaedt
*Born **1898** in Dirschau, West Prussia (now Tczew, Poland). **1906** moves to Berlin with his family. Completes senior school. First camera at 14. **1916–18** military service. Then a haberdashery salesman until **1925**. Death of his father. Turns to photojournalism. First picture published in **1927** in* Der Weltspiegel. ***1928** works freelance for the Associated Press. **1930–34** reportage in the spheres of politics. **1931** first Leica. **1935** Emigrates to the US. **1936–72** works exclusively for the newly founded pictorial* Life. ***1954** first solo show (George Eastman House, Rochester). **1958** chosen as one of the "Ten Greatest Photographers in the World" by* Popular Photography. ***1995** dies on Long Island.*

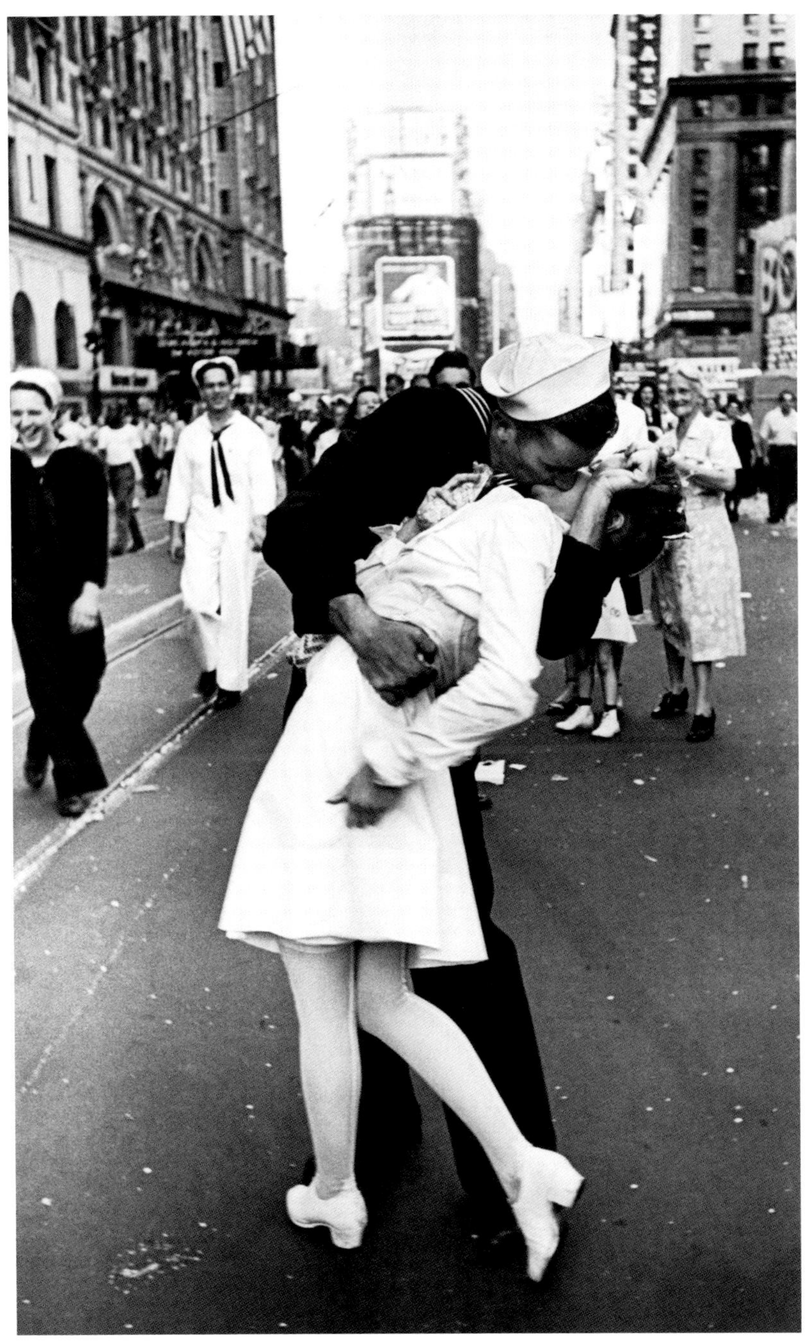

VJ Day, 1945

A SENSE OF TIMING

A photographer needs a short-circuit between his brain and his fingertips. Things happen: sometimes expected, more often unexpected. You must be ready to catch the right split second, because if you miss, the picture may be gone forever.

Fast reflexes are partly inborn, but they can be developed through practice and experience. You must know your equipment thoroughly, of course. You must be able to operate your camera quickly, automatically, without stopping to think. Life moves swiftly and unexpectedly; it won't wait for you to fumble with your focusing control or film advance.

On these pages are reproduced a number of my pictures where split-second timing was important. With some I've also included a few frames from the contact sheet, so you can see the near misses as well as the hits.

There's another element involved here, too, which I've already mentioned—luck. Often I think I've had more luck than brains as a photographer. The photograph on the facing page certainly is a good example of luck, as well as timing. I was walking through the crowds on V-J Day, looking for pictures. I noticed a sailor coming my way. He was grabbing every female he could find and kissing them all—young girls and old ladies alike. Then I noticed the nurse, standing in that enormous crowd. I focused on her, and just as I'd hoped, the sailor came along, grabbed the nurse, and bent down to kiss her. Now if this girl hadn't been a nurse, if she'd been dressed in dark clothes, I wouldn't have had a picture. The contrast between her white dress and the sailor's dark uniform gives the photograph its extra impact. Luck. But you do have to keep your eyes open, too!

56

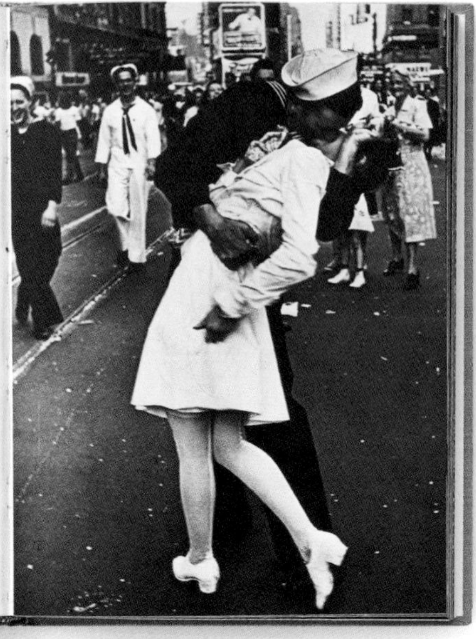

is hard to miss. The people in the background are watching, smiling, staring in astonishment. This robs the pose of some of its drama. For the picture might also be read in a different manner. As a demonstration of male power, as proof of masculine strength and dominion over women. The couple – so much is clear – dominates the center of the picture. The kiss is the message. Not a kiss of love, if we may invoke a vague typology of kissing. It is a kiss of *joie de vivre*. Of exuberance. A kiss against a historic backdrop, without which the two people would probably never have met. Seconds later they will break apart, look at each other, laugh perhaps, and then go their separate ways. For ever.

World history summed up without words

The picture was taken by Alfred Eisenstaedt, a photographer who worked for the legendary illustrated magazine *Life* and who was undoubtedly one of the most important, most active photojournalists of the 20th century. Eisenstaedt was a pragmatist. A reporter carrying out a job. A man who had to supply good, eye-catching, suggestive images. Not an artist, not a romantic. Accordingly, he spared himself flowery titles. *VJ Day in Times Square, New York City, 15 August 1945* is the official title of the picture. It would be impossible to condense

Pages 226 and 228–231:
The Eye of Eisenstaedt, *cover and double-spread pages. Detailed captions by the photographer explain the genesis of his most famous works, including probably his best-known picture,* VJ Day. *The book was published in 1969 by Viking Press, New York.*

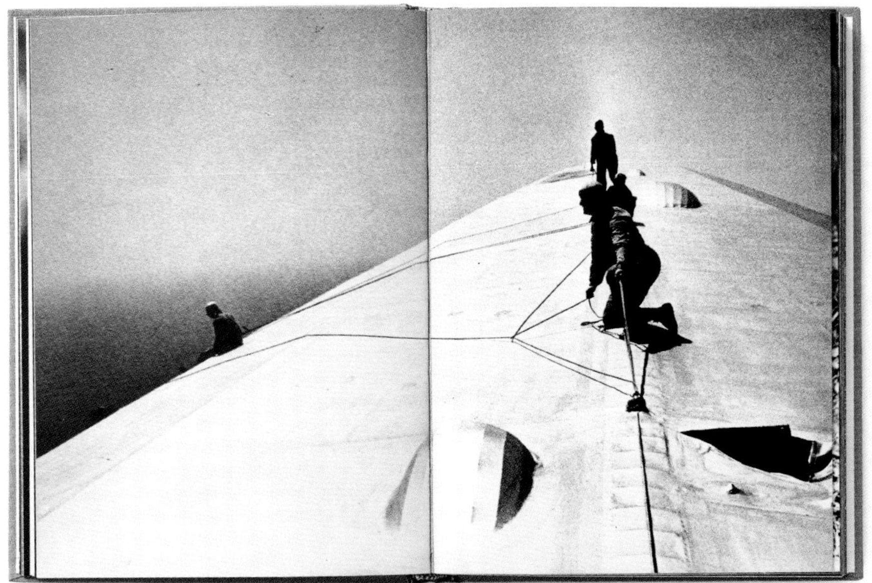

world history more succinctly. On this day, just after 12 noon Japanese local time, to be precise, Radio Tokyo broadcast a statement by Emperor Hirohito. His message was addressed to the Americans: Japan would accept the terms of the Potsdam Declaration. In other words, Japan, the last foreign power still waging war in the Pacific, had capitulated. The Second World War was over. Or, to put it more accurately, hostilities were at an end.

But the consequences, the wounds inflicted by the global campaign of killing and destruction instigated by Hitler's Germany, remain painful even today. No fewer than 58 countries were involved in the Second World War. The Soviet Union alone had 25 million dead to mourn. It thereby suffered the greatest losses of all those who took part in a conflict that lasted in total 68 months, and which was unequalled in terms of its hatred, violence, obsession with annihilation, its departure from hard-won humanitarian standards. On this point historians are agreed: the Second World War was no "normal war." It was without precedent in the history of the West.

From European war to world war

A total of more than 60 million people died in the course of the conflict: in regular action, guerrilla warfare, retaliatory measures, air raids, and through genocide. The racial fanaticism of the National Socialists claimed the lives of over six million Jews. Almost eight million people died in Germany of the consequences of forced labor, and in Japan more than two million. Cities were reduced to rubble, cultures extinguished, the achievements of the Enlightenment trampled over. War crimes became part of everyday life. The Germans and the Japanese stood out in particular: 58 percent of Soviet prisoners of war interred in German camps died,

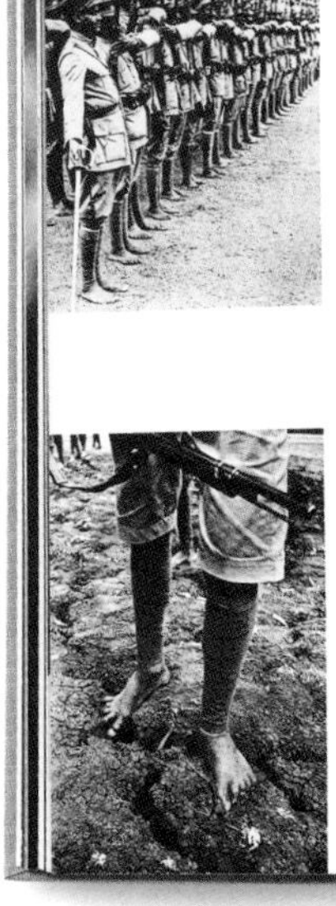

THE POWER OF THE CLOSE-UP: One of the discoveries I'd made, and which all good photojournalists must understand, is the power of a single detail to tell a story with great immediacy and impact. The three pictures reproduced here make the point clearly, I think.

The Ethiopian army was equipped in a very primitive manner and this, of course, was an important point to get across. I photographed rows of barefoot soldiers marching and at attention, as in the picture at upper left. Groups of soldiers make interesting visual patterns, and the idea that these particular soldiers are not equipped with modern arms comes across, but otherwise there is nothing very remarkable about the photograph.

Intrigued by the bare feet beneath the puttees, I moved in close to show the legs of a single soldier (lower left). This is a stronger, clearer visual statement, but it wasn't until I photographed the *soles* of a prone soldier's feet, caked with mud, in a tight close-up (opposite) that I got what I felt was the strongest statement. The soldier is not dead, as many people assume him to be; he is lying prone, firing a rifle. (The war itself didn't break out until months later.) However, I don't think this impairs the validity of the photograph. It shows a small but very significant detail which suggests much about the whole situation, the primitive condition of the Ethiopian army. The photograph certainly seems to be an unusually evocative one. It has been published many, many times, and once they have seen it, few people seem to forget it.

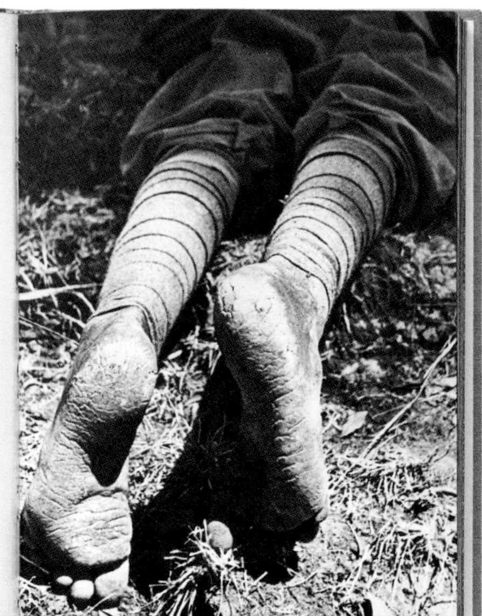

as did 27 percent of British and American soldiers imprisoned by the Japanese. Systematic torture was the order of the day. In the Pacific, in particular, the war was conducted with unimaginable brutality. "Kill or be killed" was the motto. Which meant that prisoners were taken only rarely. Japan entered the fray with the attack on Pearl Harbor in December 1941. A European war had turned into a world war. The counter-offensive began in July 1943. Step by step, General McArthur's troops conquered the parts of East Asia occupied by Japan. Flame tanks – tanks equipped with flamethrowers – were amongst the weapons commonly deployed in close combat against a Japanese army that often fought grimly to the last man. On certain stretches of the front line, the average life expectancy of an American infantryman is said to have been just three weeks. The scenario of a landing on the Japanese mainland, entailing heavy losses, was consequently hardly an attractive option at this late stage of the war. An alternative was offered by the atomic bomb, which was now ready for use. America had successfully detonated its first atomic bomb in the federal state of New Mexico on the afternoon of 16 July 1945.

An apocalypse wrought by human hand had now become a reality. On 26 July an ultimatum was issued to the Japanese. To no avail. America acted and dropped the bomb. Hiroshima on 6 August, and agasaki on 9 August. Over 200,000 people died. More than 150,000 were wounded. In the shape of the atomic bomb, the horror of war was given a new name. And the divine Emperor no other choice: on 14 August Japan surrendered. The capitulation was signed in September 1945 on board the US battleship *Missouri*.

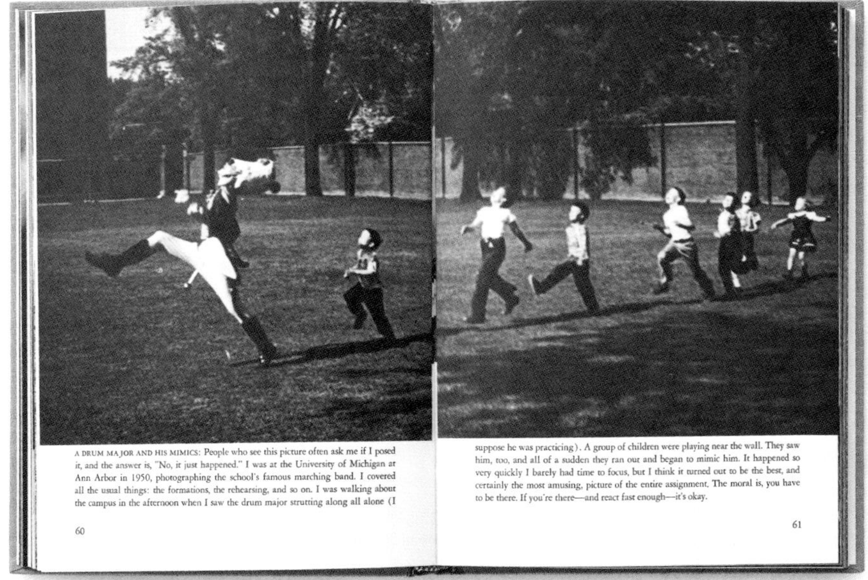

A DRUM MAJOR AND HIS MIMICS: People who see this picture often ask me if I posed it, and the answer is, "No, it just happened." I was at the University of Michigan at Ann Arbor in 1950, photographing the school's famous marching band. I covered all the usual things: the formations, the rehearsing, and so on. I was walking about the campus in the afternoon when I saw the drum major strutting along all alone (I suppose he was practicing). A group of children were playing near the wall. They saw him, too, and all of a sudden they ran out and began to mimic him. It happened so very quickly I barely had time to focus, but I think it turned out to be the best, and certainly the most amusing, picture of the entire assignment. The moral is, you have to be there. If you're there—and react fast enough—it's okay.

60

61

Capturing the moment

For us, however, it is still 15 August. The news of the end of the war spread like wildfire. Four years after the United States' entry into the war, peace was restored. The Americans called it VJ Day – "Victory over Japan Day." It was warm. It was dry. It was August. And Alfred Eisenstaedt cannot have been the only photographer out on the streets of New York with his camera during those hours. Born in 1898 in Dirschau in Germany (today Tczew in Poland), Eisenstaedt began his career as a press photographer in legendary 1920s Berlin. In 1935 he emigrated to the US and rapidly rose to become one of its busiest photojournalists. "In Times Square on VJ Day," he remembered, "I saw a sailor running along the street grabbing any and every girl in sight... I was running ahead of him with my Leica looking back over my shoulder but none of the pictures that were possible pleased me. Then suddenly, in a flash, I saw something white being grabbed. I turned around and clicked the moment the sailor kissed the nurse. If she had been dressed in a dark dress I would never have taken the picture. If the sailor had worn a white uniform, the same. I took exactly four pictures. It was done within a few seconds."

The picture appeared on the front cover of *Life*. It became Eisenstaedt's best-known photo. "People tell me," he once said, "that when I am in heaven they will remember this picture." Alfred Eisenstaedt died in August 1995. No more is known about the young sailor. One thing is sure: for him the war was over. VJ Day had granted him a second life.

Henri Cartier-Bresson
Germany, 1945
1945

Hour of Truth

Dessau, Germany, shortly after the end of the Second World War. In a camp for so-called displaced persons, a Nazi victim suddenly recognizes a former Gestapo informant. The young Henri Cartier-Bresson was on the spot and took a photograph that became an icon of liberation and a symbol for the end of the Nazi terror.

In the end, he allowed himself to be persuaded. He knew that he was not especially good at writing, nor was he by any means a theoretician. His background was rather in drawing, painting. Throughout his life he insisted that he was a painter, that he had learned from painting, and that he saw with the eyes of a painter. He felt a strong connection to Surrealism – but only as a visually oriented person, not as a formulator of theorems and programs. In the end, however, succumbing to the pressure of his Greek-born publisher Tériade, he sat himself at his desk and "in five or six days" wrote it all down. "I had it already in my head from the beginning," said Henri Cartier-Bresson, whose first great book, which also functioned as a photographic summary of decades of work, was titled thematically *Images à la Sauvette* (literally: pictures in passing). The comparatively large volume of approximately 32 × 29 cm (12½ × 11½ inches), bearing a drawing by Henri Matisse on the cover, appeared in 1952 in the Editions Verve of the legendary publisher Tériade. It would be no exaggeration to claim that it became one of the most significant and influential photographic works of the twentieth century – even if it had to wait for the English-language edition to unify Cartier-Bresson's work conceptually under an appropriated title: *The Decisive Moment*. The formula stood as a perfectly tailored banner over Cartier-Bresson's introduction that, as stressed by Wolfgang Kemp, "like no other text became the basis of an engaged photojournalism." It should be noted, however, that the title was originally drawn from a quotation by Cardinal von Retz; the American publisher Dick Simon adopted the slogan

---

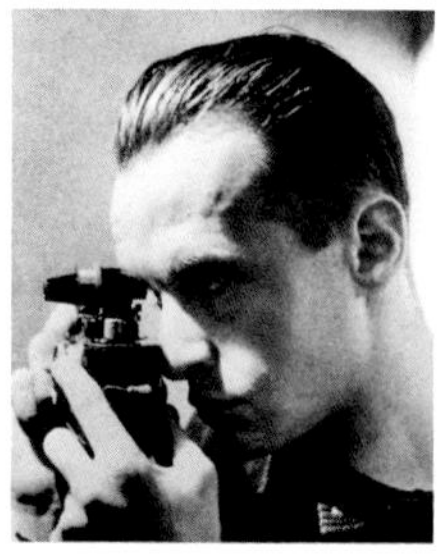

Henri Cartier-Bresson
*Born the son of a wealthy family **1908** in Chanteloup, France. **1927–28** trains under André Lhote. Discovers the works of Munkácsi, resulting in a turn to photography. **1935** trains in film technique in New York under Paul Strand. **1936–39** collaborates with Jean Renoir. **1940–43** POW in Germany. **1946** first one-man exhibition at the Museum of Modern Art, New York. **1947** founder member of Magnum. **1952** publication of his book* Images à la Sauvette. ***1954** Soviet Union. **1958–59** China. **1960** Cuba, Mexico, Canada. **1965** India and Japan. **1967** culture prize of the DGPh German photography society. **1970** marries Martine Franck. **2004** dies in Céreste (South of France).*

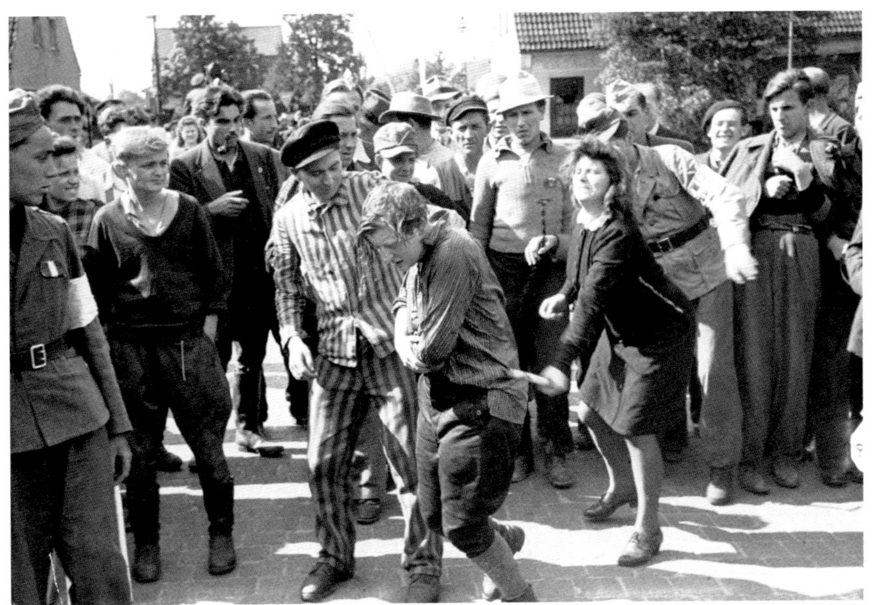

for the English-language edition, and thus introduced the phrase into photographic theory and camera practice.

Brilliant slices extracted from the stream of time

Henri Cartier-Bresson – this "giant in the history of photography" (Klaus Honnef); "God the Father, Son, and Holy Ghost" (Roger Therond); the "greatest photographer of modernity" (Pieyre de Mandiargues); and the "model for all later Leica photographers" (Peter Galassi) – was a master at intuiting critical moments. After the publication of *Images à la Sauvette*, or *The Decisive Moment*, critics have repeatedly described his work as brilliant slices extracted from the stream of time. Typically, Cartier-Bresson's photographs epitomize an event or happening just before it disintegrates or dissolves back into the flow of everyday life in a matter of seconds or split seconds. As a result, his work acquires something of a visionary, even prophetic, character. Yves Bonnefoy, for example, terms Cartier's photograph *Place de l'Europe in the Rain* (1932) nothing less than a miracle: "How was he able to recognize the analogy between the man running across the plaza and the poster in the background so quickly, how could he compose a scene out of so many fleeting elements – a scene that is as perfect in detail as it is mysterious in its totality?" He just has the feelers for it – thus Henri Cartier-Bresson explains the astounding

---

The Decisive Moment. *The English title of his book from 1952 was programmatic for Henri Cartier-Bresson's œuvre. Despite this, he also frequently produced sequences with a certain cinematic quality when closing in on an event.*

Germany, 1945, 1945

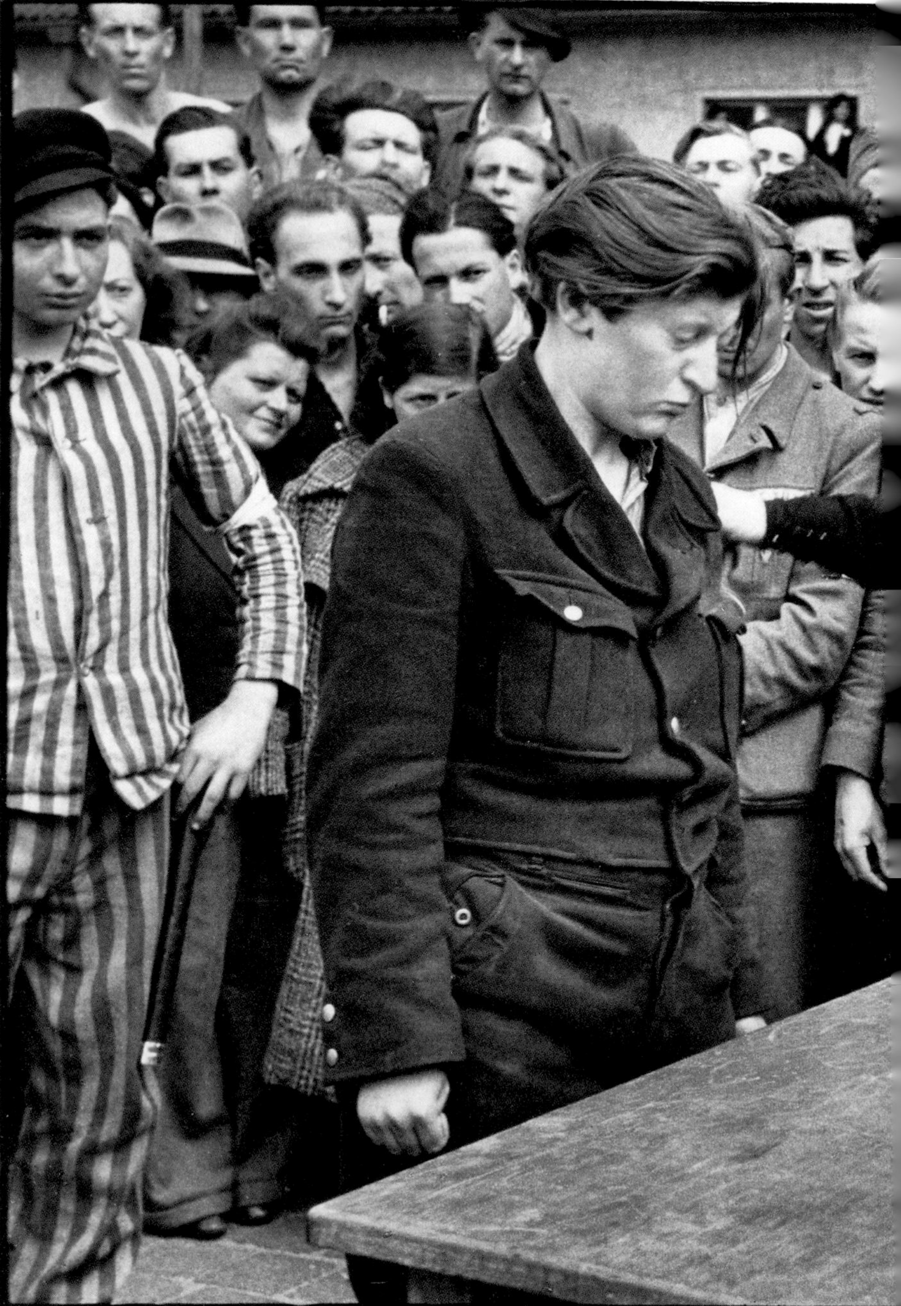

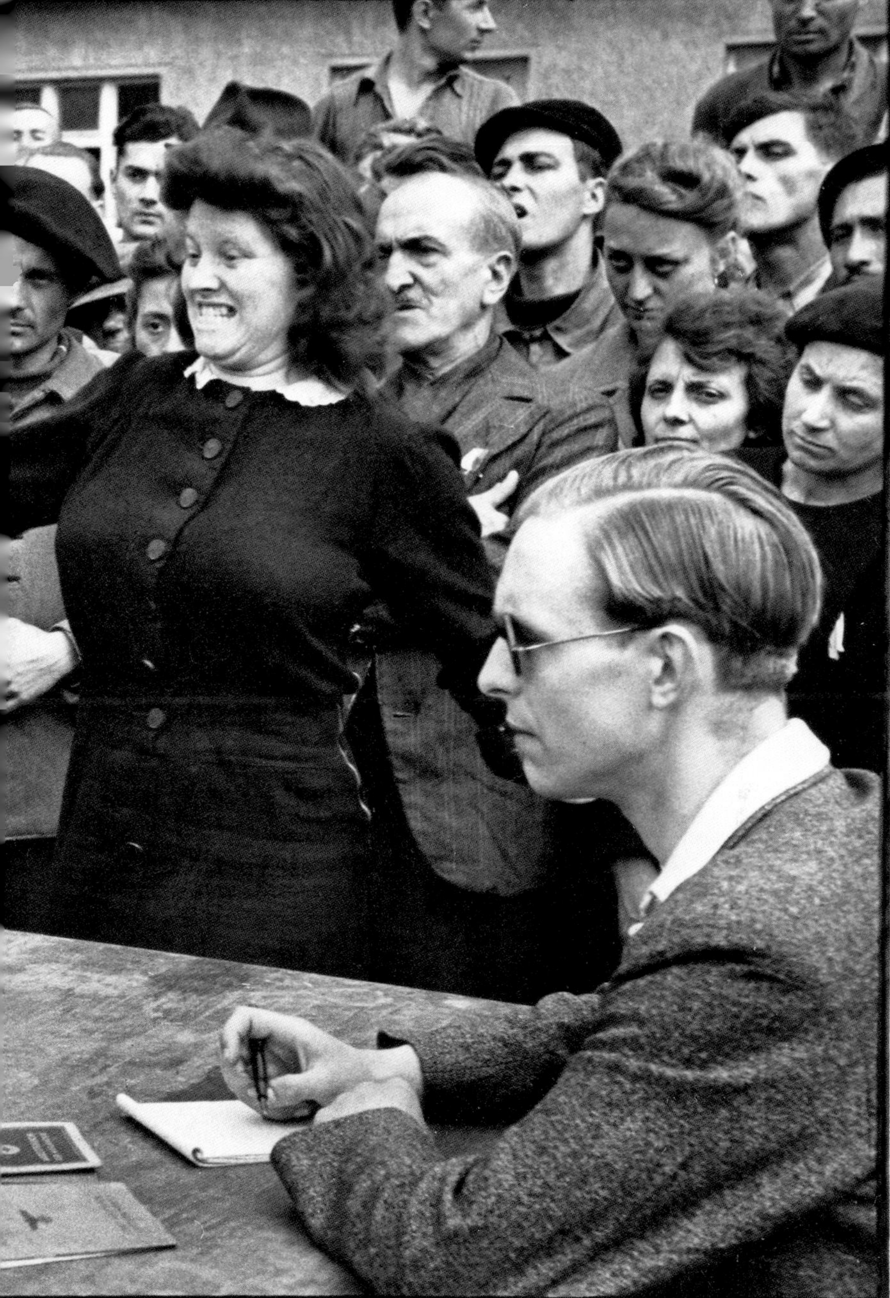

results of his photographic activity in his typical laconic manner, adding: "I love painting. As far as photography is concerned, I understand nothing."

More a matter of style

Images à la Sauvette presents a total of 132 black-and-white photographs, with the introductory text mentioned above prefacing the plates. Although this statement was not the author's sole verbal commentary on his work, it nonetheless was, or became, his most important: in it, he presents a combination of programmatic discourse, reflection, and technical manual all in one. It is, in fact, a prescription for a 'photography in passing', and as such was adopted as a bible by legions of ambitious photographers directly after the publication of the book in the 1950s – and is still followed by photographers today. Henri Cartier-Bresson, born in 1908 into a prosperous textile-manufacturing family in Chanteloup, France, studied art under André Lhote. The purchase of his first Leica transformed him into an indefati-gable chronicler of his times, and he is justly seen as one of the most influential and productive photographers of the twentieth century. Each of his published photographs appears to be an apparently effortless proof of his credo: "I like my pictures to be clear, or better, climactic… This is more a matter of style than technique." To conjure an event at its culmination point onto celluloid – this is the magic that his name still epitomizes today. Although Henri Cartier-Bresson did journalistic reports, published photo essays, and produced photographic sequences, he is above all the master of the single picture, in which a theater of the world presents itself in microcosm.

Germany, 1945 – our picture's official short title, more or less authorized by Magnum – appears on pages 33–34 of *Images à la Sauvette*. The picture is therefore a double-spread, running across the gutter. Lincoln Kirstein and Beaumont Newhall had taken note of this work as early as 1947, including it both in the first large post-war exhibition of the photographer's works at the Museum of Modern Art and also it in the slim catalogue (on page 40) accompanying the show. The photograph has also appeared in almost all subsequent retrospective monographs, the most prominent probably being Cartier-Bresson's large interim collection of photographs published in 1979 by Delpire under the simple title *Henri Cartier-Bresson photographe*. Here the famous work was of course included, along with many other classics such as *Rue Mouffetard, On the Marne*, and *Sevilla*. The ubiquity of the photograph has doubtless contributed to turning it into one of his best-known works. Moreover, the picture numbers among those deemed worthy of fuller commentary by the photographer. Thus, on the reverse of the key picture bearing the archive number HCB45003 W00115/25C one finds

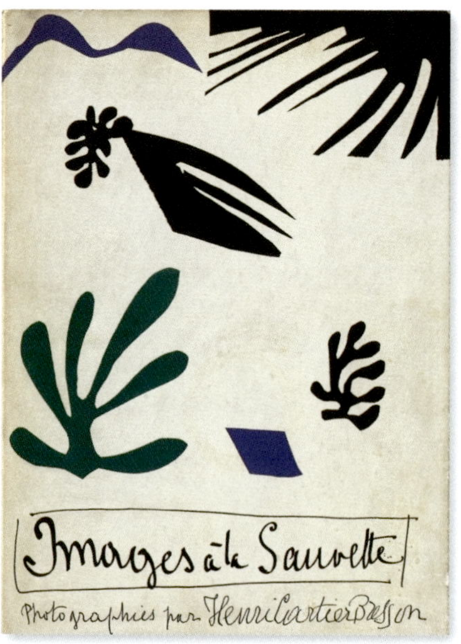

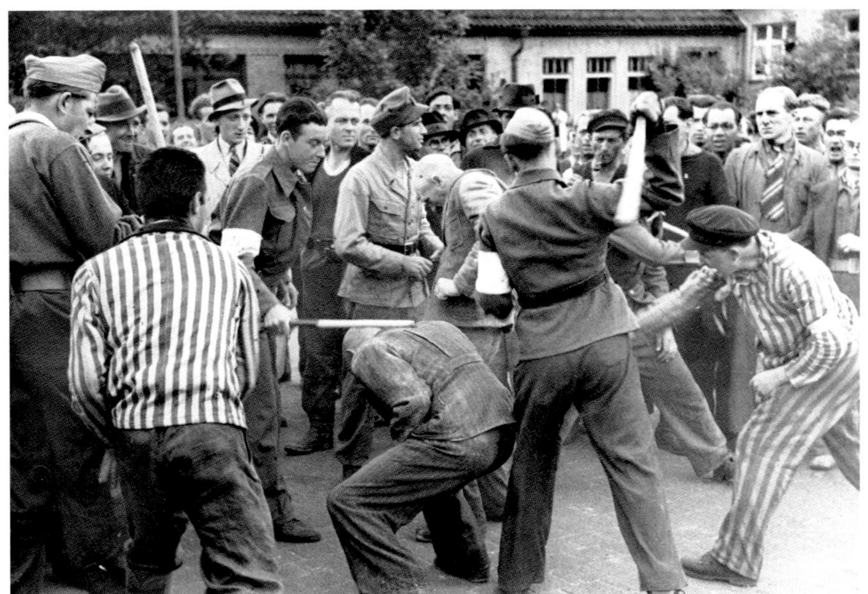

the word: "Dessau. Border between American and Soviet zone. Transit camp for former prisoners held in eastern German area: political prisoners, prisoners of war, slave labor, displaced persons. A young Belgian woman and former Gestapo informer is recognized before she can hide herself in the crowd."

Dessau, a middle-size city north of Leipzig in today's Saxon-Anhalt, which had made an international name for itself before the war as the home of the Bauhaus school. We do not know precisely when Cartier took the picture – the photographer himself never spoke willingly about his work – but the date must have been between 21 April and 2 July 1945 – that is, between the American occupation of the city and the arrival of their Russian replacements. The location is the former anti-aircraft barrack in Dessau-Kochstedt, which functioned as a transit camp during the occupation. The building, partially visible in the background, had been dedicated under the Nazis in 1937 and would later be used by the Soviets as a barrack until the unification in 1989; today the area is a housing development. On this spring day in 1945 the sky is cloudy, the light, diffuse. The sun breaks through only occasionally, casting long shadows that might indicate afternoon; more probably, however, it is morning. Cartier-Bresson in any case was carrying his Leica, fitted with a 50-mm lens. By deduction, this means he was standing about ten feet away from the protagonists – close enough to capture the event, but also far enough to satisfy his preferred policy of not intervening. "One must creep up to the subject on tip toes," he once

---

Left: Images à la Sauvette. *The French first edition of his classic book appeared 1952, produced by legendary publishers Tériade with a dust jacket from Henri Matisse.*

Above: *A further (scarcely known) motif from the Dessau-Kochstedt series dating from April to July 1945.*

said, "even when it involves a still life. One must put on velvet gloves and have Argus eyes. No pushing or crowding: an angler doesn't stir up the waters beforehand."

At the time of the photograph, Cartier-Bresson was thirty-six years old with an international reputation as a photographer, though he certainly had not yet approached the cult status that he definitively achieved with the publication of *Images à la Sauvette*. Meanwhile, in the USA Kirstein and Newhall were preparing a "posthumous retrospective" for the photographer, presuming him to have been killed in the war – an assumption not at all far-fetched, when one recalls that Cartier-Bresson had been an active resistance fighter. Captured and interned by the Germans in 1940, he had escaped only on his third attempt three years later. At this point, in 1945, however, he was in fact working with the Americans on a film for the Information Service about the home-coming of French prisoners of war. "It was a film by prisoners about prisoners," as Cartier-Bresson recalled. "The scene played itself out before my eyes as my cameraman was filming it. I had my photography camera in my hand and released the shutter. The scene was not staged. Oddly, this picture doesn't turn up in the film."

The setting for a scene that became famous

This was not the first time that Cartier-Bresson conducted filming work and photographic work in parallel. One needs only to recall his famous picnic *On the Marne*, created while he was an assistant director to Jean Renoir (*La vie est à nous, Une partie de campagne*). But whereas *On the Marne* has nothing to do directly with the filming, in Dessau the photographer and his cameraman are shooting one and the same scene simultaneously, even if the film does not contain the 'most decisive' moment captured by Cartier-Bresson. *Le Retour*, as has been mentioned, was being made at the behest of the Office of War Information and the French Ministère des Prisonniers. The black-and-white film runs 32 minutes and 37 seconds, with a commentary in French spoken by Claude Roy in the original version. *Le Retour* opens with footage taken in Dachau in late April 1945 by the American troops who had liberated the concentration camp. Following these scenes are shots of freed prisoners, straggling soldiers, refugees wandering about in a daze – all of whom, according to the narrator, were causing chaos on the roads and hindering the sweep of an Allied victory. As a result, camps to contain these people were set up in occupied barracks, factories, and private houses. Cut. The film camera now does a long shot of a large interior courtyard that is about to become a stage of the scene made famous by Cartier-Bresson's photograph. We are looking at a crowd of several hundred people. In the center, a circular area has been cleared. In the background is the high gable roof of the former barrack, some of whose windows can also be made out in Cartier's photograph. To the lower right in the picture is the table to which – cut and medium close-up – a young woman wearing dark breeches, light-colored wool socks almost up to the knee, and flat shoes is led. She walks with a stoop. With a serious expression and hanging head, she steps up to the table at which the accusation against her – whatever it is – is about to be processed. The young man on the right with sunglasses and parted hair raises his finger and seems to give a warning. His name is Wilhelm Henry van der Velden, a twenty-two-year-old Netherlander, who had been studying medicine until he, like his brother Karel, was interned in February 1943 in the Dutch concentration camp Westerbork. Now, at the behest of the Americans, he has been appointed commandant of the camp at Dessau, through which thousands of people are making their way daily, from West to East or vice versa. Above all,

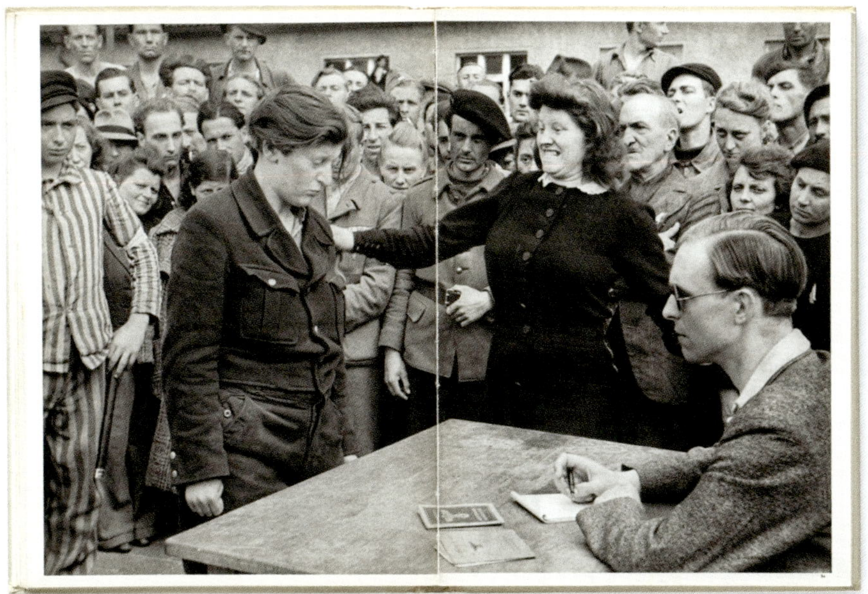

explains the commentary accompanying the film, it is necessary to be keep a careful watch out "for that handful of vile beings who were attempting to disappear amid the flood of deportees – to return home to 'business as usual'." The woman in the high-buttoned dark dress, who assumes a central position in a double sense of the word in Cartier's picture. is still standing several yards away on the right edge of the picture. But – cut and quarter close-up – now she, a Frenchwoman, moves up to the table, her arms still folded across her chest, a light colored purse dangling down. The commentary speaks of denouncers, Gestapo stooges, torturers, who will surely be turned over by those whom they had earlier betrayed. Again cut. The camera has now closed in on the two women. The one on the right addresses the other, screams at her: "Yes! You helped the Gestapo, you are an agent." She lifts her arm and strikes, hitting the other woman in the face so that the accused is literally thrown out of the picture. Seconds later she re-enters, bleeding at the nose, arranges her hair, looks briefly and confusedly at her 'torturer'. The sequence lasts exactly three seconds in the film; Cartier-Bresson's exposure may have lasted 1/60 of a second.

The decisive moment of revelation

Cartier-Bresson remembered the film correctly when he said that the scene he caught with his camera does not appear. Speculation as to whether his picture was therefore staged are quickly laid to rest, however, when one takes a closer look at the crowd of observers in

Henri Cartier-Bresson had allocated a double-page spread to his picture Germany, 1945, *even in his first major book,* Images à la Sauvette, *published in English as* The Decisive Moment.

the background. Consider for example the young man wearing his beret at a slant: in the film, his belt buckle is enclosed within his left hand – exactly in the same position that can be seen between the two women in Cartier-Bresson's photograph. A peripheral detail such as this would hardly find its way into a scene set up later. Why then did the film camera not capture the precise moment of identification? Chronologically, Cartier's photograph lies between the third and fourth scenes of the film. That is, the woman has not yet been identified as an agent, and the blow has not yet been struck, or she would be visibly bleeding from the nose in the photograph. Perhaps the critical moment fell victim to cutting and editing or, more likely, the cameraman – who must have been standing almost elbow-to-elbow with Cartier-Bresson – was changing the lens to capture what followed close-up. In any case, the cameraman caught the subsequent activity on film; Cartier-Bresson, however, got the more truly 'decisive moment': that of revelation, of identification, of the instant in which past, present, and future – the memory of sorrow, painful recognition, and furious response – come together. The distorted face of the former victim, now become a perpetrator, mirrors the tension of the tense situation.

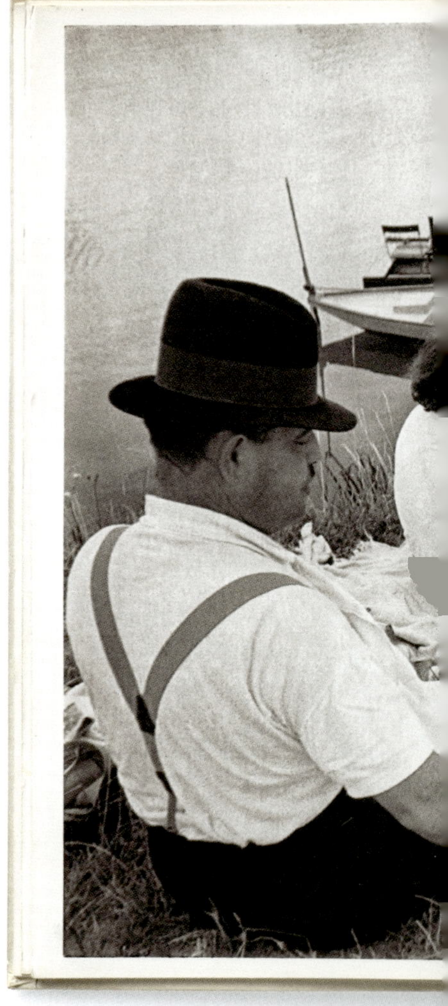

For a long time afterward, Henri Cartier-Bresson reported, he received questions and letters containing a cut-out of the photograph, with a cross over one or another of the persons in the background together with the plea: "That is my brother, that is my father – please tell us where he is now! How can we find him?" Let us look at the facts: at least ten million foreign prisoners, foreign workers, and deportees were wandering through Germany as 'displaced persons' in the years following 1945. Thus the photograph also assumed a thoroughly pragmatic function in the decades following 1945. Artistically, the picture has survived because of its "emblematic value," as Jean-Pierre Montier has expressed it. In the face of historical fact – after all, there was no concentration camp in Dessau itself – Cartier-Bresson's photograph came to function as a symbol of the Liberation: in our collective pictorial memory it has come to stand for the opening of the concentration camps and liberation from terror.

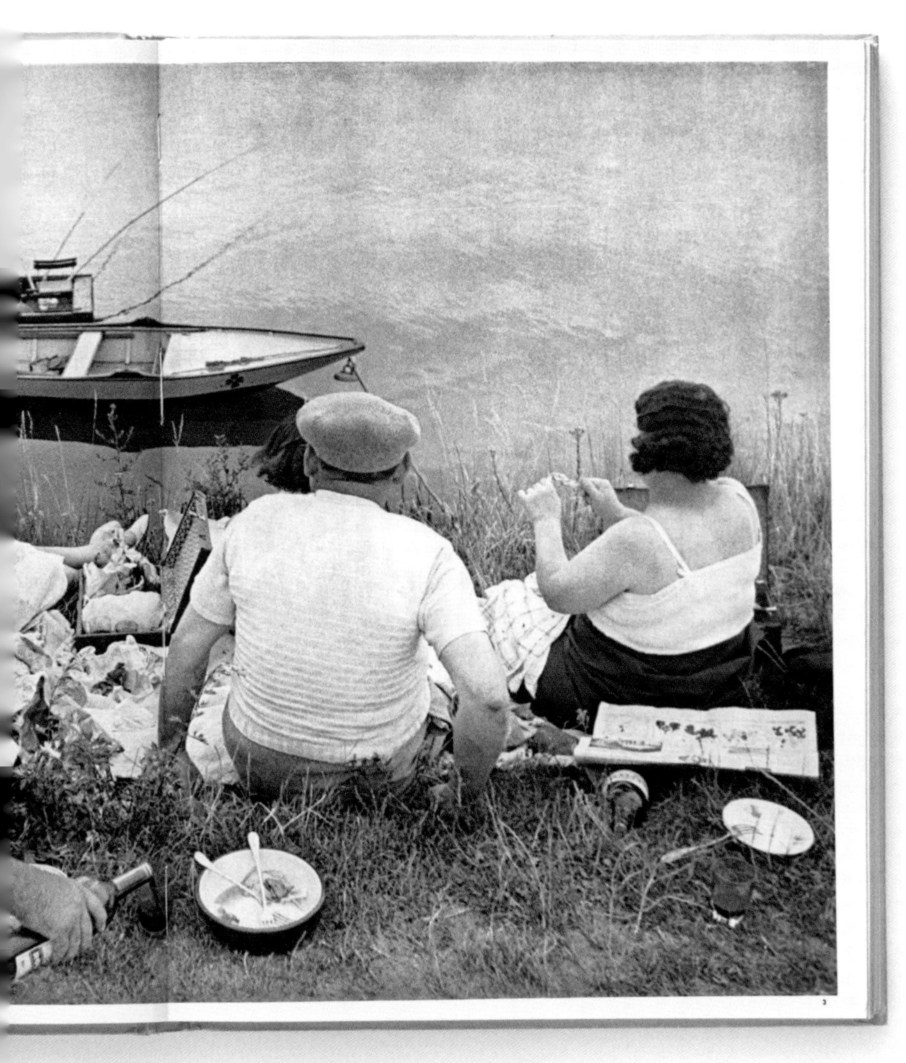

Henri Cartier-Bresson's programmatic book, Images à la Sauvette, *was published in 1952 by Éditions Verve and presents his early photographs, including such iconic images as* On the Banks of the Marne, *1938.*

Richard Peter

View from the Dresden City Hall Tower Toward the South 1945

Angel Above the City

Immediately after the end of the war, the Dresden photographer Richard Peter started an ambitious cycle on the demolished city that had once been known as the "Florence on the Elbe." By the end of the 1940s, he had taken approximately a thousand photographs, including this famed view from the City Hall Tower looking toward the south.

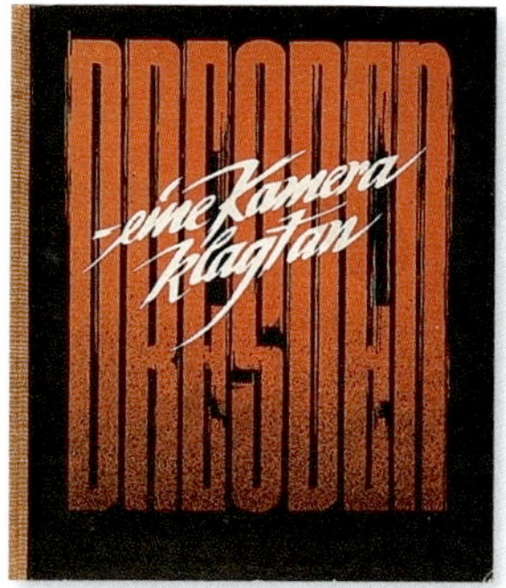

Almost miraculously, the tower of the New City Hall, dating from the mid-eighteenth century, survived the firestorm of 13–14 February 1945. Not that it had totally escaped being damaged in the inferno, of course, but compared to the Zwinger palace or the Frauenkirche, whose former glory now lay buried under the ruins, the City Hall, located between the Ringstrasse, the City Hall Square, and Kreuzstrasse, was at least reparable. The east wing of the building had been particularly heavily damaged by fire bombs and blockbusters, but the tower, visible from a great distance, still remained standing, its hands stopped at 2:30 a.m. At a height of more than 100 meters (325 feet), the tower was the tallest building in the city, but had lost its cupola. All that remained of it was a filigree-like skeleton, crowned by Dresden's recently adopted municipal emblem – a sculpted male figure in gilded bronze by Richard Guhr, which now seemed to be balancing as if on a tightrope. The famous double staircase had also survived the force of the demolition and firebombs. Richard Peter climbed these steps for the first time in the middle of September 1945.

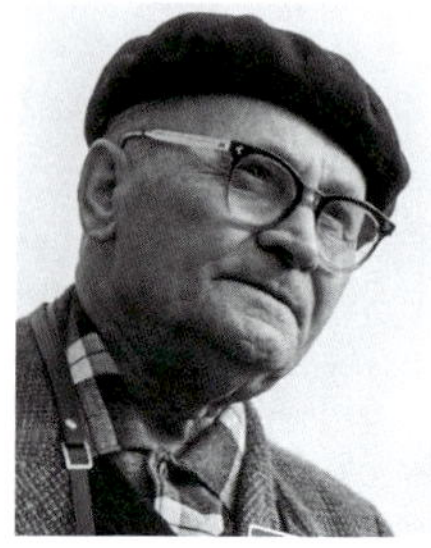

Richard Peter
Born ***1895*** *in Silesia.* ***1912*** *examination to become a journeyman smith.* ***1916–18*** *called up for First World War. From* ***1920*** *politically active in the German Communist Party.* ***1924*** *first camera reports for* Roter Stern *(later* Arbeiter-Illustrierte-Zeitung*).* ***1933*** *prohibited from practicing his profession.* ***1939*** *conscription.* ***1945*** *returns to Dresden. Archive is lost during the bombing. Involved in rebuilding the East German press. Founder editor of the glossy* Zeit im Bild. ***1946–49*** *photographic chronicles of destroyed Dresden and its reconstruction. From* ***1955*** *turns to calendar and book illustration, and trade fair photography. Dies* ***1977*** *in Dresden.*

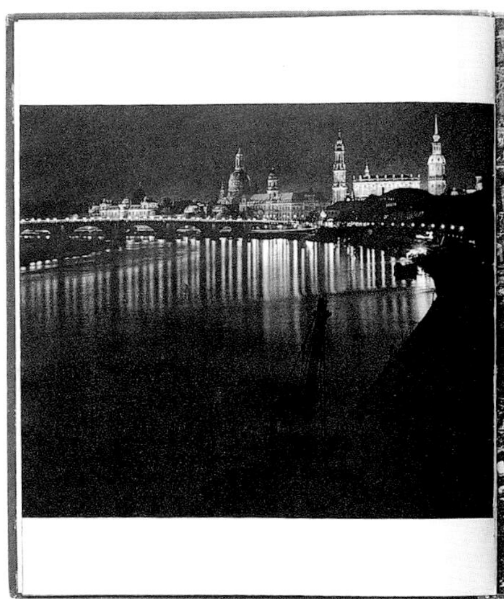

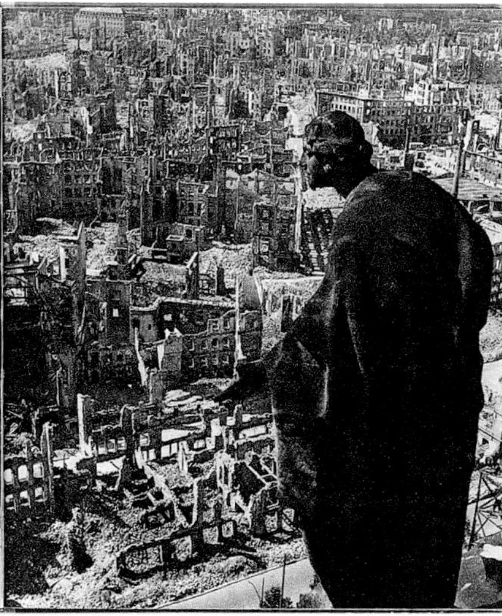

Nearly 15 square kilometers completely devastated

The photographer, well known in Dresden, was not the only one to make his way to the top of the City Hall Tower after the war had ended, however. The collection of the German Fotothek Dresden contains numerous views of the city taken from the tower – or rather, views of what remained of the "princely Saxon residence" (Götz Bergander), "famed throughout the world as a treasure chamber of art" (Fritz Löffler), the city that had once been the Florence on the Elbe. In all these photographs, the view was always shot over the shoulder of one of the figures sculpted by Peter Pöppelmann or August Schreitmüller, looking down onto the landscape of ruins. It is just this opposition – between personified virtue and death, light and darkness, proximity and distance, height and depth – that lends the photographs by Ernst Schmidt, W. Hahn, Wunderlich, Döring, Willi Rossner, and Hilmar Pabel their excitement, their suggestive power, and their memorial value.

Although some of these photographs may differ in their manner of presenting the subject, we may rest assured that it was Richard Peter's square photograph that inspired the others to find their way up the tower of the City Hall located in the south-east of the Old Town. In any case, Richard Peter's photograph was indisputably the first of an entire series of similar motifs – an image that bequeathed the world a valid pictorial formula for the horror of the bombing in general and of the destruction of the Baroque city of Dresden in particular.

The fire-bombing of Dresden is often compared with the dropping of the atom bombs on Hiroshima and Nagasaki. In the totality of the destruction and the number of victims – as well

---

Top left: **Richard Peter:** Dresden – eine Kamera klagt an (Dresden: A Camera Accuses). *Cover of the original German edition of 1949.*

Above and pages 246–247: *Double-page spreads from Peter's Dresden book. It appeared in large edition for the time – 50,000. Today it is regarded as one of the classic photo books on the war ruins.*

as in the sense of being a 'fitting' symbol for the times – all three catastrophes have much in common. On 13 and 14 February 1945, 'merely' three attacks, each by several hundred Lancaster bombers, Mosquitoes, Liberators, and Halifax planes of the Royal Air Force, sufficed to extinguish the strategically unimportant but historically unique center of the historic city of Dresden. The number of the victims is still disputed today, but estimates begin at more than 30,000; the exact figure will never be known, because many victims were instantly cremated. Furthermore, as pointed out by Adelbert Weinstein, the "already buried dead could in any case no longer be excavated from the cellars in this landscape of ruins. Because of the danger of epidemics, the rescue troops were even forced to wall up the make-shift bunkers or to burn them out with flame throwers." The damage to the buildings, on the other hand, can be statistically compiled. A surface area of nearly 15 square kilometers (6 square miles) was completely devastated. Seven thousand public buildings – museums, churches, palaces, castles, schools, hospitals – lay in ruin and ashes. Of the city apartments, 24,866 of 28,410 fell victim to the bombing attack. More than 10 million cubic meters (13 million cubic yards) of rubble had to be cleared away before reconstruction – still continuing to this day – could begin. In the years following war, Richard Peter, born in Silesia in 1895, was one of the many photographers who sought a pictorial response to the apocalypse that had ended in Europe in May 1945. Parallel to the often-discussed *Trümmerliteratur* (literature of ruins), one may also speak of a regular 'photography of ruins' – the scenes of destruction offered by every larger German city to its own pictorial chroniclers: Friedrich Seidenstücker and Fritz Eschen in Berlin, Herbert List in Munich, Wolf Strache in Stuttgart, August Sander in Cologne, Karl Heinz Mai in Leipzig. Photographically important after 1945 were especially the cycles by Hermann Claasen and Richard Peter, whose books *Gesang im Feuerofen* (1947; Song in the Furnace) and *Dresden – eine Kamera klagt an* (1949; Dresden: A Camera Accuses) were among the most-discussed publications of the post-war period.

A feeling of emptiness and stillness

Not until seven months after the inferno – that is, only on 17 September 1945 – did Richard Peter return to Dresden, his adopted city of residence. Not only did he find the city in which he had lived since the 1920s, and where he had worked as a photojournalist with the legendary *Arbeiter-Illustrierte-Zeitung* magazine, completely devastated, but also his own pictorial archive containing thousands of plates, negatives, prints, the sum of thirty years of

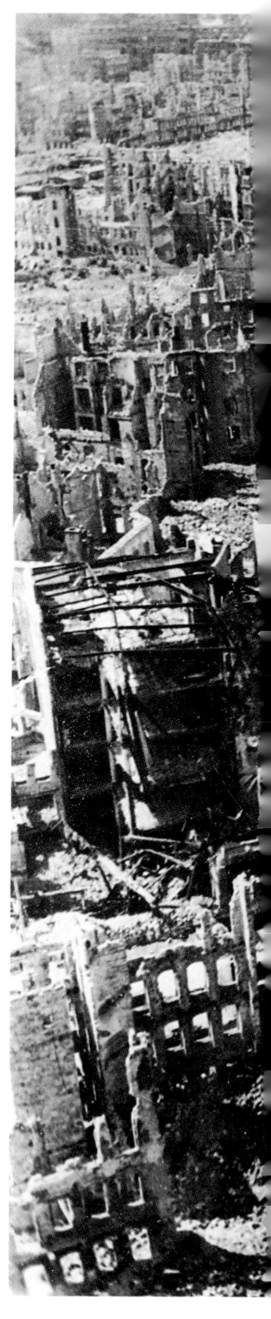

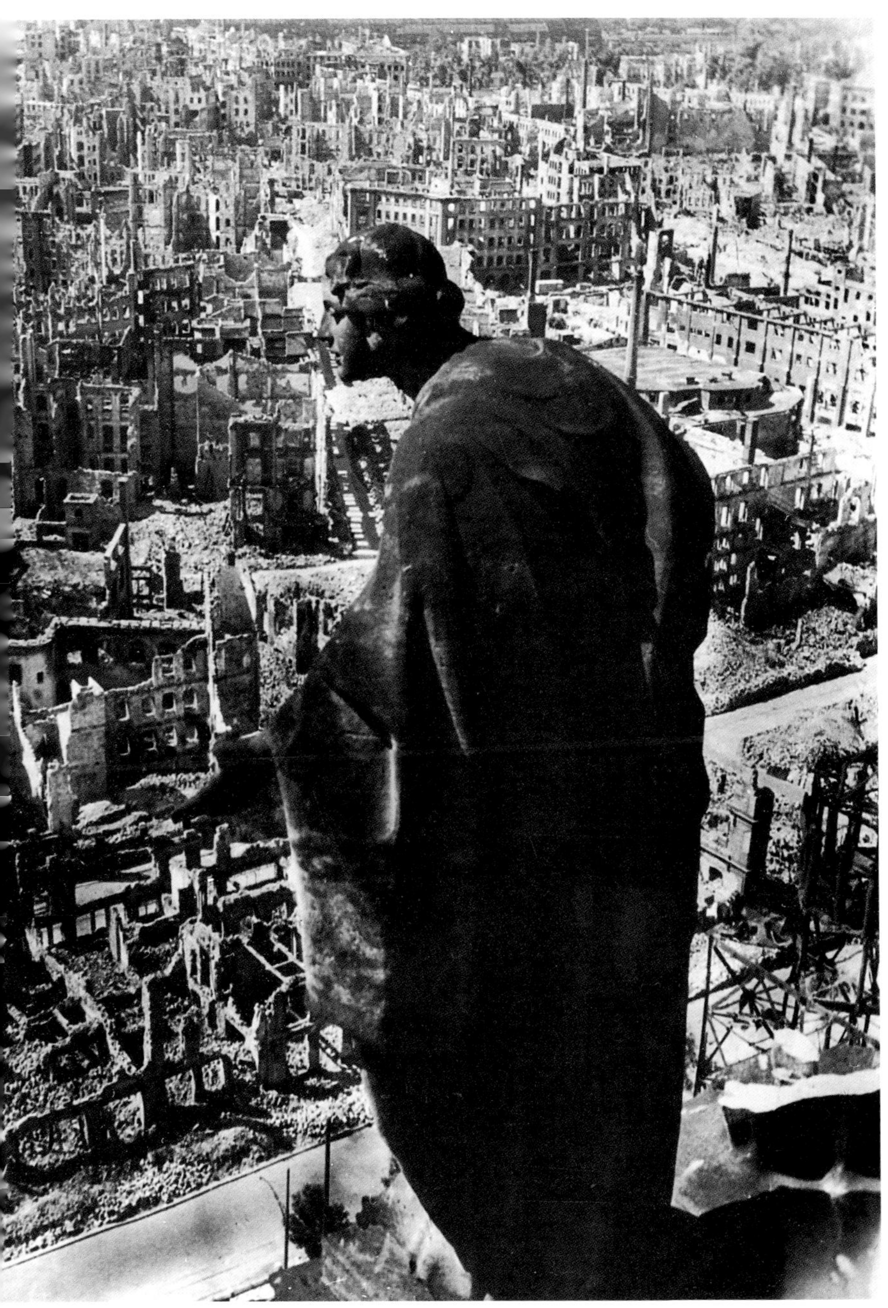

View from the Dresden City Hall Tower Toward the South, 1945

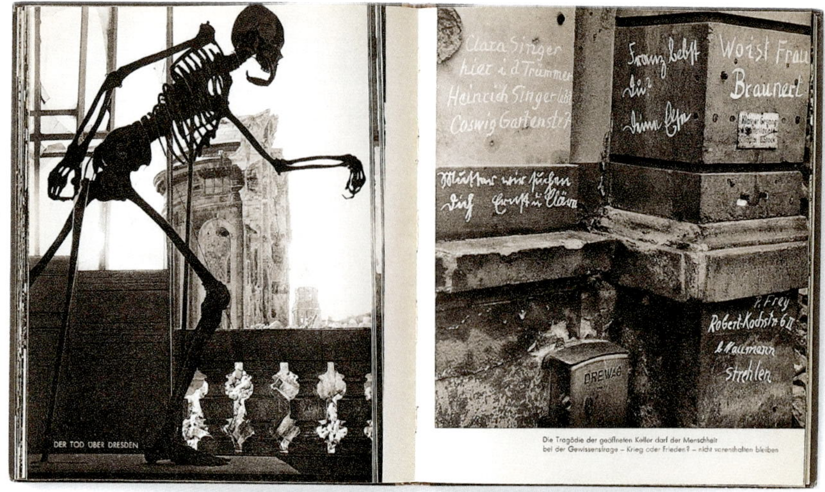

photographic work, had been destroyed beyond repair. With a Leica that someone gave him as a gift, he set out once more to photograph: ruins, urban 'canyons', car wrecks, and finally the corpses in the air raid shelters, which began to be opened in 1946. This work occupied him for more than four years. Among the thousands of pictures he created was his View from the City Hall Tower, on which Peter worked for a full week, according to his own report.

"Rubble, ruins, burnt-out debris as far as the eye can see. To comprise the totality of this barbaric destruction in a single picture," as Peter himself described the creation of the photograph, "seemed at most a vague possibility. It could be done only from a bird's eye view. But the stairs to almost all the towers were burned out or blocked. In spite of the ubiquitous signs warning 'Danger of Collapse', I nonetheless ascended most of them – and finally, one afternoon, the City Hall Tower itself. But on that day, the light was from absolutely the wrong direction, thus making it impossible to take a photograph. The next day I climbed up again, and while inspecting the tower platform, discovered an approximately 3-meter [10-foot] high stone figure – which could not in any way be drawn into the picture, however. The only window which might have offered the possibility for this was located around four meters [13 feet] above the platform, reachable only from inside the tower. Two stories down, I found a five-meter [16-foot] ladder that someone may have carried up after the fire to assess the extent of the damage. The iron stairway was still in good repair. How I managed to get that murderous ladder up the two stories remains a riddle to this day. But now I was standing high enough over the figure [to photograph] and the width of the window also allowed the necessary distance. The series of exposures made with a Leica, however, resulted in such plunging lines, that the photographs were almost unusable. In this case only a square camera could help, but I didn't own one. After two days, I finally hunted one down, climbed the endless tower stairs for the third time, and thus created the photograph with the accusatory gesture of the stone figure – after a week of drudgery effort and scurrying about."

Peter's photograph appeared in *Dresden – eine Kamera klagt an*, published in 1949 in the former German Democratic Republic with a first run of fifty thousand copies. That the cropped

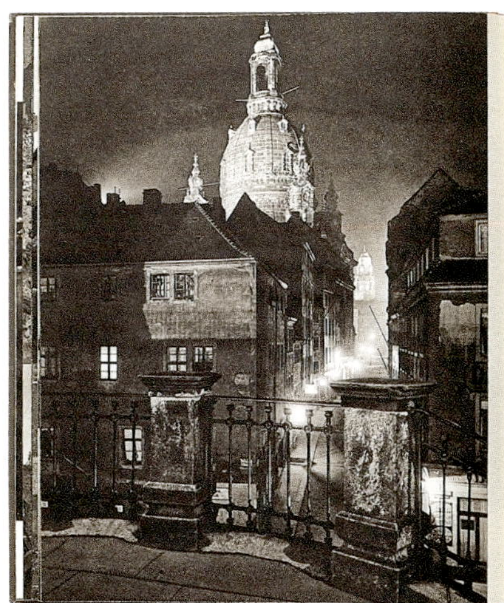

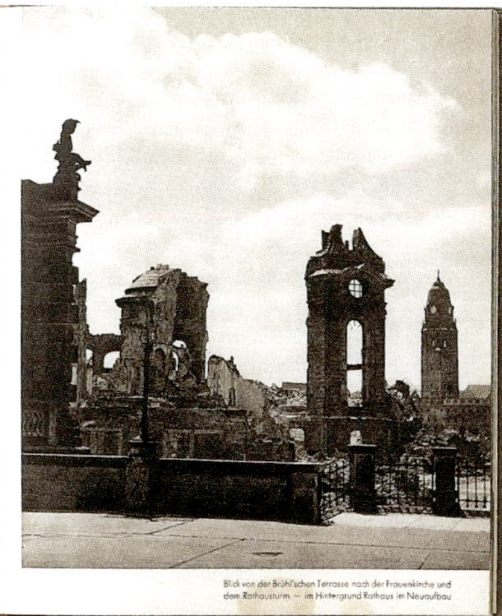

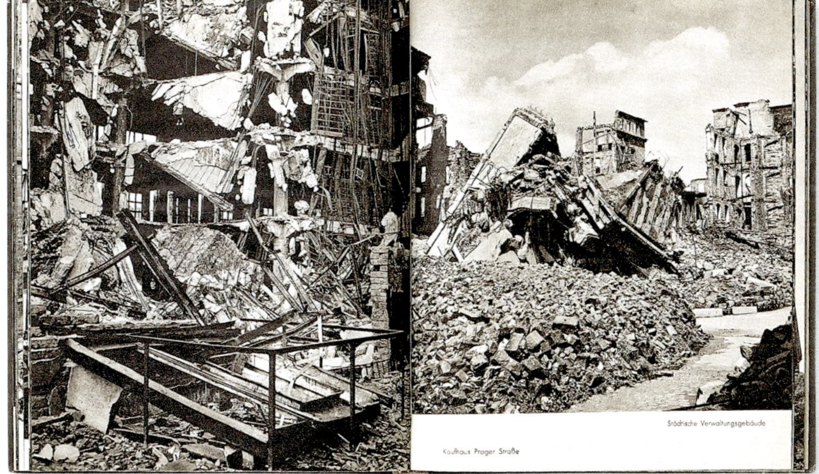

figure in the picture is not the angel of peace, but the personification of 'Bonitas', or Goodness, does nothing to diminish the symbolic character of the photograph. The fact that streets were by then largely cleared of debris and rubble even increases the feeling of emptiness as well as the stillness, which for many people was the most striking characteristic after capitulation in May 1945.

Wolfgang Kil once described Richard Peter's completely subjective images, which were intended as affective warnings, as "landscapes of the soul." In these pictures, an entire generation found their experience of the war visually preserved.

Ernst Haas
Vienna
1947

Waiting for a Miracle

Until the mid-1950s, the release of German solders from Allied imprisonment formed one of the major themes of the growing post-war press in Germany and Austria. The work of the young photographer Ernst Haas not only made an important contribution to the issue, but also carried him to international fame.

He admitted to a good many credos concerning photography. One can hardly claim, however, that the majority of his photographic declarations, delivered in numerous quotations and bon mots, are wholly free from contradiction. Nonetheless, there is one principle that may well be said to have reigned supreme throughout his professional career. Pictures, he once said, are like music: "They communicate themselves immediately, without any interpretation." The ideal and the real do not always or necessarily coincide, but in the work of the native Viennese photographer Ernst Haas, the dictum is fulfilled. His photographs – initially in black-and-white, later in color – exemplify the notion of a 'universal' photographic language, a concept which in turn helps to explain the unequalled success of his free yet firm position in the realm of applied photography – which is to say: advertising. Wherever it was necessary for pictures to operate suggestively, without an accompanying explanation, Haas was the photographer of choice. A seducer of the visual realm, Haas saw himself as an artist, as a poet-photographer, and in precisely this role he was taken as a model by an international community of amateur photographers during the 1960s and 1970. His major work, *The Creation* – the outcome of his contributions to John Huston's epic *The Bible* in book form – sold more than 350,000 copies. In 1958, *Life* devoted a segment of no fewer than thirty-six pages of Haas's photographs in an article on "Magic Color in Motion" in 1958 and, following the trend, the magazine *Popular Photography* included him in its list of the world's ten best photographers.

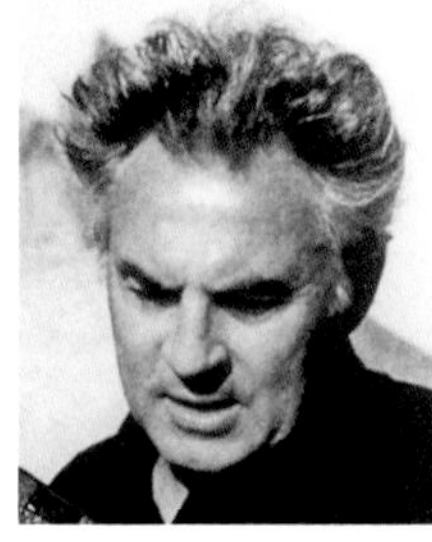

Ernst Haas
Born ***1921*** *in Vienna. Studies medicine without finishing.* ***1943–49*** *works in a photographic studio in Vienna.* ***1949*** *first large photosequence in* Heute. *Accepted in the same year by Magnum.* ***1951*** *moves to the USA. Gives up photo-reportage and turns to photographic essays in color. Publications in* Life, Look, Holiday, Vogue, Esquire, Paris Match, Queen, Stern, Geo. ***1958*** *chosen as one of the "Ten Greatest Photographers in the World" by* Popular Photography. *Film stills (from* ***1954****), cinematography (from* ***1964****) and advertising (especially Marlboro).* ***1971*** *publication of* The Creation. ***1972*** *culture prize of the DGPh. Dies* ***1986*** *in New York.*

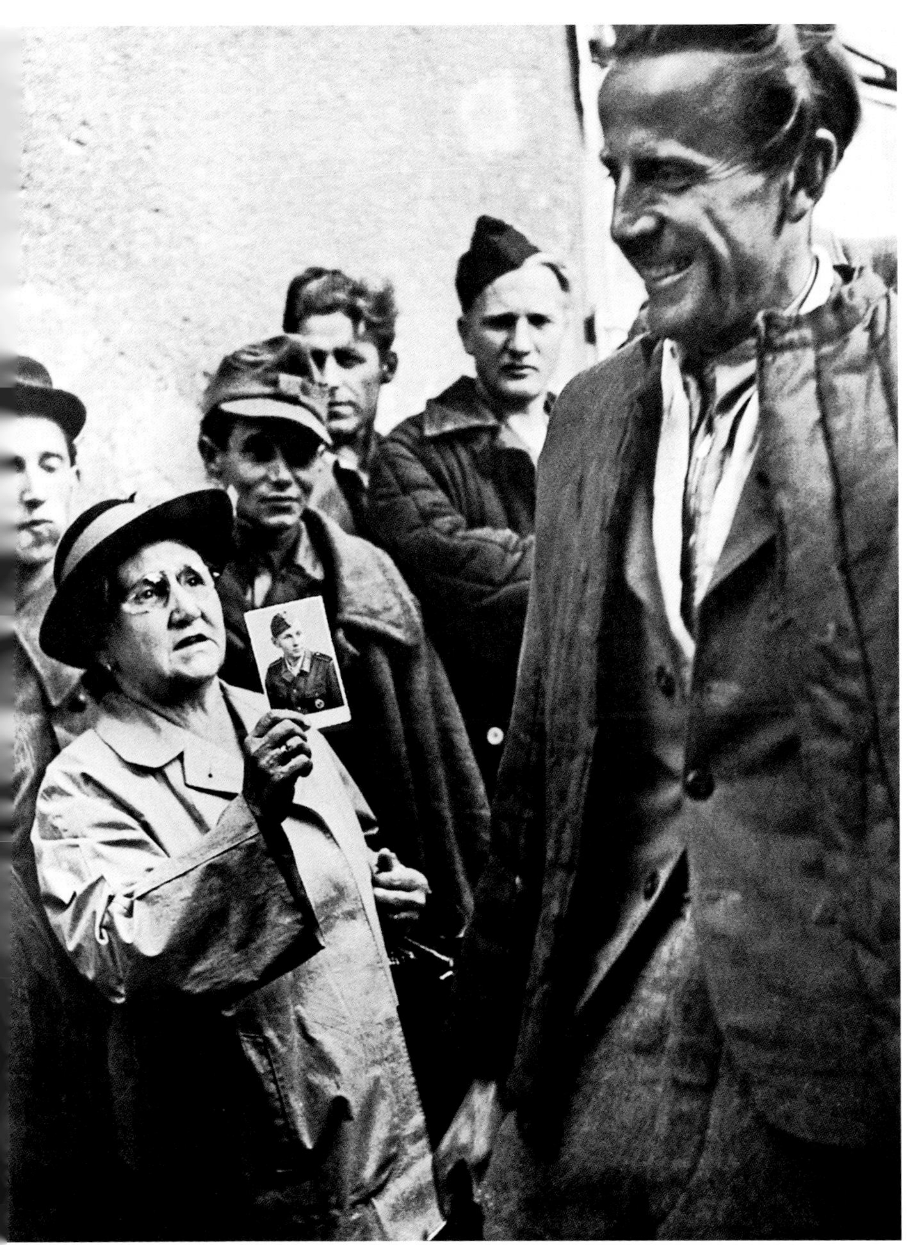

Vienna, 1947

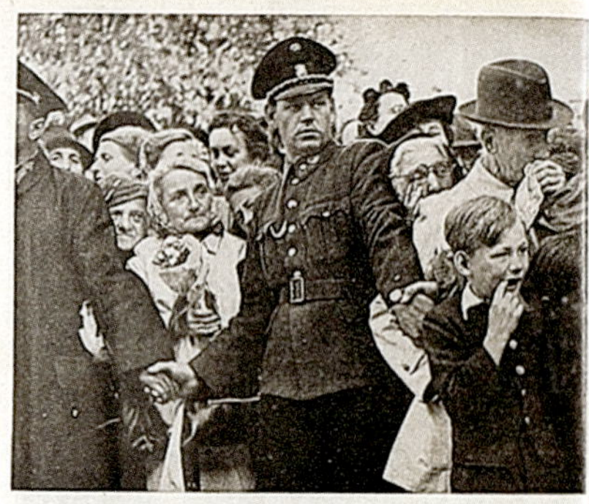

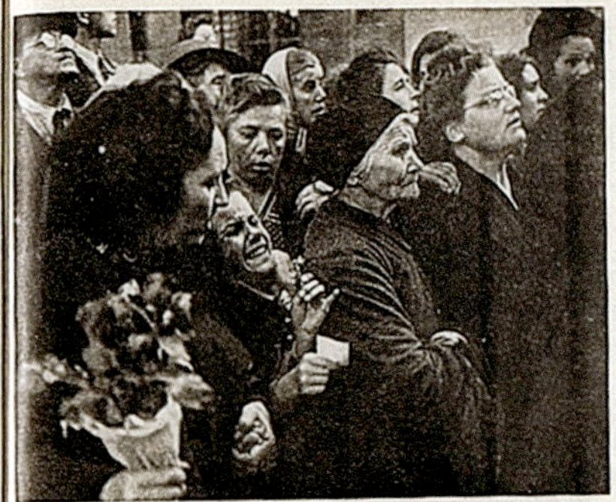

Und die Frauen warten…

Die Geschichte jedes Krieges wird mit Tränen geschrieben

Bilder für HEUTE von Ernst Haas

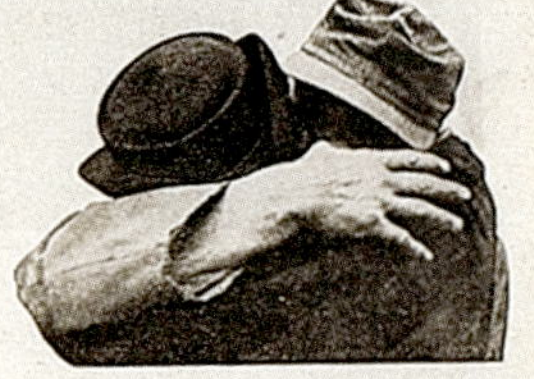

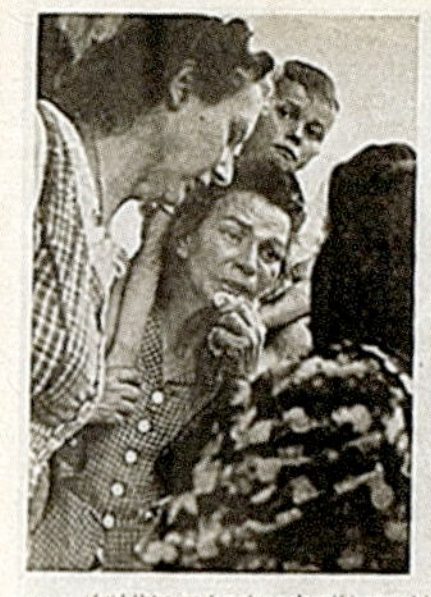

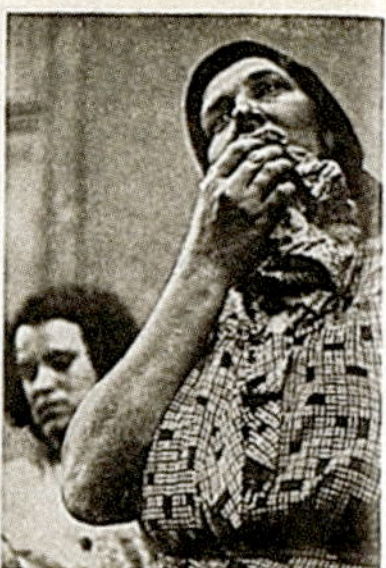

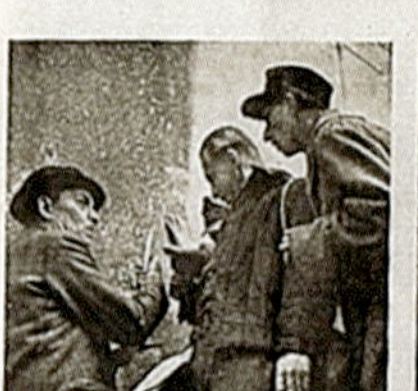

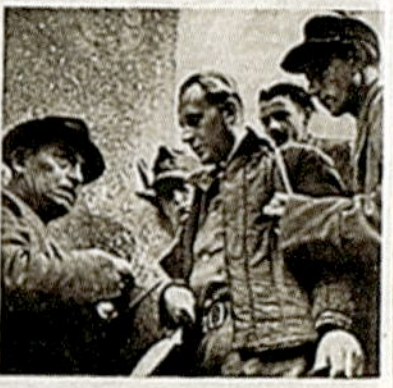

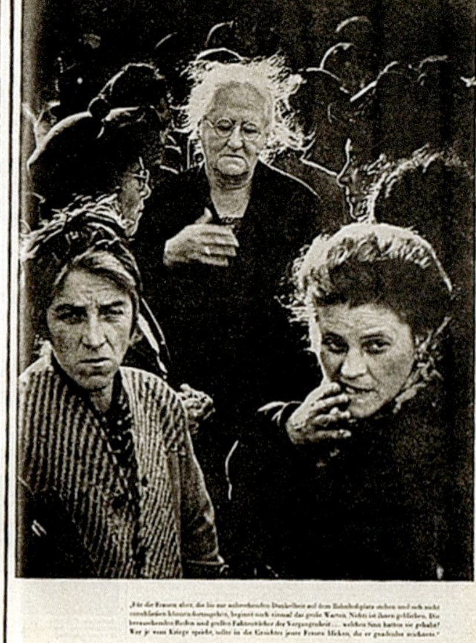

Similarly, *twen*, the German trend magazine of the 1960s, also turned to work by Haas when it decided to introduce color into its publication (6/1961).

The unheard-of success and influence of the color pioneer Ernst Haas – who was invited to present the first one-man exhibition of color photography in the history of the New York Museum of Modern Art at the initiative of Edward Steichen – make it easy to forget that Haas's roots really lay in photojournalism. Haas had, however, turned away from reportage photography in the widest sense quite early in his career, and later even took to mocking it. "The reporter," he once said, "is someone in a trench coat with a rakishly upturned collar, who runs after events, wants to capture facts, who narrates, reports on so-called reality. To be honest, I am not too interested in facts. My issues are of a more artistic nature. These are rather more the problems of the painter. I'm a painter who was too impatient to paint, and therefore became a photographer." And it is true: Haas's experimental work with color shoved his early photographic reports more or less into the background – except for his documentary work on the return of former prisoners of war, which, along with Robert Lebeck's later photo report (*Revue* 43/1955), became one of the best known of its genre, and gained Haas entry into the illustrated magazine *Life* as well as membership of the Magnum group. Critics rank his "picture-story on the first repatriated prisoners" to be among the "most powerful pictorial documents of the post-war period." The photograph of course appears in the large, two-volume history of the Magnum agency – even though Haas was not yet a member of the legendary cooperative at the time he took the picture, and was no longer a member when the book was published. In Cornell Capa's catalogue on the thematic exhibition *The Concerned Photographer 2*, Haas's photograph of the questioning mother is the feature picture to the chapter on Haas. In his own important photographic volume *Black and White*, Haas also gives prominence to the picture. The photograph has been printed numerous times and has become a part of our collective memory. It even turns up in narrative literature, as for example in Christoph Ransmayr's novel *Morbus Kitahara* (1995), where "pictures of those who disappeared are held out like trumps in a card game against death."

A remarkable humanitarian and charitable performance

A picture within a picture: the photograph of a young man or, rather, a nearly grown-up child in uniform. The photograph forms so to speak the center of the black-and-white composition, which, taken with a Rolleiflex, was originally square in format. In addition, six more faces can be made out. But the men in the background function rather like the supernumeraries in the small tragedy that was repeated thousands of times in German train stations between 1945 and 1955. The question always hanging in the air is about the whereabouts of another human being, a son. The conventional half-portrait with its traditional deckle-edge, which once had been made for remembrance, now became a kind of 'wanted' photograph, or better a search photo – a phrase that will virtually become a technical term in connection with the work of the Red Cross in the course of the largest identification campaign in history. In 1946

Heute, *3 August 1949: the illustrated magazine published by the US Military Government was the first to publish Haas' reportage.*

the photojournalist and former war correspondent Hilmar Pabel had begun to take portraits of displaced children for the sake of helping to locate their relatives; Erich Kästner published the photographs in his magazine *Pinguin*. Later, the Red Cross joined the effort with large-scale poster campaigns, and finally in 1951 began an organized research based on filing cards that were able to clarify the fates of more than a million missing persons – a remarkable "humanitarian and charitable performance" that owed much of its success to the medium of photography, and which was awarded the Culture Prize of the German Photography Society (Deutschen Gesellschaft für Photographie) in 1975 – three years after Ernst Haas himself had accepted the award.

The confidence and the desire to rebuild

Whereas the Red Cross pursued its well organized investigative work in grand style, Haas confronts us with a form of individual research that had become a routine of daily life for countless people in central Europe after 1945. Haas took his photograph in the train station Vienna South in 1947. The photographer consciously focused on a single detail of the scene and excluded the surrounding situation. This concentration has made the picture into a timelessly valid icon, in which the complex history of the period following 1933 is reduced to a simple and moving act of searching and finding. Concretely, the photograph depicts the encounter between two people. On the one hand there is the mother with her questioning and anxious gaze. On the other, there is the returnee who – so we suspect – has already identified his family beyond the edge of the picture. He is beaming. He takes a quick step forward. His posture and gestures, his facial expression, his unseen hand clutching the handle of a bag – all are expressions of confidence and the desire to rebuild. He doesn't even give a passing glance to the short woman who stands as an example for those who lost so much, perhaps all, during the war and the Nazi era. In this way the photograph unites the two realities of postwar society.

Scenes of happiness and moments of disappointment

A total of more than eighty million soldiers were involved in the Second World War. Thirty-five million, including a good eleven million Germans, were incarcerated as war prisoners between 1939 and 1945. The first German prisoners returned home in 1948, the last in 1956. These later came back to a country – or rather countries – that were already long on the way to an increasingly prosperous everyday life. Often these 'late arrivals' were disturbed by the "'normality' that had been achieved with such effort" (Kaminsky). It is no accident that Wolfgang Borchert's drama on this theme, *The Man Outside*, became one of the most discussed works of the period. But aside from this piece, the problem was treated only rarely in literature and the fine arts. The young Ernst Haas, born in 1921, also came upon the theme somewhat by accident. At that moment, he was accompanying the later Magnum photographer Inge Morath through war-ravaged Vienna looking for a location to shoot a fashion spread. At the

---

Further double-page spreads from Heute, *3 August 1949. The astonishingly spacious layout is strongly reminiscent of* Life *magazine.*

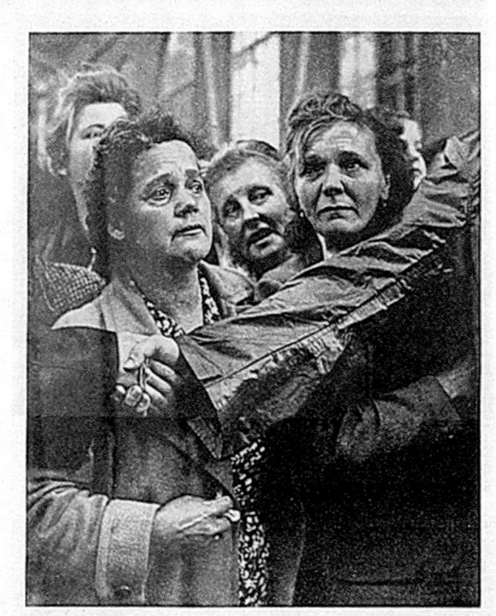

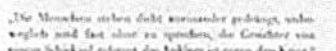
„Die Menschen stehen dicht aneinander gedrängt, unbeweglich und fast ohne zu sprechen, die Gesichter von einem Schicksal geformt, das Anklage ist gegen den Krieg."

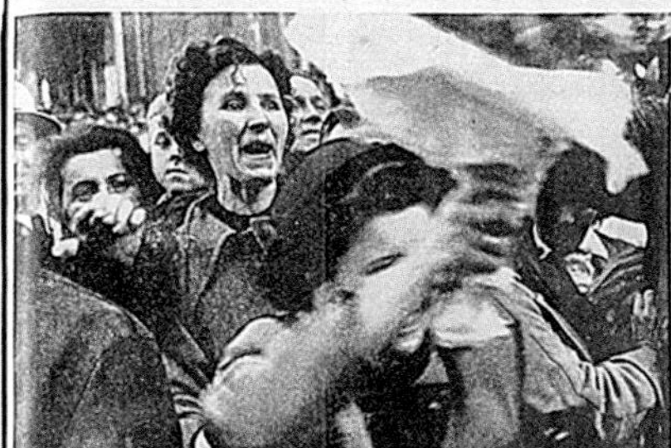

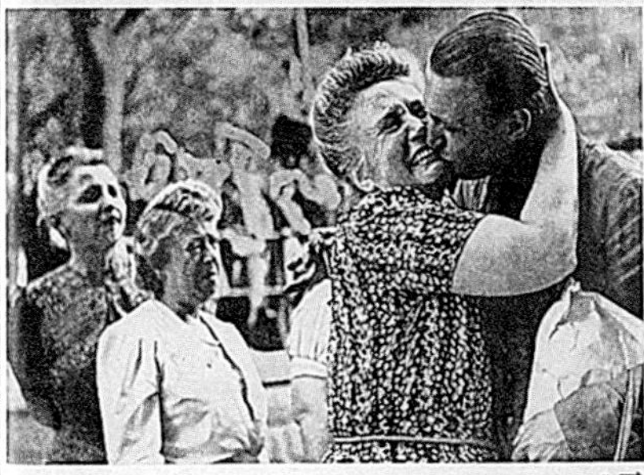

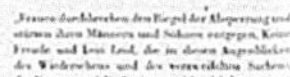
„Frauen durchbrechen den Riegel der Absperrung und stürmen ihren Männern und Söhnen entgegen. Keine Freude und kein Leid, die in diesen Augenblicken des Wiedersehens und des verzweifelten Suchens, des Fragens und Umherirrens nicht sichtbar wären."

18 19

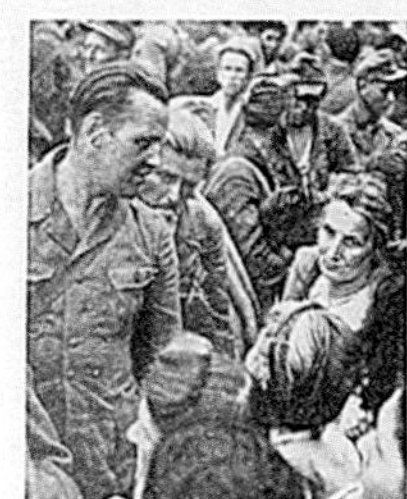

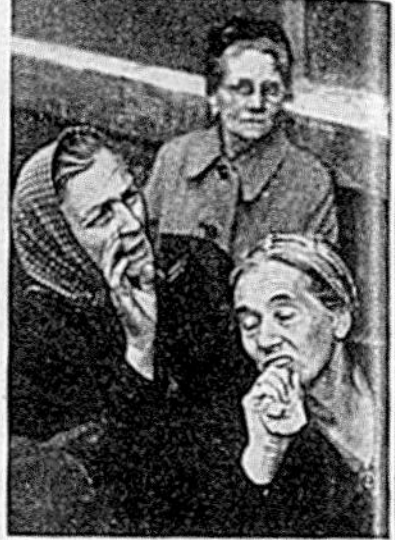

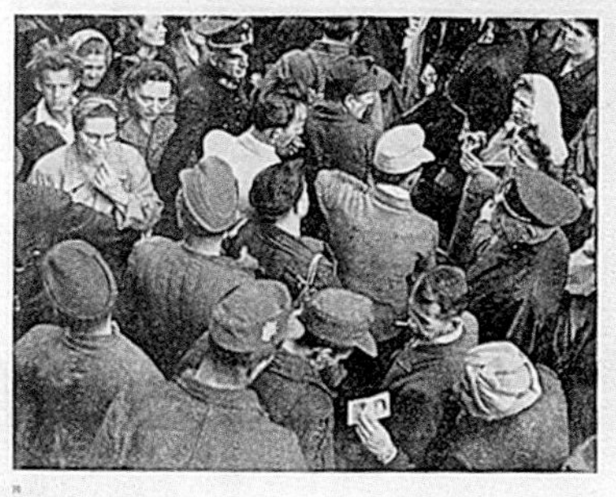

20

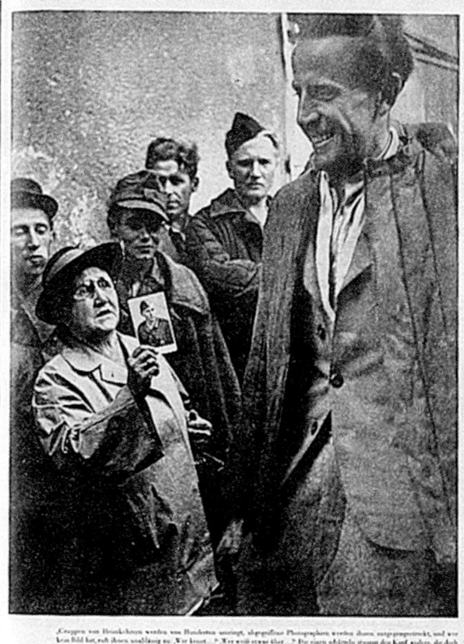
„Gruppen von Heimkehrern werden von Hunderten umringt, abgegriffene Photographien werden ihnen entgegengestreckt, und wer kein Bild hat, ruft ihnen unablässig zu: ‚Wer kennt…?' ‚Wer weiß etwas über…?' Die einen schütteln stumm den Kopf, andere, die doch noch Angehörige hinten in der Menge erspäht haben, schreiten mit Augen vorüber, die vor Glück nichts anderes mehr fassen können."

21

Vienna, 1947

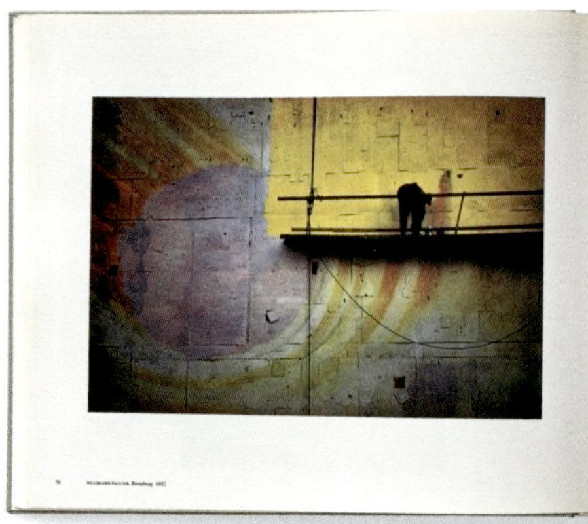

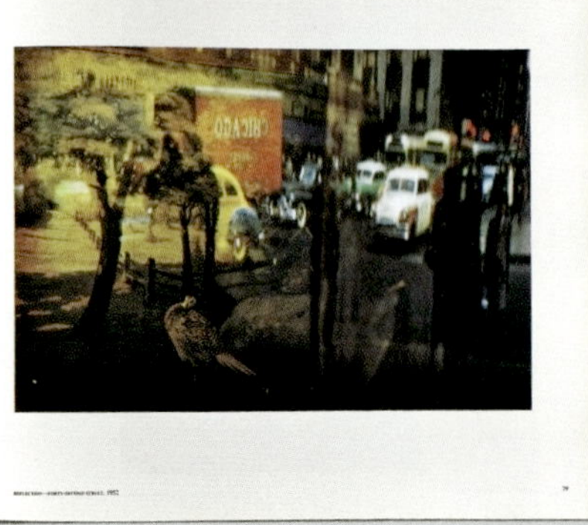

train station he ran into a crowd of people awaiting the arrival of the first six hundred Austrian war prisoners to return from Eastern Europe. "It broke one's heart," Haas later recalled. "No one knew who would be arriving. Tension and silence lay on the square until the first prisoners appeared, as if on a stage. What happened now could only be captured with the camera. I worked as if demented… Scenes of happiness gave way to moments of disappointment. Impossible to grasp all of it. Women held bleached-out photographs in the air toward the new arrivals. 'Do you know him? Have you seen my son?' They called out the names of their men. Children with pictures of fathers they had never seen compared the photographs with the faces of the arrivals. It was almost too much. I staggered home as if in a trance."

Heralded his international break-through

Haas had begun studying medicine, but his Jewish background debarred him from completing his studies. After the war, influenced by the work of Werner Bischof, his slightly older contemporary, Haas took up photojournalism. In the months after his experience at the train station, he continued to pursue the theme. As Jim Hughes writes, he accompanied transport after transport with the camera, and finally arrived at his first great photojournalistic report. Haas's work appeared for the first time in 1949 in *Heute*, an illustrated magazine published by the American military government beginning in 1945. Warren Trabant, the chief director of the magazine, was impressed with the work and devoted four double pages to it under the title "And the Women Are Waiting…" (No. 90, 3 August 1949). It was an expansive layout, clearly influenced by *Life*. Haas explained: "I did the layout myself, and because I always came with a proposal and

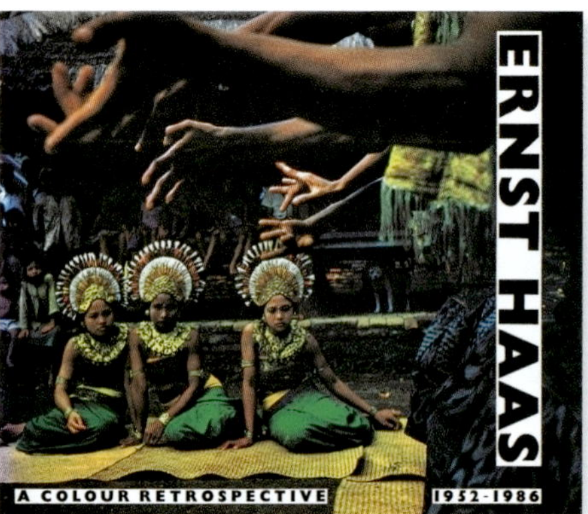

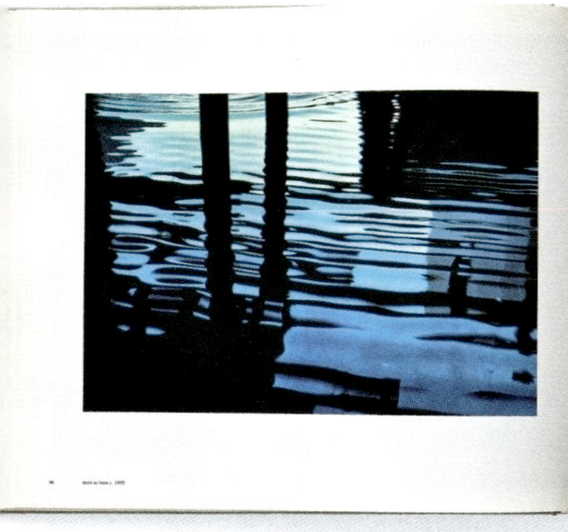
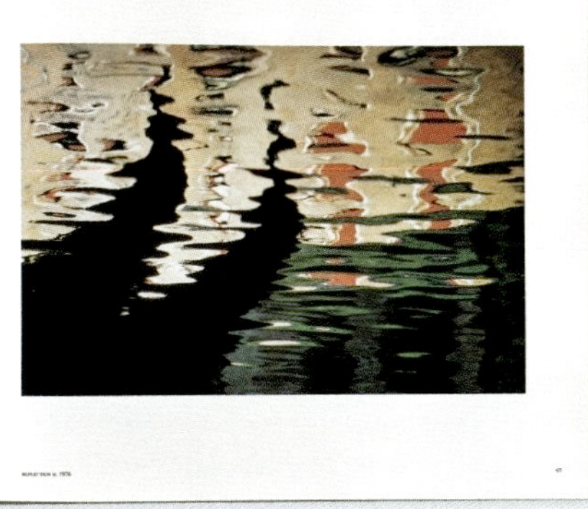

sketches, they just followed along." Trabant, who had initially worked at *Life*, passed the article on to the USA, where it appeared a week later in *Life* in a double-page spread that provided Haas with his international break-through. "Groups of the repatriated," runs the caption under the photograph in *Heute*, "are surrounded by hundreds of people; well-worn photographs are held up toward them, and those without a picture call out constantly 'Who knows so-and-so? Who knows something about…?' Some shake their heads silently, while others who have in fact spied a relative in the crowd, step across with eyes that are so happy, they cannot take in any more."

Pictures of repatriated soldiers are a natural part of the world of the post-war German and Austrian pictorial press (which remained under Allied censorship until the lifting of the license requirement in 1949). The Munich illustrated *Heute* carried an article entitled "Return from Russia" as early as 1946, and a four-page photographic report appeared in the Austrian edition of *Stern* as late as October 1958. In France, the already-mentioned photo report by Robert Lebeck on the return of the last war prisoners from Russia had appeared under the headline "Thanks Be to God" in 1955 as the title-story in *Revue*. Admittedly, none of these articles achieved the broad and enduring effect that Ernst Haas had reached with his key picture. His photograph unites joy and pain, hope and sorrow, immediate happiness and an extended waiting for a miracle as fundamental categories of human existence. Haas had wanted, he stated in a later interview, to portray "the woman as the true 'Unknown Soldier'." He did not speak to her, however, or inquire further into her fate.

Ernst Haas:
A Color Retrospective, *London 1989,*
cover and double-page spreads.

Robert Doisneau
The Kiss in Front of City Hall
1950

Love on a March Day

There is scarcely a photograph of our times that has achieved the popularity of Robert Doisneau's *The Kiss in Front of City Hall.* The image of a fleeting embrace has become an icon of Paris par excellence. Moreover, as a gripping metaphor of the sense of post-war life, the photograph brought its creator not only fame and wealth.

This time, he dared to come in closer. Usually, however, he kept his distance and tried to remain unnoticed. Robert Doisneau was fond of citing his intrinsic shyness as the reason for his restraint as a photographer. Making necessity a virtue, he had eventually transformed keeping his distance into a pictorial style that applied to the entire social and architectural environment of the city. Doisneau is the photographer of the big picture, so to speak, and is thus the antithesis of a William Klein, who consciously intermingles with the people he photographs, seeking closeness and interaction, letting it be known that he is a photographer, provoking reactions, and thus turning the very act of taking the picture into the theme of the work. But if the French term *chasseur d'images* – literally, picture hunter – is recognized throughout the world as a description for the action of the photographer, Robert Doisneau always understood himself in contrast as a *pêcheur d'images*, a fisher of images, that is, a photographer who waited patiently until the stream of life cast its more or less rich booty before his feet – a "bystander" (Colin Westerbeck), who lifted discretion to a pinnacle and placed it at the heart of all his work. In this sense, Doisneau has entered the history of photography as the master of the 'candid camera'. Or rather, he would have liked to have been so recognized, if a widely publicized series of international law suits toward the end of his life had not revealed that he – Doisneau himself – had helped set up the events that are depicted in his photographs. In any case, what is probably his most famous picture, *The Kiss in Front of City Hall*, was, as we now know, the result of a scene

---

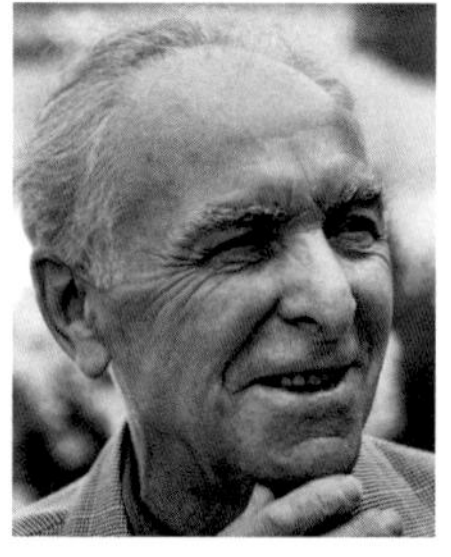

Robert Doisneau
*Born **1912** in Gentilly, Val-de-Marne, France. **1929** diploma as engraver and lithographer. **1930** commercial photographer for Atelier Ullmann. **1931** assistant to André Vigneau. **1932** first reportage in the illustrated daily* Excelsior. ***1934–39** works as advertising and industrial photographer for Renault. Active in the Résistance. **1946** joins the agency Rapho. **1949** book publication* La Banlieue de Paris *(with Blaise Cendrars). **1949–52** fashion for French* Vogue. *Afterwards freelance photographer in Montrouge near Paris. **1992** major retrospective in the Museum of Modern Art, Oxford. Dies **1994** in Montrouge.*

staged with the help of a hired actor and actress. But what does this fact mean for the reception and understanding of a photograph that functions as a 'popular icon' and is one of the most well-known photographic creations of its century?

A staple of every Doisneau retrospective

According to unofficial statistics, *The Kiss in Front of City Hall* has been sold more than two and a half million times as a postcard alone. In addition, around half a million posters bearing the same motif have found buyers. The picture decorates pillows, handkerchiefs, wall and table calendars, greeting cards, and fold-out picture series. Furthermore, it is a staple of every Doisneau retrospective, and not accidentally adorns the cover of the artist's most important publication to date, *Three Seconds from Eternity*. Visitors to Paris come across some form or another of this image on almost every street corner. The question arises: Why does this comparatively simply constructed and relatively unspectacular photograph still fascinate the public today?

At the exact center of the square photograph is a young couple, about twenty years old. Quite frankly, there is nothing at all striking about them. They are decently dressed – appropriately for the street. At most, the bright scarf tucked into the neck of the man's double-breasted suit is the only item lending a bohemian flavor to the Right Bank of the Seine. Approaching from the left, the couple are sauntering down the busily populated street. The man has placed his right arm around the girl's shoulder. Spontaneously – so the picture suggests – he pulls her toward himself and kisses her on the mouth. None of the other pedestrians visible in the picture seem to have noticed the sudden testimony of love. At most the observer in the foreground witnesses the little scene. The consciously chosen 'over-the-shoulder' shot, to borrow a term from film-making, suggests this at least.

One of those 'undecided' winter days in Paris

Why Robert Doisneau set this scene in the vicinity of the Paris City Hall (Hôtel de Ville), we don't know. In reality, the other bank of the Seine – in particular the Latin Quarter inhabited especially by students – stood for carefree happiness after the war: it was no accident that the Netherlander Ed van der Elsken chose the Rive Gauche as the location for his probably most important work in the mid-1950s: *A Love Story in Saint-Germain-des-Prés*. But Robert Doisneau determined upon the Right Bank. Blurred but clearly recognizable, the neo-Baroque Paris City Hall stands in the background of the busy street, which must therefore in fact be the rue de Rivoli. The street café from which the picture was taken may well be what is today the Café de l'Hôtel de Ville, on the corner of rue du Renard and rue de Rivoli. Doisneau shot the picture with his Rolleiflex looking out toward the street from the second row of tables. The woman walking by in the background has noticed him, her glance giving also the photographer a presence in the picture.

In monographs, the photograph has repeatedly appeared under the title *Sunday*. But in fact there is no indication in the picture itself that it is Sunday: we simply associate the idea of a stroll through the city with Sundays and holidays. Doisneau himself dated the photograph March 1950. It must, therefore, have been taken on one of those 'undecided' winter days in Paris: neither cold nor warm, certainly not sunny, but dipped rather in that diffuse light that Doisneau once described as typical of Paris – the light that is part of the perpetual "tender

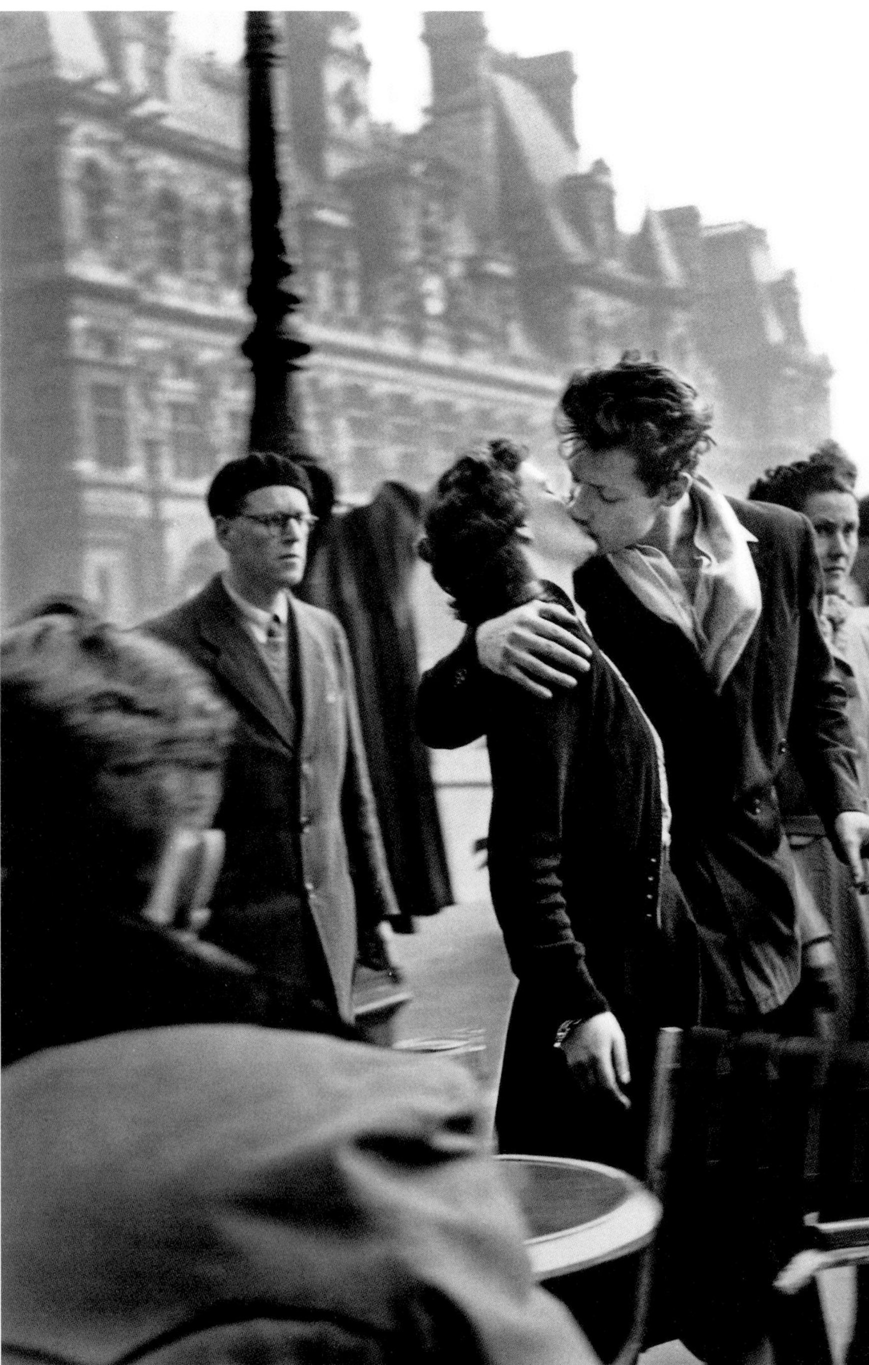

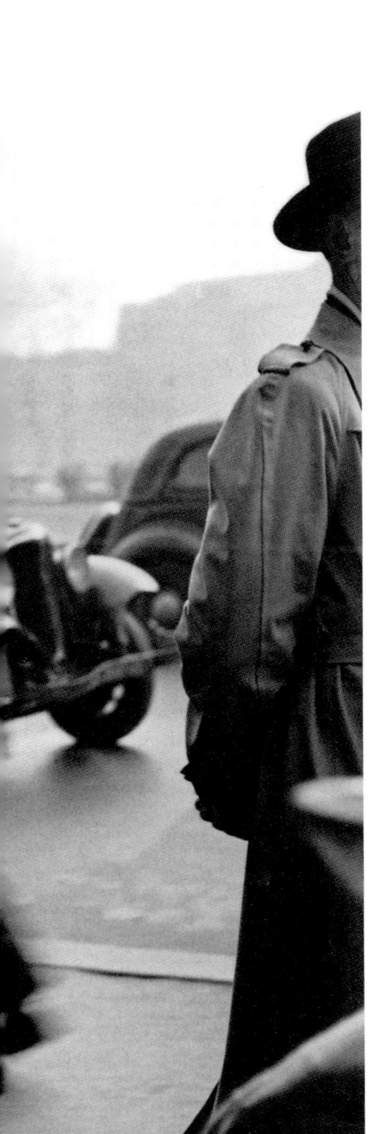

gray tent that the famed sky of the Île-de-France [begins] to unfold at daybreak as one would pull a protective cover over valuable furniture."

Always looking for an eloquent moment

Doisneau's photograph was published for the first time in the legendary illustrated magazine *Life*. At that time, this son of a petty bourgeois Parisian family was thirty-eight years old. At the École Estienne he had learned the craft of engraving, and afterwards had become acquainted with the innovative tendencies of the New Objectivity movement in photography at the studio of André Vigneau. Doisneau subsequently accepted his first position – admittedly an unsatisfactory one for him – with Renault as an industrial photographer. By 1939 he had been fired for coming to work late once too often. "So there I was on the street again, where everything was happening, I felt very happy, but also slightly worried. Five years in a factory put my initiative to sleep. But asleep or not, material need forced me to make a new beginning."

Doisneau transformed necessity into virtue, and made the street the object of his photographic explorations. It was always the Paris of the simple people who fascinated him, however – the Paris of pensioners and casual workers, of tramps and cabbies, easy women, workers, children, and of landladies peering down the hall. These are the people he sought out, always looking for the eloquent moment in which the human, and all-too-human, was concentrated. Doisneau is the story-teller among the exponents of a so-called *photographie humaniste*. Whereas Cartier-Bresson followed the Constructivist dictum and composed his photographs down to the last detail, Doisneau sought out the anecdote. His pictures evince wit, but very often there is an irony or even a slight sadness hiding behind the humor. He always defended himself against intellectualizing the taking of a picture. His camera art derived from springs of sympathy and feeling, sources which ultimately explain the unparalleled international popularity of his œuvre.

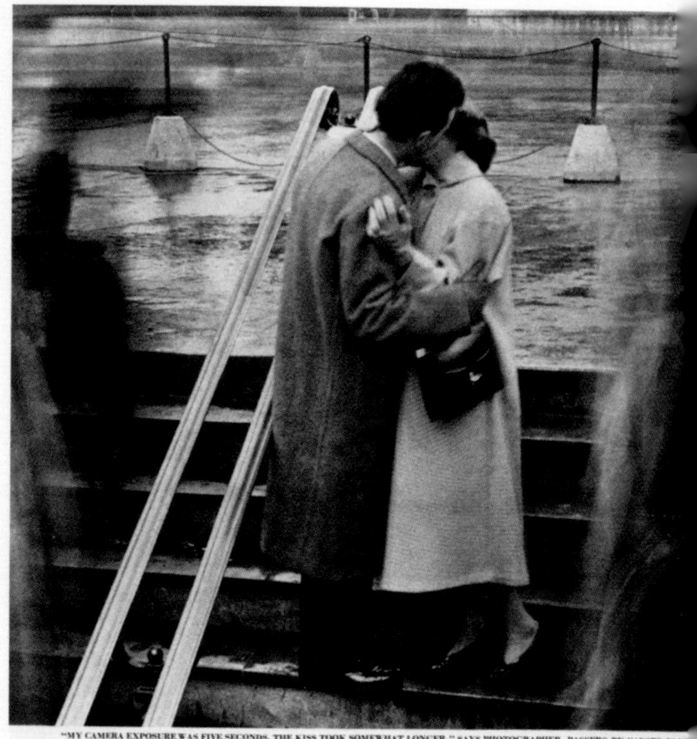

"MY CAMERA EXPOSURE WAS FIVE SECONDS, THE KISS TOOK SOMEWHAT LONGER," SAYS PHOTOGRAPHER. PASSERS-BY CAUSED BLU

SPEAKING OF PICTURES . . .

In Paris young lovers kiss wherever they want to and nobody seems to car

Paris is understandably proud of its reputation as the home of fine wines, fine perfumes—and of love. It is a reputation, so far as love is concerned, that is not left to take care of itself: constant practice keeps up the standards. In other cities bashful couples usually seek out parks or deserted streets for their romancing. But in Paris vigorous young couples, determined to uphold the municipal honor, can be observed in unabashed courting in even the most crowded parts of the city.

It goes on all day, this public kissing, and all night too. But Photographer Robert Doisneau, who took the unposed pictures on these pages, found two peaks in the day's osculation: 1) at noon, when offices, shops and universities are closed for lunch and thousands of youngsters are released into the streets, and 2) between 5 and 7 p.m., when young males make the ope ing moves in the evening's campaign. Only tou ists pay any attention to the smooching. Th French public ignores it completely, smiles ap proval even when it gets in the way. One police man explained, "It is a fine thing, and it keep these young lads out of trouble. If they weren' with their girls, they would probably be out o some hockey field where they might get hurt."

16

16a&b

First use of the *Baiser de l'Hôtel de Ville*, in *LIFE* magazine, 1950.

24

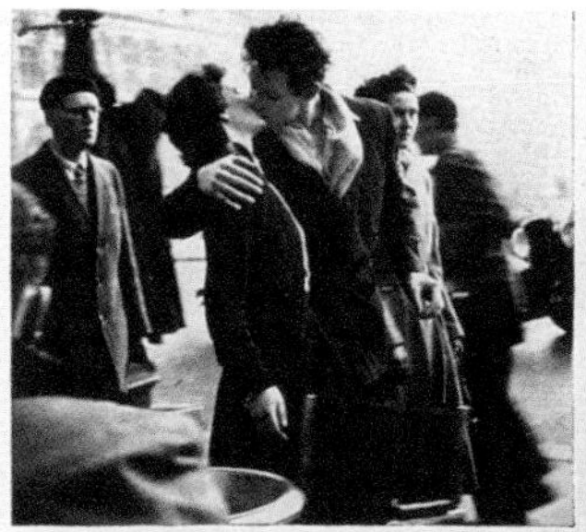

THIS WAS SHORT KISS, "A KISS RAPIDE," SAYS PHOTOGRAPHER

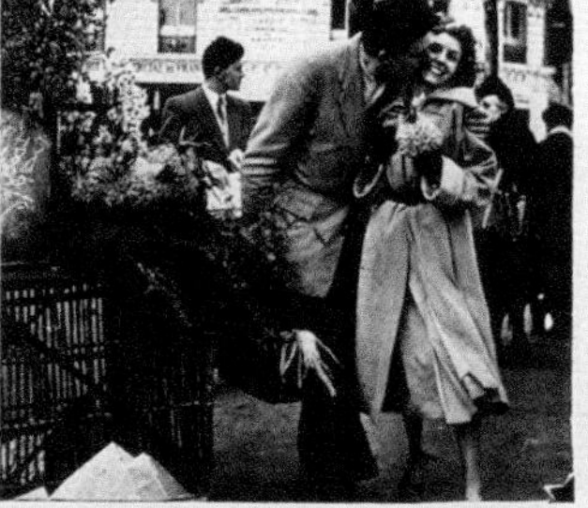

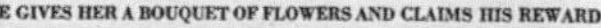

HE GIVES HER A BOUQUET OF FLOWERS AND CLAIMS HIS REWARD

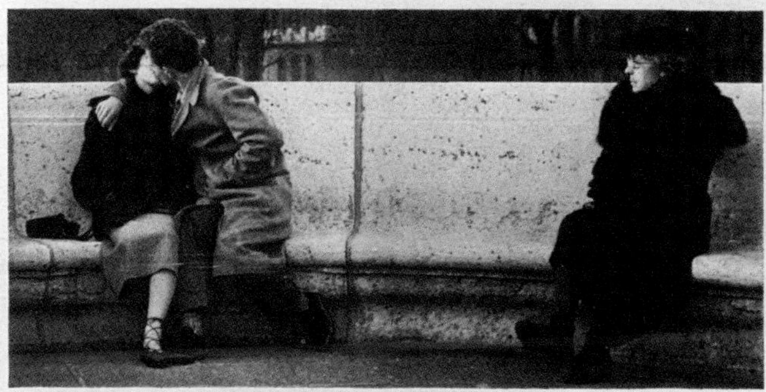

LOVERS ENJOY THEMSELVES ON PONT-NEUF. THE OLD LADY, THINKS THE PHOTOGRAPHER, IS PERHAPS REMEMBERING A TIME PAST

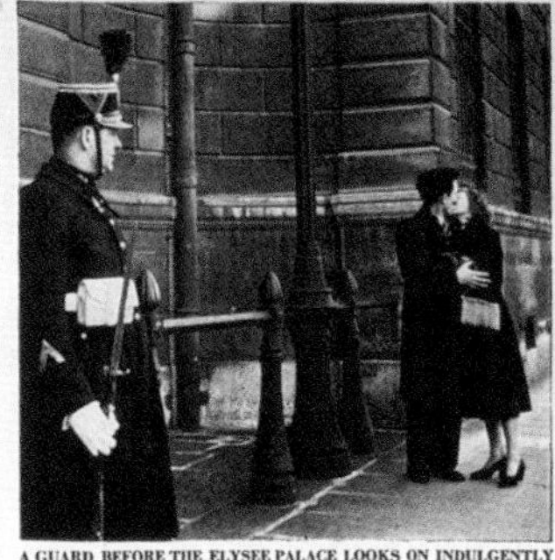

A GUARD BEFORE THE ELYSEE PALACE LOOKS ON INDULGENTLY

LOVERS ARE BLOCKING TRAFFIC BUT NOBODY SEEMS TO CARE

25

Fame came late to Doisneau – but then all the more enduringly. In the early 1970s, the market halls were torn down in Paris. For many Parisians, their demise signified not only the passing of a piece of Old Paris, but also the end of an entire era: that not-always-carefree, but always hopeful post-war era, in which the metropolis on the Seine once again had advanced to the artistic and intellectual center of the world, before the city irrevocably lost its leading position to New York. It is no accident that precisely at this painful turning point, the work of Robert Doisneau, the core of whose work largely reflected the 1940s and 1950s, underwent a literally unparalleled discovery. His friends had warned him: "Don't waste your time with these photos!" But Doisneau had held out, and in the end there was almost no other photographer of his generation who could offer such a treasury of pictures from 'better times' than the rather quiet and unassuming Doisneau. Rumor has it that his archives contained no fewer that 400,000 negatives – a visual cosmos from which innumerable never-before-seen photographs of Paris still emerge.

A city of relaxed behavior and sensual pleasure

Under the aegis of this belated acceptance of Doisneau, *The Kiss in Front of City Hall* embarked on its march of triumph after a small-format premier in *Life* as one of a total of six black-and-white photographs. The publisher had neither recognized the visual power of the picture nor seen any significance in the name of its creator: the photographer was not in fact mentioned on the double-page spread. The photograph itself was part of a story about Paris as the city of lovers. There, suggested both text and pictures, people might embrace on every street corner without anyone taking notice. Remember: we are still speaking about the 1950s, a markedly prudish era, in which a caress on the open street was hardly the rule. In this context, *Life* once more borrowed the old cliché of Paris as a city of relaxed behavior and sensual pleasure, an image also current in Hollywood films of the time. At root, *The Kiss in Front of City Hall* still functions on this level today: the picture arouses ideas of an undisturbed enjoyment of love a few years after the war. In this sense, the photograph was able to operate in a double sense as an ambassador of a peaceful, yet impetuous, harmonious relationship.

Three kisses at the City Hall, another in the rue de Rivoli, and one more at Place de la Concorde

Doisneau himself continued to maintain an ambivalent attitude toward his famous picture, once even claiming that it represented no photographic achievement. "It's superficial, easy to sell, *une image pute* [a prostituted picture]." All those who bought it, whether as a poster or a puzzle, a shower curtain or a T-shirt, saw it – and still see it – in another light. Throughout his life, Doisneau received enthusiastic letters, including some from people who thought they recognized themselves in the picture. In 1988, however, Denise and Jean-Louis Laverne from Ivry near Paris contacted the photographer with a claim of the equivalent of approximately $90,000 for lost royalties. The outcome was a much-watched court trial, during which Doisneau admitted that he had staged the picture with paid models. The photograph, according to his argument, had been made under contract with *Life* for shots of couples kissing in Paris. But for fear of judicial problems, it was decided to use actors. Doisneau seated himself in a café near Cours Simon, one of the well-known acting schools, and thus discovered "a very pretty girl… She said okay, and brought her boyfriend with her to the scheduled photographic appointment. We took three kisses at the City Hall, another in the rue de Rivoli, and another at Place de la Concorde."

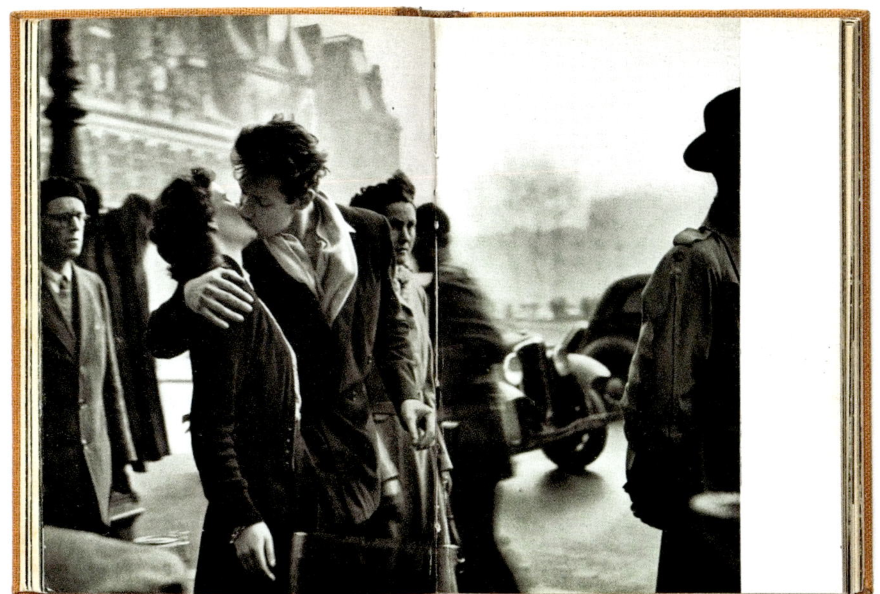

Denise and Jean-Louis Laverne walked out of the trial empty-handed – but the case had stirred up sufficient dust to rouse those who had actually posed for the picture: Jacques Cartaud, then in his mid-sixties, and the former actress Françoise Bornet, who now sued for 100,000 francs in damages. Her claim was also dismissed, even though she produced as evidence an autographed copy of the picture, which the photographer had given to her as a gift after the session. For his part, Doisneau was able to prove that he had paid the young woman what was normal at the time. He thus seemed to be out of the woods, but his artistry as a photographer had suffered damage in the larger sense. Ever since the affair, people have wondered how many of his pictures of post-war Paris Doisneau had in fact staged. The artist admitted arranging "all of my lovers of 1950" – but protested that he had very carefully observed "how people behave in certain situations," before he created the scene.

As paradoxical as it may sound, the discussion over whether the picture was set up or not did very little damage to the incriminated *The Kiss in Front of City Hall* itself: the image had long since left all concern with documentation behind. The photograph became a symbol – and symbols possess a truth of their own.

Pages 260–261: The Kiss in Front of City Hall *first appeared in 1950 in* Life *under the heading "Speaking of Pictures..."*

Above: Les Parisiens tels qu'ils sont *(Parisians as they are) was published in 1954 by Robert Delpire in Paris and proved to be one of Robert Doisneau's most successful books. In 1956 it was followed by two English editions,* Paris Parade *(London), and* Robert Doisneau's Paris *(New York), each containing a selection of 148 illustrations, including* The Kiss in Front of City Hall.

Dennis Stock
James Dean on Times Square
1955

Myth in the Early Morning

It started out as an assignment – and became a legacy. Early in 1955, the young Magnum photographer Dennis Stock accompanied the rising screen star James Dean to Fairmount, Indiana, and then to New York. The resulting photographs would prove to be the best and most intimate portrait this idol of the new youth, who was to die only a few months later in an automobile accident.

The setting is no accident, even if the weather is. But what would this picture be without the rain? It forces the bare-headed protagonist into a slight slouch, makes him pull his head into his collar. But that's what tall men do anyway. Five feet eight (173 cm) stands written on his passport – in other words, not particularly tall. And it may well be that his height at times was as much of a problem for him as his short-sightedness. In private life he had to wear glasses – and he needed them on the stage, too. But perhaps it was just this blurred perception of his environment that threw him back on himself and led to the oft-described intensity of his acting. New York. Times Square. For a few moments Broadway becomes his theater. But in reality, every place is a theater to him – a stage where in fact he doesn't act, but lives out his life, whether before an audience, or in front of the film camera. The boundary between reality and dream disappears; there is no need for him to take on another form as an actor, but rather to heighten the feelings, dreams, fears, neuroses, and phobias that already reside in him. Even now, at this moment, he is private and public at the same moment. It is not merely by chance that he is making his way across Times Square: what he is now doing for the camera is something that he has already done a thousand times before. And it's not an accident that the Chesterfield happens to be hanging from the corner of his mouth. Nonetheless, he smokes in private, too. He is acting, yes – but he is acting himself. He does it for *Life*; he does it

---

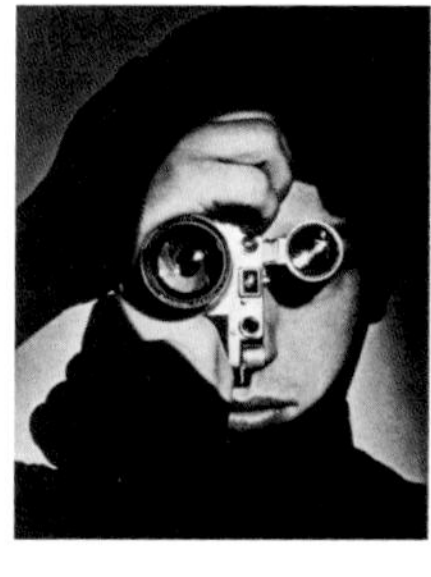

Dennis Stock
Born ***1928*** *in New York. Joins the navy at age 16. After the end of the war turns to photography.* ***1947–51*** *trains under Gjon Mili.* ***1951*** *first prize in the* Life *young photographers competition. Contact with Robert Capa. From* ***1954*** *member of Magnum. Moves to Hollywood, where friends with James Dean. From* ***1957*** *intensive photographic explorations of the jazz world.* ***1960*** *publication of his book* Jazz Street. ***1962*** *withdraws to the country. Turns to nature photography. In the late* ***1960s*** *spends several months at the Hippie communes of the American South West.* ***1970*** *publication of his book* The Alternative. *Then shows a great interest in film and video. Dies* ***2010*** *in Sarasota, Florida.*

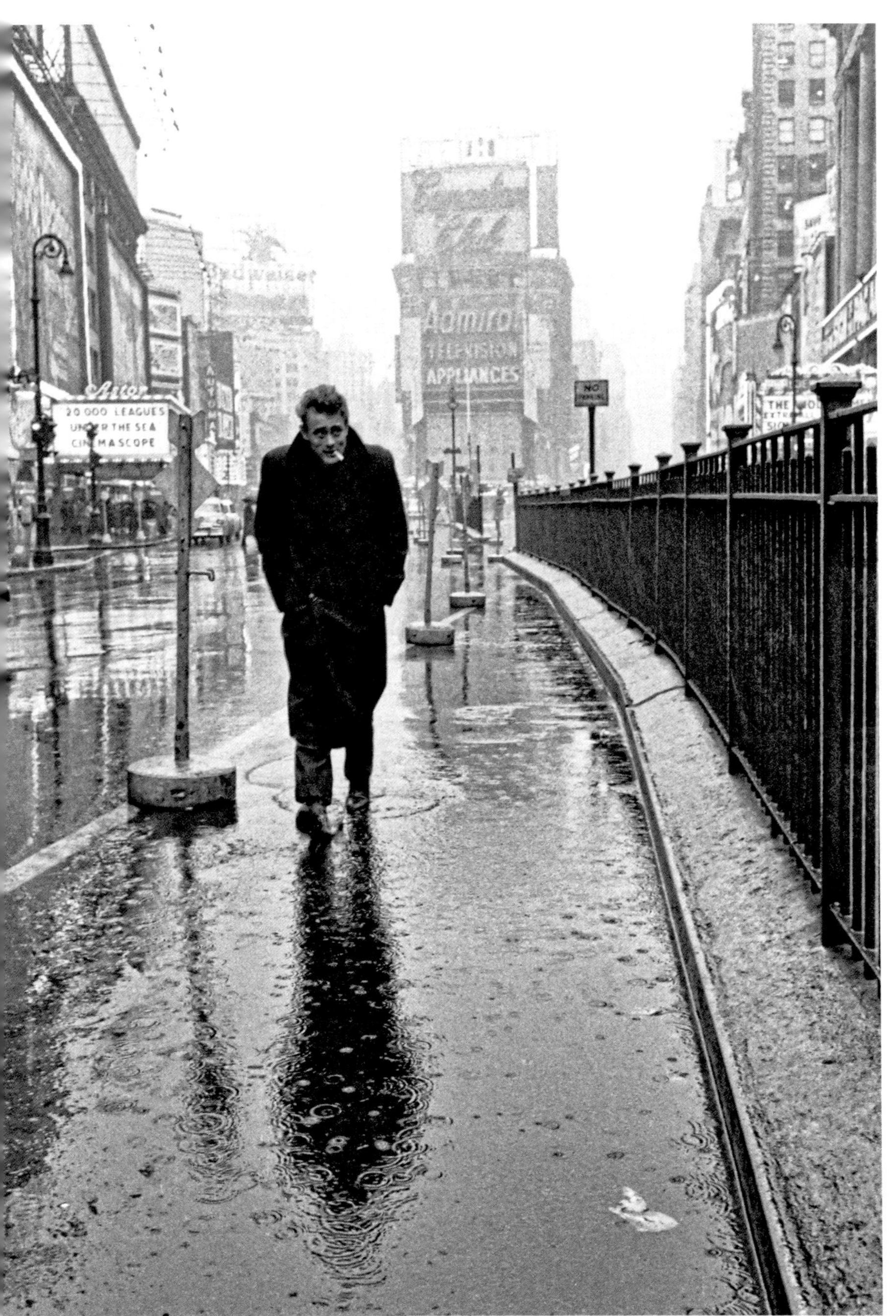

James Dean on Times Square, 1955

for the photographers; he does it for the fame and image whose structure he cannot leave to chance.

Of course he's vain. Even in photographs he sometimes gazes into the mirror, even if it is only his reflection in a frozen puddle. This time, it's a rain-slicked street. It's really quite skillful how Dennis Stock takes advantage of the puddle to double the form of his hero, as it were. In reality he should disappear between the skyscrapers of New York. Instead, the canyon of buildings sinks backward into the mist, and he, in spite of his actual stature, becomes taller. A giant with drawn shoulders – but that's the way he sees himself anyway. And how the photographer manages to convey this self-consciousness graphically is a small stroke of genius. Henri Cartier-Bresson used to look at his pictures upside down to check just how compelling they were. In this case, our picture transfers the attention of the observer from the person to the mirror image. Blurred, jittery, frayed at the edges – an image that easily becomes a metaphor for the high-strung, impatient, restless life of our hero – for his rebellious character, for his ambivalence – which concentrates all the contradictions of a satiated age into an apotheosis. "I don't know who I am," he had claimed even as a seventeen-year-old high-school student. But that doesn't matter.

With the instincts of a wild animal

Now he is twenty-four and approaching the zenith of his career – an observation that sounds strange when one realizes that he will not reach his twenty-fifth birthday. He has performed on stage and has begun to take up small roles in early television. But it is the cinema that will carry him to fame – this comparatively young, popular art form that, as he well knows, guarantees a kind of immortality even better than that of the stage. He has already made one film, and two more will follow in the coming months. His *Rebel Without a Cause* will moreover premier in the very theater, the Astor, that we see to the left at the back of the picture. Not far from here, on 68th Street West, he has a modest apartment, and Lee Strasberg's legendary Actors Studio is only a few steps away from Times Square. He had been accepted there in 1952 – certainly the most important confirmation of his talent until he won the favor of the great public. Perhaps Times Square was now no longer all that it had once been. Nonetheless, as Dennis Stock relates, before James Dean departed for Hollywood, the Square was his home where he moved about with all the instincts of a wild animal in its own territory. He could not tolerate staying inside his small apartment, and instead spent the time outdoors, pacing the streets from dusk to the early morning hours.

Anything can become a myth, as Roland Barthes once pointed out. The myth is not primarily an object, a term, or an idea, but a message. The bourgeois age is the era of technical pictures: photography, movies, and television are the vehicles of modern myths. Moving images create them, static pictures lend them stability. James Dean is one of the great myths produced by America in the twentieth century – a genius who touched the nerve of his times, a rebel who made youthful rebellion into the *basso profundo* of his artistic creativity, and who will always retain his credibility because he was saved from growing old. "Live fast," he is said to have quoted from Nick Ray's *Knock on Any Door*, "die young, and leave a good-looking corpse." Cryptic-sounding advice, but it largely reflects how he directed his own life, in which nothing was left to chance, for his life was a self-dramatization, even if the distance between being and seeming was not especially great. According to Dean's biographer David Dalton,

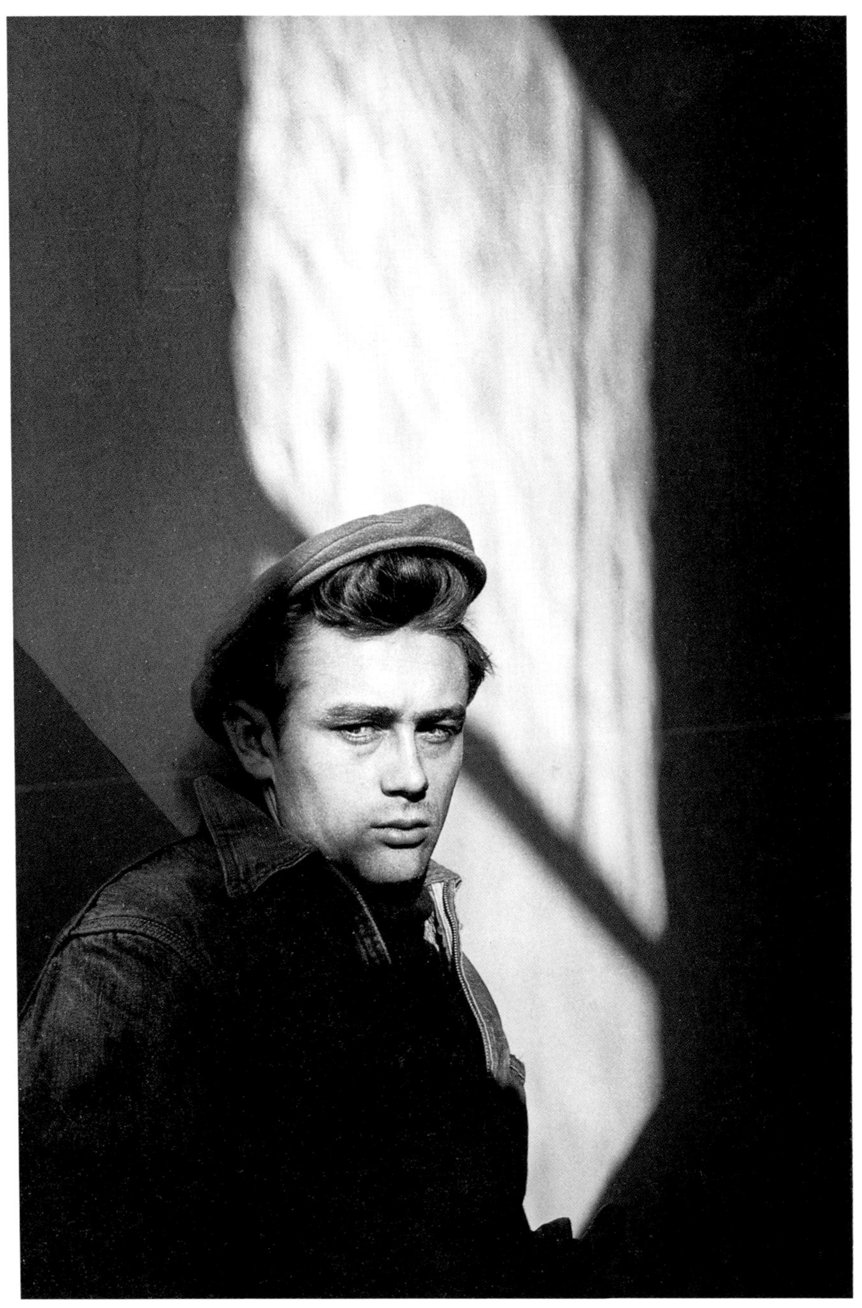

James Dean on Times Square, 1955

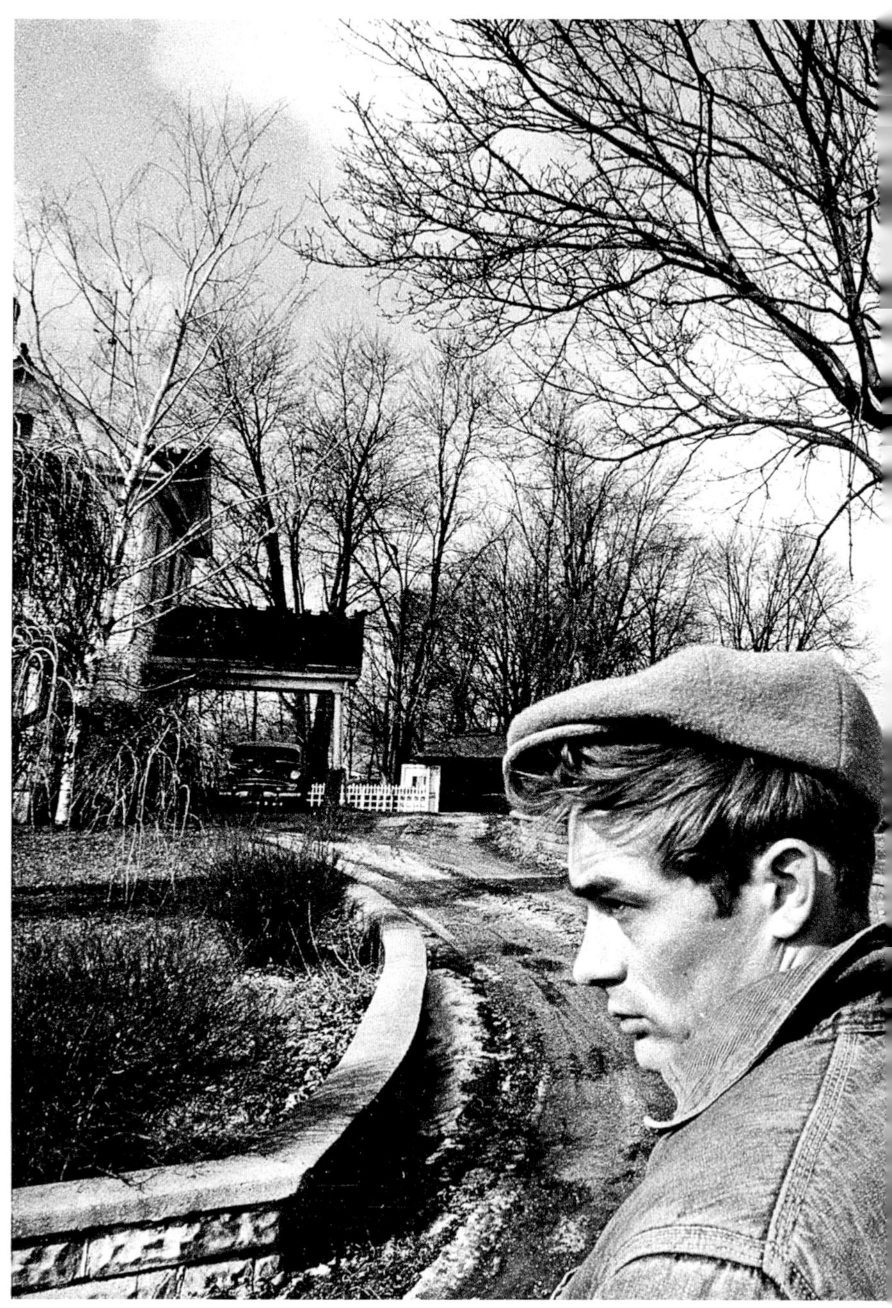

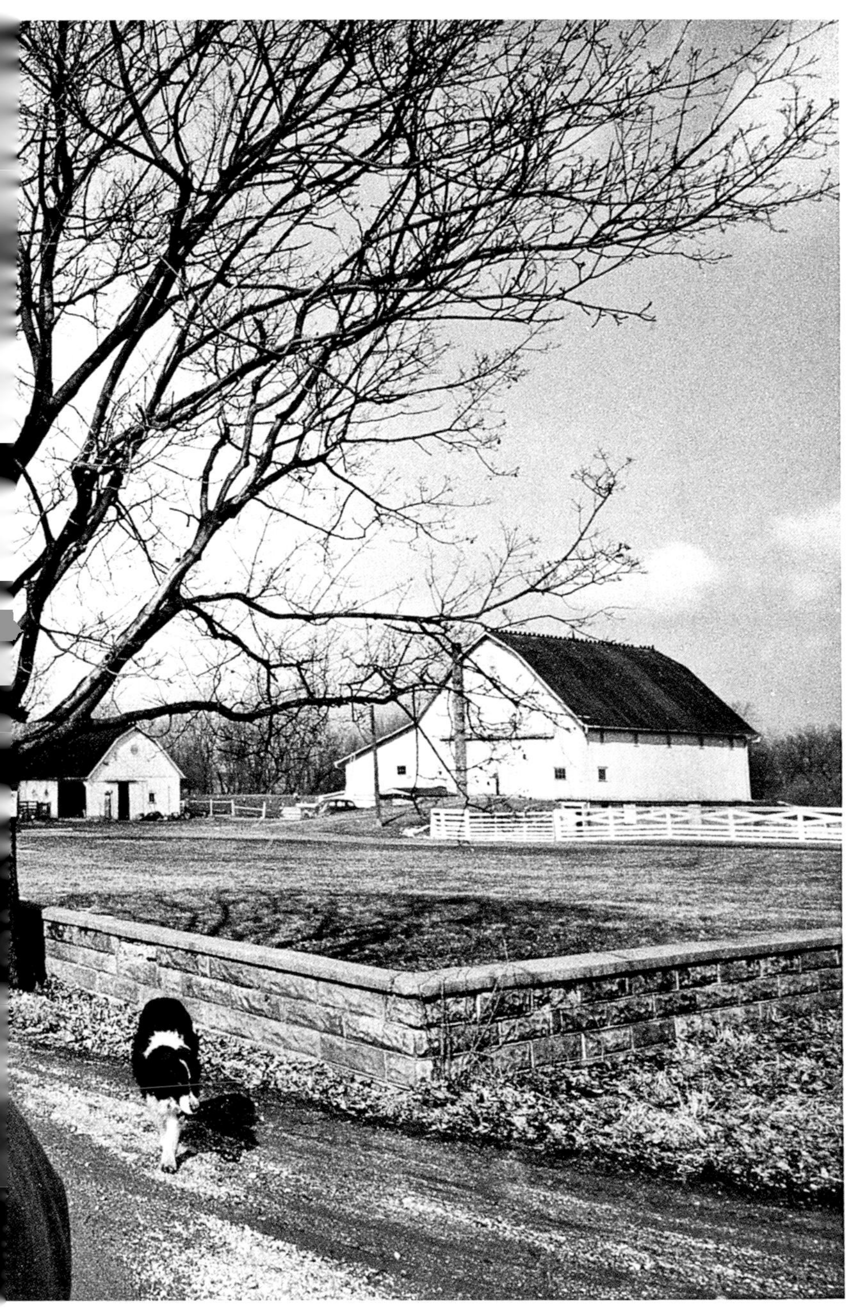

who is one of those most familiar with the actor's legend, the young actor identified totally with his characters.

The craving for pictures in the glossies and fan magazines

Dean is always said to have disliked photographs. But this can at most be only partially true. In any case, his attitude toward the medium was ambivalent, and for a while he in fact took photography lessons from the photographer Roy Schatt. There are pictures showing him with a Leica or Rolleiflex – without, however, anything worthy of notice having come out of his camera. What is more important was and remains his relation toward his own image. Schatt related how the two of them were making portraits when James Dean suddenly said that he wanted to try something. He turned his head slightly to the left and looked downwards. Schatt asked himself what on earth he was up to, and the star replied: "Can't you see? I'm Michelangelo's *David*." Dean certainly had nothing against being photographed, at least when it flattered his ego – or served his career. Star photos are as much a part of Hollywood as the star is to the film itself, even if the great age of glamour photography, characterized by warm spotlights and retouching, was already over. Now instead there were photojournalists and press photographers, who took over the job and served the craving for images in the illustrated journals or fan magazines. In Dean's case, these were names like Roy Schatt, Sanford Roth, and Dennis Stock. In other words there remained a great deal of Dean memorabilia in the form of photographs. But when David Dalton writes that our image of Dean is formed of many elements, it does not mean that there are not a few photographs standing out from the rest that have especially defined our sense of Dean.

Dennis Stock and James Dean had met in Hollywood under the auspices of Nicholas Ray, who was planning to cast Dean as the lead in his next film, *Rebel Without a Cause*. Elia Kazan's *East of Eden* was already finished, but had not yet appeared in the theaters. In other words, James Dean was still a completely unknown entity – at least for those who had not had a chance to experience him on the New York stage. The names of Marlon Brando and Elvis Presley signified the idols of a young, increasingly self-confident post-war generation that no longer accepted their youth as a synonym for immaturity, but rather as a valid state of being. In the end, however, it would be Dean who would lend the teenage cult its definitive face, even if at age twenty-three he was no longer a teen himself. As Dalton points out, Dean bequeathed a new body language to the youth of the times. Dean was a Baudelairean hero in whom the contradictions of youth – the impatience, aggression linked with vulnerability, the arrogance, nervous sensibility, shyness – were creditably lifted up to view. Stock himself was in his mid twenties, a young photographer who had studied with Berenice Abbott and Gjon Mili. Since 1951 he was a member of the Magnum group – and of course always on the lookout for a good story. "Jimmy," as the photographer later came to call him, invited Stock to a

---

Page 267: **Dennis Stock:**
In the Old Schoolhouse of Fairmount.
Photos like this made a major contribution to cementing the James Dean myth.

Pages 268–269: **Dennis Stock:**
In Front of the Driveway to Winslow Farm.
World famous star with country roots: James Dean returned to Fairmount one last time in February 1955 for a photo shoot.

preview of *East of Eden*. At the time he was not familiar with Dean's work, but the scene in the bean field convinced the photographer that the young man would become a star. Stock determined that he wanted to do something together with Dean, so he proposed a photo essay on Dean to *Life*. In February 1955, the pair set out for Fairmount, and later New York, where, among other photographs, *James Dean. New York City. Times Square* was made.

The ideal of happily lived materialism

Fairmount, Indiana. Dean biographers have consistently pointed out that this is the true East of Eden. A flat piece of earth, fields as far as the eye can see – and people whose Puritanism forms virtually the opposite pole to the American ideal of happily lived materialism. Here, or more precisely in the small town of Marion, James Byron Dean was born on 8 February 1931 – 'Byron' being a hint from his mother who, as all mothers, had great expectations for her son, and apparently wanted to underline this by a reference to the great poet. Jimmy Dean spent his early years in Marion, and later the family moved to Fairmount where, after the early and traumatic death of his mother, he grew up with his Uncle Marcus and Aunt Ortense. The pair ran a small farm, Winslow Farm.

It was here that Stock and Dean returned in 1955. The little cabin on Back Creek represented the country roots, so to speak, of the demi-god James Dean. His simple – extremely simple – background is significant; it offers hope, and at the same time belongs as much as his early, fateful death to the components of the myth, to the process of legend-making. Stock and Dean visited the local cemetery where an ancestor named Cal Dean lay buried. For his photographer, the rising star sat down again at his school desk. He wandered around Fairmount, hands in his pockets, Chesterfield in the corner of his mouth. He looked at himself absentmindedly in a frozen puddle – or tested out a coffin at the undertaker's, just to try it out. Dean's longing for death has since become the object of a great deal of speculation. In any case, Stock found a valid metaphor for his hero's necrophilic tendencies by translating Dean's isolation into pictorial form: James Dean in the midst of cows; with a dog; with a pig. The affinity for animals that the star took as a matter course can in fact be read as a metaphor for loneliness.

Dean and Stock remained a week in Fairmount. It was simultaneously a reunion and a farewell. Stock later wrote that James Dean knew that he would never see the farm again, and for that reason insisted that the last shots were taken of him before the farmhouse. James posed himself, looking straight ahead, while his dog Tuck turned away. It was, according to Stock, the actor's interpretation of 'you will never return home again'. Fairmount had formed him, New York had changed him. New York was his laboratory, in which parts of him flew apart only to form together in an arbitrary manner. In New York, he had been discovered by Elia Kazan, director of *East of Eden*, the son of the land had become a god-in-the-making. Even if it took Hollywood to form his image definitively, New York was where the career of the coming star had been launched. Blue jeans, T-shirt, and windbreaker belong to the Dean mythos just as much as the cigarette and the only partially tamed hair. Dennis Stock wrote "James Dean haunted Times Square," beneath his perhaps most famous portrait of the young actor. "For a novice actor in the fifties this was THE place to go. The Actors Studio, directed by Lee Strasberg, was in its heyday and just a block away." Dean is wearing a dark coat – because of the weather, of course. But the way in which he hides himself in it

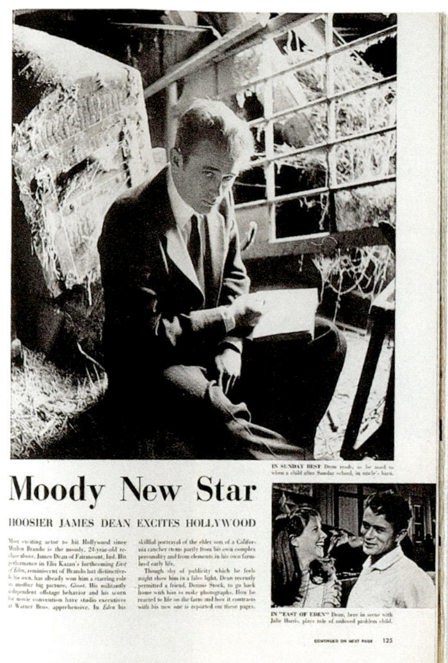

IN SUNDAY BEST Dean reads, as he used to when a child after Sunday school, in uncle's barn.

Moody New Star

HOOSIER JAMES DEAN EXCITES HOLLYWOOD

Most exciting actor to hit Hollywood since Marlon Brando is the moody, 24-year-old recluse above, James Dean of Fairmount, Ind. His performance in Elia Kazan's forthcoming *East of Eden*, reminiscent of Brando but distinctively his own, has already won him a starring role in another big picture, *Giant*. His militantly independent offstage behavior and his scorn for movie convention have studio executives at Warner Bros. apprehensive. In *Eden* his skillful portrayal of the elder son of a California rancher stems partly from his own complex personality and from elements in his own farm-bred early life.

Though shy of publicity which he feels might show him in a false light, Dean recently permitted a friend, Dennis Stock, to go back home with him to make photographs. How he reacted to life on the farm and how it contrasts with his new one is reported on these pages.

IN "EAST OF EDEN" Dean, here in scene with Julie Harris, plays role of unloved problem child.

CONTINUED ON NEXT PAGE 125

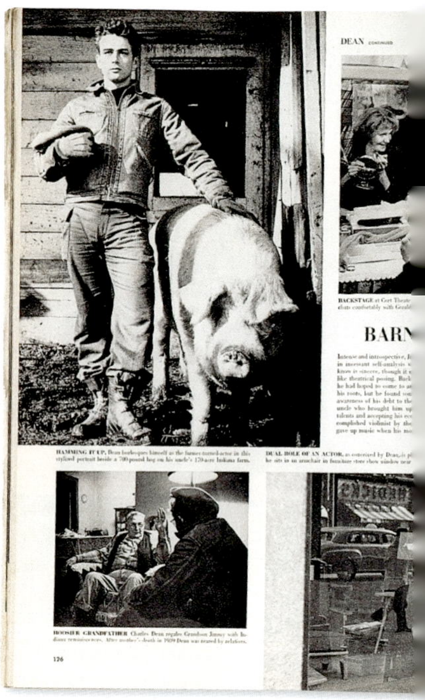

DEAN CONTINUED

HAMMING IT UP, Dean burlesques himself as the farmer-turned-actor in this stylized portrait beside a 700-pound hog on his uncle's 170-acre Indiana farm.

HOOSIER GRANDFATHER Charles Dean regales Grandson Jimmy with Indiana reminiscences. After mother's death in 1939 Dean was reared by relatives.

126

may also be interpreted as a reference to his vulnerability – it is a cocoon, even if it is in fact black. One should not perhaps over-interpret the color, even though we know that James Dean will not live to see the premier of *Rebel Without a Cause*. On 30 September 1955 at 5:45 p.m., his Porsche Speedster will crash into a Ford Sedan. It cannot be claimed that he made a "good-looking corpse"; but he had succeeded in living fast, and dying young – at twenty-four.

For Dennis Stock, his short friendship with James Dean was perhaps the most important station in his life as a photographer. If he is known for anything, then it is for his pictures of Dean, which also circulate as post cards and posters. They form a part of every retrospective of Stock. Gottfried Helnwein used our key picture as the motif for his own interpretation – and by not observing the copyright, underlined the almost universal nature of the image.

James Dean on Times Square is somewhat reminiscent of Cartier-Bresson's portrait of Giacometti (here, also, it is raining), and it is no longer possible to imagine the core of the Dean iconography without it. Even today, the photograph remains among the most often printed images of "Hollywood's ultimate god." As Richard Whelan summed it up, Dean's bequest to Stock was a certain financial independence that allowed him to dedicate himself to work that really interested him. In return, the photographer made a movie in homage to his friend: in 1991 Dennis Stock filmed *Comme une image, James Dean?* as a thirty-eight-minute documentary on the star. And what was the image of James Dean? Towards

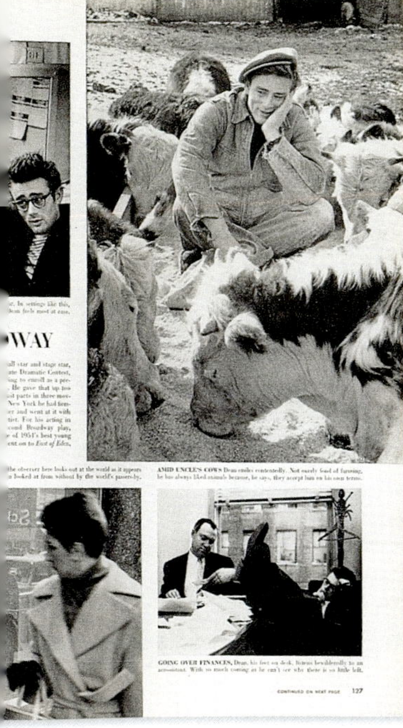

WAY

AMID UNCLE'S COWS Dean smiles contentedly. Not overly fond of farming, he has always liked animals because, he says, they accept him on his own terms.

GOING OVER FINANCES, Dean, his feet on desk, listens bewilderedly to an accountant. With so much coming in he can't see why there is so little left.

CONTINUED ON NEXT PAGE 127

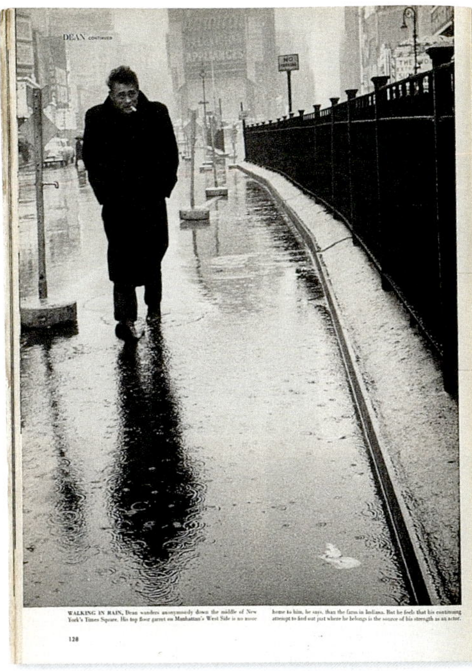

DEAN CONTINUED

WALKING IN RAIN, Dean wanders anonymously down the middle of New York's Times Square. His top floor garret on Manhattan's West Side is no more home to him, he says, than the farm in Indiana. But he feels that his continuing attempt to find out just where he belongs is the source of his strength as an actor.

128

the end of the film, Stock observes that although he was one of the last of James Dean's friends still to be alive, not one of the fans he had met during his travels had asked who Dean really was and what he had actually been like. The reason being, as Stock knew, that everyone creates their own James Dean, according to their own tastes and their own personal needs. Which allows him to be a hero in what has become a very complicated world, someone in fact who is pretty different to the twenty-four-year-old boy Stock had known and photographed.

"Moody New Star" in Life,
7 March 1955. Stock's photograph
James Dean on Times Square
was published here for the first time, albeit heavily cropped.

Will McBride
Barbara Pregnant with Shawn
1960

Signs of the Times

Will McBride's famous picture of his pregnant wife first appeared in 1960. It's an image that continues to inspire photographers today, it provoked a scandal in Germany at the end of the Adenauer years and came close to being censored.

Will McBride takes a picture of his young wife. Something no more out of the ordinary than the fact that he does so with a Leica and in black and white. It's the late 1950s. Color film is – at this stage – still too expensive and remains the exception rather than the rule among professionals and amateurs alike. Will McBride photographs "his" Barbara with the pride of a lover, a husband, and a father-to-be. He watches her with the camera while she sleeps, puts on her make-up in front of the mirror, or – by way of experiment – tries on her bridal veil. He succeeds in producing unpretentious studies of tender togetherness, mostly in a domestic setting with natural lighting. McBride documents moment of private happiness, culminating in his wife's pregnancy. As a half-length profile view in portrait format, this simple but forceful image will shortly cause a furor. An icon of the 1960s. Will McBride gives it the title *Barbara Pregnant with Shawn*. Other people, too, document moments of private happiness. Cameras and photo albums are standard features of modern life – even if, more often than not, both are now digital. But there is a difference, all the same. Will McBride, born in 1931 in the USA, and a pupil of the celebrated illustrator Norman Rockwell, takes photographs as an artist, i.e. with the trained eye of someone who can translate his ideas for a picture in a powerful way. What's more, Will McBride has a message that goes beyond the simple recording of personal memories and which might be expressed like this: "Look here, I – an American – am in love with a German woman. Together we are building a better world."

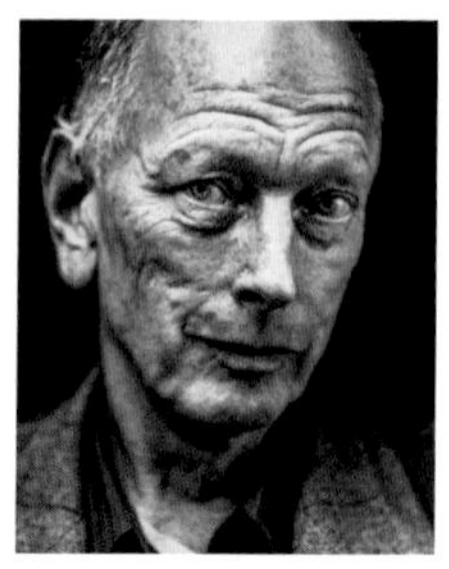

Will McBride

Born ***1931*** *in St. Louis, Missouri.* ***1948–50*** *studies English Literature at the University of Vermont and takes private courses with Norman Rockwell.* ***1950–53*** *studies painting and art history.* ***1953–55*** *Military service with the US army in Würzburg, Germany. First photographs.* ***1955–58*** *travels to Italy, France and Switzerland. Settles in Munich. Moves to Berlin, where he studies at the Free University. Continues to paint and take pictures.* ***1961*** *moves back to Munich. Works for* Quick, twen, Eltern, *and* Jasmin. *From* ***1965*** *photo studio in Munich.* ***1972*** *moves to Casoli di Camaiore (Tuscany); increased focus upon sculpture and panel painting.* ***1983*** *returns to Germany. Dies* ***2015*** *in Berlin.*

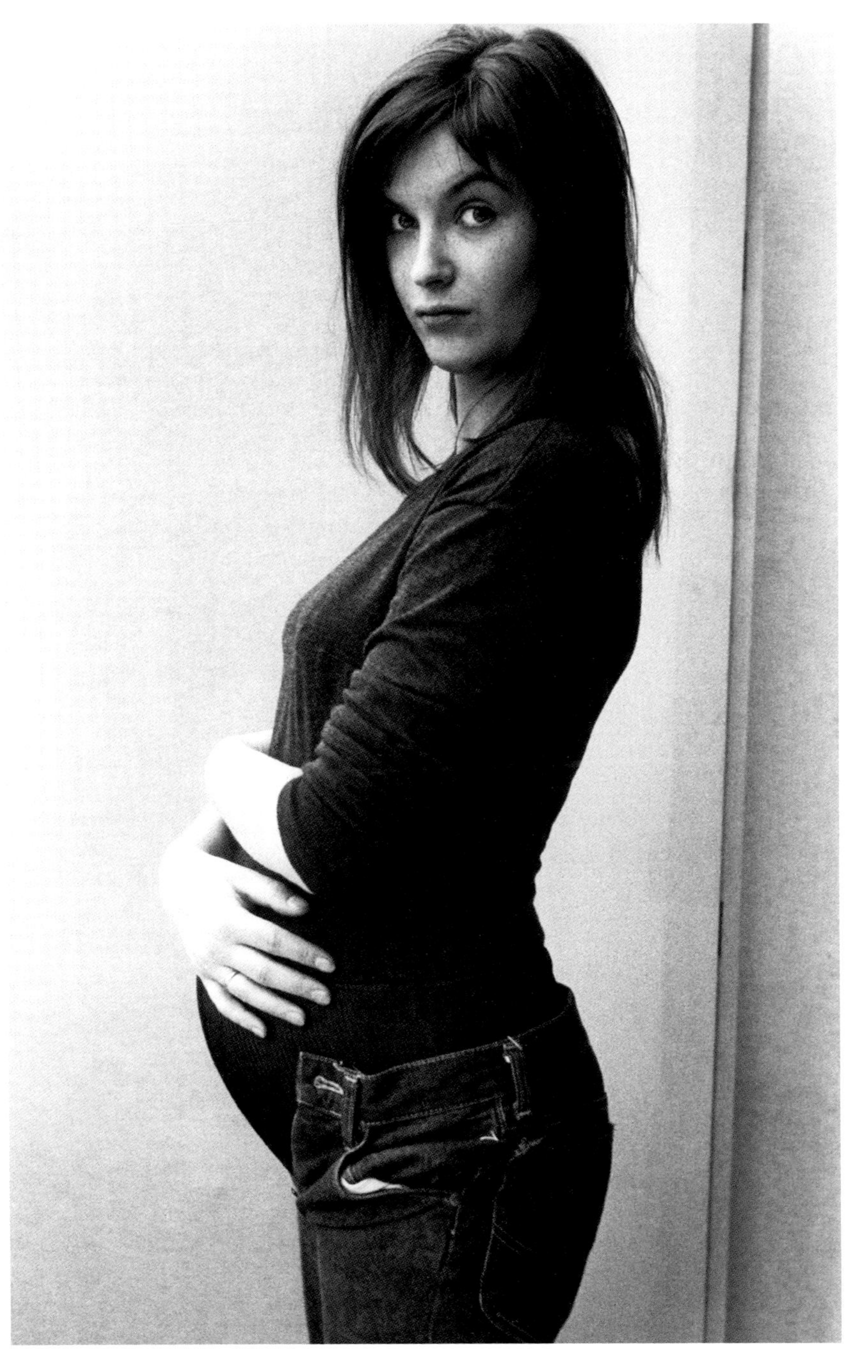

Barbara Pregnant with Shawn, 1960

Will McBride arrived in Germany at the start of the 1950s, as an American GI in a country against which his nation had waged war just ten years earlier. The young Federal Republic of Germany was no longer the German Empire, but the wounds of the catastrophe were everywhere to be seen. The country struck McBride first and foremost as gray: gray houses, gray cars, gray people – people of whom Will McBride was not alone in constantly wondering what role they might have played in the Third Reich.

It was as a GI that he started taking photographs. First in Würzburg, where he took pictures of the daily routine of his fellow soldiers, and later in Berlin, where – furnished with a scholarship from the army – he became a student. He made German friends, with whom he went swimming in the Wannsee lake, partied, listened to jazz, and jumped, literally, over barbed-wire fences. To Will McBride, this life in post-war Berlin seemed marvelously free and easy; more and more, he started to document it with the camera. Willingly or unwillingly, he became the visual chronicler of a youth about to step fully onto the stage – with the peculiar advantage that he was not an outsider, but part of this youth himself. This lends his pictures authenticity, even if McBride regularly intervenes in a directorial manner. What he shows, represents and visualizes, stands as an example of the consciousness of a generation that is resolutely starting to emancipate itself from the mores of its parents. What was originally intended to serve as a starting-point for his figural panel painting soon evolved into a project in its own right, one that demanded to be published. Towards the end of the 1950s, clearly inspired by the visual concept of the American illustrated magazine *Life*, Will McBride created a dummy that brought together his experiences and with which he presented himself to Willy Fleckhaus, art director of a new, young German magazine already causing a stir: *twen*. It was the start of an unprecedented symbiosis.

The needs of a new generation

twen appeared for the first time in April 1959. Although initially conceived as a youth magazine, the monthly pictorial soon built up a following among wider circles. Its circulation grew from 100,000 copies in the early days to around 300,000 copies towards the end of the 1960s. These figures were low compared with other popular illustrated magazines, whose circulation ran into the millions, yet *twen* shaped popular culture in the young Federal Republic like probably no other magazine of its day. The quality of its photography and the generosity of its presentation set new standards. Its layout and typography were of a radical modernity recognized as innovative even in the US on the opposite side of the Atlantic, and exerted an influence upon more or less the whole of magazine publishing in West Germany. *twen* perceived itself as a new type of magazine for a new generation, namely those who had been too young to take active part in the war, had an international outlook, and wished to turn their backs on the social customs and conventions of the Adenauer years. Whether jazz or party culture, design or fashion, leisure pursuits or the growing interest in travel, literature or cinema, politics or a more relaxed attitude to matters of love and sex – *twen* became the spearhead of a changing youth consciousness. It is against this backdrop that Will McBride's *Barbara Pregnant with*

Right and pages 278–279: *Will McBride was* twen*'s most important and most published photographer for over a decade. The magazine, under its art director Willy Fleckhaus, regularly carried features on McBride's family life. Here "Ich liebe meine Frau" in* twen *No. 12, 1962.*

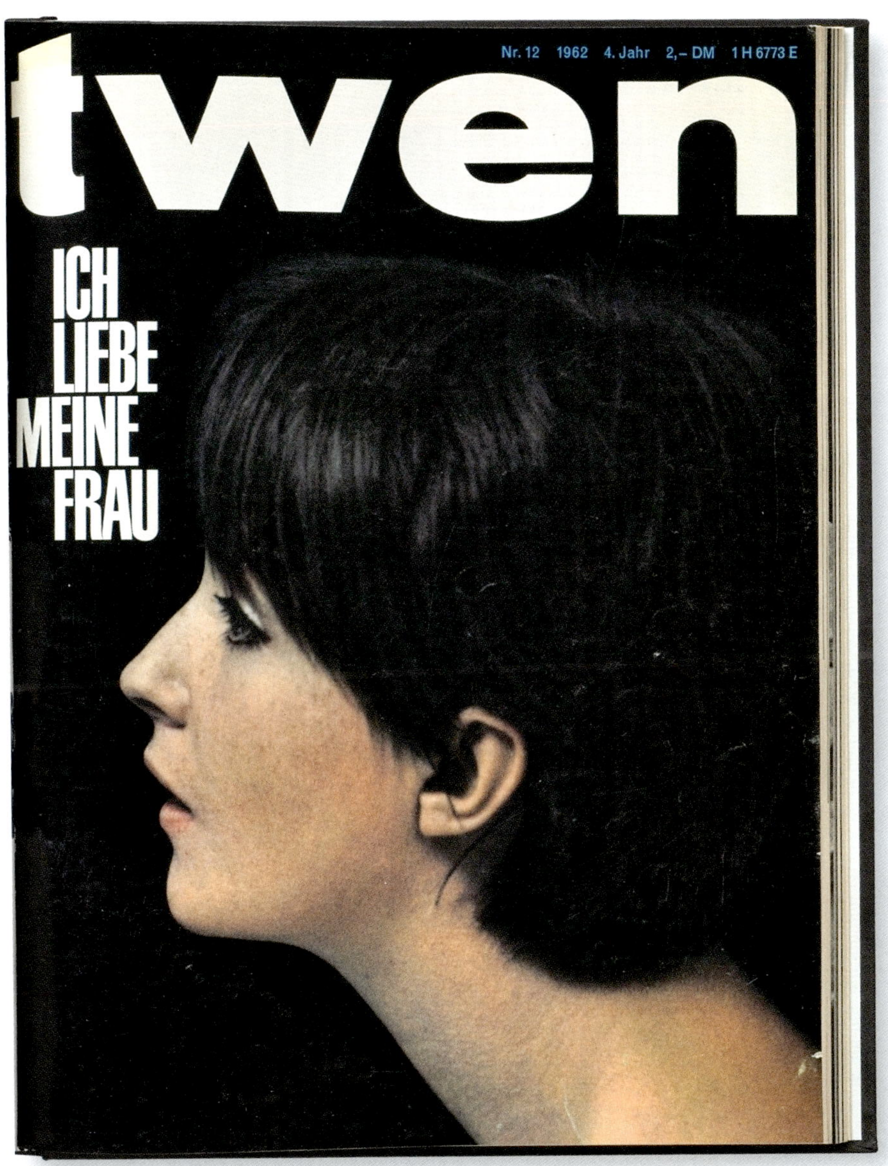

Barbara Pregnant with Shawn, 1960

Shawn must be seen. An image that deliberately wanted to make a mark.

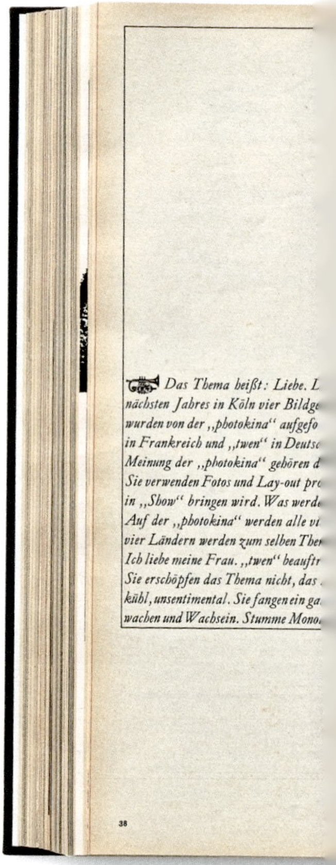

Will McBride had his first publication in *twen* in issue 6/1960. Before long, however, he had risen to become its most regular photographer, its "favorite photo," as he is at one point called, just as *twen* in turn became his most important platform. The black-and-white photo essays comprising his early work for *twen* primarily focused on youth gangs (the influence of Bruce Davidson is unmistakable here), but with his color features from Italy ("Mulis, Minne, and the Malaspina"), the Mediterranean ("Thaliai"), and India ("Siddharta"), McBride soon discovered visual formulae that encapsulated his generation's yearning for distant climes. Will McBride thus became one of the most popular and influential photographers of the legendary 1960s.

Will McBride's picture of Barbara pregnant appeared in issue 8/1960 and accompanied an article by Barbara about her pregnancy and delivery. It had been preceded in Issue 7/1960 by a ten-page feature, illustrated by photographs by Elisabeth Niggemeyer, on the former GI's marriage to Barbara Wilke. From today's point of view, the wedding of a free-lance photographer and a young woman may not seem particularly newsworthy. But this was undoubtedly no ordinary match. It was understood as a sign, a symbol, an alliance not just between two people, but also between two nations. "I had the feeling that in marrying Barbara I was marrying all of Europe plus two thousand years of tradition," Will McBride is quoted as saying in the accompanying text. *Barbara Pregnant with Shawn* appeared in the following issue of *twen* under the headline "Mein Kind kommt" ("My Child is Coming"). Will McBride not only photographed the portrait of his wife at an advanced stage of pregnancy, but – clearly inspired by Wayne Miller's book *The World is Young* – he was also present at the birth and took pictures, something certainly unheard-of in those days. The fact that the portrait of the pregnant, clothed Barbara provoked a storm of outrage seems astonishing from the perspective of an age that has grown used to seeing – naked! – pregnant women on its front covers: from Annie Leibovitz's photograph of Demi More for the August 1991 issue of *Vanity Fair* to Karl Lagerfeld's picture of Claudia Schiffer for the June 2010 edition of German *Vogue*. In the Germany of the Adenauer years, however, the photo caused a sensation.

Pages 280–281: *Barbara McBride wrote for* twen: *"Mein Kind kommt,"* twen *No. 8, 25 August 1960. One of the photos shows the pregnant Barbara in jeans. What caused a scandal at the time was not the pregnancy itself, but the fact that the top button of her jeans is undone.*

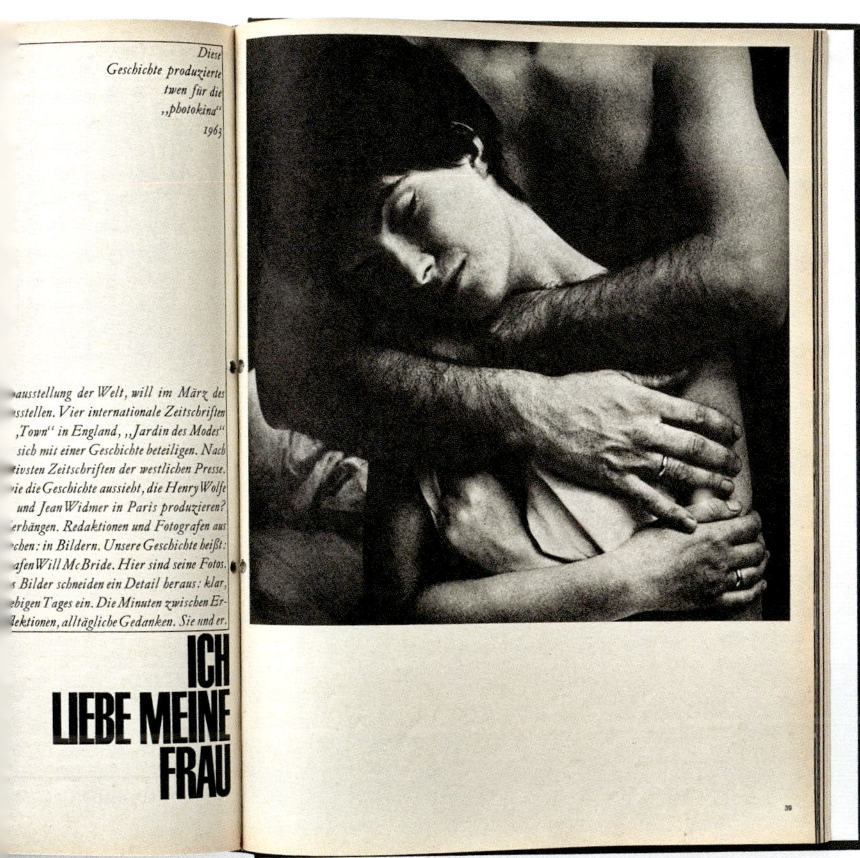

Diese
Geschichte produzierte
twen für die
„photokina“
1963

…ausstellung der Welt, will im März des
…sstellen. Vier internationale Zeitschriften
…„Town“ in England, „Jardin des Modes“
…sich mit einer Geschichte beteiligen. Nach
…tivsten Zeitschriften der westlichen Presse.
…ie die Geschichte aussieht, die Henry Wolfe
und Jean Widmer in Paris produzieren?
…erhängen. Redaktionen und Fotografen aus
…chen: in Bildern. Unsere Geschichte heißt:
…afen Will McBride. Hier sind seine Fotos.
…s Bilder schneiden ein Detail heraus: klar,
…ebigen Tages ein. Die Minuten zwischen Er-
…lektionen, alltägliche Gedanken. Sie und er.

ICH
LIEBE MEINE
FRAU

39

Will McBride has photographed his Barbara in three-quarter length against a neutral background – probably at home. With her body seen in profile, the pregnant woman turns her face towards the camera. Just as she presents her pregnancy with clear self-confidence, so her expression is one of defiance with a touch of pride. These are no longer 'different' but very 'normal' circumstances, even if they carry the disadvantage that a favorite pair of jeans – here probably pulled on just to see – no longer fit. The Free and Hanseatic City of Hamburg – along with a posse of angry readers – took a very different view. In its opinion, the "very pregnant girl in a striking pose and clothing" was clearly offensive to "young people's sense of propriety." Whatever the case: the application to have it banned was turned down by the Federal Department for Media Harmful to Young Persons in Bonn-Bad Godesberg. Which proves that the picture stands at the threshold of a new sexual ethics. The old times are not yet past – but the modern era is unmistakably announcing its arrival.

ten, um die Schande zu vertuschen! Welche Schande – ein Kind zu haben, ist das schändlich? In der Ehe soll ein Kind der Mutter schönster Lohn sein, für eine unverheiratete Mutter ist es aber eine Schande? Heiratet das Paar, ist die ‚Schande' abgewendet und die ‚Ehre' gerettet. Aber wie soll diese Ehe weitergehen?"

„Ein Mädchen mit Kind ist doch", sagt Heidrun F. aus E., „trotz Mutterschaftsgesetz ein Mensch, der fast als asozial betrachtet wird".

„Wir mögen immer wieder proklamieren, daß das uneheliche Kind dem ehelichen gleichgestellt ist", bestätigt der Sozialpsychologe Harald Focken aus Gießen, „die Tatsachen beweisen indessen, daß die Wirklichkeit anders ist. Schon in der Schule wird oft das uneheliche Kind von seinen Mitschülern gehänselt: Dich hat der Esel im Galopp verloren, du Bankert, und was dergleichen Sprüchlein mehr sind. Wenn das Kind den Namen seiner Eltern nennen muß, wird es immer wieder stocken. Es wird immer sagen müssen: Mein Vater heißt anders als meine Mutter."

Heidi Storsberg aus Düsseldorf spricht sogar von einem Zwang, unter dem die Eltern einer unverheirateten Mutter stehen, „weil sie sich wegen ihres mißratenen Sprößlings von Nachbarn und Bekannten verspottet fühlen. Aber warum sind sie dann egoistisch und denken nur an ihren guten Ruf ..."

„Die Tochter wird außer Haus gebracht oder aus der Familie verbannt", sekundiert Renate Greven aus Aachen, „diese Eltern stürzen ihr Kind dabei nur noch mehr ins Unglück!"

Ingrid Hamel zieht sozusagen die Konsequenz daraus und empfiehlt hart und nüchtern: „Keine Frau sollte mit einem Mann schlafen, wenn sie nicht die Kraft, den Willen und die Liebe fühlt, die etwaigen Folgen alleine zu tragen und auch alleine durchstehen zu können", und Antje Wiese erkennt an: „. . . daß ein Mädel, welches alleine für sein Kind sorgt, sehr viel Mut hat. Es ist alleine für das Baby verantwortlich und steht häufig ohne Hilfe dem Gerede der Leute gegenüber."

Aber der Diplompsychologe Harald Focken kennt auch die Kehrseite der Medaille: „Ich habe Frauen kennengelernt, die aus mancherlei Gründen den Mann ihrer Liebe nicht heiraten konnten, aber den brennenden Wunsch nach einem Kinde hatten. Sie waren bereit, in allen Konsequenzen die Folgen ihres Tuns auf sich zu nehmen. Sie haben ein Kind bekommen, sie haben nicht geheiratet, aber sie haben mir auch gesagt, daß sie anders gehandelt hätten, wenn sie gewußt hätten, welche sozialen, wirtschaftlichen und anderweitigen Schwierigkeiten dieser Schritt mit sich bringt."

Achtung vor der Ehe oder Angst vor Verantwortung?

Man mag den jungen Menschen von heute nachsagen, daß sie sich leichter in Liebesabenteuer stürzen, als es vielleicht ihre Eltern oder Großeltern taten. Aber diese erstaunliche Tatsache kristallisierte sich aus vielen Briefen heraus: Die jungen Menschen haben eine hohe Achtung vor der Ehe. Sie betrachten die Ehe tatsächlich als eine Bindung fürs Leben. Das Vorbild der so als Vorbild verdächtigten Filmstars scheint längst nicht so weit verbreitet zu sein, wie man annimmt: Heute heiraten, um sich vielleicht schon morgen wieder scheiden zu lassen – das lehnen sie ab. Noch nicht einmal der Gedanke an das Sicherheitsventil „. . .und dann kann man sich ja wieder scheiden lassen" kommt in unserer Leserpost zum Vorschein. Man möchte sagen: Für die jungen Menschen sind Liebeleien eine Sache, aber eine Ehe ist eine ganz andere Sache. So ernst wird der Gedanke an die „richtige" Ehe mit dem „richtigen" Partner genommen, daß man für diesen Gedanken sogar das Mädchen und das Kind opfern will, denen man sich durch eine galante Affäre verpflichtet fühlen sollte. Oder – so muß man aber auch fragen – spricht hier die Angst mit, daß man dann vielleicht nicht die Geborgenheit und das Verstehen findet, wonach man sich irgendwo innen doch sehnt? Oder ist es vielleicht sogar eine edel kaschierte Angst vor der Verantwortung? Lassen wir Briefe sprechen!

26

„Man sollte keine Ehe mit dem beruhigenden Gedanken schließen: im Falle eines Nichtverstehens ist ja Scheidung möglich", warnt Heidi Storsberg. „Falls man zu der Einsicht kommt, daß ein Zusammenleben schwierig sein würde, so wäre es besser, gar nicht erst zu heiraten, als später dann auseinanderzugehen", schreibt Rolf Runk aus Lörrach. Und Glory Life aus Gräfelfing: „Erst muß man fragen: Sind wir fähig, ein Leben lang füreinander dazustehen? Wird es uns möglich sein, immer zusammenzubleiben?"

Erfahrungen aus seiner Tätigkeit in der Amtsvormundschaft faßt Wolfgang Körner aus Dortmund so zusammen: „Lieber zehnmal ein uneheliches Kind, als eine Ehe, die von Anfang an zum Scheitern verurteilt ist!"

„Soll man ‚Verantwortung' zeigen, ein Mann sein, und das ‚Opfer' einer Ehe auf sich nehmen?" fragt René Boehm und gibt auch gleich die Antwort: „Solch ein Opfer ist weder aufrichtig noch rettet es die Misere. Solch eine Ehe wäre Betrug!"

„Es nützt nichts, als äußere Klammer des Zusammenlebens das kommende Kind zu betrachten", schreibt Jürgen Dietrich aus Hamburg. „Eine Ehe, die nur deshalb geschlossen wird, muß zwangsläufig eine hohle Einrichtung bleiben, weil ihr die echte Erfüllung, die gegenseitige Geborgenheit, mangelt. Unter der äußerlichen Fassade einer ehelichen Gemeinschaft bliebe weiterhin die unerfüllte Sehnsucht nach Geborgenheit, Verständnis, dem echten Partner, bestehen."

„Eltern, die sich nicht lieben", gibt Heidi Volk aus Darmstadt zu bedenken, „können ihrem Kind keine Eltern sein. Eine Mutter aber liebt ihr Kind und wird es besser erziehen können, wenn sie sich vom Vater gleich trennt und vielleicht einen liebevolleren, verständigeren Vati findet."

Ein Mädchen mit 17

„Nein, gezwungen durch ein Kind würde ich nicht heiraten, da ich weder mir mit meinen siebzehn Jahren noch meinem zweiundzwanzig Jahre alten Freund die nötige Reife zutraue. Ich will nicht riskieren, mich später mit ihm vor dem Scheidungsrichter zu sehen. Oder sogar, was vielleicht noch schlimmer wäre, ein Leben lang in gegenseitigem Nichtverstehen zuzubringen", schreibt Tris aus Düsseldorf. Und ähnlich Karin Labe aus Hamburg, zweiundzwanzig Jahre alt: „Auf keinen Fall wäre für mich ein Kind, das unterwegs ist, ein Grund zum Heiraten – unter Umständen einen Mann, den ich nicht liebe. Mit dem Kind würde ich schon irgendwie durchkommen. Denn jedes junge Mädchen hat ja heutzutage einen Beruf und verdient Geld, also warum sich da noch einen Mann einhandeln – noch eine Sorge mehr!"

Nun, nicht alle Mädchen sind so selbstbewußt und stehen so lebenstüchtig auf eigenen Füßen! Darf man dann einfach ein Mädchen, das ein Kind erwartet, mit der – vielleicht sogar als billige Ausrede mißbrauchten – Erklärung sich selbst überlassen, man liebe sich ja nicht, und deshalb sei eine Ehe sinnlos? Natürlich darf man das nicht. „Der Mann sollte seine Pflicht nicht in der Erfüllung des Gesetzes sehen", meint zwar Siegfried Oesterle, aber er schreibt auch: „er würde schwere Schuld auf sich laden, wenn er die junge Frau nicht unterstützen würde."

Wenigstens einmal versuchen

Thomas Weinstock aus Zürich bejaht sogar eine Heirat, „um der Frau während der Schwangerschaft einen Halt zu geben". Er hat dabei die Hoffnung, daß „ja nicht jede Zwangsheirat wieder geschieden werden muß. Warum also nicht wenigstens einmal probieren?"

Diesem letzten Satz scheint ein Erlebnis recht zu geben, das Isabella Rechner aus Eislingen/Fils uns berichtet. Sie begegnete einem Bekannten namens Rainer. Sie sah seinem Gesicht an, daß

(Fortsetzung Seite 89

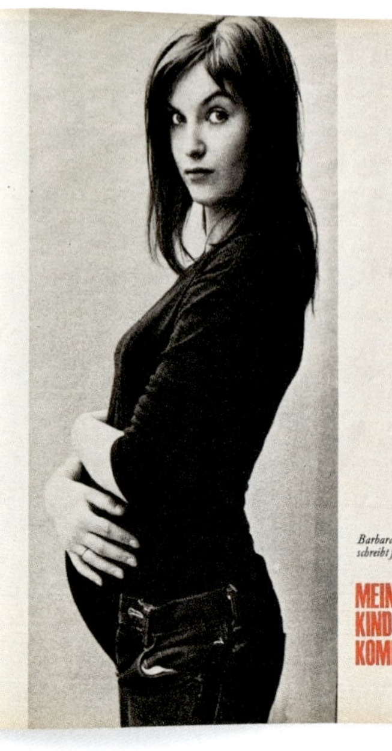

Barbara schreibt für twen

MEIN KIND KOMMT

27

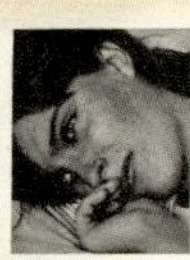

Das Gesicht seiner Frau während der Minuten, in denen sie ihr Kind gebar, fotografierte der amerikanische Reporter Will McBride. In vier Bildern hielt er die Phasen des sich steigernden Schmerzes und der erlösenden Erschöpfung fest. Das Gesicht auf dem ersten Bild hat noch Raum für Reflektionen: wie weit der beginnende Schmerz sich noch steigern mag, wie lange es noch dauert – und wie es wohl sein wird, das erste Kind, dessen Ankunft nun unmittelbar bevorsteht. Doch nun wächst die Qual. Die Hand, die vorhin neben dem Gesicht auf dem Kissen

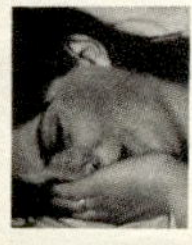

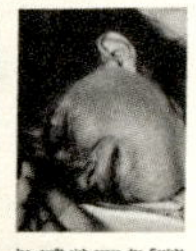

lag, preßt sich gegen das Gesicht. Abwehr, der Versuch, Schutz zu finden, liegt in dieser Geste. Dann aber wird auch sie sinnlos. Der Schmerz muß durchgestanden werden. Das Gesicht verzerrt sich zur Grimasse, alle Nerven des gepeinigten Körpers ziehen sich zusammen. Das ist der Augenblick, von dem Barbara McBride später schreibt: „Am Ende der Geburt, als der Kopf des Kindes schon halb geboren war, hatte ich einen Traum." Ohnmächtig fällt die Hand über das Kissen. Als der Körper des Kindes den Körper der Mutter verlassen hat, entspannen sich Muskeln und Nerven. Das Gesicht gewinnt sein früheres sanftes Aussehen zurück, die von der Gewalt des Geburtsschmerzes breit über den Kiefer gezogenen Lippen finden sich allmählich wieder in ihre anmutig sanft geschwungene Form zurück. Jugendlich glatt gibt sich wieder das Gesicht, das eben zerfurcht und verformt die Wehenwellen ertrug. Will McBride sagte später: „Als ich den in die Breite verzerrten Mund sah, mußte ich an Bilder von Düsenpiloten bei Geschwindigkeitsversuchen ohne den Schutz der Druckkammern denken. Nur bei ihnen, wenn sie die Gewalt der Fliehkraft auf sich wirken ließen, sah ich eine ähnliche Veränderung des Gesichts." Die Wehen sind vorbei, die Anstrengungen der Geburt überstanden – aber das Gesicht wird nie mehr wieder dasselbe sein. Barbara ist nun wirklich kein Mädchen mehr. Nun ist sie tatsächlich eine Frau. Sie ist Mutter.

36

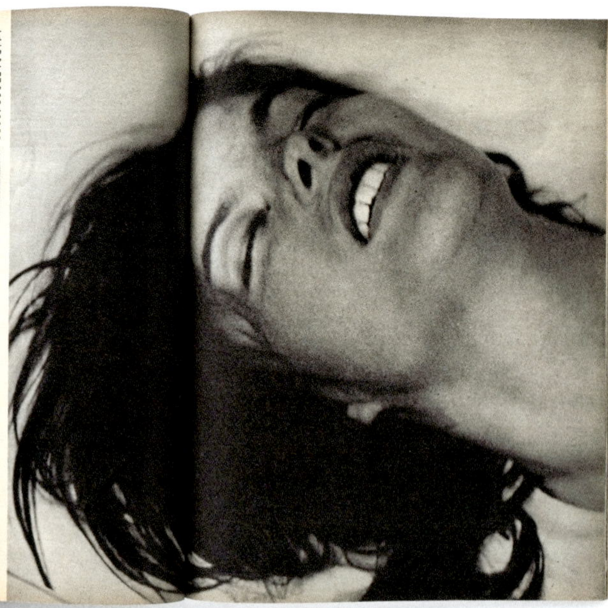

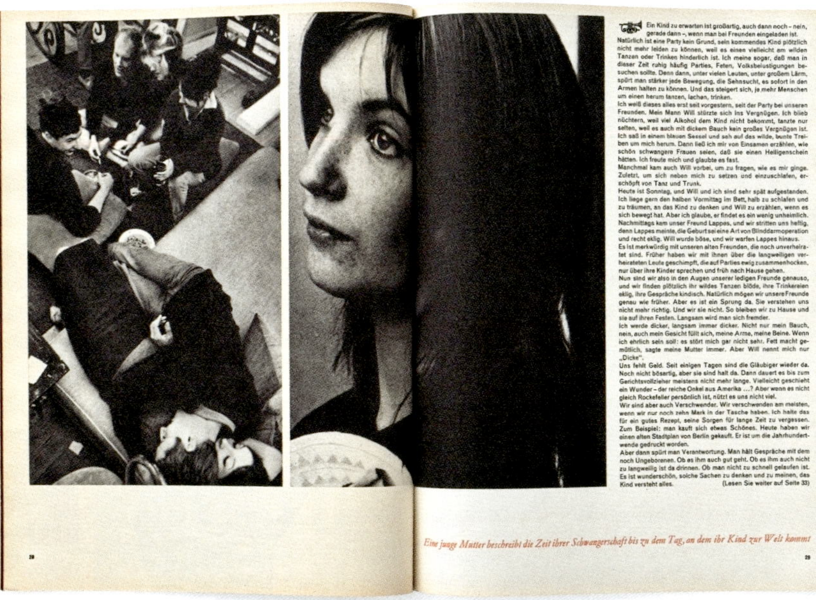

Ein Kind zu erwarten ist großartig, auch dann noch – nein, gerade dann –, wenn man bei Freunden eingeladen ist. Natürlich ist eine Party kein Grund, sein kommendes Kind plötzlich nicht mehr leiden zu können, weil es einen vielleicht am wilden Tanzen oder Trinken hinderlich ist. Ich meine sogar, daß man in dieser Zeit ruhig häufig Parties, Feten, Volksbelustigungen besuchen sollte. Denn dann, unter vielen Leuten, unter großem Lärm, spürt man stärker jede Bewegung, die Sehnsucht, es sofort in den Armen halten zu können. Und das steigert sich, je mehr Menschen um einen herum tanzen, lachen, trinken.

Ich weiß dieses alles erst seit vorgestern, seit der Party bei unseren Freunden. Mein Mann Will stürzte sich ins Vergnügen. Ich blieb nüchtern, weil viel Alkohol dem Kind nicht bekommt, tanzte nur selten, weil es auch mit dickem Bauch kein großes Vergnügen ist. Ich saß in einem blauen Sessel und sah auf das wilde, bunte Treiben um mich herum. Dann ließ ich mir von Einsamen erzählen, wie schön schwangere Frauen seien, daß sie einen Heiligenschein hätten. Ich freute mich und glaubte es fast.

Manchmal kam auch Will vorbei, um zu fragen, wie es mir ginge. Zuletzt, um sich neben mich zu setzen und einzuschlafen, erschöpft von Tanz und Trunk.

Heute ist Sonntag, und Will und ich sind sehr spät aufgestanden. Ich liege gern den halben Vormittag im Bett, halb zu schlafen und zu träumen, an das Kind zu denken und Will zu erzählen, wenn es sich bewegt hat. Aber ich glaube, er findet es ein wenig unheimlich. Nachmittags kam unser Freund Lappes, und wir stritten uns heftig, denn Lappes meinte, die Geburt sei eine Art von Blinddarmoperation und recht eklig. Will wurde böse, und wir warfen Lappes hinaus.

Es ist merkwürdig mit unseren alten Freunden, die noch unverheiratet sind. Früher haben wir mit ihnen über die langweiligen verheirateten Leute geschimpft, die auf Parties ewig zusammenhocken, nur über ihre Kinder sprechen und früh nach Hause gehen.

Nun sind wir also in den Augen unserer ledigen Freunde genauso, und wir finden plötzlich ihr wildes Tanzen blöde, ihre Trinkereien eklig, ihre Gespräche kindisch. Natürlich mögen wir unsere Freunde genau wie früher. Aber es ist ein Sprung da. Sie verstehen uns nicht mehr richtig. Und wir sie nicht. So bleiben wir zu Hause und sie auf ihren Festen. Langsam wird man sich fremder.

Ich werde dicker, langsam immer dicker. Nicht nur mein Bauch, nein, auch mein Gesicht füllt sich, meine Arme, meine Beine. Wenn ich ehrlich sein soll: es stört mich gar nicht sehr. Fett macht gemütlich, sagte meine Mutter immer. Aber Will nennt mich nur „Dicke".

Uns fehlt Geld. Seit einigen Tagen sind die Gläubiger wieder da. Noch nicht bösartig, aber sie sind halt da. Dann dauert es bis zum Gerichtsvollzieher meistens nicht mehr lange. Vielleicht geschieht ein Wunder – der reiche Onkel aus Amerika ...? Aber wenn es nicht gleich Rockefeller persönlich ist, nützt es uns nicht viel.

Wir sind aber auch Verschwender. Wir verschwenden am meisten, wenn wir nur noch zehn Mark in der Tasche haben. Ich halte das für ein gutes Rezept, seine Sorgen für lange Zeit zu vergessen. Zum Beispiel: man kauft sich etwas Schönes. Heute haben wir einen alten Stadtplan von Berlin gekauft. Er ist um die Jahrhundertwende gedruckt worden.

Aber dann spürt man Verantwortung. Man hält Gespräche mit dem noch Ungeborenen. Ob es ihm auch gut geht. Ob es ihm auch nicht zu langweilig ist da drinnen. Ob man nicht zu schnell gelaufen ist. Es ist wunderschön, solche Sachen zu denken und zu meinen, das Kind versteht alles. (Lesen Sie weiter auf Seite 33)

Eine junge Mutter beschreibt die Zeit ihrer Schwangerschaft bis zu dem Tag, an dem ihr Kind zur Welt kommt

28

29

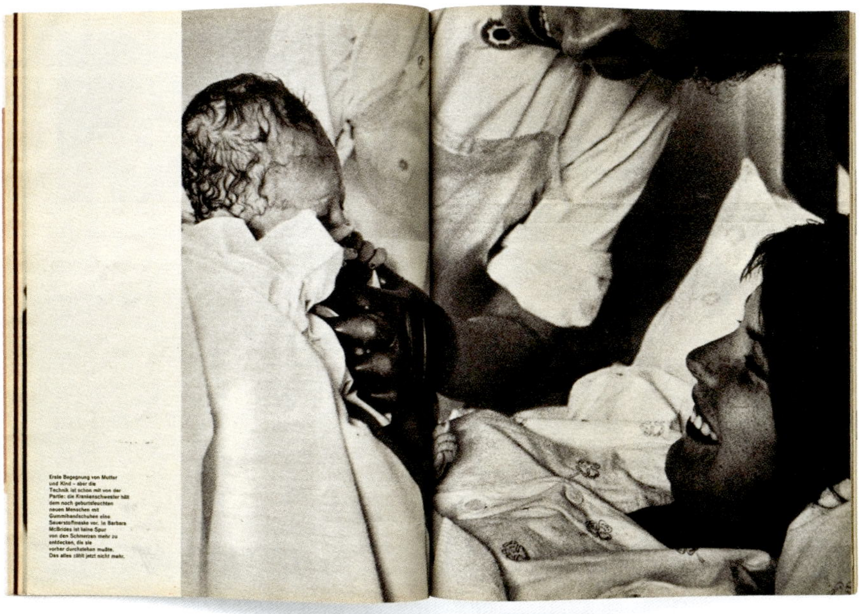

Erste Begegnung von Mutter und Kind – aber die Technik ist schon mit von der Partie: die Krankenschwester hält dem noch geburtsfeuchten neuen Menschen mit Gummihandschuhen eine Sauerstoffmaske vor. In Barbara McBrides ist keine Spur von den Schmerzen mehr zu entdecken, die sie vorher durchstehen mußte. Das alles zählt jetzt nicht mehr.

Robert Lebeck
Leopoldville
1960

Dagger in a Black Hand

This photograph quickly made its way around the world: a young Congolese man stealing the ceremonial sword of the Belgian King Baudouin. Robert Lebeck, at the time working in Africa for the illustrated magazine Kristall, captured the picture with all its symbolic character during the freedom celebrations in the Belgian Congo in June 1960.

Being at the right place at the right time, a working camera in hand, fitted with the correct lens and loaded with sufficient film: a patent recipe for creating a 'photograph of the century' – providing, of course, that the scene is not staged. But even if the photographer also knows what he or she is doing professionally, and the 'tool' is in good working order, there still remains something that needs to be explained – something that the 'picture hunter' terms the luck of the chase; the lay person, chance; the romantic, fate.

Leopoldville, 1960. Robert Lebeck is not the only photojournalist who has come to Africa to follow the independence process of the Congo with his camera. In one picture, we recognize Hilmar Pabel, equipped with two Leicas with lenses of different focal lengths. The escort has already passed by Robert Lebeck on the right. Others have hurried out in front of the limousine carrying President Kasavubu and Belgian's King Baudouin. According to the rules of the trade, they catch the approach of the protagonists, either not realizing or only suspecting that at this moment the decisive scene is being played out elsewhere. Namely, a few steps further to the left, where 'fate' places the decisive picture into the hands of Robert Lebeck, whose position already seemed to have been 'written off': a young black man suddenly sees his chance. He has already been running for some time alongside the open, dark-colored limousine. On the rear seat he spots the royal sword which the king has laid aside, grabs it, and runs directly toward

---

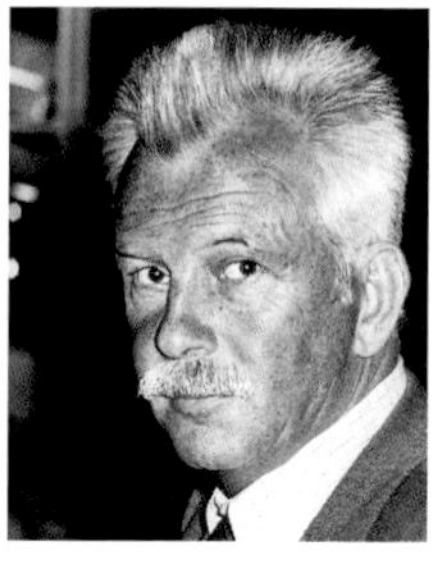

Robert Lebeck
Born ***1929*** *in Berlin.* ***1944–45*** *military service on the Eastern Front. POW until summer* ***1945****. Studies in Zurich and New York.* ***1951*** *returns to Germany. From* ***1952*** *first photographic experiments, first photos published. Freelance photojournalist for various newspapers in Heidelberg. From* ***1955*** *director of the Frankfurt office of* Revue. ***1960*** *changes to* Kristall. ***1966–77*** *photoreporter for* Stern. ***1977–78*** *chief editor of* Geo. *From* ***1979*** *works once more for* Stern. ***1991*** *awarded the Dr. Erich Salomon Prize by the DGPh German photography society.* ***2007*** *Henri Nannen Prize. Also prominent in his role as a collector of historical photographs and illustrated periodicals. Dies* ***2014*** *in Berlin.*

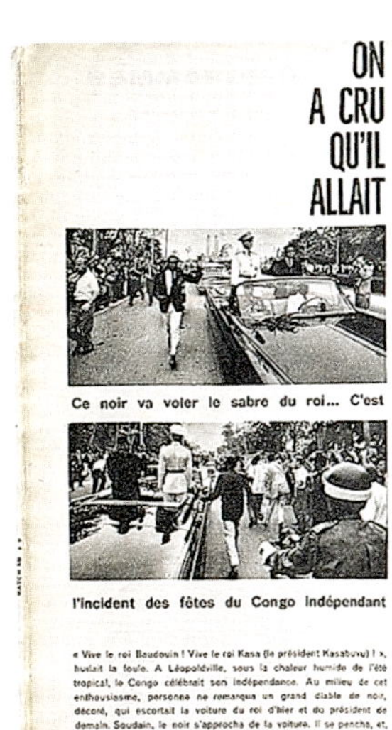

ON A CRU QU'IL ALLAIT

Ce noir va voler le sabre du roi... C'est

l'incident des fêtes du Congo indépendant

« Vive le roi Baudouin ! Vive le roi Kasa (le président Kasabuvu) ! », hurlait la foule. A Léopoldville, sous la chaleur humide de l'été tropical, le Congo célébrait son indépendance. Au milieu de cet enthousiasme, personne ne remarqua un grand diable de noir, décoré, qui escortait la voiture du roi d'hier et du président de demain. Soudain, le noir s'approcha de la voiture. Il se pencha, et, l'instant d'après, s'enfuit vers l'arrière du cortège, serrant dans sa main un objet scintillant : le sabre de Baudouin ! Le roi n'avait rien vu.

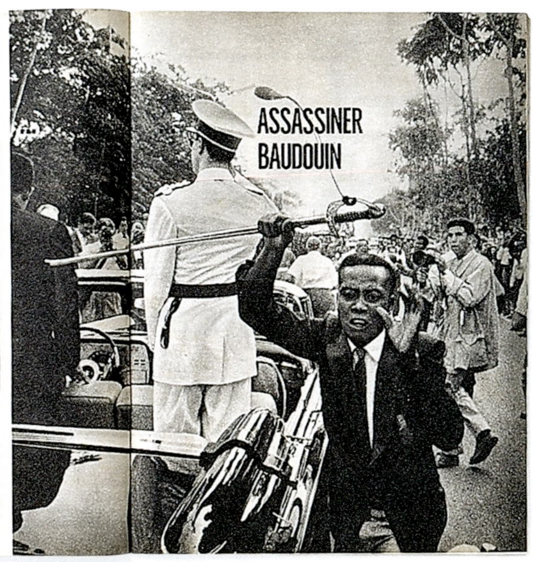

ASSASSINER BAUDOUIN

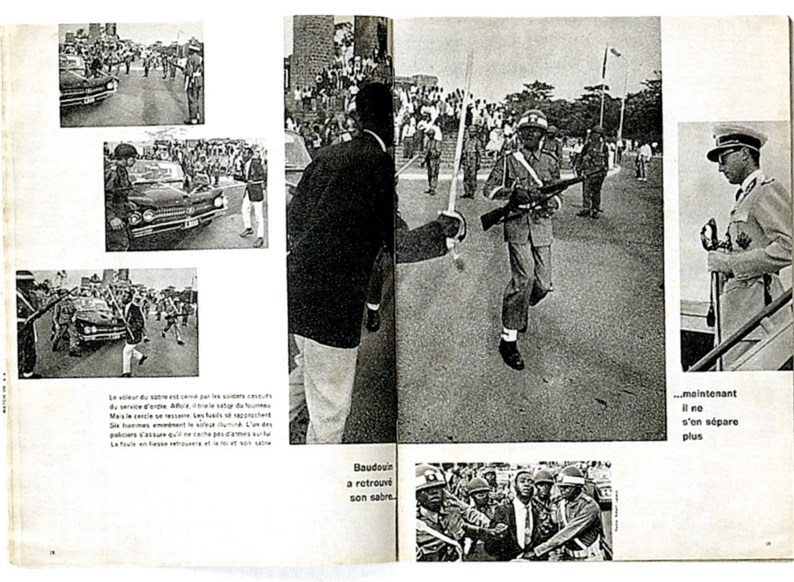

Le voleur du sabre est cerné par les soldats casqués du service d'ordre. Affolé, il tire le sabre du fourreau. Mais le cercle se resserre. Les fusils se rapprochent. Six hommes emmènent le voleur illuminé. L'un des policiers s'assure qu'il ne cache pas d'armes sur lui. La foule en liesse retrouvera et le roi et son sabre.

Baudouin a retrouvé son sabre...

...maintenant il ne s'en sépare plus

Paris Match, *9 July 1960. The French illustrated was the first to publish Lebeck's sensational photo report.*

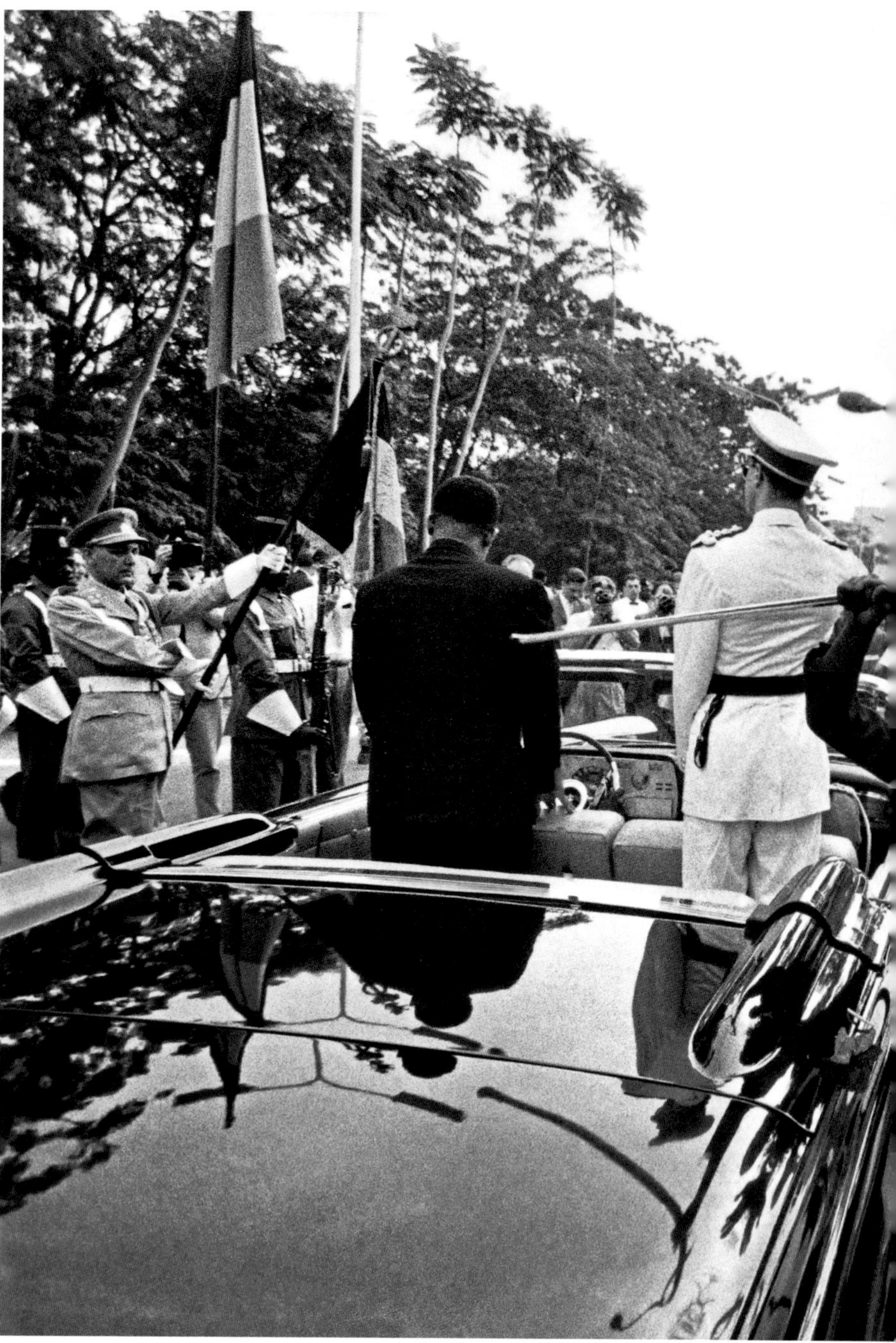

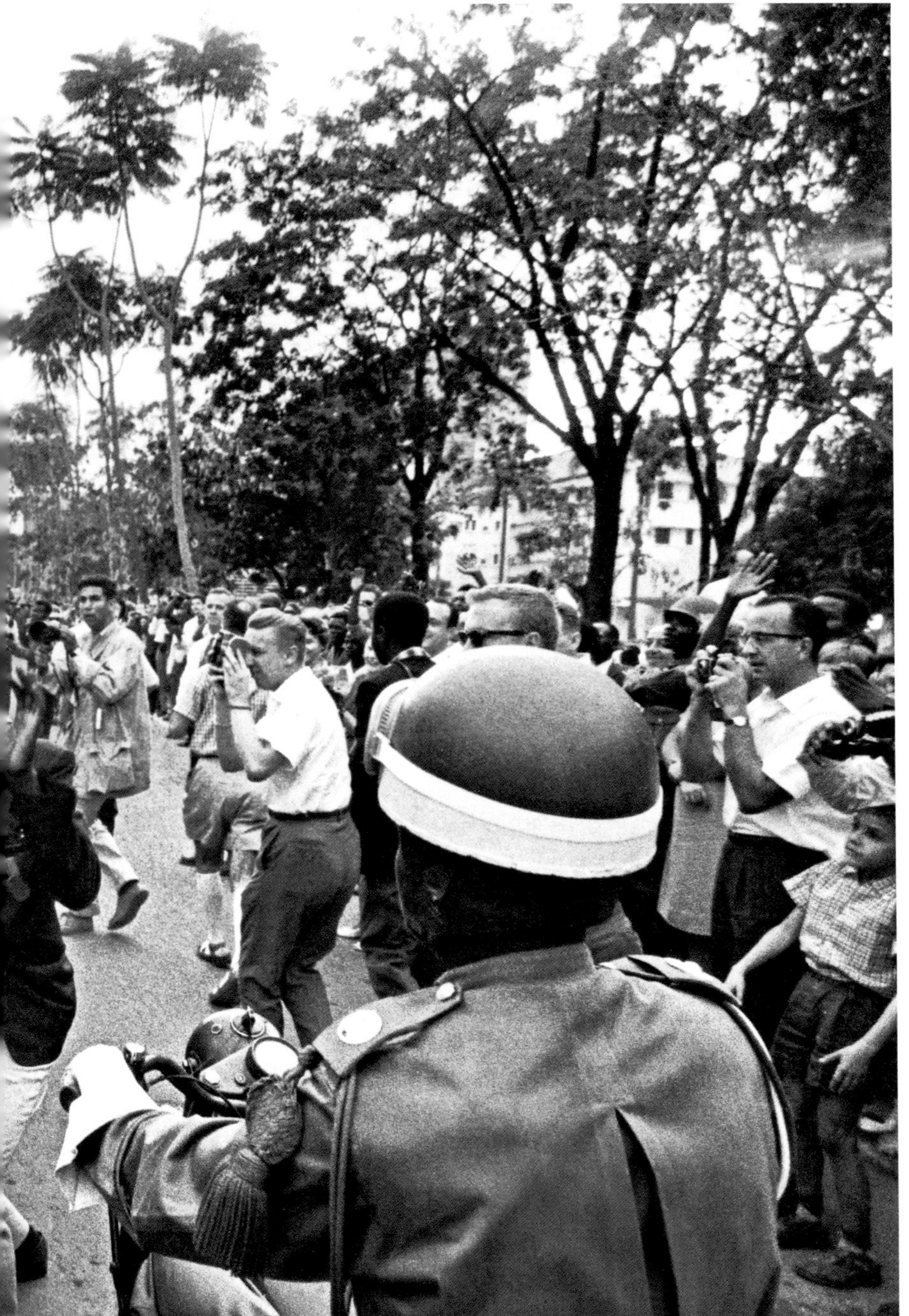

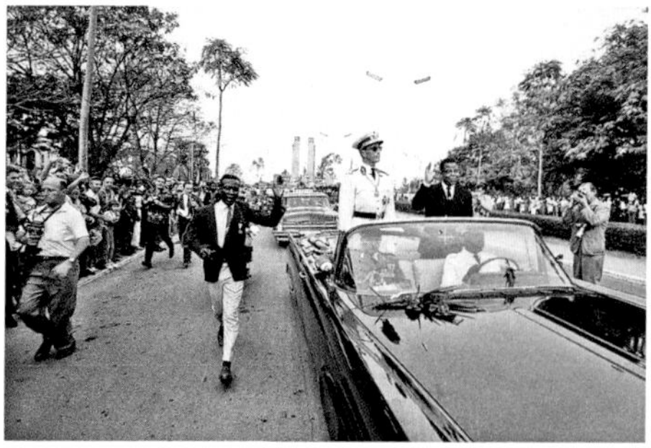

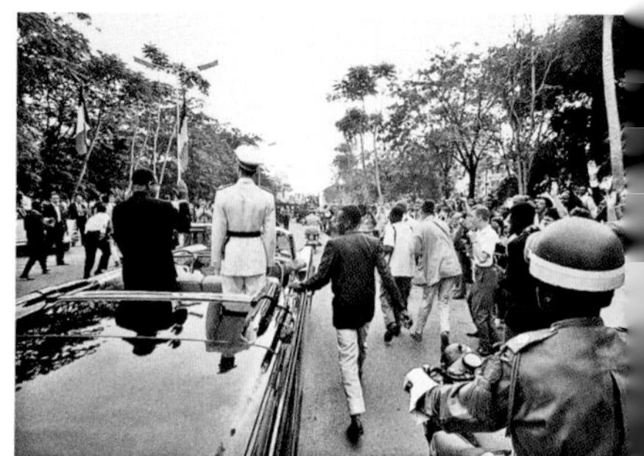

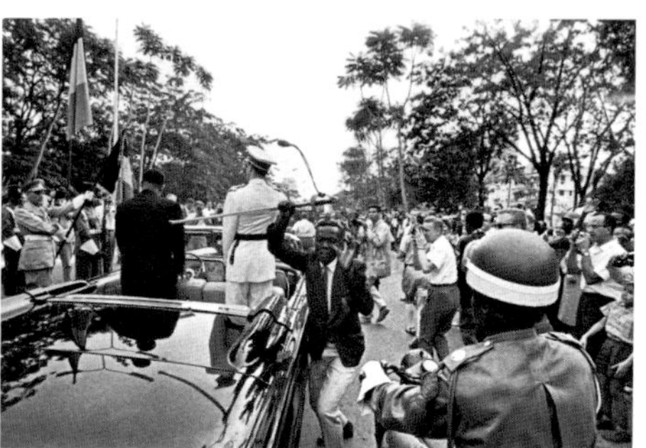

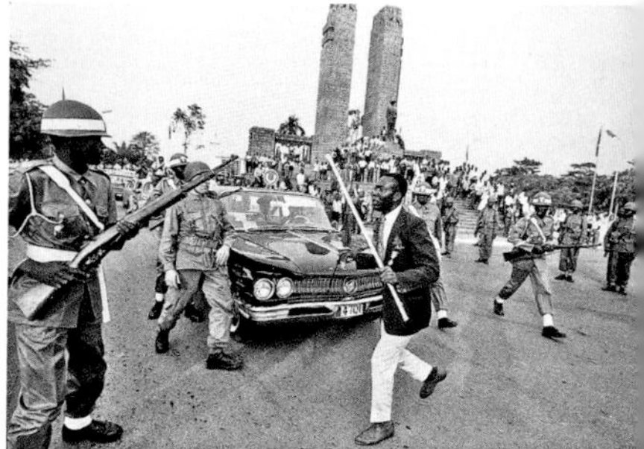

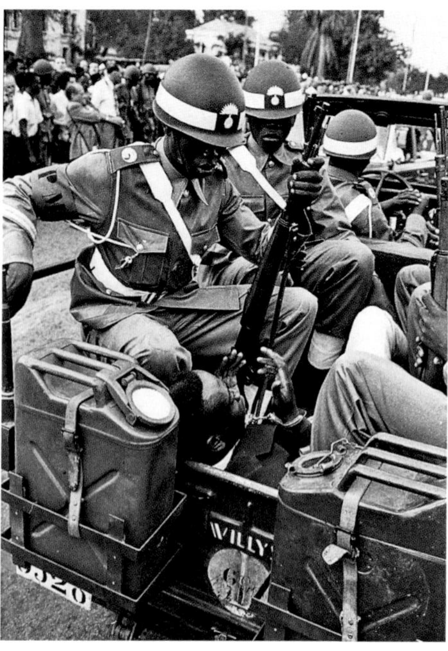

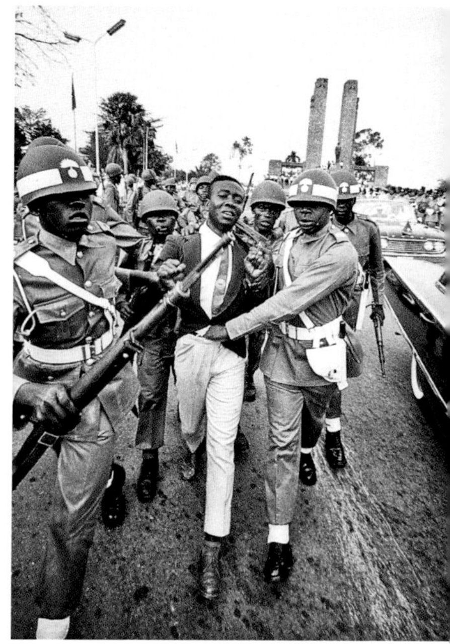

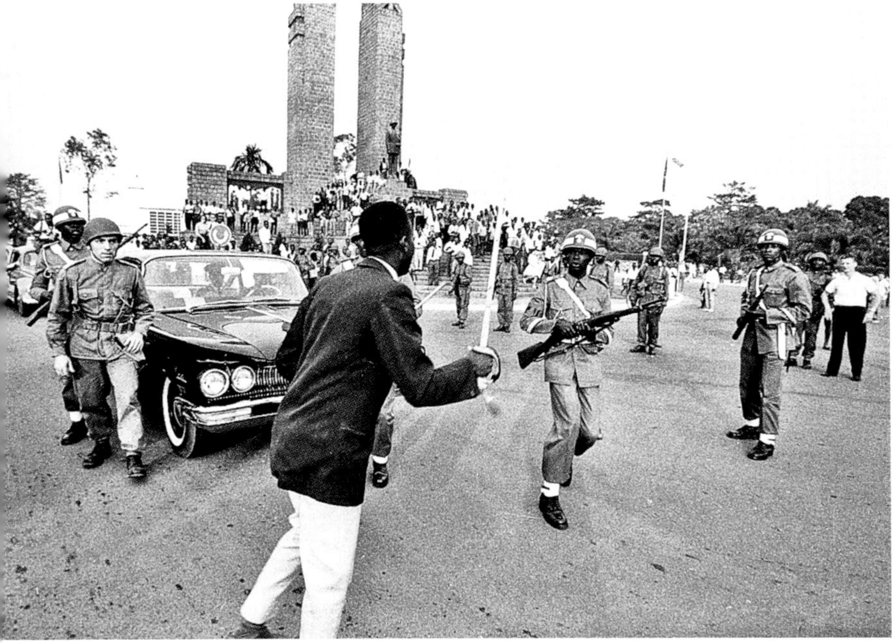

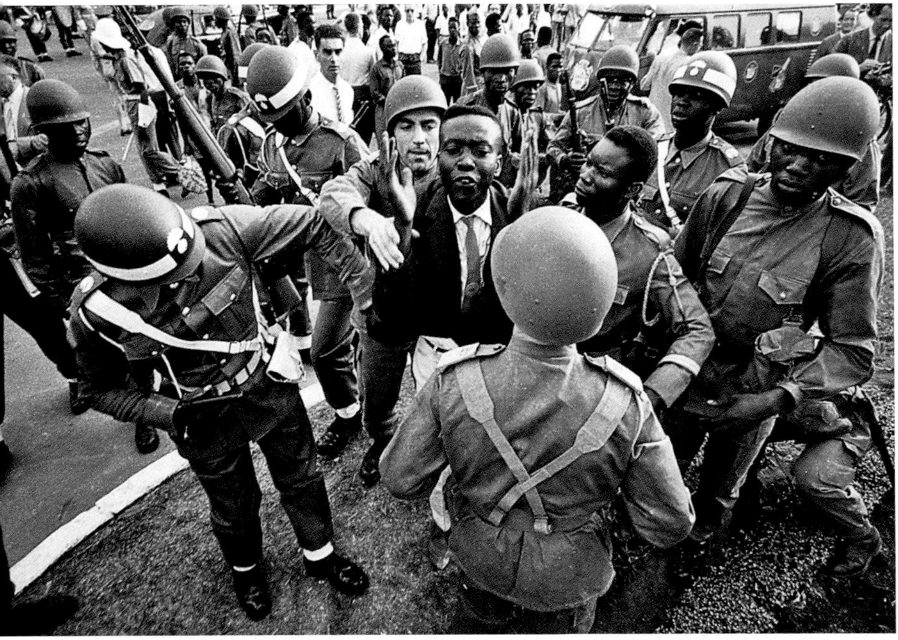

Leopoldville, **1960**

Robert Lebeck, who now – in a certain sense as the culminating point of a sequence of before-and-after pictures – succeeds in capturing the key picture.

Zero hour of the Dark Continent

"King's Sword in a Black Hand." Lebeck's report first appeared in *Paris Match*, No. 587 (9 July 1960). Two days later, *Life* published the crucial motif under the title; *King gives up a colony – and his sword*, followed by *Kristall* and the Italian magazine *Epoca* – not to mention the many books, anthologies, exhibitions, and catalogues that have pushed Lebeck's image again and again into our consciousness and assured its position as a kind of icon, a symbolic metaphor for the end of colonialism and Africa's entry into a new age. 1960 was an important year for the African continent, bringing as it did independence to a series of largely west and central African states: Cameroon and Togo, Mali, Dahomey, Niger and Upper Volta, the Ivory Coast, Gabon and Mauritania. The Belgian Congo, too, by far the largest of the group of colonies, received its independence. The talk was already of an 'African year', and of the 'zero hour' of the Dark Continent – phrases signaling confidence in the political future and expressing a strong and independent Africa.

Beautiful, and rich in mineral resources

The Congo was 'given' to Belgium at the end of the nineteenth century. King Leopold II had been attempting to acquire the colony with the support of Bismarck in Germany, which sought to halt the advance of Britain and France across the Dark Continent. Then at the Berlin-Congo Conference of 1884/85, the territory left of the Congo River was finally allotted to Belgium. Thus the history of the Belgian Congo began: beautiful, rich in mineral resources, and, with its more than 1.5 million square kilometers (half a million square miles), approximately eighty times larger than its so-called mother country. In 1960, the Congo contained about two and a half million inhabitants, including eighty thousand Whites; of the native population, at the time, not more than fifteen had a university diploma – testimony to how ill-prepared the land was for independence. In fact, it had long been assumed that independence would not come until the 1980s, or at the earliest the 1970s. As late as 1957, the Antwerp academic A. A. van Bilsen had set up a "Thirty-Year Plan for the Political Emancipation of Belgian Africa." But in the end, everything happened far quicker than was planned.

The riots in January 1960 had set the process in motion. From today's standpoint, it looks as if Belgium could not have ridded itself of its colony more quickly. King Baudouin set the day of independence for 30 June 1960, and already in early July the first mutinies started in portions of the Force Publique, the 23,000-man army of the Congo. Then came plundering and attacks on the white officers, which resulted in the flight of thousands of Belgians from the land. Belgian paratroopers attacked, and Moise Tshombé took advantage of the opportunity of the moment to declare independence for the mineral-rich province of Katanga. UN troops landed in Leopoldville. Taking advantage of the rivalry between President Kasavubu and Prime Minister Lumumba, Colonel Mobutu came to power through a putsch – and delivered Lumumba over

---

Pages 286–287: *The complete sequence underlines the advantages of 35-mm cameras for dynamic series of shots.*

Right and page 291: *"Turmoil in the Congo." The German illustrated* Kristall *devoted more space to this series than any other magazine.*

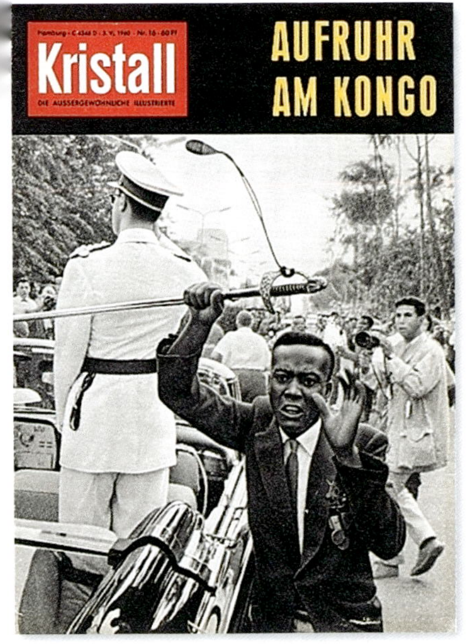

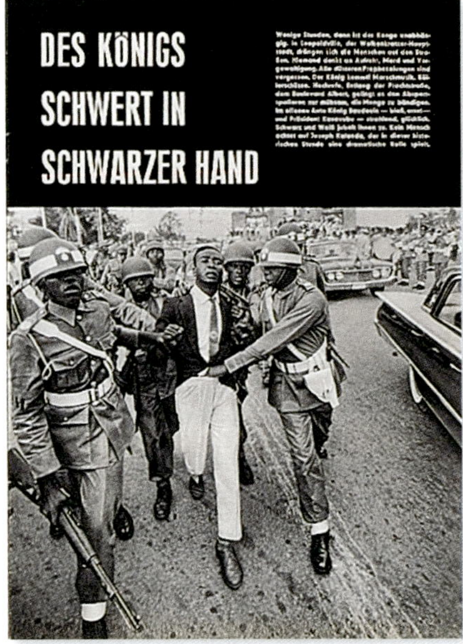

to Katanga, where he was shortly found dead. The Congo, according to the headlines in the world press, was sinking into chaos.

But at the moment our photograph was taken, there was no trace of all that was to come. It is 29 June 1960 – a warm and sunny Wednesday morning. The entire country is rushing deliriously toward independence. In the streets, crowds are gathering, church bells are tolling, flags are flying everywhere. King Baudouin is due to arrive any moment at the airport of the capital city of Leopoldville, and tomorrow, Thursday, there will be a festive Te Deum service in the church of Notre Dame du Congo. Observers from all over the world are present to report on the historical event. At the end of the church service, a ceremony is scheduled in which President Kasavubu will address "the slow awakening of the Congo's sense of nationhood" and praise "the wisdom of Belgium… which did not stand in the way of history." Then Premier Patrice Lumumba will take the podium, whose description of "the sufferings of the native population during the colonial period" will have the effect of a diplomatic bombshell. At 11 o'clock, the colonial history of the Belgian Congo will come to an end, and with the words "May God protect the Congo" King Baudouin will send the land on its way into independence. "Of all the new states that are being founded, the most exciting experiment is beginning," according to the correspondent of the German newspaper *Süddeutsche Zeitung*, "here in the middle of the heart of Africa."

The frozen symbol of the end of an era

So much for Thursday, 30 June. But today is still only Wednesday, and the King has not yet landed. Robert Lebeck is sitting with his colleagues in a Belgian restaurant enjoying a leisurely lunch. Some of his companions have left in order to catch Baudouin at the airport, but Lebeck is taking his time. After all, nothing important is going to happen at the airport. He goes instead directly to the city, to Boulevard Albert, where the convoy containing king and president is awaited. A crowd of people is already lining the main street with its monument to Leopold II, which has now become the frozen symbol of the era approaching its definitive end. Lebeck passes through the barriers: he wants to place himself exactly by the guard of honor and the waving flags, where the convoy will probably slow down. Finally the cavalcade approaches. Standing in an open automobile, Baudouin and President Kasavubu receive the ovation of the multitude. A young black man, elegantly dressed, is running in tempo at the side of the automobile. Through the viewfinder of his Leica M3 with its 21-mm Super Angulon lens, Robert Lebeck is tracking the action. Supposing the man to be one of the many a security guards, the photographer expects to be chased any moment from his position in the street. Instead, the young man runs past him, followed by a motorized police escort. Lebeck begins shooting again. At this point, the young man seems to have spotted the sword lying on the back seat of the car. A second later, he reaches for it, snatches it up and brandishes it in his right hand. A spontaneous gesture, over in a moment, yet caught by the camera.

Story-teller in pictures

Once asked by a British publisher to define his understanding of himself as a photographer, Robert Lebeck gave a short, clear answer: "I am a journalist." Lebeck sees himself as a craftsman – someone who is sent out on a job and returns with usable photographs. His model for this approach has always been Alfred Eisenstaedt, a photographer for all seasons. But there are others with whom Lebeck feels himself tied: Felice Beato, for example, or Robert Capa, Eugene Smith, and Erich Salomon, whose discreet manner continued to define the standard for Lebeck.

Born in 1929 in Berlin, Robert Lebeck sees himself in the tradition of the 'classic' photojournalism that assumed the task of providing visual information along with the rise of the illustrated magazines in the 1920s. More precisely, Lebeck, who first published his reports in the mid-1950s in *Revue*, and then moved on to *Kristall*, and finally in 1966 to *Stern*, numbers among the mid-twentieth-century generation of well-known international photojournalists. The impact of the large – primarily American – magazines after the war aroused his curiosity, and Lebeck succeeded in building on the achievements of modern reporting, without having to fear the overly powerful competition of today's television.

Lebeck is a story-teller in pictures, and is loath to let himself be classified according to a certain style, strategy, or aesthetic. Nor does he pursue a single theory of reporting. At most, one might speak of a certain cinematic approach that structures its theme, dissects it, circles around it, and describes it from various standpoints. His reporting on the Congo can be taken as exemplary of his approach: from the first appearance to the arrest of the young enthusiast whom the *Kristall* editors arbitrarily dubbed "Joseph Kalonda," the story is told in a mere dozen pictures.

That Lebeck in fact took an interest in the people who appeared in his reports and in the circumstances of their lives is certainly not one of the necessary and self-evident properties of his profession. But these are in fact the characteristics of a photographer who numbers today among the most famed of the post-war photojournalists. On a later trip to Africa, Robert Lebeck sought to discover from President Mobutu the whereabouts of the young man who had been carried away under military guard. But there are times that one may search without finding an answer: the fate of "Joseph Kalonda" remains sealed in the depths of history.

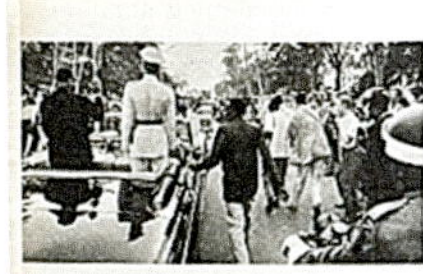

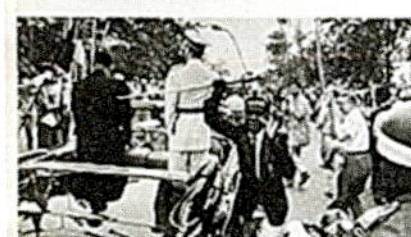

Hundert Meter war Joseph Kalonda neben dem Wagen hergelaufen, hatte „Es lebe der König" gerufen. Plötzlich sah er Baudouins Degen auf dem Rücksitz liegen. Blitzschnell riß er ihn heraus und stürmte davon. Er kam nicht weit. Was der Menge entgangen war, hatten die Soldaten der Force Publique entdeckt. Sie kreisten den Dieb ein, der in der Zwischenzeit den Degen aus der Scheide gerissen hatte.

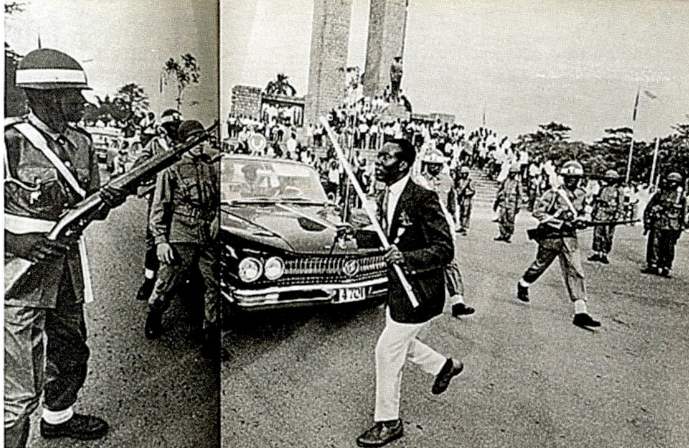

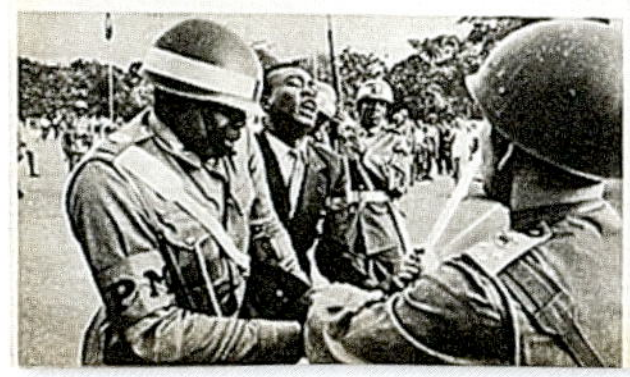

Kalonda ist rasch überwältigt. Der Degen wird ihm aus der Hand gerissen. Er brüllt auf.

Die ersten Schläge fallen. Die Pistolen sind entsichert. Schützend hebt der Mann die Arme.

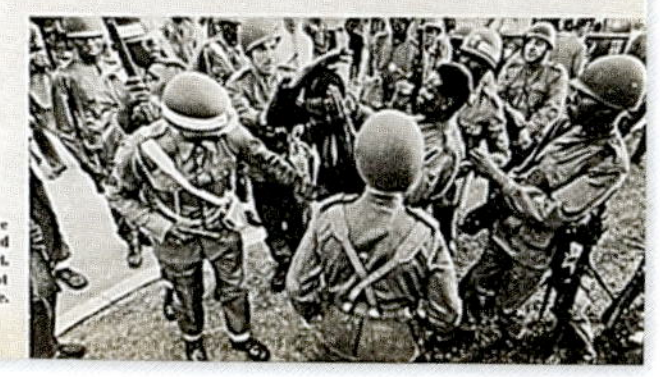

„Hört doch auf! Gnade!" Ein Offizier rettet den Täter vor den Mißhandlungen der Soldaten.

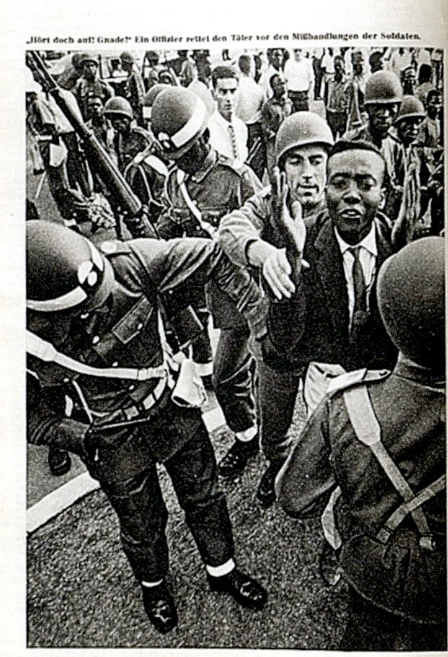

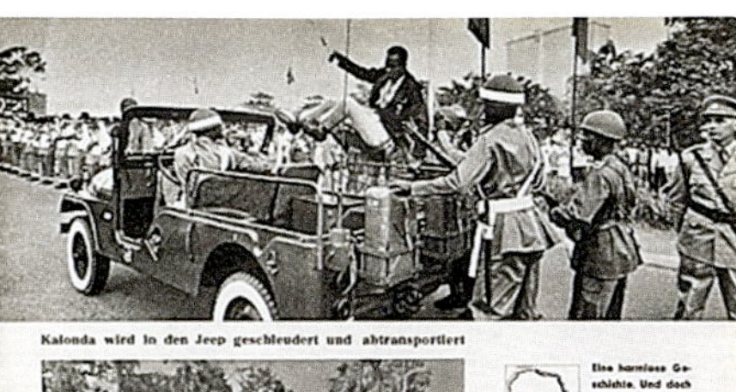

Kalonda wird in den Jeep geschleudert und abtransportiert

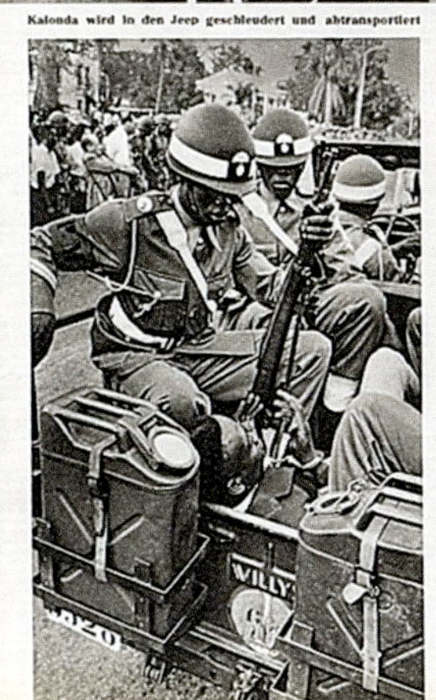

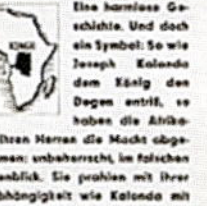

Eine harmlose Geschichte. Und doch ein Symbol: So wie Joseph Kalonda dem König den Degen entriß, so haben die Afrikaner ihren Herren die Macht abgenommen: unbeherrscht, im falschen Augenblick. Sie prahlen mit ihrer Unabhängigkeit wie Kalonda mit seiner Beute. Beide Male ein verhängnisvoller Triumph. Die Freiheit ist in den Händen der Kongolesen. Kaum gewonnen, scheint sie unter den eigenen Gummiknüppeln zu enden. Der König bekam seinen Degen wieder. Diesmal kein Symbol, nur eine Geste. Die Macht bleibt in schwarzer Hand. Und im Kongo herrschen Aufruhr und Chaos.

Wieder mit Degen: Baudouin

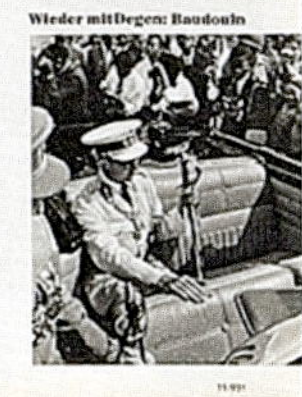

Peter Leibing
Leap to Freedom
1961

An Afternoon Change of System

The border was new, and in many places still temporary, when twenty-year-old Peter Leibing took the picture of his life. The fact that it showed a uniformed guard leaping with one valiant bound into the West lent his picture the particular explosiveness that made it, in Western eyes, an ideal testament to the weakness of the East. There would subsequently be many escape attempts and many pictures of the Berlin Wall. Peter Leibing's photo became an icon – because it showed not just a divide but a vision of its defeat.

The sentence is one of the classics of political rhetoric. Not that it is formulated in a particularly eloquent manner. No verbal puns. No thundering phrases. But short enough to be quoted again and again in the years to come. And even now it seems to confirm an old prejudice that says: for the sake of holding on to power, politicians are fully prepared to say the opposite of what they really think. Or to put it more bluntly: people in such circles are not so particular about the truth. East Berlin, June 1961. Within the framework of an international press conference, the female correspondent of the *Frankfurter Rundschau* has to opportunity to put a question to the German Democratic Republic's head of state, Walter Ulbricht. The reply begins in a meandering fashion. Ulbricht favors a somewhat pompous style of speech, which – delivered in his Saxon soprano – has spurred on the political cabaret for years. At last, however, the politician gets to the point: "No one," he says, "no one has the intention of erecting a wall."

It sounded dogmatic and was a downright lie. Two months later, during the night of 12/13 August, armored tanks drove up. At 2 o'clock in the morning, members of the national police, the People's Army, and workers' militia set to work. Roads were torn up. Barbed wire unrolled. On Sunday morning, East Berlin woke up to find itself cut off from the West. In the

---

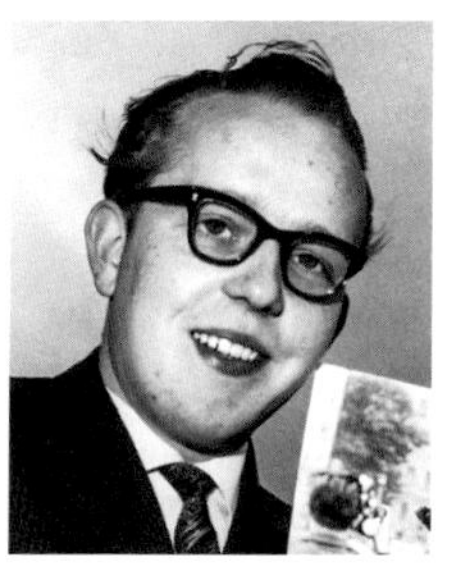

Peter Leibing
Born ***1941*** *in Hamburg. Starts as a trainee at the Hamburg photo agency Conti-Press. In August* ***1961*** *sent by Conti-Press to Berlin, where he takes his most famous picture. First published on 16 August* ***1961*** *in the* Bild *newspaper. The picture wins him the Overseas Press Club Best Photograph Award.* ***1970*** *joins the* Hamburger Abendblatt *newspaper, where he works as a photo editor until* ***2001.*** *Dies* ***2008*** *in Oerel, near Bremervörde, Germany.*

language of GDR propaganda, a firm end had been put to the "political agitation against the countries in the Socialist camp."

The Berlin Wall, naturally, was primarily a wall. In reality, however, it was more than that. From a technical point of view, it was a system – refined over the years – of concrete and barbed wire, anti-tank obstacles and mines, watchtowers and a no-man's-land in which a wealth of flora and fauna somewhat atypical for big cities was gradually able to spread. But that is the romantic side of a border that, with a rare pitilessness, divided one country, but two systems, one people, but two political creeds. Berlin, with its four-power status, brought the on-going East–West conflict to a topographical head: here capitalism, the West, prosperity; there communism, the East, the planned economy. Nowhere in Europe were the differences between the systems more glaringly apparent. And the Wall granted physical expression to their opposition. It divided Good from Evil. Which side was which depended on one's ideological perspective.

In political terms, Berlin had a special status. The former imperial capital functioned as the simultaneous representative of two rival forms of government, which, following their adoption of separate currencies in 1948, had drifted ever further part. A race developed between the systems, one that for many East Germans, it is true, was long since decided. Against the oft-cited "economic miracle" taking place in the West, the communist East could offer only a lack of freedom, a planned economy, and institutionalized shortages. The situation was compounded by the ideologically fed curbs placed on the former elite, whom the workers' and peasants' state had consigned to the lower end of the social hierarchy. It was hardly a coincidence that university lecturers, engineers, doctors, and intellectuals departed the GDR in droves, thereby threatening to drain the country of its life blood. Over three million people are said to have left the GDR prior to the building of the Wall. A safe barrier against the migration of its own citizens was thus only a question of time. On 13 August 1961 the first stone was laid. The finished wall ran a length of 43.1 km (nearly 27 miles). A mark of infamy for some. A protective shield for others. At all events, a powerful symbol of the political disintegration of Europe and the world.

Coming to terms with a divided Germany

That August of 1961 saw dramatic scenes unfold along a border that everyone knew was only going to become more final, more perfidious, and more impermeable with time. People leapt out of houses overlooking the border and landed, if they were lucky, in the blankets stretched out by West Berliners who had hurried up to help. People attempting to flee were left entangled in the barbed wire. Families waved to relatives and friends on the other side of the border. Overnight, the idea of 'over there' took on a new meaning. The protest voiced by the Western allies was limited to diplomatic notes. At the end of the day, the division of Germany was quietly accepted. There was no question of increasing hostilities over a few meters of barbed wire.

It's now 15 August. Assembled along the border, together with police and onlookers, is the press. One of the journalists is called Peter Leibing. He has traveled across from Hamburg and is working for Conti-Press, a relatively small agency. It would be exaggerating to call Leibing a professional. He is just twenty years old, and if we look through his portfolio to date, we will find chiefly photos of horses – Leibing's main job was to cover horse racing. Who could have suspected that his eye, trained on the racecourse, would help him to frame the shot of his life within the space of a few moments? But Leibing has luck on his side – alongside technical proficiency, patience, flexibility, and instinct, one of the key requirements of successful photojournalism. And he is also – it goes without saying – carrying a decent camera. Ironically, an East German Exacta with a 200-mm telephoto lens. Leibing is watching events from Bernauer Strasse. He is divided from the East by a waist-high fence of barbed wire. On the right-hand side, a sign marks the end of the sector. On the other side of the border, a uniformed *Volkspolizist*. He's smoking. He seems nervous. It's 2 in the afternoon. He starts running, jumps, clears the barbed wire and lands in the West, immediately disappearing into a waiting police car.

Countless pictures were taken during those days. Peter Leibing's picture traveled around the world. He had tripped the shutter at the right second. Frozen the leap to freedom at the decisive moment. The fact that the escapee is wearing a uniform and a steel helmet, and carrying a carbine of the type issued to East German border guards, lends the image a particular explosiveness, and probably contributed significantly to the photo's fervent embrace by the Western media. The message was clear: now even the East's own troops were running away. Prior to the building of the Wall, Conrad Schuhmann had in fact been something of a loyal citizen of his country. Nineteen years of age and, it is said, a staunch communist. But his days patrolling the border had sewn doubts in his mind, said Schumann: "There was a little girl, four or five years old, who came from her grandparents in East Berlin, and her parents were standing on the West Berlin side. The little girl wanted to go to her parents. But she wasn't allowed to. She was held back by GDR officers in the East. That was my worst experience on the border." Leibing was not only photojournalist who watched Schumann jump. But his photo captures the flight to freedom in the clearest fashion. It did not make him rich. The rights to the picture belonged to the agency. As for Conrad Schumann: in 1998 he committed suicide in Kipfenberg, Bavaria. The "Prussian Icarus" had never truly made the crossing to the West.

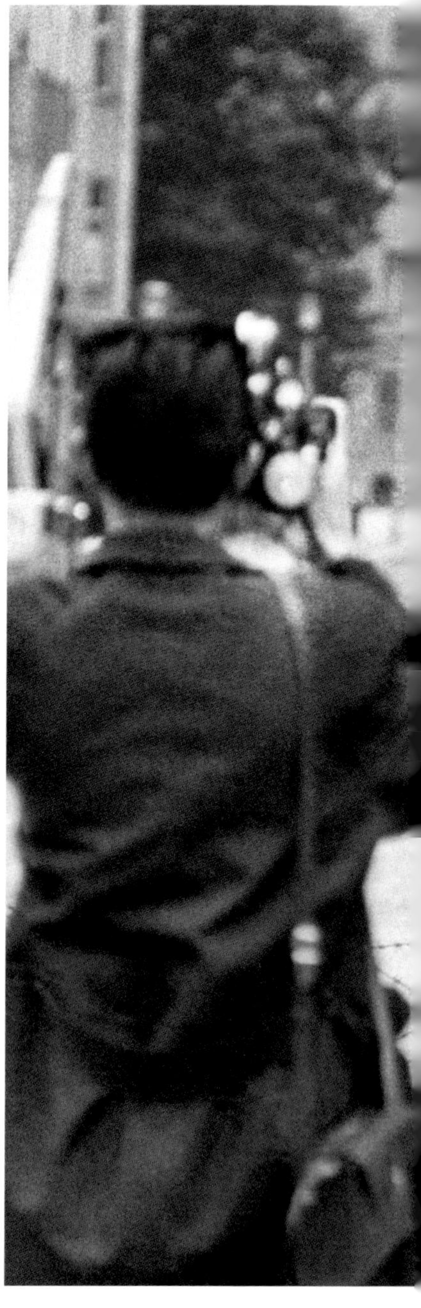

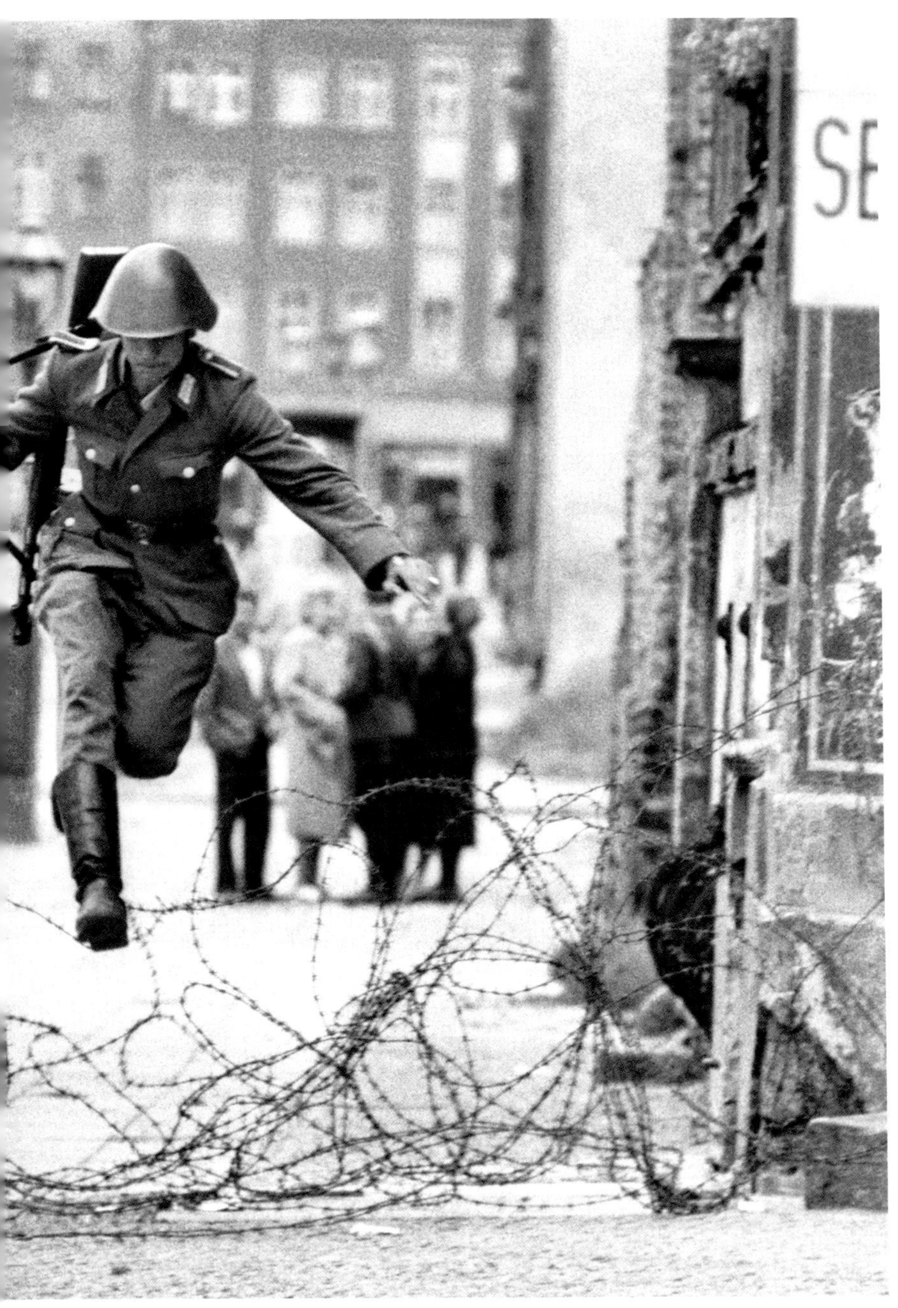

Leap to Freedom, 1961

Bert Stern
Marilyn's Last Sitting
1962

Epitaph in Ektachrome

He may not have been the first to photograph her, but he was certainly the last. In July 1962, the young photographer Bert Stern succeeded in three sittings in capturing a many-faceted portrait of an unusually relaxed and playful, close and direct Marilyn Monroe. A few weeks later she was dead. What had begun as an eight-page homage to the screen star in *Vogue* became an obituary, and has entered photographic history as *Marilyn's Last Sitting.*

His first words upon meeting her were short and simple: "You're beautiful" – perhaps not exactly the most original start to a conversation, but Bert Stern does not seem to have been a man of many words. Moreover, what does a man say when he suddenly finds himself face to face with a woman whose screen presence and sex appeal have already caused millions of men throughout the world to lose their reason? A true "Stradivarius of sex," as Norman Mailer once described her. And as such, she might just as well have been a mere invention of film, a creation of make-up and curlers, light and direction. Seen in this way, Stern's entrée was nothing less than the translation of a myth into reality. Furthermore, the words were honest, spontaneous – and they seemed to have pleased her. "Really? What a nice thing to say," she answered – which also sounded self-confident: not the content, but the manner in which it was said, evoked her comment – not the 'what' but the 'how'. For she knew that she was attractive. And she also knew that the way she looked was her capital in a world which in other respects had hardly treated her well. After a comfortless childhood with bigoted foster-parents came three broken marriages and a round dozen abortions and miscarriages. Finally an unhappy affair with the American president. She had tried to challenge the omnipotence of the studios – and lost. Nonetheless, she had succeeded in making fifteen films – admittedly

---

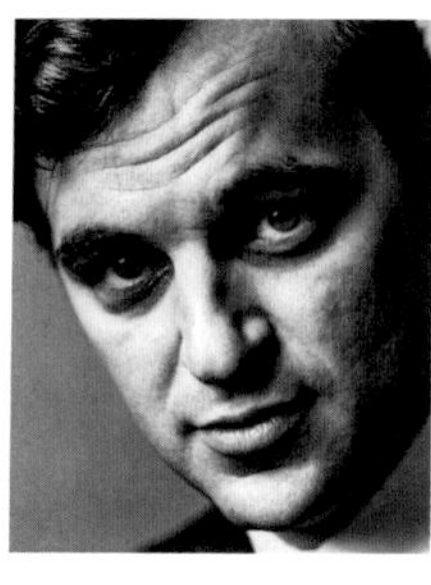

Bert Stern
Born ***1929*** *in Brooklyn, New York. Self-taught as a photographer.* ***1946–47*** *Wall Street Bank, New York.* ***1947*** *moves to* Look *magazine, where he works in the postal department. From* ***1948*** *assistant to art director Herschel Bramson.* ***1951*** *art director of the magazine* Mayfair. *Photographer in New York. Campaigns for, among others, Smirnoff, DuPont, IBM, Pepsi-Cola, VW. Editorial photography for* Vogue, Esquire, Look, Life, Glamour, *and* Holiday. ***1974*** *moves to Spain. Since* ***1976*** *active again as advertising photographer in New York, working for Polaroid and Pirelli. Editorial work for American* Vogue. ***1982*** *publication of the book* The Last Sitting. *Dies* ***2013*** *in New York.*

none of them productions that critics considered worth entering in the annals of film history. Furthermore, she was not even fairly paid for her work, in comparison with the brunette Liz Taylor, who was in a sense Marilyn's opposite number throughout her life. For filming *Cleopatra*, Liz received as much in one week as Marilyn did for an entire film. It may be that for Marilyn Monroe a glance in the mirror compensated for a great deal. She was beautiful, in fact, and no one could take her beauty away from her – or at any rate, only time, alcohol, and sleeping pills, which in this phase of her life had already formed into an unholy alliance. And perhaps it was really true, as Clare Booth Luce formulated in her obituary in *Life*, that Marilyn Monroe was moved by the fear of becoming old and ugly when she took that mixture of Dom Pérignon and barbiturates that carried her from a state of drowsiness to an eternal sleep on the night of 4 August 1962. Or perhaps it was indeed murder, as many still whisper today, ordered from on high – from the very highest levels – to hide something or other? The death of Marilyn Monroe remains until today one of the great unsolved riddles of the twentieth century.

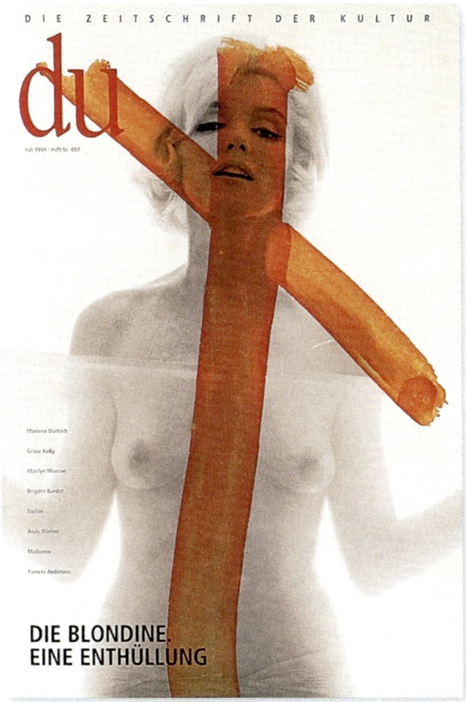

But now it is still only July. We find ourselves in the Bel Air Hotel in Los Angeles. Not a bad address, and presumably the most suitable location to realize an idea that the photographer Bert Stern hardly dares to dream about. At the time of the photograph, he was thirty-six years old and already one of the best-paid photographers in New York, which is to say, the world. Ever since he had helped a brand of vodka named Smirnoff to truly sensational profits through a spectacular advertising photograph – no small feat at the time of the Cold War – he had become one of the most sought-after photographers in the branch. In addition, he had a lucrative contract with the American *Vogue*, both then and now the Olympia of all those for whom the camera is the true medium to lend a certain durability to the appearance of beauty. Stern had been eighteen years old when he saw a still life by Irving Penn that opened a door in his mind. Nonetheless, it would not be still lifes that would inspire him and finally drive him to a career in photography, but rather life itself, especially in those places where it is sensual and full, exciting and erotic. Here Stern reflects precisely the pattern that Michelangelo Antonioni had made into an ideal in the 1960s with his film *Blow Up*. In this sense, Bert Stern dreamed his dream, although even before Antonioni he had discovered the camera to be the ideal "dream machine" that it became for at least a generation of photographers who followed upon David Hemmings. And as he noted, it was amazing all the things it allowed him to get and the people he was able to get, as long as he had a camera on him. In this way, some of his boldest dreams came to be realized.

Lighthouse on the horizon

And the boldest of bold ideas? To photograph Marilyn Monroe – naked. One must place oneself mentally back in the 1950s or early 1960s – furnished with a good measure of fantasy and sympathy – to evaluate the full audacity of Stern's longing. In addition, the photographer was, in spite of his promising career in photography, still a nobody – at least compared with Monroe, the superlative, who could claim to be "America's greatest sex symbol" (Joan Mellen). And that would probably be an understatement. She was already long an international idol, a global pin-up girl, and the lighthouse on the horizon of male fantasies around the globe. She was, as Normal Mailer phrased it, "the sweet angel of sex… Across five continents the men who knew the most about love would covet her, and the classic pimples of the adolescent working his first gas pump would also pump for her, since Marilyn was deliverance." Innumerable photographers had done her portrait in more or less provocative poses. And they were an impressive group: André de Dienes, for example, who can claim the credit for discovering Marilyn; or Cecil Beaton, the master of glamour in fashion; or Alfred Eisenstaedt, Ernst Haas, Henri Cartier-Bresson – in other words, the top rung of international photojournalists. In addition, she had modeled for Richard Avedon and Milton Greene. Philippe Halsman, not to mention Frank Powolny or Leonard McCombe, had done her portrait. She liked to be photographed. She loved the presence of a camera. She knew how to pose. Completely without clothes, however, she had been photographed only once. That was in 1949; and when Tom Kelley's photograph appeared years later in a pin-up catalogue in March 1952, it almost brought her Hollywood career to an end. Her films crackled with intense eroticism; she was always playing the easy girl. And the most memorable scene from *The Seven Year Itch* – that is, Marilyn standing on the subway vent – became one of the most famous in movie history. But then, after all, an ambivalent attitude toward sexuality was one of the many contradictions endemic to the 1950s.

Bert Stern was exactly twenty-six years old when he met Marilyn Monroe for the first time. That was the upstroke, so to speak, to a fixed idea that would take shape on this late July day in 1962 in the most beautiful sense of the word. After Dienes and Beaton, Avedon and Green, now he, Bert Stern, was allowed to photograph Marilyn Monroe – that same Marilyn who had given wings to his thoughts ever since 1955, and whom he had 'desired' since that time, as he himself admitted. "The first

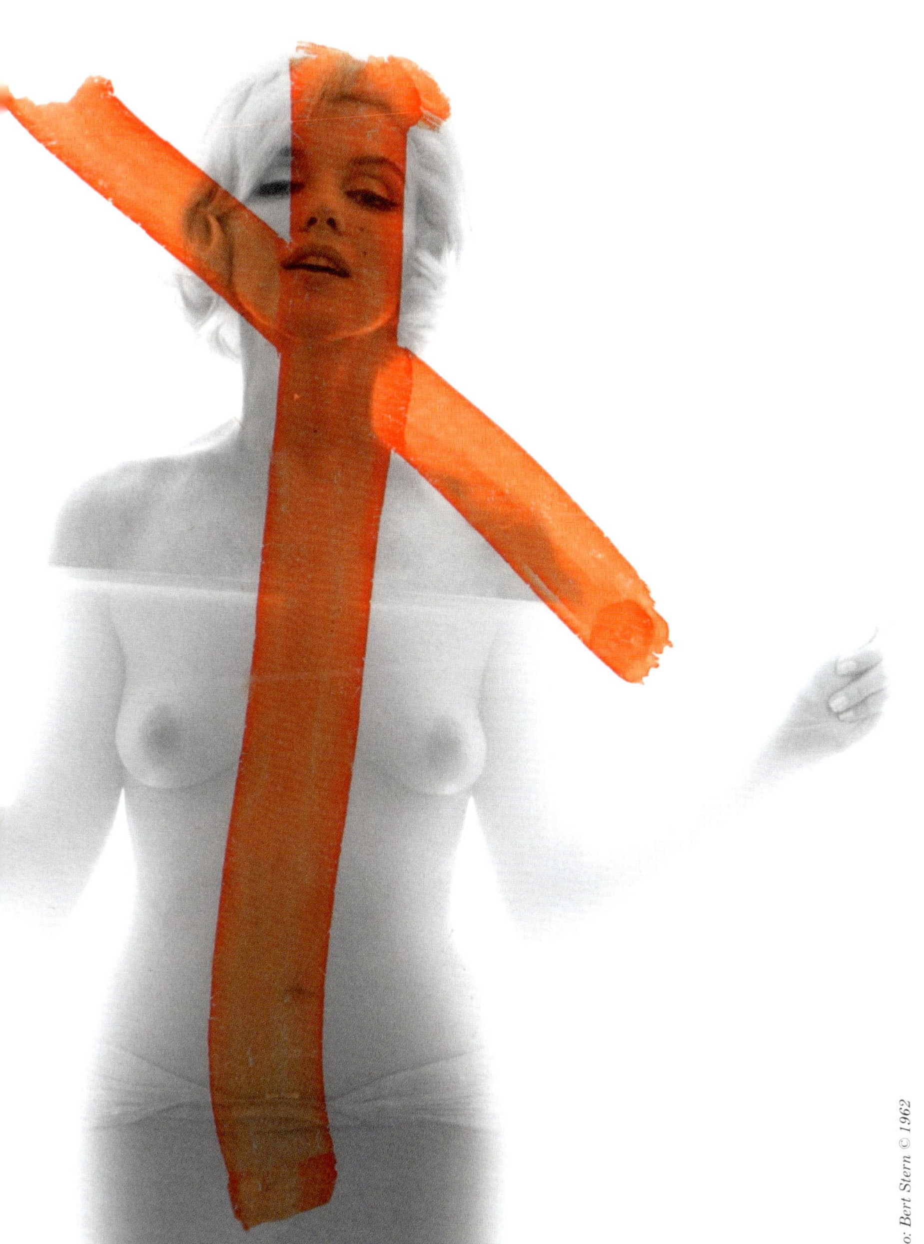

Foto: Bert Stern © 1962

time I saw her," he relates, "was at a party for the Actors Studio, in New York City. It was 1955. A friend and I had been invited, and when walked in, there was Marilyn Monroe. She was the center of attention. All the men were around her, and all the light in the room seemed focused on her. Or was the light coming from her? It seemed to be, because she glowed. She had that blond hair and luminous skin, she wore a gleaming sheath of emerald-green that fit her body like a coat of wet green paint. 'Look at that dress,' I said to my friend. 'I hear they sew her into it,' he said. How could you get her out of it, I wondered, with a razor blade? I'd laid eyes on Marilyn Monroe only moments before and already ideas about taking her clothes off were going through my mind."

The goal of his dreams and secret fantasies

Now, however, it's 1962, and Bert Stern is about to reach the goal of his dreams and secret fantasies. The Dom Pérignon vintage 1953 has been chilled, and Suite Number 261 in the upper floor of the Bel Air has been transformed into a temporary studio. The lighting is in place, the portable hi-fi set up. He wanted not only to create a space out of light, as he said, but also an environment of sounds. In this case, it was not Sinatra, as Avedon had used, but the Everly Brothers. The people at *Vogue* had done him a favor and gotten him some gauze-thin cloths. That the editors had accepted his proposal to supply a portrait of Monroe had been no less surprising than the spontaneous "yes" from Marilyn Monroe herself. The luxury liner among the magazines had never published anything about Marilyn – who, it was known, really was named Norma Jean Baker, an illegitimate child hardly stemming from the social sphere to which *Vogue* usually devoted its attention and its pages. But in the meantime, Marilyn had become such an integral part of the American Dream that even *Vogue*, where dreaming was naturally at home, could no longer ignore her. The photo session was intended as her entry into Condé Nast. It became her epitaph.

It was getting toward seven o'clock and Bert Stern was beginning to get restless. He knew that Marilyn Monroe was notoriously unpunctual, but he had already been waiting for a good five hours now. What if she came only for a short time? he began to ask himself. What if the dream Marilyn had little to do with the real Marilyn Monroe? After all, the fact was that she was "well into her thirties, and she really was a little chubby," as he had seen in *The Misfits*. Still on the evening before, alone in the atmospheric illumination of the Bel Air garden, the wildest ideas had coursed through Bert Stern's head – thoughts that a married man and father of a little daughter had better not entertain. "I was preparing for Marilyn's arrival like a lover," Stern recalled, "and yet I was here to take photographs. Not to take her in my arms, but to turn her into tones, and planes, and shapes, and ultimately into an image for the printed page." The photographer found himself back in reality as the phone finally rang: Miss Monroe had arrived. "I slowly put down the phone and took a deep breath."

Better than the full-blooded girl I had seen in the movies

He met her in the lobby of the hotel. To his great surprise, she had come alone. No bodyguards, no press agents, not even her PR girl, Pat Newcomb, had accompanied her. "She had lost weight, and the loss had transformed her. She was *better* than the full-blooded, almost over-blown girl I had seen in the movies. In her pale-green slacks and cashmere sweater she was slender and trim, with just enough softness in the right places – all of it hers. She had wrapped a scarf around her hair, and wore no make-up. Nothing. And she was gorgeous. I had expected – feared – an elaborate imitation. No. She was the real thing." A moment later he asked her whether she was in a hurry. "No," she answered, "Why?" – "I thought you were going to have like five minutes," he replied. "Are you kidding," she smilingly said, entirely the professional. "Well," he carefully enquired, "How much time have you got?" "All the time that we want!"

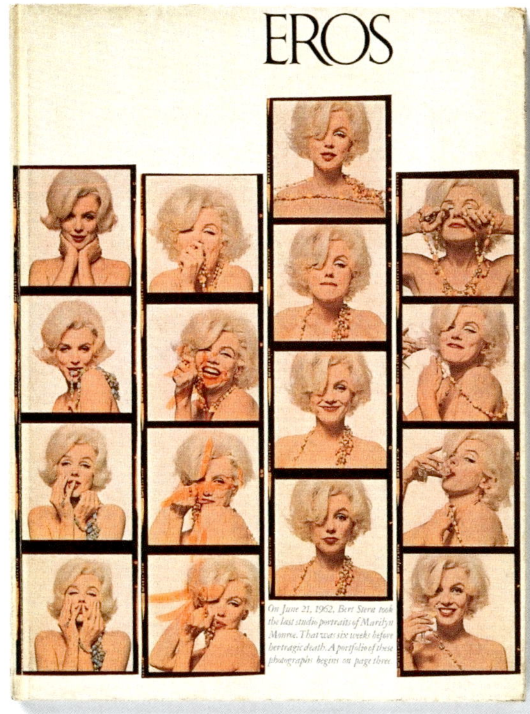

In the end, it would amount to almost twelve hours. And Bert Stern, the child of a lower middle-class Brooklyn family, as he described himself at one point, is able to get what he hoped for. Everything. Almost everything. At his request, Marilyn does without make-up, or applies at most a bit of eye-liner and lipstick; under his direction, she drapes herself in a boa. Even the transparent veils come into play. "You want me to do nudes?" she asks, and the stammering Stern replies: "Uh, well I – I guess so!" adding "… it wouldn't be exactly nude. You'd have the scarf." – "Well, how much would you see through?" – "That depends on how I light it." And will her scar be visible? Stern does not understand what she is referring to, but she explains that six weeks ago, her gall bladder was removed. Bert Stern assures her that it will be no problem to retouch it, and recalls a statement of Diana Vreeland that "…a woman is made beautiful by her scars." Marilyn is like putty in the photographer's hand. "I didn't have to tell her what to do," as he later recalled. "We hardly talked to each other at all. We just worked it out. I'd photographed a lot of women, and Marilyn was the best. She'd move into an idea, I'd see it, quickly lock it in, click it, and my strobes would go off like a lightning flash – PKCHEWW!! – and get it with a zillionth of a second."

Vogue liked the pictures. Alexander Liberman, at that time still the all-powerful art director of the magazine, pronounced them "fabulous" – but Stern knew that with Liberman, everything was "divine." This time, however, he seemed to be serious: *Vogue* devoted eight pages to

---

Page 297: *"The blonde – a revelation." Title page of the Swiss magazine* Du, *July 1999, using Bert Stern's picture.*

Above: Not the first, but to date the loveliest magazine feature on Bert Stern's cycle: the lead in Eros, *Autumn 1962.*

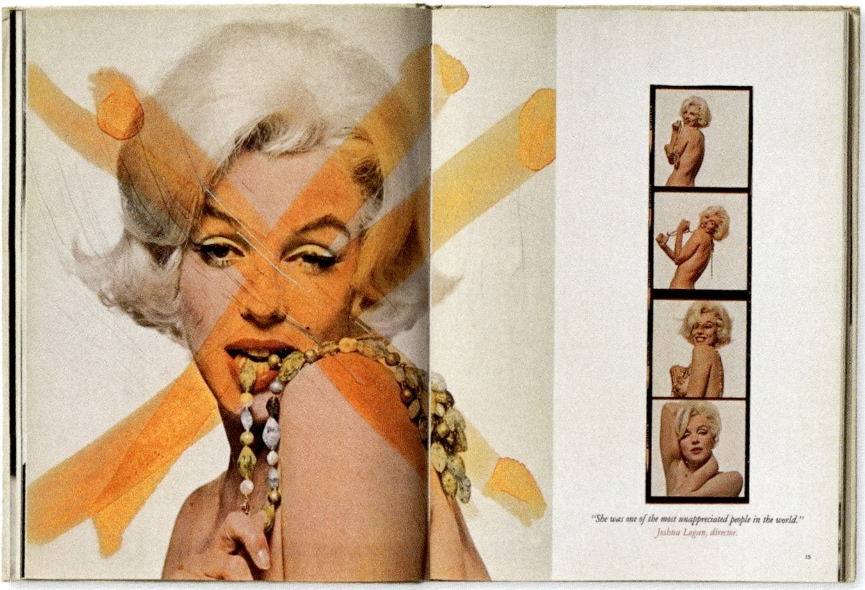

"She was one of the most unappreciated people in the world."
Joshua Logan, director.

15

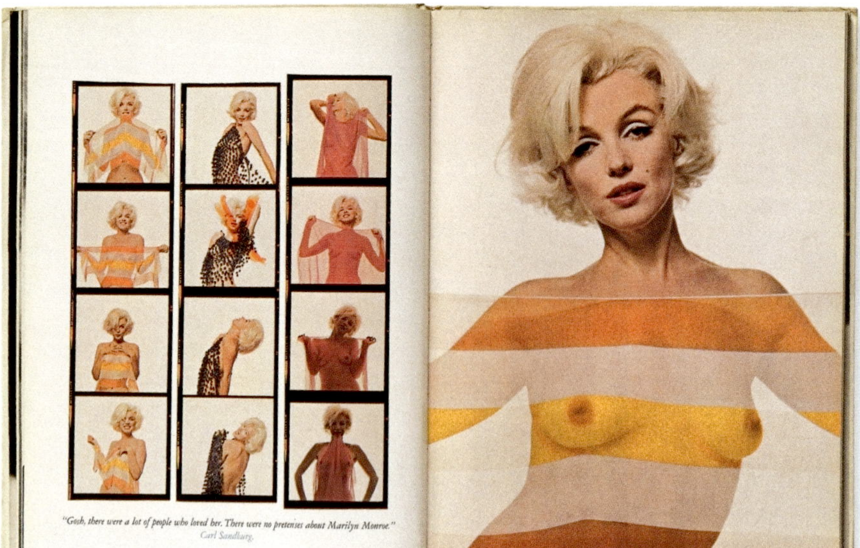

"Gosh, there were a lot of people who loved her. There were no pretenses about Marilyn Monroe."
Carl Sandburg.

10

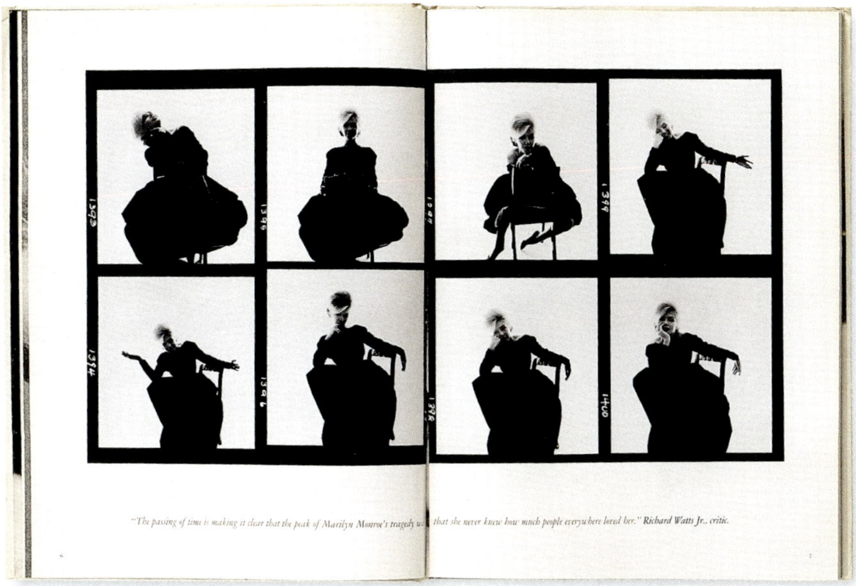

"The passing of time is making it clear that the peak of Marilyn Monroe's tragedy was that she never knew how much people everywhere loved her." Richard Watts Jr., critic.

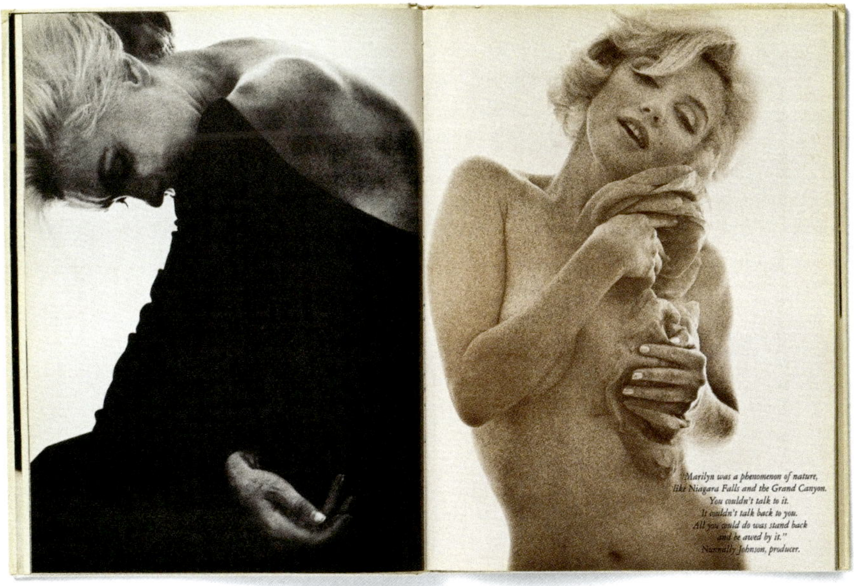

"Marilyn was a phenomenon of nature,
like Niagara Falls and the Grand Canyon.
You couldn't talk to it.
It couldn't talk back to you.
All you could do was stand back
and be awed by it."
Nunnally Johnson, producer.

Double-page spreads from Eros *(Autumn 1962): even some of the shots Marilyn that rejected were published here for the first time.*

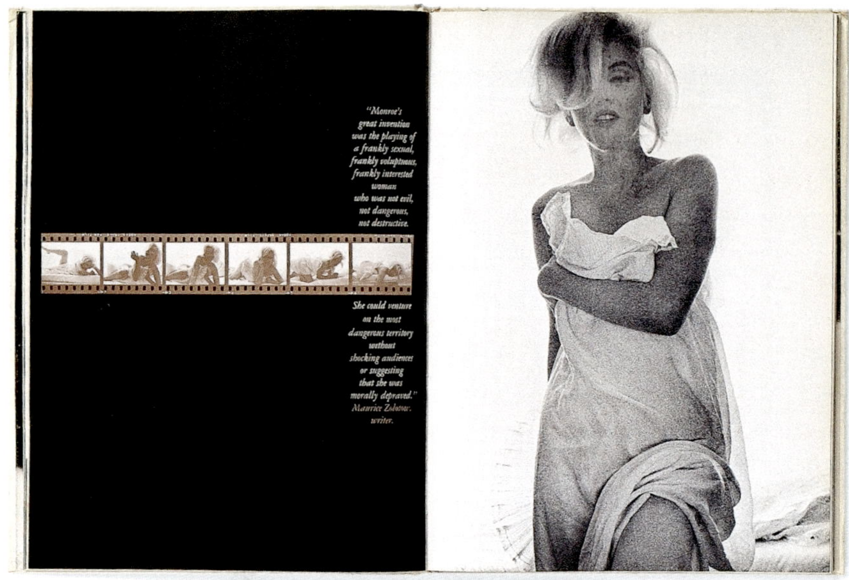

Stern's pictures. The magazine apparently realized that it had gotten onto something good – and wanted more. But, as *Vogue* let Stern know, they needed more black-and-white. Stern understood immediately: "That meant fashion pages. And that meant that they didn't want to run just nudes. They were probably going to get a lot of clothes, cover her up." There were in fact two more photo sessions in the Bel Air, to which *Vogue* sent along its best editor – a sign Stern interpreted as meaning that the magazine was indeed serious about the project. And so once again, the Everly Brothers sounded forth on the portable hi-fi, and once more the lightning storm of flash bulbs blitzed down on a tender Marilyn, whose weight coroner Dr. Thomas Noguchi would determine just three weeks later at 115 lb – further describing her in his report as a well-nourished woman, 5′5″ (166 cm) tall. But for now, the *Vogue* editor Babs Simpson had brought mountains of fashion clothing and furs along with her. And the Dom Pérignon is present once again as Bert Stern takes his photographs. In the end, he suddenly remembered the "picture I came for – that one black-and-white that was going to last for ever. Like Steichen's Garbo." Stern entered "that space where everything is silent but the clicking of the strobes." Then all at once, as he recalled, Marilyn tossed her head, "laughing, and her arm was up, like waving farewell. I saw what I wanted, I pressed the button, and she was mine. It was the last picture."

Not only the photos were crossed through

Vogue decided in the end for the black-and-white photographs, and by the beginning of August, the chosen pictures were in the layout, and the text had been composed. It was scheduled to be printed on Monday 6 August. Stern had sent Marilyn a set of pictures, but

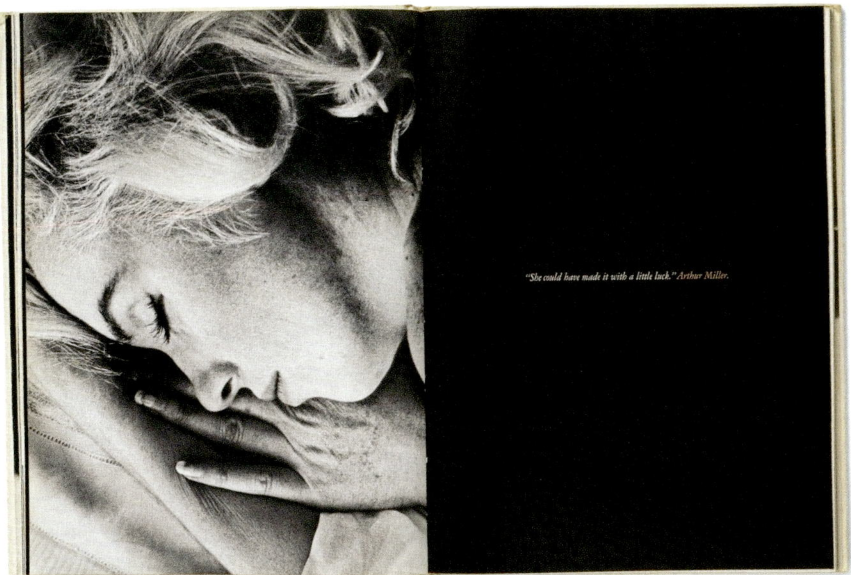

received two thirds of them back crossed out: "On the contact sheets she had made x's in magic marker. That was all right," as he later reflected. "But she had x-ed out the color transparencies with a hairpin, right on the film. The ones she had x-ed out were mutilated. Destroyed." Bert Stern was upset, even felt "some anger"; but as he later realized "she hadn't just scratched out my pictures, she'd scratched out herself." Weeks later, friends invited him to brunch. It was Saturday, 4 August, and the television in the hallway was beaming out the usual American interiors. Suddenly the program was interrupted: "Marilyn Monroe," the speaker announced, "committed suicide last night."

"I didn't know what I felt," Stern recalled. "I was just paralyzed, shocked in a dumb, numb way." But the photographer claims that "there was some way in which I was not surprised… I'd smelled trouble." And *Vogue*? They stopped the weekend presses in order to create a new headline and compose another text. "Greetings" became "a last greeting from Marilyn," at the end of which Bert Stern's final portrait came to stand. It was in any case the last large picture of the series, just as Stern's cycle is the last of the great series on the "American love goddess" who still calls to us through these pictures, as Bert Stern phrased it, like to "a moth flying around a candle."

Too daring for the times: Eros *publisher Ralph Ginsburg was charged and sentenced for disseminating pornography – "The last thing the magazine was about" (David Hillman).*

René Burri
Che
1963

Mythic Moments

When Ernesto (Che) Guevara met his death at the hands of the Bolivian army in October 1967, he was transformed from a living legend into a true cult figure. Four years earlier, René Burri had made a portrait of Che which, together with the portrait by Alberto Korda, is probably the most-reproduced icon of this 20th-century martyr.

January 1963: the two men who met in the Havana ministry office could not have been more different from each other. Nonetheless, one can, as usual, cite a number of elements they shared in common: a middle-class background, for example; a solid education, including university diploma; and a love of German literature – although in the one case it tended more toward Goethe, and in the other toward Brecht. Furthermore, both men were markedly urbane, curious about the world at large, enthusiastic about traveling and, last but not least, more or less strongly skeptical toward everything having to do with North America. In short, they had a basis for their conversation, which was conducted in French, since René Burri could not speak Spanish, and Ernesto Guevara's knowledge of German was too meager. Conversing with Che, however, was not the assignment of the young Swiss photographer. The interviewer was the then well-known journalist Laura Bergquist, who, as René Burri recalled, went at her job with a pointedness bordering on provocation. After all, wasn't she sitting here next to the man whom the USA hated more than any other in South America – except for Fidel Castro himself?

Fully human in such moments

We are in the Ministry of Industry in Havana, Cuba, specifically in the office of Ernesto Guevara, familiarly known – and not only to his friends, comrades, and disciples – as Che. It is a sunny January afternoon in 1963. A glance out the window should provide a peaceful

---

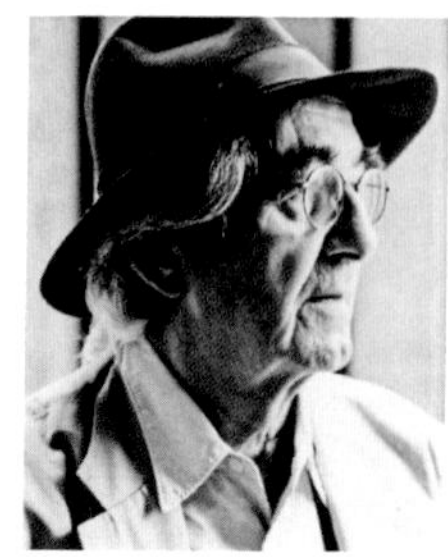

René Burri
Born ***1933*** *in Zurich.* ***1949–53*** *studies at the Arts and Crafts School in Zurich.* ***1953–54*** *military service. Growing interest in 35-mm photography.* ***1955*** *first photo published in* Life. *Becomes an associate member, in* ***1959*** *full member of Magnum.* ***1962*** *publication of his book* Die Deutschen. ***1963*** *Cuba trip. Meets Fidel Castro and Che Guevara. Pictures are published in* Life, Look, Bunte, Stern, Paris Match, Schweizer Illustrierte, Du, *among others. Films, including* The Two Faces of China *and* Jean Tinguely. ***1984*** *retrospective at the Kunsthaus Zurich.* ***1998*** *Dr. Erich Salomon Prize of the DGPh German photography society.* ***2004*** *retrospective in Paris (MEP). Dies* ***2014*** *in Zurich.*

CUBA Communist giants like China, Russia madly court little Cuba. Say the Cubans: "We are the spoiled child of the Socialist world."

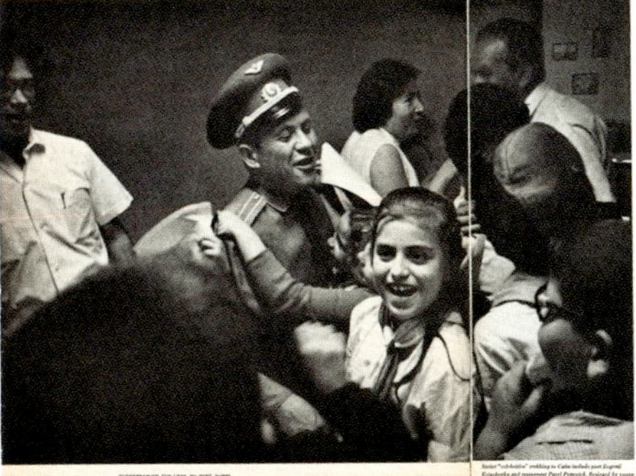

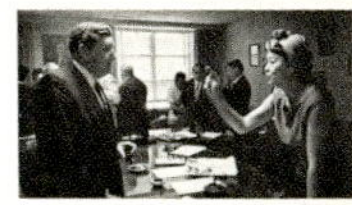

In Havana, you meet the most interesting people—from Pravda editor Zhukov, with whom I argued at a TASS press conference, to apolitical Irish engineers, beguiled leftist Greek moviemakers and friendly Poles and Yugoslavs. Harshest anti-U. S. talk I heard came from the Canadians!

16 17

CUBA Miami, in current Cuban slang, is referred to as "90 miles."

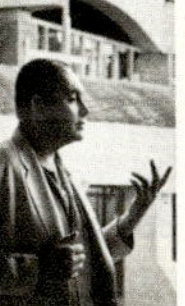

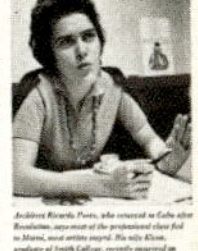

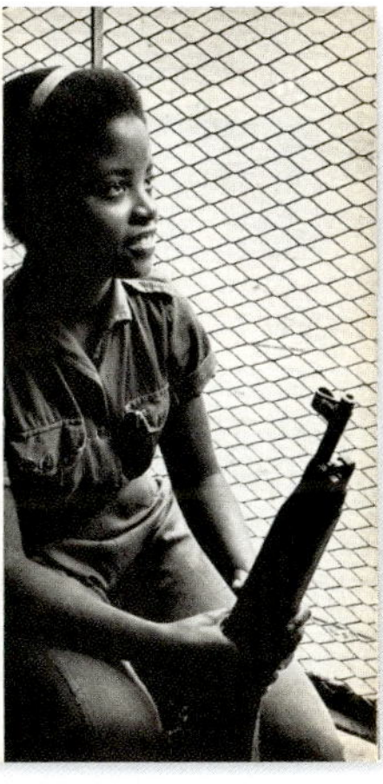

20

CUBA Tropical Marxism: Bongo drums are stored in old U. S. bank vaults; cane cutters go off to Leningrad

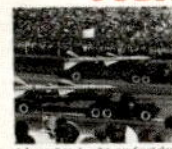

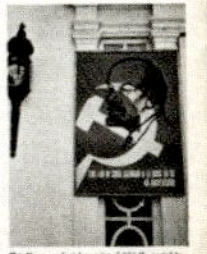

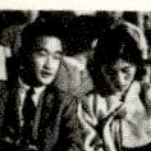

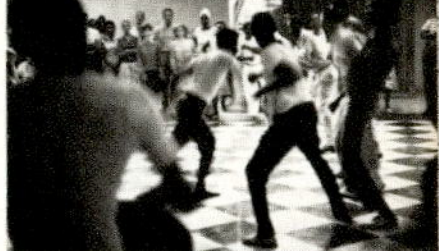

18 19

panorama of the roofs of the capital city, but the Venetian blind remains decidedly closed, allowing only a milky light to enter the room. But the gleam of several ceiling lamps is sufficient to mean that Burri, who on principle rejects the use of flashbulbs, does not have to work against the light. To the session he has brought two Leicas and a Nikon fitted with 35-, 50-, and 85-mm lenses, and in the course of the three-hour discussion, he will shoot a total of six rolls of film. This occasion will not be Burri's only chance to photograph Che, however; a few days later the photographer will join Ernesto Guevara at a festival in honor of especially worthy workers. On this second occasion, the minister will in fact make a much more jovial impression, winking at the photographer; Che seems fully human in such moments. Nonetheless, it is not a relaxed photograph that the course of time will designate as the valid icon of the Che. But it takes time to become a myth, and Burri's portrait, appearing on page 27 of the article in *Look* dated 9 April 1963, is too small and strongly cropped to serve as an icon. The cover of the magazine features a photograph of Fidel Castro – also taken by Burri – who remains America's number-one nightmare. Only later will the square-format portrait of a self-confident Che forge itself into an icon in its own right and, transformed into the sanctified image of a martyr, be found on postcards, posters, book covers, and catalogues.

Model of a classless, communist society

Che is smoking. The large Havana, still bearing its label, is perhaps what first strikes the eye of the unprejudiced observer. The cigar appears to have just been lit, and tobacco smoke is curling its way toward the ceiling. Ernesto Guevara is leaning back, looking self-confidently and even defiantly at his interview partner, who presumably has just posed a question. Notably absent from the face is any trace of self-doubt. Other photographs from this sequence present a Che who is tired or excited, or who uses his hands to express his agitation or to explain something. But in this picture he seems completely relaxed as he peers almost arrogantly past the camera into the face of his questioner. Clearly, here is a man who looks the world squarely in the face – and thus will the photograph be later interpreted by those who reproduce it over and over again.

As usual, Che Guevara is wearing a uniform; more precisely, he is wearing those same inconspicuous combat fatigues that transform even a powerful Minister of Industry – his post at present – into a battle-ready guerrilla at a moment's notice. His hair is shorter than in other photographs, his beard longer; on either side of his chin, the two patches of almost bare skin have virtually disappeared. Out of focus but unmistakable in the background are the closed Venetian blinds. In a moment René Burri's question whether they might be opened a bit will call forth an unusually gruff answer from Che: the blinds remain closed! What is he afraid of? Or is his irritation rather the response to the pointed questions of the equally self-confident Laura Bergquist?

Burri and Che had met for the first time during 1962. Che – at that time thirty-four years old and already a legend – was in New York visiting the United Nations. Together with Fidel Castro,

---

Right, pages 307, 312–313: Look, *9 April 1963: double-page spreads and cover. Burri's iconic image only appeared on the last page of the 13-page article, quite small and heavily cropped.*

CUBA Big culture buildup: Free ballet lessons for peasant children, with Marxist overtones, of course

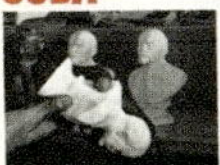

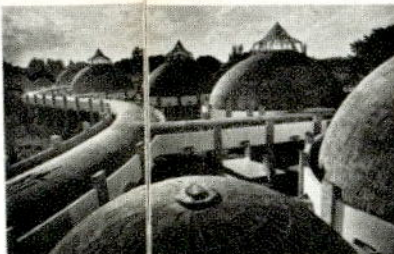

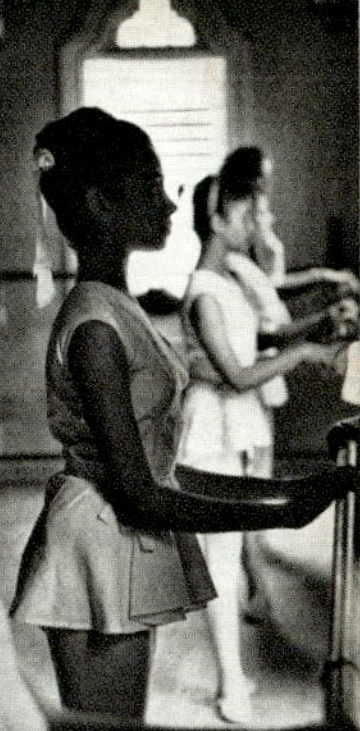

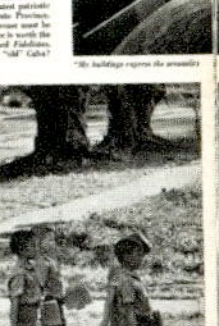

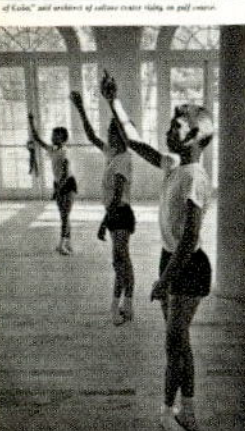

22 23

CUBA Havana's women now cut cane, wear militia uniforms and go to "Socialist" beauty parlors

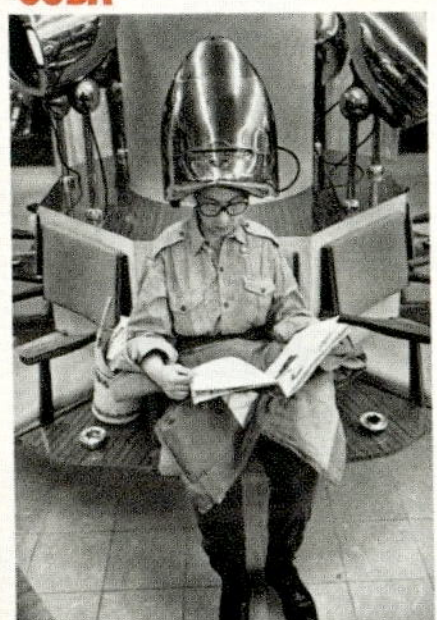

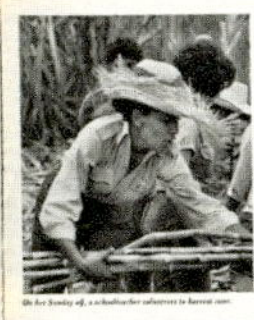

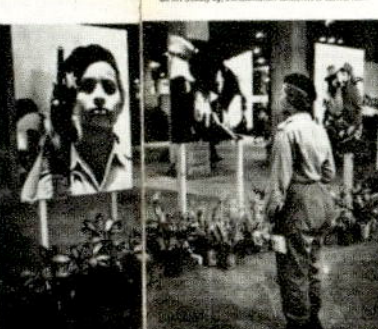

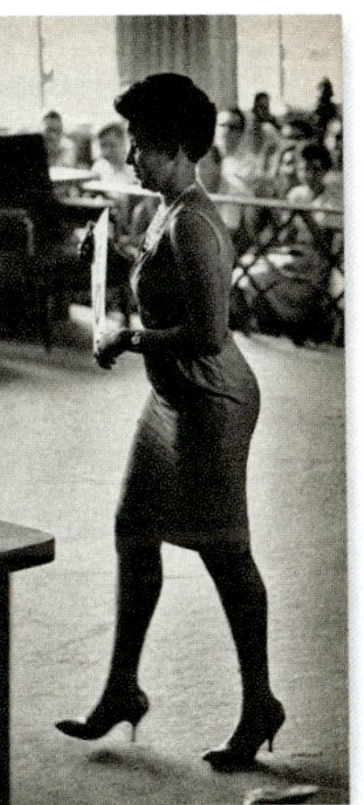

24

CUBA A revisit with "Che" Guevara, guerrilla turned industrialist, but still very much the No. 2 power of the regime

Yes, he said, a Marxist revolution was what he personally had in mind for Cuba, even back in the Sierra Maestra. No, he couldn't have served a "moderate" government. He remains the regime's "crudely explicit" critic and Castro's intellectual mentor.

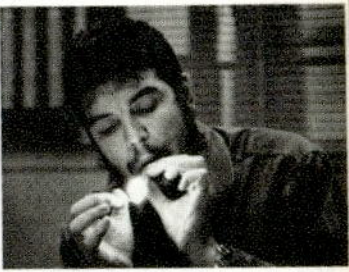

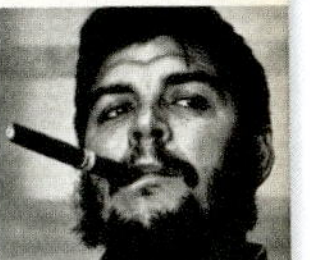

26 27

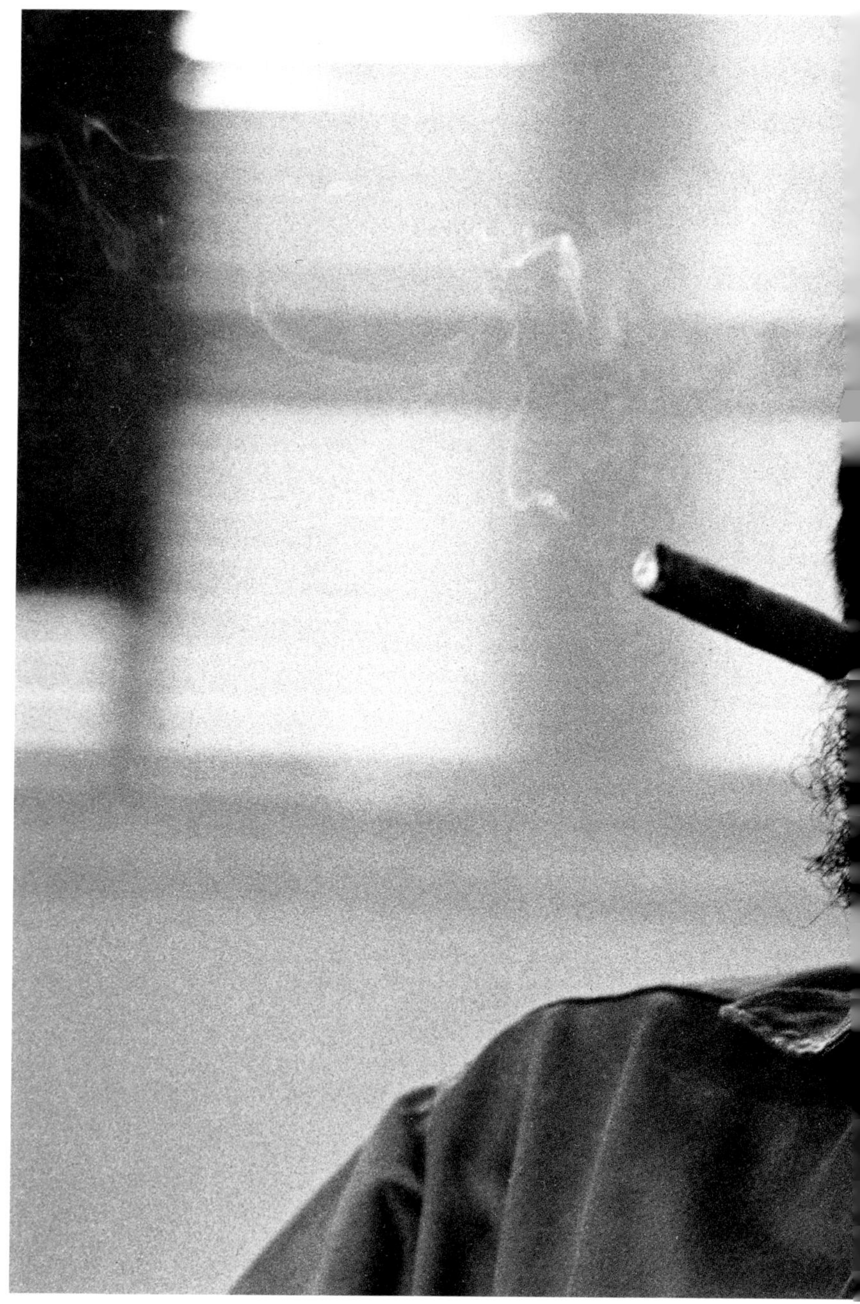

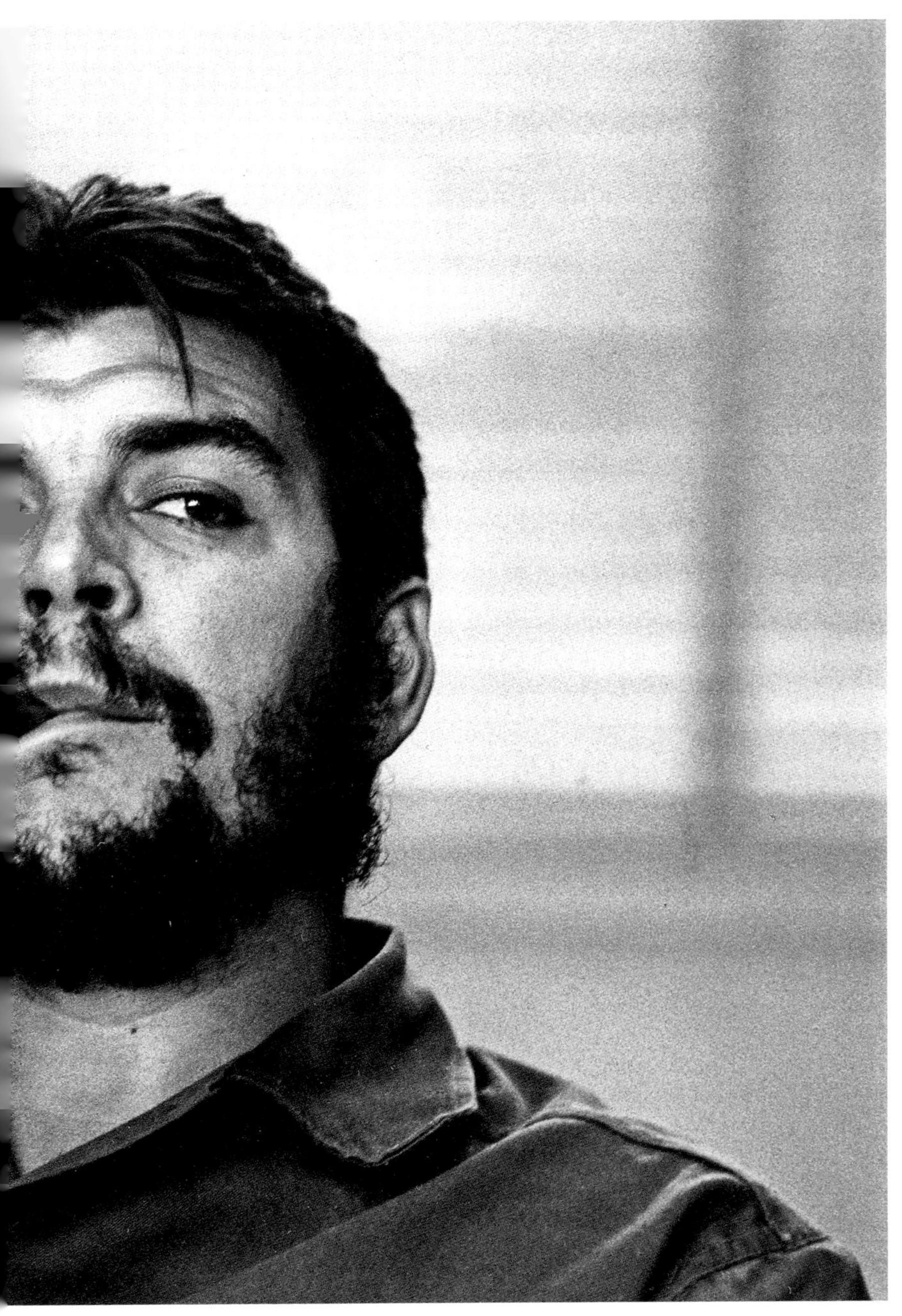

Che, 1963

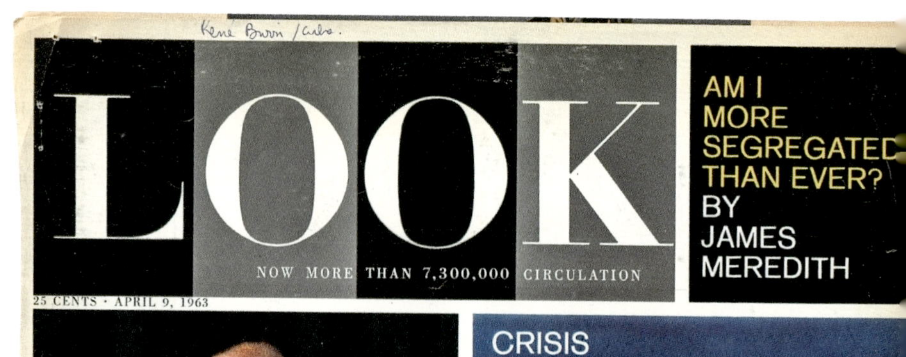
René Burri / Cuba.
LOOK
NOW MORE THAN 7,300,000 CIRCULATION
25 CENTS · APRIL 9, 1963
AM I
MORE
SEGREGATED
THAN EVER?
BY
JAMES
MEREDITH

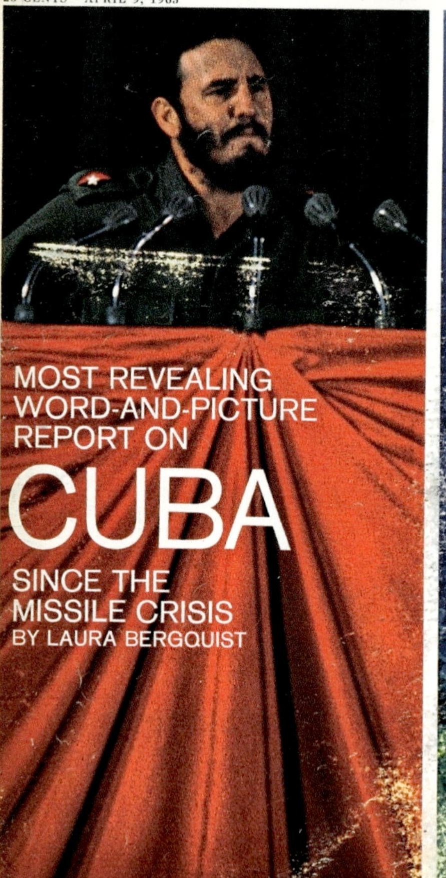
MOST REVEALING
WORD-AND-PICTURE
REPORT ON
CUBA
SINCE THE
MISSILE CRISIS
BY LAURA BERGQUIST

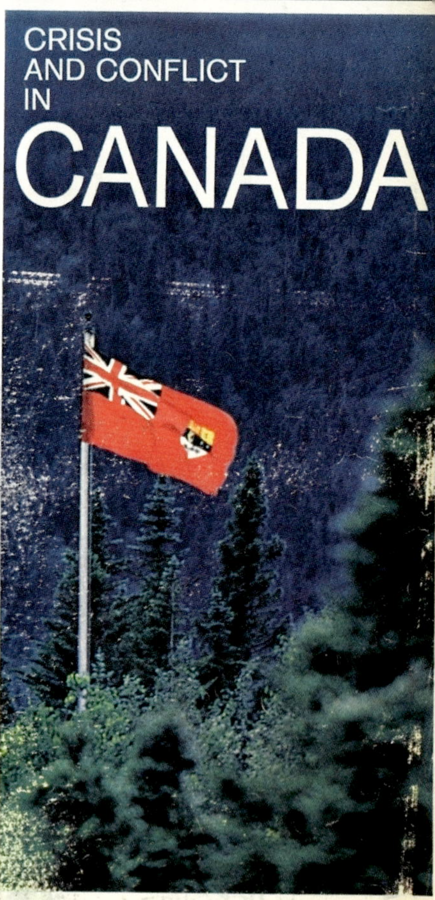
CRISIS
AND CONFLICT
IN
CANADA

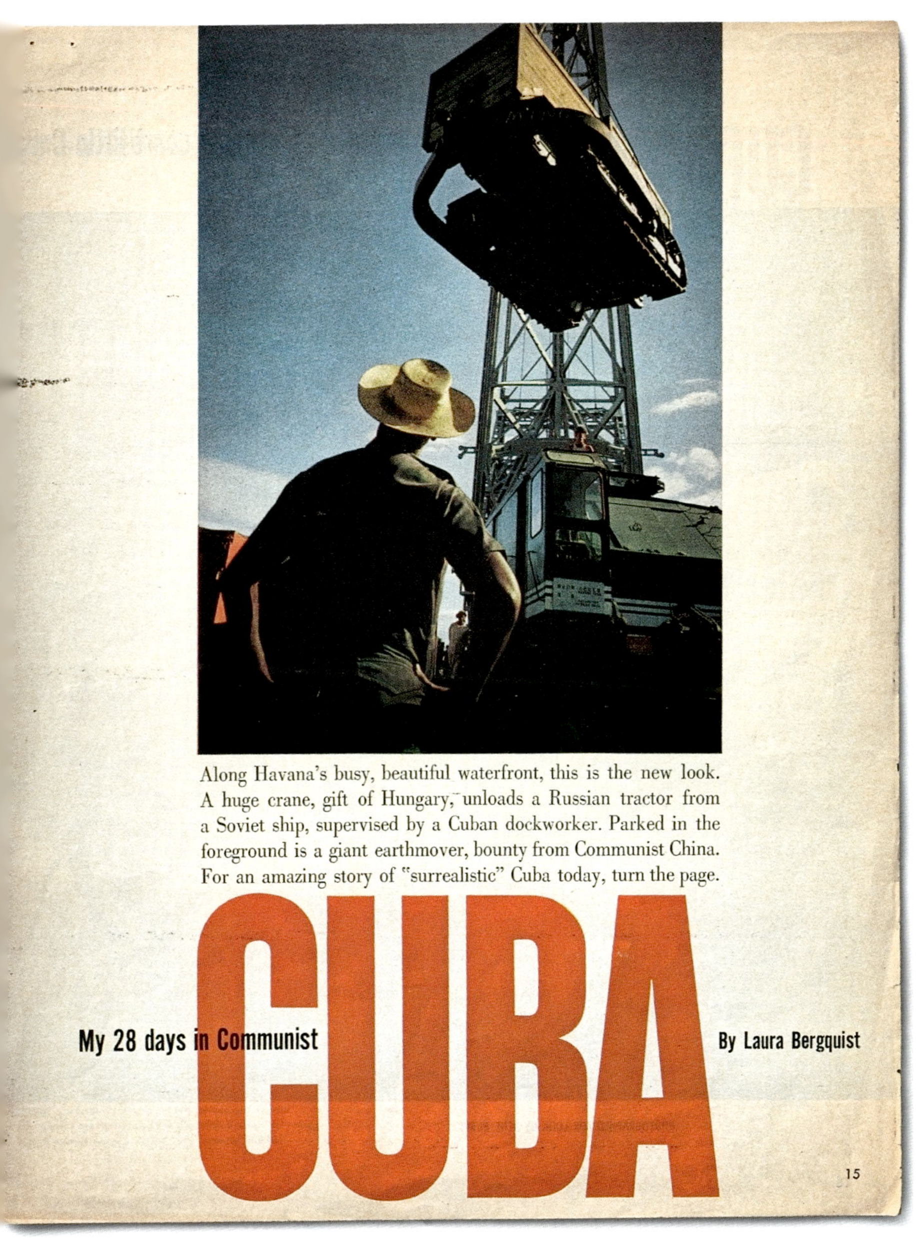

Along Havana's busy, beautiful waterfront, this is the new look. A huge crane, gift of Hungary, unloads a Russian tractor from a Soviet ship, supervised by a Cuban dockworker. Parked in the foreground is a giant earthmover, bounty from Communist China. For an amazing story of "surrealistic" Cuba today, turn the page.

My 28 days in Communist CUBA

By Laura Bergquist

15

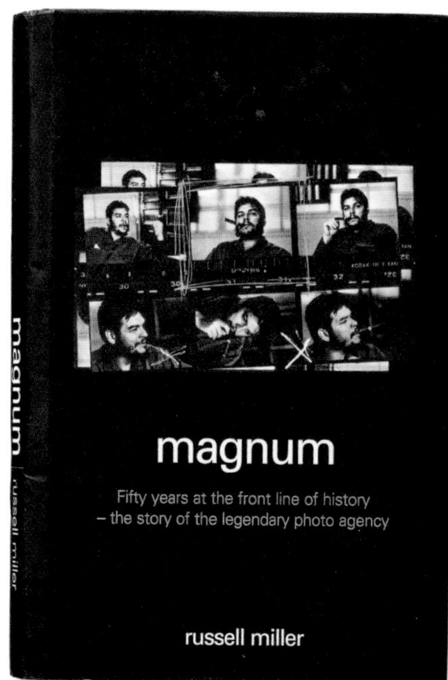

he had managed to carry off a successful revolution on the very doorstep of the USA, whose active support for the counterrevolution culminated in the debacle of the Bay of Pigs landing in 1961. The American failure served only to enhance the glory of Castro and the Argentina-born Ernesto Guevara, a medical doctor who had taken his leave of middle-class life in order to establish his model of a classless communist society not only in South America, but throughout the world. Whether in the role of a revolutionary or national bank president (which he became immediately after the revolution), or as Minister of Industry – his assignment since February 1962 – Che was at the peak of his power during these months.

A *Yanqui* journalist on the Communist island

Laura Bergquist had also been present as one of the reporters in New York in 1962. Blond and good-looking, a skilled and critical interviewer, she seems to have made a particular impression on Che with her unusually direct, not to say aggressive, questions. In any case, she subsequently received an invitation to inspect the successes of the Cuban revolution herself. Note well: it is only a few months after the end of the so-called Cuban Crisis, which had carried the world to the brink of nuclear war – a fact which makes the twenty-eight-day research visit of a *yanqui* journalist to the island all the more remarkable. *Look* intends to publish the results of this visit – which is, moreover, a visit without restriction, as Bergquist has insisted. With a circulation of 7.3 million, *Look*, together with *Life*, was at the time the most important illustrated journal. Accompanying Bergquist as photographer on the tour is the young photojournalist René Burri, whose Swiss citizenship has the advantage of raising him above ideological suspicion.

Burri, who was born in 1933, had studied under the legendary Hans Finsler at the Zurich School of Commercial Art, and was the author of a highly respected photographic volume entitled *Die Deutschen* (The Germans), which he also compiled in 1962. He had begun his photographic career in the late 1950s with a report on deaf children – a sensitive work in the tradition of humane photojournalism that soon led to publication in *Life* and inclusion in the

---

Above: *Russell Miller,* Magnum: Fifty Years at the Front Line of History. *Published in 1997 by Secker & Warburg, Miller's book represents the first critical study of the legendary agency.*

Right: **René Burri:** Che, *1963. Rarely published variant of his iconic image.*

famous photographic group Magnum. Later Burri not only served as reporter in practically all the world's crisis spots, but also supplied photographs to illustrate essays and current news reports, took portraits of artist friends, and shot individual pieces whose formal austerity are reminiscent of Finsler's school. A reviewer once termed him a "complete photographer." Although his square portrait of Che Guevara is only one of many thousand pictures in his archive, it is his most famous work.

Burri had landed in Cuba on the day before. Even en route from the airport to the hotel, he had turned his camera on tanks returning from a parade. From this moment on, Cuba became a lifelong subject for him. But the high point of the visit nonetheless was the personal meeting with Ernesto Che Guevara – who in fact hardly paid attention to the photographer at his work. Che made, in fact, a nervous, driven impression on the photographer. Later Burri would compare him to a caged animal, a metaphor which supports the closed Venetian blind. Che saw his place as being in the armed struggle, not behind a desk, and it would not be much longer before a speech critical of the Soviet Union would marginalize him politically at home and make him decide to leave Cuba. His last public appearance would be in the middle of March 1963. At this point, Che went underground, turning up in Bolivia in 1966 under an assumed name. Barely one year later, in October 1967, Ernesto Guevara was tracked down in the jungle by the Bolivian military, captured, and executed. But the photographs of the dead revolutionary caught the public's eye for only a relatively short period of time. The student revolt of 1968 brought other pictures to the fore, namely the portraits by René Burri and Alberto Korda, both of which became ubiquitous icons of the protest movement. Commandante Che, returning as myth, had thus made himself immortal.

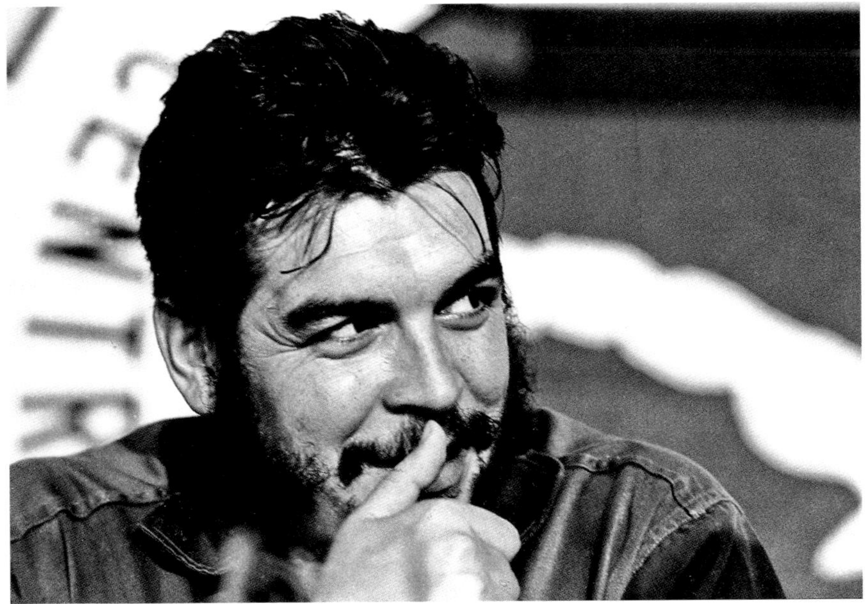

Gerard Malanga
Andy Warhol and The Velvet Underground 1966

Group Portrait with Nico

May 1966: Andy Warhol is making a guest appearance in Los Angeles together with the pop group The Velvet Underground and Nico. This is hardly his first visit to the city, but it marks his premier as a band 'member'. Also present on the occasion is Gerard Malanga, who can hardly have imagined that his rather relaxed group portrait will go down in the history of photography as proof of Andy Warhol's short but passionate excursion into rock music.

The arrangement of the group expresses a historical reality, as it were: it reflects the actual dynamics of the band, even if the photographer, Gerard Malanga, has always stressed that nothing was set up or staged. "This picture almost didn't happen," says Malanga, by which he means that he stumbled into it almost by accident. That is, it was nothing more than a mere snapshot, a quick press of the button without any attempt at making 'art'. But this very artlessness is probably what lends the photograph its intrinsic charm. From left to right: Nico, Andy Warhol, and The Velvets in a relaxed atmosphere – cool and at ease because, after all, they are just posing for their friend with a Nikon given to him by his dad, not for eternity. All that Gerard Malanga wants is a small photograph, for as a poet, performance artist, and co-worker in Andy Warhol's Factory, Malanga has not yet felt the call to become a photographer, and he picks up a camera only on rare occasions. But even so, he is nonetheless conforming to one of Henri Cartier-Bresson's famous dicta: "You can't photograph a memory." In other words: when should you photograph something, if not now?

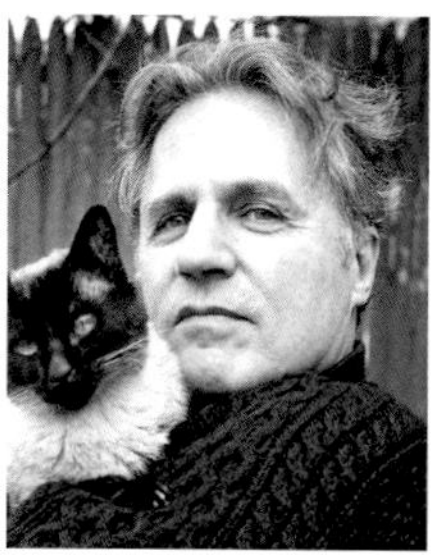

Gerard Malanga

Born ***1943*** *in New York. Collaborates closely with Andy Warhol in the* ***1960****s. Designated by the* New York Times *"Warhol's most important associate."* ***1964–66*** *collaboration on over 500 different 3-minute* Screen Tests. ***1967*** *publishes book of the same name. Publishes his own photographic works in four monographs (to date), the last being* Resistance to Memory *(****1998****), and* Screen Tests, Portraits, Nudes 1964–1996 *(****2000****). In addition, a dozen literary works and two CDs.* ***1999*** *major retrospective in Brussels. Lives as photographer and Warhol expert in New York.*

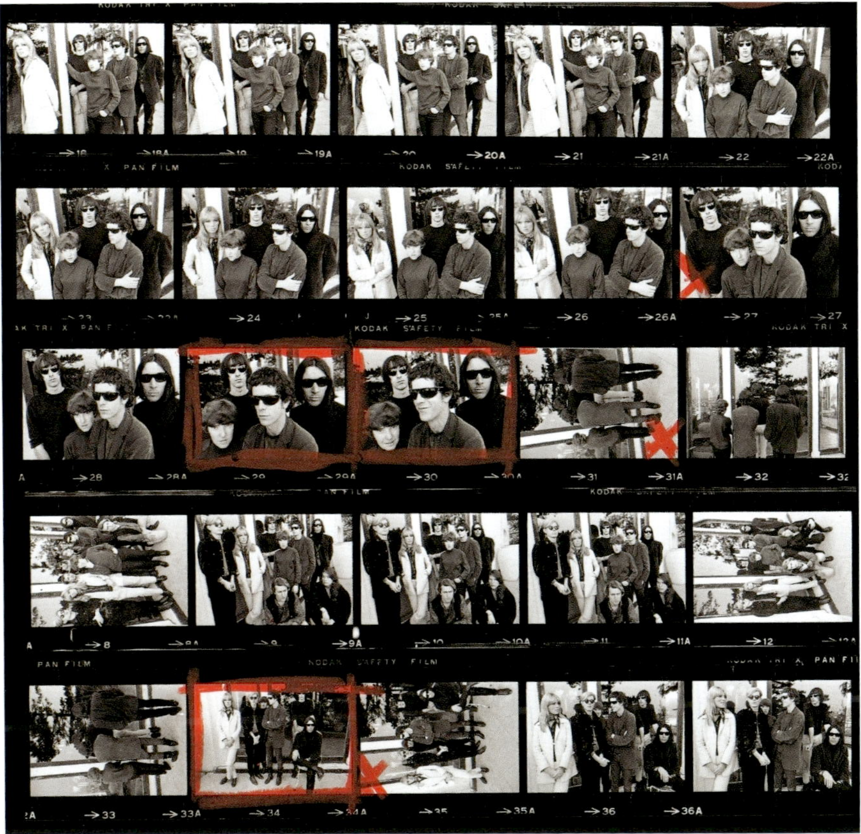

Career in the Land of Unlimited Opportunity

It's May 1966. They've all come together on the terrace of the 'Castle': Lou Reed, the only one refusing to look into the camera; behind him, almost hidden, the androgynous-looking Maureen Tucker; standing to the right of Lou is Sterling Morrison. John Cale is seated. It is obvious that he and Lou Reed form the great antipodes of the group. Without their even wishing it, the conflict between them is palpable in the photograph, which almost brilliantly reflects the deep rift within the band. To the far left and completely in white is the beautiful Nico, the lead singer of The Velvet Underground. She is a discovery of Andy Warhol's whom he has described as weird and silent. "You ask her something, and she answers you maybe five minutes later." Warhol has cast himself once again in the role of a little boy, a game that he greatly enjoyed, according to Malanga. Warhol's pose in the photograph might be described as awkward, even inhibited. But one shouldn't be fooled by appearances, for with Andy Warhol everything was calculated, including the mannered way he held his hands. Malanga says that it's a style that he picked up from Cocteau, and adds: "Andy was very aware of this."

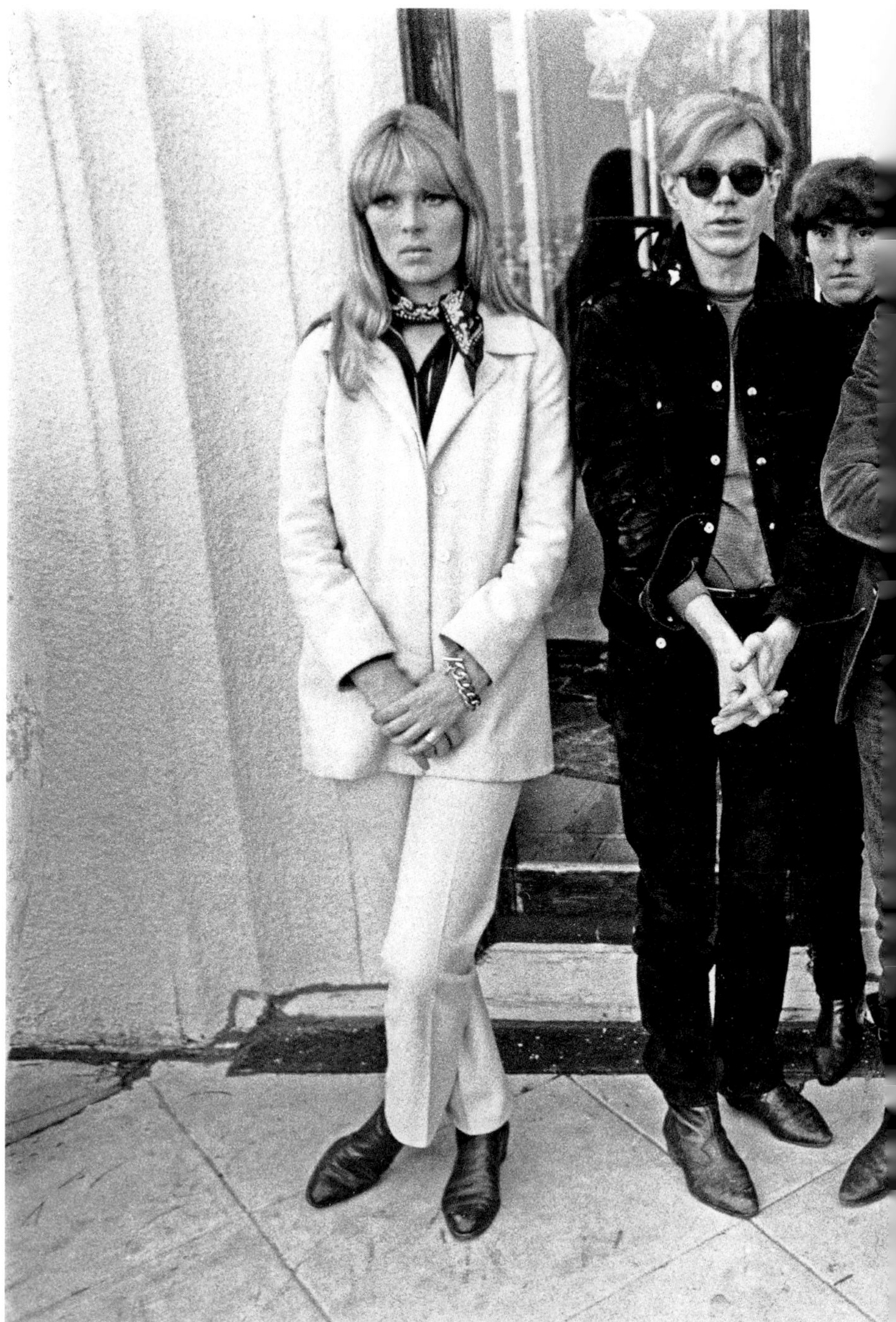

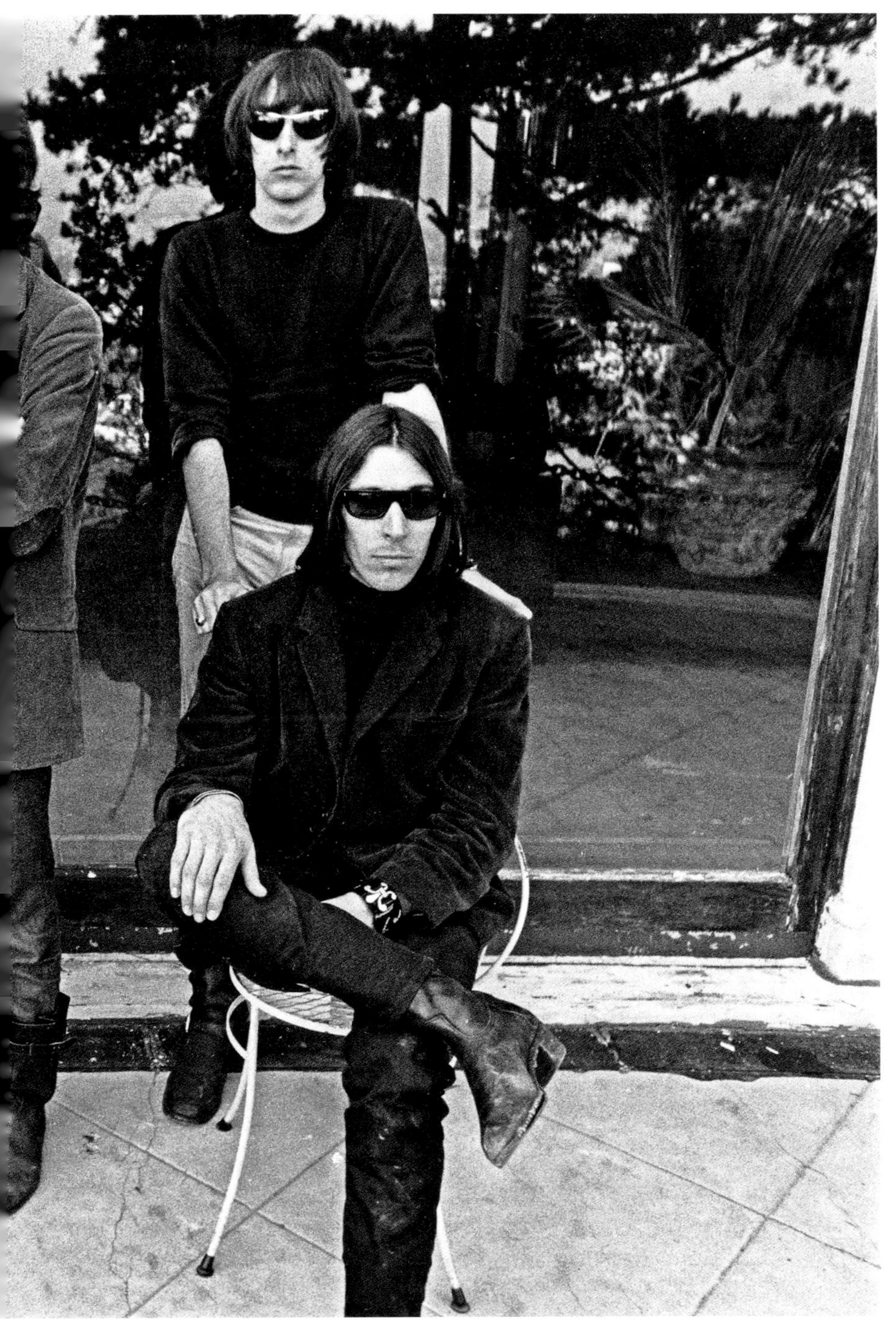

Andy was aware of everything. And as befits this consciousness, he began to work on his image early in his career, and the first step was a change of name. An appellation like 'Andrei Warhola' scarcely provides a ticket to success in the Land of Unlimited Opportunity, and the man who was described by John Lennon as the world's best publicity star was aware of this from the beginning. 'Warhola' pointed back to his Slavic roots, stamped him as a weird stranger, underlined his origins as a poor immigrant. And this was precisely what Andy wanted to get away from – the entire milieu, and in particular the city where he spent his childhood: Pittsburgh, a dirty, soot-filled Moloch, center of America's vast iron and steel industry, with all the charm of the notorious Ruhr Valley, or Manchester at the height of the Industrial Revolution. He wanted to escape from all that, to get out into the great land beyond, to share in the 'American Dream', to make his mark and become rich and famous – it really didn't matter how.

Typical symptoms of a poor-boy-made-good

When he finally 'arrived' – after he had gotten rich and became a star – Warhol manifested the typical symptoms of a poor-boy-made-good. During the week, he took on the role of provocateur, but on Sunday he crept back into church. Warhol donated alms to ensure himself a place in heaven, but was irresponsible in paying his employees and helpers. A consummate Scrooge who appreciated nothing more than the crinkle of a crisp new dollar bill. An artist who loved money so much that he even painted it. A petty bourgeois who slept on pillows filled with crumpled greenbacks. A pack rat who couldn't let anything go, who checked every bit of trash for fear that someone might comb through it and start selling the contents as souvenirs. A peacock who let himself be chauffeured around in a Rolls Royce, all the while complaining about his financial troubles. And yet at the same time, Andy Warhol was an extremely creative spirit who left almost no field of art untouched. He was a writer and poet, a film-maker and photographer, and the founder and publisher of the now-legendary magazine *Interview*.

Through his engagement with The Velvet Underground, he even fulfilled his dream of having his 'own' rock band. With some degree of success he also designed album covers: for The Velvets, of course, but also for the Rolling Stones' famous album *Sticky Fingers*. And, if one takes his constant self-staging into account, Andy Warhol was also an actor – or rather, a twenty-four-hour performance artist. And of course, above all he was a painter.

One has to admit, whatever he took up, he rubbed it against the grain. Every discipline to which he submitted himself (if the word 'submission' can be applied to Warhol's approach), he grasped with the naive intuition of a child – and ended up doing whatever he wanted with it, flaunting every rule of the game in the process. Thus, as a matter of principle, the book that he wrote had to be bad; that is, it was intentionally full of spelling errors and other problems. His numerous underground films transgressed not only the rules of narrative

---

Page 317: **Gerard Malanga:** Andy Warhol with The Velvet Underground & Nico, *The Castle, 1966 (contact sheet, detail).*

Gerard Malanga: Patti Smith on a Platform in the 68th Street/Lexington Ave. Subway Station, New York City, *1971.*

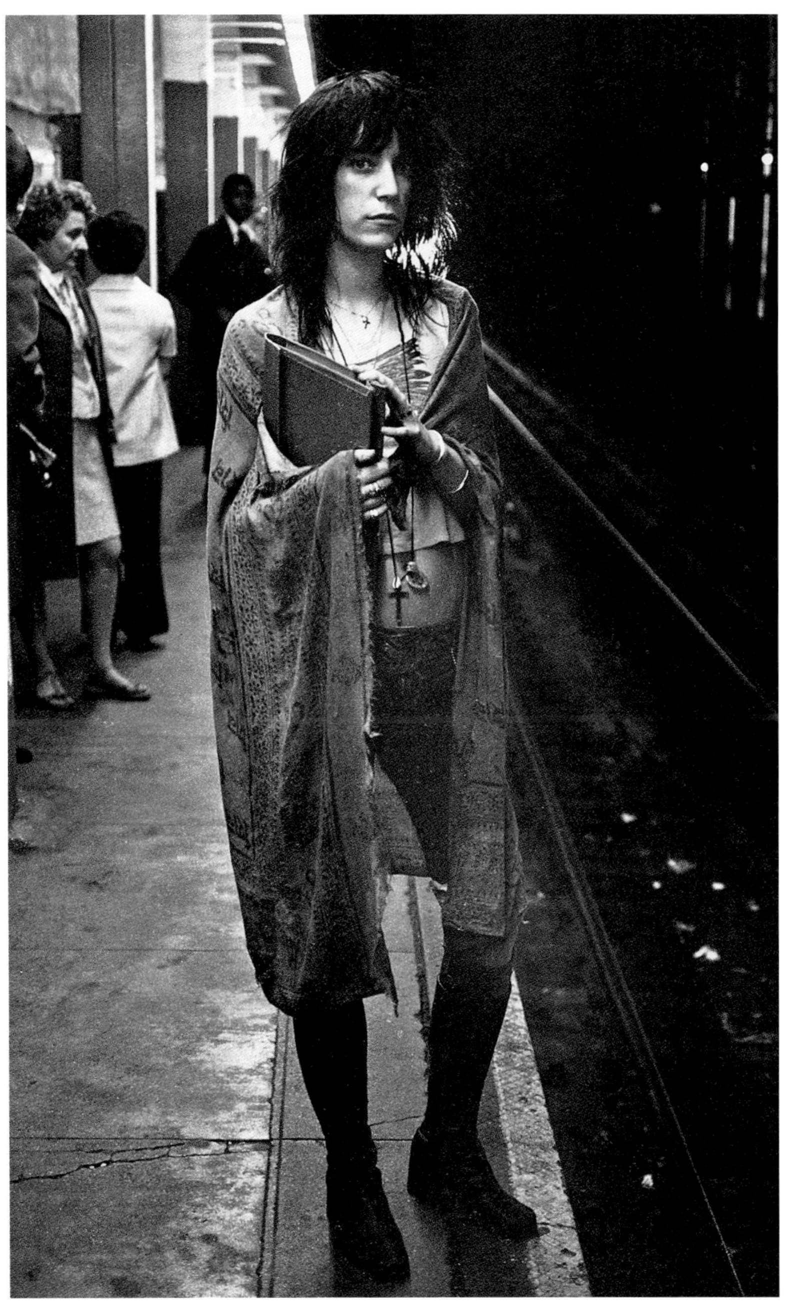

cinematography but also the sitting power of the average movie-goer. And naturally the rock group that he joined was something which, as Cher phrased it at the time, "will replace nothing – except maybe suicide" – a critique that The Velvets of course immediately conscripted into their own PR. Last but not least, Warhol was a painter; but also here, his 'painting' had nothing to do with the canvases created by the ingenious hand of the traditional artist.

Adoption of everyday, banal objects

Andy Warhol's first coup was the creation of a new canon of motifs. Truly revolutionary for the early 1960s, a period still stamped by the Abstract Expressionism of a Pollock or de Kooning, Warhol's adoption of everyday, banal objects, his interest in the trivial myths of America from Coca Cola to Campbell's Soup, was truly revolutionary. But Pop – that is, the artistic treatment of everyday objects – had had its practitioners before Warhol. His true significance for recent art history lies elsewhere: Warhol taught us to redefine the concept of the artist, artistry, and art itself. In this sense, he in no way saw himself as an ingenious artist-individualist, but rather as the boss of a fractious troupe. Significantly, Warhol did not maintain a studio, but a 'Factory'; and the Marilyns, Elvis Presleys, dollar bills that were produced there on the assembly line had more to do with photo-mechanic reproduction than with talented brush strokes. Lawrence Guiles describes Warhol's somewhat complicated process: first the artist searched through newspapers and magazines for a picture that intrigued him; he cut it out, and reproduced it to whatever size he wanted. Then he coated a silk screen with a light-sensitive layer and produced a stencil that enabled him to make innumerable copies of his image. As Guiles points out, photography lay at the root of the process.

Photography as a mode of artistic expression

But in May of 1966, neither Andy Warhol nor his 'student' and co-worker Gerard Malanga had yet discovered photography as a mode of artistic expression. As a child, the latter had used his Kodak box camera to shoot a photo of his beloved Third Avenue El – the New York elevated railway – before it was torn down, and later, in 1965, he had worked with Andy Warhol on his so-called 'screen tests', activities which in a sense served as an entrance into the medium. But not until 1969 did his portrait of the writer Charles Olson and the multiple prints that he immediately produced from it become the starting point for Malanga's intensive engagement with the art of photography. Meanwhile, Warhol for his part began increasingly to take Polaroids – probably as an outgrowth of his work for Jimmy Carter, Willy Brandt, and Golda Meir – and then to produce screened patterns from them. Warhol also carried his small-format Minox along with him, but, as the photographer Christopher Makos explains, a Minox requires focusing, which was not at all of interest to Warhol. As a result, Makos introduced the artist to the new auto-focus cameras.

Warhol acquired a modern Canon in addition to his small Minox camera. According to the historian David Bourdon, it was the Canon that enabled Warhol to take his notoriously indiscreet snapshots of, for example, Truman Capote visiting a plastic surgeon, or Liza Minelli stepping out of the shower. In all, there were several hundred of these candid photographs that Warhol did not hesitate to publish in his book *Exposures*. In other words, in the early 1970s Andy Warhol emerged a diligent photographer. His importance to the history of photography, however, does not lie so much in his prima facie assemblage of photographs in itself. As paradoxical as it may sound, his real significance as a photographer arises from his painting: insofar as Warhol won recognition in the field of art through his pictures created with mechanical means and produced (i.e. printed) in great numbers, he also broke the ice for a new photography based on mechanical production and 'endless' reproducibility.

And yet, as everyone knows, Andy Warhol had begun his career in the early 1950s as a commercial and advertising artist. The work that he produced during this period for Condé Nast (*Vogue*) and I. Miller (shoes) is among his best. But Warhol wanted to be more than a simple, anonymous 'hand', and he felt himself drawn toward art without, however, having any particular theme in mind, let alone a message. Even later he managed without 'messages', of course; and in fact many critics found his pictures fascinatingly empty – candy-colored nothings. On the other hand, Warhol's biographer Guiles argues that Warhol presented this 'nothing' in such a bold and striking manner that it was impossible to overlook. At the end of the 1950s, Warhol decided to turn to Pop, that is to the artistic translation of popular objects – such as comics. But here it was already too late, for comics were already the domain of Roy Lichtenstein. Depressed, Andy complained to his friend Muriel Latow that he didn't know where to begin, and asked for some inspiration. Latow's answer: he should choose a common object, something ordinary that one sees every day, but takes for granted – for example a can of soup. Andy Warhol's face lit up in a smile: the suggestion proved the turning point both of the evening and of the history of painting.

Thus, Andy Warhol took up painting Campbell's Soup: Noodle, Tomato, Chicken. And he became famous – but such fame was still a far cry from recognition as an artist. Until the end of his life, many considered him no more than a seasoned charlatan: a talented draftsman, certainly, but as an artist, a dud – and as a human being, the dregs. The New York Museum of Modern Art, for example, stubbornly refused to mount a retrospective of his works. Only after his death – and then without hesitation – did the Museum of Modern Art finally mount the show that the artist had so long wished, and afterwards it moved on to Chicago, London, Cologne, Paris, and Venice. In other words, the curve of Andy Warhol's career was anything but steep and continuous. His beginnings as an artist were in fact rather discouraging; for many years, his attempts to find a niche in respected galleries remained unsuccessful. "Andy, lay off," the *New York Times* advised at regular intervals; "you're not real art." Willem de Kooning, the exponent of an Abstract Expressionism that in many way constituted the antithesis to Warhol, spoke out even more clearly, screaming out his hatred of the Pop artist in public, and accusing him of killing beauty and joy.

Everybody's plastic, but I love plastic

Andy Warhol understood very well how to polarize anything he touched – including his comparatively brief excursion into rock music. He had set out searching for a band already in late 1965. Theater producer Michael Myerberg was in the process of opening a new club in an abandoned airplane hangar in Queens, and declared himself ready to christen the shed "Andy Warhol's Up," on the condition that the Pop artist would provide the music. Before Christmas, on a lead from Barbara Rubin, Warhol listened to a rock group called The Velvet Underground in the New York café *Bizarre*. Right from the start, Warhol got along brilliantly with Lou Reed, as Warhol's biographer Victor Bockris reports. And thus, several days later, negotiations began in the Factory. Bockris tells how the 'coked-up' Velvets felt almost magically drawn to Warhol, and that Lou Reed was hit the hardest, because, like Billy Linich and Gerard Malanga, he had simply been waiting to be formed by a master hand. Andy gave Lou ideas for songs, and hammered the importance of work into him. The appearances that Warhol organized and directed turned into multimedial events. In short, he professionalized the Velvs and made them famous. But as to the identity of the true star of the show, Bockris leaves no doubt. After all, almost no one had heard of The Velvet Underground or Nico, but Andy was already a celebrity. And there he sat, elevated high above the dance floor, operating the projectors and exchanging the light filters.

At the beginning of May, the group had a gig in Los Angeles, and 3–15 May, Warhol and The Velvets were scheduled to appear with Nico in the club *The Trip*. The group was staying in what was known as the Castle, a private house modeled along medieval lines, and probably conforming fairly well to Warhol's taste. "I love L.A.," he once announced, "I love Hollywood. They're beautiful. Everybody's plastic, but I love plastic. I want to be plastic." Our picture was taken on the terrace of the Castle. Gerard Malanga set the Nikon on a stand, which accounts for his own inclusion in several variants of the photograph. In the first versions of the picture, The Velvets are laughing, or at least smiling. Here, however, they are serious, almost ill-humored. After only a few weeks, *The Trip* had been closed down by order of the local sheriff. The local press expressed a less negative response to The Velvets, calling the arrival of Andy, the super-hippie, on Sunset Strip the greatest match since French fries discovered ketchup.

Enter Valerie Solanas, radical feminist

Thirty-seven years old in 1966, Andy Warhol was almost at the height of his international fame – which is not, however, to be mistaken for popularity. The manner in which he stylized himself – his gay affectations; his waxy, elfin-like being; his almost albino coloring, accented by pimples and nylon wig; his feeble charm combined with an eloquence that hardly rose above "Uhmm," "Crazy!" and "Super!" – these were not the sort of things to turn him into a national favorite. On the contrary, he had enemies, including some who were not content to leave the matter at verbal attacks. On 1 June 1968, for example, exactly two years after our picture was taken, Valerie Solanas, a radical feminist, turned up at Warhol's New York Factory and in a state of fury laid the artist low with several bullets. Warhol, although given up by the doctors, nonetheless survived. Robert Kennedy, also the victim of an assassination attempt in the summer of 1968, died. "That's the way things are in this world," Warhol's artist colleague Frank Stella is reputed to have said.

There's no question: two bullets from the gun of a crazed feminist would have been precisely the fitting end for the publicity-seeking Warhol – at any rate more suitable than the simple gall bladder operation that Warhol in fact succumbed to at age fifty-nine in 1987. A few days after his unexpected death, his body was carried back to Pittsburgh, where he was buried. The city of his childhood had claimed him once again – and the local grave-digger reveled in what he termed his first famous burial.

Andy Warhol's chapter in history by no means ended with his death, however. The mountain of pictures, antiques, and knickknacks that the social climber – forever plagued by insecurity about the future – had collected in his various domiciles now awaited new owners: on 23 April 1988, Sotheby's in New York began a ten-day auction of Warhol's estate. The five volumes of the catalogue comprised 3,429 items, and more than 6,000 people wanted to

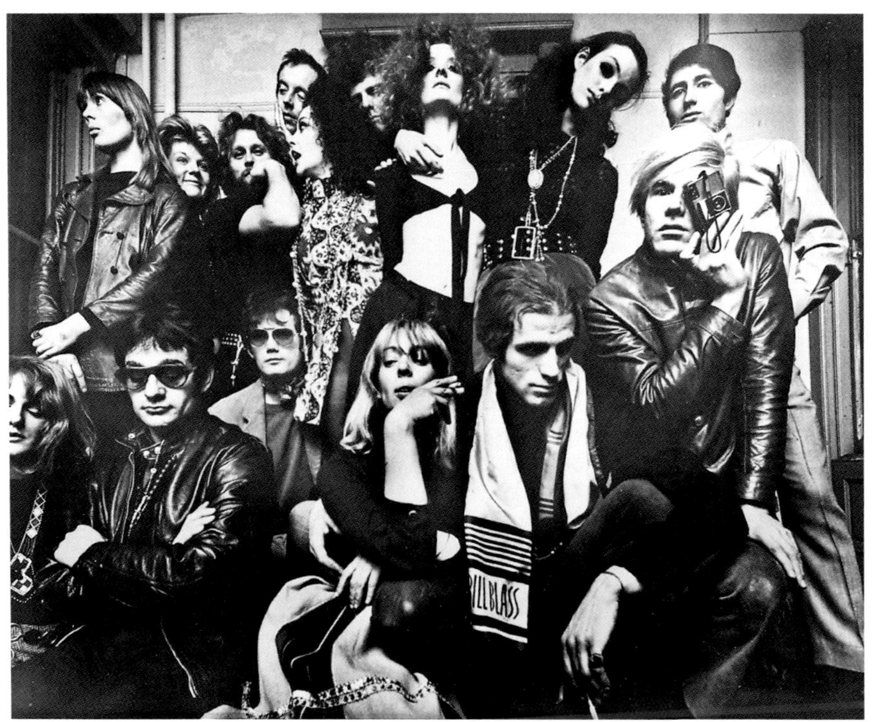

attend. These figures were harbingers of what was to come. As Victor Bockris reports, the auction house had underestimated the hammer price in almost every case. For example, at $77,000, Warhol's Rolls Royce brought in more than five times what had been reckoned; a ring estimated at $2,000 went for $28,000; and a Cy Twombly was taken up to a record price of $990,000. Last but not least, Andy Warhol's candy jars, with a market worth of perhaps $2,000, were sold for a total of $247,830. The entire estate, which Sotheby's had estimated at a value of $15 million brought in more than $25 million. And what would Warhol have said to all this? Fran Lebovitz, a friend and co-worker on *Interview*, is reported to have glanced heavenward and said: "Andy must be furious that he's dead."

Photo Archives Malanga:
Andy Warhol/"Factory" Group Photo, New York City, *1968.*
Top row, left to right: Nico, Brigid Polk, Louis Waldon, Taylor Mead, Ultra Violet, Paul Morrissey, Viva, International Velvet, unknown.
Below, left to right: Ingrid Superstar, Ondine, Tom Baker, Tiger Morse, Billy Name, Andy Warhol.

Nick Ut
Kim Phúc – Napalm Against Civilians
1972

The Face of War

The picture of Kim Phúc running down the road covered in burns certainly did not bring the Vietnam War to an end. But the image, rapidly broadcast by the world's media, strengthened doubts about a conflict that has gone down in the history of the 20th century not least as a huge media spectacle. But although the fighting was covered primarily by television, no corresponding TV images have lodged themselves enduringly in our minds. Yet again, it is classic reportage photos that have entered our global consciousness. The picture by Nick Ut is one of them.

Her name is Kim Phúc. In full, Phan Thi Kim Phúc. But it is as Kim Phúc that she has gone down in history. In Vietnamese, Phúc means "good luck." In view of her fate, this might sound bitterly ironic. But it can be interpreted in a different light. Kim Phúc was lucky because she came from an intact family. She was lucky, because she was well nourished, which in view of her injuries proved to be a vital factor in her survival. She was lucky because she came running towards a war reporter who – after he had taken her picture – administered first aid. She was lucky because she received basic medical care relatively quickly. And she was lucky because not every nine-year-old child is equipped with the strength to endure a martyrdom of pain, fourteen skin grafts, disfigurements, and the knowledge that the scars would mark her out for the rest of her life. Kim Phúc survived. She is now over 50 and lives in Canada. An energetic woman who is fully aware of her role in contemporary history. Perhaps it was she who ended the war in Vietnam, as has sometimes been claimed. Her photo nevertheless – and this much is sure – helped multiply doubts, above all in the US, about a war that was increasingly affecting the civilian population.

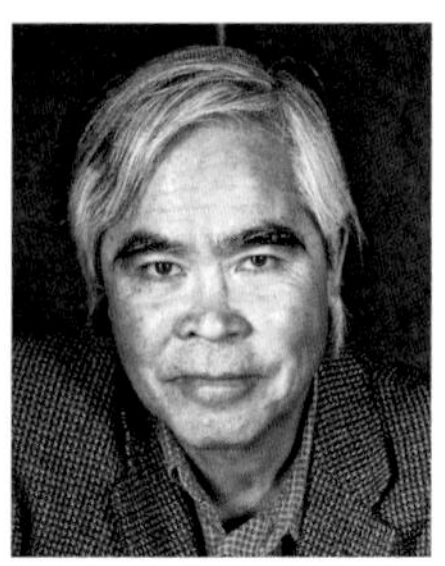

Nick Ut

Born Huynh Cong Út in ***1951*** *in Long An, Vietnam. Photojournalist in the Vietnam War. Works for the Associated Press (AP) agency.* ***1972*** *(8 June) photo of the nine-year-old Phan Thi Kim Phúc after a napalm attack. The image was released by Horst Faas, AP chief in Saigon. The motif is subsequently seen around the world.* ***1972*** *voted press photo of the year.* ***1973*** *Pulitzer Prize.* ***2012*** *Leica Hall of Fame Award. Lives in Los Angeles.*

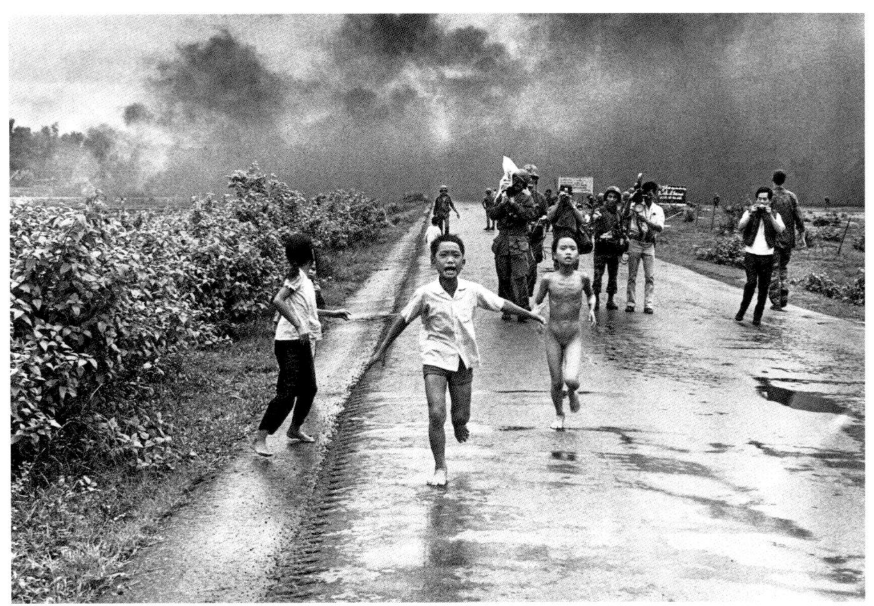

The longest war of the 20th century

A war that was making peasants into cripples, wives into widows, children into orphans, and inflicting lasting devastation on a country that already ranked among the poorest in the world. "I wonder," the then US President Richard Nixon is supposed to have said at the sight of the picture, "I wonder if that was a fix." It was a logical suspicion for a warring nation that thought it had everything under control. And especially the propaganda accompanying and legitimizing events. There is a myth according to which the Vietnam conflict was the first war in which reporters were allowed full freedom of movement. This is only partly true. Reporting even in Vietnam was already largely 'embedded'. It started with accreditation and finished with censorship. In between, the reporters followed in the tracks of the military, used their means of transport, and acted on their tips. It was not their closeness to the action that was new. It was their conscious emotionalizing of this closeness, encouraged by an illustrated press that offered a brand new form of coverage combining humanitarian appeal, documentary objectivity, and sensationalism. In this area, the politicians had indeed somewhat lost control of the helm. And if America has learned one lesson from Vietnam, it is that it needs to pay closer attention to the pictures being taken in tandem with its operations.

Hoang Van Danh:
Vietnamese children fleeing near Trang Bang.
Nick Ut's colleague has captured the scene at a slightly later moment and from a different angle. A pack of reporters in the background lends the scene something oddly voyeuristic.

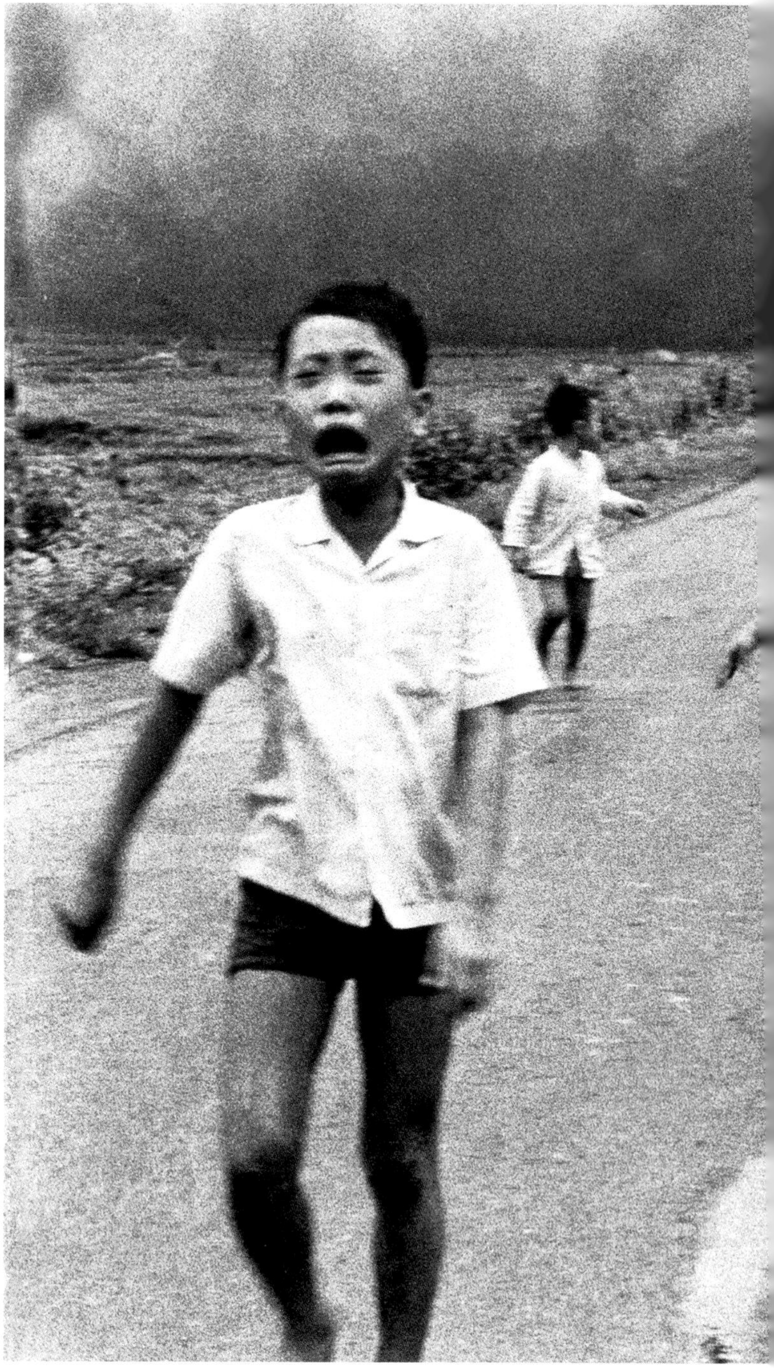

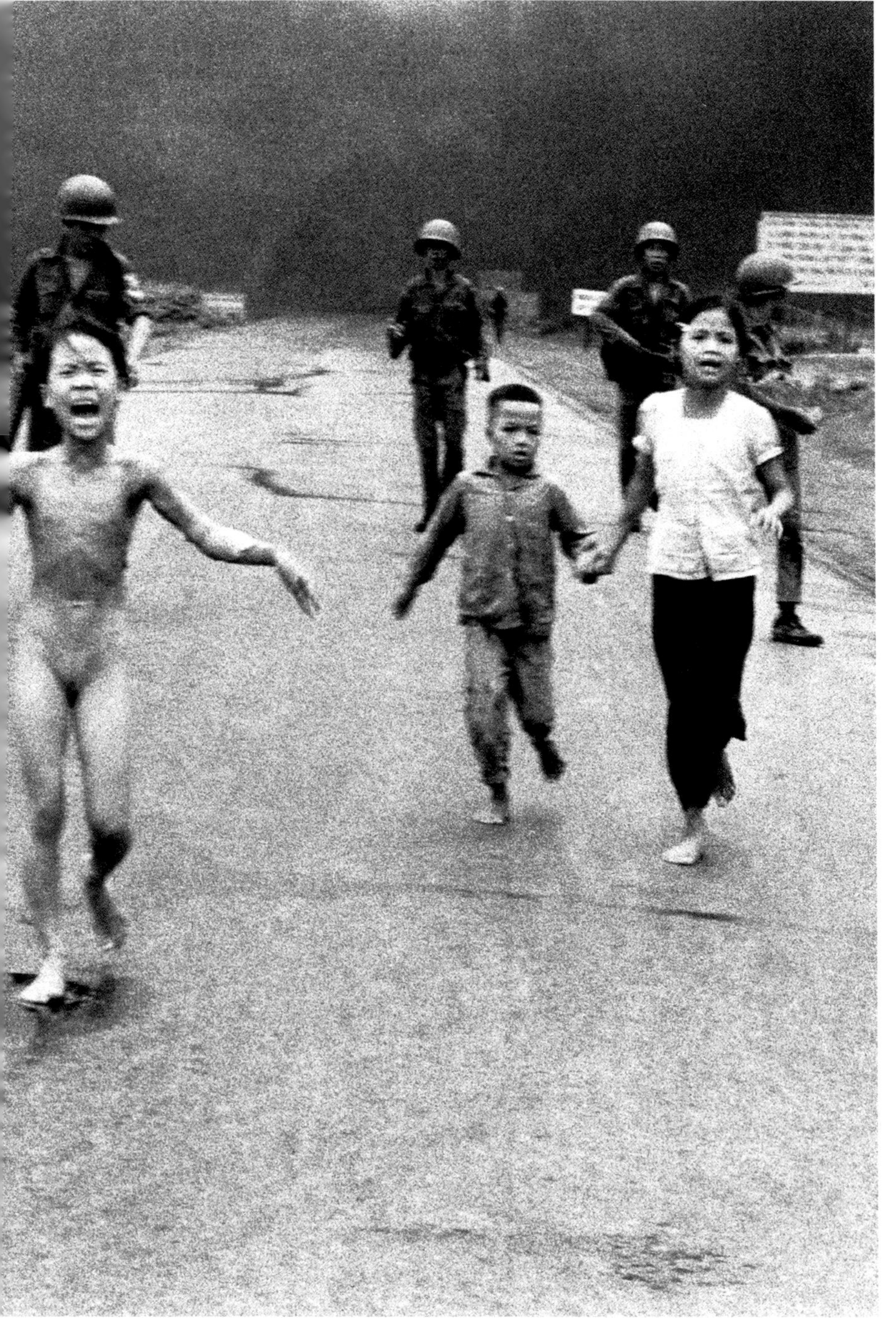

Photographing war

Vietnam is first and foremost a country. A culture. But when we think of Vietnam, our first thought is of war. That's no coincidence. The Vietnam War was the longest war of the 20th century. If we take the engagement of the French as the beginning and the capture of Hanoi by North Vietnamese troops on 1 May 1975 as the end, it lasted a good thirty years.

With Vietnam, the positive American myth that sprang up in Europe, and in particular Germany, after the Second World War, suffered lasting damage. Vietnam became the feeding ground for a global wave of youth protest and provoked in the US a 'Vietnam syndrome' that continues to influence American foreign policy right up to today. In our minds, Vietnam has mutated into a negative myth, one that conjures up little in the way of concrete facts or historical insights but instead invokes a series set of nightmarish images that have branded themselves upon the global consciousness. Eddie Adam's photo of the Southern Vietnamese head of police Nguyen Ngoc Loan shooting a suspected Vietcong collaborator in the middle of the street is one of them.

And of course Nick Ut's picture of Kim Phúc fleeing amongst a group of children after a napalm attack: crying, naked, injured. The picture traveled around the world and across an illustrated press that played a truly important part in communicating photographic images for the last time, before the role of supplying the very latest 'infotainment' was definitively taken over by television. How do you photograph war? When the young Vietnamese photographer Nick Ut documented a Buddhist monk setting himself on fire in the mid-1960s, the response of his teacher and mentor, the well-known *Stern* reporter Horst Faas, was critical: the pictures were too distasteful. The newspapers would not carry anything like that. "It would be better," according to Faas, "to have a photo of someone covering up the dead man, with onlookers weeping in the background."

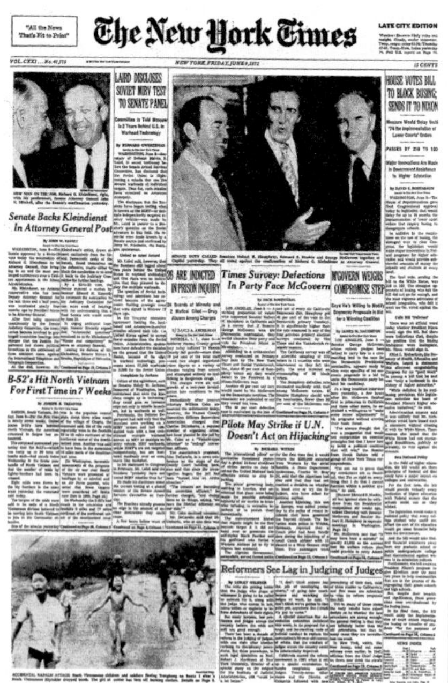

"All the News That's Fit to Print"

The New York Times

LATE CITY EDITION

NEW YORK, FRIDAY, JUNE 9, 1972

15 CENTS

LAIRD DISCLOSES SOVIET MIRV TEST TO SENATE PANEL

Senate Backs Kleindienst In Attorney General Post

HOUSE VOTES BILL TO BLOCK BUSING; SENDS IT TO NIXON

26 ARE INDICTED IN PRISON INQUIRY

Times Survey: Defections In Party Face McGovern

McGOVERN WEIGHS COMPROMISE STEP

B-52's Hit North Vietnam For First Time in 7 Weeks

Pilots May Strike if U.N. Doesn't Act on Hijacking

Reformers See Lag in Judging of Judges

Giving the war a name

Nick Ut had learned his lesson. On 8 June 1972, 65 kilometers (40 miles) north of Saigon, he was in the right place at the right time to capture, from the right angle, a scene that satisfies all the unwritten conditions of a good war photo. The composition, whose original title is *The Terror of War,* conveys drama without being too complex. Even if we are ignorant of the exact circumstances of the event, the picture's message remains clearly legible: the war in Vietnam is also – and above all – affecting children, in other words the most innocent members of human society. And lastly, the picture visualizes terror, shock, and pain without thereby becoming 'distasteful'. What the picture does not tell: an attack has just taken place outside the village of Trang Bang. Was it the Americans, as is soften said, or was it the South Vietnamese themselves who flew this attack?

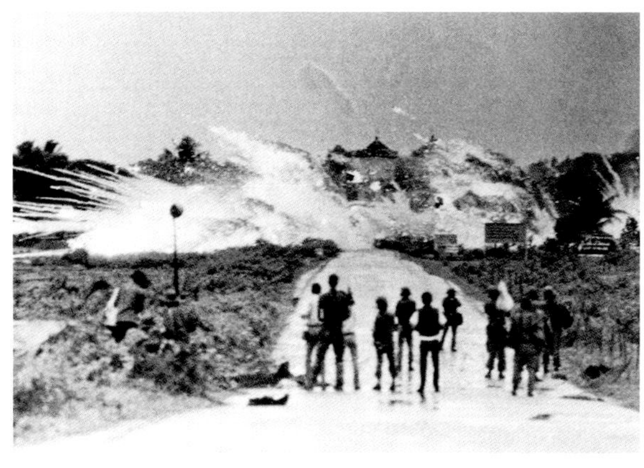

It is now known that it was skyriders from South Vietnam who dropped four napalm containers not over enemy locations but directly over the village. The photograph of an unknown 'stringer' captured the moment. Several reporters were near Trang Bang at the time: David Burnett was one of them, as was Fox Butterfield, the head of the *New York Times* offices in Saigon. Then there were Hoang Van Danh, Christopher Wain, Arthur Lord from NBC, Le Phuc Dinh, Alexander D. Shimkin and Don Kirk. Everything happened very quickly. Ut had a mere 15 seconds to capture the crucial scene with two images (negatives 7a and 8a) with his Leica. A group of children is running towards the photographers. The girl in the middle of the picture has already ripped the burning clothes off her body. Barefoot and completely naked, she is running towards the camera. What we can't see is that her entire back is covered in burns. The culprit is napalm. A weapon that remains as indelibly associated with Vietnam as mustard gas with the First World War and nuclear weapons with the Second. Dropped in firebombs, the incendiary material sprays itself over the surrounding area. If it hits the body, it glues itself to the skin, burning at a temperature of up to 1,200 °C and eating its way into the flesh. A third of its victims are dead after thirty minutes. The girl was lucky. The napalm hit her in the back, not in the face. And the nine-year-old was met by Nick Ut, who took her to the nearest hospital directly after the photo.

Nick Ut's photo gave the Vietnam War a face. And a name. Such details reinforce the credibility of an image and make it of interest to a press eager to personalize political messages. That same day the photograph was wired to New York. Evening newspapers such as the *Toronto Star* were the first to publish the cropped picture (the photographer Hoang Van Danh is missing on the right-hand side of the image), followed by the *New York Times,* the *NY Daily News, the Indianapolis Star* and the *Los Angeles Times.* After that "the photo that shocked the world," as it was later called, was rapidly seen around the globe.

Just three years later, America's military involvement in Vietnam was over. In one and a half decades, 1.7 million people had died; 5 million were seriously injured or scarred for life. Amongst the victims, Kim Phúc remains the one whose name is known to the world.

Left: *World events on the front page of the* New York Times, *9 June 1972, with Nick Ut's photo at the bottom of the page.*

Above: *The Associated Press picture shows the moment of the attack: napalm as fireworks.*

Barbara Klemm

Leonid Brezhnev, Willy Brandt, Bonn 1973

A Visit to the Rhine

In May 1973, Leonid Brezhnev, Chairman of the Soviet Communist Party, visited Bonn, Germany. This first appearance of a Kremlin leader in West Germany since the end of the war had been preceded by a controversial visit of German Chancellor Willy Brandt to the Soviet Union. Now, after so many years of Cold War, the road finally seemed to be cleared for good neighborly relations, in the words of the Soviet journalist Valentin Falin.

The small group of three has retired into a room in the Bonn Chancellery. The date is Saturday, 19 May 1973. Actually, a standing reception had been scheduled to take place before lunch, but owing to circumstances the men had now settled down into the dark-upholstered suite of chairs. The figures are easy to identify: from left to right are the Soviet Communist Party Chairman Leonid Brezhnev, German Chancellor Willy Brandt, and the German Foreign Minister Walter Scheel. Undoubtedly, there were other people also present in the room, but the camera concentrated on the protagonists of a meeting that appears to have entered the critical phase at just this moment. The atmosphere seems tense in the photograph, even though none of the participants are indicating any agitation or excitement by means of wild gestures. Quite the contrary, in fact: Brezhnev appears to be thinking something over; Willy Brandt, whose suit jacket has slipped up somewhat, looks at him questioningly; and Scheel, Foreign Minister and chairman of the liberal Free Democratic Party, seems at this moment more or less relegated to the role of an onlooker. Looking at this picture, one might be inclined to say that there is a sense of excitement emanating from the group of five translators and advisers who are whispering together as they stand or bend over the protagonists.

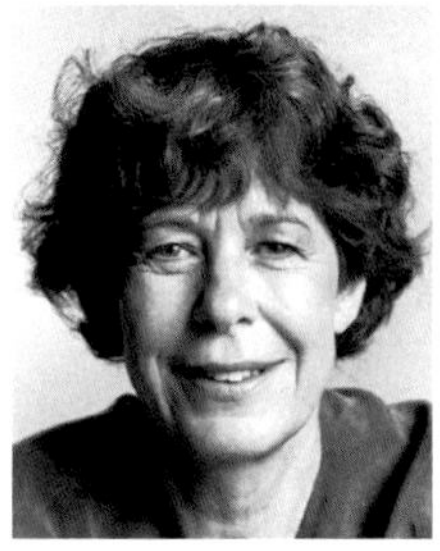

Barbara Klemm
*Born **1939** in Münster, Germany. Trains in a studio for portrait photography. From **1959** works for the* Frankfurter Allgemeine Zeitung *(*FAZ*). Since **1970** editorial photographer for the* FAZ. *Elected member of the DGPh German photography society. Member of the Academy of Arts Berlin-Brandenburg since **1992**. **1989** Dr. Erich Salomon Prize of the DGPh German photography society. **1989** Hugo Erfurth Prize. **1998** Maria Sibylla Merian Prize. **2000** Hessian Culture Prize. **2010** nominated a member of the Order Pour le mérite for Arts and Sciences. **2012** Leica Hall of Fame Award. Lives in Frankfurt am Main.*

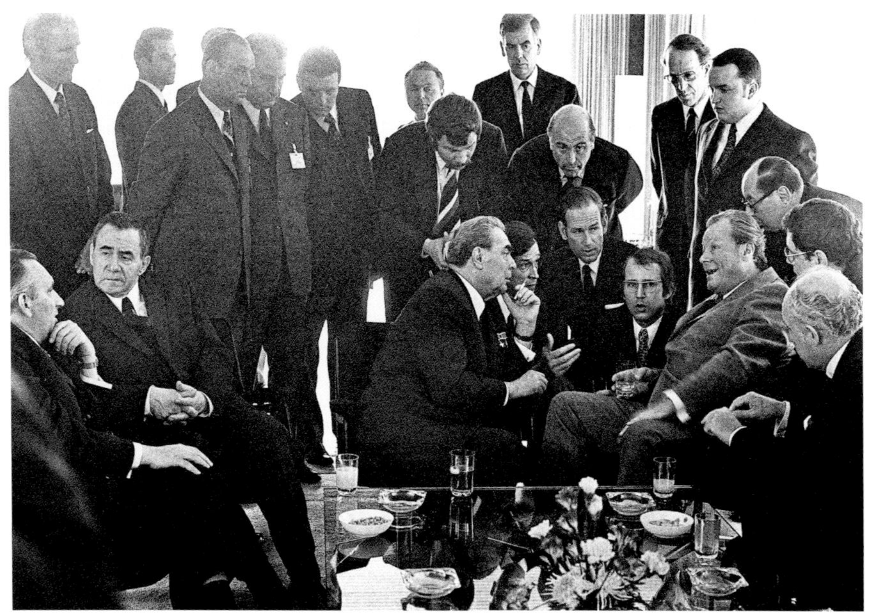

Guests from the fields of politics, economics, and culture

The press had been regularly reporting on what the group was eating and drinking; in the picture, we see only water and what appears to be orange juice; to the right, someone finds a moment to munch on some nibbles. But the leaders had been able to pamper their palates the previous evening at a banquet in Brezhnev's honor in the Palace Schaumburg, to which the chancellor had invited more than sixty guests from the fields of politics, economics, and culture. Helmut Kohl, then the Christian Democratic union (CDU) opposition leader in parliament, had turned down the invitation, however; officially the reason was his displeasure that Rainer Barzel, CDU party chairman, and Gerhard Stoltenberg, chairman of Foreign Relations Committee in the Bundesrat, had not also been invited. In general, however, the German press had treated such internal political concerns as side issues.

The newspaper headlines devoted themselves to what they felt was a historic visit, even if it was not at all clear what the political results might be. The arrival of the General Secretary of the Communist Party of the Soviet Union in Bonn on 18 May marked the first official state visit of a Soviet party chief since the Second World War. In terms of internal Soviet politics, Brezhnev had laid the groundwork for his journey carefully. The Germans in turn had had to be particularly careful, lest a relaxed German-Soviet dialogue cause ripples among the Western Allies. In addition, there were doubts from diplomatic quarters as to whether Brezhnev – who was the

---

Barbara Klemm: Brezhnev and Brandt in Bonn, *1973. One of the lesser-known variants of the shot, with Egon Bahr and Andrei Gromyko left of the picture.*

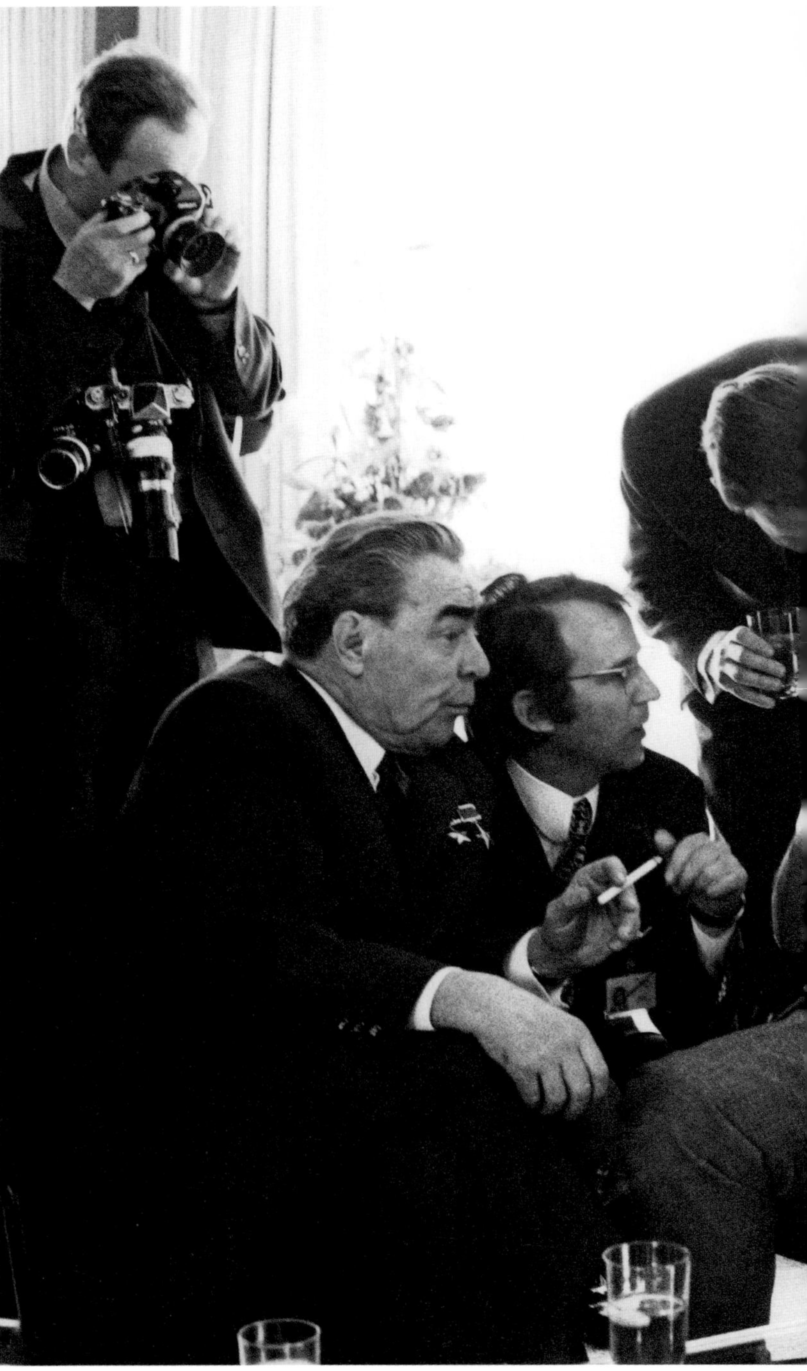

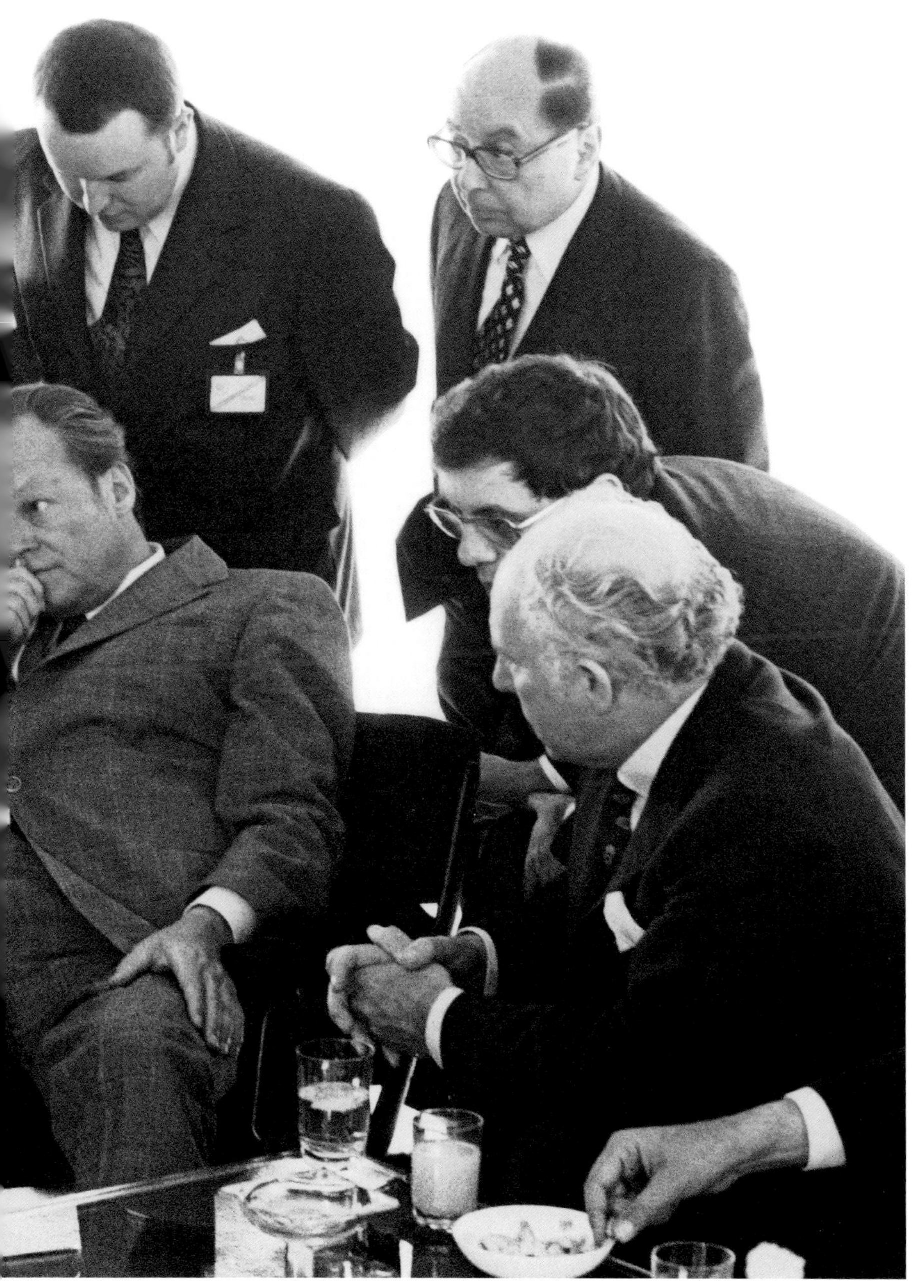

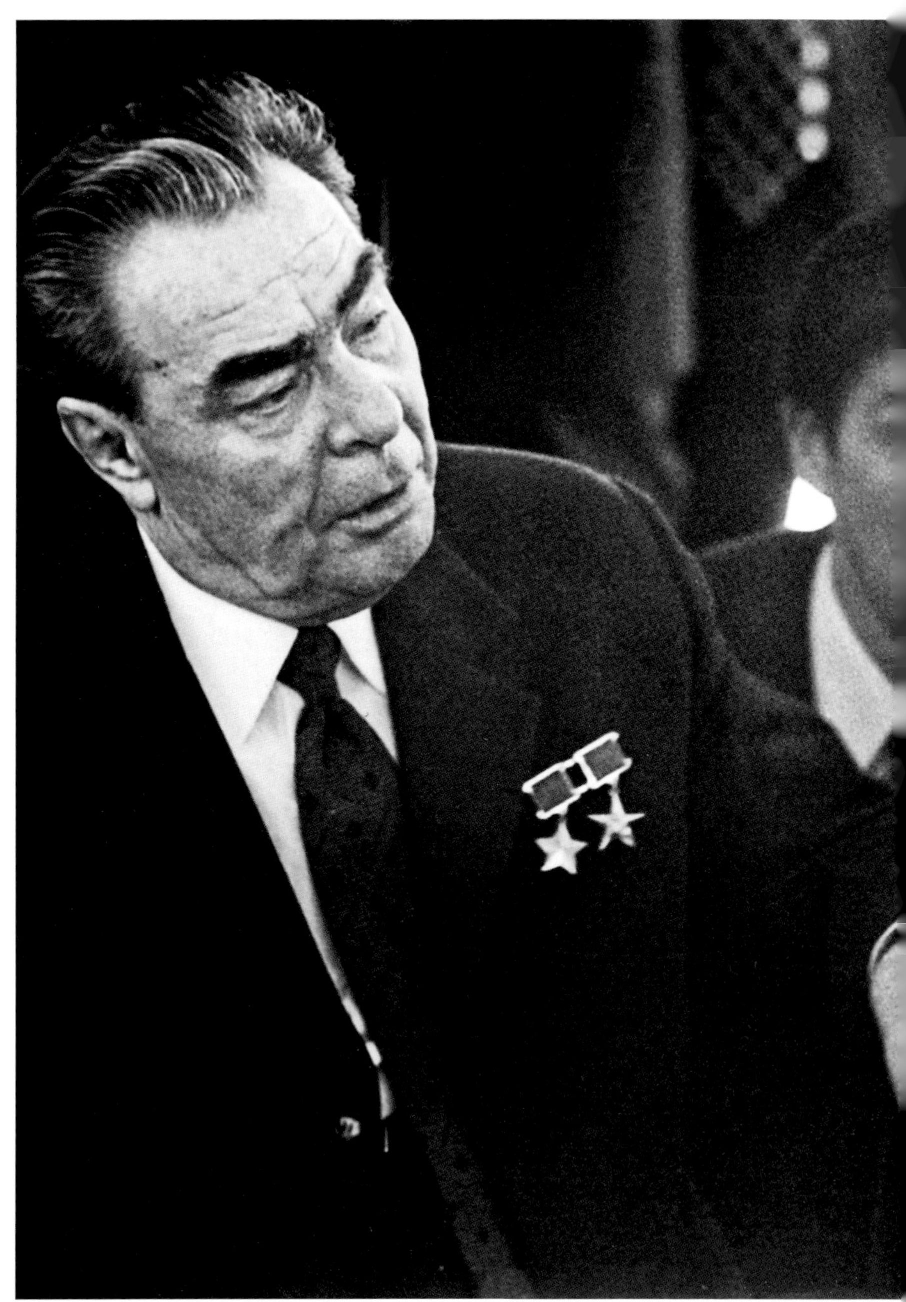

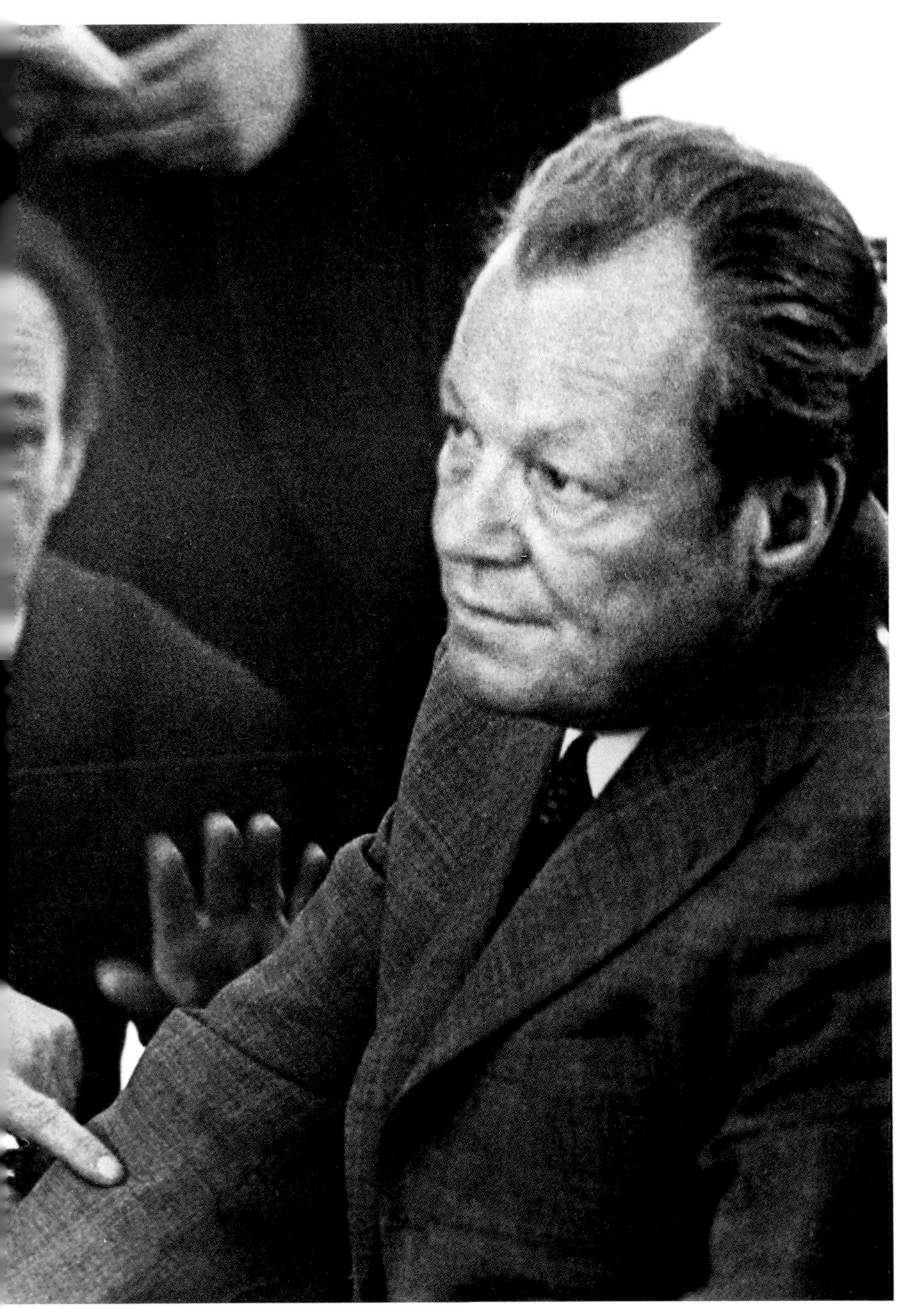

Leonid Brezhnev, Willy Brandt, Bonn, 1973

head of the Communist Party, but not of the Soviet state – was the right political partner for discussion. But here, too, pragmatism ruled the day. The conservative *Frankfurter Allgemeine Zeitung* (*FAZ*) for example, granted in its end-of-the-week edition of 18 May that in meeting with Brezhnev, Brandt was in fact conferring with the top Soviet official. According to the paper, Brezhnev had in fact as much competence as the West might wish for – "and not only because he had unobtrusively begun to co-sign international treaties for the Soviet Union."

On the whole, the signs looked favorable. The headline of the Moscow newspaper *Novge Vrenia* announced that the barometer forecast good weather, and expressed the hope for a lasting peace between the peoples of the West and the East. Fifty-one percent of the Germans rated the visit as "good and useful" – a judgment which might well have been called forth by Brezhnev himself, who behaved in a markedly jovial manner, and seemed much more open and 'Western' than any of his predecessors, ranging from Beria to Khrushchev. Even the Party's chief's "well-fitting gray suit" won praise from the press, which described Brezhnev as being a head shorter than the German chancellor, and went on to comment that in spite of the Russian's broad face, he was in fact thinner than Willy Brandt – who was in turn described as having acquired a "rather portly figure" since he had given up smoking.

Aware of the special significance of the visit

All the participants were undoubtedly aware of the particular significance of the visit. According to the *Frankfurter Allgemeine Zeitung*, "the most powerful man in the Eastern World is now on the soil of the Federal Republic of Germany." The security measures were correspondingly high: there were reputed to be approximately twenty-thousand security police, both in uniform and plain clothes, protecting the Soviet party chief so closely "that even the vast majority of the journalists were hardly able to see the whites of his eyes."

For the occasion, nine hundred journalists had gathered in Bonn. Among them was Barbara Klemm, born 1939 as the daughter of the well-known painter Fritz Klemm. Since 1970, she had been the editorial photographer for the *FAZ*, and Brezhnev's visit was her first assignment in the West German capital. She and three colleagues were the only photographers to gain admission to the room with Brezhnev, Brandt, and Scheel; film and TV cameras were

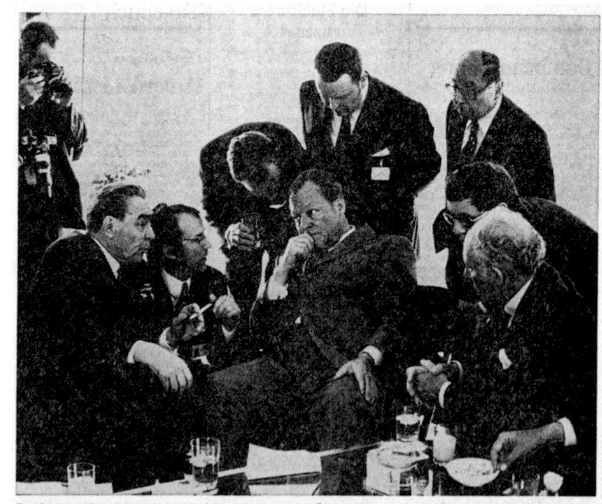

Breschnew und Brandt bei den deutsch-sowjetischen Verhandlungen 1973 im Bundeskanzleramt. Man meint das Bild schon einmal gesehen zu haben, wie es als aktuelles Pressefoto die Berichte von der Begegnung illustrierte. Wenn man es heute aus einer historischen Distanz betrachtet, fällt seine Intimität auf: Die Politiker scheinen hier die Rituale der Öffentlichkeit, das Lächeln und die großen Worte überwunden zu haben. Sie sind zu einer Gruppe zusammengerückt und versuchen, aus dem Mienenspiel und der übersetzten Rede die Absichten des Gegenübers herauszulesen. Durch die unpathetische Genauigkeit, mit der das Bild die Situation fixiert, bewahrt es auch seine Glaubwürdigkeit über den Tag hinaus: der Schnappschuß verwandelt sich in ein vielsagendes Dokument. Diese Aufnahme unserer Fotografin Barbara Klemm wird bis zum 12. Mai mit etwa neunzig anderen Bildern, die sie für diese Zeitung anfertigte, vom Hamburger Museum für Kunst und Gewerbe ausgestellt. P.

forbidden. In total, Klemm shot three or four rolls of film, and in the process caught the attention of the Communist Party leader. Brezhnev expressed surprise, so the story goes, that in Germany a woman was able to pursue "the difficult profession of a news photographer."

At the moment of the shot, however, Brandt and Brezhnev are deep in conversation. Their initial optimism appears to have given way to a skeptical reserve. At any rate, there is no trace of the hearty laughter with which Brezhnev had rung in his visit of state. What is remarkable is that the *FAZ* did not publish the key picture until several years later, namely in 1976 in connection with a report on an exhibition of Barbara Klemm's work in Hamburg. The rotogravure weekend supplement for 26–27 May 1973 gave preference instead to a total of four rather less impressive photographs.

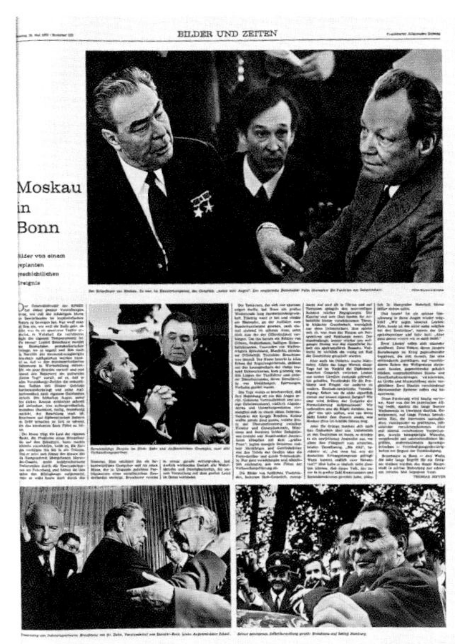

BILDER UND ZEITEN

Moskau in Bonn

ilder von einem eplanten eschichtlichen reignis

The beginning of day-to-day German-Soviet cooperation

The discussions between Brezhnev and Brandt – between Russians and Germans – turned out in fact to be more difficult than originally expected. Two years after the initial meeting in Crimea, which had been termed a milestone on the road to normalization, and one year after the signing of the Moscow Treaty, the constructive dialogue ground to a halt once again over the status of Berlin. The leaders by no means reached a consensus on the issue; on the contrary, negotiations were tough: ten hours on Sunday alone in order to turn the visit into a political success. The tense atmosphere so palpable in Barbara Klemm's picture, however, arises from a much more mundane cause. According to reports, the Communist Party Secretary had begun to suffer from a toothache; thus a change of schedule needed to be discussed. For this reason, a press photograph came to mirror a meeting whose political results were thin, but whose long-range significance can hardly be overestimated in terms of subsequent history – in the words of the *Frankfurter Allgemeine Zeitung*, neither more nor less than an age of "day-to-day German-Soviet cooperation" had begun.

Left: Frankfurter Allgemeine Zeitung, *9 April 1976: the first publication of the motif today considered a photo icon.*

Pages 336–337: **Barbara Klemm:** Brezhnev, Falin, and Brandt, *1973. The supplement of the* Frankfurter Allgemeine Zeitung *on 26–27 May 1973 had this group portrait as the lead.*

Above: *"Moskau in Bonn": Barbara Klemm's iconic image was not among the four motifs chosen to illustrate the photogravure supplement of the* Frankfurter Allgemeine Zeitung *of 26–27 May 1973.*

RAF
Hanns Martin Schleyer, Prisoner of the RAF 1977

Hopes and Fears

The man was not uncontroversial, but was irrefutably part of the elite of the old Federal Republic. Nicknamed the "boss of the bosses," Hanns Martin Schleyer ranked among the most influential figures in post-war West Germany. His kidnapping remains a key date in the national calender, his picture as a prisoner and victim the most profoundly disturbing portrait in media history. This isn't someone simply looking with a serious expression at the camera. This is someone looking death in the face.

The picture's small. It measures 7.8 × 7.8 cm (3 × 3 inches) from corner to corner. It's carefully composed, but without any claim to aesthetic quality. Its formal appearance is ultimately in inverse ratio to its effect. In 1977 it was a bombshell. Photography has the potential to be art. That seems to be generally agreed. Often enough, however, a photographic image makes an impact precisely because it does not glance sidelong at the museum but exploits the strengths that take it beyond the sphere of art. Namely its capacity to serve as a document. As proof of something. As evidence. A clue. A testament. Our picture is a simple Polaroid. The photographic process came onto the market in 1972 under the name SX-70 produces instant pictures that measure roughly the size of the palm of the hand and are garbage-free, thanks to their integral film. Compared with conventional photography, the SX-70 has two unbeatable advantages: the picture is delivered instantly, and the image it bears does not need to pass before the eyes of a laboratory technician. Amateurs loved it. Especially if they had betaken themselves into the domain of erotic photography. So did terrorists.

Portrait under compulsion

Millions of Polaroid photos were taken in the 1960s, '70s and '80s. Digital photography still lay in the future. And Polaroids were the fastest and most intimate way of taking one's own pictures. Millions of Polaroid photos fill frames, albums, shoeboxes. This is probably the most famous one. Almost everyone knows it. Almost everyone in Germany has stored it in their memory. Probably in black and white. Because the picture broadcast to a horrified public in virtually every paper after 6 September 1977 was printed, as a rule, in black-and-white halftone. It might be termed a portrait, if by portrait we mean simply the likeness of a person. In its narrower sense, a portrait captures essence, character, and individuality. It is also a picture that arises with the voluntary participation and active cooperation of the sitter. This was most certainly not the case here. The picture was taken under duress, to put it mildly. And here it was not a matter of capturing character or essence, but simply a likeness. Which brings the image close to police mug shots. It,

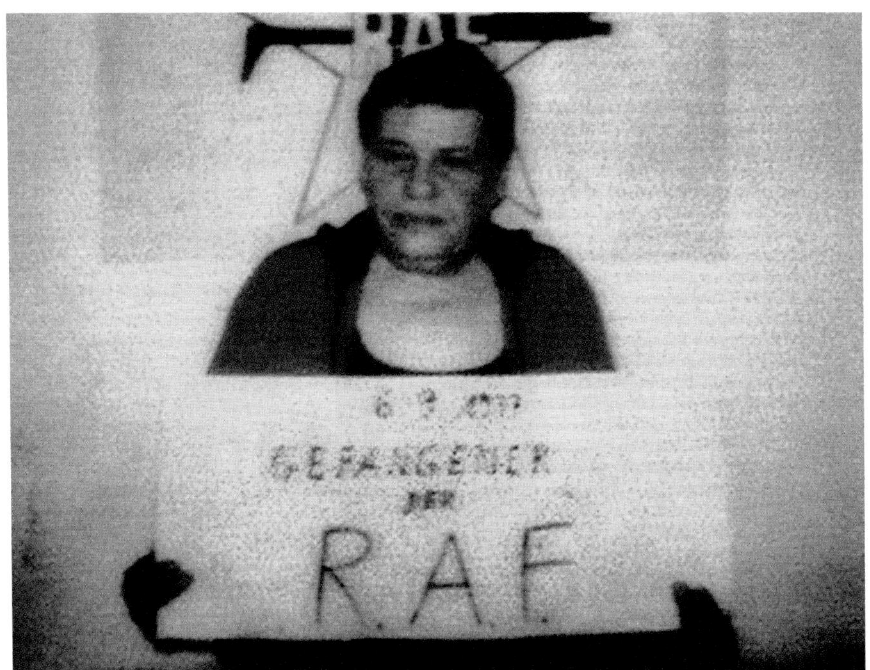

too, is all about recognition. With one vital difference: we are dealing here not with a perpetrator, but a victim. His name: Hanns Martin Schleyer.

On 5 September 1977 the Siegfried Hausner Commando, part of the so-called Red Army Faction (RAF), kidnapped Hanns Martin Schleyer, Employers' Association president. Imagine the circumstances: a small group of young people from middle-class backgrounds, armed and describing themselves as "urban guerrillas," successfully seize one of Germany's most powerful, influential, and heavily guarded top executives, drag him off to an unknown location and use their hostage as a tool with which to bargain for the release of comrades sitting in jail. Active since 1970, the RAF – often called the Baader-Meinhof Gang by politicians and the media – had already proven on several occasions that it was serious. Murder was factored into the equation right from the start, and the execution of defenceless prisoners an accepted part of what they termed "armed resistance." On 1 April 1977 the "Ulrike Meinhof Commando" had murdered Federal Prosecutor General Siegfried Buback, in Karlsruhe. In July, Jürgen Ponto, chairman of the Dresdner Bank, was shot in his home in Oberusel. Schleyer was thus not simply looking into the lens of a whirring Polaroid camera. He was facing a possibly imminent death.

Hanns Martin Schleyer, photographed on 6 September 1977. The picture is one of two put out by the RAF on the same day.

Message in capital letters

The man seems astonishingly collected. As collected as in the hand-written statement attached by the kidnappers to their own letter of blackmail to the German government. He is fine for the moment, writes Schleyer. He is unharmed and he believes he will be released if the demands are met. He wears a serious expression, and holds up a board bearing a message scrawled in capital letters: "6. 9. 1977 – GEFANGENER DER R.A.F." ("6. 9. 1977 – Prisoner of the R.A.F."). Schleyer: a figure from public life. Usually he would probably have appeared in a shirt, tie, and expensive suit. This time, surely not by choice, he's wearing some sort of dark jacket or bath robe. His chest is bare, his hair a little unkempt. How one might normally emerge from the sauna. Schleyer may have emerged from the soundproofed cupboard in which he was sometimes locked up. The picture exudes force and humiliation. One of the most powerful men in the Federal Republic imprisoned, subjugated, robbed of his dignity and freedom. Above his head appears the Red Army Faction logo, consisting of a five-pointed star and a Kalashnikov. The picture is a document of hatred. And equally of triumph. With the kidnapping of Schleyer, the RAF had carried off its most spectacular coup to date.

Schleyer was undoubtedly one of the most glittering figures within the German world of commerce and industry. In 1977 he was aged 62 and for many people the embodiment of a capitalist. And then there were the black marks, too, on his CV: he had joined the SS in as early as 1933 and joined the Nazi Party in 1937. Schleyer's Nazi past was unable, however, to check his meteoric rise to the very top of the Federal German economy. In 1951 he joined the senior management of Daimler-Benz and in 1963 was appointed a member of the board. He held important offices in employers' associations and in 1973 was elected president of the Federal Association of German Employers. The media treated him as the boss of the bosses. Union leaders perceived him as a ruthless industrialist. For Brigitte Mohnhaupt, Chistian Klar, Peter-Jürgen Book, Rolf Klemens Wagner, and Adelheid Schulz, he was nothing short of the "Frankenstein" of German capitalism. His name had been on their list of possible targets for quite a while. Why? With Schleyer's help, the German government was to be pressured into releasing members of the first generation of the RAF – Andreas Baader, Gudrun Ensslin, and Jan-Carl Raspe amongst them – incarcerated in Stuttgart's Stammheim prison. On 5 September 1977 they acted. In Cologne's Vincenz-Statz-Strasse, Schleyer's car and the vehicle escorting him were forced to a halt by members of the RAF. The terrorists lost no time. Chauffeur and body guard were killed at close range. The unharmed Schleyer was bundled into a VW van and driven off to the Liblar district of neighboring Erftstadt. His first prison. It was here, on the third floor of a highrise building that guaranteed anonymity, that the Polaroid photo was taken. A picture that symbolizes, like no other, the terrorist threat posed by the RAF for nearly three decades.

Body in the boot

There now followed weeks of negotiation and tactical maneuvering. Should a government allow itself to be blackmailed? No, argued Federal Chancellor Helmut Schmidt. He was supported in his stance by opposition leader Helmut Kohl. While Schleyer was still in the hands of his kidnappers, four Palestinians hijacked a Lufthansa plane, the *Landshut*, and issued their own demand for the release of imprisoned members of the RAF. The storming of the *Landshut* by a GSG 9 counter-terrorism unit in Mogadishu has gone down in legend. So, too,

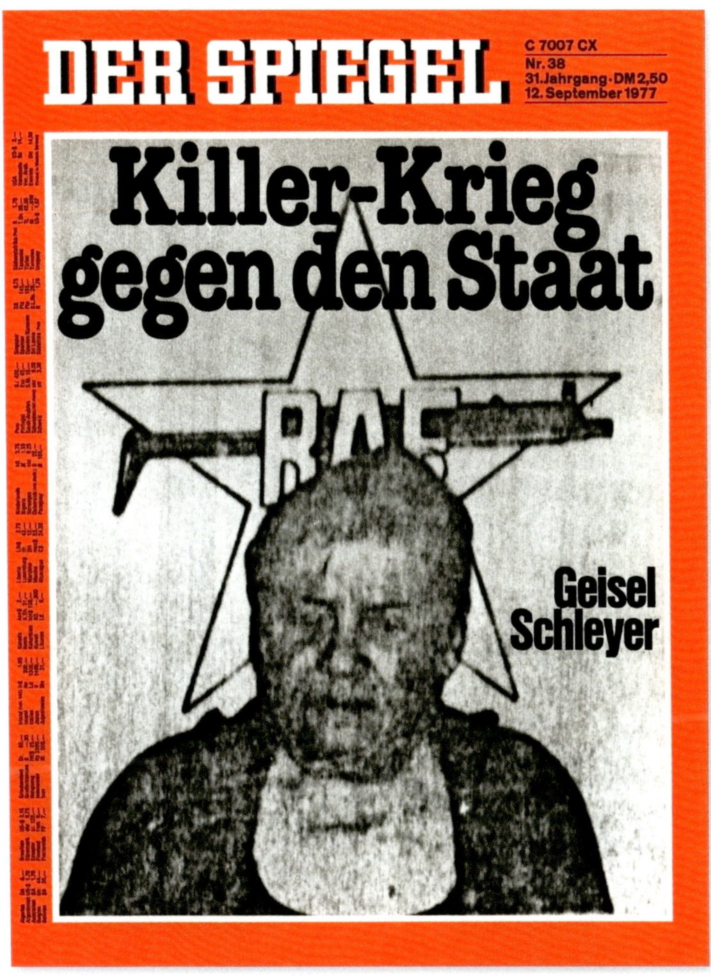

have the subsequent suicides of Baader, Ensslin, and Raspe in Stammheim. One day later, on 19 October 1977, Schleyer's body was found in the boot of an Audi 100 in Mulhouse in the Alsace. In 1998, after twenty-eight years of existence, the RAF announced the end of its urban guerrilla "project" and its own dissolution. The balance: thirty-four murders. Its most prominent victim was called Hanns Martin Schleyer.

A man caught in the wheels of history: the cover of Spiegel, *12 September 1977.*

Helmut Newton
They're Coming!
1981

Ice-Cold Self-Consciousness

The photograph marked a turning point - and it was, of course, intended to be provocative. In fact, not until 1981 did the French edition of Vogue feel ready to publish Helmut Newton's diptych They're Coming! as an erotic metaphor for the changing image of woman.

This time there were no Italian gardens or fin-de-siècle hotel rooms, no beaches on the Côte d'Azur, no promenades, no New York apartments with a view, or well-appointed rooms in the 16th arrondissement. In their place, only the sober, empty chamber of a professional studio. That was unusual for Helmut Newton, who loved to stage scenes, especially in settings that exuded life and vitality (or at least he did at one time). His photographs, which many believe to have been schooled in the German cinema between the wars, were sometimes even set on bridges or in underground passageways, in train stations or airports. It all depended on what Newton's fat notebook - that irreplaceable storeroom bursting with ideas that have feasted on reality - proposed. Newton was a realist - if one accepts the idea that dreams, desires, and fantasies also belong to the inventory of reality. But his inventory had one important difference from the world of things that surround us: namely, one does not need a drawer for them. Helmut Newton provided images for those forces that move the world beneath the skin, as it were - our collective passions, fantasies, suppressed desires, and sublime wishes. And he did this not for the sake of the public, but for his own sake. If he had concerned himself about what the public might like, he would never have created another picture, he said. "No, I do only what pleases me."

Helmut Newton was a gardener of our secret desires. And without doubt he was the best-known gardener of the kind, and was therefore automatically the most controversial botanist

---

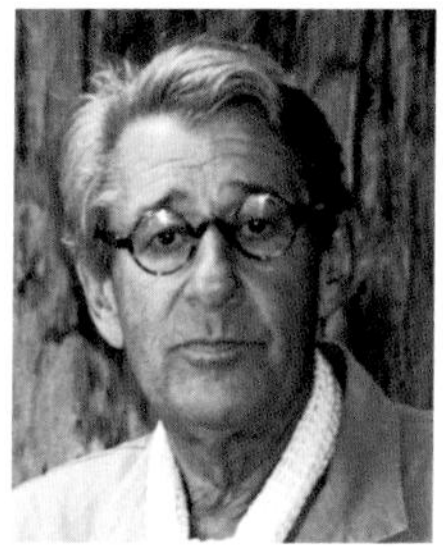

Helmut Newton
Born Helmut Neustädter in ***1920****, the son of a button manufacturer in Berlin.* ***1936–38*** *Apprenticeship under Else Simon (Yva).* ***1938*** *flees from Germany. From* ***1940*** *in Australia. Australian citizen from* ***1944****. Marries June Browne (alias Alice Springs).* ***1956*** *returns to London.* ***1957*** *moves to Paris. Works for* Vogue, Elle, Marie Claire, Jardin des Modes, Nova, Queen. *From* ***1971*** *works on an increasing number of autonomous projects.* ***1975*** *first solo show in the Paris Nikon Galerie.* ***1976*** *publication of his first book,* White Women. ***1987*** *retrospective in the Rheinische Landesmuseum, Bonn.* ***1992*** *awarded the Order of the Federal Republic of Germany. Dies* ***2004*** *in Los Angeles.*

of our collective longings. He was a latter-day pupil of Freud, whose medium was of course not the couch but the camera. Whether small format or 6 × 6 inch, whether ring flash or daylight – technical data are of little help in mapping the rich idea-landscape of a Helmut Newton. He created a cosmos enclosed within itself, subject to its own rules, which Newton, with his aversion to all theories, never attempted to organize into a program, but which nonetheless allow themselves to be distilled in retrospect. Newton's 'film stills', his frozen scenes, are clearly artificial, but at the same time thoroughly consistent with the interior world created by the photographer; the scenes revolve around power and submission, around force and passion, seduction, pleasure, and physical love. His arrangement of his realm is unmistakably vertical: there is no sense of egalitarian togetherness among his figures, but rather clear hierarchies of power, although – and we will return to this point later – the woman is clearly given the determining role. Boots and whips, saddles and spurs, German shepherd dogs, chains, high heels, are recurring symbols in a complex system of visual symbols always set against mirrors and broad corridors, stairs and balconies that rise to dizzying heights, swimming pools and bridge balustrades: in other words, flight and fall, falling and death are always at least implicated in Newton's pictorial world.

Fashion as an excuse for something else

Helmut Newton loved to arrange scenes and thus to achieve absolute control over his picture. Moreover, the writer Michael Stoeber finds this to have been a tendency throughout the artist's life. Anyone who, like Newton, has been cheated out of a life plan – however it may be defined – in the course of time may compensate for the loss by searching for some form of "absolute control over his own life." Born the son of a Berlin button-factory owner in 1920, Newton left – that is, felt compelled to leave – Germany at age eighteen for Australia. His decision proved correct, as the fate of his photography teacher Yva (Else Simon) in Auschwitz demonstrates, even though both his journey to Australia and his entry into the field of professional photography were difficult. In the early 1960s, Newton returned to Europe, where he found a congenial platform for his work, particularly with the French *Vogue* under its courageous editor-in-chief, Francine Crescent. Note well: at this point in time, moral boundaries were still quite narrow. Nevertheless, the unmistakable signs of change were beginning to emerge – at first (cautiously) in Ed van der Elsken's volume of photography, *Love on the Left Bank*, in 1956, and later (openly) in the much-cited 'sexual revolution' around 1968. In a certain sense, Helmut Newton was, or became, a part of this movement. On the one hand, he and the pictorial world he created profited from the increasingly liberal morality of the age. On the other hand, his constant exploration of the possibilities also led to an expansion of the limits of tolerance. Newton thus simultaneously functioned as a catalyst and an exploiter of the development.

Helmut Newton was a fashion photographer – and nothing less than that. He photographed clothes or, as one calls them in the industry, 'collections'. The cut or the fabrics – the 'buttons and bows' in the language of the fashion editors – interested him only peripherally, however. For Newton, fashion was rather a pretext for something else, although – and this makes his work easier – the path from fashion to his passion was not a long one, when one recalls that fashion, in the sense of the age-old game of revealing and concealing, lies also at the core of all sensuality. Newton's visualizations may have been connected with

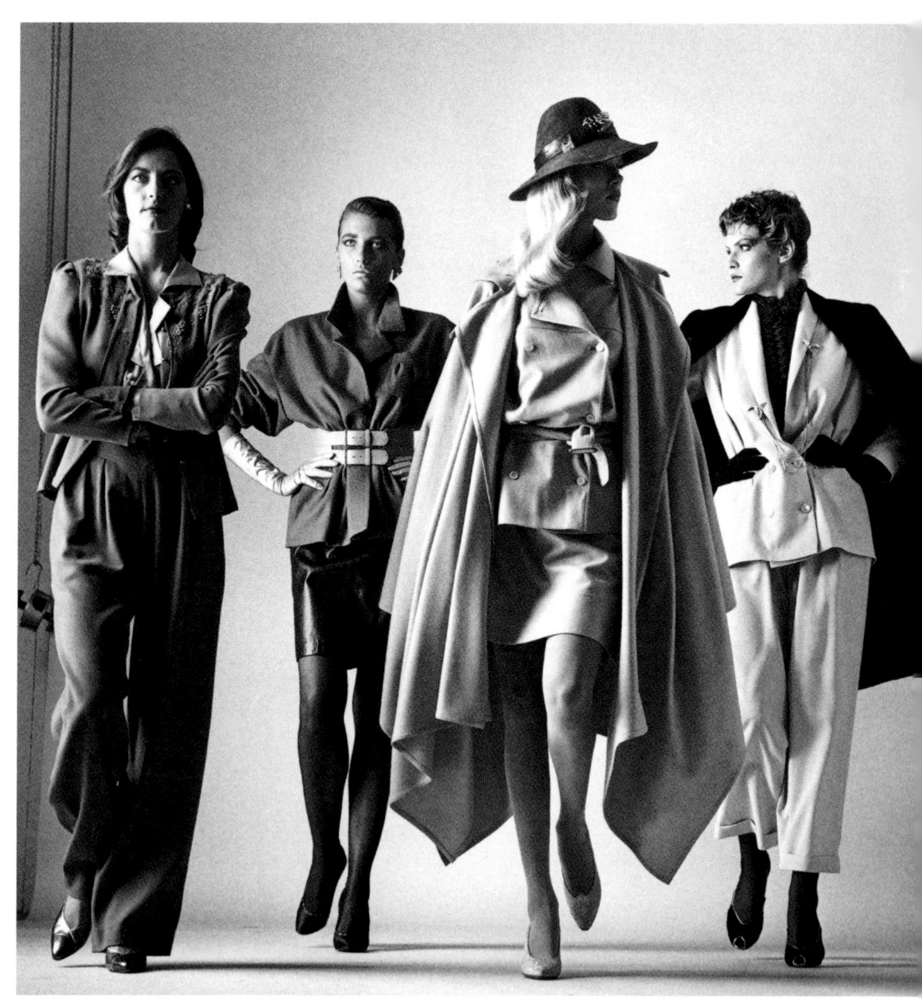

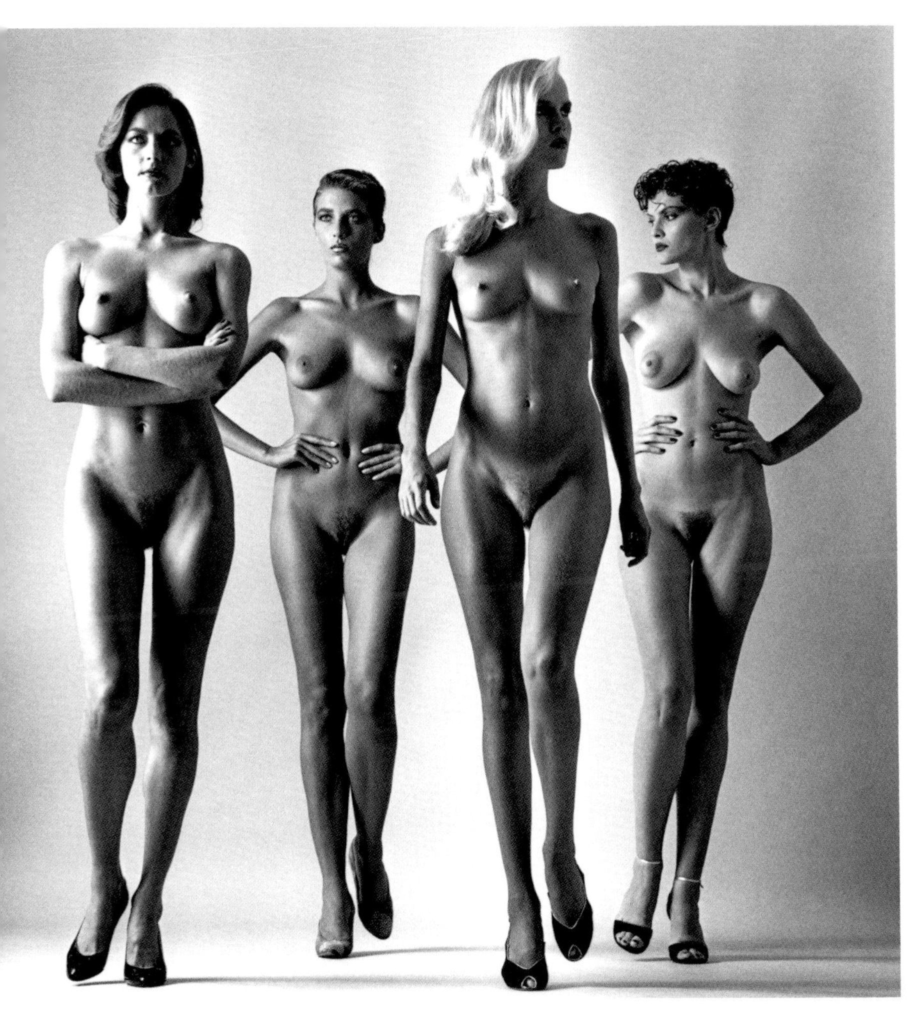

They're Coming!, 1981

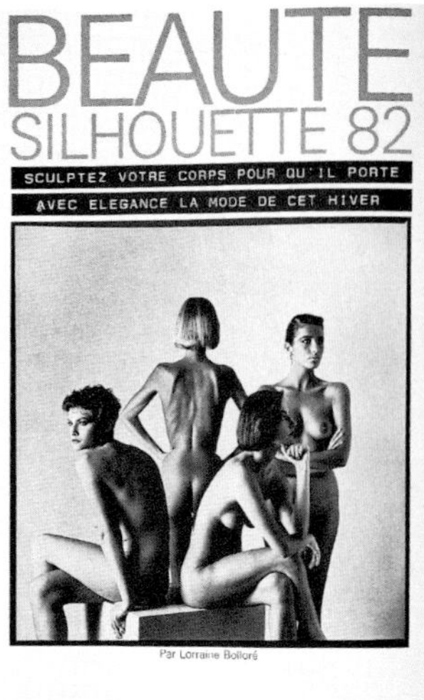

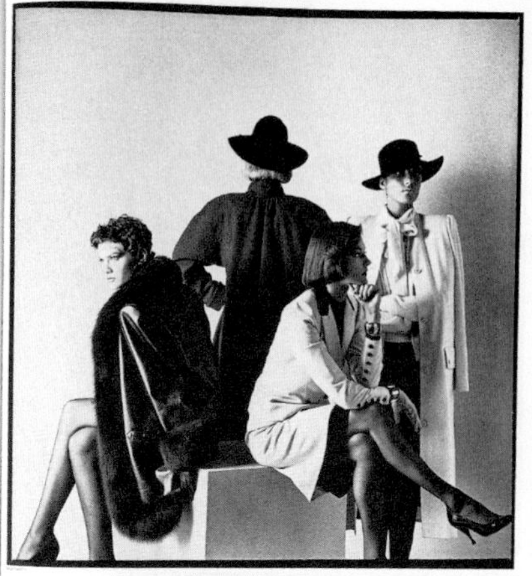

a contract, but they are nonetheless steeped in his personal desires, wishes and dreams, delights and fears. Furthermore, his success only goes to show that his photographs touch the depths of collective longings. Newton translated into pictures that which many hardly dare to think.

The voice whispering to Newton was that of reality. He loaded his creative batteries, so to speak, from everyday life. He always insisted that he was little more than a voyeur, a claim which coquettishly borders on understatement, but nonetheless reveals the conceptual core of his photographic work – an art, moreover, which is schooled in life at its fullest, gaudiest, and most pleasurable, or conversely when it radiates on lighter and softer frequencies. Newton's powers of perception were both alert and selective: the "bad boy of photography," as he liked to call himself, picked up the lascivious signals that he then translated into pictures that succeed in being provocative even in an age that is largely without taboos. "I am," as Helmut Newton pointed out, "a good observer of people." That is, he was a seismographer of those waves which people – preferably 'cool girls' – emit through gestures, glances, their way of walking, or even their clothing. The street was the costume room for his pictorial ideas,

---

"Beauté – Silhouette 82." Double-page spreads in the French Vogue, *November 1981, the first publication of the images commonly known as* They're Coming!

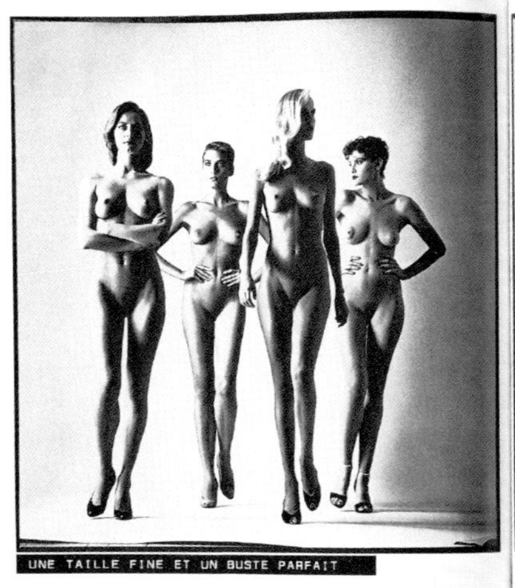

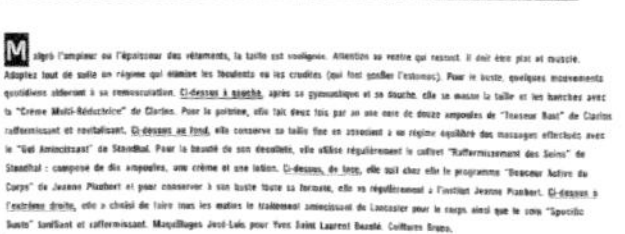

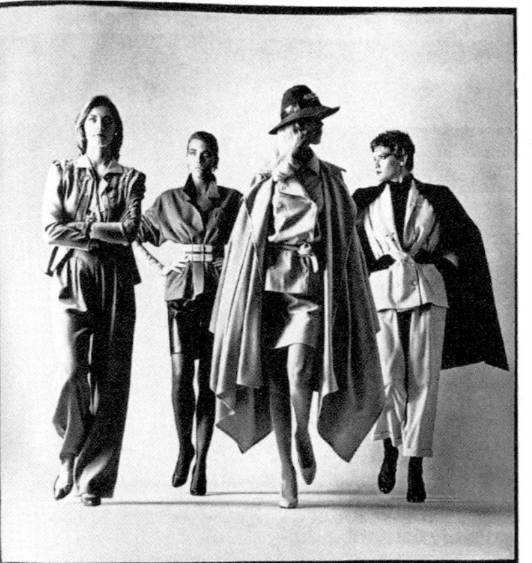

enriched through a bit of *haute-volée* that transcends the trivial and passes into the fabulous. "The people in my pictures," according to Helmut Newton, who did not at all attempt to hide the parameters of his creations, "have been 'arranged', as on a stage. Nonetheless my pictures are not counterfeit; they reflect what I see in life with my own eyes."

In this connection, Newton liked to refer to a photograph titled *Eiffel Tower* (1974), initially published in *White Women* – Newton's first book, which was particularly important in laying the groundwork for the later reception of his photographs. *Tower* is a late-evening view into the rear seat of a limousine that has been transformed into a 'bedroom'. A beautiful young blonde woman is lounging In the midst of the black leather cushions; apart from her leather jacket, which is already pulled open, she is wearing only transparent undies embroidered with an Eiffel Tower – images that sing of Helmut Newton's penchant for double meanings and ambiguity, in the words of Klaus Honnef. In the background, an anonymous man has begun to work on her, fumbling with the zipper and helping her out of her high-heeled boots. "The scene," according to Newton, "undoubtedly takes place after work – a business man has a date with his girlfriend. He is wearing a blue suit, handsome cuff-links, and drives a black Citroën DS – the typical auto of the bourgeoisie and of civil servants in France. Lying on the seat next to the woman is a copy of the establishment newspaper *Le Monde*. And what the man is doing before he drives home – he has not yet gotten to the stage of going to a hotel with his girlfriend – is undressing her in the automobile. That happens all day long in the Bois de Boulogne," explained Helmut Newton; "the autos are lined up as in an American Lover's Lane."

***They're Coming!*, 1981**

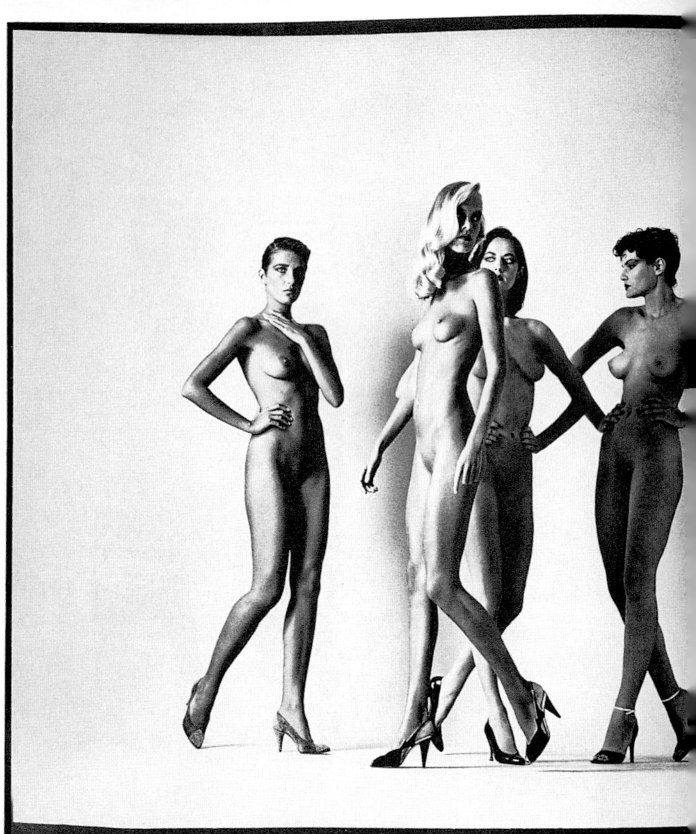

L'ALLURE D'UN CORPS EN MOUVEMENT

Le corps doit se mouvoir avec grâce, avec ou sans vêtements. Pour retrouver l'harmonie physique, vous pouvez vous inscrire dans un cours de danse classique à la salle Mozart, de danse moderne à Pleyel ou chez Joseph Russillo. Ci-dessus à gauche, elle entretient sa ligne avec la gamme "Elancyl". A l'institut Revlon, elle confie ses mains et ses pieds à vernir et ses jambes qu'elle fait parfaitement épiler à la cire chaude. Ci-dessus de face, elle aide son corps à conserver fermeté et élasticité avec le "Masque Modelant" à l'institut Maria Galland. Elle complète son action avec la Crème Raffermissante pour le corps de Maria Galland, riche en oligo-éléments. Ci-dessus au fond, elle aime le programme de revitalisation de l'épiderme du corps fait à l'institut Orlane en trois étapes : le bain de parafine amincissant aux algues qui élimine les toxines, le gommage des coudes et des genoux et le brossage du corps avec la Crème Fluide Hydratante B 21. Ci-dessus à droite, elle utilise la crème "Objectif Minceur" Les Corporelles de Jeanne Gatineau, conçue en fonction des dernières connaissances scientifiques. Les jambes sont douces et parfaitement épilées à l'institut Adrienne. Maquillages José-Luis pour Yves Saint Laurent Beauté. Coiffures Bruno. Chaussures de gauche à droite : Carel, Maud Frizon, et Charles Jourdan.

162

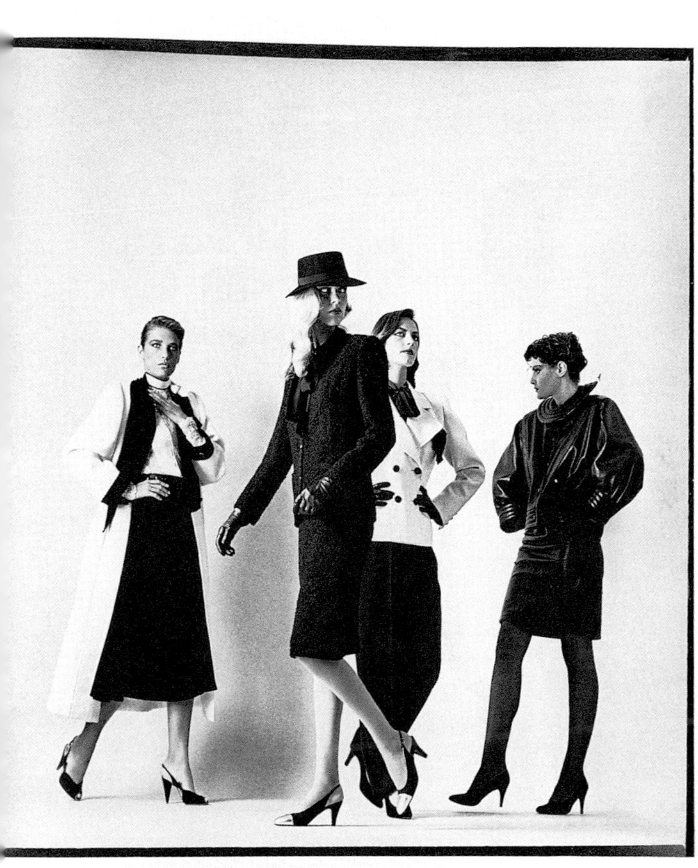

Le noir est la couleur de l'hiver, associé souvent avec le blanc ou le clair. Il exige une coupe raffinée. Classique ou sophistiqué, il est l'un des meilleurs amis des femmes. Elancée, on le reste. Moins élancée, on le devient, affaire d'optique. A gauche, manteau en lainage blanc de Gandini, à col écharpe et poignets en velours de soie noir de Gandini et blouse de dentelle ivoire de Marescot, sur une jupe ample en velours de soie noir de Clément. Emanuel Ungaro. Au premier plan, tailleur en bouclette noire d'Agnona, à veste et jupe droite, sur une blouse à col noué, en soie de Cattin. Chanel Boutique par Philippe Guibourgé. Accessoires Chanel. Au fond, blazer croisé en lainage jaune de Hurel, sur une blouse à col cravate en satin de soie noir de Besson-Corisia, et un pantalon droit en flanelle noire de Moreau. Yves Saint Laurent. Accessoires Yves Saint Laurent. A droite, tailleur en cuir noir : blouson à col disque et poignets surpiqués, sur une jupe courte droite. Pierre Cardin. Escarpins Pierre Cardin. Coiffures Bruno.

163

"Bodies in motion." The caption is highly understated, the images themselves anything but. Even today, naked women in stilettos are hardly the everyday stuff of sophisticated fashion magazines. French Vogue*, November 1981.*

Basso continuo to his performance with the camera

Helmut Newton was fascinated by the idea that hiding under every woman in 'full dress' is a more (or less) well-formed body. Fashion was the theater curtain that must be pulled aside. And possibly – no, certainly – this nakedness, this ceremony, remained something of a *basso continuo* to his performance with the camera. Already in the mid-1970s, Newton started photographing girls in the Paris Métro: stark naked under a fur coat. An undertaking not entirely without danger, as the photographer admitted. "You can land in jail for something like that, because the Métro has very strict rules." But Newton loved to test the borders of the possible, in daily life as in art – which for him in any case flowed together. That these borders have clearly moved since the 1970s has a good deal to do with Newton himself, as mentioned earlier. Opening the curtain slowly, Newton radically altered our idea of what is allowed and what is forbidden. At the end of this process of development, his models were completely naked – without coat or furs – provided at most with the black stilettos that are a staple of his iconography: "When I look at a woman," said Newton, "my first glance goes to her shoes and I hope that they are high. High heels make a woman very sexy and give her something threatening."

An increasing obsession

Helmut Newton was an artist whose work has found its way into the sacred halls of international art museums – which is all the more surprising considering that most of his photographs have a commercial background, and that he did not at all attempt to hide his origins in editing and advertising. Newton succeeded in blurring the distinction between 'free' and 'applied' art for us – just as he himself never took the border seriously. "Whenever I've worked on a commission, whether editorial or advertising, I have always found my inspiration," he admitted. "Not all, but almost all of my best photographs stem from these assignments." Newton's ideas, as Sotheby curator Philippe Garner once noted, were elaborate; they demanded the noblest raw materials and masterly skill from experts – makeup artists, hairdressers, stylists. Newton, in other words, needs a 'back office' that could be offered only by large newspapers and publishing houses, with all the logistic and financial support they provide. Therefore, the humus from which his work grew was the commission – even if not everything thrived in this soil, at least not in the early years. This was a situation that bothered Newton, at least in the official legend. "A dream of a contract," the photographer recalled; "I'm supposed to take photographs in this grand hotel for the magazine *Réalités*. I've got two interesting models, but I've also got a problem: my first book, *White Women*, is almost done – just a few pictures are missing. For the book, the pictures should be rather daring nudes, but for *Réalités*, I need elegant photos to fit in with the character of the magazine. I decided to make two versions: one nude, the other clothed." From then on, Newton admitted, his interest in the opposition between 'naked' and 'dressed' became an increasing obsession.

They're Coming! was published for the first time in the November issue of the French *Vogue*, and naturally represented the high point, and even in a sense the crowning moment, of a passion which seemed hardly capable of being carried any further. The editor-in-chief Francine Crescent devoted a bold eight pages to Newton's series, a decision which, as Karl Lagerfeld recalls, "placed her job at risk" once again. Admittedly, complete nakedness combined with stilettos is almost part of the basic vocabulary of Newtonian photographic art; one needs only think of *Rue Aubriot* (1975) or *Mannequins quai d'Orsay II* from Newton's second book, *Sleepless Nights*, which twice took up the opposition between 'naked' and 'dressed' (not to mention the photographer's explorations of lesbian love, a theme which always intrigued him). But the one picture was taken under the cloak of darkness, so to speak, and the other in the seclusion of a salon. Both photographs therefore exude something of an intimacy that Newton's pictorial vision clearly passed beyond – from his *Big Nudes* to the sequence discussed here. The title *They're Coming!* – applied to the photographs only after their appearance in *Vogue* – underlines the resolution behind a nudity that is now 'worn' as a matter of course, but which also and especially signifies vulnerability. Seen in this way, Newton's women of the 1980s are 'big nudes' in a double sense: large, strong, goal-oriented, and – whether 'dressed up' or unclothed – ready to conquer the world of men.

A horror of too much smoothness, too much perfection

The idea of dissolving the opposition between 'naked' and 'clothed' in diptychs is one Newton had already experimented with earlier in Brescia during the summer of 1981, in a seaside Fascist-style villa. "The same situation, the same woman," recalled Karl Lagerfeld; "once dressed and once naked (but with high heels – for Newton, a woman isn't naked unless she's wearing high heels). The reconstruction is perfect; only one thing could not be replicated – the light. The sun had changed, and the unique hours were gone forever." Helmut Newton learned from his work in northern Italy; afterwards, he exchanged the admittedly charming ambiance of a summer villa for the antiseptic atmosphere of a Paris studio. The single model furthermore gave way to a group of well-built graces. The haziness of motion that had been suggested in the Italian sequence was now replaced in favor of a truly 'frozen' entry in *They're Coming!*. Careful observers will note, however, that not all the details are logically followed through. Somehow, the shoes have gotten mixed. And the model on the back left has reversed the stationary and moving leg. In film one would say that the continuity is missing. Oversight – or intention deriving from a horror of too much smoothness, too much perfection?

Newton emulated his women. He always valued dominant femininity. The high-heeled shoes, the strong upshot, the light, neutral background against which the contours of the women stand out as if chiseled all strengthen the impression of the threat, especially in the 'undressed' version. In the magazine business, the right side is usually considered to be the more important. In the *Vogue* premier, the naked variant is to the left, the clothed to the right – a layout that seems logical as long as one follows the direction of reading and reckons that the human being is initially naked and only afterwards clothed. When, however, Newton was responsible for the order of the sequence, as in his *Big Nudes*, he reversed them – perhaps indicating which of the motifs held more importance for him. At the same time, the charm of the two photographs clearly resides in their character as a diptych: only in terms of such a thesis and antithesis does the theme develop its full interest. *Vogue* presented the sequence under the title "Beauté – Silhouette 82." The lead-in was brief: "Work on your body so it can wear the fashions of the coming season with grace." Interestingly, in the autumn of 1939 a similar theme had appeared in the French *Vogue*: looking toward the coming lines that were fitted to the contours of the body: the corset had been reinvented and was now being recommended once more to women. Today, they have the fitness studio and hand-weights. Helmut Newton was without a doubt a witness of the dramatically changing role of women in society. And he was their important, if often misunderstood, iconographer.

Sandy Skoglund
Revenge of the Goldfish
1981

The Mellowest of Nightmares

Since the 1980s, photographic artists have increasingly taken to 'designing' their pictures. Consciously following the trail blazed by advertising, they have used imagination and wit to overcome the strictures of the Classical Modern. Rather than seeking themes in reality and 'taking' it straight, they invent new pictorial worlds. They often manipulate their pictures in the name of brilliant and outrageous ideas, and thereby take up the challenges posed by the postmodern. Along with Cindy Sherman and David LaChapelle, Sandy Skoglund, based in Jersey City, numbers among the outstanding exponents of this so-called 'staged photography' – though she also wishes her constructed environments to be understood as art in their own right.

Revenge of the Goldfish: it's impossible not to feel the contradiction in the name given by Sandy Skoglund to the work she created in 1981. Her later tableaus would feature foxes or dogs. The viewer may well be overcome by disgust on seeing *Germs are Everywhere* (1984), or succumb to a sense of discomfort in the face of the shimmering green felines in *Radioactive Cats* (1980). Even the fidgety squirrels in *Gathering Paradise* (1991) somehow seem more threatening than the over-sized goldfish that have somehow found their way into a middle-class bedroom. In fact, the two protagonists of the scene – mother and son (or is it brother and sister?) – seem to not even have noticed the arrival of the fish. The woman is sleeping, the boy is dozing as he sits on the edge of the bed. The scene oscillates oddly between the real and the surreal. What sounds threatening in the title reveals itself in the picture to be markedly peaceful and relaxed. At most, it is the mass of the reddish-orange creatures taken as a whole that creates a rather alarming effect – fish that somehow have mistakenly wandered into an environment where they really do not belong. Much easier to understand is the room, in which we find

---

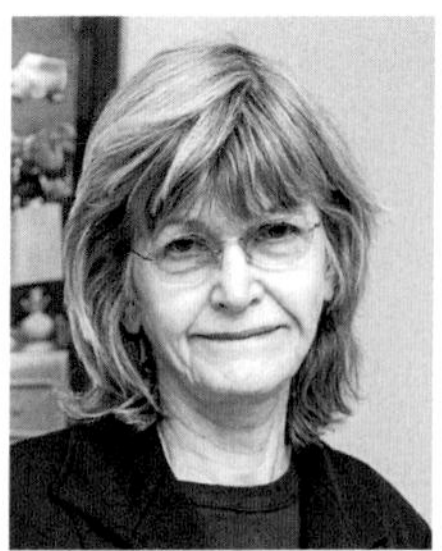

Sandy Skoglund
*Born **1946** in Quincy, Massachusetts. **1964** high school degree. **1964–68** Smith College, Northampton, Massachusetts. One year in France studying art at the Sorbonne. **1969–72** studies Film and Multimedia Art at University of Iowa (MFA). **1972** moves to New York. Panel painting along the lines of Minimal Art. **1979** move to photography. Breakthrough **1981** at the Whitney Biennale with* Radioactive Cats *(1980) and* Revenge of the Goldfish *(1981). Numerous solo shows. Lives in Jersey City, New Jersey.*

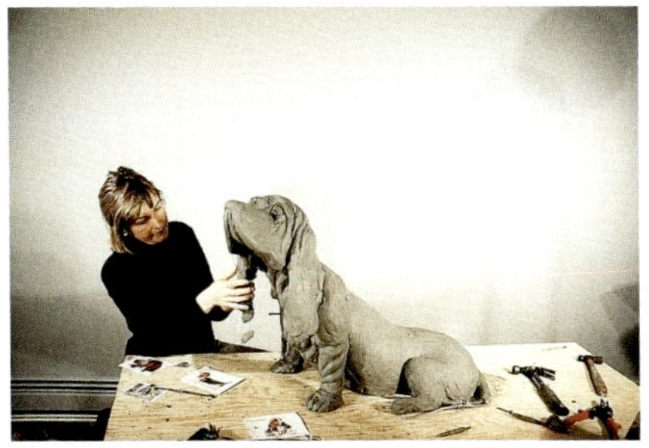
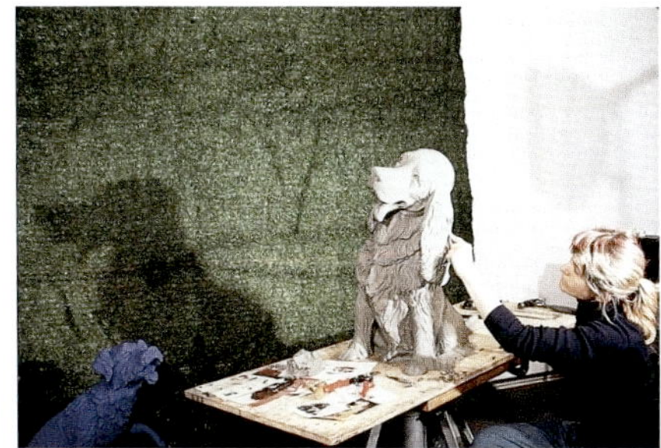
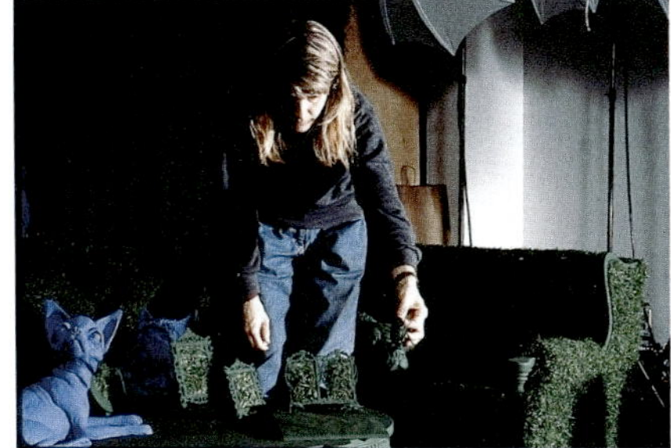
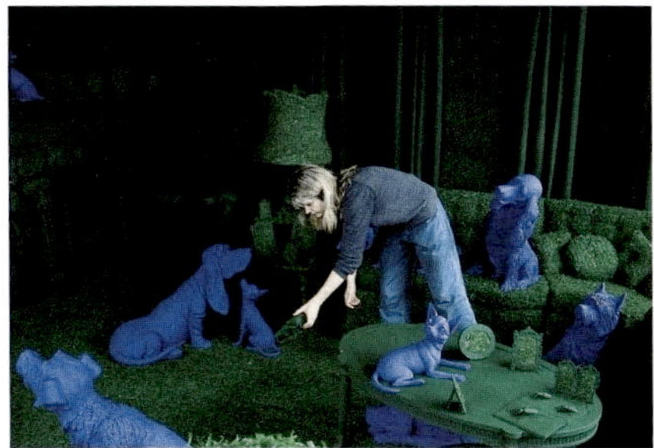

everything that a bedroom ought to offer: bed, dresser, lamp, mirror, sash window. Admittedly, everything has been dipped into a swampy green wash – the whole scene is somewhat reminiscent of an oversize aquarium. Can it be that the picture is thematizing the reverse of a standard assumption? Namely, that the people have become captives of nature, caught as it were in a foreign environment, just as in a 'normal' household aquarium, nature has been imprisoned by people?

Sculptures of papier-mâché, plaster, or polyester

Anyone confronting the photographic works of the American artist Sandy Skoglund for the first time – anyone who has recovered sufficiently from the trompe-l'œil effects of her minutely detailed installations to make out her goldfish, squirrels, cats, dogs, or babies for what they in fact are, namely sculptures made from papier-mâché, plaster, or polyester – will inevitably ask how she does it. In other words, once viewers realize that the scenes are amazing theater sets, located somewhere between fact and fiction, reality and artifice, they inevitably inquire after the technical and artistic processes she employs. To set things straight right from the beginning: Sandy Skoglund is responsible for all the creative steps involved in her work; she is consummately the author of her photographs, in the sense introduced by the French Nouvelle Vague.

Above and page 359: **Sandy Skoglund:** The Green House © 1990. *Preliminaries to this work ended in 1990. The artist began to document the growth of her elaborate installations only in the late 1980s. Still more or less alone at the time, Sandy Skoglund now has her own team to help her in the realization of her complex ideas.*

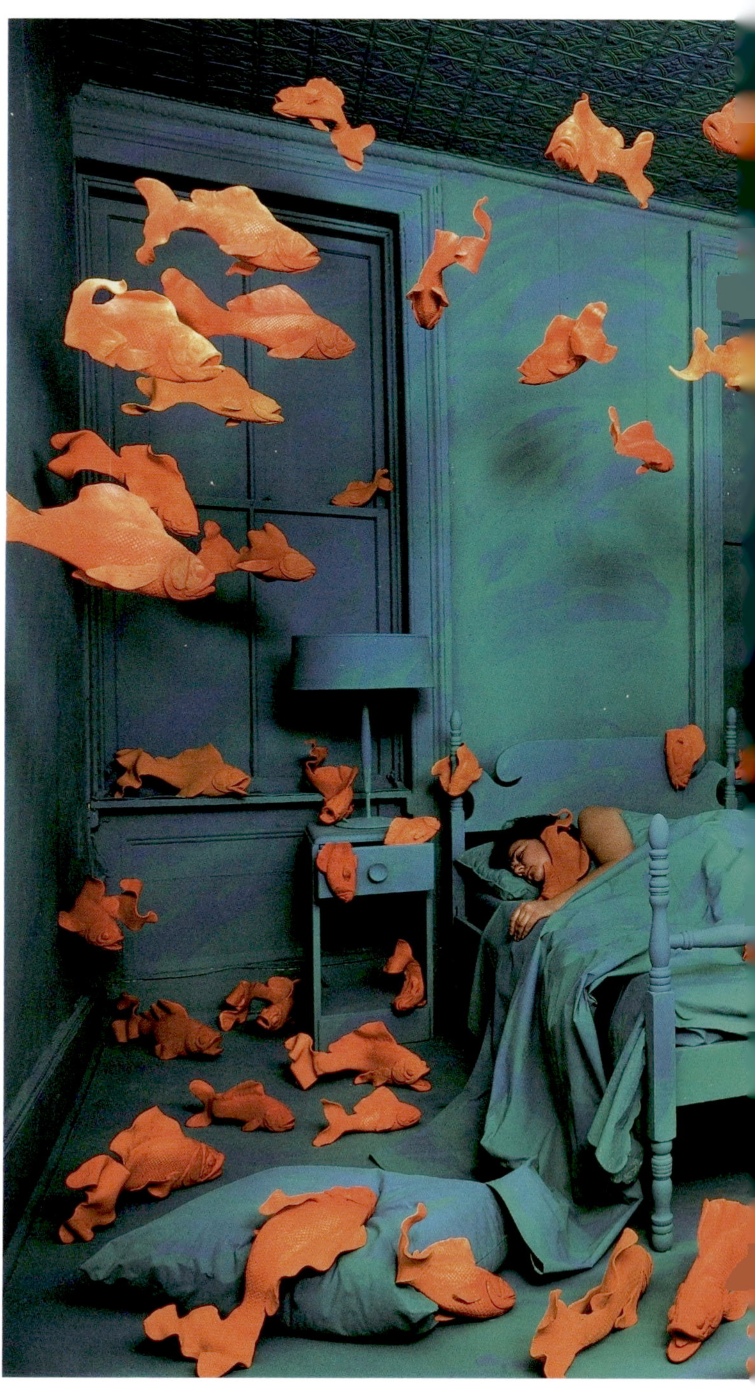

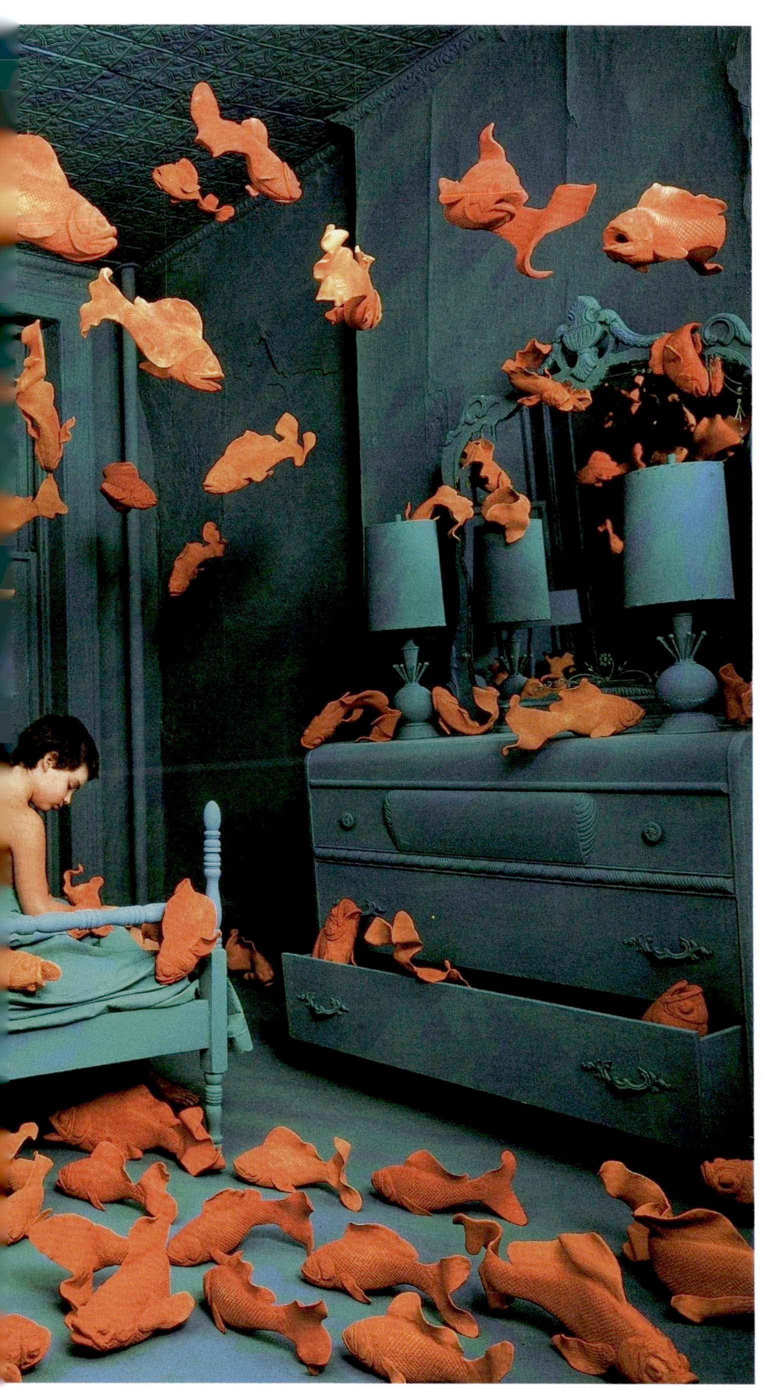

Skoglund develops her ideas and constructs her worlds in her gigantic Soho studio located in Jersey City. Here she designs and models her figures from photographic patterns that she has abstracted from magazines and other printed matter; she sets up her 8 by 10 inch (20 × 25.4 cm) large-format camera, checks the development of her 'scene' through the focusing screen, arranges the lighting – and then takes her photograph.

A plethora of photographic 'power acts'

According to her own understanding, Skoglund is neither sculptor, nor painter, nor photographer. Douglas Crimp once denoted the phenomenon of her work as a 'hybridization' of the arts. More precisely, Skoglund belongs to the generation of artists who are applying intellectual skills originally acquired in the areas of sculpture or painting to what has become known since the beginning of the 1980s as 'staged photography'.

The photographer may either find or invent what appears before the lens. The resulting picture may be a documentation, or a reaction to a situation specially created or arranged for the camera. "Document and discovery" – thus Jörg Boström has termed (1989) the two fundamentally divergent paths that photography has unconsciously pursued ever since Niépce's *View from the Study Window* (1827), on the one hand, and Daguerre's *Still Life* (1837) on the other. Whereas the Classical Modern apotheosized Paul Strand's definition of absolute objectivity as the ultimate task of all photography, including 'artistic' photography, the postmodern photographer has in contrast shown a fascination with design. "Right now we are experiencing a plethora of photographic 'power acts' within the original medium of photography," Gottfried Jäger points out concerning the trend. He enumerates "staged works, montages, decollages, expansions of every sort that run directly and completely against the original intentions of the photographic process, and begin to undermine it, dissolve it. The picture's truth-to-reality is thus shaken and confronted with radical questions that make this 'truth' itself into the theme."

Cindy Sherman, Jeff Koons, and Teun Hocks 'stage' themselves before the camera; Joel-Peter Witkin and Joe Gantz on the other hand create narrative tableaus of sometimes shocking character. Arthur Tress and David Levinthal have meanwhile specialized in miniature stages; Calum Colvin and Victor Schrager, in still lifes. In a highly respected analysis published at the end of the 1980s, Michael Köhler comprehensively addressed these various approaches to staged photography, and brought Sandy Skoglund's work to the attention of a European audience, which in fact tended to be surprised, particularly by the fineness of the details. In America, Skoglund's work has been praised as towering over anything else being done in the pictorial field. Skoglund herself admits that her work demands much effort – not only on her part, but also on that of her viewers. "Obsession and repetition in the process of making things is one constant element in my work," the artist has noted.

Traces of the American horror film

Oscillating as it does between the witty and the ridiculous, Skoglund's œuvre has been hard to place. Critics have variously attempted to locate it somewhere between dream and nightmare, or within the art-historical tradition of Duchamp and Magritte, or under the categories of Dada and Surrealism. But strictly speaking, Skoglund's œuvre reveals the inspiration of much more trivial influences. Disneyland and the colorfulness of American West-Coast photography in general have made their mark on Skoglund. Also present are traces of the American

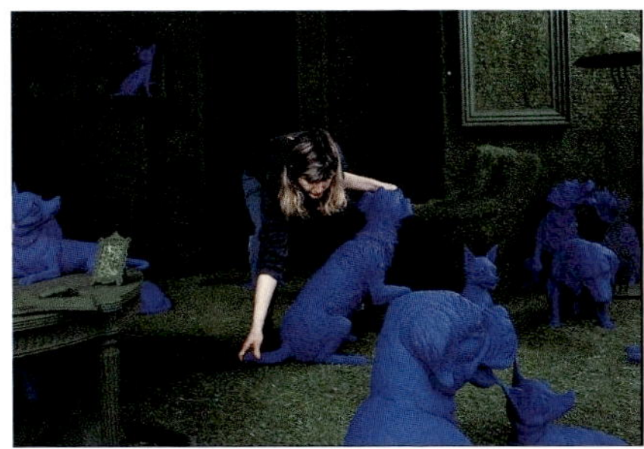

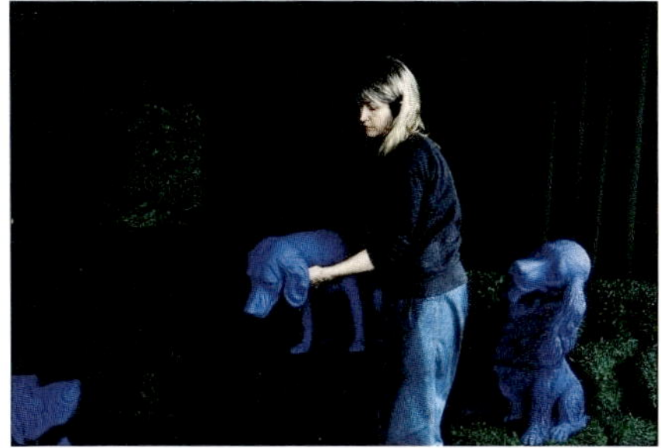

horror film and, naturally, the anxieties of middle-class America, which Skoglund handles with ironic flair. A breath of suburban *tristesse* wafts unmistakably through her work. She admits that mediocrity interests her, and "My own background is middle class, and class perceptions in terms of taste are at the root of a lot of the choices that I make."

Skoglund, the descendant of Swedish immigrants, knows what she is talking about. Born in Quincy in 1946, she grew up in California and went to school in the Midwest. 'Middle America' – the lower-middle-class under-side of the U.S. – is thus as familiar to the artist as the back of her hand. Hitchcock sent forth his flocks of gulls and crows in an attempt to crack open deadening small-town assumptions; Skoglund does the same with the cats, foxes, squirrels, and new-born babies that swarm forth to transform middle-class dreams into nightmares. Skoglund has been strongly influenced not only by American cinema, but also by European. As a nineteen-year-old art student, she spent a year in Paris, where she became fascinated by the possibilities of film. She acquainted herself with the Nouvelle Vague, watched movies by Chabrol and Godard, and flirted with the idea of film herself, but the division of work and responsibility in film-making contradicted her perfectionist impulses. Sandy Skoglund requires absolute control over every step, every detail. She ended her studies in the US, moved to New York, and took up minimalist painting. After years of searching and experimentation, she finally turned to photography. But she found herself thoroughly bored by the work of traditional masters such as Steichen, Stieglitz, or Weston – even commercial art seemed preferable to that! What she basically values in photodesign is the calculability and manipulability of the end product – the contradiction between being and seeming, reality and artificiality. Skoglund feels that turning to natural images for stimulation is deeply embedded somehow in the American culture.

With her first, full-colored still life in hand, Skoglund approached a gallerist, Marvin Heifermann, who at the time was director of photography for Castelli Graphics. In spite of his interest in color photography, he initially found the artist's work exaggeratedly shrill. Skoglund did not give up, however, and Heifermann soon found himself fascinated and genuinely amused both by the detailed realism and the eclectic content he discovered in Skoglund's photographs – everything from Walt Disney to horror films. With *Ferns* and *Radioactive Cats* at the end of the 1970s, Skoglund had in fact discovered an art strategy for herself that corresponded equally to her affinity for painting, film, and photography. Now she could successively take on the role of scriptwriter, stage designer, painter, sculptor, director, and, ultimately, photographer. "In this approach," remarks Michael Köhler, "the whole point is to use photography as an aid in presenting imaginary worlds, inventing pictures. Out of this, an interesting double-layered base is called into

***Revenge of the Goldfish,* 1981**

existence, because observers assume that what has been photographed is real, but by looking more closely, they notice that they have been fooled. This whole trend plays with this reverse, or flip-flop, effect."

Environments with unparalleled attention to detail

As mentioned earlier, Sandy Skoglund is by no means the sole exponent of staged photography, but she is the only artist who conceives, constructs, and sells her installations as works of art alongside their photographic representations. Skoglund's procedure is correspondingly exact; she is not satisfied to make a sham just for the camera, but instead creates complete environments with unparalleled attention to detail, working a half year to produce a single scene. So her work is extremely labor intensive, requiring far more effort than would be needed to produce a photograph alone. Today, viewers may respond to Skoglund's elaborate tableaus with fascination, shock, or amusement, but in the early days, her scenes chiefly elicited confusion and irritation in the art world. Diane Vanderlip, curator of the Denver Museum of Art, recalls a conversation with Lucas Samaras and Philip Tsiaras in the early 1980s in which she asked for their opinion of two of Skoglund's works. They pronounced it highly intelligent, but questioned whether it was serious art. Vanderlip let the works go; later she discovered her errors and purchased *Fox Games* for the Denver Museum of Art – at a price of $40,000.

Cindy Sherman has staked out media and cultural criticism as the special areas for her self-stagings. Skoglund, by contrast, does not pursue any similarly identifiable intention with her pictures. The artist denies that her works reflect a single intention. Nonetheless, many viewers sense a connection between *Radioactive Cats* and the debates on the atom, or interpret *The Green House* as a contribution to the discussion about the greenhouse effect, and take *Maybe Babies* as a comment on the abortion debate. According to the artist, however, similarities with contemporary problems are, so to speak, merely accidental. She defends a less narrow approach, arguing: "If the politics are open rather than closed, the piece adapts to the environment rather than the other way around." Skoglund's works appeal more to the senses than to the intellect. As an artist, she relies upon

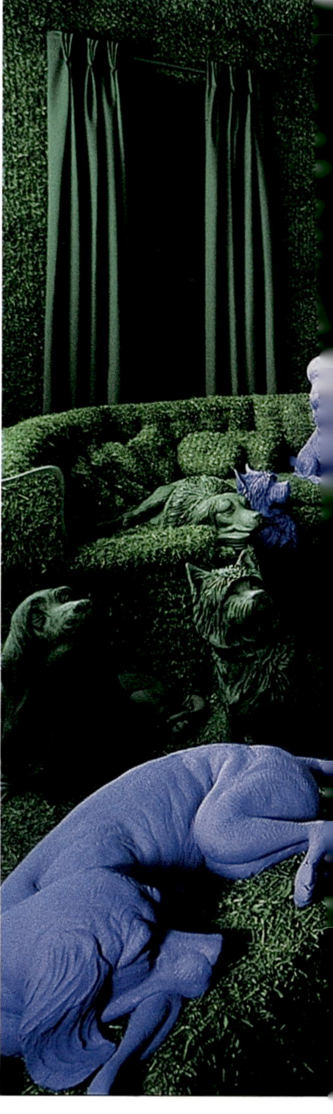

Sandy Skoglund:
The Green House © 1990.

The finished piece. Skoglund's works exist both as installations as well as on celluloid.

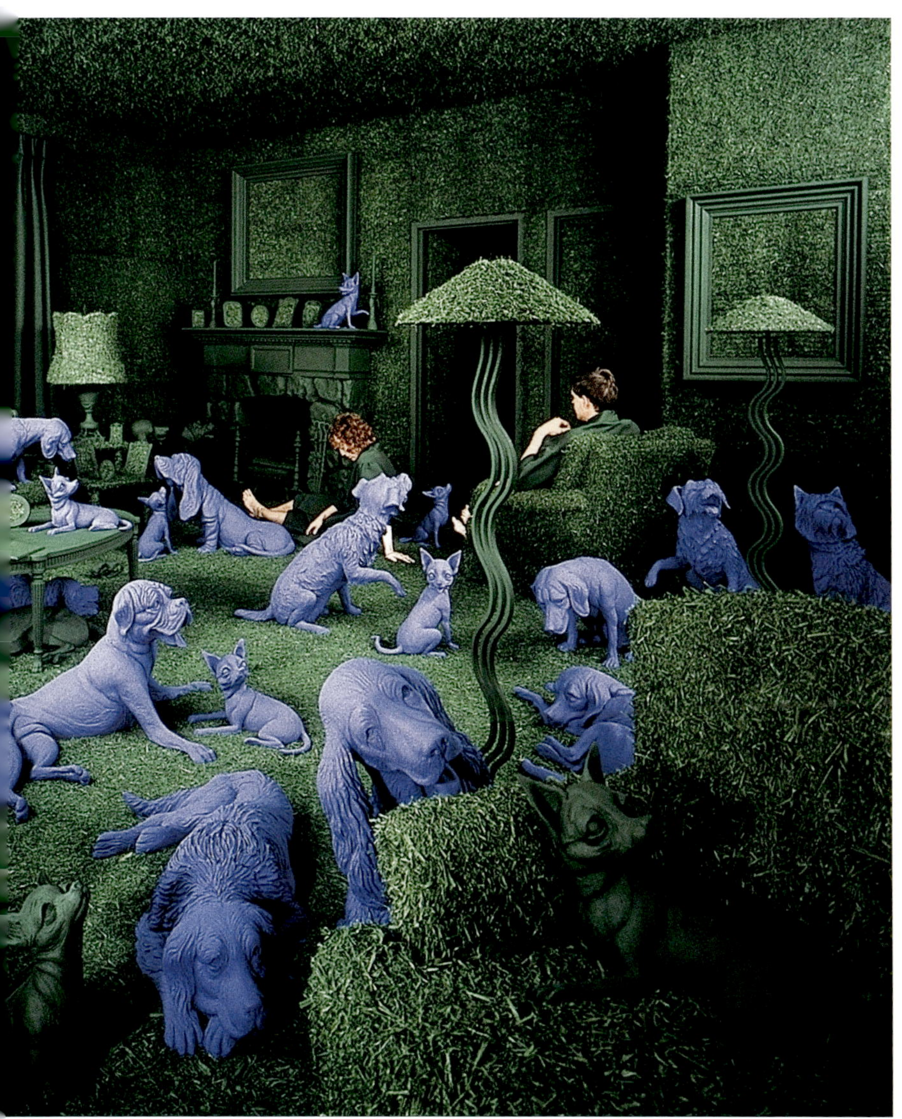

the emotional intensity of her work and finds a similarity between their effect and the manner in which Hollywood films manipulate emotions. So-called 'high art' does not interest her. In a moment of epiphany early in her career, she realized "the idea of making [conceptual] art was not a good way to approach things… Instead, I saw myself as trying to make something that my relatives could understand." This direct approach has been her trademark through the decades.

***Revenge of the Goldfish*, 1981**

Robert Mapplethorpe
Lisa Lyon
1982

Portrait of a Lady

The most-talked-about photographer of the 1980s, Robert Mapplethorpe was a belated classicist who understood how to present provocative themes in catchy visual images. After his photographic work with the New York leather scene, male nudes, and erotically charged flower studies, Mapplethorpe turned his lens on the first female world champion in body-building. The resulting cycle is probably his most comprehensive work, and at the same time constitutes an homage to the new, strong woman, who is aware of her body.

The name of the woman is Lyon. Lady Lisa Lyon. The alliteration is no accident. The same holds for the reference – at least phonetically – to the king of the beasts, for this, too, is part of a broader strategy. The young woman has a sense for effective publicity gestures. Furthermore, the physical strength of a wild animal – natural, untamed, and by no means the sole province of the male sex – has in any case always been her ideal. And it has aided her in defending women's body building when she has had to it in the face of a generally skeptical public. As she admits in 1981 in her best-selling *Lisa Lyon's Body-Building*, she feels like an animal. For her, physical signs of strength, charm, and suppleness do not have to be limited to a single sex. This association only exists in people's limited conception of things.

A new ideal of beauty

Lisa Lyon is admittedly not the first woman to take pleasure in strikingly well-developed biceps. In her book, she reminisces about the Viennese strong-woman Caterina Baumann, one of the greatest athletes in history, who was able to lift ten times her own weight in the 1920s. But it was Lisa Lyon who brought the discipline out of the ghetto of the circus, removed it from

---

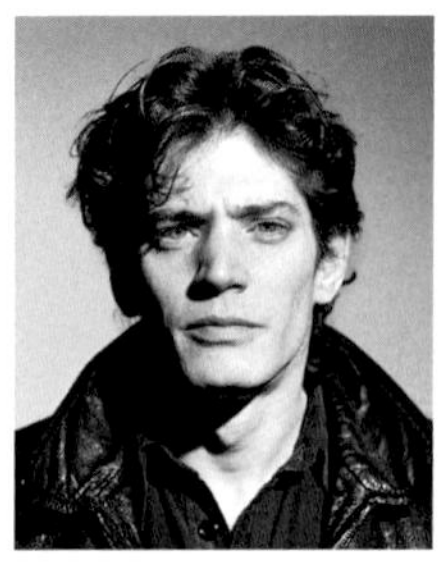

Robert Mapplethorpe
*Born **1946** in Queens, New York. **1963–69** studies fine art at the Pratt Institute, Brooklyn. From **1970** a growing interest in photography. First instant photographs. **1973** first exhibition in the New York Light Gallery. **1976** changes to square medium-format photography. **1977** included in the* documenta VI *at Kassel. **1980–83** cycle* Lisa Lyon. *Films, book projects, and exhibitions. **1988** major retrospective in the Whitney Museum of American Art in New York. In the same year the Robert Mapplethorpe Foundation is inaugurated to support AIDS research and artistic photo projects. Dies **1989** in Boston.*

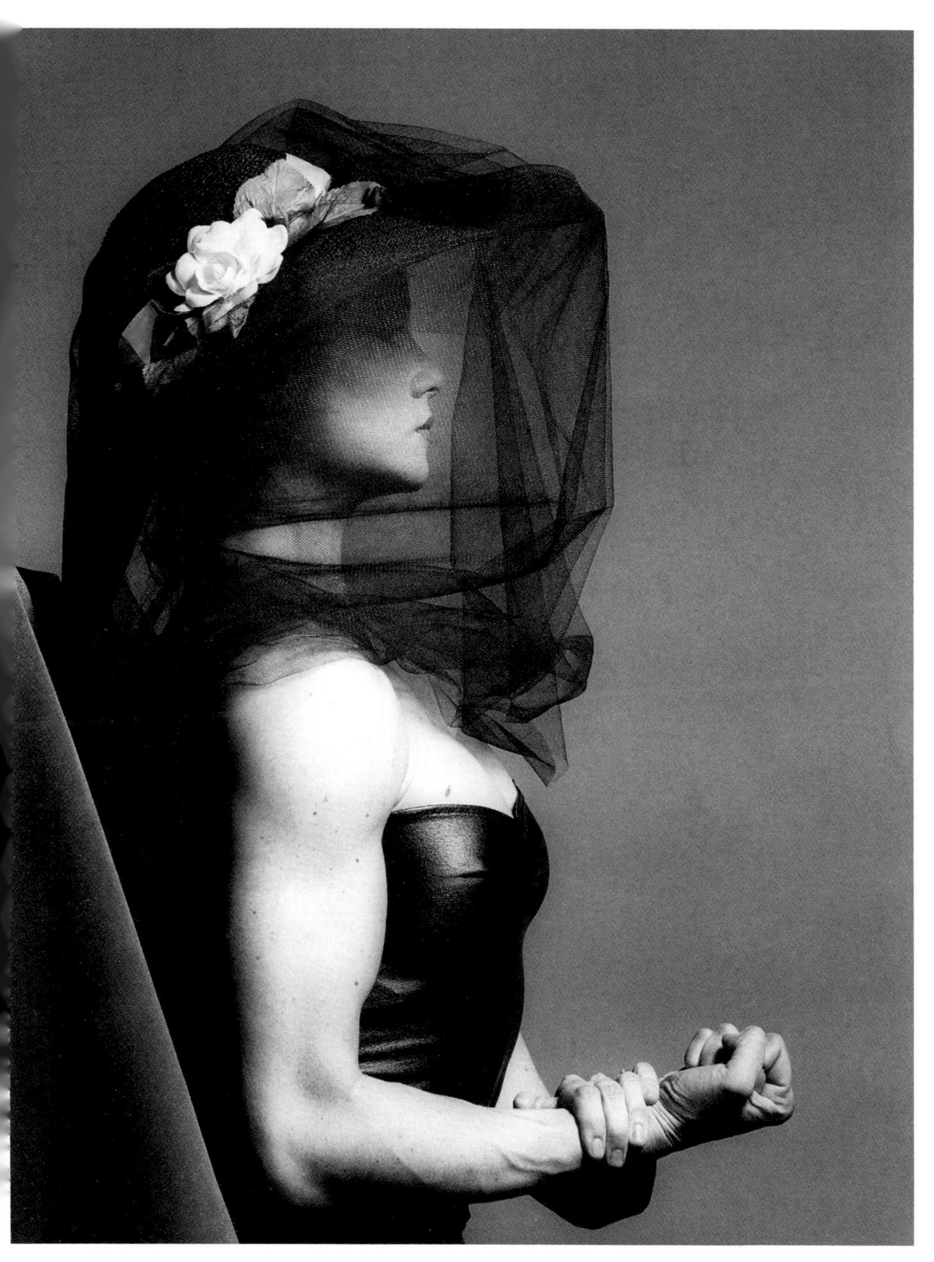

Lisa Lyon, 1982

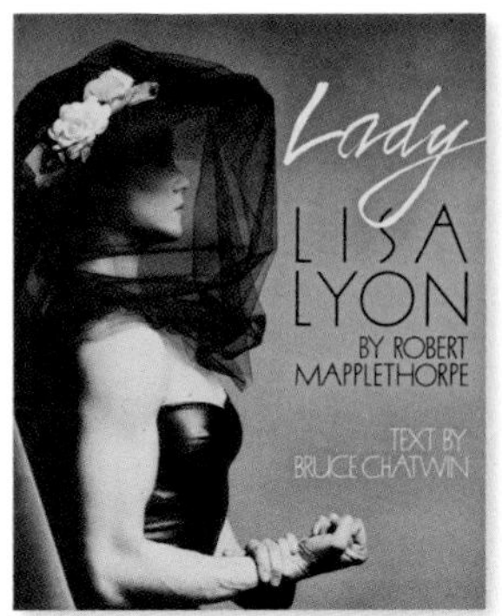

its historical niche in middle-class reform movements, and declared it to be a matter of course in the life of the 'new woman'. Her timing was unquestionably right. The utopian ideals of the 1960s were now history; the 1970s were nearing their end, and values were once again undergoing a turnover. It was a good moment to introduce a fresh concept: that of a new, physically conscious, and above all physically powerful woman, and to integrate this ideal into the developing consciousness of the 1980s. In this sense, Lisa Lyon is unmistakably a child of the Reagan era, even if at first glance her entry, armed with dumbbells, seems not precisely to coincide with the ultraconservative spirit of the times. But in the struggle for wealth and success, in the glorification of power and the fetishism of material happiness (it's no accident that *Dallas* and *Dynasty* are ruling the air-waves at this time), there was a meeting of the minds. As part of her fitness program, Lisa Lyon recommends zero tolerance towards what she designates as losers. As cynical as it may sound, the advice corresponded fairly well to the political climate of the day.

Lisa Lyon is dressed in mourning. But that doesn't signify anything – except that the creator of the picture, Robert Mapplethorpe, had been raised a Catholic and throughout his life retained an affinity with everything smacking of Catholicism. Robert Mapplethorpe is also obsessed with sex – a combination which may appear to be a self-contradiction, but on the other hand, explains his approach to his own homosexuality: an unusually long road marked by repression and denial. To claim that precisely the artist who had made homosexuality the theme of his photography at the end of the 1970s had once been a rather uptight individual is therefore not far from the truth. But Mapplethorpe, who had so many problems with his own coming-out, discovered in photography a medium for self-exploration – and applied it excessively. The cold smoothness of his emphatically formalistic photography, so well-schooled in principles of design, has made it easy to overlook this exploratory aspect of his work. His pictures give the impression of being finished pieces, at least at first glance. But they are just the opposite. His work abounds in contradictions – along with a good shot of irony – all of which indicate that his creations are in fact children of postmodernism.

Lisa Lyon, 1982. What do we see here? A young woman, perhaps in her early twenties. One could call it a profile portrait – to be more exact, a half-length portrait – but with this difference: the side-view is rather unusual within the genre of portrait photography. A traditional professional photographer would invariably choose the more flattering half- or quarter-profile, all the while giving the subject precise instructions on the direction in which to turn their gaze – above all, course, to look past the camera. But our young woman is standing or sitting with an admirably erect posture, looking straight ahead. One is almost reminded of the photographs of criminals systematically taken by the French photographer Alphonse Bertillon

---

Above: *Cover of* Lady Lisa Lyon. *The original edition of the book was published 1983 by The Viking Press, New York.*

Page 363: **Robert Mapplethorpe:** Lisa Lyon, *1982 © Copyright The Robert Mapplethorpe Foundation. Courtesy Art + Commerce.*

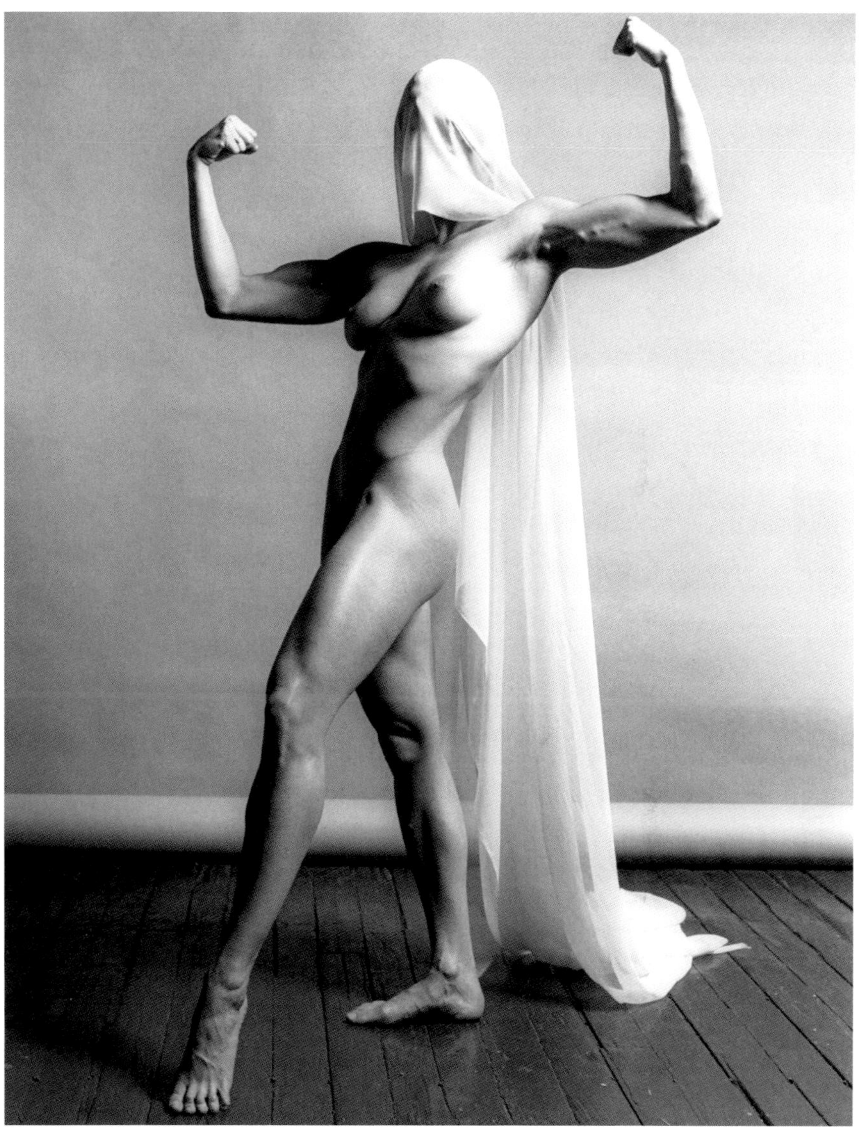

Robert Mapplethorpe:
Lady Lisa Lyon Viewed Slightly from Below. *This view point was consciously employed by the artist in order to lend heroic stature to the comparatively short athlete.*

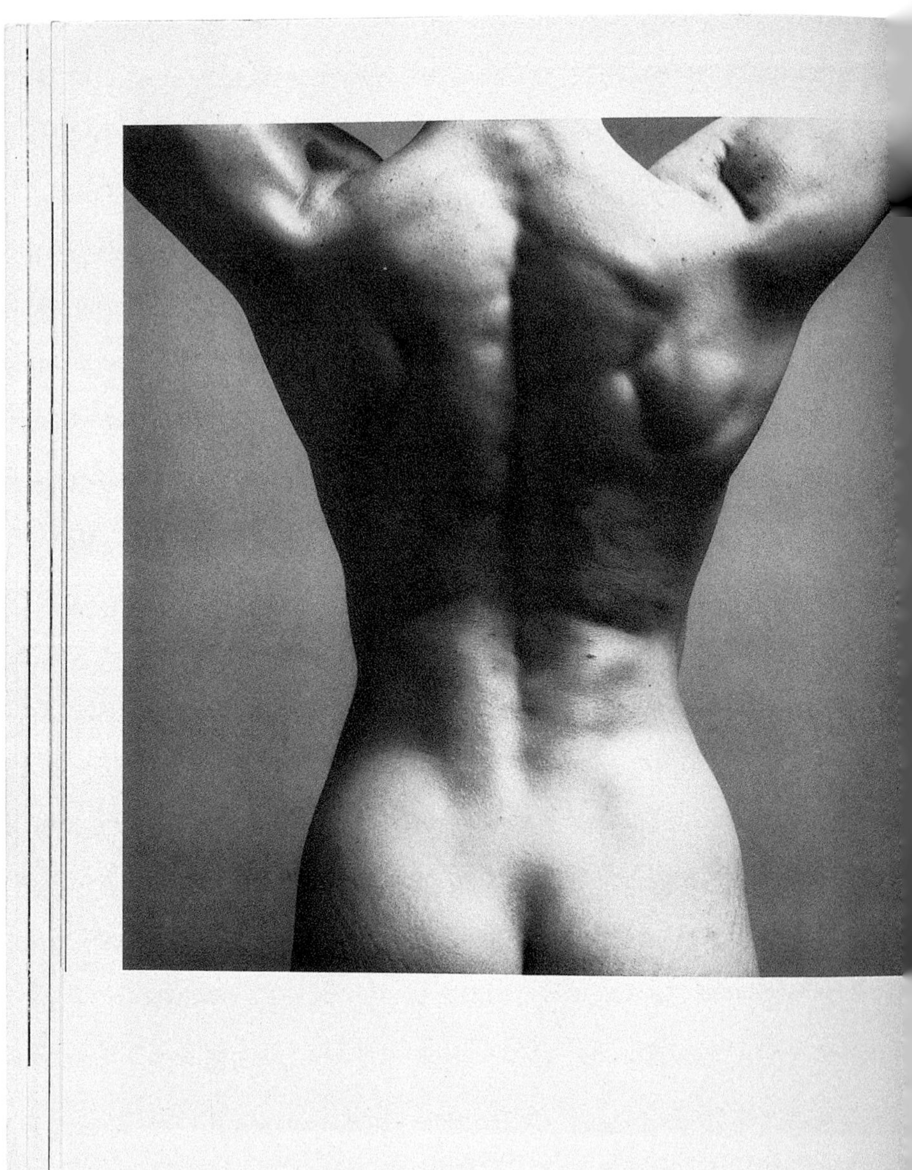

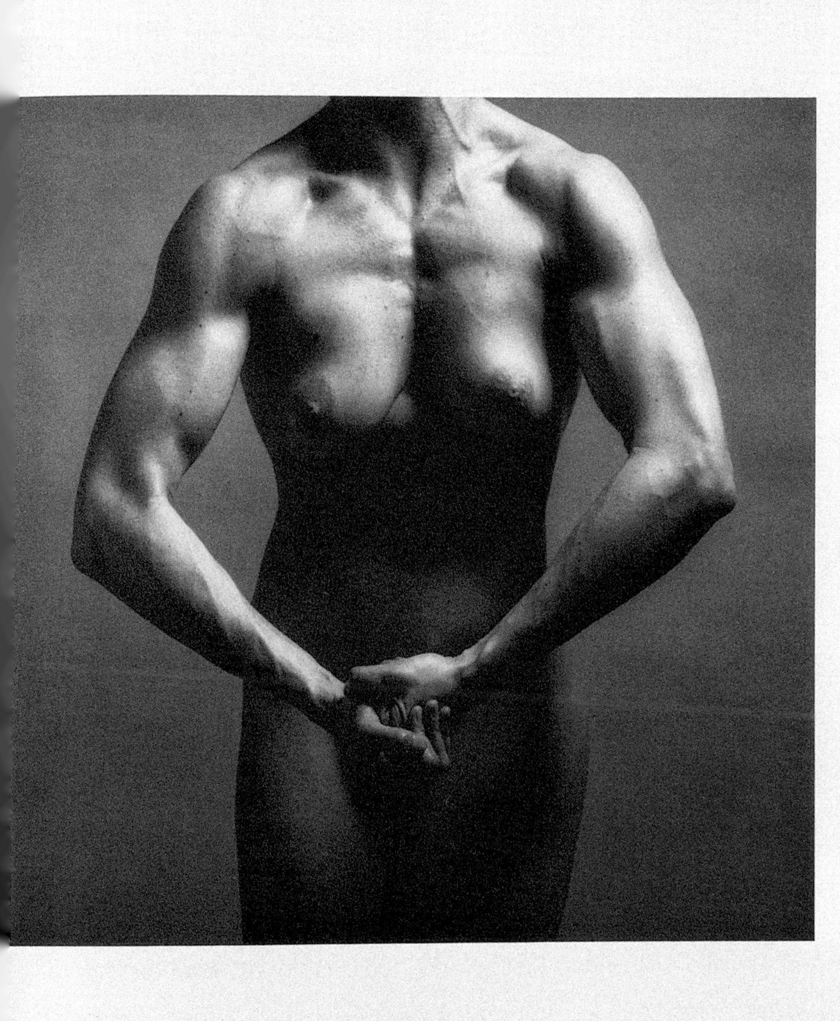

Lisa Lyon, **1982**

around 1890: his strategy for identification rested on only two exposures, one of which was precisely this 'hard' profile. The dark veil with its suggestion of sorrow, however, provides an ironic comment on this association. What we can make out under the veil is correspondingly little. For example, that the subject has carefully painted lips, and seems to be waiting without expression for whatever might come her way. That she is looking straight ahead, we have already noted – but is this really true? Hasn't she in fact closed her eyes? The veil obscures her gaze and, together with the elegant hat decorated with artificial flowers, stands in clear contradiction to the erotic appeal of the gleaming black bustier. The picture, one might say, splits into a 'serious' upper half and a less 'serious' lower half. It is the combination of the two that gives the scene its fascination. In addition, what the observer will certainly notice first and then give more attention to: the steely upper arm with its large number of unretouched moles – certainly a contradiction to the ideal of the self-confidently presented, beautifully formed body? Or can it be that these 'impurities' not only belong to the iconography of the image, but also to the ideology of a new ideal of beauty?

Someone from a different planet

Depending on the version one follows, they met for the first time in 1979 or 1980 at a party in Soho. Lyon was wearing a leather jacket and black rubber pants, an outfit that Mapplethorpe, with his unwavering interest in bizarre eroticism, could not help but notice. "Mapplethorpe," according to his biographer Patricia Morrisroe, invited her to Bond Street the following afternoon for a photo session, and she appeared at his door in a miniskirt, thigh-high leather boots, and a wide-brimmed hat decorated with feathers. He immediately responded to what was then an exotic notion – a muscle-packed woman – by photographing her in the frilly hat, flexing her biceps. Never before, as Morrisroe relates, had he seen such a woman: "It was like looking at someone from another planet."

Robert Mapplethorpe was thirty years old at the time – not yet a star, but well on his way to becoming the most internationally known photographer of the 1980s. Born in Queens, New York, in 1946, he had, so to speak, photographed his way out of his lower-middle-class background and over the rim of the New York subculture, all the way to the top – an amazing trajectory that is only partially explained by the active support of his influential friend Sam Wagstaff. With his simple but elegant, classically oriented interpretation of the 'unspeakable', Mapplethorpe had touched the nerve of the age – an era in which the emancipation of homosexuals had already advanced considerably, without the increased gay self-confidence having yet developed an appropriate aesthetic of its own. Precisely herein lies the importance, and moreover the achievement, of Robert Mapplethorpe. Certainly, there had been photographers with homosexual interests earlier; one needs only to recall Fred Holland Day, Thomas Eakins, or George Platt Lynes. The illustrations of Tom of Finland might also be considered here. But what these artists had created under cover, or at best in the context of the subculture, Robert Mapplethorpe made palatable, consumable, for wider circles, and thus moved the theme into the mainstream of art. But the protection provided by the success of

---

Pages 366–367: *Double-page spread from the book* Lady Lisa Lyon, *1983.*

his work fostered more that a broader recognition of gay eroticism. The move in the understanding of photography in the 1980s from merely a technical picture-producing medium to an art form with a place in the museums is very largely thanks to Robert Mapplethorpe. The only other artist to achieve such a strong and international reception was Mapplethorpe's original model, Andy Warhol.

The erotic force of the body

To the same extent that Mapplethorpe defined a new image of the male, who was now allowed to be black and horny, strong and beautiful, physically conscious of his body, sexy, and capable of taking pleasure in himself, he also participated in the transformation of the contemporary image of woman. The artist's black-and-white portraits of the rock poet Patti Smith, whom Mappelthorpe had lived with for an extended period at the beginning of his artistic career, provide an example. Smith's pale, elf-like being flew in the face of all standard ideals of beauty, extending from Veruschka to Raquel Welch. Mapplethorpe took numerous photographs of Smith, the most famous probably being an androgynous manifestation with unkempt hair, a white man's shirt, and tie. The record company is said to have repeatedly refused to use the photograph on the cover of Patti Smith's first record, *Horses*. Years later, when the pop music magazine *Rolling Stone* made a list of the 100 best covers of all time, *Horses* was number twenty-six on the list.

Mapplethorpe's liaison with Patti Smith had already come to an end when he met Lisa Lyon in 1979/80. For the photographer it was, so to speak, like the continuance of a fascination by other means. Where Patti Smith clearly represented the ideals of the 60s generation in her life and art, Lisa Lyon was an unmistakable product of the 1980s: ambitious, success-oriented, goal-directed and, last but not least, clever in a very pragmatic way. While still at university, the five-foot-three young woman – not precisely tall – had become acquainted with kendo, the traditional Japanese martial art. She enjoyed discovering what her body could do, testing it to its very limits, and eventually joined Gold's Gym in Los Angeles, the center of body-building in the USA – initially, in must be said, with the opposition of her male environment. Hormonal differences, so it was then assumed, would prevent a woman from developing her muscles. Furthermore, Lyon faced doubts about her perseverance. But inspired by her great example Arnold Schwarzenegger, and guided by well-known body-builders like Franco Colombo or Robbie Robinson, she threw herself into training, "rigorously counting bicep curls and leg lifts" (Morrisroe). In the evening, she trained in her apartment – taking, instead of steroids, LSD in order to "reprogram her cellular structure." In 1979, in the virtual absence of competition, Lisa Lyon won the first world championship in women's body-building; the following year, she did not even bother to enter. From this perspective, she had a short but effective career. Even before the sport had been properly born, Gaine and Butler claim in their 'bible' of heavy athletics, Lisa Lyon was not only the leading protagonist for female body-building, but also its media star, making numerous appearances on television and radio, and presciently extolling the virtues of (strong) girl-power.

Homage to the erotic power of the human body

For Robert Mapplethorpe, Lisa Lyon offered a welcome opportunity to at least balance out his image as a gay or sado-masochistic photographer. He took the first pictures in his loft at 24 Bond Street, with others to follow in an unnamed fitness studio and outdoors under the Californian sun. It is probably fitting that the Lisa Lyon cycle is considered the most comprehensive of all Mapplethorpe's works. Just how many exposures were made between 1980 and 1982 we do not know; in any case, 117 black-and-white, largely square, pictures found their way into the first volume of *Lady Lisa Lyon*, published in 1983. Some of the images are obviously drawn from the fashion photography of Horst P. Horst, others refer to the Art Deco pictorial language of Hoyningen-Huene. Borrowings are also recognizable from Weston's dune nudes as well as the early photography of the nudity movement. Mapplethorpe likes to quote. In return, his pictorial style had an influence on photodesign and on the advertising of the 1980s. Contemporary art criticism, however, looks at his work rather critically. Ulf Erdmann Ziegler speaks of "technoid pomp," A. D. Coleman of "warmed-over Pictorialism." However it may be, Mapplethorpe's work remains an expression of its time. In retrospect, his pictorial homage to the erotic force of the human/male body seems almost like a futile protest against the latter-day plague that in the end also claimed his life. Robert Mapplethorpe died of AIDS early in 1989. By then, Lisa Lyon had already long since fallen back into anonymity. Their meeting was short, but powerful – and not without results for our understanding of the being and appearance of the modern woman.

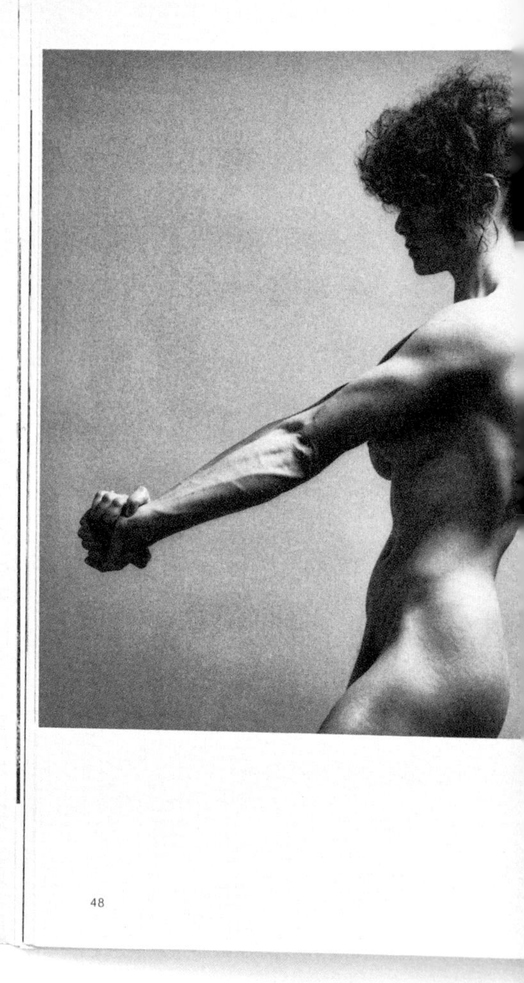

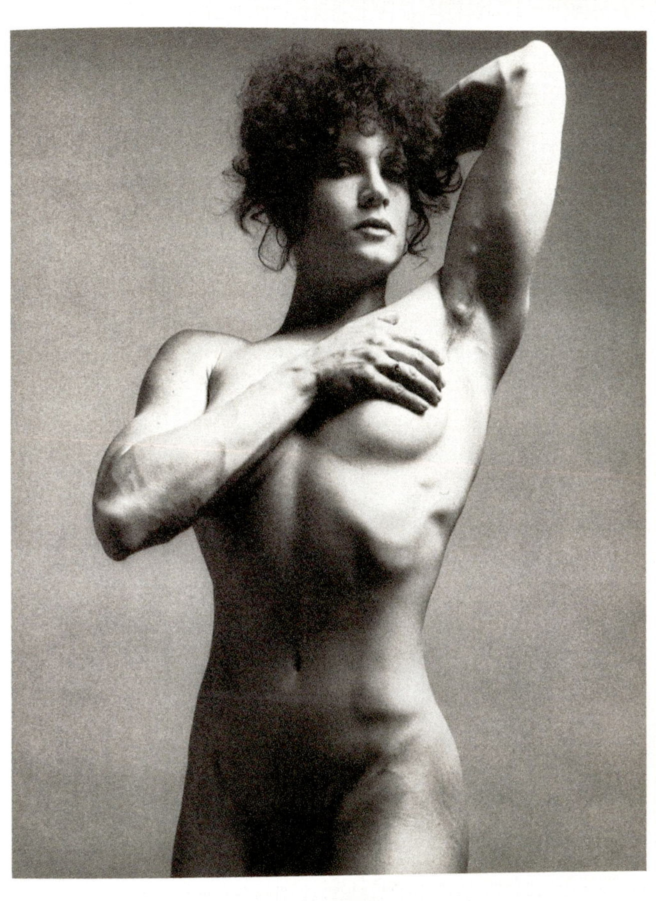

A remarkable wealth of fantasy and variety distinguishes Robert Mapplethorpe's pictures of Lisa Lyon's body, whereby he orients himself less towards the functional specifications of the body-building scene than towards earlier examples of erotic photography. Double-page spread from the first edition of Lady Lisa Lyon, *1983.*

Joel-Peter Witkin
Un Santo Oscuro
1987

A Martyr of Life

Some see his bizarre allegories as the quintessence of Western decadence and moral decline; others compare him to Goya or call him the Hieronymous Bosch of photography. No other photographer of our age has polarized both art critics and the general public more than the American artist Joel-Peter Witkin.

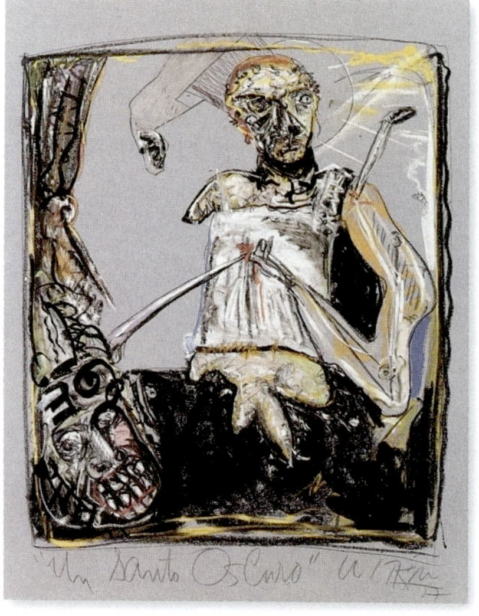

Taken unaware, the unprepared gaze finds itself looking at what seems quite unbelievable. What are we looking at? A man? A human figure? Or simply a masquerade? A nightmare from another age, or perhaps an image created by contemporary postmodernism? The uncertainties are multi-layered, resulting in alienation coupled with curiosity and a vague sense of horror.

As a rule, we are able to assign a photographic image spontaneously and confidently to a certain time frame or epoch – the nineteenth or early twentieth century, the 1950s, or a more recent date. This picture, however, seems to want to withdraw grotesquely from all temporal parameters. On the one hand, the observer has the impression that the image stems from a strange, sinister world, which has somehow left its traces on the photograph as it journeyed

---

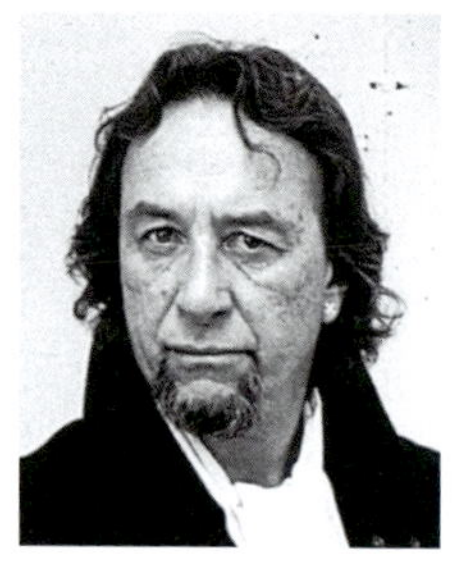

Joel-Peter Witkin

*Born **1939** in Brooklyn, New York. **1961–64** military service as war correspondent. Studies sculpture at the Cooper Union School of Fine Art. **1969** first solo show at the Moore College of Art, Philadelphia. **1975** moves to Albuquerque. **1976** studies photography at the University of New Mexico. **1984** a much acclaimed solo exhibition at Pace/MacGill, New York. **1985** publication of his first book,* Joel-Peter Witkin. *Also edits various works on the history of medical photography:* Masterpieces of Medical Photography, ***1987**, and* Harms Way, ***1994**. Lives in Albuquerque, New Mexico.*

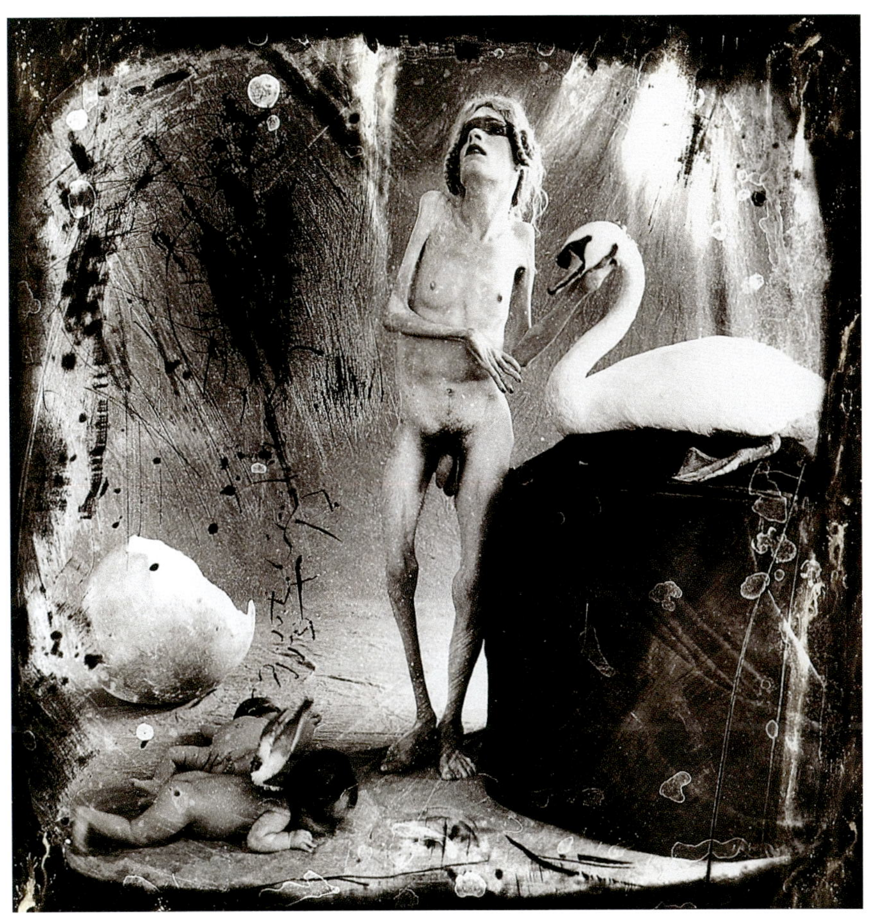

to the present: spots, scratches, a 'leap', such as one identifies with the age of the glass negative. On the other hand, the prosthesis, at least, points to the late twentieth century. Ergo, a digitally created horror vision, using the most modern technology to present a stifling variation of St. Sebastian, pierced with arrows – an image which has been a part of Christian art since the Renaissance and Baroque?

To set matters straight right from the start, the American photographer Joel-Peter Witkin does not work with a computer, but with traditional photographic means. A twin-lens Rolleiflex vintage 1960 remains his camera of choice; he uses conventional roll film, and rarely shoots more than two frames per motif. And nor does he make collages or montages. The sole way in which

Top left: **Joel-Peter Witkin:** *Sketch for* Un Santo Oscuro.

Above: **Joel-Peter Witkin:** Leda, *Los Angeles, 1986.*

he distances himself from the normal photography that takes 'straight' shots of its subjects is the way he works the negative – but more on that later. And, of course, by the way he creates scenes, a process in which he does not simply take the world as seen through the viewer, but creates rather a universe according to his pre-formulated ideas, visions, and fantasies – a cosmos rich with allusion, references, quotations – whose 'inhabitants' Witkin discovers in those places from which the proponents of more conventional ideals of beauty normally shy. And what is he interested in? Witkin unashamedly calls a spade a spade, and lists: freaks of every kind, idiots, dwarves, giants, deformations, pre-op trans-sexuals… All the people who were born without arms, legs, eyes, breasts, genitals, ears, noses, lips. All those with unusually large genitals, dominas and slaves… Recently, Witkin has added dismembered bits of corpses to his list, which he arranges in the manner of seventeenth-century Flemish still lifes – an approach which must seem incredible even to his more tolerant contemporaries – and which especially in the USA has repeatedly stirred up the ire of district attorneys and self-appointed cultural censors. Without a doubt, Joel-Peter Witkin is one of the most controversial artists of his time. But where fundamentalist preachers stamp him as a monster in front of millions of TV viewers, the art world has come to recognize him as one of the most original and profound of contemporary artists. Accordingly, the prices of his limited editions, rarely consisting of more than a dozen prints, are the highest that postmodern photography commands.

The extraordinary as part of everyday life

Anyone who looks will find that Witkin's biography gives more than enough evidence for what at first glance seems to be a morbid obsession, but which is in fact nothing more than an attempt to examine the basis of earthly existence, to take issue with categories of norms and deviations, to transgress boundaries with open eyes, in order to discover pictorially what Witkin likes to term the 'divine'.

As a child, equipped with a used Rolleicord, he once tried to photograph God: someone had told him of a rabbi who had seen God. Witkin visited the rabbi, but God remained invisible. Where was God to be found, he asked himself. In people, as the Christian message teaches? And if so, then in which people? Might it not be that God reveals himself in a special way precisely thorough those beings who are clearly different from the majority bodily or mentally? It is, in fact, philosophical-religious reflections like these which lie at the core of Joel-Peter Witkin's œuvre.

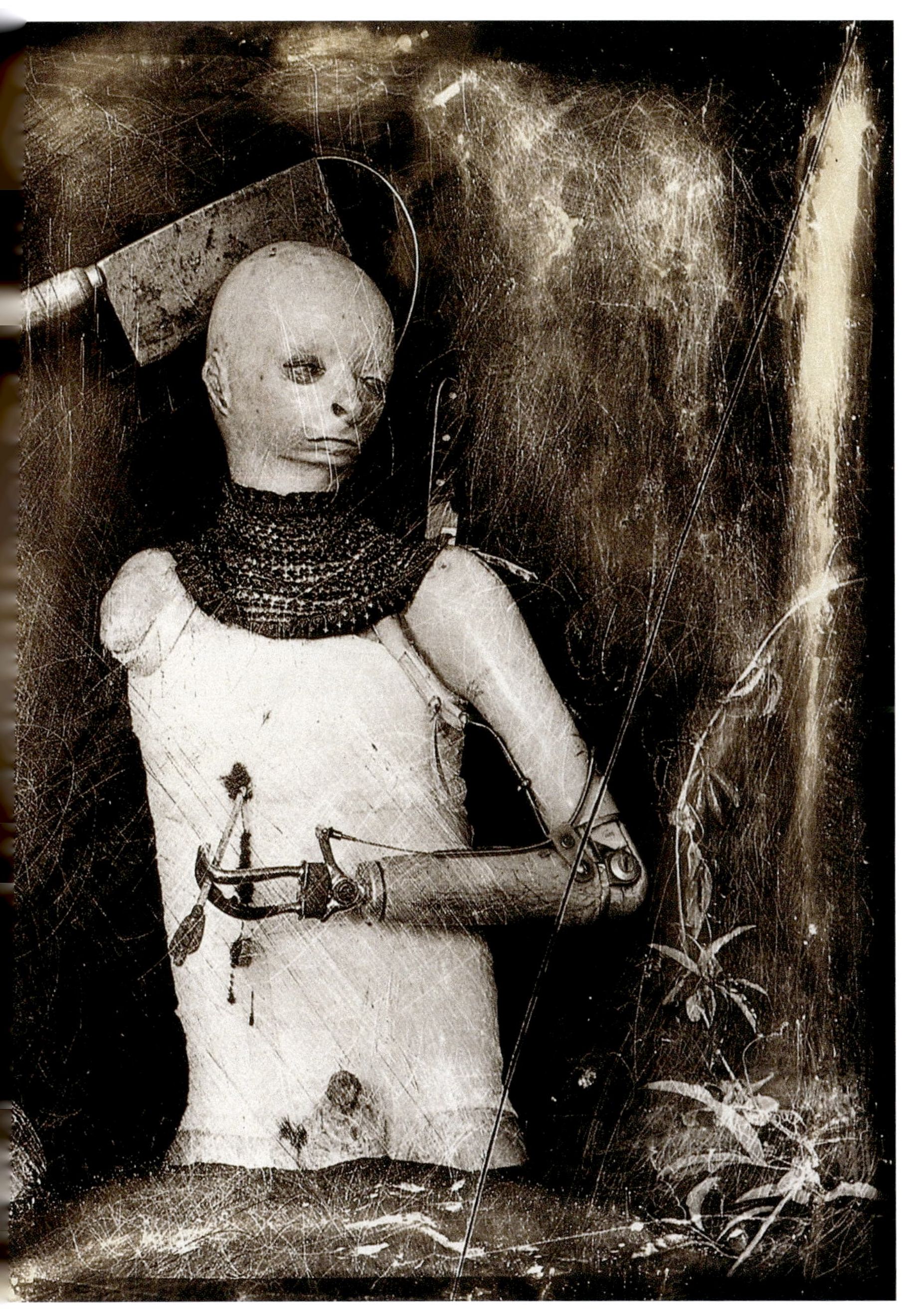

Un Santo Oscuro, 1987

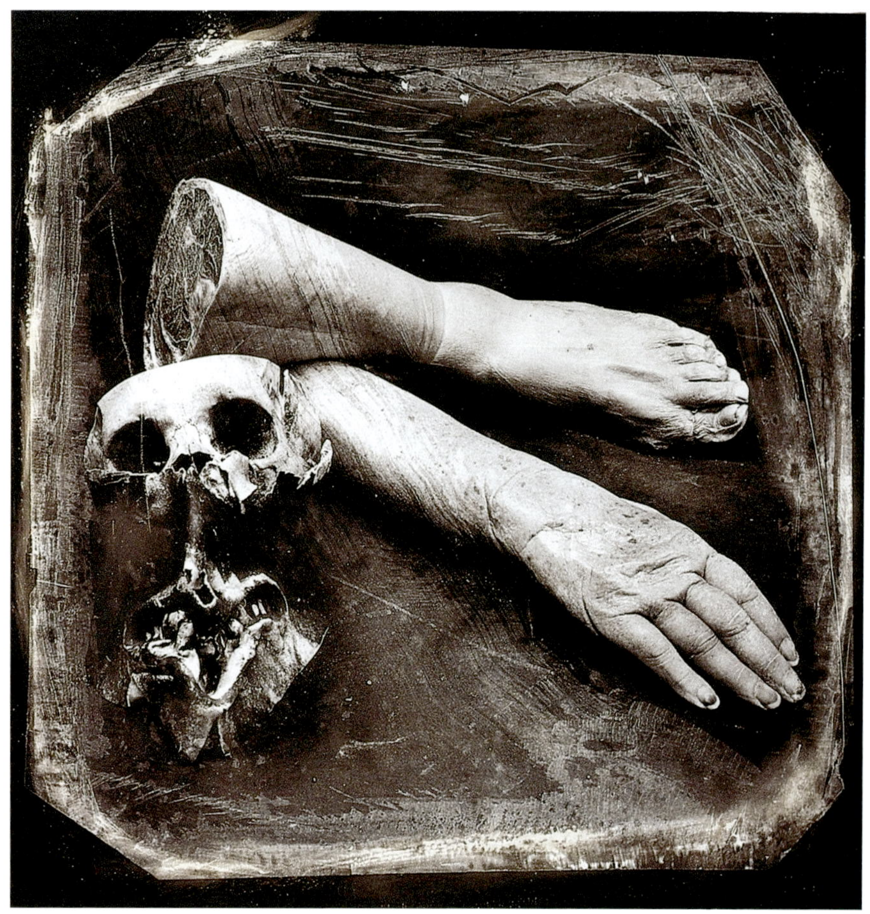

Witkin was born in Brooklyn in 1939 as the son of poor immigrants. His father was an Orthodox Russian Jew, his mother an Italian with strong Catholic beliefs – differences that were to become the primary reason for the couple's separation. Joel-Peter and his twin brothers were raised by his mother and his grandmother. "My grandmother had only one leg," Witkin recalls, "and in the morning I would wake up and smell her gangrenous leg. Where most kids would wake up and smell coffee, I would wake up and smell grandmother's rotting leg." Witkin thus became early acquainted with the strange, and the extraordinary became a natural part of everyday life. He learned to accept illness and suffering in life, of which death was also necessarily a part, even if the thought is often suppressed. "My first conscious recollection occurred

Joel-Peter Witkin: Poet: From a Collection of Relics and Ornaments (Berlin), *1986.*

when I was 6 years old. It happened on a Sunday when my mother was escorting my twin brother and me down the steps of the tenement where we lived. We were going to church. While walking through the hallway to the entrance of the building, we heard an incredible crash mixed with screaming and cries for help. The accident had involved three cars, all with families in them. Somehow, in the confusion, I was no longer holding my mother's hand. At the place where I stood at the curb, I could see something rolling from one of the overturned cars. It stopped at the curb where I stood. It was the head of a little girl. I bent down to touch the face, to ask it – but before I could touch it – someone carried me away."

His own world of personal fantasies

Already at age sixteen, Joel-Peter Witkin began taking a serious interest in photography. At the Museum of Modern Art, he introduced himself to Edward Steichen, who in fact accepted one of his pictures into the permanent exhibit. This experience motivated him to become a photographer. Witkin made a trek to Coney Island, where a freak show particularly caught his interest. He photographed the three-legged man, the 'Chicken Lady', and the hermaphrodite, with whom he claimed he had his first sexual experience. The freak show became his 'home', the true environment where his lively fantasies could play themselves out. Unfortunately, they didn't need a photographer, and nor was he a freak, for otherwise Witkin would have gone on the road with them. So he remained in New York and worked in commercial studios, while at home he began to create my own world of personal fantasies that he could photograph.

Witkin was drafted into the army in 1961, where he documented accidents that occurred on maneuver – and the fatalities they sometimes resulted in. He volunteered for Vietnam, attempted suicide, and was released from the army. He then took up studies at the Cooper Union School in New York, switching later to the University of New Mexico, where he graduated in 1981 with a Master of Fine Arts degree. By 1980, with his first one-man show curated by Sam Wagstaff in New York, Witkin became the object of passionate and controversial discussion.

Christian taboos of Eros and the body

"Witkin's philosophical/spiritual beliefs," according to Hal Fisher, "are exceptionally complex, a not particularly decipherable synthesis of Jewish cabalistic thought, Roman Catholic practice, Eastern philosophy and 1960s counterculture consciousness." Last but not least, Witkin's work can be read as an artistic revolt against both traditional Jewish iconoclasm and the Christian taboos of Eros and the body. Witkin mistrusts established norms and places them consciously in question. He even uses his own medium 'against the grain': for Witkin, recognition and understanding do not grow out of the mere duplication of reality, but only from the creation of an artificial world at whose center hermaphrodites, dwarves, cripples, Siamese twins, and amputees function as the catalysts of an expanded spiritual horizon. Probably the most common protest against Witkin's photography is that he misuses the handicapped to create a macabre spectacle. Jackie Tellalian, New York theatrical agent and lead actress in Witkin's *Woman in the Blue Hat* (1985), who is herself confined to a wheelchair, reacted to these charges saying: "I've had many people say: 'Didn't you feel exploited by that?' and I always said no, because first of all he never made me feel as though he was using my disability as a sensational aspect in the picture."

***Un Santo Oscuro*, 1987**

Others have also reacted in a similar manner, openly speaking of the humane manner in which Witkin treats them, how he makes them into the subject of his art, and thereby open to public view with full dignity, in contrast to the society which had hidden them away and pushed them aside. And in fact, in Witkin's photographic creations, deficiencies acquire a metaphysical power. "The formless and misshapen, the lowly and that which causes shudders are brought back into the light" (Germano Celant).

Created in 1987, *Un Santo Oscuro* exemplifies Witkin's artistic approach. As so often, in this case also it was a person with a physical handicap who inspired the photograph. Friends had told him about a man in a wheelchair who lacked a face and arms. On the spur of the moment, Witkin made a first draft – a scribble or sketch – of an idea. But where in Los Angeles could he possibly find the man? "With my friend," Wirkin recalls, "we went down to the area where we thought he lived. There was an old run-down hotel, and when we got inside we finally saw him, because the door was open on the room he lived in. He was asleep. What we saw was this kind of plastic head, this little body, and we didn't want to disturb him. It was our conviction that we had to wait for other people to arrive, and sure enough they did. Two men actually arrived to take care of him. We got into the room and talked. We found out from our conversation that this man was a Thalidomide victim. He was Canadian. His mother took Thalidomide, and he was born without skin, without arms or legs, without hair, eyelashes or eyelids. Early on, from the time he was a child, he was the subject of ridicule and curiosity and wanted by side-shows and freak-shows. I talked about how I wanted to photograph him. I wanted to photograph him as clerics would have been depicted, mostly in seventeenth and eighteenth-century Spain, as martyrs, and I told this man that he was a martyr to life."

A popular subject for religious painting commissions

Joel-Peter Witkin's photographs are the result of elaborate staging in the studio, during which an interior image, a vision, finds its outward expression. Often works of the great masters – Velásquez, Cimabue, Giotto, Rembrandt, Arcimboldo, Picasso, Goya, Delacroix – stand at the start of Witkin's artistic creations. Without hesitation, he reaches back to myths, fairy tales, the traditions of western art history, all of which he seems to know well. The titles of works like *Sander's Wife, Courbet in Rejlander's Pool*, or *Von Gloeden in Asia* make the sources of his inspiration clear. In addition to painting and graphics, the photography of Ernest James Bellocq, Eadweard J. Muybridge, and Charles Nègre also provided stimulation. *Un Santo Oscuro*, however, does not draw from a particular individual picture, but rather from a pictorial genre that was a popular subject for religious painting commissions, in particular during the Spanish Baroque. Priests appeared in the pose of honored saints in order to increase their own power by association, their social position, and their clerical aura. What remained a mere travesty, however, in the historical panel painting, Witkin creates from real earthly torture. "Instead of a voluntary, playful masochism, Witkin cites real pain" (Chris Townsend).

The darkroom becomes a sanctum

Witkin may arrange his scenes, but he does not manipulate his pictures. The photographs are called into being without any technical tricks; they are therefore 'straight'. All the elements of the given scene are components of an often slowly and painstakingly arranged ensemble. Only later is the negative reworked to acquire the patina that gives Witkin's pictures the aura

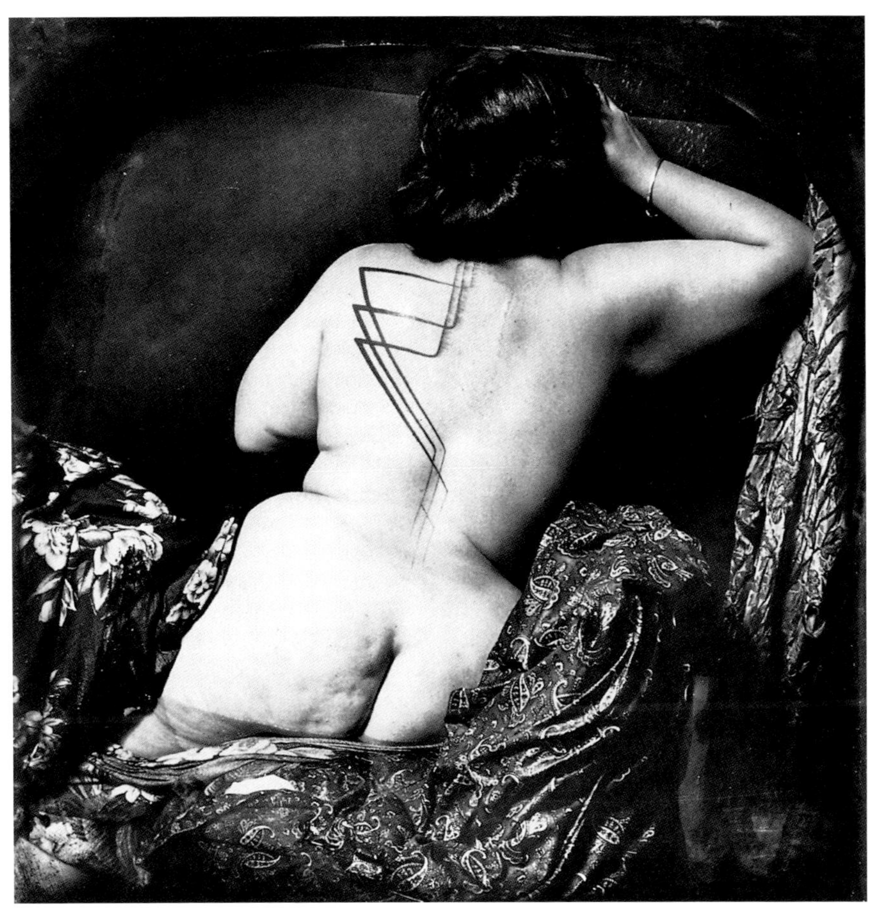

of being withdrawn from time. In the author's own description, he becomes a kind of priest of aesthetics. "I work alone during printing and begin by communicating with my equipment and chemistry, thanking them in advance. I place a negative in the enlarger and the darkroom becomes a kind of holy house, a refuge for phenomena..." By changing the texture of the picture, Witkin effectively moves it in time and space. As if through a hidden crack, we catch a glimpse into a strange cabinet. Witkin's pictures, as the writer Ludwig Fels states, are "Witnesses of a profound spirituality that creates from archaic sources." Witkin's art takes up the basic categories of human existence: love and pain, joy and suffering, Eros and Thanatos. He is the philosopher among the photographers of our age.

Joel-Peter Witkin:
Courbet in Rejlander's Pool, *1985.*

Sebastião Salgado
Kuwait
1991

Apocalypse in Oil

Saddam Hussein's troops were defeated, but Kuwait is in flames: the Iraqis set approximately 900 oil wells on fire. Now international specialists are trying to extinguish the fire. Sebastião Salgado observed them – labor heroes in an age of automation.

Like every well-made play, this drama too has three acts, and we find ourselves at the beginning of the third. No one knows how it will end. It's April 1991. The man who staged it left the ending open – with an option for a *Götterdämmerung.* Dictators seem to like binding their personal finale to a universal apocalypse. Saddam Hussein remains, as before, in power. Somewhere beneath Baghdad, he's holed up in a bunker built by German or British or American specialists. And this is not the only cynical aspect of a conflict that will go down in the annals of the 1990s as the Gulf War, and that will cost an estimated hundred to hundred and fifty thousand lives before it's over. Much of Iraq was destroyed. The newest technical weapons – cluster bombs, smart bombs, and cruise missiles – threw the cradle of Middle Eastern culture back to the Middle Ages. But beyond this, the war changed little, if we take Saddam's attack on Kuwait on 2 August 1990 as its starting point. It has certainly brought about no changes in the map, nor in the tendency of human beings to turn to violence in settling disputes, nor even in the balance of power in the region. Saddam was weakened, but he's not yet been banished to oblivion, as America's president George Bush would gladly see, without knowing precisely who he would set up in Saddam's place. And the Kuwaiti rulers are also back on their old thrones as if nothing had happened. Apart from which, the balance stands at 138 dead and 66 listed missing on the side of the Allied forces – along with a series of new experiences. For example: in the psychology of conducting a war. Or in the way the military

---

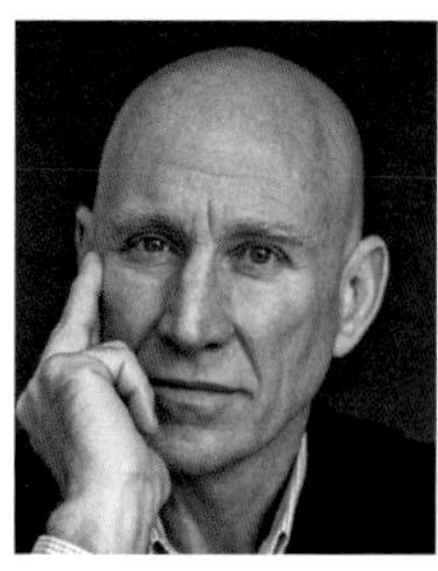

Sebastião Salgado
*Born in **1944** in Aimorés, Brazil. **1964–67** studies economics at Vitoria, Brazil. **1968** employed at the Brazilian Ministry of Economic Affairs. **1969** Research studies in Paris. **1971–73** works from London for the International Coffee Organisation. Turns to photography. **1973** reports on the Sahel zone begin his international acclaim. **1974** member of Sygma. **1975** changes to Gamma. **1979–94** member of Magnum. Subsequently sets up his own agency (Amazonas Images). Numerous prizes, including **1985** and **1992** Oskar Barnack Prize, **1988** Dr. Erich Salomon Prize, and **1989** Hasselblad Prize. **2019** Peace Prize of the German Book Trade. Dies **2025** in Paris.*

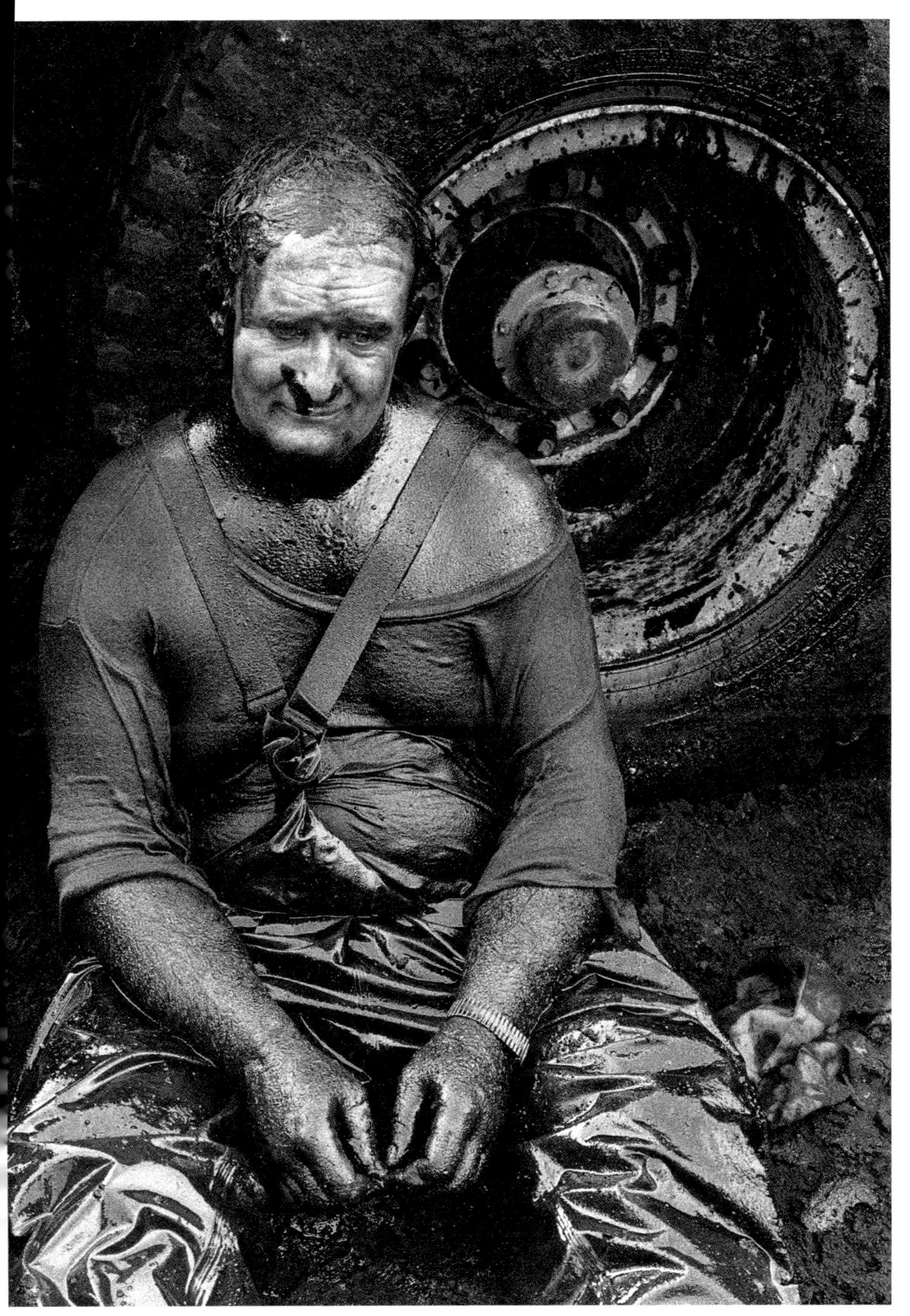

Kuwait, 1991

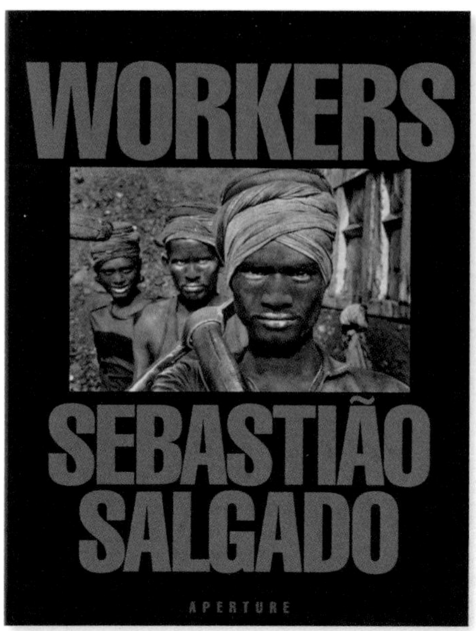

deals with the media. Or in the question how one gets the upper hand over almost 1,000 burning oil wells.

On 28 February, after exactly 210 days of combat, the Gulf War comes to an end – at least the military part of the drama. Saddam's troops more or less withdrew from Kuwait, but not before fulfilling the threat the Iraqi dictator had made from the beginning, namely, "to set the whole region, including the oil fields, on fire." Before the war, Kuwait had the world's highest average income; its oil reserves, the third-largest in the world, overflowed, creating prosperity for the approximately one million Kuwaitis. Now the liquid gold was in flames: the advancing Allied troops were greeted by a single vast inferno. The German news magazine *Der Spiegel* was moved to comparison with the Bible to describe the extent of the catastrophe: the destruction of Sodom and Gomorra, so it seemed, could now be assigned a date, namely March–April 1991. Everything was on fire. At least nine hundred of the once wealth-producing oil wells – pessimists spoke of up to a thousand torches in the desert sands – were burning up to a height of nearly 300 meters (1,000 feet). A cloud of soot and smoke darkened the heavens, causing a decline in temperatures throughout the Gulf region. In Kashmir, nearly 2,700 kilometers (1,700 miles) away, black snow was falling; in the deserts and savannas of East Africa, dirty rain. A natural catastrophe of unimagined dimensions seemed to be approaching. Scientists prognosticated abnormal weather patterns and questioned whether India would still receive its critical monsoon rains. If not, the result would be hundreds of thousands of deaths by famine on the subcontinent. Health risks were discussed, including possible delayed reactions after people had breathed in the poisonous soot particles. By the middle of the year, according to the estimates, forty million tons of raw oil had been burned, releasing two hundred and fifty thousand tons of nitrous oxide into the atmosphere, along with thirty millions tons of carbon dioxide. And no end of the catastrophe was in sight. Asked by the German magazine *Stern* in early 1991 whether all of the Kuwaiti oil fires could be extinguished within a half year, the American fire expert Paul Neal Adair, nicknamed 'Red', had a simple answer: "Nonsense." Cautious estimates reckoned two to three years would be needed. Even more skeptical was Ali Qabudi of the Kuwait Oil Company at the end of March, who spoke of a worst-case scenario of ten years before all the fires were extinguished.

Cover of Workers. An Archeology of the Industrial Age, *probably Salgado's most important book. It was originally published in 1993 by Aperture in New York.*

Additional problems in extinguishing the fires

What made the situation so difficult was not merely the number of fires. The area had been studded with mines, which greatly restricted the mobility of the fire-fighting troops who had been sent to the region. Furthermore, the oil flowed from the Kuwaiti wells under natural pressure. The force which had once made it easy to obtain the raw material now caused additional problems in extinguishing the fires. In addition, there was the problem of the proximity of the burning wells to each other: some were less than a mile apart. This concentration increased the temperatures to infernal levels, causing the desert sand to turn to glass. Red Adair joked that they had not even brought a thermometer along with them, because if they knew how hot it really was, no one would stay there to work. Texas-born Red Adair is already a legend among fire-fighters, "the most famous fireman in the world" (*Stern*). His specialty is blowing out burning shafts with a carefully placed load of dynamite, but Kuwait seems to be more than even an expert can handle. In the end, other teams from the USA and Canada, Romania, Italy, France, China, Hungary, Iran, and Russia also arrive to help solve the problem – attracted naturally by the impressive rewards that are being offered. And they try everything – every conceivable idea or plan – for time is money. Three million barrels – that is, ten per cent of the world's daily oil consumption – is going up in flames every day; which in turn means a forty-three billion dollar loss in two years for the Kuwait oil industry. "Big job, big money," as Red Adair succinctly phrases it. In other words: no matter how much it costs, the work of his team will not be too expensive for the country. After all, as he and his co-workers realize – and only for this reason are they willing to face these hellish temperatures – every one of them will return home a millionaire. That is, those who return home at all – for, as the *Spiegel* emphasizes, "the work is fraught with mortal danger."

An inferno of oil and mud, heat and gas

A man is taking a break. Possibly waiting for supplies. As reported by the western media, there's not enough of anything here. Not enough water for extinguishing and cooling – instead, it must be pumped for miles through pipelines from the sea. Not enough specialized equipment and machines, nor welding gear and bore heads. Red Adair speaks of a Mickey Mouse job, a remark which sounds like a bad joke. But he doesn't mean it comically. The issue is survival: for the firefighters on the job, for the country, for the region. There's nothing funny about it. And if we think we see something like a smile on the face of the man in the picture, then it arises more likely from complete exhaustion than from any sort of amusement. The worker is clearly at the end of his strength. Kaput. Dreaming of nothing as he stares into space – minutes of regeneration amid an inferno of oil and mud, heat and gas, soot and stench. He is covered from head to toe in slippery oil. Anyone who worked on an automobile will wonder how he will ever get himself clean again. But it's even worse, for he stands under this shower of oil every day. The observer's response to such a filthy layer of oil might be disgust. But here the opposite is the case. What we are looking at is an anonymous labor hero – no ordinary human being, but an icon: not a mere 'hand', but a monument, cast in bronze for eternity.

With the passion of an adherent of liberation theology

Sebastião Salgado is a specialist in icons. Whatever he photographs becomes a formula for pathos. His pictures – always in black and white – are well-composed, suggestive, direct, and believable in their depiction of the world's misery. Salgado is a master at making the

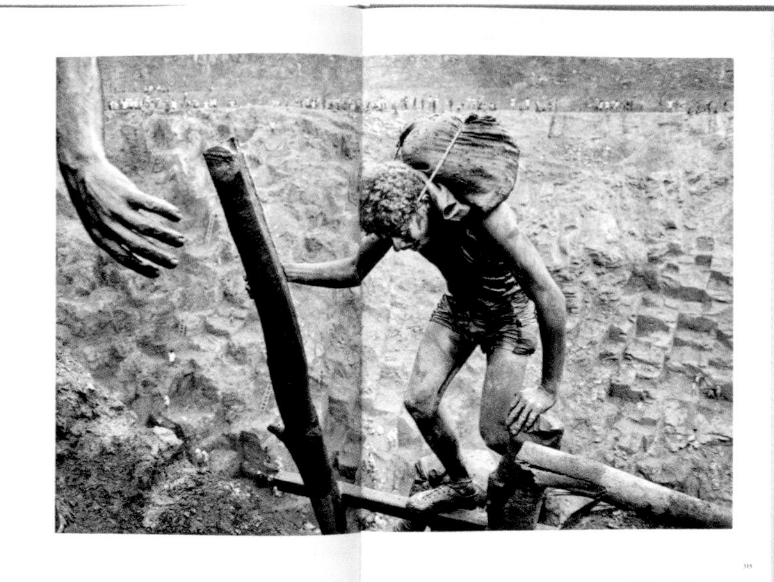

frightening into something beautiful, and as a result is certainly one of the most admired international photographer today. In terms of his influence on present-day photojournalism – his function as a role model – one can designate him justly as the most important camera artist of the times – a kind of Cartier-Bresson of the late twentieth century. But whereas Cartier-Bresson approached his work with the knife-sharp calculation of the Constructivists, Salgado pursues the emotions. Compared to what one finds in the sensational press, his pictures do not look spectacular; rather, their effect lies in the manner in which they lift up an event. Every one of his photographs thus becomes something special: "Their pathos," says the *Zeit* author Peter Sager, "their elegiac gesture derives from the subject itself, but also from the way it is presented. Mother-and-child groups, scenes of passion, masses of people caught up in a great movement – such pictures narrate biblical stories, and Salgado quotes them with the passion of a Marxist-oriented adherent of liberation theology."

Salgado sees himself as a documentary photographer, and he can celebrate his success not only in the illustrated press throughout the world, but also in the realm of galleries and museums – a unique and much admired triumph in the world of photography. It's sometimes said that he aestheticizes suffering, that he exploits the misery of others for the sake of his art. But one thing is certain. There are few who got as close as he, and with such an alert and interested eye, to misery. Salgado, as the writer Márcio Souza points out, brought a completely new element to photography, one which is perhaps traceable to his Brazilian origins: namely, the complete absence of a bad conscience in relation to poverty, suffering, and social injustice. This does not mean, however, that Salgado feels no sympathy for what he sees. What distinguishes him from others is his attitude toward those he photographs. As oil engineer Dave

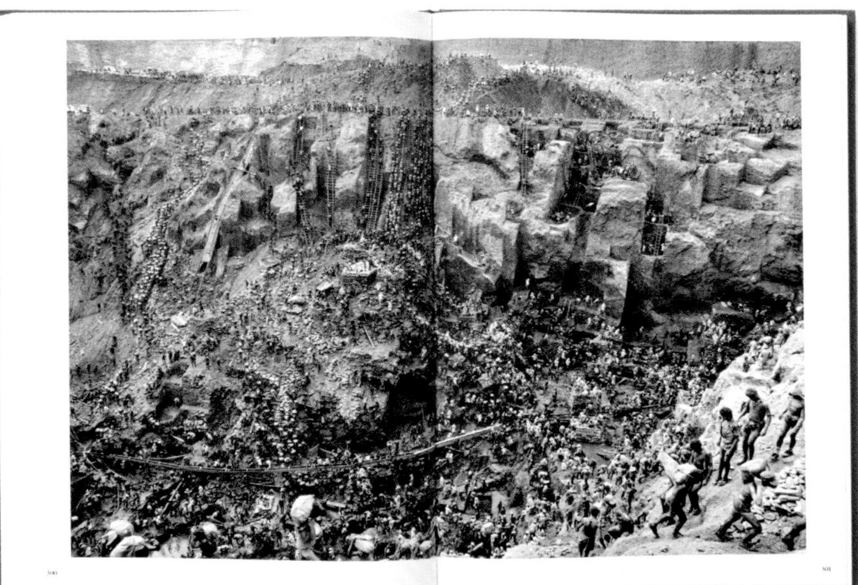

Wilson puts it: "It's kind of an aggressive act to take someone's picture. Somehow or other, he melts all that away."

Salgado was born in 1944 in southwestern Brazil, the only boy in a family of eight children. He studied in São Paulo and Paris, and seemed to be headed for a career with the World Bank. But then, almost overnight, he changed his mind. Inspired by the engagement of photographers such as Lewis W. Hine and Dorothea Lange, Salgado took up the camera and set out for Africa to document the famine in the desert regions of the Sahel. That Salgado was the photographer who caught the attempted assassination of Reagan in 1981 seems today to be almost a mistake, for Salgado – the global player with a touch of Marx – is primarily interested in the Third World. At the core of his engagement stand the peoples of Latin America, Asia, and Africa, or the International Union of Manual Workers, about whom he was working on a major cycle since 1980, calling his project on the dignity of labor simply *Workers*. According to Salgado, he is not necessarily directing criticism at a certain development, but rather trying to "portray the disappearance of the community of laborers."

This is not his first excursion into the Near East. At the end of the 1980s, he had accompanied a troop of Iraqi military actors at the front during the war between Iraq and Iran. Western media had actually been denied access to the war, but on occasion a Brazilian passport can have its advantages.

Above and pages 386–389: *Double-page spreads from Salgado's book* Workers, *1993.*

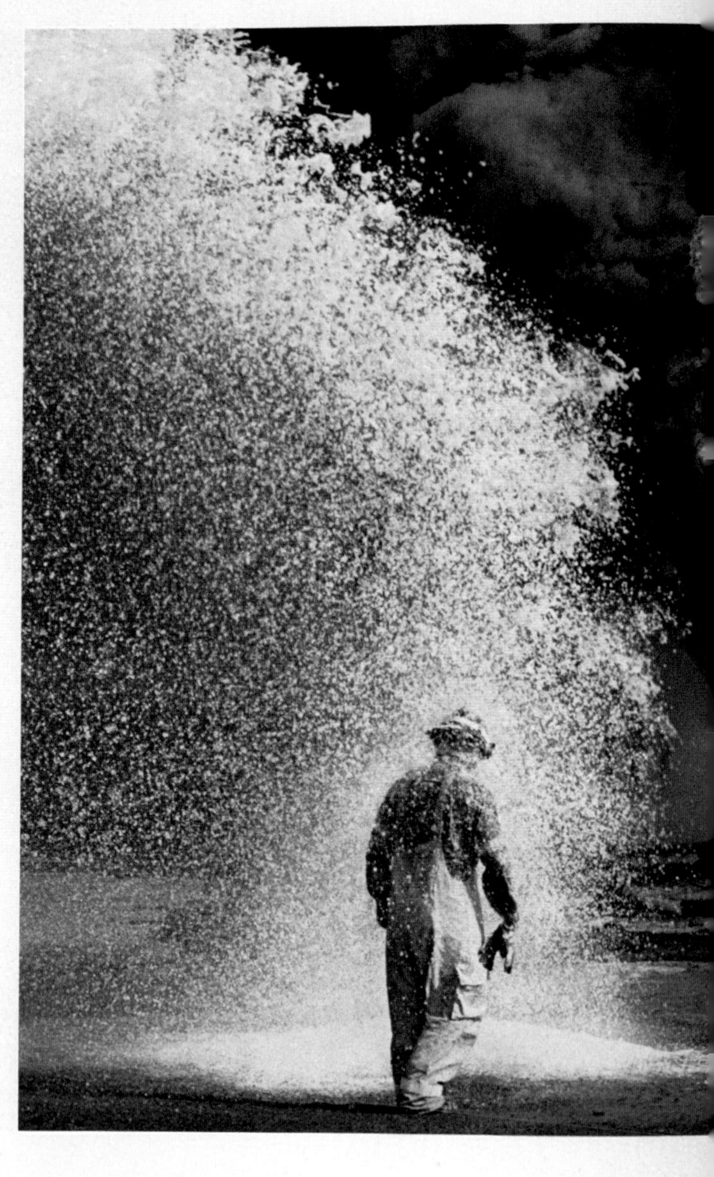

336

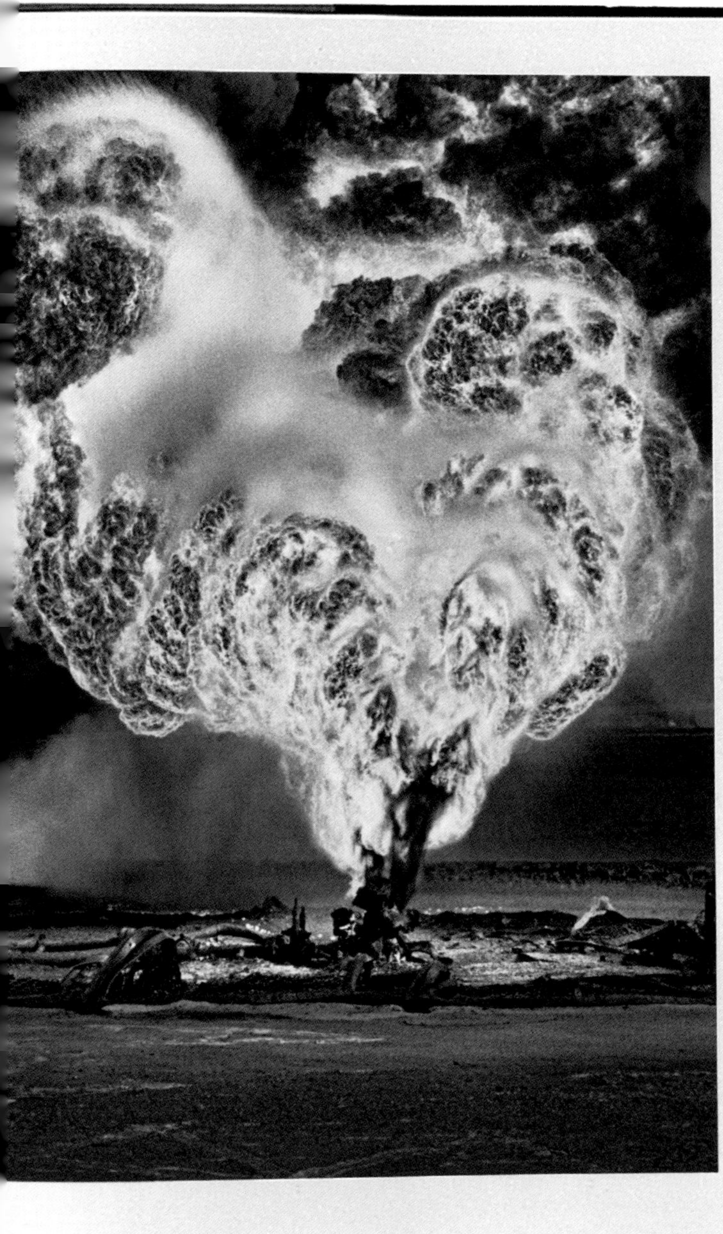

Kuwait, 1991

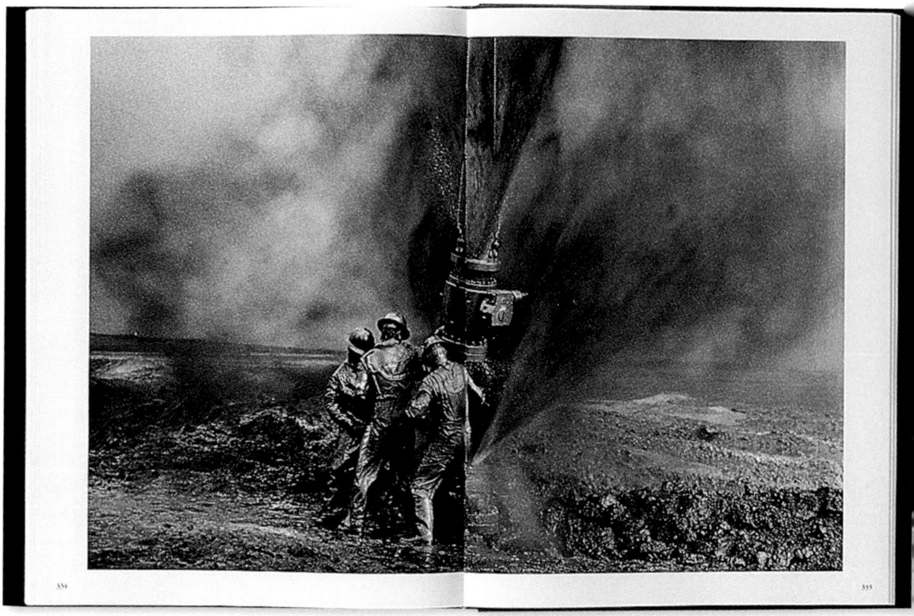

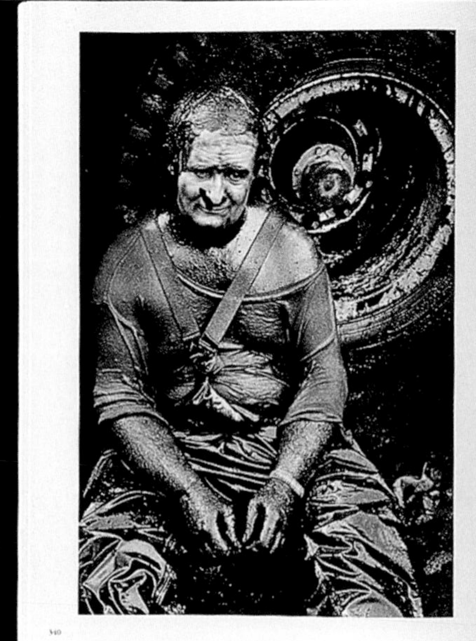

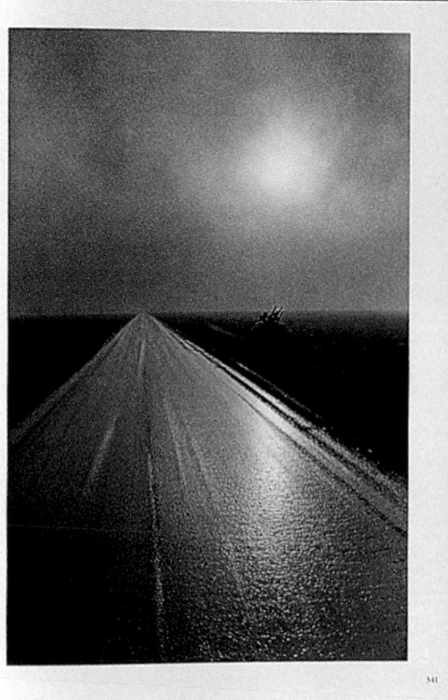

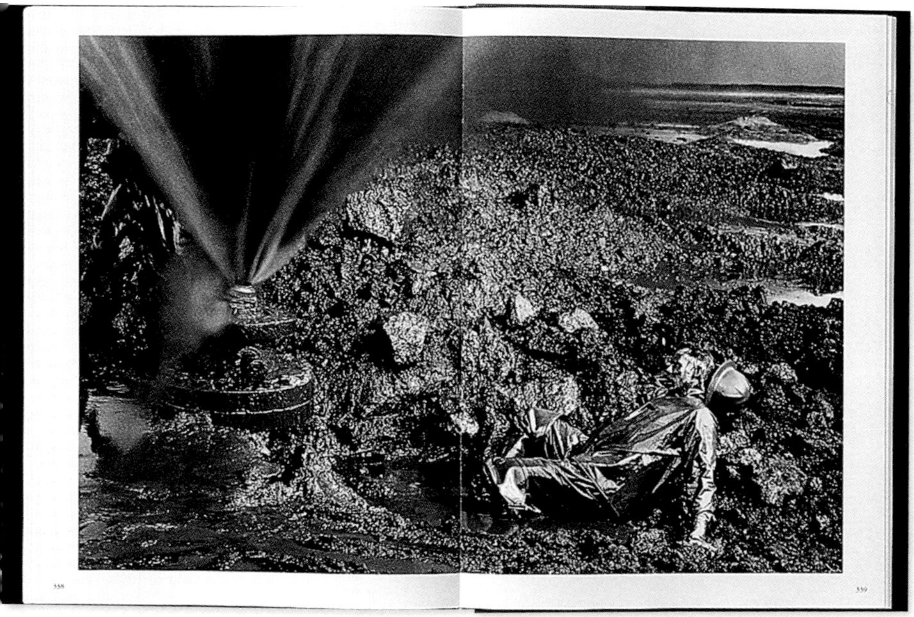

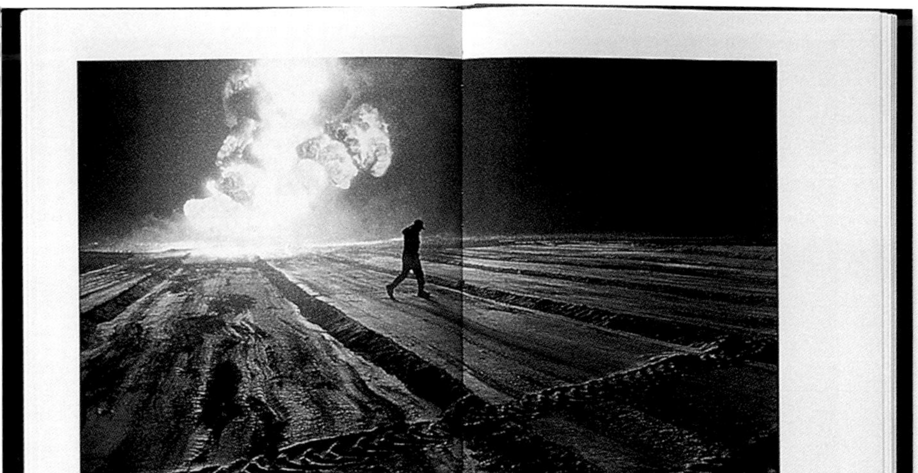

Kuwait, 1991

On average twelve rolls of film per day

Here, in the midst of the burning oil fields, Salgado is of course not the only reporter. Stephane Compoint is present, and will eventually receive a photography prize for his work. Also the Magnum photographer Bruno Barbey is on the scene, as well as the photographers Steve McCurry (*National Geographic*) and Peter Menzel (*Stern*). What distinguishes Salgado from the others, though, is that he photographs in black and white. Equipped with three Leicas and 28-mm, 35-mm, and 60-mm lenses, he shoots on average twelve rolls per day. In Kuwait, he made approximately seven thousand exposures, from which six per roll are processed as work prints. On average he presents fifty photographs to magazines, who then make their selections. Salgado's report, with the working title *Oil Wells* appeared for the first time in the *New York Times Magazine* on 9 June 1991 under the title *The Eye of the Photojournalist*. The *Spiegel* published several samples of his work in issue 24 of the same year (10 June). In the World Press Contest, Salgado's work secured him the Oskar Barnack Prize. And the Kuwait cycle is also represented in his thematically oriented book *Workers: An Archaeology of the Industrial Age* (1993): our picture occurs as a full-page print on page 340.

At the beginning of November 1991, against all expectations, the last fire in Kuwait was extinguished. Red Adair and his workers, the gang from Boots & Coots, Wild Well Control, and Safety Boss returned to their various homes. In the meantime, the catastrophe became history, and as such, is (almost) forgotten. What still remains are the photographs by Sebastião Salgado: icons that transcend time, made not for the daily press, but for the collective pictorial memory. Salgado's pictures are a visualized Bible which extol the core of all that we find human. This is why his pictures are understood – and treasured – around the world.

Sebastiao Salgado:
Kuwait. A Desert on Fire, *TASCHEN, Cologne, 2016. The abstractive power of classic black-and-white photography forms the foundation of Salgado's work right up to the present. In the layout of his book, he renounces graphic effects in favor of a calm design celebrating the large, tranquil picture.*

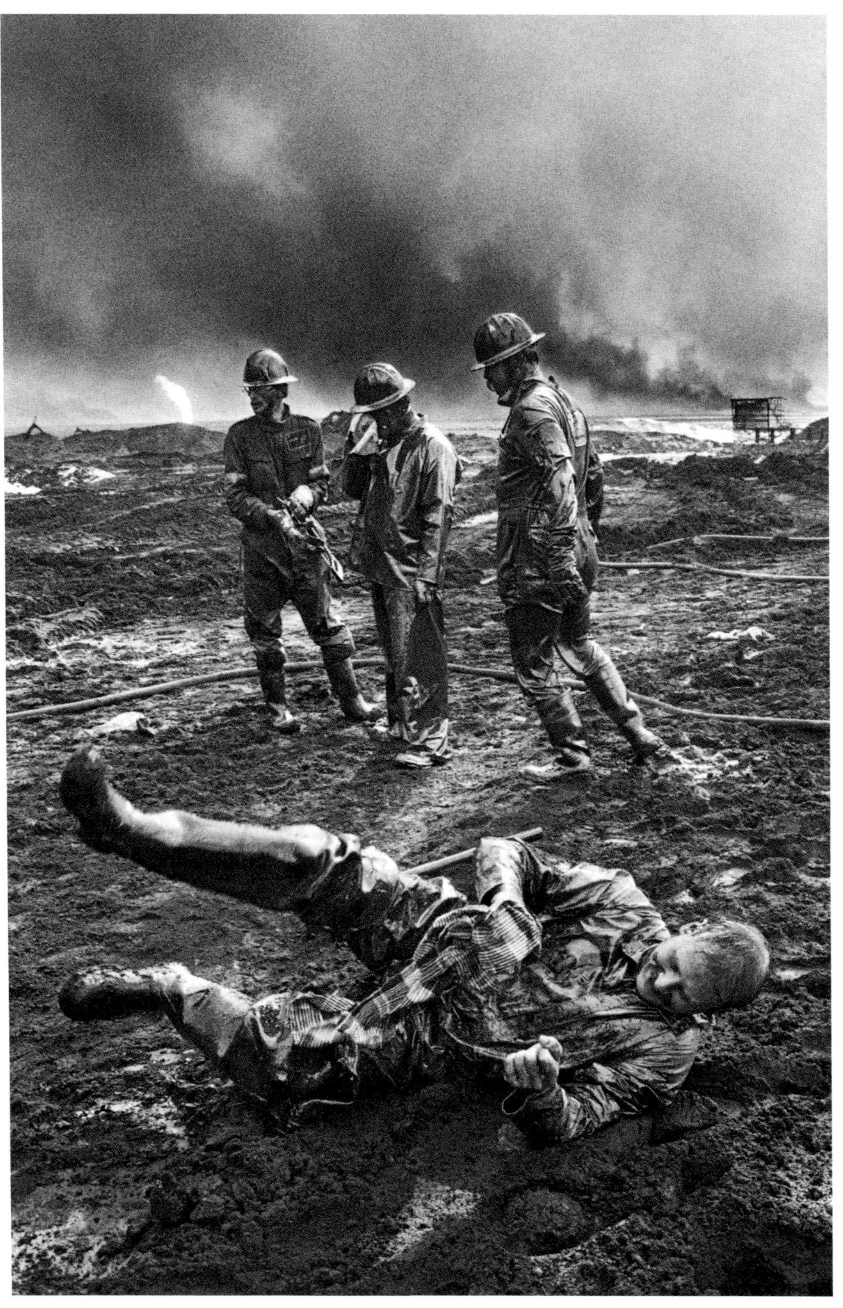

Kuwait, **1991**

Martin Parr
Acropolis, Athens, Greece
1991

A Temple in the Viewfinder

The British photographer Martin Parr is seen as a leading representative of the new European color photography. Since the late 1970s he was documenting postmodern everyday life in Britain and elsewhere. With a mixture of dismay and satire, he turns his lens on the world we know so well. And makes it appear - literally - in a new light.

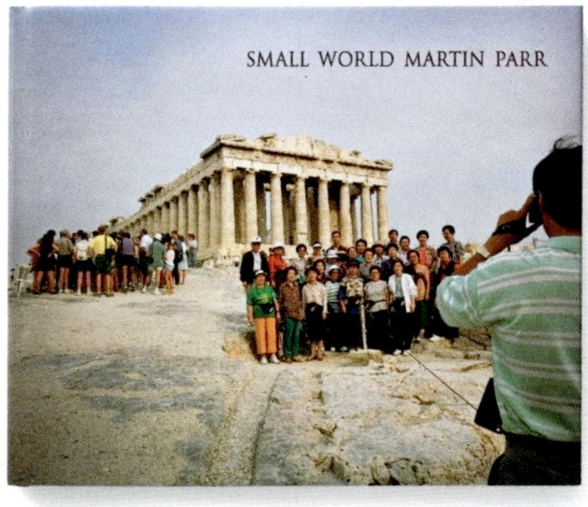

The irony is impossible to miss – even if it's not easy to identify from where, exactly, it draws its source. What are we looking at? The Acropolis. Or, more accurately, the Acropolis in Athens as the backdrop for little more than an automatic reflex in the post-modern age. People are having their picture taken. Posing nicely. Not moving for a few seconds. Freezing for a sense of 'eternity' in Kodachrome, with behind them – observant viewers will have spotted it – the object to which the collective interest should really be addressed: the temple for which they have jetted half way round the world. Japanese! The fact that the group in the foreground is made up of tourists from the Far East does not automatically make the scene an odd one. The Japanese are the Germans of the East. Comfortably off and to be found everywhere – and thus part of what we might describe as tourist normality. In their clothing, too, there is nothing

---

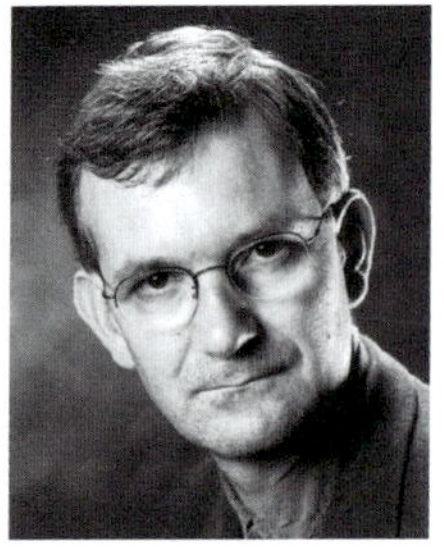

Martin Parr
*Born **1952** in Epsom, England. **1970–73** studies at Manchester Polytechnic. Influenced by the works of Tony Ray-Jones and William Eggleston, he develops a distinctive pictorial style. **1982** publication of his first book,* Bad Weather. ***1986*** The Last Resort. ***1989*** The Cost of Living. ***1991** included in the exhibition* British Photography from the Thatcher Years *in the Museum of Modern Art (New York). **2004–06** joint editor with Gerry Badger of* The Photobook: A History *(3 vols.). **2004** artistic director of the Rencontres d'Arles. **2006** Dr. Erich Salomon Prize by the DGPh German photography society. **2008** Baume et Mercier Award at the PhotoEspaña festival. Dies **2025** in Bristol, England.*

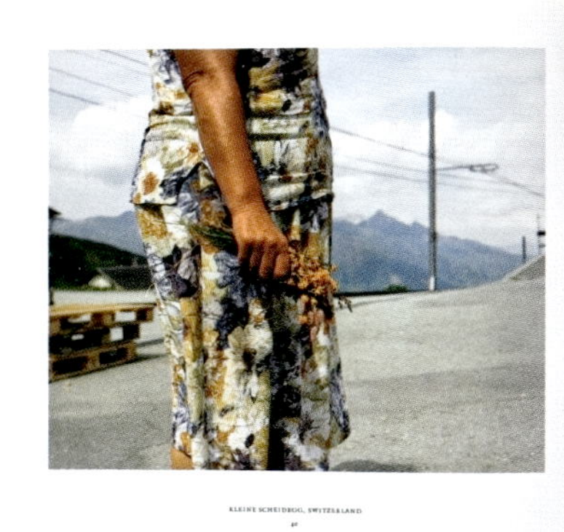

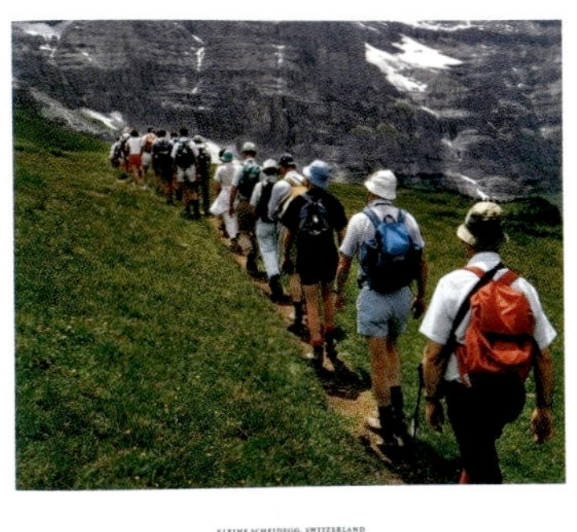

special to be found, even upon closer inspection. It is light, appropriate for the climate, colorful without being too bright, and – without revealing too much in the way of flesh – reflects the 'international style' that found its way into 'casual' and 'leisure' fashions.

The sky feels leaden. At any event, it spares us the standardized Mediterranean blue of industrially produced iconography. The Acropolis under the pale blue canopy looks clean, as if it were recently sandblasted. On the left of the picture, a second group of tourists appears to be listening to the explanations of a guide. This group may indeed be made up of Germans, whose affinity with shorts and bulging Cullmann camera bags must have got around. A woman in the left-hand background and a lone man in jeans and a white shirt at the foot of the temple underline the fact that a form of travel also exists outside the group. As for the rest, they cluster together, look at the camera with a mixture of happiness and self-consciousness, or wear the archetypal "I, too, was in Arcadia" smile that became a fixed component of the international tourist industry. The picture reflects a cliché: a wonder of the world reduced to a theatrical prop. Ignorance as standard. Photography as a ritual that has to be performed. We are all familiar with it, which is perhaps what makes us smile in amusement. Once our sense of *déjà vu* passed, however, it is rapidly succeeded by a sense of superiority, a sort of critical aloofness. However paradoxical it may sound, this, too, belongs to the phenomenon of tourism. The tourist is always someone else – the one we are smirking at, making fun of. The photo reinforces this distinction. As if through a window, we are looking at a scene that is familiar to us. And from which, at the same time, we are all too eager to distance ourselves.

Travel is as old as the human race. By instinct sedentary, people migrate in search of food and to escape from epidemics, wars, and famines. Or journey to cement family ties. Trips to thermal baths were a feature of life even in Ancient Rome and were made possible

---

Top left and above: *Martin Parr's cycle* Small World *developed during trips he took between 1987 and 1994. The* Acropolis, Athens *appeared on the front cover of both the English (Dewi Lewis) and the French (Marval) editions.*

not least by the relative degree of domestic stability and a comparatively well-developed road network. In the Middle Ages, travel was the privilege of itinerant scholars, beggars, robbers, and pilgrims – if privilege is the right word, considering the poor roads and the dangers that lurked on all sides. Travel correspondingly remained the exception rather than the rule, a deviation from the norm, right up to more modern times. Those who traveled thus journeyed into new territory in several respects. They left themselves exposed to the new, to the unknown, to danger. Exchanged 'civilization' for 'nature'. Whereby the perception of the latter as purely menacing began to change as from the Renaissance epoch. Lord Byron made the Rhine popular, Jean-Jacques Rousseau the Alps. The aristocratic Grand Tour evolved into an educational trip for the well-to-do, a 'romantic' or 'sentimental' journey into a compulsory exercise completed by every self-respecting member of the middle classes. Travel gained steadily in popularity from about 1830 onwards – even though it remained arduous, expensive, and not without danger, and thus the reserve of the privileged few.

What social scientists like to call 'secularized tourism' began to emerge only in the wake of the industrial revolution of the late 19th century, the expansion of the rail network, and the growing purchasing power of broader social strata. Even teachers, minor officials, and employees could now enjoy the chance to travel, initially understood first and

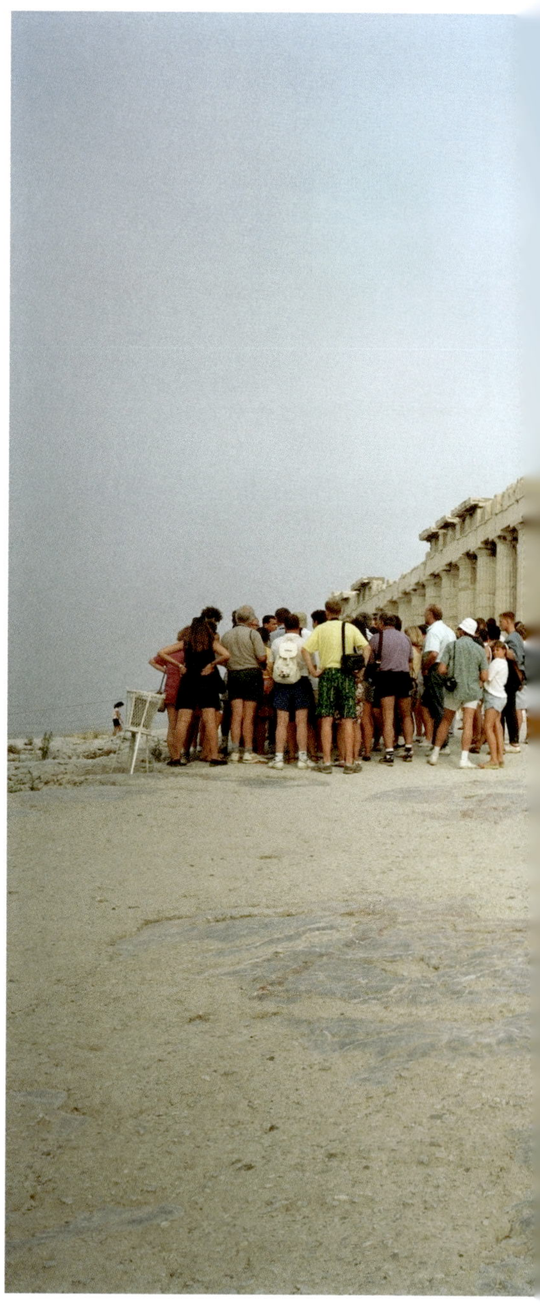

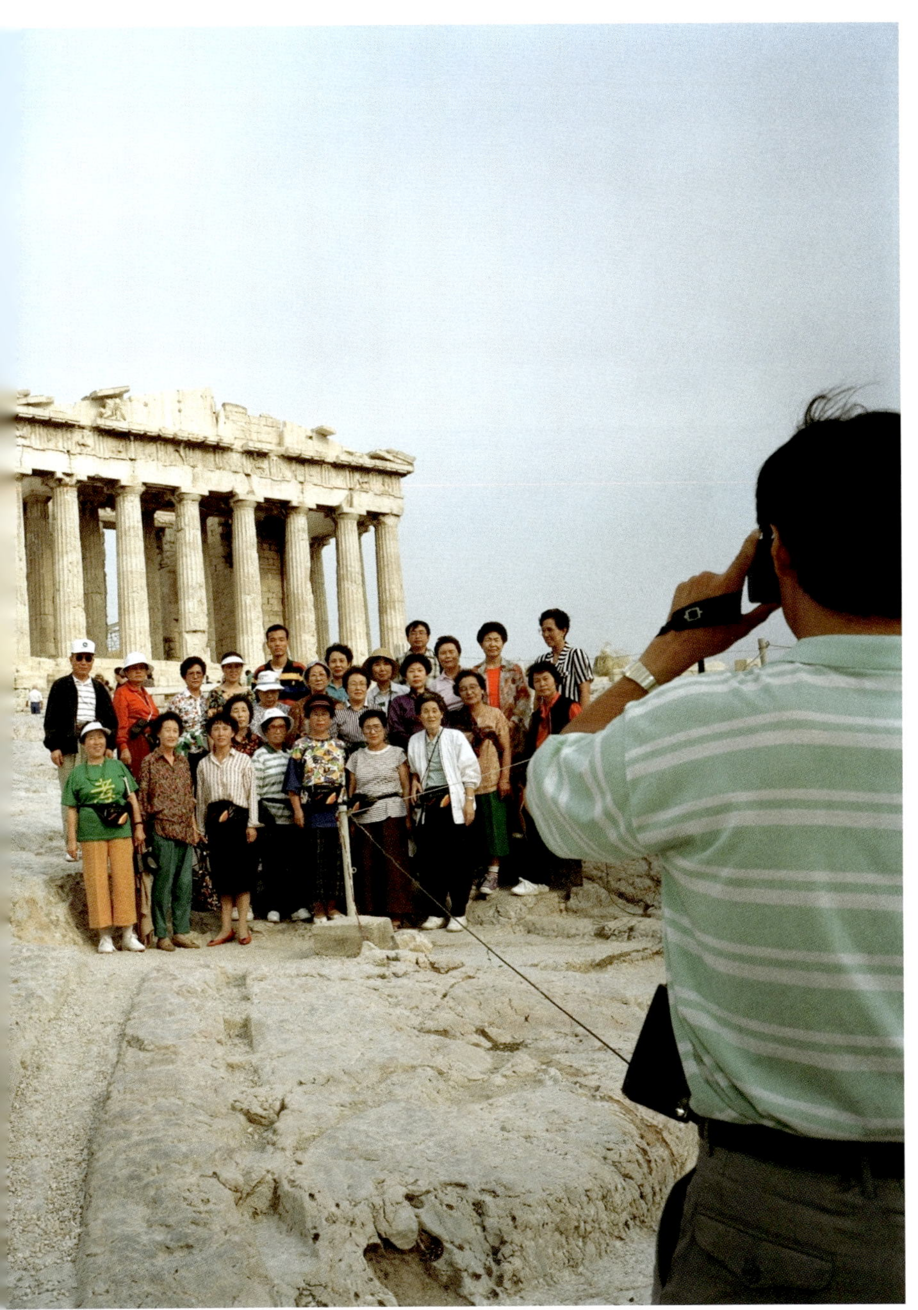

Acropolis, Athens, Greece, 1991

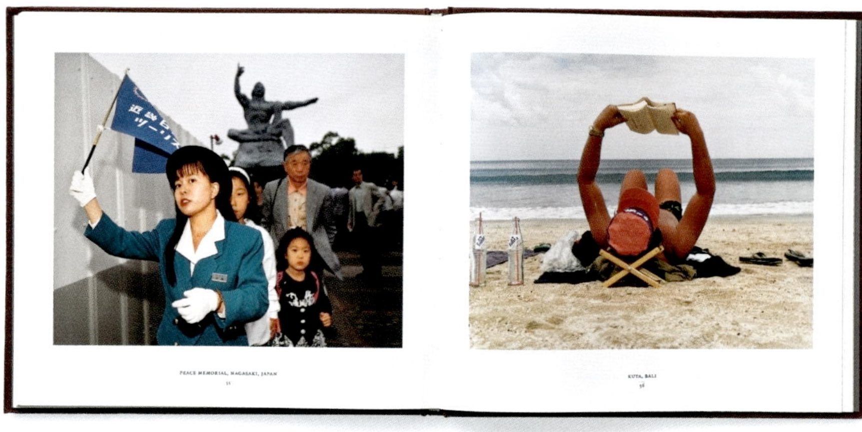

foremost as an opportunity for intellectual regeneration. People traveled alone. Or, as from 1845, as part of an organized group. The Englishman Thomas Cook is considered the inventor of the package holiday and the travel agency, the German Karl Baedeker the pioneer of standardized, succinctly written guide books that quickly supplanted the flowery travel writing of the past. The practice of giving sights a hierarchical rating by means of stars or asterisks was already in use in 1813. The rationalization of group travel, in conjunction with the gradual introduction of paid leave, were major factors in the development of modern mass tourism. Hiking and camping trips were particularly popular in the inter-war years. Collectively agreed paid leave was extended during this period to workers on the shop floor, whose unions wanted to make holidays affordable by setting up their own travel organizations. Under National Socialism, 'relaxation' became an obligation and was provided for – up to the start of the war, at least – by the semi-governmental Nazi organization Kraft durch Freude (Strength through Joy). A model that the later German Democratic Republic would adopt in the shape of state-organized ocean cruises. In the Federal Republic, the number of people holidaying abroad exceeded those vacationing at home for the first time in 1968. Charter holidays are not the only type of tourism that boomed. Travel switched from being a rare experience to being a regular part of life, a ritual that none wish to forego. None in the industrialized, wealthy countries of the North, at all events.

Small World: *Double-page spreads from the first edition, with a comparatively static layout, based on classic volumes of plates.*

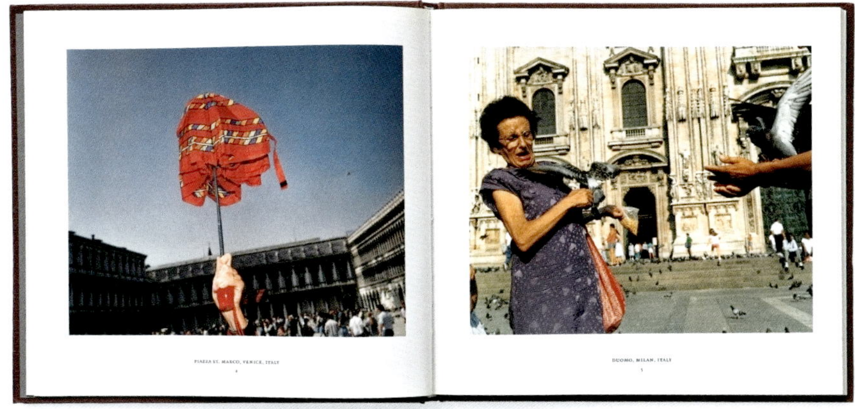

Package tours as an annual must

Modern tourism is a mass phenomenon. What exactly makes people head off for distant destinations is a matter of dispute amongst social scientists. "Escape from the stresses of industrial society" is the current reasoning. Travel, writes Christoph Hennig, represents "one of the most effective means of temporarily getting away from the established social order – not in blind flight, but as a productive human achievement that makes new experiences possible." Travel as an opportunity to bypass current restrictions, to step outside the norm; group travel as a ritual, as the "low-brow side of medieval festivities"; camping as fun or as "relief from social pressures" – whatever the motivation may be for fleeing one's familiar surroundings: what is certain is that travel is perceived as something desirable by the whole of the industrialized hemisphere. A trip abroad is declared an annual "must" for everyone who can afford it, and who willingly makes savings in other areas for its sake. Around 150 million people holidayed away from home in 1995. By 2009 this figure had soared to 880 million and reached over 1.5 billion in 2025. The number of people employed in the tourism sector rose to over 370 million in 2025. To talk about tourism is thus to talk first and foremost about a sector of the economy which – with annual international receipts of over US$ 900 billion (€600 billion) – overtook the classic branches of industry, from cars to chemicals.

Mass tourism disturbs nature. Drains natural resources. Harms the environment. Levels cultures. In short: to go in search of something special is to destroy it. This criticism of tourism is as old as tourism itself. Those who pass judgment on tourism for the masses are both distancing themselves from it and at the same time seeking to portray themselves as the representatives of a different, better, 'alternative' style of travel. It is in this light that author Christoph Hennig sees the complaint voiced by Lord Byron, who in 1817 described Rome as "pestilential with English, a parcel of staring boobies." Ever since the days of late-Enlightenment invectives against tourism, the negative aspects of mass travel have been a standard theme of cultural criticism. Tourism creates jobs. It brings much-needed cash to poor, underdeveloped regions. It encourages the protection of the environment and of species, for without a healthy

***Acropolis, Athens, Greece,* 1991**

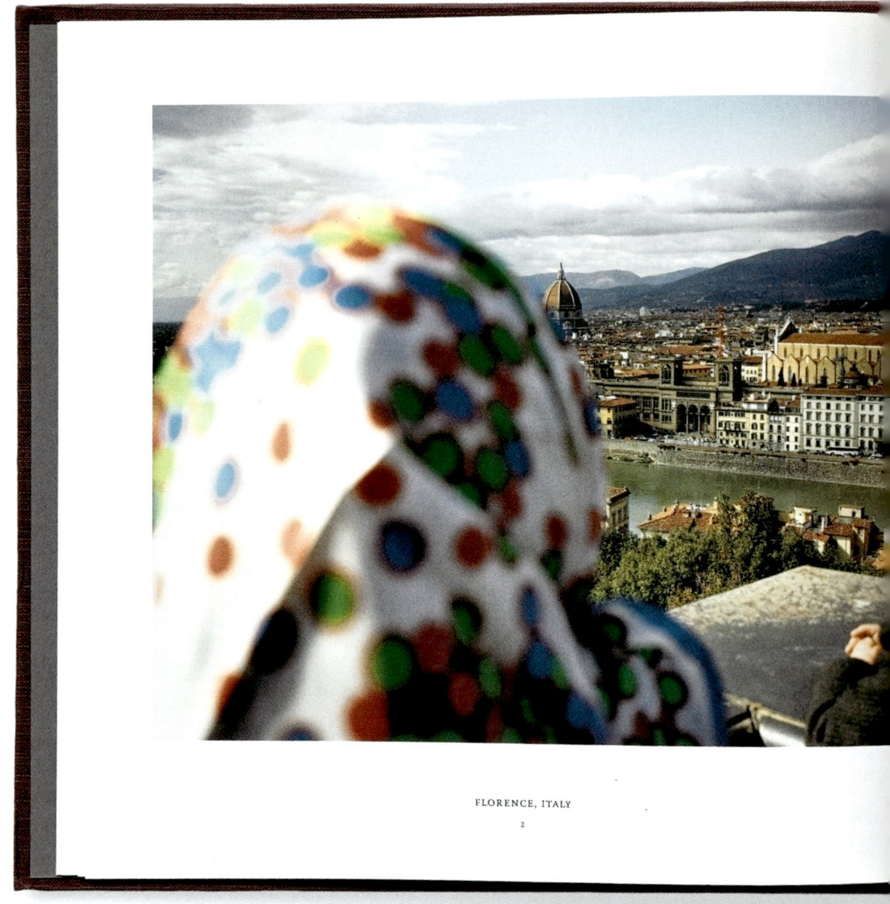
FLORENCE, ITALY

2

environment there is no tourism. However many the arguments presented by apologists for travel, doubts over the purpose and benefits of tourism escalate in line with the latter's growing appeal – the arguments heard today are the same as those of 150 years ago. "The tourist, in short," as the traveler Leslie Stephen wrote back in 1869, "is notoriously a person who follows a certain hackneyed round; who never stops long enough before a picture to admire it or fix it in his memory."

Martin Parr's photo *Acropolis* falls unmistakably into the tradition of such criticism. His view is the view of one who visualizes the farcical and at times bizarre aspects of mass tourism from a 'loftier' standpoint. He counters the negative and at times cynical attitudes of many of his photographer colleagues with irony. Martin Parr is an accurate observer of the phenomena of popular culture, a seismograph with a pronounced interest in the trivial. The photograph is strictly speaking part of a larger project Parr embarked on in 1987 and completed

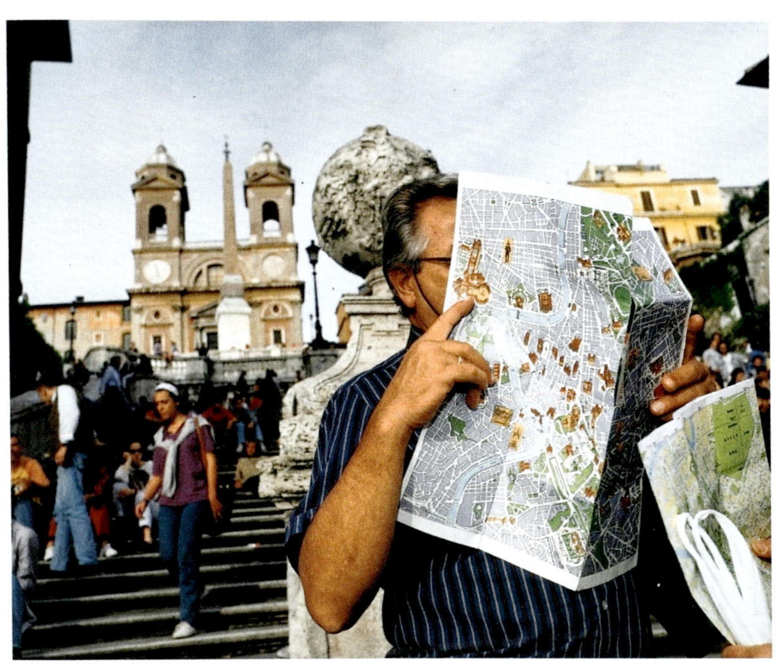

SPANISH STEPS, ROME, ITALY

3

in 1994, which was published in book form one year later under the title *Small World*. Exactly when *Acropolis* was taken, Parr can no longer say. Probably 1992 or 1993. But the British photograph remembers, nonetheless, that he traveled especially to Athens for four days in order to take the picture. According to Martin Parr, the Acropolis had featured on his 'informal list' of sights to be photographed right from the start. Like the Pyramids, the Giza Sphinx, Florence, Rome, Venice, Milan, Las Vagas, Paris, and Barcelona. Parr photographs hordes of tourists in front of the real wonders of the world. Or in front of their copies in Japan, Holland, and the USA. Everything became interchangeable. What seems to count is simply getting away, going somewhere different, having a change of scene. Parr goes up close. Emphasizes, through his framing, the frequently absurd condition of being a tourist. As Diane Arbus before him, Parr often combines daylight with flash as a means of exposing the loud in an ordinary scene. Equipped with a Plaubel 6 × 7, he nods at clichés: tourists are fat, wear printed T-shirts, take photos rather than look. For Parr, it is true, things seem turned upside down. It has long been the world that adapts itself to fit the clichés. Parr acknowledges this with a wink. In taking photographs, he is himself part of the circus. Even if he is watching not from the front stalls but – in part – from the balcony.

The vocabulary of the banal

Martin Parr, born in 1952 in Epsom, long ranked among the most prominent photographers of the present day. He studied at the Faculty of Art and Design at Manchester Polytechnic, graduating in 1973. Parr himself remembers this time as a phase characterized by a certain lack of orientation. The Swinging Sixties were only recently past and the influence of the 'big three' – David Bailey, Brian Duffy, and Terence Donovan – was still palpable. Parr was part of the first generation to rebel. Unwilling to go down the commercial route of 'applied photography', he started exploring his own ideas. The New British Photography is often causally linked with the Thatcher era, which dawned in 1979. In fact, however, the search for new forms of photographic expression that lay outside the spheres of fashion, advertising, and photojournalism had begun much earlier than this. Parr's friendship with Bill Jay, chief editor of the magazine *Creative Camera*, was highly significant in this respect. Jay pointed the young photographer towards alternatives and introduced him to names such as David Hurn, Ian Barry, and Tony Ray-Jones. For Parr this was "a real moment of inspiration." The William Eggleston exhibition staged at the Museum of Modern Art in New York in 1976 also made a profound impact upon him. Firstly because it focused resolutely on the banal and the trivial. And secondly because it no longer acted as if the world was black and white. Color, in other words, had made its entry into contemporary photography and thereby appeared to overturn the verdicts of Old Masters from Walker Evans to Edward Weston, who had denigrated color for being too ordinary and too close to reality. These, however, were precisely the properties that interested the young photographers. Here the ground was undoubtedly prepared by Pop Art. Post-war popular culture was colorful, indeed brightly so, and any contemporary art form wishing to explore it in a playfully critical manner had to employ – at least up to a certain point – the vocabulary of the banal. At all events, the world at the end of the 20th century could no longer be measured in black-and-white Tri-X film. Photographers (not only in Great Britain) thereby had a thoroughly ambivalent attitude to the products of trivial culture. Having themselves grown up with color television, fast food, and disposable goods, this generation felt thoroughly at home in the modern world of plastic – and at the same time repulsed by it. This vacillation between criticism and an affinity tinged with irony, with the trivial, with the mass culture of a postmodern present, also determines the photography of Martin Parr. The most trivial objects, as he says himself, provide both the inspiration and the raw material for his work. He thereby sees his task as elevating the ordinary to the level of the extraordinary.

Pages 398–399: *A medium-format camera, daylight and flash are the technical ingredients of Parr's* Small World*: Another spread from his 1995 book.*

Cross-over between art and advertising

Since 1994 Martin Parr was a full member of the legendary Magnum photo agency, founded in the late 1940s by Henri Cartier-Bresson, Robert Capa, David Seymour, and a number of other press photographers. This may astonish those who still associate this photo co-operative with the black-and-white ideal of a 'humane photojournalism'. Not that Magnum does not continue to uphold this ideal. But the media world changed. And with it the concept of photojournalism, which is today understood in a considerably broader sense. Firstly with regard to the form and content of its images. The pictorial language of photojournalism and the themes conveyed with its help may thus now fall well outside the bounds of what was formerly considered camera worthy by press and news photographers. And secondly with a view to the forums in which photojournalism is now found. Thus Martin Parr publishes in fashion and lifestyle magazines such as *W* and *Amica*. He makes adverts, smoothly transferring his distinctive visual language into the commercial sector – fully in the spirit of a post-modern cross-over. Like Jürgen Teller or Nan Goldin, Parr's "entire *modus operandi*," writes Gerry Badger, "depends on slipping deftly between photographic worlds, thereby instinctively addressing such issues as the role of the photographer, the status of the photographic image in our culture, and indeed the very nature of contemporary culture itself." The boundaries crossed by Parr's works are blown up for inspection in the signed color laser copies he exhibits in museums and galleries. He also creates books: for many photojournalists today, the most important vehicle – apart from the museum wall – through which to publicize their photo essays and reportages.

Martin Parr's first book was *Bad Weather*, published in 1982. In 1986 he bought out his first book in color, *The Last Resort*. The title, it goes without saying, is intended ironically. Just as irony runs as a constant theme through all his work, providing the *basso continuo*, so to speak. Parr's lens reveals the absurd dimension lying underneath everyday life. We gaze, spellbound, at a world that is at once familiar and foreign. Parr provokes by presenting craziness as normal and vice versa. But as he insists himself, he is not trying to preach. He is not saying, for example, that hamburgers are disgusting; he even admits to eating them himself, now and again. He recognizes that life is not simply black and white. Even if his work is misinterpreted by some as cynical or negative, Parr himself tries to adopt a balanced stance. His second book in color, *The Cost of Living*, came out in 1989. Overladen barbecues and finger food being eaten from limp cardboard plates are already present. Parr developed this interest in contemporary dining culture into a large and highly regarded cycle in *Common Sense* (1999). His technique of macro lenses and ring flash – here employed for the first time – make the plastic-wrapped, industrially prepared food look even more artificial and unappetizing. Parr, no question about it, is a visual satirist. He exaggerates the familiar. He relocates our normal madness into the realm of Surrealism. In his pictures, the world becomes a stage. And we know that we are the actors. That Parr's work contains an "essential pessimism" is recognized by Gerry Badger. But while the photographer's vision might be "sharp and sceptical," Badger continues, "it is also playful and whimsical, even surprisingly gentle at times if one looks closely enough. He lies much more within the mainstream English comic tradition of self-deprecating irony. Unlike the true satirist, Parr is not disaffected. He is assuredly a part of the world he photographs, and if clearly not sharing all its values, he is not seeking to demolish it totally. After all, it furnishes him with endless raw material."

***Acropolis, Athens, Greece,* 1991**

Bettina Rheims
Chambre Close
1992

Daydream in a Private Room

Plain Parisian hotel rooms. Young women adopting erotic poses to please an aging voyeur. Serge Bramly wrote the 'script' for a series of photographs by Bettina Rheims that would lead to a downright scandal in Germany in the early 1990s.

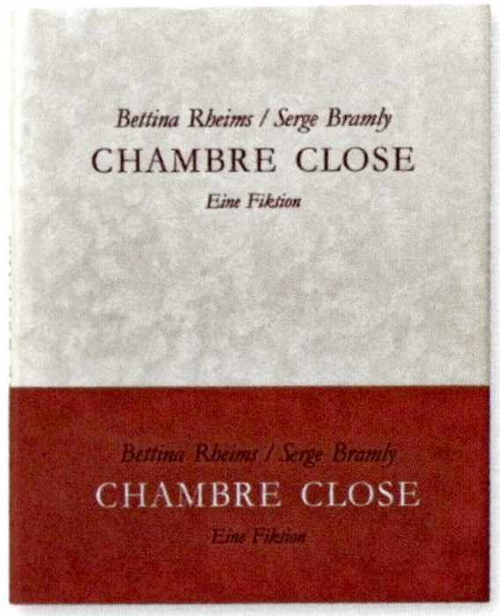

She doesn't look happy; anxious, rather, if not upset. And the way in which she is hiding her breasts speaks more of defensiveness than of relaxation at her toilette. The bidet in the background is proof that we are in a bathroom. Black and a constantly recurring red – in the curtain, the lips, the fingernails, and the tap – nevertheless dominate as pronouncedly aggressive colors. There is nothing amusing about the scene. Were it taken from a film, it would surely have to be a crime movie. Who the young, attractive, flawlessly made-up woman is looking at, we do not know. The scene thus right away conceals – more than anything else – an erotic secret. But it is precisely this that lends the photo its fascination.

The picture forms part of a larger cycle that the French photographer Bettina Rheims first released to the public in 1992 in the form of a much talked-about 'photographic novel': *Chambre Close*. The inspiration for the book had come from a friend, the writer and art critic Serge Bramly, who told her about his idea for a plot at the end of the 1980s. At the center of the story: an elderly gentleman, well-groomed, discreet, in a high-ranking job, married. Suddenly, in the autumn of his life, an astonishing libido awakens

---

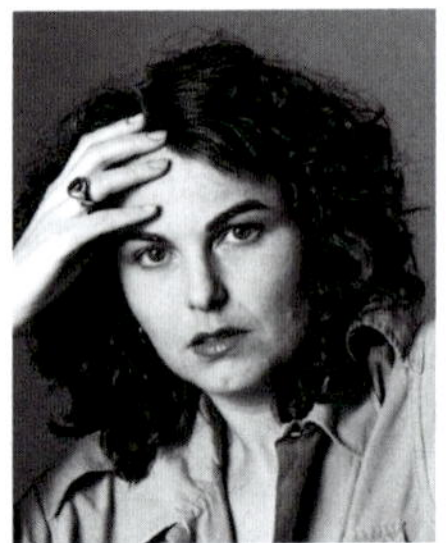

Bettina Rheims

*Born **1952** in Paris, the daughter of art expert Maurice Rheims. First photos while still at school. Works as a model in New York at the start of the **1970**s. **1975** returns to Paris. **1978** becomes a professional photographer. **1981** first solo show, at the Centre Georges Pompidou. **1982** series of stuffed animals. First advertising photos, fashion photos, record covers, film posters, and portraits of prominent personalities for international magazines. **1990*** Modern Lovers *cycle. **1991–92*** Chambre Close *cycle. As from **1992**, film commercials (incl. for Chanel). Campaigns for Ferré. **1994** Grand Prix de la photographie de la ville de Paris. **1995** official portrait of French President Jacques Chirac. Lives in Paris.*

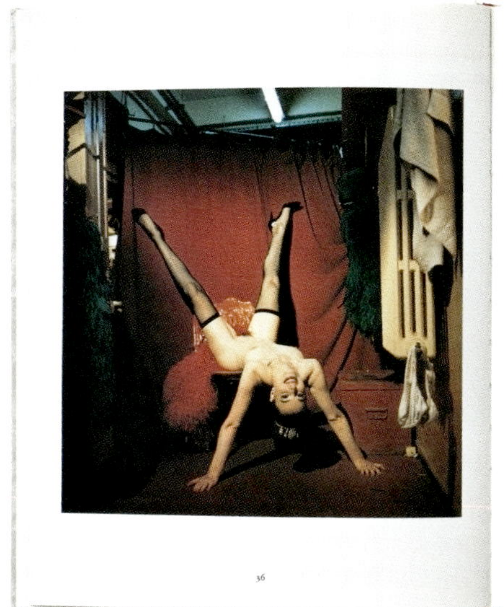

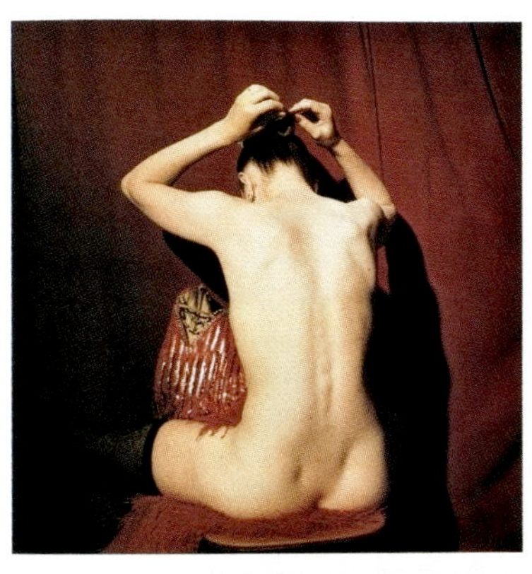

in this quiet figure. Walking down the street, riding in buses or seated in cafés, he addresses young women and asks them to pose for him. These assignations take place in cheap hotels. Photographic assignations. For the protagonist of the story is interested only in images, in photographs, in manifestations on paper of his fantasies. The images are developed and enlarged secretly, in the attic of his home. Beauty appears next to beauty, pin-up next to pin-up. In the end, the collection is handed over to a neutral acquaintance. "My secret," notes the old man, "must be kept safe, for the sake of the peace of mind of my nearest and dearest and my own reputation."

Bettina Rheims, who was born in 1952 in Paris, began translating Bramly's idea for a novel into images at the beginning of the 1990s. She had been struck by the prominent role regularly played by the background wall-paper in erotic and pornographic photography. So an assistant was dispatched from the photo studio on a bike. The hotel room was to cost no more than 120 francs – and be decorated with a distinctive wall-paper. According to Rheims, "it was harder to find the wall-paper than the girls." The latter were all amateurs. Young actresses, waitresses, shop assistants, girls from the Métro. "I would never work with professional nude models." Nor would they suit the way she likes her pictures to be, as the photographer admits. She values shyness and occasional awkwardness, a touch of embarrassment. "I think that comes through in the pictures."

Top left: *Cover of the first edition of* Chambre Close. *The book was first published in 1992 by Gina Kehayoff in Munich.*

Above and pages 406–409: *Spreads from* Chambre Close. *The series, developed jointly with writer Serge Bramly, undoubtedly ranks among Bettina Rheims' most powerful works.*

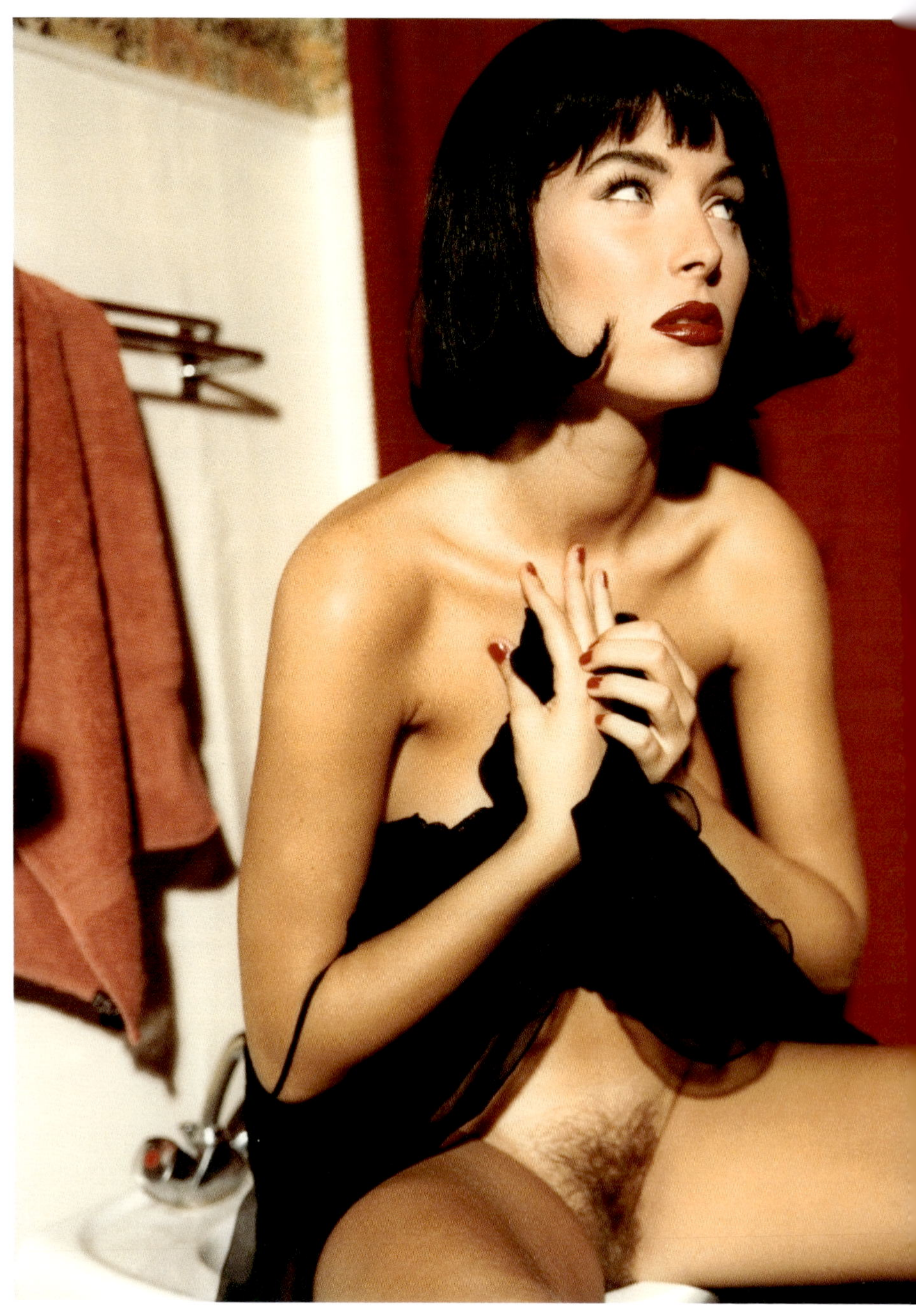

Bettina Rheims

Initially, says Bettina Rheims, she took refuge behind the fiction. "I said to myself, these aren't my pictures. They're the old man's pictures. He's the voyeur. He's taking the dirty pictures." More and more, however, this game of revealing and concealing became her own affair. The male fantasy became a visual dialogue amongst women. A square format and color film were decided upon from the start. Rheims: "I don't know why. There was no logical reason behind it. Nevertheless, it was immediately clear: it had to be square and in color." The lighting was provided by a single 1,000-watt spotlight. According to Rheims, there was no room for anything more in the tiny rooms.

Game of revealing and concealing

Chambre Close – the title refers both to the institution of the brothel (in French, a *maison close*) and the medium of photography (cf. *La Chambre Claire*, a collection of essays on photography by Roland Barthes, translated as *Camera Lucida*). As a series published in 1992, the cycle is complete and self-contained. And yet it represents the logical continuation of an œuvre that can already be described as representing one of the most interesting contributions to the subject of the nude. Bettina Rheims acknowledges that nudes have always been what interested her, right from the start. Even if, in her early days, she was constantly having to justify herself. In 1981, her first cycle of photographs, devoted to strip-tease artists from the Pigalle district in Paris, was exhibited in the Centre Pompidou and the Texbraun gallery in Paris under the placatory title of *Portraits nus* (Nude Portraits). Rheims: "I was criticized by feminists all the same. I had tomatoes thrown at me. The whole thing, I was told, was an offense against female dignity." Today, some three decades later, Bettina Rheims is seen as the protagonist of a new understanding of what it is to be a woman. In a manner more pointed than others, she visualizes erotic dreams that are not simply the dreams of men. A new age has dawned for women, says Bettina Rheims. "They know that they can have a career, that they can be successful and sexy, and are allowed to show a little *décolleté*." And there is another constant in the work of Bettina Rheims: she loves ambiguity. This is true above all of her portraits of stuffed animals, taken at the start of the 1980s. They look at the camera with a strange air of sadness and, although long dead, still seem to live and feel. It is also true of her cycle *Modern Lovers*, fragile but nonetheless self-confident elfin beings situated somewhere between child, man, and woman. It is true of the transsexuals whom she photographed in *Les Espionnes*, published as a small catalogue in 1992. And it is true of *Chambre Close*, a work which – even in the age of a civilization fed a surfeit of sex in every medium and on every channel – still succeeded in provoking an outright scandal.

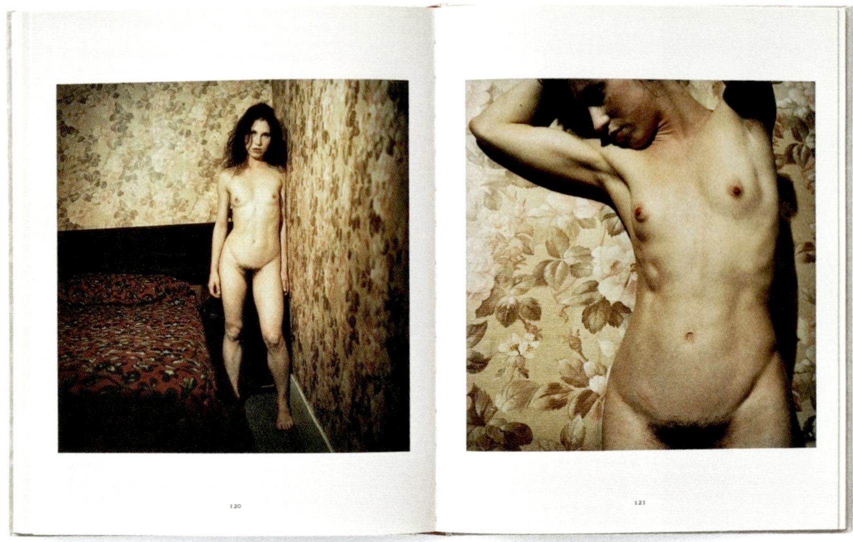

Photographic positions all about the nude

Frankfurt am Main. August 1993. Under its then director, Peter Weiermair, the highly regarded Frankfurter Kunstverein art association stages the exhibition *Das Bild des Körpers* (The Picture of the Body). Works by Robert Mapplethorpe and Bruce Weber, Jeff Koons and Cindy Sherman, Dieter Appelt, and Thomas Florschuetz mark different positions in the artistic approach to a subject that seems little likely to trigger the emotions, let alone protests. Even if Nobuyoshi Araki should present male and female genitalia with a rare directness. Or Rainer Leitzgen photograph human organs – heart, spleen, small intestine, brain – against a neutral background with a complete lack of emotion, as if they were simply spare parts. Or John Coplans deliberately touch upon one of perhaps the last taboos: the depiction of the aging, withered body. Bettina Rheims provided one of the two motifs for the exhibition posters (the other came from Robert Mapplethorpe). A young woman in a green trench coat, smiling faintly and with her breast exposed. In the background, a red telephone, which in conjunction with the yellow living-room sofa lends the picture – unmistakably – a certain irony. The anonymous beauty in her coat and nylons was supposed to advertise the show in the Steinernes Haus am Römerberg exactly 433 times. On billboards and advertising pillars. But it was not to be.

War was raging in those days. War in Bosnia. War in the Balkans. Which at first sight had nothing to do with Bettina Rheims and her photography. For the manager of the German Cities Advertising company, however, Rheims' photo reminded him of images of "raped Bosnian women." Even though there had "never been any press photos of raped Bosnian women in which these women were shown naked," as one critic rightly observed. This did not prevent the management of the publicity company from finding Rheims' motif "offensive," "primitive" and "obscene" and – therefore – logically to insist on pasting it over. Frankfurt thus had its scandal. And the press its topic for the summer. "Does Frankfurt face a re-opening of the debate on

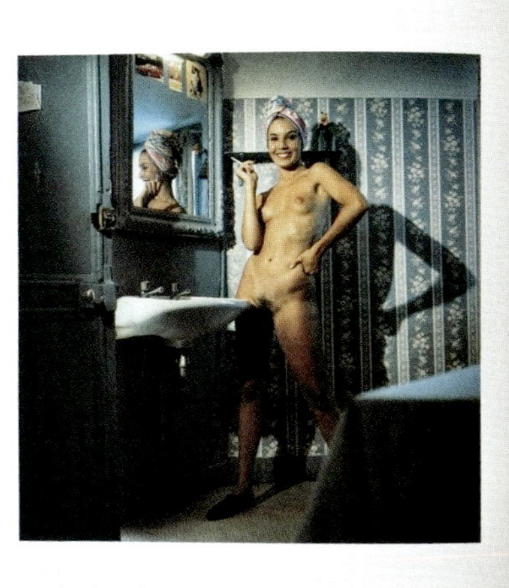

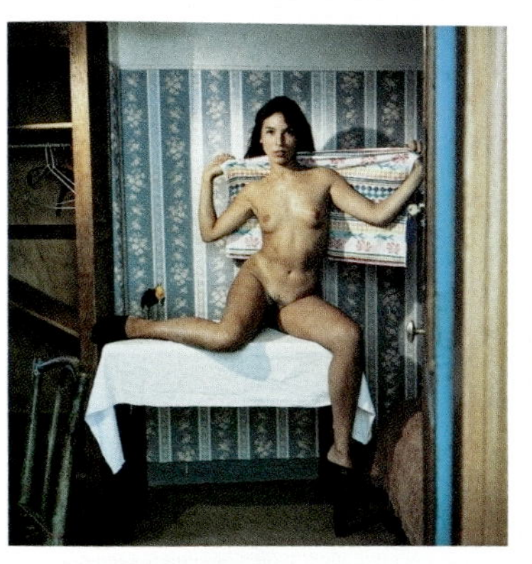

pornography?" asked the *Handelsblatt*, for example. "Chastity belt for sex poster" was the headline in *Bild*. The *Frankfurter Allgemeine Zeitung* found it "understandable that the picture offends against propriety, causes indignation, and can be perceived as threatening." In the weekly magazine *Die Zeit*, meanwhile, Ulrich Greiner reflected: "Isn't it marvelous that the illustration of human nakedness can still arouse such heated feelings? Might it not have been feared that the omnipresence of the sexually charged body in advertising and the media would lead to complete inertia, to eunuch-like indifference? Erotic provocation still functions; the cunning of irrationality is unrivalled."

It goes without saying that a scandal such as this one has two sides. Here, indisputably, it was a case of censorship. A form of tutelage believed long since dead and gone. On the other hand, the storm of protest attracted a level of interest in the exhibition that the poster alone could never have generated. Indeed, the Rheims motif was sold out at the Kunstverein within just a few days. The catalogue sold in numbers that catalogues rarely achieve. And elegantly groomed men sporting ties and briefcases turned up during their lunch hour: a public not otherwise often seen at the Steinernes Haus am Römerberg, either then or now. The Frankfurt scandal also illustrated yet again, moreover, that those who try to draw a line between the permissible and the impermissible, between art and pornography, are treading on extremely shaky ground. For what is "obscene" continues to depend upon the cultural climate and above all upon the subjective opinion of the individual. What the German Cities Advertising company judged to be a "clear offence against decent morals" was, for the then head of Frankfurt's Department of Women's Affairs, indubitably art. Women, it was to be heard from this corner, do indeed have pubic hair and breasts. And, it might be added, they are proud of it. Something unmistakably proclaimed by Bettina Rheims with *7 November, Paris*, as this image is officially titled.

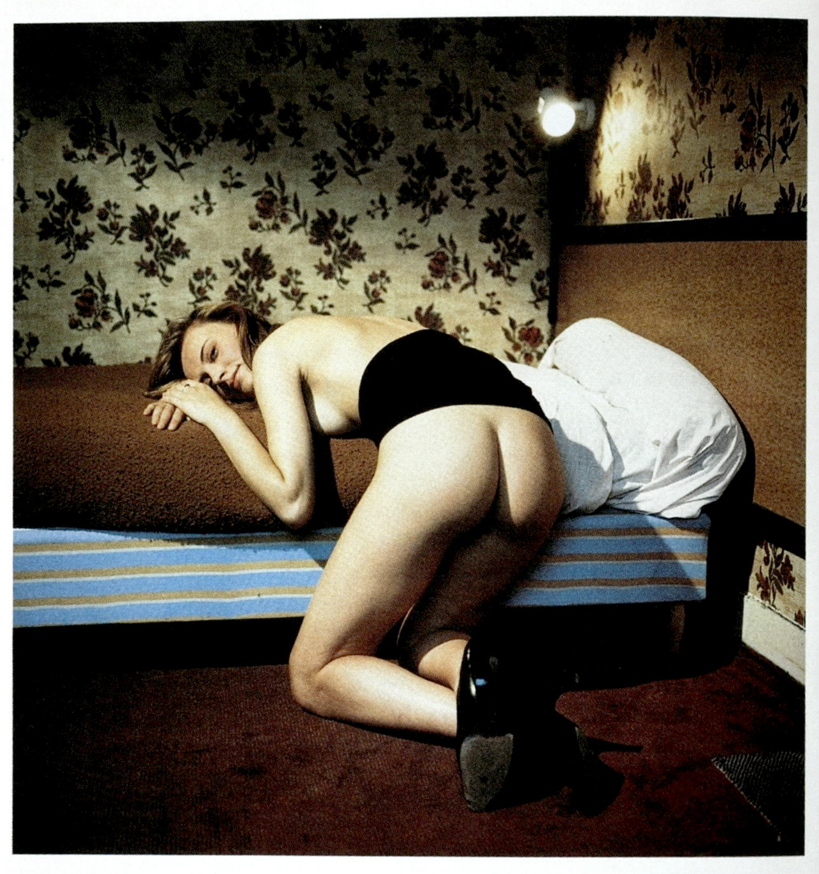

90

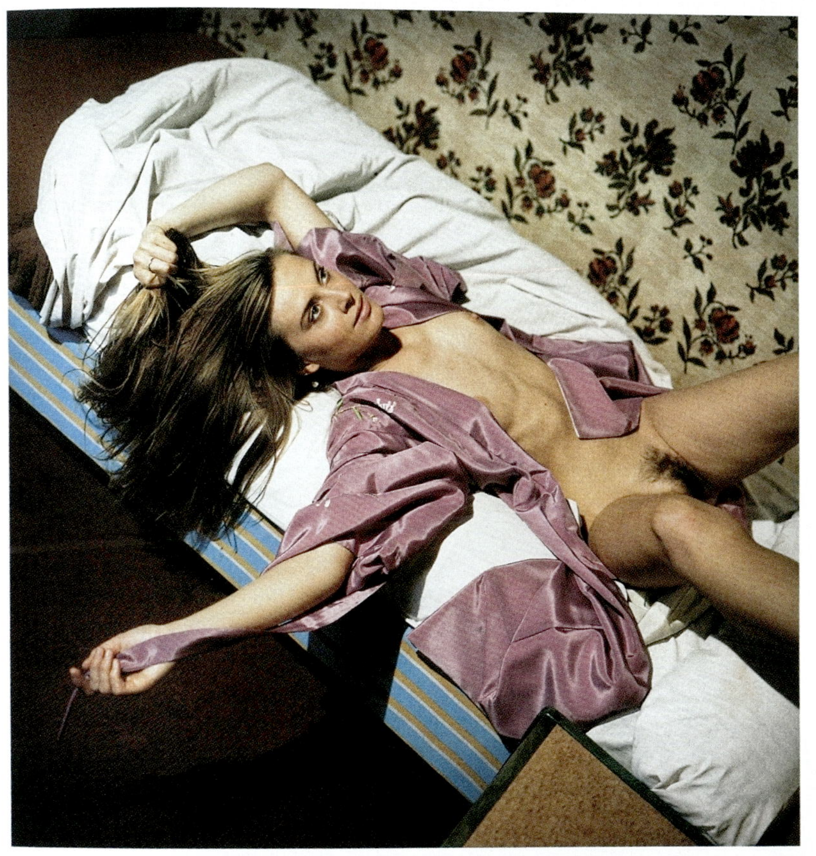

91

Thomas Hoepker
View of Manhattan from Williamsburg, Brooklyn September 11, 2001

Apocalypse Now

September 11, 2001, was also and above all a media event. America was being attacked – and the world was watching. From this point of view, the terrorists' calculations were doubly correct. Not only had they struck right at the economic heart of the US, but their purposes were further served by the response – still reluctant to end – of TV, Internet and press. Such instrumentalization of the media became a significant facet of attention-seeking acts of terrorism.

The motto is clear: "Reading Makes a Country Great." In the presence of a president who candidly admits that he reads rarely, if at all, the words assume a touch of wry humor. But on this September 11, 2001, the most powerful man in the world indeed picked up a book. It's 9 o'clock in the morning and George W. Bush is reading fairytales to elementary-grade pupils in Sarasota, Florida. TV cameras, naturally, are also present, in order to broadcast a double message to the world. Firstly, that reading makes a country great; that, at any event, is what is written on a blackboard in the background. And secondly, that the President gets along well with children and they with him. A message whose publicity value the 43rd President of the United States is not the first to exploit but which regularly goes down well – assuming that it is not overshadowed by an event that causes others to pale into insignificance, or even appear ridiculous, by comparison. At the same moment, or to be precise at 8.45 a.m. New York time, an American Airlines Boeing 767 crashed into the North Tower of the World Trade Center. An accident? Human error? Or an act of terrorism? Once before, in the 1980s, a private sports plane had drifted off course and bored its way into the top of the Empire State Building. But at the latest by 9.03 a.m., when a second passenger plane hit the South Tower of the World Trade Center between the 77th and 85th stories, the question had been answered: a calculated plan

---

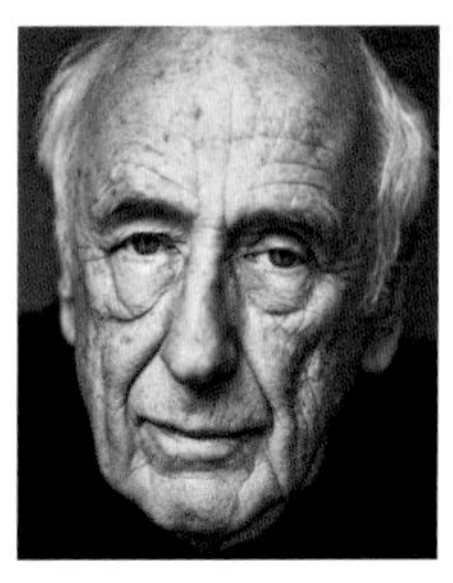

Thomas Hoepker
Born ***1936*** *in Munich.* ***1942–56*** *attends school. First photos.* ***1954*** *and* ***1956*** *first photos shown at* photokina *(junior photography competitions).* ***1956–59*** *studies art history and archaeology in Göttingen and Munich. Photojournalist for* Münchner Illustrierte *and* Kristall. *From* ***1964****, photo reporter for* Stern *in Hamburg. From* ***1972****, also works for TV.* ***1974–76*** *GDR correspondent for* Stern. ***1976*** Stern *correspondent in New York.* ***1978*** *deputy chief editor (pictures) for* Geo *(USA).* ***1981*** *gives up post at* Geo. ***1986*** *works freelance for various magazines, incl.* Stern *and* Geo. ***1968*** *Prize from the DGPh German photography society.* ***1975*** *German Federal Cross of Merit. Dies* ***2024*** *in Santiago de Chile.*

was in operation. A bloody cynicism in a previously unknown form. "An overt terrorist attack on our country," as a visibly shaken George W. Bush announced in a first statement at around 9.30 a.m. in front of running cameras. He had meanwhile abandoned his fairytale class to do what millions of other people were doing all over the world: turn on the television.

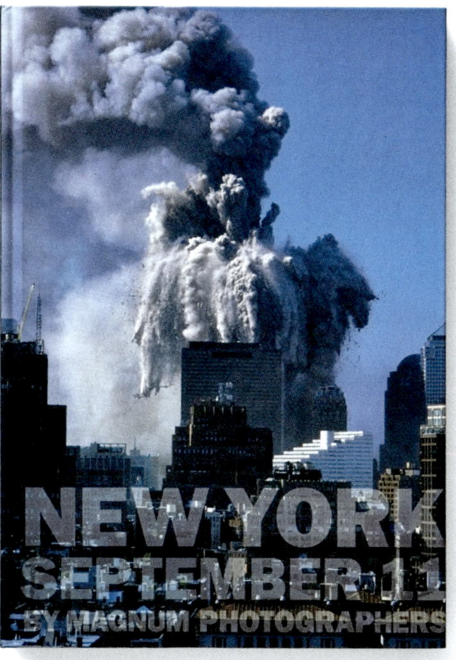

The September 11 attack was not the first catastrophe to be transmitted almost simultaneously on television. New technologies have long since made it possible to carry out live broadcasts, which for many people are the true criterion of television quality. Let the printed media analyze and explore matters in depth: the attraction of television lay and lies in the immediacy of its reporting. As Latin scholars know, the word 'interest' is derived from *interesse*, 'to be present at'. It is in this spirit that ever greater numbers of state-funded, semi-privatized and private television channels compete globally to satisfy an international clientele: as directly as possible, as rapidly as possible, and if possible from right in the thick of things. Whereby bad news is regularly good news if judged in terms of the number of viewers tuning in. On September 11, 2001, it was just the same. With the difference, however, that the quality and quantity of the pictures reached a new level. From about 9 a.m. local time onwards, more and more TV crews trained their cameras unswervingly on the scene. Everyone who wanted to and was able to, stared at the screen. The North Tower was ablaze at roughly the height of the 96th story. The gleaming tower soared like an ominous torch into a beautiful, brilliantly blue New York sky. This image alone would have sufficed as a metaphor. As a parable of our high-tech and thereby vulnerable civilization. But worse was to come. The fact that Mohammed Atta, the deadly pilot of the first plane, had already summoned the attention of the media with his direct flight into the heart of the global financial world, meant that the second pilot would be sure of a previously unprecedented audience. Millions of people would become first-hand witnesses to the second crash at 9.03 a.m. It would have been impossible for terrorism to stage itself with greater effect.

Terror equals violence and fear. The goal of terrorism in the age of communications technology is to inflict maximum terror with means that are plain to see. And the images yielded by

---

The anthology New York September 11 by Magnum Photographers *was published in the immediate aftermath of the September 11 attack on the initiative of Thomas Hoepker, who was at that time Magnum's vice-president. Hoepker's iconic photo is missing from this early selection.*

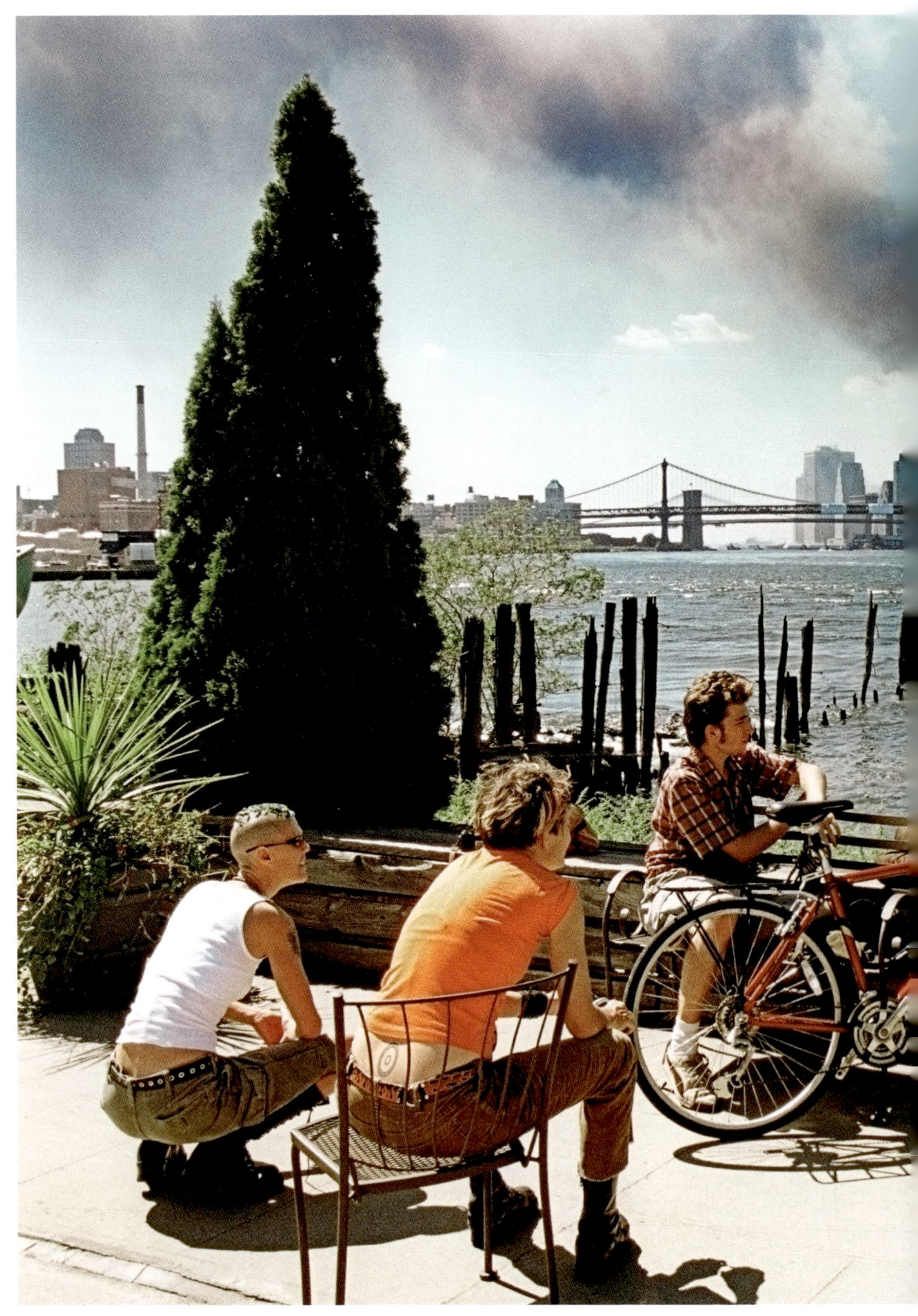

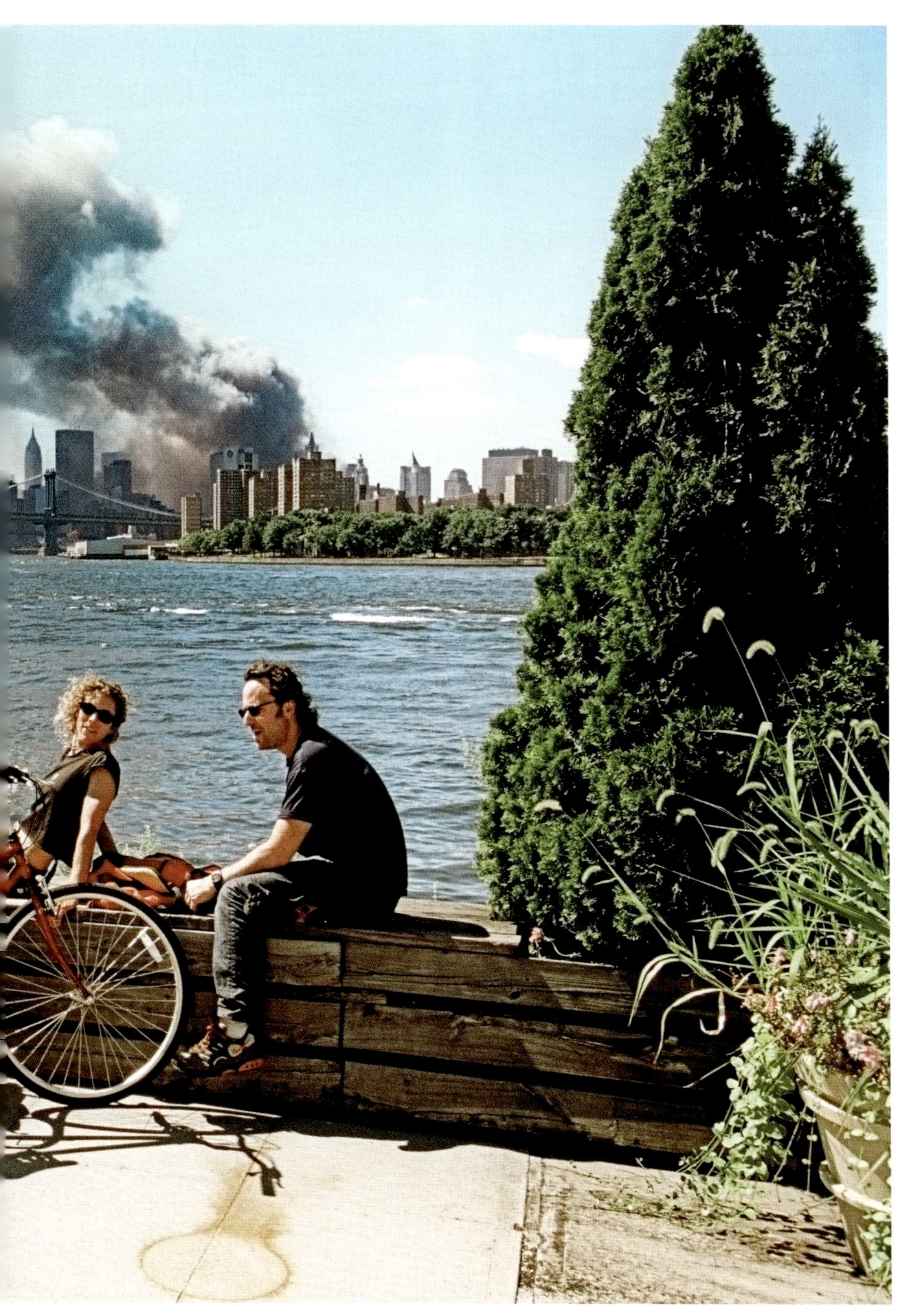

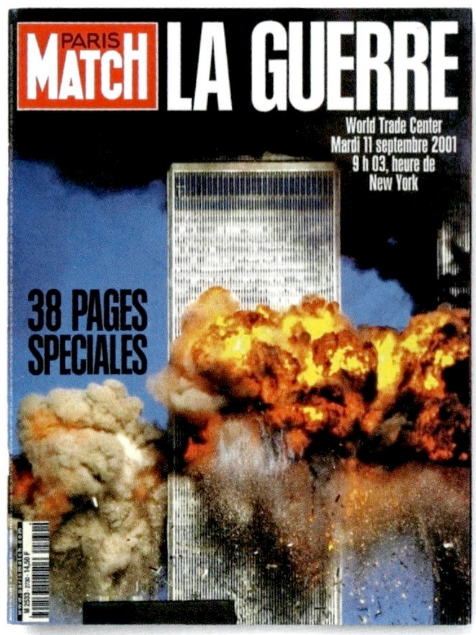

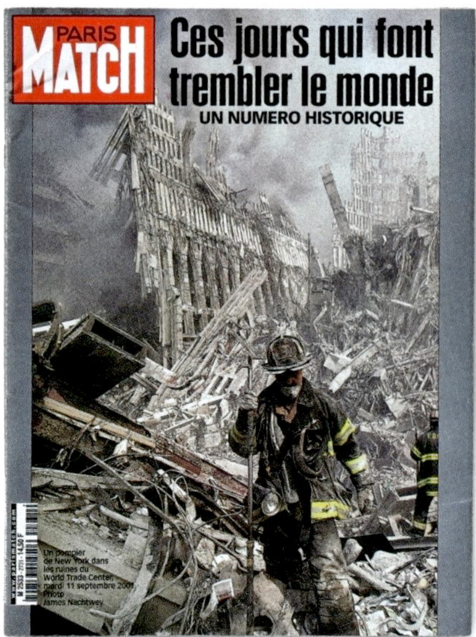

technology help it to do so. From this point of view, September 11 was also and above all a war of images. As we oscillated between curiosity and sympathy, our eyes were fed a previously unknown flood of visual messages both from television and classic photography. Those behind the terror had thereby also given thought to their timing and location. Their act was carried out not in the depths of night but in the fresh, clear air of morning. And with New York they had selected not only a famous, famously capitalist, Western and American city, but also a media city in which practically everyone owns a photo or video camera. They could thus be assured of triggering a massive wave of visual footage. Literally hundreds of private recording devices proceeded to focus, from every possible angle, on events as they unfolded. Amateurs as well as professionals rushed out to capture the scene. Almost no other event in our recent history had been photographed, documented and interpreted with such intensity as September 11. Whether in private snapshots or by the cream of international photojournalism, including names such as Steve McCurry, Larry Towell, Gilles Peress, Alex Webb, David Alan Harvey, Eli Reed, Susan Meiselas, and Thomas Hoepker, who took one of the most unsettling images.

Tragedy and titillation

Hoepker, born in 1936 in Munich, lived in New York since 1989. A seasoned photojournalist and film-maker, he worked for many years for the German magazine *Stern* and is a member of Magnum. He was told of the catastrophe relatively early on the morning of September 11. "I had just sat down for breakfast and the phone rang," the photographer remembers. "Magnum's editorial director, Rebecca Ames, was calling, about five minutes after the first plane hit. She lives in Brooklyn and had just seen smoke coming from the World Trade Center from her window. She was totally shaken. In a way, I didn't really believe what she said. It took a while to sink in. Then I switched on the TV, and only when I saw the pictures did it become a reality." Millions of people all over the world had now also turned on their televisions. And like them, Thomas Hoepker proceeded to witness the attack by the second plane as it happened: "I saw the second plane hit the building on the screen, and for a moment I was totally helpless. I didn't know what to do. I just sat there in shock for a moment thinking, what to do now? What's the right thing to do?" As a successful photojournalist who worked all over the world, Thomas Hoepker is a true pro with an instinctive feel for subjects and stories. As a member of the venerable photographic cooperative Magnum, however, he is also conscious of the ethical side of his job. It strikes him that this might not be the moment to be thinking about taking pictures: "It's so horrific, it's not decent to photograph that." And there is the speed of television, which long since seems to have secured the interpretive monopoly over events. To set off now, armed with nothing but a simple 35-mm camera, in order to take stock images? But at some point, as Hoepker says, the professional starts to take over: "You have to do something. You simply have to go out and take pictures."

The subway, he discovers, stopped running. Car seems to be the only way reach the scene. It becomes clear even on Second Avenue, however, that reaching downtown Manhattan is going to be impossible. Hoepker decides to cross Queensboro Bridge, which soon turns out to be a mistake: "I was trapped on the other side of the East River and couldn't drive back into Manhattan. So I shot most of my pictures from Brooklyn and by walking over the Manhattan Bridge." Thomas Hoepker unwillingly becomes a distant witness to events. He watches the catastrophe from a distance, photographs it sooner according to the rules of a battle painting attempting an overview than from the immediate proximity of modern reportage. In particular, his picture of a group of young people relaxing and chatting with the towers burning and collapsing in the background would become a key visual in the series – and ultimately one of Hoepker's best-known photos full stop. It was no coincidence that it was chosen for the cover of the large retrospective monograph on Hoepker that appeared in 2005. Even though it must be said that the photographer hesitated for a long time about releasing the image to the public. It was not included, for example, in the book *New York September 11 by Magnum Photographers* published immediately after September 11 and edited by Hoepker himself. The contradiction between apocalypse and a sort of *Déjeuner sur l'herbe*, between a good-humored get-together and the end of the world, was too gaping. What Hoepker in fact thematized is the great daily lottery of life, also known as fate, which constantly ensures that different things happen at the same time for reasons that are often difficult to comprehend. Insofar as the photographer portraits the disaster as part of a distant tragedy, one that we observe – via a relaxed group of young people – to a certain extent from a comfortable seat, he furthermore delivers a commentary on his modern media society: one person's tragedy is always, at least in part, the titillating thrill of those who are consuming it in images.

Broadcast, shown, printed and published over and over again, the events of September 11 conveyed by the media have made their way into our visual memory. Images of the towers

---

Opposite left and pages 416–417:
Cover and double-page spreads, Paris Match, *20 September 2001.*

Opposite right: *Two weeks after the attacks on the United States,* Paris Match *magazine brought out a special issue in its* Numéro historique *series, entitled "Ces jours qui font trembler le monde" (The Days that Shook the World).*

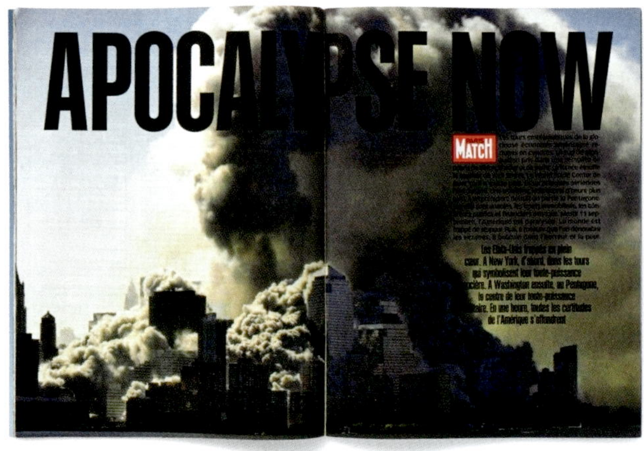

APOCALYPSE NOW

PARIS MATCH

Les Etats-Unis frappés en plein
cœur. A New York, d'abord, dans les tours
qui symbolisent leur toute-puissance
cière. A Washington ensuite, au Pentagone,
le centre de leur toute-puissance
taire. En une heure, toutes les certitudes
de l'Amérique s'effondrent

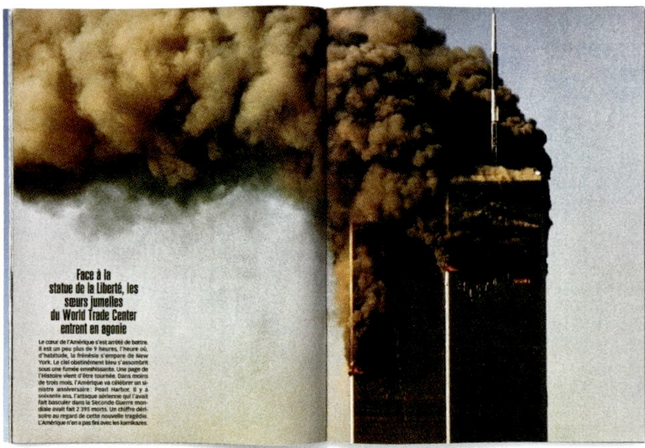

Face à la
statue de la Liberté, les
sœurs jumelles
du World Trade Center
entrent en agonie

Le cœur de l'Amérique s'est arrêté de battre. Il est un peu plus de 9 heures, l'heure où, d'habitude, la frénésie s'empare de New York. Le ciel obstinément bleu s'assombrit sous une fumée envahissante. Une page de l'Histoire vient d'être tournée. Dans moins de trois mois, l'Amérique va célébrer un sinistre anniversaire : Pearl Harbor. Il y a soixante ans, l'attaque aérienne qui l'avait fait basculer dans la Seconde Guerre mondiale avait fait 2 395 morts. Un chiffre dérisoire au regard de cette nouvelle tragédie. L'Amérique n'en a pas fini avec les kamikazes.

en train de brûler. Celles des tours en train de s'effondrer, comme dans ces films qui montrent des démolitions contrôlées. Les images des personnes enfermées dans les étages supérieurs, à 400 mètres de hauteur, et qui savaient ne pouvoir être sauvées. Ou celles de ces gens qui se jetaient dans le vide. « Je ne peux plus fermer les yeux », dit un témoin, « sans voir ces virgules qui tombent du ciel, ces corps tordus, comme des virgules noires. Quelquefois ils se tenaient par la main. Ils n'avaient que le choix entre brûler ou sauter. »

Environ 3 300 personnes ont perdu la vie le 11 septembre à New York, ce chiffre incluant les pompiers et les passagers des avions. Le nombre de victimes aurait pu être dix fois supérieur. Environ 50 000 New-Yorkais travaillaient au World Trade Center qui abritait 350 sociétés et accueillait chaque jour 100 000 visiteurs. Mais le nombre des victimes reste effroyable. L'attentat perpétré à New York a fait plus de victimes que tous les attentats terroristes à ce jour. C'est la première fois que des avions civils ont été transformés en véritables engins meurtriers. Le concept de l'attentat-suicide a acquis une toute nouvelle dimension. Même sur le plan de la

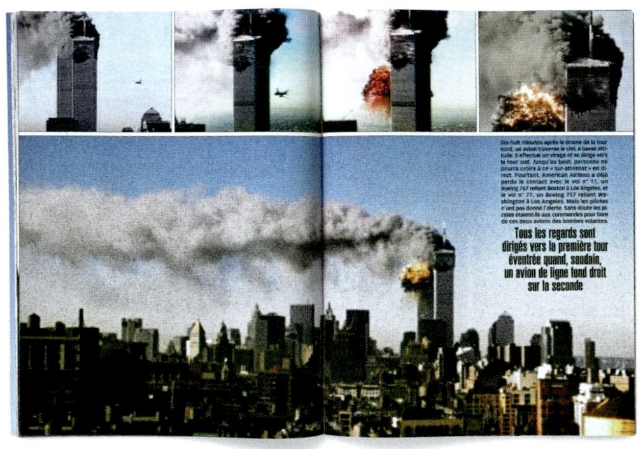

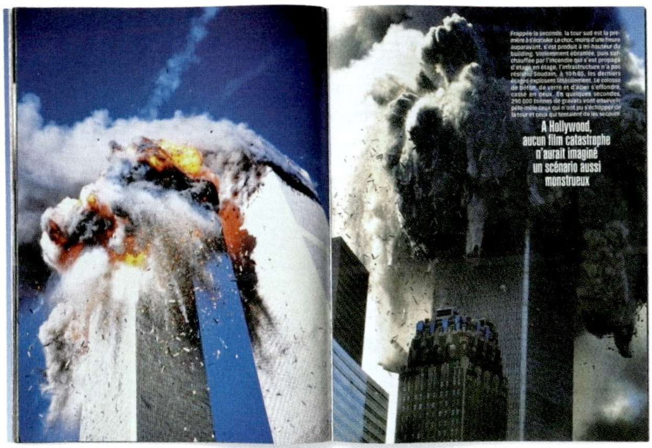

assumed a whole new dimension. In terms of planning and logistics, too, the 19 hijackers involved in the September 11 plot attained a previously unknown level of organization. Let's not forget: the terrorists had attacked the most powerful country in the world, the nuclear-armed superpower that was the USA, on its own territory. The lead article in the Frankfurter Rundschau summed it up: "The World Trade Center a vast heap of rubble, the Pentagon badly damaged, the White House vacated, the President on the run, the US government in a nuclear bunker in Nebraska – a superpower could not suffer a more comprehensive humiliation." September 11 changed the United States. And indeed the world as a whole. Without "9/11" things in Afghanistan, in the Near East, in Iraq would look very different. And in our daily lives, which since 2001 have been accompanied by ever new security laws. September 11 is a historic date. Like Pearl Harbor. And like 22 November 1963, the day that John F. Kennedy was assassinated. The terrorist attacks inflicted a lasting trauma on northern America. One that is accompanied by countless images – right up to today.

Bibliography

Aubert, François

Reinke, Jutta/Wolfgang Stemmer (ed.): *Pioniere der Kamera. Das erste Jahrhundert der Fotografie 1840–1900.* Exh. cat., Fotoforum Bremen, Bremen 1987

Bayard, Hippolyte

Dewitz, Bodo von: *La Bohème. Die Inszenierung des Künstlers in Fotografien des 19. und 20. Jahrhunderts.* Exh. cat., Museum Ludwig, Göttingen 2010

Duca, Lo: *Bayard.* Paris 1943

Frizot, Michel: *La Parole des primitifs. À propos des calotypistes francais.* In: *Études photographiques,* No. 3, November 1997, pp. 43–63

Gautrand, Jean Claude/Michel Frizot: *Hippolyte Bayard – naissance de l'image photographique.* Amiens 1986

Girardin, Daniel/Christian Pirker: *Controverses. Une histoire juridique et éthique de la photographie.* Arles 2008

Jammes, André: *Hippolyte Bayard. Ein verkannter Erfinder und Meister der Photographie.* Lucerne/Frankfurt am Main 1975

Potonniée, Georges: *Histoire de la Découverte de la Photographie.* Paris 1925

Steinert, Otto: *Hippolyte Bayard. Ein Erfinder der Photographie.* Exh. cat., Museum Folkwang, Essen 1959

Bisson, Auguste Rosalie

Die Brüder Bisson. Aufstieg und Fall eines Fotografenunternehmens. Exh. cat., Museum Folkwang, Essen 1999

Leroy, Marie-Noelle: "Le monument photographique des frères Bisson." In: *Études photographiques,* No. 2, 1997, pp. 82–95

Stenger, Erich: *Die beginnende Photographie im Spiegel von Tageszeitungen und Tagebüchern.* Würzburg 1943

Blossfeldt, Karl

Blossfeldt, Karl: *Photographien.* Munich 1991

Blossfeldt, Karl: *Photographien 1865–1932.* Cologne 1993

Blossfeldt, Karl: *Urformen der Kunst. Wundergarten der Natur. Das fotografische Werk in einem Band.* Munich 1994

Van Deren Coke, Frank: *Avantgarde-Fotografie in Deutschland 1919–1939.* Munich 1982

Ewing, William A.: *Flora Photographica: Masterpieces of Flower Photography from 1835 to the Present.* London 1991

Herzog, Hans-Michael (ed.): *Blumenstücke – Kunststücke. Vom 17. Jahrhundert bis in die Gegenwart.* Exh. cat., Kunsthalle Bielefeld, Bielefeld 1995

Nierendorf, Karl (ed.): *Urformen der Kunst.* Berlin 1928

Photographische Sammlung/SK Stiftung Kultur (ed.): *August Sander, Karl Blossfeldt, Albert Renger-Patzsch, Bernd und Hilla Becher – Vergleichende Konzeptionen.* Cologne 1997

Wilde, Ann and Jürgen (eds.): *Fotografie.* Exh. cat., Kunstmuseum Bonn, Ostfildern 1994

Wilde, Ann and Jürgen (eds.): *Karl Blossfeldt – Photographien.* Munich 1991

Burri, René

Burri, René: *One World.* Zurich 1984

Burri, René: *Impossible Reminiscences.* London 2014

Burri, René: *Mouvements.* Göttingen/Zurich 2015

Burri, René/François Maspero: *Che Guevara.* Paris 1997

Che. Fotografisches Album. Berlin 1991

Look, 9 April 1963

"Los Cubanos. Metamorphosen einer Revolution. Aufnahmen von René Burri." In: *Du,* No. 12, 1993, pp. 12–73

Koetzle, Hans-Michael: *René Burri. Photographs/Fotografien.* London/Berlin 2004

Loviny, Christophe: *Che. Die Fotobiografie.* Munich 1997

Ulmer, Brigitte: "Ich dachte, Burri, du spinnst." In: *Cash Extra,* No. 49, 5 December 1997

Capa, Robert

Born, Katharina/Rita Grosvenor: "Dem die Stunde schlug." In: *Stern,* No. 41, 1996

Capa, Cornell (ed.): *The concerned photographer.* New York 1968

Capa, Cornell/Richard Whelan: *Robert Capa. Photographien.* Cologne 1985

Capa, Robert: *Death in the Making.* New York 1938

Capa, Robert: *War Photographs.* Exh. cat., Museum of Modern Art, New York 1960

Fabian, Rainer/Hans Christian Adam: *Bilder vom Krieg. 130 Jahre Kriegsfotografie – eine Anklage.* Hamburg 1983

Girardin, Daniel/Christian Pirker: *Controverses. Une histoire juridique et éthique de la photographie.* Arles 2008

Heart of Spain: Robert Capa's Photographs of the Spanish Civil War. New York 1999

Kershaw, Alex: *Blood and Champagne. The Life and Times of Robert Capa.* Boston 2002

Lavoie, Vincent: *L'affaire Capa. Le procès d'une icône.* Paris 2017

Lavoie, Vincent: *Falling soldier: Préambule au procès d'une icône.* In: *Études photographiques,* Nr. 35, 2017, pp. 4–25

Squiers, Carol: "Capa is Cleared: A famed photo is proven authentic." In: *American Photo,* May/June 1998

Whelan, Richard: *This is War! Robert Capa at Work*. Exh. cat., International Center of Photography, Göttingen 2007

Cartier-Bresson, Henri

Burri, René: "Alter Meister." In: *Süddeutsche Zeitung Magazin*, No. 31, 1998
Cartier-Bresson, Henri: *Images à la Sauvette*. Paris 1952
Cartier-Bresson, Henri: *Die Photographien*. Munich 1992
Cartier-Bresson, Henri: *Europäer*. Munich 1997
Cartier-Bresson, Henri: *Auf der Suche nach dem rechten Augenblick. Aufsätze und Erinnerungen*. Munich 1998
Chéroux, Clément: *Henri Cartier-Bresson*. Paris 2014
Eger, Christian: "Schnappschuss wurde eine Fotolegende." In: *Mitteldeutsche Zeitung*, 27. 7. 1995
Galassi, Peter: *Henri Cartier-Bresson. The Modern Century*. Exh. cat., Museum of Modern Art, New York 2010
Kirstein, Lincoln/Beaumont Newhall: *The Photographs of Henri Cartier-Bresson*. Exh. cat., Museum of Modern Art, New York 1947
Montier, Jean-Pierre: *Henri Cartier-Bresson. Seine Kunst – Sein Leben*. Munich 1997

Daguerre, Louis Jacques Mandé

Bajac, Quentin/Dominique Planchon de Font-Réaulx: *Le daguerréotype français. Un objet photographique*. Exh. cat., Musée d'Orsay, Paris 2003
Gernsheim, Helmut and Alison: *L. J. M. Daguerre: The History of the Diorama and the Daguerreotype*. New York 1956
Gunthert, André: "Daguerre ou la promptitude. Archéologie de la réduction du temps de pose." In: *Études photographiques*, No. 5, 1998, pp. 4–25
Haugsted, Ida: "Berichte aus Paris, 1839. Zu den Briefen Christian Falbes an den dänischen Kronprinzen." In: *Fotogeschichte*, No. 31, 1989, pp. 3–14
Pohlmann, Ulrich/Marjen Schmidt: "Das Münchner Daguerre-Triptychon. Ein Protokoll zur Geschichte seiner Präsentation, Aufbewahrung und Restaurierung." In: *Fotogeschichte*, No. 52, 1994, pp. 3–13
Reynaud, Françoise: *Paris et le Daguerréotype*. Exh. cat., Musée Carnavalet, Paris 1989
Starl, Timm: *Ein Blick auf die Straße. Die fotografische Sicht auf ein städtisches Motiv*. Berlin 1988
Starl, Timm: "Sicht und Aussicht. Zu den Aufnahmen Pariser Boulevards von Daguerre und Talbot." In: *Camera Austria*, No. 24, 1987, pp. 81–86
Stenger, Erich: *Die beginnende Photographie im Spiegel von Tageszeitungen und Tagebüchern*. Würzburg 1943

Disdéri, André Adolphe Eugène

Barret, A.: *Die ersten Fotoreporter 1848–1914*. Frankfurt am Main 1978
La Commune photographiée: Exh. cat., Musée d'Orsay, Paris 2000
Le Corps et son Image. Photographies du dix-neuvième siècle. Exh. cat., Bibliothèque nationale, Paris 1986
McCauley, Elizabeth Anne: *André Adolphe Disdéri and the Carte de Visite Portrait Photograph*. New Haven/London 1985
Neumann, Thomas: "Fotografie zur Zeit der Pariser Kommune." In: *Pariser Kommune 1871*. Exh. cat., Neue Gesellschaft für Bildende Kunst, Berlin 1971, pp. 152-159

Doisneau, Robert

Anon.: "Ein Klassiker unter den Küssen." In: *Süddeutsche Zeitung*, 24. 12. 1992
Anon.: "Der Kuss der Küsse." In: *Süddeutsche Zeitung*, 4. 6. 1993
Anon.: "Der schönste Kuß – nur ein Bluff." In: *Abendzeitung München*, 4. 6. 1993
Atelier Robert Doisneau (ed.): *Doisneau Paris*. Paris 2005
Doisneau, Robert. Paris 1983
Doisneau, Robert: *Trois Secondes d'Éternité*. Paris 1979
Doisneau, Robert: *A l'imparfait de l'objectif. Souvenirs et portraits*. Paris 1989
Doisneau, Robert: *Drei Sekunden Ewigkeit*. Munich 1997
Gautrand, Jean Claude: "Au revoir Monsieur Doisneau!" In: *Le Photographe*, No. 1514, May 1994, pp. 8–11
Girardin, Daniel/Christian Pirker: *Controverses. Une histoire juridique et éthique de la photographie*. Arles 2008
Hamilton, Peter: *Retrospective Robert Doisneau*. London 1992
Hamilton, Peter: "Robert Doisneau. Born Gentilly, 14 April 1912, died Paris, 1 April 1994." In: *The British Journal of Photography*, 13 April 1994, pp. 16–17
Koetzle, Hans-Michael: *Eyes on Paris. Paris im Fotobuch 1890 bis heute*. Munich 2011
Koetzle, Hans-Michael (ed.): *Robert Doisneau – Renault. Die Dreißiger Jahre*. Berlin 1990
Langer, Freddy: "Das Flüchtige des Glücks. Zum Tod des französischen Fotografen Robert Doisneau." In: *Frankfurter Allgemeine Zeitung*, No. 78, 5 April 1994
Mandery, Guy: *Robert Doisneau. Un photographe et ses livres*. Paris 2013
Ollier, Brigitte: *Doisneau Paris*. Paris 1996
Zollner, Manfred: "Der Foto-Poet." In: *Foto-Magazin*, No. 5, 1992, pp. 34–41

Duchenne de Boulogne
À corps et à raison. Photographies médicales 1840–1920. Exh. cat., Mission du Patrimoine photographique, Paris 1995
Burns, Stanley B.: *A Morning's Work: Medical Photographs from The Burns Archive & Collection 1843–1939.* Santa Fe 1998
Ewing, William A.: *Faszination Körper.* Leipzig 1994
Guilly, Paul: *Duchenne de Boulogne.* Paris 1936
Marbot, Bernard/André Rouillé: *Le Corps et son image. Photographies du dix-neuvième siècle.* Bibliothèque nationale, Paris 1986
Mathon, Catherine: *Duchenne de Boulogne 1806–1875.* Exh. cat., École nationale supérieure des beaux-arts, Paris 1998

Durieu, Eugène/ Delacroix, Eugène
L'art du nu au XIXe siècle. Le photographe et son modèle. Exh. cat., Bibliothèque nationale de France, Paris 1997
Aubenas, Sylvie: "La collection de photographies d'Eugène Delacroix." In: *La Revue de l'Art,* 1999
Heiting, Manfred: *At the Still Point: Photographs from the Manfred Heiting Collection.* Vol. I, 1840–1916. Los Angeles/Amsterdam 1995
Jobert, Barthélémy: *Delacroix. Le trait romantique.* Exh. cat., Bibliothèque nationale de France, Paris 1998
Koetzle, Hans-Michael/Uwe Scheid: *1000 Nudes. Uwe Scheid Collection.* Cologne 1994
Paviot, Alain: *Le Cliché-Verre. Corot, Delacroix, Millet, Rousseau, Daubigny.* Exh. cat., Musée de la vie romantique, Paris 1994
Sagne, Jean: *Delacroix et la photographie.* Paris 1982
Vaisse, Pierre: "Delacroix et la photographie, un livre de Jean Sagne." In: *Photographies,* No. 3, December 1983, pp. 96–101
Zerner, Henri: "Delacroix, la photographie, le dessin." In: *La revue du musée d'Orsay,* No. 4, 1992, pp. 83–87

Eisenstaedt, Alfred
Dewitz, Bodo von/Robert Lebeck: *Kiosk. Eine Geschichte der Fotoreportage/A History of Photojournalism.* Exh. cat., Museum Ludwig/Agfa Foto-Historama, Göttingen 2001
Eisenstaedt, Alfred: *Witness to Our Time.* New York 1966
Eisenstaedt, Alfred: *The Eye of Eisenstaedt.* New York 1969
Eisenstaedt, Alfred: *Eisenstaedt's Guide to Photography.* New York 1978
Fulton, Marianne: *Eyes of Time: Photojournalism in America.* Boston/Toronto/London 1988
The Great LIFE Photographers. New York 2004.
Honnef, Klaus/Frank Weyers: *Und sie haben Deutschland verlassen ... müssen.* Exh. cat., Rheinisches Landesmuseum, Bonn 1997
Die Internationale Bibliothek der Photographie: Photojournalismus. Zurich 1985

Guibert, Maurice
Adhémar, Jean: "*Toulouse-Lautrec et son photographe habituel.*" In: *Aesculape,* No. 12, December 1951, pp. 229–234
L'art du Nu au XIXe siècle. Le photographe et son modèle. Exh. cat., Bibliothèque nationale de France, Paris 1997
Dewitz, Bodo von: *La Bohème. Die Inszenierung des Künstlers in Fotografien des 19. und 20. Jahrhunderts.* Exh. cat., Museum Ludwig, Göttingen 2010
Schimmel, Herbert D.: *Die Briefe von Henri de Toulouse-Lautrec.* Munich 1992
Toulouse-Lautrec. Exh. cat., Galeries nationales du Grand Palais, Paris 1992

Haas, Ernst
After the War was over … London 1985
Andies, Helmut/Ernst Haas: *Ende und Anfang.* Vienna/Hamburg/Düsseldorf 1975
Campbell, Bryan: *Ernst Haas. The Great Photographers.* London 1983
Capa, Cornell (ed.): *The Concerned Photographer 2.* New York 1972
Eskildsen, Ute: *Fotografie in deutschen Zeitschriften 1946–1984.* Exh. cat., Institut für Auslandsbeziehungen, Stuttgart 1985
Gruber, L. Fritz/Renate Gruber: *Große Photographen unseres Jahrhunderts.* Darmstadt 1964
Haas, Ernst: *In Black and White.* Boston/Toronto/London 1992
Langer, Freddy: *Ernst Haas.* Hamburg 1992
Mauracher, Michael: "Heimkehrer. Ein Gespräch mit Ernst Haas." In: *Wiener Zeitung,* 31.7.1987 (Part 1) and 7.8.1987 (Part 2)

Hine, Lewis Wickes
America & Lewis Hine: Photographs 1904–1940. Millerton, New York 1977
Doherty, R. J.: *Sozialdokumentarische Photographie in den USA.* Lucerne 1974
George Eastman House (ed.): *Portfolio.* Rochester, New York, 1970
Gutmann, Judith Mara: *Lewis W. Hine and the American Social Conscience.* New York 1967
History of Photography, No. 2, 1992 (special issue on Lewis W. Hine)
Kaplan, Daile: *Lewis Hine in Europe: the Lost Photographs.* New York 1988
Kemp, John R. (ed): *Lewis Hine: Photographs of Child Labor in the New South.* Jackson 1986
Lunn Gallery (ed.): *Lewis W. Hine. Child Labor Photographs.* Washington, DC, 1980

Orvell, Miles: "Lewis Hine: The Art of the Commonplace." In: *History of Photography*, vol. 16, No. 2, 1992, pp. 87ff.
Rosenblum, Naomi: *The Lewis Hine Document*. Brooklyn 1977
Rosenblum, Naomi/ Walter Rosenblum: *Lewis W. Hine*. Paris 1992
Steinorth, Karl (ed.): *Lewis Hine. Die Kamera als Zeuge. Fotografien 1905–1937*. Kilchberg 1996
Victor, Stephen: *Lewis Hine's Photography and Reform in Rhode Island*. Providence 1982

Hoepker, Thomas

Deutsche Fotografie. Macht eines Mediums. Exh. cat., Kunst- und Ausstellungshalle der BRD, Bonn. Cologne 1997.
Die großen Fotografen: Thomas Höpker. Munich 1985 Hoepker, Thomas: *Yatun Papa*. Stuttgart 1963
Gundlach, F. C. (ed.): *Das deutsche Auge. 33 Photographen und ihre Reportagen – 33 Blicke auf unser Jahrhundert*. Exh. cat., Deichtorhallen Hamburg, Munich 1996
Hoepker, Thomas: *Photographien 1955–2005*. Exh. cat., Fotomuseum im Münchner Stadtmuseum, Munich 2005
Hoepker, Thomas: *Wanderlust. 1954–2013*. Kempen 2014
Hoepker, Thomas (ed.): *New York September 11 by Magnum Photographers*. New York 2001
Hoepker, Thomas/Günter Kunert: *Berliner Wände*. Munich/Vienna 1976
Hoepker, Thomas/Heinz Mack: *Expeditionen in künstliche Gärten*. Hamburg 1977
Hoepker, Thomas/Eva Windmöller: *Leben in der DDR*. Hamburg 1976
Hoepker, Thomas/Eva Windmöller: *New Yorker*. Schaffhausen 1987
Zeitprofile. 30 Jahre Kulturpreis DGPh 1959–1988. Exh. cat., photokina, Cologne 1988

Horst, Horst P.

Brugger, Ingried (ed.): *Modefotografie von 1900 bis heute*. Exh. cat., Kunstforum Länderbank, Vienna 1990
Devlin, Polly: *Vogue Book of Fashion Photography: The First Sixty Years*. New York 1979
Ewing, William A./Nancy Hall-Duncan: *Horst P. Horst. Photographs 1931–1984*. Milan 1985
Honnef, Klaus/Frank Weyers: *Und sie haben Deutschland verlassen ... müssen. Fotografen und ihre Bilder 1928–1997*. Exh. cat., Rheinisches Landesmuseum, Bonn 1997
Horst P. Horst: Photographs of a Decade. New York 1944
Horst P. Horst/George Hoyningen-Huene: *Salute to the Thirties*. New York 1971
Horst. Exh. cat., Münchner Stadtmuseum et al., Milan 1987
Lawford, Valentine: *Horst: His Work and His World*. New York 1984
Tardiff, Richard J./Lothar Schirmer (ed.): *Horst. Photographien aus sechs Jahrzehnten*. Munich 1991
Vogue (France), Nos. 9 and 12, 1939

Howlett, Robert

Buckland, Gail: *Reality Recorded – Early Documentary Photography*. London 1974
Haworth-Booth, Mark: *The Golden Age of British Photography 1839–1900*. New York 1984
Hiepe, Richard: "Industrie und Maschine in der Weltanschauung der Fotografie." In: *Tendenzen*, Nos. 106 and 107, 1976
Naef, Weston: *The J. Paul Getty Museum Handbook of the Photographs Collection*. Malibu 1995
The Waking Dream. Photography's First Century. Selections from the Gilman Paper Company Collection. Exh. cat., The Metropolitan Museum of Art, New York 1993

Kertész, André

Aperture Masters of Photography: André Kertész. New York 1993
Borhan, Pierre: *André Kertész. La biographie d'une œuvre*. Exh. cat., Pavillon des Arts, Paris 1994
Frizot, Michel/Annie-Laure Wanaverbecq: *André Kertész*. Exh. cat., Jeu de Paume, Paris 2010
Kertész, André: *Day of Paris*. New York 1945
Kertész on Kertész: A Self-Portrait. New York 1983
Kertész, André: *A. K. in Paris. Photographien 1925–1936*. Munich 1992
Lemagny, Jean-Claude: *L'ombre et le temps*. Paris 1992
Phillips, Sandra S.: *The Photographic Work of André Kertész in France 1925–1936: A Critical Essay and Catalogue*. The City University of New York 1985
Phillips, Sandra S./David Travis/Weston J. Naef: *André Kertész. Of Paris and New York*. Exh. cat., The Art Institute of Chicago, Chicago 1985

Klemm, Barbara

Frankfurter Allgemeine Zeitung, issues of 18–22 May 1973, 26 May 1973 and 9 April 1976
Hess, Hans-Eberhard: "Die Zeitungsfotografin." In: *Photo Technik International*, No. 6, 1995, pp. 74–83
"Ihr lächelt die Welt zu." In: *Frankfurter Allgemeine Zeitung – Bilder und Zeiten*, No. 299, 24.12.2009
Klemm, Barbara: *Bilder*. Frankfurt am Main 1986
Klemm, Barbara: *Blick nach Osten*. Frankfurt am Main 1995
Klemm, Barbara: *Unsere Jahre*. Exh. cat., Deutsches Historisches Museum, Munich 1999
Klemm, Barbara: *Fotografien 1968–2013*, Wädenswil am Zürichsee 2013
Pohlert, Christian-Matthias (ed.): *Bilder in der Zeitung. Journalistische Fotografie 1949–1999*. Munich 1999

Lange, Dorothea
Davis, Keith F.: *The Photographs of Dorothea Lange*. Kansas City 1995
Dixon, Daniel: *Dorothea Lange: Eloquent Witness*. Chicago 1989
Doherty, R. J.: *Sozialdokumentarische Photographie in den USA*. Lucerne 1974
Elliott, George P.: *Dorothea Lange*. Exh. cat., Museum of Modern Art, New York 1966
Heyman, Therese Thau/Sandra S. Phillips/John Szarkowski: *Dorothea Lange: American Photographs*. San Francisco 1994
Lange, Dorothea: *American Photographs*. San Francisco 1994
Dorothea Lange. Exh. cat., Caisse nationale des monuments historiques et des sites, Paris 1998
Lange, Dorothea: *Politiques du visible*, Paris 2018
"Lange, Dorothea: An Assignment I'll Never Forget." In: Liz Heron/Val Williams (eds.): *Illuminations: Women Writing on Photography from the 1850s to the Present*. London 1996, pp. 151–153
Lange, Dorothea/Paul Schuster Taylor: *An American Exodus. A Record of Human Erosion*. New York 1939
Levin, Howard M./Katherine Northrup (eds.): *Dorothea Lange: Farm Security Administration Photographs, 1935–1939*. Glencoe 1980
Meltzer, Milton: *Dorothea Lange: A Photographer's Life*. New York 1978
Partridge, Elizabeth: *Dorothea Lange: A Visual Life*, Washington/London 1994
Steichen, Edward: *The Family of Man*. Exh. cat., Museum of Modern Art, New York 1955
Stryker, Roy Emerson/Nancy Wood: *In this Proud Land: America As Seen in the FSA Photographs*. Greenwich 1973

Lartigue, Jacques-Henri
Astier, Martine/Mary Blume: *Lartigue's Riviera*. Paris/New York 1998
Avedon, Richard: *Diary of a Century*. New York 1971
Chapier, Henry: *Jacques-Henri Lartigue*. Paris 1981
Lartigue, Florette: *Jacques-Henri Lartigue. La Traversée du siècle*. Paris 1990
Lartigue, Jacques-Henri: *Jacques-Henri Lartigue et les autos*. Paris 1974
Lartigue, Jacques-Henri: *Mémoires sans mémoire*. Paris 1975
Lartigue, Jacques-Henri. Photo Poche 3, Paris 1983
Lartigue, Jacques-Henri. Munich 1984
Lartigue, Jacques-Henri: Album. Exh. cat., der Stiftung für die Photographie, Bern 1986
Life. 29 November 1963
Sprung in die Zeit. Bewegung und Zeit als Gestaltungsprinzipien in der Photographie von den Anfängen bis zur Gegenwart. Exh. cat., Berlinische Galerie, Berlin 1992
Szarkowski, John: *The Debut of Jacques-Henri Lartigue*. New York 1991 (unpublished typescript, archives of the Association des Amis de Jacques-Henri Lartigue)
Szarkowski, John: *The Photographs of Jacques-Henri Lartigue*. New York 1963

Lebeck, Robert
Glasenapp, Jörn: *Die Deutsche Nachkriegsfotografie*. Paderborn 2008
Koetzle, Hans-Michael: "Zeitzeuge mit der Kamera." In: *foto-scene*, No. 6, 1991/92
Koetzle, Hans-Michael: "Von der Propaganda zur Kunst, vom Journalismus zum Design. Anmerkungen zur Fotografie in Deutschland 1939 bis 1970." In: *Fotogeschichte*, No. 117, 2010
Koetzle, Hans-Michael (ed.): *Augen auf! 100 Jahre Leica Fotografie*, Heidelberg 2014
Lebeck, Robert: *Afrika im Jahre Null. Eine Kristall-Reportage*. Hamburg 1961
Lebeck, Robert: *Begegnungen mit Großen der Zeit*. Schaffhausen 1987
Lebeck, Robert: *Rückblende*. Düsseldorf 1999
Lebeck, Robert: *Vis-à-vis*. Göttingen 1999
Lebeck, Robert: *Unverschämtes Glück*. Göttingen 2004
Lebeck, Robert: *Fotoreporter*. Göttingen 2008
Lebeck, Robert: *Tokyo, Moscow, Leopoldville*. Göttingen 2008
Lebeck, Robert/Harald Willenbrock: *Neugierig auf Welt. Erinnerungen eines Fotoreporters*. Göttingen 2004
Steinorth, Karl/Meinrad Maria Grewenig (eds.): *Robert Lebeck – Fotoreportagen*. Ostfildern 1993
Tabel-Gerster, Margit: *Durchschnitt fotografiert sich (nicht) doch! Ein Gespräch mit Robert Lebeck*. Hamburg 1988

Leibing, Peter
Paul, Gerhard (ed.): *Das Jahrhundert der Bilder. 1949 bis heute*. Göttingen 2008
Pett, Saul: *The Instant it Happened*. New York 1975

Löcherer, Alois
Dewitz, Bodo von/Reinhard Matz (eds.): *Silber und Salz. Zur Frühzeit der Photographie im deutschen Sprachraum 1839–1860*. Exh. cat., Museum Ludwig, Cologne 1989
Dewitz, Bodo von/Museum Ludwig/Gesellschaft für Moderne Kunst am Museum Ludwig (eds.) *Tatsachen/Facts. Fotografien des 19. und 20. Jahrhunderts. Die Sammlung Agfa im Museum Ludwig Köln*. Exh. cat., Museum Ludwig, Göttingen 2006

Gebhardt, Heinz: *Königlich Bayerische Photographie 1838–1918.* Exh. cat., Münchner Stadtmuseum, Munich 1978
Pohlmann, Ulrich (ed.): *Alois Löcherer. Photographien 1845–1855.* Exh. cat., Fotomuseum im Münchner Stadtmuseum, Munich 1998
Wiegand, Wilfried: *Frühzeit der Photographie 1826–1890.* Frankfurt am Main 1980

Malanga, Gerard

Avedon, Richard: *Evidence. 1944–1994.* Exh. cat., Whitney Museum of American Art, New York 1994
Avedon, Richard/Doon Arbus: *The Sixties.* Munich 1999
Bockris, Victor/Gerard Malanga: *Up-tight. Die Velvet Underground Story.* Augsburg 1988
Malanga, Gerard: *Selbstportrait eines Dichters.* Frankfurt am Main 1970
Malanga, Gerard: *Genesis of an Installation.* New York 1988
Malanga, Gerard: *Screen Tests, Portraits, Nudes 1964–1996.* Göttingen 2000
McShine, Kynaston (ed.): *Andy Warhol. Retrospektive.* Exh. cat., Museum Ludwig Köln, Munich 1989
Steinorth, Karl/Thomas Buchsteiner (ed.): *Social Disease. Photographs '76–'79.* Exh. cat., Kodak Kulturprogramm, Ostfildern 1992
Andy Warhol: Photography. Exh. cat., Hamburger Kunsthalle, Schaffhausen 1999
Andy Warhol's Exposures. New York 1979

Man Ray

Billeter, Erika (ed.): *Skulptur im Licht der Fotografie. Von Bayard bis Mapplethorpe.* Exh. cat., Wilhelm Lehmbruck Museum Duisburg, Bern 1998
Ecotais, Emmanuelle de l'/ Alain Sayag: *Man Ray. La photographie à l'envers.* Exh. cat., Centre Georges Pompidou, Paris 1998
Girardin, Daniel/Christian Pirker: *Controverses. Une histoire juridique et éthique de la photographie.* Arles 2008
Jaguer, Edouard: *Surrealistische Photographie. Zwischen Traum und Wirklichkeit.* Cologne 1984
Krauss, Rosalind/Jane Livingston/ Dawn Ades: *Explosante-Fixe. Photographie & Surréalisme.* Exh. cat., Centre Georges Pompidou, Paris 1985
Man Ray: Photographien 1920–1934. Munich 1980
Man Ray: Photograph. Munich 1982
Man Ray: Selbstporträt. Eine illustrierte Autobiographie. Munich 1983
Man Ray: Sein Gesamtwerk 1890–1976. Schaffhausen 1989
Man Ray. Exh. cat., Galerie der Stadt Stuttgart, Ostfildern 1998

Mapplethorpe, Robert

Coleman, A.D.: *Critical Focus,* Munich 1995
Dunne, Dominick: "Robert Mapplethorpe's proud finale." In: *Vanity Fair,* February 1989, pp. 124–132, 183–187
Gaines, Charles/Butler, George: *Pumping Iron II: The Unpredecented Woman.* New York 1984
Lyon, Lisa: *Lisa Lyon's Body Magic.* New York 1981
Mapplethorpe, Robert: 1970–1983. Exh. cat., Institute of Contemporary Arts, London 1983
Mapplethorpe, Robert: *The Black Book.* Munich 1986
Mapplethorpe, Robert: *Ten by Ten.* New York 1988
Mapplethorpe, Robert. New York 1992
Morrisroe, Patricia: *Robert Mapplethorpe. Eine Biographie.* Munich 1996
Weiermair, Peter: "Homosexuelle Sehweisen in der Fotografie des 19. und 20. Jahrhunderts. Einige Anmerkungen unter besonderer Berücksichtigung des Werks von Robert Mapplethorpe." In: *Fotogeschichte,* No. 19, 1986, pp. 23–28

McBride, Will

Gundlach, F. C. (ed.): *Das deutsche Auge. 33 Photographen und ihre Reportagen – 33 Blicke auf unser Jahrhundert.* Exh. cat., Deichtorhallen Hamburg, Munich 1996
Honnef, Klaus: *Will McBride. My Sixties.* Cologne 1994
Koetzle, Hans-Michael: *twen. Revision einer Legende.* Exh. cat., Münchner Stadtmuseum, Munich 1995
Koetzle, Hans-Michael: "Von der Propaganda zur Kunst, vom Journalismus zum Design. Anmerkungen zur Fotografie in Deutschland 1939 bis 1970." In: *Fotogeschichte,* No. 117, 2010
Koetzle, Hans-Michael/ Carsten M. Wolff: *Fleckhaus. Deutschlands erster Art Director.* Munich/Berlin 1997
Koetzle, Hans-Michael/ Carsten Wolff: *Willy Fleckhaus. Design – Revolte – Regenbogen,* Stuttgart 2017
McBride, Will: *Knips. Berliner Bilder aus den 50er Jahren.* Berlin 1979
McBride, Will: *Foto-Tagebuch 1953–1961.* Berlin 1982
McBride, Will: *I, Will McBride.* Cologne 1997
Peter Weiermair (ed.): *Will McBride. 40 Jahre Fotografie.* Schaffhausen 1992

Nadar

Aubenas, Sylvie/Anne Lacoste (eds.): *Les Nadar. Une légende photographique.* Paris 2018

Barret, André: *Nadar. 50 photographies de ses contemporains.* Paris 1994
Gosling, Nigel: *Nadar.* Munich 1977
Hambourg, Maria Morris/Françoise Heilbrun/Philippe Néagu: *Nadar.* Munich 1995
Honnef, Klaus (ed.): *Lichtbildnisse. Das Porträt in der Fotografie.* Exh. cat., Rheinisches Landesmuseum Bonn, Cologne 1982

Newton, Helmut

Haenlein, Carl (ed.): *Anton Josef Trčka, Edward Weston, Helmut Newton. Die Künstlichkeit des Wirklichen.* Exh. cat., Kestner Gesellschaft Hannover, Zurich 1998
Honnef, Klaus: "Die Lust zu sehen. Mehr als ein Fotograf – Ein Meister der Bilder: Helmut Newton". In: idem: *Nichts als Kunst ....* Cologne 1997, pp. 447–457
Newton, Helmut: *White Women.* Munich 1976
Newton, Helmut: *Big Nudes.* New York 1982
Newton, Helmut: *Welt ohne Männer.* Munich 1984
Newton, Helmut: *Sleepless Nights.* Munich 1991
Helmut Newton. Aus dem Photographischen Werk. Exh. cat., Deichtorhallen Hamburg, Munich 1993
Newton, Helmut: *Pages from the Glossies. Facsimiles 1956–1998.* Zurich 1998.
Newton, Helmut: *SUMO.* Cologne 1999
Newton, Helmut: *Autobiographie.* Munich 2002
Newton, Helmut: *A Gun for Hire.* Cologne 2005
Vogue (French), No. 621 (November) 1981
Vogue (German), No. 11 (November) 1979

Niépce, Nicéphore

Fage, Jean: *La Vie de Nicéphore Niépce.* Bièvre 1983
Harmant, Pierre.-G./Paul Marillier: "Some Thoughts on the World's First Photograph." In: *The Photographic Journal,* No. 107, April1967, pp. 130–140
Jay, Paul: *Nicéphore Niépce. Lettres et documents choisis par P. J.* Paris 1983
Jay, Paul: Niépce. *Genèse d'une Invention.* Chalon-sur-Saône 1988
Jay, Paul: *Niépce. Premiers outils – Premiers résultats.* Chalon-sur-Saône 1978

Parr, Martin

Boot, Chris (ed.): *Magnum Stories.* London 2004
Goldberg, Vicki: *Light Matters: Writings on Photography.* New York 2005
Lange, Andrea: *On the Bright Side of Life. Zeitgenössische Britische Fotografie.* Exh. cat., Neue Gesellschaft für Bildende Kunst (NGBK), Berlin 1997
Lardinois, Brigitte (ed.): *Magnum Magnum.* London 2008
Mellor, David Alan: *No Such Thing As Society: Photography in Britain 1967–87. From the British Council and the Arts Council Collection.* London 2007
Phillips, Sandra: *Martin Parr.* London 2007
Roberts, Pamela: *A Century of Colour Photography.* London 2007.
Williams, Val: *Martin Parr: Photographic Works 1971–2000.* London 2002
Williams, Val/Susan Bright: *How We Are: Photographing Britain.* London 2007

Peter, Richard

Derenthal, Ludger: *Bilder der Trümmer- und Aufbaujahre. Fotografie im sich teilenden Deutschland.* Marburg 1999
Domröse, Ulrich (ed.): *Nichts ist so einfach wie es scheint. Ostdeutsche Photographie 1945–1989.* Exh. cat., Berlinische Galerie, Berlin 1992
Frühe Bilder. Eine Ausstellung zur Geschichte der Fotografie in der DDR. Exh. cat., Gesellschaft für Fotografie im Kulturbund der DDR, Leipzig 1985
Glasenapp, Jörn: *Die Deutsche Nachkriegsfotografie.* Paderborn 2008
Honnef, Klaus/Ursula Breymayer (eds.): *Ende und Anfang. Photographen in Deutschland um 1945.* Exh. cat., Deutsches Historisches Museum, Berlin 1995
Peter, Richard: *Dresdener Notturno.* Dresden 1961 Peter, Richard: *Dresden – eine Kamera klagt an.* Dresden 1949. 2nd edn. Leipzig 1982
Peter, Richard: "Gute Fotos kosten Zeit und Mühe." In: *fotografie,* No. 4, 1960
Pommerin, Rainer/Walter Schmitz: *Die Zerstörung Dresdens am 13./14. Februar 1945. Antworten der Künste.* Dresden 1995
Wurst, Werner (ed.): *Richard Peter sen. Erinnerungen und Bilder eines Dresdener Fotografen.* Leipzig 1987
Zervigón, Andrés Mario: "Le Wiederaufbau de la perception. La photographie allemande dans l'après-guerre, 1945–1950." In: *Études photographiques,* No. 29, 2012, pp. 82–108

Priester, Max/Wilcke, Willy

Anon.: "Bismarck auf dem Sterbelager." In: *Die Welt,* No. 270, 19. 11. 1974
Girardin, Daniel/Christian Pirker: *Controverses. Une histoire juridique et éthique de la photographie.* Arles 2008
Kempe, Fritz: "Ein Bild, das vernichtet werden sollte." In: *Zeitmagazin,* No. 32, 4. 8. 1978
Franz von Lenbach. Exh. cat., Städtische Galerie im Lenbachhaus, Munich 1987

Lorenz, Lovis H.: *Oevelgönner Nachtwachen.* Hamburg 1974
Machtan, Lothar: *Bismarcks Tod und Deutschlands Tränen. Reportage einer Tragödie.* Munich 1998
Ruby, Jay: *Secure the Shadow: Death and Photography in America.* Cambridge, Mass./London 1995

Ressler, Konrad
Bormann, Hans-Friedrich: "Masken des Schreibers. Bertolt Brecht als Akteur und Zuschauer in einer Porträtserie Konrad Reßlers." In: *Fotogeschichte,* No. 101, 2006
Debold-Kritter, Astrid: *Augsburg in frühen Photographien 1860–1914.* Munich 1979
Gebhardt, Heinz: *Königlich Bayerische Photographie 1838–1918.* Exh. cat., Münchner Stadtmuseum, Munich 1978
Koetzle, Hans-Michael: *Bertolt Brecht beim Photographen. Porträtstudien von Konrad Reßler.* Siegen 1987. 2nd edn. Berlin 1989. 3rd edn. Munich 1998

Rheims, Bettina
Misselbeck, Reinhold (ed.): *Photographie des 20. Jahrhunderts, Museum Ludwig Köln.* Cologne 1996
Rheims, Bettina: *Female Trouble.* Exh. cat., Münchner Stadtmuseum. Munich 1989
Rheims, Bettina: *Chambre Close.* Munich 1992
Rheims, Bettina: *Les Espionnes.* Exh. cat., Galerie Apicella. Cologne 1992
Rheims, Bettina: *Animal.* Munich 1994
Rheims, Bettina: *I.N.R.I.* Munich 1998
Rheims, Bettina: *More Trouble.* Munich 2004
Rheims, Bettina: *Retrospective.* Munich 2004
Rheims, Bettina/Serge Bramly: *Rose, c'est Paris.* Munich 1992

Sabau, Luminita (ed.): *Das Versprechen der Fotografie. Die Sammlung der DG Bank.* Munich 1998
Weiermair, Peter (ed.): *Das Bild des Körpers.* Exh. cat., Frankfurter Kunstverein, Schaffhausen 1993

Salgado, Sebastião
Salgado, Sebastião: *Workers: An Archaeology of the Industrial Age.* New York 1993
Salgado, Sebastião: *Serra pelada.* Paris 1999
Salgado, Sebastião: *Kuwait. A Desert on Fire.* Cologne 2016
Der Spiegel, Nos. 10, 11, 17, 24, 26, 1991
Stern, No. 46, 7. 11. 1991
Wald, Matthew L.: "The Eye of the Photojournalist." In: *The New York Times Magazine,* 9 June 1991
World Press Photo 1992. Düsseldorf 1992

Sander, August
Berger, John: *About Looking.* London 1980.
Keller, Ulrich/Gunther Sander: *August Sander – Menschen des 20. Jahrhunderts. Portraitphotographien 1892–1952.* Munich 1980
Molderings, Herbert: *Fotografie in der Weimarer Republik.* Berlin 1988
Photographische Sammlung/SK Stiftung Kultur (ed.): *August Sander, Karl Blossfeldt, Albert Renger-Patzsch, Bernd und Hilla Becher – Vergleichende Konzeptionen.* Cologne 1997
Powers, Richard: *Three Farmers on Their Way to a Dance.* London 1989
Sander, August: "In der Photographie gibt es keine ungeklärten Schatten!" Exh. cat., August Sander Archiv Köln, Berlin 1994
Scholz, Christian: "August Sander, Photograph aus Deutschland." In: *Neue Zürcher Zeitung,* No. 159, 12/13. 7. 1997, pp. 57–59

Shere, Sam
Carlebach, Michael L.: *American Photojournalism Comes of Age.* Washington, DC, 1997
Faber, John: *Great Moments in News Photography: From the Historical Files of the National Press Photographers Association.* New York 1960
The Great LIFE Photographers. New York 2004
Loengard, John: *Life – Classic Photographs: A Personal Interpretation.* London 1996
Paul, Gerhard (ed.): *Das Jahrhundert der Bilder. 1900 bis 1949.* Göttingen 2009
Scherman, David Edward: *The Best of Life.* New York 1973

Skoglund, Sandy
50 Jahre Moderne Farbfotografie. Exh. cat., photokina, Cologne 1986
Hülsewig-Johnen, Jutta/Gottfried Jäger/J. A. Schmoll (J. A. Eisenwerth): *Das Foto als autonomes Bild. Experimentelle Gestaltung 1839–1989.* Exh. cat., Kunsthalle Bielefeld, Stuttgart 1989
Köhler, Michael: *Das konstruierte Bild.* Schaffhausen 1989
Lemagny, Jean-Claude/Alain Sayag: *L'Invention d'un Art. Simulacres et Fictions.* Exh. cat., Centre Georges Pompidou, Paris 1989
Picazo, Glòria/Patrick Roegiers: *Sandy Skoglund.* Exh. cat., Paris Audiovisuel, Paris 1992
Piguet, Philippe: *Sandy Skoglund.* Exh. cat., Galerie Guy Bärtschi, Geneva 2000
Skoglund, Sandy: Reality Under Siege: A Retrospective. Exh. cat., Smith College Museum of Art, New York 1998

Stern, Bert
Eros, No. 3, Autumn 1962
Greene, Milton H.: *Milton's Marilyn. Die Photographien von Milton H. Greene.* Munich 1994

Marilyn Monroe und die Kamera. 152 Photographien aus den Jahren 1945–1962. Munich 1989
Stern, Bert: *Marilyn Monroe – The Complete Last Sitting.* Munich 1992

Stieglitz, Alfred
Eisler, Benita: *O'Keeffe & Stieglitz: An American Romance.* New York 1991
Finsler, Hans: "Das Bild der Photographie." In: *Du*, No. 3/1964
Greenough, Sarah/Juan Hamilton: *Alfred Stieglitz. Photographs & Writings.* Exh. cat., National Gallery of Art, Washington, DC, 1983
Stieglitz, Alfred: Aperture Masters of Photography. New York 1989
Stieglitz, Alfred: Camera Work. The Complete Illustrations 1903–1917. Cologne 1997
"Stieglitz, Alfred: Wie es zu 'The Steerage' kam." In: Wilfried Wiegand (ed.): *Die Wahrheit der Photographie. Klassische Bekenntnisse zu einer neuen Kunst.* Frankfurt am Main 1981, pp. 173–177
Whelan, Richard: *Alfred Stieglitz.* New York 1996

Stock, Dennis
Boot, Chris (ed.): *Magnum Stories.* London 2004
James Dean. Photographien. Munich 1989
Lardinois, Brigitte (ed.): *Magnum Magnum.* London 2008
Roth, Sanford and Beulah: *James Dean. Ein Porträt.* Munich 1984
Schatt, Roy: *James Dean. Ein Porträt.* Munich 1984
Stock, Dennis: *James Dean Revisited.* Munich 1986
Stock, Dennis: *Made in USA. Photographs 1951–1971.* Ostfildern 1994

Strand, Paul
Burns, Stanley B.: *A Morning's Work: Medical Photography from the Burns Archive & Collection 1843–1939.* Santa Fe 1998
Fleischmann, Kaspar (ed.): *Paul Strand.* Vol. I. Zurich 1987
Fleischmann, Kaspar (ed.): *Paul Strand.* Vol. II. Zurich 1990
Hambourg, Maria Morris: *Paul Strand circa 1916.* Exh. cat., Metropolitan Museum of Art, New York 1998
Haworth-Booth, Mark: *Paul Strand.* New York 1987
Hill, Paul/Thomas Cooper: *Dialogue with Photography.* New York 1979
Lyons, Nathan: *Photographers on photography.* Englewood Cliffs, NJ, 1966
Stieglitz, Alfred: Camera Work. The Complete Illustrations 1903–1917. Cologne 1997
Strand, Paul: Photographs 1915–1945. Exh. cat., Museum of Modern Art, New York 1945
Strand, Paul: A Retrospective Monograph: The Years 1915–1946. New York 1971
Strand, Paul: Sixty Years of Photographs. New York 1976
Strand, Paul: An American Vision. New York 1990
Strand, Paul: Essays on His Life and Work. New York 1990
Strand, Paul: The World on My Doorstep. New York 1994
Strand, Paul: Circa 1916. Exh. cat., Metropolitan Museum of Art, New York 1998
Tucker, Ann W.: *Five American Photographers.* Exh. cat., Museum of Fine Arts, Houston 1981

Ut, Nick
Chong, Denise: *Das Mädchen hinter dem Foto. Die Geschichte der Kim Phúc.* Hamburg 2001
Ebert, Michael: "Nein, es waren nicht die Amerikaner. Die ganze Wahrheit über ein Foto, das jeder kennt." In: *Camera in Conflict.* Marburg 2018, pp.176–197
Girardin, Daniel/Christian Pirker: *Controverses. Une histoire juridique et éthique de la photographie.* Arles 2008
Grewenig, Meinrad Maria (ed.): *Augenblicke des Jahrhunderts. Meisterwerke der Reportagefotografie von Associated Press.* Exh. cat., Historisches Museum der Pfalz, Ostfildern 1999.
Leekley, Sheryle & John: *Moments: The Pulitzer Prize. Photographs.* New York 1978
Panzer, Mary: *Things as they are.* London 2005
Paul, Gerhard (ed.): *Das Jahrhundert der Bilder. 1949 bis heute.* Göttingen 2008
Stahel, Urs (ed.): *Darkside II. Fotografische Macht und fotografierte Gewalt, Krankheit und Tod – Photographic Power and Violence, Disease and Death Photographed.* Exh. cat., Fotomuseum Winterthur, Göttingen 2009

Witkin, Joel-Peter
Celant, Germano: *Witkin.* Zurich 1995
Enfers, No. 1. Biarritz 1994
Fels, Ludwig: "Grimassen der Lust." In: *Süddeutsche Zeitung Magazin*, No. 40, 1995
Glanz und Elend des Körpers/ Splendeurs et Misères du Corps. Exh. cat., Musée d'art et d'histoire de Fribourg/ Musée d'Art Moderne de la Ville de Paris, Fribourg/Paris 1988
Thijsen, Mirelle: "Die Form Gottes. Interview mit Joel-Peter Witkin." In: *European Photography*, No. 42, 1990
Witkin, Joel-Peter. Paris 1991

Witkin, Joel-Peter. Exh. cat., Stedelijk Museum, Amsterdam 1983
Witkin, Joel-Peter: Forty Photographs. Exh. cat., San Francisco Museum of Modern Art, San Francisco 1985
Witkin, Joel-Peter. Exh. cat., Forum Böttcherstrasse. Bremen 1989
Witkin, Joel-Peter. Exh. cat., Centre National de la Photographie, Paris 1989
Witkin, Joel-Peter. Exh. cat., Galerie Baudoin Lebon, Paris 1991
Witkin, Joel-Peter: *Gods of Earth and Heaven.* Altadena, CA, 1991
Witkin, Joel-Peter (ed.): *Masterpieces of Medical Photography: Selections from the Burns Archive.* Pasadena 1987
Witkin, Joel-Peter (ed.): *Harms Way: Lust & Madness: Murder & Mayhem.* Santa Fe 1994

Zille, Heinrich

Das alte Berlin. Photographien von Heinrich Zille 1890–1910. Munich 2018.
Bohne, Friedrich: *Heinrich Zille als Fotograf.* Exh. cat., Wolfgang-Gurlitt-Museum, Linz 1968
Brost, Harald/Laurenz Demps: *Berlin wird Weltstadt. Mit 277 Photographien von F. Albert Schwartz, Hof-Photograph.* Stuttgart 1981
Van Deren Coke, Frank: *The Painter and the Photograph from Delacroix to Warhol.* 2nd edn. Albuquerque, NM, 1972
Fischer, Lothar: *Heinrich Zille.* Reinbek bei Hamburg 1979
Flügge, Gerhard: *Mein Vater Heinrich Zille.* Berlin 1955
Flügge, Matthias: *Heinrich Zille. Fotografien von Berlin um 1900.* Leipzig 1987
Flügge, Matthias: *Heinrich Zille. Berliner Photographien.* Munich 1993
Kaufhold, Enno: *Heinrich Zille. Photograph der Moderne.* Munich 1995
Luft, Friedrich: *Mein Photo Milljöh. 100 x Alt-Berlin aufgenommen von Heinrich Zille selber.* Hannover 1967
Photographie als Photographie. Zehn Jahre Photographische Sammlung 1979–1989. Exh. cat., Berlinische Galerie, Berlin 1989
Ranke, Winfried: *Vom Milljöh ins Milieu. Heinrich Zilles Aufstieg in der Berliner Gesellschaft.* Hannover 1979
Ranke, Winfried: *Draughtsman and Photographer.* Exh. cat., Goethe Institut, Munich 1982
Ranke, Winfried: *Heinrich Zille. Photographien Berlin 1890–1910.* Munich 1975. 2nd edn. Munich 1979. 3rd edn. Munich 1985

Credits

Agfa Foto-Historama, Cologne / Rheinisches Bildarchiv, Cologne: *63, 64–65, 66–67, 77, 82–83, 88, 89*

Aperture Foundation Inc., Paul Strand Archive: *159*

Alamy Stock Photo: *84, 94*

Bayerische Staatsbibliothek, Munich: *99, 101 left and right*

BBC Hulton Picture Library, London: *126*

Berlinische Galerie, Photographische Sammlung / © VG Bild-Kunst, Bonn: *111, 112–113, 116–117*

Bettmann / Corbis / Hoang Van Danh: *327*

Bibliothèque Nationale de France, Paris: *41, 45, 47, 71, 96–97*

bpk / Will McBride, Berlin: *275*

René Burri / Magnum Photos / Agentur Focus: *310–311, 315*

Caisse nationale des Monuments historiques et des sites; Félix Nadar © Arch. Phot. Paris: *75*

© Robert Capa © International Center of Photography / Magnum Photos / Agentur Focus: *194–195*

Henri Cartier-Bresson / Magnum Photos / Agentur Focus: *233, 234–235, 237*

Collection Manfred Heiting, Amsterdam: *55*

Collection / Archive Hans-Michael Koetzle, Munich; reproductions by Hans Döring, Munich: *11, 57, 73, 90, 91, 92, 93, 103, 106–107, 109, 114 top and bottom, 120, 121, 123, 140, 141 top and bottom, 156, 161 top and bottom, 167, 175 top and bottom, 181, 189, 190, 191 top and bottom, 193, 196, 197, 198, 211 top and bottom, 214, 217 top and bottom, 223, 226 top, 228, 229, 230, 231, 236, 239, 240–241, 242 top, 243, 246, 247 top and bottom, 250 top and bottom, 253 top and bottom, 260–261, 263, 264, 272–273 left, center and right, 277, 278–279, 280 top and bottom, 281 top and bottom, 297, 301, 302 top and bottom, 303 top and bottom, 304, 305, 307 top, center and bottom, 309 top, center and bottom, 312, 313, 314, 338, 339, 348, 349, 350–351, 364, 366–367, 370–371, 382, 384, 385, 386–387, 388 top and bottom, 389 top and bottom, 392 top, 393, 396, 397, 398–399, 402 top, 403, 406, 407, 408–409, 411, 414 left and right, 416 top and bottom, 417 top and bottom*

Collection Robert Lebeck, Berlin: *282, 283 top and bottom, 284–285, 286–287 all images, 289 left and right, 291 top and bottom*

Collection Horst Moser, Munich; reproductions by Hans Döring, Munich: *147, 148, 149*

Collection Musée de la Photographie, Charleroi: *79*

Collection Uwe Scheid: *42, 43, 46*

Les Publications Condé Nast Paris S.A., Courtesy Vogue Paris: *220, 221*

ddp images / Associated Press / Nick Ut: *328–329, 331*

École nationale supérieure des beaux-arts, Paris: 49, 51, 53

Archiv Fotomagazin, Munich: *14–15*

Fotomuseum im Münchner Stadtmuseum: *19, 20–21, 22*

Photo Jean Claude Gautrand: *256*

George Eastman House, Rochester © Lewis W. Hine / Courtesy George Eastman House: *134–135, 137*

Gernsheim Collection, Harry Ransom Humanities Research Center, University of Texas at Austin: *12–13, 85*

Getty Images / Alfred Eisenstaedt: *227*

Getty Images / Ernst Haas: *249*

The J. Paul Getty Museum, Los Angeles: *26, 70, 166*

Thomas Hoepker / Magnum Photos / Agentur Focus: *412–413*

Horst P. Horst / courtesy Hamiltons Gallery, London: *219*

Barbara Klemm, Frankfurt: *333, 334–335, 336–337*

Hans-Michael Koetzle, Munich: *306*

Kunst- und Museumsbibliothek Cologne / Rheinisches Bildarchiv, Cologne: *200, 201*

laif, Cologne / Rapho, Agence photographique, Paris: *258–259*

Landesmedienzentrum Hamburg: *104–105*

J. H. Lartigue © Ministère de la Culture, France / Association des Amis de J. H. Lartigue: *142 top, 143, 144–145*

Library of Congress, Washington D.C. – p.203: LC-USZ62-95653

© Library of Congress, Washington D.C.; pp.206–207: LC-USZ 62-58355
© Library of Congress, Washington D.C.; p.208: LC-USZ62-9097-C
© Library of Congress, Washington D.C.; p.209: LC-USZ62-9093-C
© Library of Congress, Washington D.C.

Gerard Malanga, New York: *317, 318–319, 321, 325*

Man Ray Trust, Paris / VG Bild-Kunst, Bonn: *168–169, 171, 172–173*

© The Robert Mapplethorpe Foundation. Courtesy Art + Commerce, New York: *363, 365*

The Metropolitan Museum of Art, New York: *18*

© Ministère de la culture – Médiathèque du Patrimoine / Kertész Andor (1894–1985), André Kertész (dit) / dist.RMN: *183, 185, 187*

Münchner Stadtmuseum, Sammlung Fotografie: *33, 35, 36, 37, 177*

Musée Carnavalet, Paris – © Photothèque des Musées de la Ville de Paris: *86–87*

Musée Toulouse-Lautrec, Albi-Tarn, France (tous droites reservés): *95*

Museum Ludwig Cologne / Rheinisches Bildarchiv, Cologne: *224–225*

The Helmut Newton Estate / Maconochie Photography: *346, 347*

© Georgia O'Keeffe Museum: *127, 131*

Martin Parr / Magnum Photos / Agentur Focus: *394–395*

Die Photographische Sammlung / SK Stiftung Kultur – August Sander Archiv, Cologne / VG Bild-Kunst, Bonn: *151, 153, 155*

Atelier Gebr. Martin / Konrad Reßler (Collection Hans-Michael Koetzle): *178 top, center and bottom*

Bettina Rheims, Paris: *402 bottom, 404–405*

Rheinisches Bildarchiv, Cologne: *133, 138*

Royal Photographic Society, Bath: *128, 163, 164, 165*

Rue des Archives / SZ Photo: *212–213*

Sächsische Landesbibliothek – Staats- und Universitätsbibliothek Dresden, Deutsche Fotothek; unknown photographer: *242 bottom*; Richard Peter sen.: *244–245*

Sebastião Salgado / Amazonas Images: *391*

Sebastião Salgado / Amazonas Images / Agentur Focus: *381*

© Sandy Skoglund, New Jersey: *355 all images, 356–357, 359 left and right, 360–361*

Societé française de Photographie, Paris: *27, 28–29*

Sotheby's, London: *31*

Der Spiegel, Hamburg: *343*

Staatsarchiv Hamburg: *294–295*

Bert Stern, New York: *2–3, 298–299*

Dennis Stock / Magnum Photos / Agentur Focus: *265, 267, 268–269*

TASCHEN, Cologne: *10, 32, 40, 48, 54, 62, 76, 110, 118, 132, 142 bottom, 150, 176, 182, 192, 202, 210, 218, 226 bottom, 232, 248, 254 top and bottom, 255, 274, 292, 296, 316, 326, 332, 344, 354, 362, 372 bottom, 380, 392 bottom, 410*

Universität München, Institut für Kommunikationswissenschaft: *108*

The Board of Trustees of the Victoria & Albert Museum, London, V&A Picture Library: *56, 59, 61*

Joel Peter Witkin, courtesy Pace / MacGill Gallery, New York: *374–375*

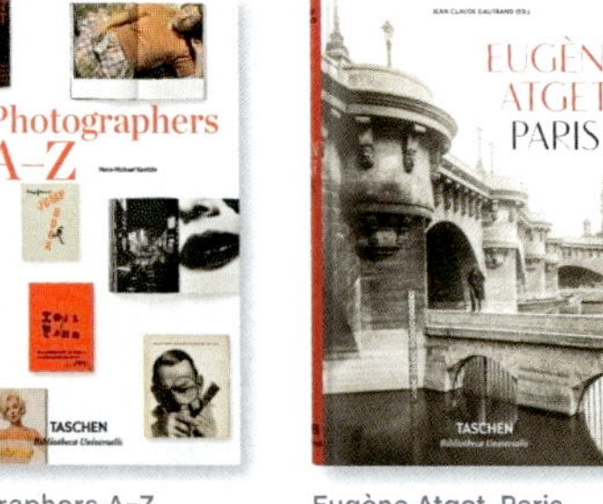

Photographers A–Z

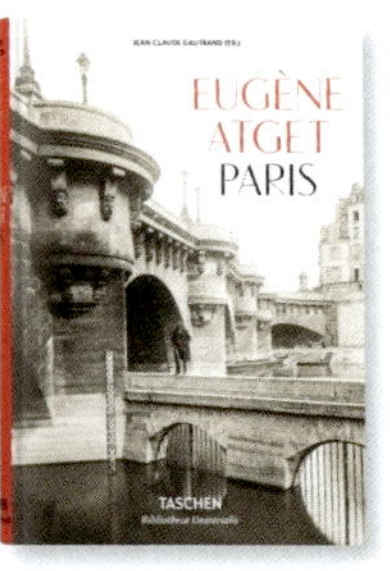

Eugène Atget. Paris

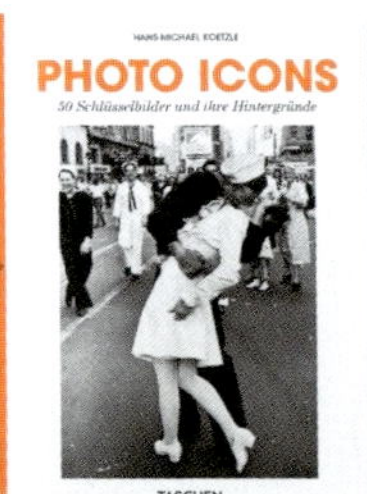

Photo Icons

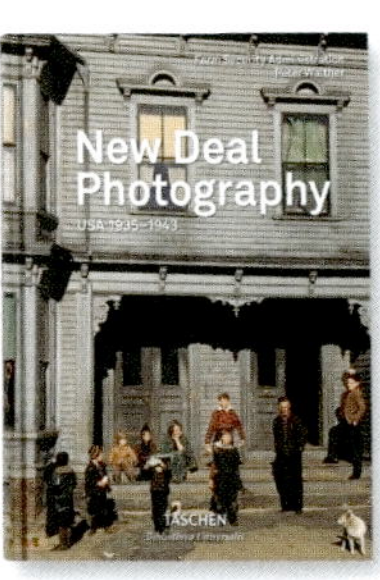

New Deal Photography

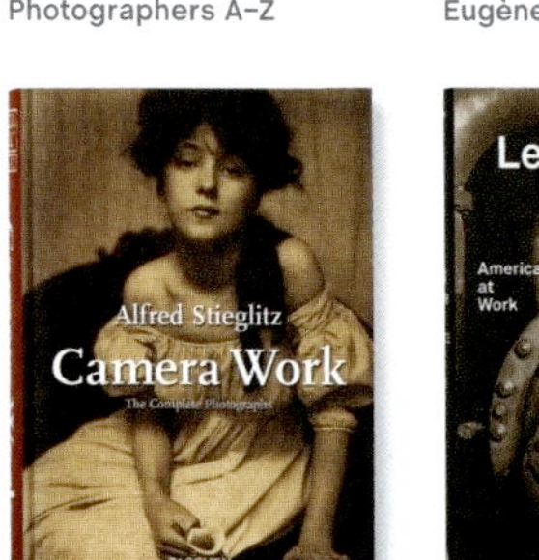

Stieglitz.
Camera Work

Lewis W. Hine

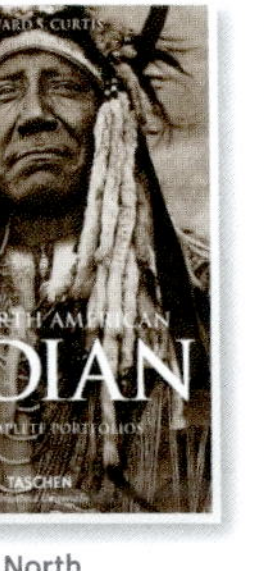

Curtis. The North
American Indian

Tiki Pop

Film Noir

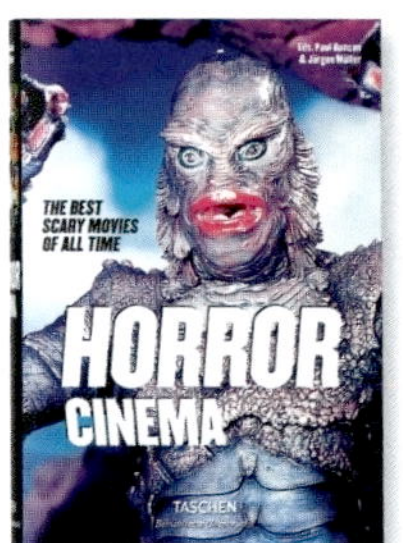

Horror Cinema

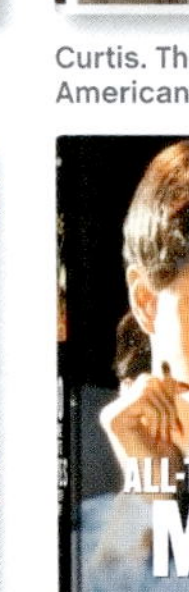

100 All-Time
Favorite Movies

The Stanley Kubrick
Archives

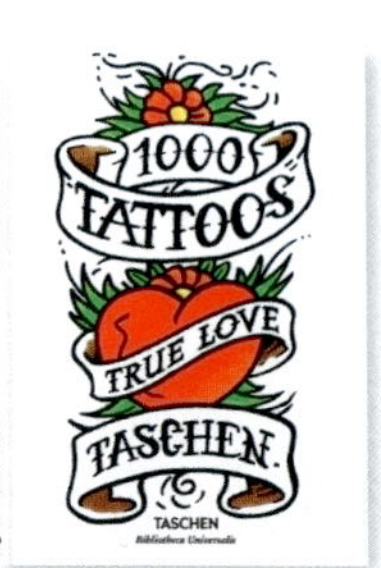

1000 Tattoos

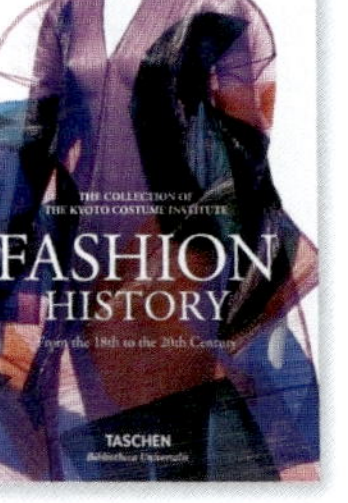

Fashion History

20th Century Fashion

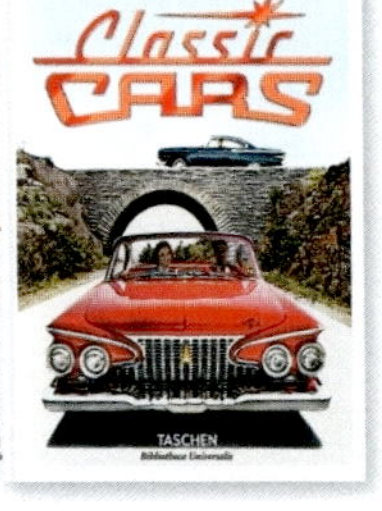

20th Century Classic Cars

Imprint

EACH AND EVERY TASCHEN BOOK PLANTS A SEED!
Each year, we offset our annual carbon emissions with carbon credits at the Instituto Terra, a reforestation program in Minas Gerais, Brazil, founded by Lélia and Sebastião Salgado. To find out more about this ecological partnership, please check: www.taschen.com/institutoterra.
Inspiration: unlimited. Carbon footprint: (almost) zero.

Want to see more? Visit taschen.com to view our current publications, browse our latest magazine, and subscribe to our newsletter.

Hohenzollernring 53
D-50672 Köln
www.taschen.com

Translation: Karen Williams, Rennes-le-Château

Printed in Bosnia–Herzegovina
ISBN 978–3–8365–7774–8

Front cover: **Alfred Eisenstaedt**: *VJ Day*, 1945

Back cover: **Man Ray**: *Noire et blanche*, 1926

Pages 2–3: **Bert Stern**: *Marilyn's Last Sitting*, 1962 (detail)

The author: **Hans-Michael Koetzle**, born in 1953, is a Munich-based freelance author and journalist, focusing mainly on history and the aesthetics of photography. He has published numerous books on photography, including *Die Zeitschrift twen* (1995), *Photo Icons* (2001), *Das Lexikon der Fotografen* (2002), *René Burri* (2004), *Photographers A-Z* (2011), and *Dr. Paul Wolff & Tritschler* (2019).

The Poetry of Hanshan (Cold Mountain), Shide, and Fenggan

Translated by
Paul Rouzer

Volume edited by
Christopher M. B. Nugent

De Gruyter

This book was prepared with the support of the Andrew W. Mellon Foundation.

ISBN 978-1-5015-1056-4
e-ISBN (PDF) 978-1-5015-0191-3
ISSN 2199-966X

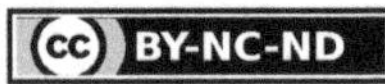

Library of Congress Cataloging-in-Publication Data
A CIP catalog record for this book has been applied for at the Library of Congress.

Bibliografische Information published by the Deutsche Nationalbibliothek
The Deutsche Nationalbibliothek lists this publication in the Deutsche Nationalbibliografie; detailed bibliographic data are available in the Internet at http://dnb.dnb.de.

Typesetting: Asco Typesetters, Hong Kong
Printing and binding: Hubert & Co. GmbH & Co. KG, Göttingen
∞ Printed on acid-free paper
Printed in Germany

www.degruyter.com